ROUTLEDGE LIBRARY EDITIONS:
INTERNATIONAL BUSINESS

INTERNATIONAL BUSINESS
HANDBOOK

INTERNATIONAL BUSINESS
HANDBOOK

Edited by
V. H. (MANEK) KIRPALANI

Volume 23

Routledge
Taylor & Francis Group

LONDON AND NEW YORK

First published in 1990

This edition first published in 2013
by Routledge
2 Park Square, Milton Park, Abingdon, Oxfordshire OX14 4RN

Simultaneously published in the USA and Canada
by Routledge
711 Third Avenue, New York, NY 10017

First issued in paperback 2014

Routledge is an imprint of the Taylor & Francis Group, an informa business

© 1990 The Haworth Press, Inc.

British Library Cataloguing in Publication Data
A catalogue record for this book is available from the British Library

ISBN: 978-0-415-65763-1 (Volume 23)
ISBN: 978-1-138-00788-8 (pbk)

Publisher's Note
The publisher has gone to great lengths to ensure the quality of this reprint but points out that some imperfections in the original copies may be apparent.

Disclaimer
The publisher has made every effort to trace copyright holders and would welcome correspondence from those they have been unable to trace.

International Business Handbook

V. H. (Manek) Kirpalani
Editor

The Haworth Press
New York • London

International Business Handbook is Volume Number 1 in the Haworth Series in International Business.

The Haworth Press, Inc., 10 Alice Street, Binghamton, NY 13904-1580
EUROSPAN/Haworth, 3 Henrietta Street, London, WC2E 8LU England

Library of Congress Cataloging-in-Publication Data

International business handbook / Vishnu H. (Manek) Kirpalani, editor.
      p.   cm. — (Haworth series in international business, ISSN
1041-2565 ; #1)
   Includes bibliographical references.
   ISBN 0-86656-862-X
   1. International trade—Case studies. I. Kirpalani, V. H. (Vishnu H.), 1928- . II. Series.
HF1379.I567 1990
281—dc20
                                                89-26682
                                                  CIP

CONTENTS

Contributors

Dr. Osman A. Atac is Associate Professor of Marketing. University of Massachusetts — Boston, Harbor Campus, Boston, Massachusetts.

Dr. Nizamettin Aydin is Associate Professor of Marketing. Suffolk University, Boston, Massachusetts.

Dr. Jozsef Beracs is Associate Professor of Marketing, Karl Marx University of Economics, Budapest, Hungary.

Dr. Joseph O. Eastlack, Jr. was Group Marketing Research Manager at Campbell Soup Company and has recently become Associate Professor of Food Marketing, St. Joseph's University, Philadelphia, Pennsylvania.

Dr. Robert E. Grosse is Associate Director, International Business and Banking Institute, Graduate School of International Studies, University of Miami, Coral Gables, Florida.

Dr. Razaul Haque is Associate Professor of Marketing, University of Windsor, Windsor, Ontario, Canada.

Lisa R. Hearne is a Master of Science candidate, Pennsylvania State University, University Park, Pennsylvania.

Dr. Erdener Kaynak is Professor of Marketing, Pennsylvania State University at Harrisburg, Middletown, Pennsylvania, and Editor-in Chief, *Journal of Global Marketing*.

Dr. Eugene J. Kelley is Dean, College of Business Administration, Pennsylvania State University, University Park, Pennsylvania, and a Past President of the American Marketing Association.

Dr. V. H. (Manek) Kirpalani is Professor of Marketing and International Business, Concordia University, Montreal, Canada, and is Past Vice-President of the American Marketing Association.

Dr. William Lazer is Eminent Scholar in Business Administration, Eugene and Christine Lynn Chair, Florida Atlantic University, Boca Raton, Florida, and a Past President of the American Marketing Association.

Dr. Essam Mahmoud is Associate Professor of Management Science, University of North Texas, Denton, Texas.

Dr. James C. Makens is Associate Professor of Marketing, Babcock Graduate School of Management, Wake Forest University, Winston-Salem, North Carolina.

Dr. Jacob Naor is Associate Professor of Marketing, University of Maine, Orono, Maine.

Dr. Nicolas G. Papadopoulos is Associate Professor of Marketing, Carleton University, Ottawa, Canada.

Dr. Samuel Rabino is Associate Professor of Marketing, Northeastern University, Boston, Massachusetts.

Dr. Gillian Rice is a marketing consultant and researcher at Rice Mahmoud Associates, Denton, Texas.

Dr. Midori Rynn is Professor of Sociology, University of Scranton, Scranton, Pennsylvania.

Dr. Ronald Savitt is John L. Beckley Professor of American Business, University of Vermont, Burlington, Vermont.

Dr. Chin Tiong Tan is Head, School of Management, National University of Singapore, Singapore.

Soo Jiuan Tan is Research Associate, National University of Singapore, Singapore.

Susan Kraemer Watkins, MBA, is Senior Supervisor of Accounting-Capital Investment Systems, Campbell Soup Company, Camden, New Jersey.

Dr. Jehiel Zif is Associate Professor of Marketing at Tel Aviv University, Tel Aviv, Israel.

Dr. Leon Zurawicki is Associate Professor of Marketing, University of Massachusetts-Boston, Harbor Campus, Boston, Massachusetts.

Dr. Peter Zurn was Partner, John Stork and Partners International GmbH, Frankfurt, West Germany and has recently become Director, Deutsches Institut zur Forderung des Industriellen Fuhrungsnachwuchses, Baden-Badener Unternehmergesprache, Koln, West Germany.

Acknowledgments

My deepest appreciation is expressed to the people who have helped in the development of this book. The first group are the numerous talented professionals who have contributed various chapters and those whose names are noted in the text. I also wish to thank my institution, the Faculty of Commerce and Administration at Concordia University, especially for the encouragement given by Steven Appelbaum, Dean of the Faculty.

I am indebted to Susan Krieger who helped to organize the manuscript. I am grateful to Laurie St. John, Supervisor of the Commerce Academic Support Staff, and her assistants who provided the requisite secretarial help.

My sincere appreciation and thanks are offered to Linda Cohen, Executive Editor, Kathyrn Rutz, Managing Editor, and their team at the Haworth Press for their thoroughness and efficiency in bringing the manuscript to publication.

It is my pleasure to mention two other people. One is Erdener Kaynak, Senior Editor for International Business at The Haworth Press and my good colleague, who significantly contributed to this project by his interest and sustained confidence in me. The other is Paul Donnelly, Vice President-Books, Warren, Gorham and Lamont, Inc., for actively encouraging me to embark on the project and carry it through.

Finally, my warmest thanks to my wife, Pachi, and my two children, Tara and Arjun, for their understanding throughout the project.

Foreword

In recent years, we have witnessed tremendous changes in the socioeconomic, technological, legal, and competitive environments of the global marketplace. These perpetual changes have had their profound effects both at micro (individual firm) and macro (country or regional) levels. At the micro level, firms of all sizes are not only trying to enter into more foreign markets, but are also doing their utmost to be cost-effective and consumer-oriented while operating in foreign markets in the face of changing international business circumstances. At the macro level governments from both the developed and developing world are actively seeking better and more lucrative market opportunities for their firms and products in the international marketplace. The attainment of higher economic performance by countries and their citizens' improved standards of living are measured against how successful the countries have been in the international market arena.

To be able to be more successful in international markets, businessmen as well as public policymakers should be more knowledgeable about the workings of international business practice. To facilitate this, higher educational institutions all over the world are charged with the yeoman's task of educating the business leaders of tomorrow about international business realities. In the words of the editor of this volume, we should create a very favorable environment in which "understanding international influences that affect international business, and relevant aspects of the world environment" become a reality.

As the first volume in The Haworth Press book series on International Business, I am very pleased to present to our readers, *International Business Handbook*. It is a very carefully prepared volume that contains practically oriented contributions from a group of very knowledgeable and experienced international business scholars and academicians. All of the country or regional chapters contain eye-opening information on facets of international business pertaining to the selected countries. As such, the book is mainly targeted at the international business practitioner working in manufacturing, trading, banking, and service industries. In this book, in particular, international influences affecting nations, national economic and physical environment, sociocultural environment, political and legal systems, technological environment, organizational culture, national control of international trade, business opportunities, sources of information, methods of entry into national business, areas of conflict, conflict resolution, corporate strategy and planning for foreign firms, corporate organization and control for foreign firms, and future business opportunities and scenarios are examined critically and with insight.

When we decided to commission a capstone type of book in the international business area, Professor V.H. (Manek) Kirpalani as editor and contributing author of the volume was the immediate choice. A highly respected scholar, Professor Kirpalani combines his past industry experience and vast talents with his sound and very successful academic and consulting experiences. The result has been an outstanding collection of essays which, I am sure, will have far-reaching impact on current international business literature and thinking.

Over a period of one year, I have observed and witnessed the tremendous effort and time that Professor Kirpalani has spent to bring this important project to a successful completion. He deserves our heartfelt thanks and appreciation. I think the profession is very lucky indeed to have scholars of his caliber. I also take this opportunity to thank the other contributors for their fine works.

I am certain that this volume will be a great addition to our growing body of knowledge in international business. I am very pleased and honored to be able to offer this volume of our book series in International Business for the use of international business practitioners, public policy makers, and scholars.

Erdener Kaynak
Hummelstown, Pennsylvania

Preface

This book is for those who do or intend to do international business. It emphasizes the informative and practical implementation of such business. The book is designed to inform succinctly about global trends, different regions and their consumer cultures and business customs, methods of entry, and global strategies. It also emphasizes the relatively new concept of global marketing: world-class products marketed to global segments that overarch national boundaries. Lastly, it discusses the future in relation to international business opportunities and how to capitalize on them through strategic management, and comments on the important vehicle of countertrade.

The focus of the book is understanding international influences that affect international business, and relevant aspects of the world environment. These aspects are economic, physical, sociocultural, political, legal, and technological, and include the cultures of foreign business organizations. It is necessary that one learns about the various national controls on international trade, international business opportunities, sources of information, and knowledgeable organizations and people. It is also useful to know the favored methods of entry for doing business in different countries. Moreover, international business managers are helped by the identification of past areas of conflict abroad, and the mechanism and mechanics of the resolution of such conflicts. One can meaningfully profit from the study of corporate strategy and planning adopted in international business and the organization systems that are in vogue. Finally, successful management requires information about future international business opportunities and scenarios of possible divergences.

The chapters in this informative book basically follow the above pattern. The first chapter gives a global overview, the epilogue deals with the future, and each other chapter is about one country or region. The coverage of the book is global. However, global does not mean that the 170 countries in this world are each covered. Many are small and can be subsumed within the study of a region. The attempt has been to provide a selection that is global in scope. The criteria for selection has been threefold:

— importance of nation or region
— a range which gives global coverage
— the availability of sufficient information about a nation/region to give a meaningful picture

The chapters on the Americas deal with the United States, Central America, and the Andean Group comprising Bolivia, Chile, Colombia, Ecuador, and Peru. Western Europe chapters include Great Britain and West Germany. Reference to East Germany and chapters on Hungary, Poland, and Romania are the Eastern Europe representatives. The Arab Middle East is covered as a region. There are also separate chapters on Egypt, Israel, and Turkey. Asia has four entries: China, Japan, and Singapore with its ASEAN Group relations: Indonesia, Malaysia, Philippines, and Thailand.

Each chapter is written by an expert in the field who has been involved in international business in that area. The purpose of each chapter is to enable effective performance in the international business arena. An integrated system view of the country or region and how international business managers can obtain success in that area are provided. The content of these chapters is not easily found, and nowhere else is it compiled in a collection like this. The expert opinions of the authors add a unique dimension which will be useful to every international business practitioner and reader.

Part 1

An Overview

Chapter 1

Doing International Business: A Global Overview

V. H. (Manek) Kirpalani

The world marketplace is receiving increasing attention from governments and business. Exports have been growing faster than gross world product as the world becomes more interdependant. Products and services from abroad are flooding into most national domestic markets. It is becoming obvious to all businessmen that they have to become more aware, and if necessary take participative action in this tidal wave of foreign commerce and investment.

The international businessman must know the dimensions, structure, and potential of the foreign economies with which he wishes to do business and of the international marketplace. He has to have a clear picture of international trade and the reasons why trade flows between nations occur. Furthermore, it is crucial that he properly understands what is causing change in the world marketplace and in nations. This comprehensive knowledge is essential for the strategy, planning, and commitment of international business effort. It is the basis for optimal performance and choice of foreign markets. Accordingly, this first chapter gives a global overview of doing international business; strategy and management are dealt with after delineating the environment. The chapter starts with international influences affecting nations, then covers the environment for international business, including the important topics of consumer behavior for international business and business behavior. It proceeds to outline international business opportunities and sources of information, and the emphasis then shifts to practical methods of entry into the arena, conflict areas, and ways of resolving such conflicts.

Finally, it explains how effective corporate strategies, planning, organization, and control have resulted in success. So, the international business manager can profit from knowing how others have done such business.

INTERNATIONAL INFLUENCES
AFFECTING NATIONS

These influences emanate from three basic sources: trade, capital flows, and international agreements.

International Trade

About 20% of gross world product (GWP) is internationally traded. Five basic causes are influencing the massive growth in international trade, which is increasing at a trend rate of 7% a year, compared with the world economy's growth rate at about half this pace. These causes are likely to maintain the continued growth of world trade. The five basic causes are outlined without order of priority because they are interlinked: (a) Government decisionmakers and multinational corporations (MNCs) realize that international trade based on comparative advantage is a major stimulant to economic growth. (b) The technological improvement in the efficiency of production processes often results in an economic output level that cannot be absorbed by single nation markets. (c) Production is internationalized on a worldwide scale. (d) Global shopping center markets for many products have grown since rising affluence has brought relatively similar standards of living across large parts of the world economy. (e) Large MNCs have proliferated whose revenues are greater than the economies of most countries, and whose cash flow is far higher than most governmental budgets.

The automobile industry can be used to illustrate. In the context of what has been stated above, it is interesting to note that General Motors (GM) has been involved in international business since the corporation's formation in 1908. By 1920 GM had successfully entered the competitive European auto market. Mass production techniques in the U.S. had lowered costs compared to the European manufacturers' low volume and high unit costs. Today, GM operates worldwide with many auto and component plants manufacturing abroad. Not only has it internationalized its production, but a worldcar has been developed. This auto, using standard components, is being sold in many countries.[1] Thus GM, a present-day giant MNC whose annual revenues of close to $120 billion are larger than the Gross National Product (GNP) of all but 15 countries in the world, has taken advantage of the global shopping center and technological efficiency of its production processes. Where advantageous, it has formed joint ventures, for example, with Toyota in the U.S. for small car development expertise. Furthermore, it has internationalized its production and, driven by the search for comparative advantage, has sought out cheaper cost locations. Many small companies have also globalized their operations. Pierre Cardin has clothes made of his design in countries like Hong Kong and India where manufacturing is cheaper. He now puts his name on many other products, such as belts, ties, and shoes. His products are marketed in all countries of the Western world and quite a few other relatively affluent lands.

Trading Patterns

World trading patterns have changed considerably in the past 20 years. In 1970 there was nearly twice as much trans-Atlantic as trans-Pacific trade. Today it is about the same. The major cause of this shift is the impact of U.S. imports. The U.S. has become a huge importer, gobbling up 63% of the growth of world imports in the mid 1980s, with the rest being relatively equally shared between Western Europe, Southeast Asia, Japan, and others. Japan and Southeast Asia have been the main beneficiaries. In the mid-1970s the U.S. took only 23% of world import growth, with 50% being taken by Western Europe.[2]

Japan and West Germany vie as the world's largest exporters of manufactured goods. Some 50% of West German exports go to the Common Market, whereas Japan seeks outlets everywhere. But the Western World is not about to stop Japan, which has become a world lender of a size unparalleled since Britain in the nineteenth century and America in 1920-1982. Much of this lending is to the

U.S. which has a huge trade deficit that in 1987 amounted to about $150 billion.

The U.S. has been going into external trade debt faster than any other major industrialized country has ever done before. A fall in the value of the dollar is not an answer. The dollar has dropped by more than 40% against the Deutsch Mark and the Yen since its peak in February, 1985. But Europe and Japan account for only 40% of U.S. trade and little more than half its trade deficit. Almost all the balance of the latter comes from four Asian newly industrializing countries (NICs), Canada, and Latin America. The currencies of the NICs and Canada are basically unchanged against the dollar, but those of Mexico and others in Latin America have sharply devalued by more than enough to compensate for the dollar's fall.

The U.S. trade deficit may well persist, although on a smaller scale, into the 1990s. It may not need to vanish if the U.S. can maintain a surplus on services trade and continue to attract a flow of foreign capital. The U.S. government seems to recognize that a long-term global solution must be found. Parties to the General Agreement on Tariffs and Trade (GATT) are pledged to bring services within their purview. This is an important step that will slowly lead to reduction of barriers to the international flow of services. This is vital for the Western industrialized world where manufacturing now accounts for only about a quarter of all jobs. This is also vital for the less developed countries (LDCs) which, by and large, are entering the manufacturing phase and lack the support of sophisticated services, particularly technology, finance, and transportation.

The world's largest trader is the Common Market. Table 1 is broadly descriptive of who trades with whom, and Table 2 shows merchandise exports and imports by major trading region/country. It should be realized that the Common Market trade has expanded precisely because it is a Common Market; the more it becomes one market without barriers, the more its trade is likely to increase. Netherlands trade is so high precisely because Rotterdam is the largest port in Europe and much of Europe's imports and exports flow through it. As these products cross Netherlands boundaries they are registered as imports and exports. The same is true for Belgium with its major port, Antwerp.

Table 1-1 1986: Who Markets to Whom (Percentages of World Exports = 100)

Exports ──▶ To From	Industrial Countries	OPEC	Other Third World	Soviet Bloc & China	Total
Industrial Countries	53%	4	8	3	68
OPEC	4	-	3	-	7
Other Third World	8	1	4	2	15
Soviet Bloc & China	3	-	2	5	10
World	68	5	17	10	100%

Source: Adapted from data in **U.N. Statistical Yearbooks, U.N. Monthly Bulletin of Statistics** (various issues).

Trade in Services

The global market for services is difficult to measure. It has been estimated that one-quarter of world trade is made up of services and is therefore "invisible."[3] Recently some 26% of this was receipts from an amalgam of services, the principal of which was probably technology transfer, 32% from international banking and charges on transfers of investment income, 19% from tourism, and 23% from transport.

Services trade is dominated by the industrial countries that regularly run a large surplus. This is probably underreported due to lack of adequate statistics, although OPEC and the LDCs show big deficits.

Opportunities for the international transfer of technology/skills are continuously escalating as countries become richer and desire ever more economic growth. Global research and development (R & D) is highly unbalanced. Just six countries, the U.S., U.K., France, Japan, U.S.S.R., and West Germany, account for nearly 85% of all R & D spending. Relatively recently, GM and IBM each spent more on R & D than India, Spain, and South Korea com-

Table 1-2: World Trade by Regions and Selected Countries (1986: Billion Dollars)

Regions	Exports (f.o.b.)	Imports (c.i.f.)
World	2166	2250
Industrial Countries	1463	1529
Oil Exporters	118	93
Non-Oil LDCs:	371	416
Centrally Planned Economies: U.S.S.R. & Europe	184	172
Centrally Planned Economies: Asia	30	40

Selected Countries		
U.S.	217	387
West Germany	243	191
Japan	210	128
France	124	129
U.K.	107	126
Italy	98	99
U.S.S.R.	90	78
Canada	90	85
Netherlands	79	75
Belgium	69	69
Sweden	37	33
Switzerland	37	41
South Korea	35	32
Hong Kong	35	35
China	30	40
Brazil	22	16
Singapore	22	26
Saudi Arabia	20	25
South Africa	18	13
Indonesia	15	11
Nigeria	13	9
Poland	12	12
Iran	7	11
Kuwait	7	6
India	6	8

Source: **U.N. Monthly Bulletin of Statistics** (various issues), **IMF International Financial Statistics** (various issues).

bined. The industrialized countries generate 90% of the new technology in the world and 90% of this is traded among these countries themselves.[4] A high proportion of that trade occurs within the intracompany network of MNCs. Expertise has been one of the fastest growing items within the world marketplace and this will continue. Although LDCs account for only 10% of all technology trade, virtually all of that is imported. LDCs increasingly recognize that the critical resource for the productive utilization of land, labor, and capital is knowledge. Moreover, technology/skills are essential catalysts during the change of traditionally static societies into those capable of rapid growth. North-South technology transfer is vital to their growth and, from an international businessman's viewpoint, vital to peaceful coexistence.

International trade in financial services is escalating. Much of the OPEC surplus on current account went into the Eurocurrency markets; national currencies deposited outside their own borders. Many unidentified funds also found their way into Eurocurrency markets as well. Almost every major bank in the world is an international bank. Today, half of the Bank of America's deposits are foreign, as are 75% of Citicorp's. In the 1980s, the main international banks had foreign deposits of over $1,000 billion, representing roughly half of world export revenues today. The Eurocurrency market is unregulated and a 2-3% profit on $1,000 billion translates into $20-$30 billion in earnings, but the market is overlent. Only 20 LDCs account for more than 80% of Eurocurrency borrowing and five of these for over 40%. Thus international banks have unhealthily concentrated loan portfolios, and some borrowers have stretched their debt-servicing facilities to the limit. International businessmen in Brazil, for example, should know that Brazil's oil imports and interest payments cost over 65% of its export earnings.[5]

Two polarized scenarios pinpoint the present dilemma. In the first, lending dwindles with concomitant defaults. The LDCs will buy less goods from the industrialized countries and the rich countries will stagnate. In the second, politicians in rich countries, unwilling to impose austerity, will encourage their banks to provide plenty of liquidity both at home and to the LDCs. The resulting inflation, with its attendant disruptions, will end up paralyzing the international capital flows upon which everybody's trade and prosperity depend. The way out is to strengthen the International Monetary Fund (IMF) and the International Bank for Reconstruction and Development (World Bank), and many nations will have to accept a bearable slowdown in the growth rate of their economies while money supply is brought under control. The emphasis must be on competition and productivity. International businessmen must understand the structure of the evolving international financial system and the changes being proposed in order to incorporate risk probabilities into their planning.

Tourism is the fastest growing industry in the world; annual growth has averaged 15% over the last two decades. Some 250 million people, over 6% of the world's population, cross international frontiers every year. Many look for familiar products – a Colgate user would like to buy Colgate toothpaste even when abroad. Also, the tourist tends to be more of a free spender; tourists spend over $100 billion, some 1% of GWP. Alert international businessmen should monitor tourist trends to decide how best to cater to this rapidly growing group of consumers.

For several countries, tourism is an extremely important foreign exchange earner. In Spain, for example, it has made up a quarter of all export revenues. Also, the tourist business is labor intensive: close to 3% of France's labor force is directly employed in it. Proximity has led to two-thirds of the world's tourists traveling within Western Europe and 80% of these are West Europeans. Another large group is in North America, where the bulk of tourism emanates from the cross traffic at the U.S.-Canada and U.S.-Mexico borders. Rapid growth of tourism should increase the market share of LDCs from the present meager 7%. As traditional resorts get more crowded, exotic places like the Seychelles, Bali, and Goa will beckon wealthier tourists. There is next to no possibility of tourism slowing down. International business growth, affluence, globe-spanning communications technology which introduces the people of the world to the world, and the growing number of people living abroad all help to foster tourism. At this stage, even if the growth rate of business travel slows down because of improved telephone and computer communications technology, the rate of vacation travel is rising so fast that the overall growth will probably continue unabated.

International transportation services are a function of world trade, the growth rate of which is unlikely to diminish. But in to-day's world, international businessmen often face uncertain demand and rapidly changing trade patterns as a result of political developments, raw material shortages, or advances in technology. The increased uncertainty has hastened the trend toward decentralized warehousing, smaller multipurpose carriers, and containerization. Here, the industrialized world leads. Much of the world's international trade involves shipping. Rail and road transportation play a major role, primarily within Western Europe, North America, and the COMECON* region. But between continents and in many regions, shipping is the major means of international transportation. The bulk of the primary products and fuels trade in the international marketplace travels by ship, as does a significant proportion of manufactures.

The top 10 shipping nations in terms of tonnage are Liberia, Panama, Greece, Japan, Norway, U.S.S.R., U.K., U.S., France, and Italy. The first three are so-called flags of convenience, where low taxes and low-paid foreign sailors have attracted international shipowners from the other nations, excepting the U.S.S.R., to register their vessels there. A substantial amount of foreign exchange is earned by these nations from shipping. The LDC share in seaborne trade for goods reaching or leaving their ports is about 4%, although they generate about one-third of the world's bulk cargo. The U.S.S.R. fleet of about 2,500 merchant ships has been invading both cargo and cruise markets, underbidding competitors by 40% or more, especially the liner conferences which are legally accepted price-fixing cartels. Today the Russians have 42% of the British cruise market, carry 80% of France's imported oil, and have 10% of the cargo trade between Japan, Australia, and New Zealand. They underbid because they are state insured, fueled by cheap domestic oil, and manned by low-paid sailors. They earn more than $2 billion hard currency for the U.S.S.R. annually.[6] Passenger air carriage is dominated by the Western World, as is air-

---

*COMECON is the Council of Mutual Economic Cooperation, that is, the East European countries controlled by the U.S.S.R. This region is sometimes also called CMEA, or Council for Mutual Economic Assistance.

freight cargo. The latter is still small but growing rapidly. Minimization of total physical distribution system costs which include transportation plus storage and the efficiencies of just-in-time inventory are behind the aircargo boom.

NATIONAL ECONOMIC AND PHYSICAL STRUCTURE

International business is fueled by the economic differences between nations. These differences are based on the physical resources of nations, levels of human population, and the creativity and skills of their peoples. These differences have caused economies to evolve at varying speeds. For the international businessman it is important to know those differences because they govern both present and potential growth of national markets. This section will first outline the economic differences and then focus on the physical differences.

Today's world has over 4.5 billion people and a GWP of over $16 trillion. Figures 1 and 2 depict the size of regional population and GNP, respectively.

Economic Structure

The world economic structure is distributed unevenly. About 30% of gross world product is concentrated in North America: the U.S. and Canada. Another 25% is concentrated in Western Europe. An additional 20% is roughly evenly divided between the U.S.S.R. and Japan. The rest of the world shares the remainder. Of this remainder, the large economies in order of size are China, India, Brazil, and Nigeria. There are also a number of NICs, Singapore, Hong Kong, South Korea, Taiwan, and Malaysia, that are relatively affluent on a per capita basis. Gross national products are important for gauging the size of industrial markets. But international businessmen are also greatly interested in per capita income as this indicates consumer buying power. The average level of such income is documented in Table 3.

Some caveats are in order. The figures above are in nominal dollars, using current exchange rates to convert estimates of GNP in

Figure 1-1 Estimated Percentages of World 1987 Population (4.9 Billion)

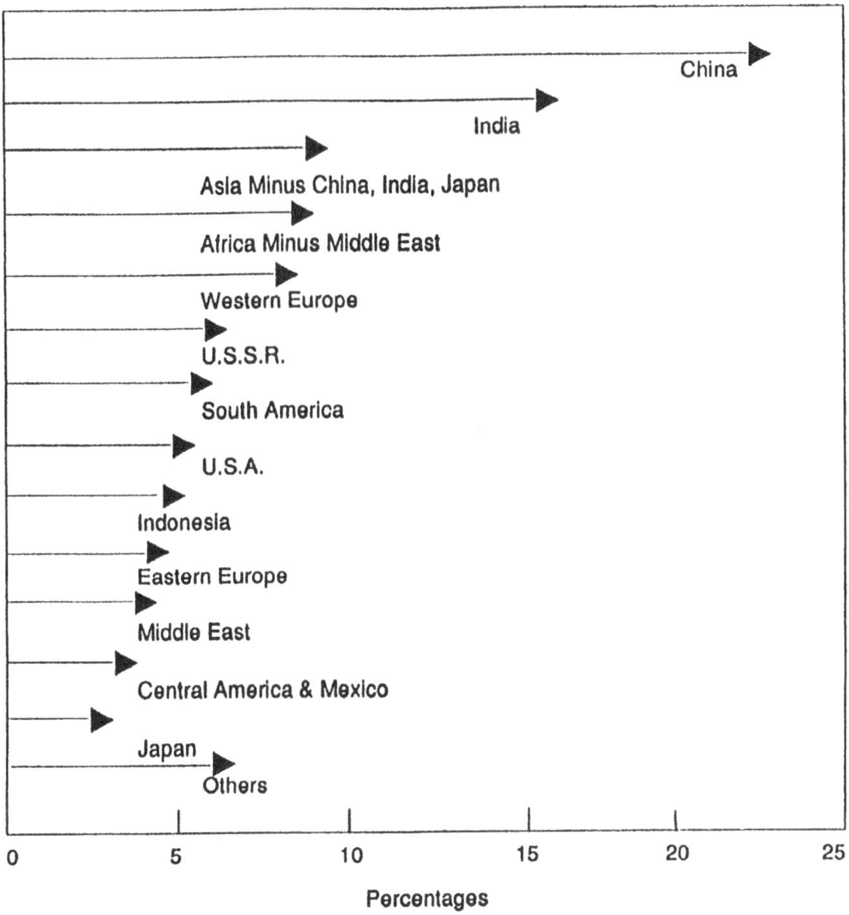

China

India

Asia Minus China, India, Japan

Africa Minus Middle East

Western Europe

U.S.S.R.

South America

U.S.A.

Indonesia

Eastern Europe

Middle East

Central America & Mexico

Japan

Others

| 0 | 5 | 10 | 15 | 20 | 25 |

Percentages

Source: **U.N. Monthly bulletin of Statistics** (various issues).

local currencies to dollars. The exchange rates reflect internationally traded goods and services; they do not take into account the prices of local goods and services such as housing, education, and medicine, which are not exported or imported. Thus, a difficult but more realistic comparison would be on the basis of purchasing power parities or direct real product comparisons of what currency

Figure 1-2 Estimated Percentages of 1986 Gross World Product ($12 Trillion at Market Prices)

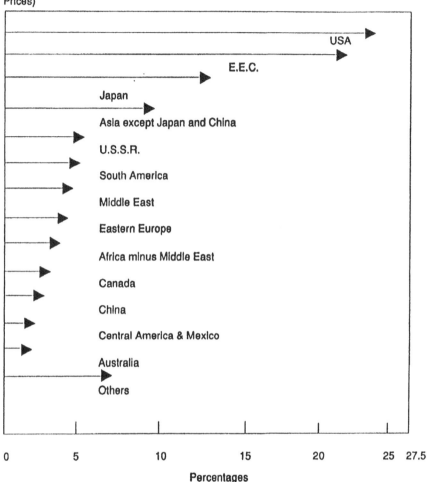

Source: U.N. Yearbook of National Accounts and U.N. Monthly bulletin of Statistics
(various issues).

units buy in the different countries. Such a comparison would tend to lift the real income of the poorer country versus the richer since in a poor country the costs of shelter and of the simpler services usually are cheaper. The Hudson Institute real per capita gross product estimates show that the estimate for the poorer countries

Table 1-3　Per Capital Gross Domestic Product (GDP) by Regions and Selected
Countries

(1985: Dollars) Regions	Per Capita GDP $
World	2570
Market Economies	3310
Developed Countries	11000
Developing Countries	870
Centrally Planned Economies	800
North America	16350
E.E.C.	8310
Africa	690
Latin America	1790
Middle East	2970
Asia, East and South-East excluding Japan	380
Eastern Europe	2420

Selected Countries

U.S.	16636
Switzerland	14555
Canada	13698
Sweden	12003
Japan	10975
Kuwait	10902
West Germany	10226
France	9343
Netherlands	8620
U.K.	8069
Belgium	7985
Saudi Arabia	6858
Singapore	6843
Italy	6259
Hong Kong	6162
Israel	5776
Iran	3766
Iraq	2942
South Korea	2089
South Africa	1693
Brazil	1673
Nigeria	625
Indonesia	511
India	259
China	227

should be tripled compared to the nominal, and that of the middle income countries increased by 50%.[7]

The Unrecorded Economy

In today's world there is an important undercurrent to these statistics. Income arises out of the parallel economy, at times referred to as the underground economy or the "black market" economy. Many have participated in this at some time, either as a customer who pays the plumber in cash, or as a practitioner who does not report some income to the taxman.

In the West, the spirit of free enterprise does not always mesh with government revenue demands. The U.S. Internal Revenue Service reported recently that almost half of 50,000 independent contractors checked had reported not one cent of earnings for income tax and over 60% had paid no social security taxes.[8] Another reported find is that there are 8 to 10 million illegal immigrants in the U.S., many from Mexico. Presumably, some of the income and output of these people is not reported. The underground economy appears to be on the rise in Western Europe due to the larger numbers of self-employed and unemployed. A recent British study concludes that the underground economy there is between 3-5% of GNP, in the U.S. it is thought to be 10-15%, in West Germany 10%, and Italy's may be as high as 30%.[9] Generally, one would expect the underground economy to flourish in the European Economic Community (EEC), where unrestricted travel across national boundaries is the norm. In the LDCs, which have relatively limited statistical systems and where the majority of the people are engaged in agriculture, the underground economy must be extensive. Besides, in price-controlled economies and/or scarcity economies, which predominate in LDCs, there are obvious rewards for producing and marketing goods off-the-record. In India and Kenya it has been estimated that about 30% of the economy is unrecorded. Finally, significant economic activity in some nations comes from the output of illegal goods and services; drugs and prostitution are the most typical.

International businessmen are also initially interested in the distribution of income in order to gauge the size of specific product markets. In most of the developed, industrialized economies the bulk of the distribution is within a relatively narrow band. These economies are built on mass consumption. In contrast, in LDCs the distribution resembles a pyramid with a few very rich people at the top and the majority of the people below the poverty line. In most LDCs the development consists of urban port cities with an agricultural hinterland where most of the population lives barely inside the monetary economy. But with the growth of bureaucracy and industry the middle-classes are growing – the estimate for India is 70 million people. This is creating noticeable demand for consumer durables.

National Resources and Skills

Population and income do not provide sufficient information for international business planners to assess a country's growth potential. It is also necessary for them to consider resources and skills. Utilizing all of these variables, the international market can be divided usefully into four sectors: the industrial countries, the OPEC countries, other LDCs that are rich in resources but poor in skills, and the remainder of the Third World which is poor in both resources and skills. These sectors have very different foreign exchange capabilities and varying needs for particular product categories.

Sector A, the industrial countries, can be subdivided into two groups: the resource rich-skill rich and resource poor-skill rich.[10] The U.S., Canada, Sweden, and West Germany – where high incomes are buttressed by comparatively good economic prospects based on possession of raw materials and manufacturing strength – are in the top group of the "rich-rich." Many other industrial countries may be called the "poor-rich," although the extension of coastal state jurisdiction to 200 nautical miles from shore has given ownership of potentially extensive ocean resources to a number of them, including Japan.

Sector B comprises the OPEC countries. This sector is oil rich-skill poor but because of foreign exchange earning possibilities has the probability of continued rapid economic growth in a number of its member countries. Their real gross domestic product (GDP) grew at about 9.5% a year in the 1970s but mismanagement has slowed growth in the 1980s. Sector C consists of perhaps 30 middle-income countries that are rich in commodities other than oil and/or have a reasonable manufacturing base. These include most Mediterranean countries, a few Soviet satellites, the NICs, some other Southeast Asian countries, and some South American countries. Their annual average GDP growth rate in the last decade was about 6.25%. Sector D consists of the world's poorer lands. These low-income countries range from tiny Bhutan and Togo to gigantic India, Pakistan, and Indonesia. Their average growth rate is only 4% and they are burdened with rapidly increasing populations. It should be noted, however, that India and Indonesia, among others, gain potential resources by the 200 nautical miles ownership agreement.

In educational terms, the spread of skills is worldwide but depth only exists in the industrialized countries; large numbers of skilled people also exist in countries with historical cultures and huge populations like India and China. The U.S.S.R. maintains skill levels through planned educational systems. For international businessmen it is important to know where skills are available and to judge the potential economic growth of nations. In general, a combination of skills and physical resources are necessary for economic growth to occur.

The pattern of world economic activity since the commencement of the industrial revolution has been that major economic activity is centered in the industrialized nations. The LDCs were organized by the West through empires into cash crop producers whose output flowed to industrial nations for processing, consumption, and export of finished products. However, in recent years LDCs have become independent, their markets offer inviting opportunities for international businessmen, and there has been a shift to the internationalization of production as MNCs seek lower cost manufacturing locations for labor intensive operations. Concurrently LDCs are attempting to add value to their primary products on site. The world structure, therefore, is changing. The leading industrialized nations are creating a semi-global market among themselves. They are also developing knowledge centers that can provide technology at the same time they are sending products for further processing, and contracting out component manufacture to LDCs. The LDCs are basically entering the industrial age and their markets are expanding. Thus, it is important for international businessmen to know how to function effectively in the world cultural topography.

CULTURAL ENVIRONMENT

How can one best study world cultures? The chapters on individual countries provide details, but here a broader sweep is made based on religions, since these have had and continue to have a powerful effect on cultures. Consumer and business cultures are discussed. Then an overview of major trends that are permeating the global shopping center are outlined.

Religions

Religious beliefs and values affect culture through architecture, art, and music, among other things. The international businessman's planning is affected directly by different cultures in terms of the product that must be provided and the services that should be offered. Moreover, these facets of culture combine with others to influence attitudes toward time, space, the meaning and tone of words, nonverbal communications, written and verbal contracts, and attitudes toward friendships. It is only in some societies, notably the Western, industrialized, urbanized, commercialized world, that religion has become a relatively subordinate matter in the life of many people.

Christianity and Islam today claim an estimated 40% of the world's population as their followers. There are three main branches of Christianity: Protestantism, which prevails in the West, Australia, and South Africa; Roman Catholicism, which prevails in Southern Europe, Central and South America, and in the Philippines; and Eastern Orthodoxy, which prevails in Russia, parts of Eastern Europe, and Ethiopia. The Christian faith has always been characterized by aggressive proselytism by its missionaries.

Islam dominates Northern Africa and Southwestern Asia, and it extends slightly into the Soviet Union. In many ways the precepts of Islam constituted a revision and embellishment of Judaic and

Christian beliefs and traditions. Although Jesus is acknowledged as a prophet, Mohammed is considered the ultimate prophet. There is but one all-powerful God. What is earthly and worldly is profane, and only Allah is pure. This is translated through repeated expressions of the basic creed, frequent prayer, a month of daytime fasting, alms giving, and at least one pilgrimage to Mecca in Saudi Arabia. Alcohol, smoking, and gambling are frowned upon. Ultimately, the Arab empire extended from Morocco to India, from Turkey to Ethiopia.

Hinduism is primarily the religion of India, although the faith also extends into Nepal, Bangladesh, Burma, and Sri Lanka. Hinduism is the oldest of the major religions. The fundamental doctrine of the faith is Karma, which involves the concept of the transmigration of the soul. All beings are in a hierarchy and all have souls. The principle of reincarnation is a cornerstone of the religion. Karma expresses the notion that one moves upward or downward in the next life according to one's behavior in the present. Hinduism's doctrines are closely related to the caste system, for castes themselves are steps on the universal ladder. The system, however, locks people in this life into social classes, reducing mobility. Like Islam, the Hindu religion is a way of life. India is an agricultural land. The cow pulls the plow and gives milk and other fats for sustenance, and, therefore, Hindu practice decrees that the cow not be killed, beef not be eaten. For health reasons, Islam and Judaism decree that the pig is not to be eaten.

Another religion that had its source in India, Buddhism, is now a minority faith in that country, but is still strong in Southeast Asia, China, and Japan. Buddhism was founded by Prince Siddharta as a reaction to the less desirable features of Hinduism. The Prince, known as Gautama Buddha, renounced his fortune and sought salvation through meditation and teaching. He preached that salvation could be attained by anyone no matter what his or her caste. Enlightenment would come to a person through self-knowledge, the elimination of consciousness and desire, the principle of complete honesty, and the determination not to hurt another person or animal.

The Chinese religions are a mixture of Confucianism, Taoism, and Buddhism, with Confucianism dominant. Confucius (551-479

B.C.) and his followers constructed a blueprint for Chinese civilization in almost every field, including philosophy, government, and education. Confucius postulated that the meaning of life lies in the present and that service to one's fellows should supersede service to spirits. The main precept of Taoism is that people should learn to live in harmony with nature, viewing themselves as but insignificant elements in the great universal order. Confucianism dominated with its emphasis on the present. It became the state ethic, as worship of and obedience to the state leader constitute central elements of Confucianism.

Shintoism prevails in Japan. It is a national religion, unifying state and faith, which emphasizes emperor worship, a reverence for nature, and a strong feeling for land and nation. Religion and government are indivisible. Since Japan's defeat in World War II, Shintoism is no longer the official state religion, and the emperor's divine descent doctrine has been rejected. However, the basic Shinto influence prevails, sustaining the Japanese in their objectives of rejecting external domination and building up their national power.

Judaism has some 14 million followers. Despite this relatively small number, Judaism has the honor of being the oldest major religion of the Western world. Through history, the Jews have been persecuted but the strong faith in their one God and their determination not to be assimilated by other cultures culminated in the establishment of Israel in 1948. The Jews are spread throughout the world, with the greatest concentration in North America and in Israel.

Cultural Facets and Selected Business Practices

The international businessman must be alert to cultural influences and idiosyncracies. These affect the product configurations and the whole process of negotiations in the international marketplace. Furthermore, for MNCs, it is important for head office people to know how to handle employees of different cultures who are working with and for them. Here, the discussion will center on certain points related to business practices.

Time Consciousness

International businessmen should be aware of the differing sense of time in various cultures. In the Christian/Protestant Western world, time is very important. The people believe in achievement in this life. Efficiency is important for this achievement and for economic growth. Moreover, services are expensive so paid work, the enjoyment of leisure, and the do-it-yourself jobs that most people must attend to create enormous demands on time. People are annoyed if they are kept waiting for appointments and in business discussions, one tries to make one's point quickly, efficiently, and neatly.

In the Hindu culture, the belief in reincarnation creates the thinking that time, although valuable, is not in such short supply, and that it is important to make a right decision rather than a fast one.

Latin American and Arab cultures have only recently evolved from an agricultural society in which time had little meaning. In these cultures and those in similar stages of economic development, much time is spent in an idle but pleasant way.

The Japanese have a different attitude. They are very precise people, and this also applies to their concept of time. A meeting is meant to start exactly at the appointed time, but the meeting may take twice as long as in North America. This is because there is a long sequence of formal pleasantries, which includes the Japanese questioning on various general subjects, such as the state of the foreigner's economy, about which they feel the foreigner should be knowledgeable. This is actually a testing period during which the Japanese assess the foreigner.

The Chinese are also prompt about business engagements but, like the Japanese, they want to assess the foreign marketer before closing the deal. They and the Japanese seem to have found out that North American impatience is a weakness on which they can play. They obtain a better agreement if they can make the North American wait long enough.

Contracts and Negotiations

The Western world in general attaches much importance to written contracts. To the Westerner, the contract is a clear statement of the obligations and considerations of the contracting parties, and it is employed as a basis for minimizing misunderstandings and enforcing compliance. In Latin America, the written contract is viewed more as an expression of intent at the time the agreement was made, thus its applicability and value may deteriorate over time. The Latin Americans seem to place much more emphasis on friendship for assurance that an agreement will be kept, rather than on a written contract. In the Arab world, also, friendship dominates over reliance on written contracts. In many cultures, personal gift giving is part of the negotiation process. A study has found that U.S. executives find it difficult to establish rapport through gifts or through the flattery of asking advice and opinion.[11] The need for clearly understanding communications is obviously fundamental.

Negotiating within a complex culture like Malaysia, the problem is further complicated. By government regulations, a significant percentage of equity must be in Malay hands. However, the real driving force behind the Malay owners are still the Chinese administrators. In negotiation one always directs questions to the Malay owner. To do otherwise would be to cause the Malay to lose face and risk loss of the order. But the Chinese administrators who work for the Malays really decide who gets the order. Chinese businessmen are known to be among the toughest bargainers because they are clever and have a great capacity for remembering details.

The Japanese tend to see a contract as binding only as long as the conditions under which the contract is signed do not change, rendering the contract unfair. There are numerous instances in which the Japanese have insisted that written contracts be renegotiated in view of changed conditions. Attention to detail is essential when negotiating with the Japanese, for they are an extremely well-educated and precise people. It is also important to remember that they generally come in a group. It should be noted that in Japanese management, advancement often takes place by seniority and older members of a company may at times be moved to head a department of which they know very little. Thus, the people to be convinced are those in the group who have expertise on the subject. The development of personal rapport and the use of pros and cons when presenting arguments may be quite effective in Japan, whereas power plays are generally unacceptable because one party may lose face.[12]

Words, Familiarity, and Place

The way words are used differs across cultures. In Western culture, people generally say what they mean and mean what they say. For people in Japan, however, one must develop a feel for when "Yes" means affirmative and when "Yes" means they would like to. In North America it is common in business dealings to be on a first name basis from the first meeting of the individuals. Most other cultures would consider such familiarity presumptuous and rude. In most traditional and hierarchical cultures one must continue to call a person by his last name until the other person asks that the relationship be on a first name basis.

The place where it is appropriate to discuss business is also important. In Western culture business can be discussed anywhere, in an office or in a restaurant. In almost any other culture in the world, business is discussed mainly in business settings. It is considered an invasion of one's privacy and one's leisure time to discuss business in social settings.

Organizational Culture

Western Civilization, with its prevalent philosophy of individualism and achievement in the present, has spawned the largest corporations and the most developed infrastructure. The organizational forms are a combination of international, regional, and product division structures. These allow for better communication, more delegation, and a better balance of interest and power. This is the creativity of the industrial culture at its best. At the same time, small business flourishes in the West. A significant amount of total output is the outcome of small business efforts. The dynamism and vitality of small business is a powerful feature of the constantly renewing economic landscape of Western business.

Parallel to this Western scene is the rise of Japanese corporations which today have the same size dimension and vitality. The explanation lies in the combination of its monolith Shinto religion, the island nature of its people, the comparatively limited topography and physical resources, and the traditional culture of a few dominant families who retained their status from warlord times. The continued determination of this nation, where the state/organization/ group is far more important than the individual, is an unmatched marvel of modern times. Decisions are based on consensus. This slows down the decision process, but once decisions are made the implementation process is swift. In contrast, in individualistic societies there is a constant need for motivation and a need to control the focus of individual efforts so that a common goal may be achieved.

In both the Western and Japanese systems the importance of good information for decision-making is well recognized. In the larger companies computer data and information banks are in place and much marketing research is carried on. Organized information flows link the different parts of the organization. Decision-making is influenced by a two-way flow: bottom-up and top-down.

In LDCs and centrally planned economies, however, marketing and international business data and information are, in general, sketchy. The decision-making patterns are based on a hierarchical structure and tend traditionally to originate from the top down. Decision-making is usually conducted without good data and information. Much reliance is placed on people and their roles, which tends to make the system inaccurate and slows down the response function. It also means that international businessmen must have patience; the time taken to reach agreements will be much longer.

Behind the Iron Curtain and China

International businessmen have to identify the role structure within the organizations they are dealing with and the power distribution. In Communist, centrally planned economies there are two power distribution systems: the administrative hierarchy within every ministerial and business organization, and the key personnel of the ministry/business organization who specifically report to the Communist party. These key personnel do not have a functional role in the organization. Their role is to see that the decisions taken by the personnel within the organization conform to the Communist party guidelines. They report back to the Communist party, thereby exerting power and control over the usual decisionmakers within the organization.

Qualities Helpful to Success

To be successful, the international businessman must possess personality traits that allow accommodation to other cultures. A number of such qualities can be identified. First, the international businessman must accept that others also have the right to do as they please. When we go abroad to do business we are the foreigners and we must conform. The second quality is flexibility. Mannerisms, attitudes, even business approaches and the product itself, may have to be adjusted to the foreign environment. Humility is the third quality needed in dealing abroad. To patronize or to condescend is to invite hostility. Modest terms must be used to describe one's products rather than excessive praise. Sensitivity is essential and sincere curiosity and interest are required to comprehend fully another people and area. The curiosity must be sincere, as insincerity can only be viewed with distrust by people from the other culture. Finally, the international marketer should enjoy working with foreigners.

The international businessman's key to understanding cultural differences lies in the use of systematic research procedures to understand the cultural values of any particular society. The businessman cannot attend to stereotypes or use nationals of a particular foreign country for more than their personal opinion.[13] A few key variables that usually create problems are the cultural differences in time, space, material possessions, friendship patterns, and agreement on a definitive plane. One must also study consumption habits, tasks, and promotion, and the degree of desire for material goods and quality products. Other factors are the preference for foreign versus local products and the we-they attitude.

The problem for international businessmen is to find out the importance of cultural differences and their influence on the business task. To do so, businessmen must be able to analyze the differences between their own culture and others. They must know their own cultural pattern and how it influences their approach. It has been pointed out that the ethnocentric, self-reference criterion, the unconscious use of one's own cultural values, has been the root of most international business problems.[14] The self-reference habit is very difficult to break, especially when one is not consciously aware of its existence. Once broken, however, the international business task is to align one's behavior and attitude to satisfy cultural needs in the foreign country.

Bribery

Where is the fine line between a reasonable act to facilitate business and an immoral payoff? In many cultures, making facilitating payments is a standard, acceptable practice. Americans call these bribes or payoffs. In many Latin American countries the word is *mordilla*, a lyrical adaptation of the word to bribe, or *el solomo*, a payoff. Some Africans call it *dash*, a takeoff on the Portuguese word meaning to give, or *chai*, which is tea in Swahili and Hindi. In the Middle East, India, and Pakistan, *baksheesh* is widely used; this is a Persian word meaning a tip or gratuity given by a superior. The Germans call it *schimergeld*, grease money; the French refer to it as *pot-de-vin*, a jug of wine. The Italians call it *bustarella*, a little envelope. The Japanese word is *wairo*, but corruption is *kuroi kiri*, a black mist.

A Fact of Life

Bribery is a fact of international marketing life in deals for large projects in industries that are highly competitive where it is easy to justify supplier selection for a variety of different reasons. Such conditions are present in the international marketing of telecommunications, aircraft, heavy industrial or drilling equipment, and in bidding for large construction programs. Actually, commercial corruption of government and business is looked upon as acceptable in many cultures. Many business people outside the U.S. practice it, if necessary, when doing international marketing. The West European countries either condone bribery or look the other way. Such expenses are tax deductible up to a certain amount in West Germany.

Italy passed a law in 1980 stating that payments to foreign officials to get business are perfectly legal for Italian companies. France has no law regarding foreign bribery. In Japan, paying off foreign officials to secure business is regarded as normal practice.[15]

Such payments put U.S. MNCs in a moral bind. By concealing payments abroad, are U.S. MNCs violating the Securities and Exchange Commission's (SEC) disclosure regulations? Not surprisingly, U.S. MNCs would like to see self-policing and self-regulation rather than federal investigations and interference. The concept of ethical relativism, or relating any decision about right and wrong to the specific situation at hand, seems appealing in today's context.

In traditional terms, if either the end, the means, the motive, or the foreseeable consequences is wrong, the entire action is immoral. For instance, an American shirt manufacturer in a poor village in Puerto Rico brings a higher standard of living to the locals by providing work in a new factory. Although the firm is producing a quality shirt at a price the middle classes can afford, it must also pay a kickback to local government officials in order to operate. Even though the motive, the ends, and the foreseeable consequences are good, the means involve an immoral act. Therefore, by the traditional system defined above, the manufacturer's action could be considered immoral, but the situationist might well say that the kickback was right, good, and moral.[16]

No other event in the area of international marketing drew more attention in the late 1970s and early 1980s than questionable payments to generate overseas sales. These payments led to a variety of charges against monarchs and politicians around the world, including Prince Bernhard of the Netherlands for his dealings with the Lockheed Corporation, and Prime Minister Tanaka of Japan who was also involved with Lockheed. In the 1970s, Lockheed confessed to paying $202 million in commissions and fees abroad to obtain $3.8 billion in foreign sales. Of that $202 million, $22 million eventually reached officials of foreign governments or airlines.[17] Can one categorize bribes into those that are "permissible" and others? The "permissible" category of bribes, facilitating payments, usually involves small sums of money and perhaps can be ignored. In many countries, such facilitating payments are part of the culture and visitors must live with them to expedite bureaucratic operations and paperwork, and trim the inherent delays. They include the universal tip, or customary payment in appreciation of especially efficient or prompt services rendered. This minor category is not part of the serious concerns about MNC behavior. But in the second category, perhaps one could make the distinction between a bribe and an agent's fees. The good agent is often a necessary liaison between an MNC and a foreign country in which it is doing this operation. By definition, its fees are not considered bribes or kickbacks. It is the additional fees in excess of adequate compensation for the normal commercial services performed that are ethically questionable. Such commissions and political contributions or direct cash disbursements are the categories of bribes that continue to stimulate concern about MNC behavior.

What causes bribery? Among various scholars who have speculated about corruption in LDCs, there is some unanimity about its causes. They mention inadequate salaries paid to public officials, the proliferation of bureaucratic controls and regulations, and strong loyalties among public officials toward their particular groups. These groups include their extended families, political parties, and the relevant linguistic community. The social punishment for having neglected one's responsibilities to the particular group is feared more than the possibility of suffering legal punishment for violating a law.[18]

The Official Response

One response to the bribery question is demonstrated by the U.S., where legislation makes it a possible criminal offense for corporations to bribe public officials overseas. Britain has not passed any such law, nor has France, West Germany, or Japan. Also, in the U.S. the Securities and Exchange Commission is interested from the viewpoint of corporate disclosure and financial information. At the international level, the Organization of Economic Cooperation and Development (OECD) and the United Nations have been developing codes of conduct.

Since the passage of the U.S. Foreign Corrupt Practices Act in 1977, the effects on U.S. MNCs have been twofold. The first involves organizational restructuring. The second is the issue of company actions governing corporate ethical questions. Companies can avoid the bribery regulations in the U.S. by exporting through their foreign subsidiaries in Western Europe where bribery statutes are less stringent. Alternatively, some companies have organized some distributorship arrangements overseas to shield themselves. Boeing, for example, is not selling aircraft directly to the ultimate user in the Middle East. Instead, it sells planes to a distributorship overseas which is an international distribution company. This distributorship is registered in the Netherlands, primarily for tax purposes, but it operates from Geneva. It buys the aircraft from Boeing after obtaining orders for the aircraft in the Middle East. It seems that the Boeing Corporation followed this course of action because the Act was not clear about the involvement of a U.S. firm's foreign subsidiaries.[19] The problem is highlighted in the following example. A company pays a bribe that does not appear to be directly covered by the bribery prohibition, for instance, a bribe made by a foreign subsidiary. The bribe could be recorded in the subsidiary's records accurately or inaccurately. If it is recorded inaccurately by the subsidiary, the U.S. records might then consolidate the inaccuracy. If it is recorded accurately, knowledge of the bribe may be attributed to the U.S. parent.

The congressional objective in passing the act was to bolster the moral image of U.S. MNCs abroad. This may not have been achieved. The effect has been to saddle those companies with restrictions their foreign competitors do not face.[20]

POLITICAL SYSTEMS, LAW, AND NATIONALISM

Although a country may appear appealing, an international businessman must understand that in a nationalistic world, individual governments have the power to allow the businessman to operate or not and to determine the conditions. The usual pattern in a Communist country is to refer all foreign business proposals applicable to its jurisdiction to the state-owned industries. In addition to the main Communist nations, there are the socialist countries, most of them LDCs, which believe that public enterprise is inherently more suitable to their conditions than private enterprise. But, being underdeveloped, these countries have to compromise. They leave whole sectors for local and foreign private development. For example, India is willing to allow private investment in a wide range of industries. There is a third group of nations, which might be termed the free enterprise capitalistic states, which are generally favorable to private enterprise and usually willing to allow considerable foreign investment. Included in this third group of countries are a number of dictatorships. Overall, there is a fairly broad mainstream of business-government relationships in the non-Communist world which encourages free private enterprise, but counterbalances this with overall directions and control from the national government. Of particular interest to international businessmen are the national economic plans of states, special inducements to investments through tax incentives, foreign trade regulations, and direct government investments in certain sectors of the economy.

Nationalism

Citizens of every nation typically have some sense of national identity. This manifests itself in national feelings, pride, and attitudes toward foreign businessmen. These attitudes have two kinds of impact on international firms. The first kind of impact is the effect caused by laws, rules, and regulations that reflect national attitudes.[21] The second impact is emotional, and ranges from kidnapping MNC representatives to regarding cartels as the only sound and rational way to organize and control large enterprise.

A study of attitudes is relevant. If the general Mexican trend is toward nationalization and socialism, one international business decision might be made. On the other hand, if it is thought that Mexico will mature toward the political system of the developed, Western, private-property democracies, quite another will be endorsed. The French strongly believe that they should be responsible for their own national defense forces, which implies that as much of defense material as possible should be manufactured by French firms. Thus, rarely does a foreign-owned firm in France make any serious effort to market purely defense material to the French government.

How do international businessmen assess the influence of nationalism? First, they study political and nationalist facts about the relevant countries, including the kind and stability of the political system, and the importance of government's national economy planning and the control system for private sector business. In particular, they must look at the controls on foreign business and on direct foreign investment. There is also the question of the overall degree of support given by the government to the free market. Only after this kind of study can it be determined whether the opportunity is worth the cost imposed by the constraints on operating abilities.[22]

When examining centrally planned economies, two sets of restriction are important to consider. The first includes restrictions on trade as established by the exporting country, such as the restrictions embodied in the U.S. Trading with the Enemy Act. The second includes the restrictions by the importing country. Those restrictions will necessitate dealing with a government department and coping with import policy as an appendage of a long-term plan. Other restrictions are currency control and the insistence on bilateral agreements.

Assessment of Political Risk and Conflict Resolution

How does one assess political risk? Two studies that covered 284 takeovers of U.S. overseas investments in LDCs indicate that past patterns were not a very good guide.[23] Further, they showed that large numbers of takeovers occurred in only a few countries. Thus, in other countries there was no pattern to serve as a guide. One could ascertain the opinions of local leaders and other people who may influence political events that affect foreign business and try to obtain the opinions of embassy officials and persons who are active in the business sector, including foreign business people who have been working in the host country for some time. Another suggested method is to assess the level of frustration or the difference between the level of aspiration and the level of expectations in the country. The premise is that a high level of frustration will lead to future measures, including perhaps expropriation, against foreign investment. Clearly, one must evaluate this risk within the combined contexts of regional and economic national development. The role of MNCs in LDCs may be transitory, and expropriations and divestments can always occur.[24] The basic point is that one must inquire and assess rather than cling to subjective misconceptions about political risk.[25]

Some key questions about the host government that need to be asked are: Where does power lie? How many people are involved in the control of power? What is the attitude of oppositions who may become the future government?

With reference to the specific product line that an MNC may be thinking of manufacturing, the following questions require consideration: Is the product necessary from an economic viewpoint? Is it essential to agriculture? Does it affect defense capability? Which other industries depend upon these products? Is there competition from small-scale local industry? Does the product use slack local inputs or will manufacture induce a net drain on foreign exchange reserves? And will production volume be so large as to give the foreign company a new monopoly position?

What steps can an MNC take to reduce conflicts that could arise from political and nationalistic forces? One strategy is accommodation. This means taking every opportunity to minimize misconceptions that the MNC is operating against the national interest. The MNC must avoid public exposure of any areas of actual conflict. Furthermore, host nationals, both employees and others, who may have been educated in the MNC home country or who are favorable to its culture should be cultivated whenever feasible. The MNC must continually try to renew the major benefits it provides to the host country by introducing new products, expanding output, and/or developing export markets.[26]

The other strategy is a balance of power approach, provided one has the power. IBM has been allowed 100% ownership in a number of countries because of the local need for their technology. By 1980, Saudi Arabia had purchased 100% of Aramco. However, the four Aramco partners, Exxon, Socal, Texaco, and Mobil, continue to obtain favorable treatment in crude oil supplies because of their refining, transportation, and marketing capabilities. It is reported that Aramco assets were sold to Saudi Arabia at prices above net book value. Moreover, the four oil companies continue to supply foreign workers, infuse technology, and train Saudi personnel.

Law

The legal environment in international business is becoming increasingly complex. The legal environment that prevails within the host country must be considered, as well as the legal environment which extends its coverage to take account of the activities of firms abroad. Also significant is the international dimension, which is the collection of agreements, treaties, and conventions between two or more nations.

The domestic legal environment within a country is a facet of its culture. The international legal environment, however, is a reflection of the increasing complexity of our interdependent world, including the various regional groupings of nations such as the European Economic Community (EEC). The speed of modern technology which bridges national frontiers is bringing international codes into operation, and the rising significance of MNCs has led to an additional stream of international law.

There is a considerable amount of domestic legislation surrounding business in most countries. The term legislation is used here to include written law and government rules and regulations. Legislation in this sense, which affects business systems and operations fairly directly, concerns the following areas: taxation, including import and export duties; restrictions on entry, products, packaging, pricing, advertising and sales promotion, trademarks, labeling, and product liabilities; and laws/regulations affecting distribution agreements and labor practices. The international businessman is well advised to employ a good local lawyer and to get familiar with the legal environment of the foreign country of interest. In addition to the legislation that governs marketing within each country, many nations enact legislation that affects the foreign firm alone. This is most often true where:

— protection is accorded, particularly to small-scale industries,
— regulations restrict the number of foreigners that can be employed,
— taxation is specific to foreign firms, and
— foreign exchange restrictions apply.

The extent of U.S. regulatory impact abroad is mainly in its antitrust regulations, export controls, and taxation systems. For the

U.S. Justice Department, the key to antitrust action is whether it has reason to believe that competition will be lessened, either in U.S. markets or between U.S. firms engaged in foreign commerce. Even an action that eliminates potential competition risks an antitrust suit. In contrast, foreign governments are willing to overlook some lessening of domestic competition if they think that the overall national interest will be furthered by their firm's competing abroad. The Japanese seem to be the most pragmatic in this respect.

The EEC founding agreement, the Treaty of Rome, embodies antitrust restrictions in its Articles 85 and 86. The stipulations therein are tighter than most of the individual countries' restraint of trade laws, and they do have an extraterritorial reach. But it is argued by American business and others that they have not been enforced as rigorously as the U.S. laws. For instance, the EEC countries have tolerated agreements to restrict markets or to set prices in cases where a particular industry needs to be built up or protected from U.S. competition. Japan's case is also interesting. Japan's antimonopoly law allows exemptions for rationalization cartels or antidepression cartels. The rationalization cartel applies to industries that may produce a product made of many components. Through the cartel, each firm is told to produce what it makes most efficiently, thus the product can be put together and exported at the lowest cost.

NATIONAL CONTROL OF INTERNATIONAL TRADE

Every country has a foreign trade policy, although in free market economies it may be not articulated, but rather is manifested through various regulations. National controls exist for a variety of reasons, one of which is economic. Nations wish to protect their local industries, although they have to abide by GATT agreements. Tariffs are set through GATT, as are some constraints on nontariff barriers, but other non-tariff barriers abound, e.g., product standards, customs procedures, health and safety regulations, and testing requirements. Philips, the Dutch electronics company, manufactures 29 types of electrical outlets, 10 kinds of plugs, and 12 varieties of cords to meet the multiple national standards.[27] Government procurement policies almost always favor their domestic firms. This is true worldwide, although GATT has now agreed on nondiscrimination by governments for purchases covered by their code. This opens up a $20 billion market which had hitherto been closed to international competition. Some barriers are dormant but can be activated at will, such as customs officers dragging out the paperwork needed to let in imports. Further barriers can be agreed on through multinational agreements such as the Multifiber Arrangement. This arrangement effectively limits the amounts of low cost clothing and textiles that can be exported. Beyond all these means, GATT permits member countries to impose surcharges and quotas under certain hardship conditions with GATT permission.

A modern answer to trade problems is a voluntary quota. The exporting country agrees to impose a voluntary export quota on its exporting firms. This is done with the agreement of the importing country, so the importing country avoids having to seek GATT permission to impose a quota. The modern approach is built on the concept of fair trade rather than free trade. Implementation of this concept occurs through what might be termed "managed trade"; international trade increases but industries are not disrupted. The Japanese, for example, have agreed to voluntary quotas on their export of automobiles to the U.S, and on exports of quartz watches, hi-fi equipment, and computer-controlled machine tools to the EEC. Brazil and the EEC have agreed to limit steel exports to the U.S.

Other reasons for export controls in the rich industrialized nations are to protect national security, to regulate participation in the international arms traffic, and to restrict exports of high technology products and the expertise required to make them. There are also controls designed to achieve geopolitical goals such as trade embargoes. The U.S. goes further. It has used export controls as a lever to further the cause of human rights, or to force U.S. environmental goals on certain countries.

Centrally planned economies maintain export and import controls, which is a necessary extension of the planned economy. Another major causal region for controls are also implemented in communist regimes who work to be independent of capitalistic countries. Communist nations prefer to keep exports and imports in balance, and not to take foreign exchange loans. LDCs are capital short and therefore also impose export and import controls. In most LDCs, major exports are conducted by state owned and/or state-controlled enterprises, therefore the state exercises direct control over international trade in these important sectors. International businessmen are usually best off employing local agents in such LDCs.

Foreign Trade Zones

International businessmen should also know about a modern phenomenon: the foreign trade zone. Many countries have established foreign trade zones, which attract foreign investment, create local employment, raise economic activity, and often help the balance of payments. Even the U.S. has some 30 such zones. The foreign trade zone helps consignment and re-export trade, and manufacture within the zone. For example, a foreign exporter may forward its products to a foreign trade zone in the U.S. until a favorable market in the U.S. or a nearby country is available. The products are not subject to customs entry, payment of duty or tax, or bond. Products can also be sorted, assembled, or manufactured within the foreign trade zone. Another benefit is that users of the zone may display products, establish showrooms, and may also sell from stock in wholesale quantities. Upon entering the zone, domestic goods for export are considered to be exported for purpose of excise and other internal revenue tax rebate. Thus, a manufacturer of domestic goods does not need to wait until it finds a foreign customer before obtaining duty rebates. Foreign trade zones are therefore really duty-free transshipment and manufacturing points. There is a big foreign trade zone in Rotterdam, the largest port in Europe, and is used heavily for warehousing by exporters to Europe. The zone at Kandla, India is used by Western firms for manufacturing and trading output with the U.S.S.R. This trading is possible because of the Indian-U.S.S.R. bilateral trading agreement, without which firms cannot export to the U.S.S.R. because the Russians do not have the hard currency to pay them. Foreign trade zones can be of immense help to international businessmen.

INTERNATIONAL BUSINESS OPPORTUNITIES

How do international businessmen become aware of opportunities? In centrally planned economies, including the Communist nations and many LDCs, there are national five year and annual plans. A study of these reveals information about planned growth, exports, and imports. This information plus whatever is available on industry trends gives a relatively informed idea of business opportunities within those nations. Industry trends can be identified in two basic ways: by analyzing available statistics, and by talking to industry experts in that nation.

In many free market nations there are no formal national plans, although publicized fiscal policy measures indicate industries and regions that are receiving incentives. However, statistics on industry and market trends are more valid and reliable, industry and market experts are more accessible, and this data is much easier to collect.

SECONDARY DATA AND INFORMATION SOURCES

The international businessman has available to him a vast array of data and information sources, but one must know exactly where to look. An essential step for an organization engaging in international business or trade is the development of an effective international information system. To build such a system, it is necessary to have extensive secondary data sources by country or market in the areas in which the organization is interested (see below).

There are a wide variety of secondary data and information sources available from international organizations; for example, the United Nations, the OECD, and the IMF. At the national and private sector level, readily available international market information sources for organizations include:

1. National governmental sources, such as
   a. U.S. Department of Commerce
   b. U.S. Department of Agriculture
   c. U.S. state agencies
2. Commercial banks and other service organizations
   a. International banks, e.g., Bank of America, Citibank, Credit Suisse, and Deutsche Bank
   b. Airlines, freight forwarders, and other transport firms

    c. Major public accounting firms (primarily the Big Eight) and international advertising agencies
3. Private sector intelligence sources, such as
    a. Business International
    b. The Economist Intelligence Unit[28]

The U.S. federal government sources mentioned have a variety of services and programs, especially for firms interested in exporting. Among the U.S. Department of Commerce offerings are individual country reports, overseas business reports, technical trade seminars, and its new computer-based World Information and Trade System, plus the Bureau of Census international data base, which is a computerized data bank of demographic, economic, and social data. These are all provided at little or no cost. Similarly, many U.S. states have export or industrial development organizations, which generally complement federal efforts while promoting their own particular interests. Ohio, for example, maintains an office in Brussels to stimulate and facilitate foreign direct investment in the state as well as to assist the international sales efforts of Ohio firms.

Major international banks have long been an important source of information and advice for the international business community. These major banks maintain a presence in the principal financial centers of the world, such as New York, London, Zurich, Hong Kong, and Singapore. Their foreign offices provide a continued source of information for these international banks, which may even publish periodic newsletters or reports for their clients. To a lesser extent the other service sources, such as the international public accounting firms, also can provide useful country market data. Finally, the two important private sector professional sources, Business International and the Economist Intelligence Unit, are noted in particular for their extensive overseas network of offices and reporters. They not only provide information that is available to all subscribers to their general reports, but also will conduct special individual studies for customers as requested.

The U.N. statistics have more complete global coverage than any other organization since no other has such universal relationships. Because of its uniquely central international position and as a result of its activities in ensuring global coverage and comparability, the U.N. Statistical Office is able to publish important regional and world totals, e.g., value of trade, commodity and industrial production, population, and energy consumption/production. A large number of indicators also are prepared. In the specific case of trade statistics one will find value indexes, unit values, quantum indices, and percentage shares of world market.[29]

The U.N. Statistical Office works with national governments on the development and application of international statistical standards, applies conversion factors, and estimates data when national governments are unable or unwilling to supply them. For example, sometimes exports from a country can be estimated by aggregating imports from that country reported by its trading partners. In other cases, estimates may be made by projecting trends. Overall the U.N. Statistical Office strives continuously through personal visits, international meetings, and correspondence to improve the comparability, reliability, scope, coverage, and timeliness of statistics collected. The U.N. Statistical Office also publishes the *Directory of International Statistics*, which contains a listing of statistical series published by international agencies, as well as an inventory of machine-readable data bases. OECD and IMF publications are also listed therein.

In addition to the above, there are other information collection possibilities. The U.S. Bureau of the Census is a very informed source. Also helpful are index publications, of which the most important in this field are the *U.S. Business Periodicals Index* and *The International Executive* which also gives some abstracts. Another useful way to extend an international business secondary data source base is through a computer search into an existing data base.

It is both effective and efficient for any organization or researcher considering business opportunities overseas to consult a number of readily available secondary information sources before undertaking extensive travel or incurring the research costs of gathering primary data. Many of the secondary data and information sources cost little or nothing, but provide generally high quality materials. This is true of much information from the U.N. Statistical Office, the U.S. Department of Commerce, and international banks. Private sector sources, such as Business International and the Economist Intelligence Unit, are primarily engaged in the collection, interpretation, and discrimination of international business data, and charge directly for their services. Industry sources of information exist but are often not public, and have to be tapped by developing knowledgeable expert contacts within the industry. In addition, major importers and distributors are knowledgable expert sources for many industries and markets. Owners of these trading and distributing firms are entrepreneurs and know their fields well. Service sources can be very useful, as well. Bank managers, legal firms, and major accounting firms located in any nation/territory have a vast amount of information about firms. Introduction to such service firms through their offices in the international businessman's country of working origin can save a considerable amount of time abroad.

METHODS OF ENTRY

What method of entry does one adopt in doing international business? Various methods of entry differ in commitment and risk levels. They are adopted for different purposes, but trade-offs always exist. For example, to enter with a wholly owned subsidiary will usually optimize control, but the trade-off is that one probably increases the exposure to political risk.

A firm can conduct its international business in five basic ways: ownership through foreign investment abroad, contractual arrangements with other firms, licensing, franchising, and exporting. A number of combinations of these five are also possible.[30]

The propensity of an MNC to establish production abroad through foreign direct investment depends on the extent to which the firm possesses ownership-specific advantages, whether it wishes to use these assets itself by internalizing them, and the extent to which it is profitable to exploit these assets in conjunction with indigenous resources abroad. The more ownership-specific advantages possessed, the greater the inducement to internalize them.[31] The inputs that can give an ownership specific advantage may include patents, brand names, and trademarks, or the size and technical characteristics of the firm. They could also rise from a commercial monopoly, such as a particular raw material or exclusive control of a particular market outlet. When firms combine these with different foreign locations, other ownership advantages are derived. These include the ability to engage in international transfer pricing to shift liquid assets to take advantage of exchange fluctuations, to reduce risks in general by diversifying investments, to operate parallel production capacity in different countries, and to engage in international product or process specialization.

The basic incentive for a firm to internalize its ownership endowments is to avoid the disadvantages or to capitalize on the imperfections of one or the other of the two main external mechanisms – the market or price system and public authority fiat. Where either of these factors creates conditions in which the economies of interdependent activities between independent firms cannot be fully captured and benefits diminish, then the firm will internalize. Also, whenever the firm wishes to avoid the full impact of government legislation and differential tax or exchange rate policy, there is a tendency to internalize.

Joint Ventures, Mergers, and Acquisitions

Ownership may take the form of a wholly owned subsidiary, a joint venture, a merger, or an acquisition. A wholly owned subsidiary affords maximum flexibility in determining the subsidiary's power, including market division. Joint ventures, mergers, and acquisitions are all ways of expanding rapidly. An international joint venture is an association between two or more firms to carry on a separate legal entity established and controlled by the participants. In the communist bloc countries, the only possible direct foreign investments may be in a joint venture with local governments or paragovernment organizations. The term joint venture has also been applied to direct investment by the MNC in acquiring equity in a local foreign partner. In many LDCs, government regulations dictate that foreigners must form joint ventures with local firms. Taking a majority equity position is usually less risky than acquiring only a minority interest. In either case, MNC managerial commitment is equally high. It should be noted that part of the investment can be nonmonetary, i.e., through the exchange of assets such as used machinery, for equity.

A joint venture gives an MNC three main advantages. One advantage is that since the local foreign partner knows the host environment well, the quality of information flow is good. The second is that market penetration can be achieved with less foreign direct investment. The third is that the products of joint ventures may be better received by customers with nationalistic attitudes.[32]

The risk is that the partners might not agree or be able to reach consensus on strategic and operating decisions. The local foreign partner may be selected for its complementary resources; in LDCs, it may be because of its financial strength or political influence. The partners may have differing views on whether to plow back the cash flow for expanding the business or to extract it as dividends. A major study showed that there is a high divorce rate among U.S. MNCs and their foreign joint venture partners. It was found that of 1,100 U.S. MNCs surveyed, 30% of their joint ventures ended in divorce or in an increase in the U.S. partner's apparent power.[33] As the product's foreign market matured and its sales volume increased there, the MNCs started to centralize decisions at corporate headquarters, causing conflict with the local partner. Even joint ventures of two foreign MNCs to set up a wholly owned subsidiary in a third country have problems.

Joint ventures are common when a very high input activity level has to be surpassed to obtain any significant output or result. A case in point was the building of the Concorde, where the minimum commitment amounted to close to $1 billion. An analogous situation exists in the exploitation of North Sea oil, where the drilling stage is very costly. Technological linkages or cases where certain resources are not available through free markets — in distribution networks, for instance — also may necessitate joint ventures.[34]

Joint Venture Strategies

If a firm chooses the joint venture alternative, it has the option of three different strategies: the spider's web, go together-split, or successive integration. A spider's web strategy is for a firm to have joint ventures with many other firms. Thus, the firm obtains economies of scale but avoids the dangers of excessive dependence on any individual partner. An example of this is the strategy followed by DAF, the Dutch auto firm. DAF has concluded an equity joint venture with International Harvester. DAF benefits from International Harvester's worldwide sales outlets, whereas the latter acquires an important addition to its product range and access to DAF's European sales network. DAF is also involved in a joint venture as a member of the Club of Four, a group of four truck manufacturers which also includes KAT of West Germany, Saviem of France, and Volvo of Sweden, to develop a new medium-weight truck outside the DAF-International Harvester deal. Further, DAF has a marketing and R & D agreement with Volvo's auto division in which the Swedish firm began with a 33% share.

A more dynamic joint venture strategy is the go together-split. This refers to a strategy where two or more firms cooperate over a certain period of time and then separate. It is particularly applicable to situations where firms work together on a limited project. It is typical of large consultancy projects in Third World countries; for example, SNC of Canada, the Danish Hydraulic Institute of Denmark, and a local Nigerian company banded together on the Warri Port project feasibility study done for the Nigerian Ports Authority over a period of three years.

The successive integration strategy begins with weak interfirm linkages then develops toward more interdependence, and may end in a takeover or merger. The DAF-Volvo agreement is an example of successive integration strategy. In 1974 Volvo increased its share to 75%, with the remaining ownership being transferred to the Dutch government. In an interview, Volvo Managing Director Pehr Gyllenhammar stated:

> A closer cooperation and an increased participation in DAF was anticipated from the start. However, it was not until spring that discussions were started to increase our participation, when DAF experienced sales setbacks and losses. Volvo wanted to inject more money, but also wanted more control. Hence, we increased our participation to 75%, at which level certain minority restrictions are no longer affected.[35]

Contractual Joint Venture

The new contractual joint venture is gaining popularity. The only difference from the normal joint venture is that there is more than one contract between the partners, increasing the partners' flexibility to negotiate separately the conditions of contract for different sectors and to handle each sector through an independent contract. Hoechst, the German chemical giant, has 49% participation in a joint venture called *Jugodisperzija*, with Yugoslav partner Iplas having 51% participation. Hoechst has five contracts. The first two deal with the terms of investment: costing and profit, and management and profit transfer. The third deals with the number of directors, the fourth with technical assistance, and the fifth covers marketing and brand names.[36]

A specialized form of contractual joint venture, contractual nonequity, is becoming increasingly popular. The advantage of having the joint venture legal entity, rather than a standard contract, is that liability may be restricted to the entity. It is widely used in industrial cooperation with the communist bloc countries and with LDCs. The most common types are formed for coproduction, contract manufacturing, turnkey projects including management contracts, joint entry into third countries, technical agreements, and a service and consulting contract. Coproduction may involve an MNC furnishing equipment and technology to a local foreign firm so that the entity they have together can produce a product for the host country. The production of Bell Helicopters in Iran is an example of this arrangement.

East-West Joint Ventures

East-West ventures are often the contractual nonequity type under which an identifiable organizational entity is established specifically for the purpose of joint production, marketing, or related activities such as R & D. The venture must be export oriented to earn the hard currencies required to purchase whatever may be needed or to pay the western MNC for services rendered.

The East European governments are naturally most anxious to form such ventures with large integrated western MNCs as this facilitates production and marketing abroad. The Romanians, for ex-

ample, first approached IBM to produce computer peripherals under a joint venture arrangement, but IBM's principle is full-control,
not minority holdings. The Romanians later linked with Control
Data.

Joint Ventures: The West and China

In 1979 the Chinese National People's Congress passed the new
joint venture law. The law permits the establishment of limited liability companies between Chinese entities and foreign corporations,
but the Chairman must always be Chinese and the foreign corporation can have only a minority interest. This law also provided for
the creation of a Foreign Investment Commission and the China
International Trust and Investment Corporation, which are responsible for administration of the law and negotiations of agreements
with foreigners.

The Chinese seem to be primarily interested in joint ventures that
will help them earn foreign exchange and meet relatively short-term
goals. The production of irrigation equipment, tractors, combines,
and improved seed technology would be welcome joint venture
schemes. Also, the Chinese want to concentrate on industries that
can be developed rather quickly, require a relatively small investment, and produce goods for sale through government cooperatives. Desirable schemes would include production of canned and
processed foods, shoe manufacture, textile plants, and electronic
products. It should be noted, however, that recently the Chinese
canceled $1.5 billion worth of major contracts with Japanese firms,
so though there are opportunities for profit, there are also risks.[37]

The joint venture can be thought of as space on the plane of risk
versus control, below the wholly owned subsidiary. This plane extends below the joint venture to turnkey operations and exporting.
The latter involves no equity risk and minimal foreign control.[38] The
host country, especially if it is an LDC, views a turnkey arrangement as a means of acquiring a complete operational system together with skills transfer. The MNC often regards the turnkey part
as a marketing necessity, a prerequisite to the more important objective of selling equipment. In practice, the skills transfer is often

provided as an afterthought rather than as an integral part of the product.

The management contract is varied and applicable to a large number of circumstances. For instance, MNCs have used it when setting up some assembly operations on imported semifinished goods and components in many LDCs. The MNC receives contractual fees plus the output of a high unit value, lightweight product which is exported back to its rich home country. The MNC also saves because import duty on these products applies effectively only to the value-added plus transportation costs. The LDCs benefit through economic activity and foreign exchange; the value of the assembled product is more than the components. Even if the final product is sold in the LDC domestic market, the LDC benefits by having paid only the cheaper imported value of the components. At times after an LDC has nationalized or taken over an MNC operation, it offers a management contract to the MNC to keep the plant operating efficiently.

Another form of joint venture is very close to what might be termed contract manufacturing, exemplified by Seabrook and its Israeli partner, Sun Frost Frozen Foods.[39] Sun Frost has modern manufacturing facilities and easy access to vegetables and fruits. The bulk of the joint venture's output is marketed internationally through Seabrook. Seabrook has contented itself with 25% of Sun Frost equity, but it has a 50% vote on the board of directors and the right to name the managing director. It is sometimes difficult for the contracting partner to find a satisfactory foreign manufacturer, especially in an LDC; the arrangement reduces control over product quality, and it trains a potential competitor. This last risk can be reduced if the MNC's product range continuously advances technologically so that the foreign contractee is faced with obsolescence if it breaks off the relationship.

Licensing: An Expansion Alternative

A license is simply a contract to use some intellectual property, such as a patent. It can also embrace copyrights and trademarks. Many companies do not patent all their technology, believing that it is more profitable to keep it confidential, but they have been known to license such confidential technology. There is growing interest in licensing within the international marketplace as another means for foreign diversification and growth. To be more effective, licensing needs to be viewed as part of a global marketing strategy which is coordinated with other key elements. Licensing can increase and/or safeguard return through other modes such as joint venture and contract manufacturing. Situational factors may at times favor licensing, including the foreign market's being too small, unstable economic conditions, and rapidly changing technology, when the firms can specialize and exchange technology by cross-licensing each other. Licensees are usually selected on the basis of technical ability.

Licenses may be granted on an exclusive or noninclusive basis. They can also be limited in various ways to reflect legitimate strategies of the patent owner or other international realities. A firm may occasionally grant a patent or know-how license to another firm that could design around the problem anyway. Others grant such licenses as a safeguard against infringement. Trademark licenses are granted with stringent quality control often imposed on the licensee.

Licensing offers rapid access to global markets for a firm's products and services, often at low risk without great investment of money or time. The licensor receives market share as well as fees. This market share might be very useful if the licensor decides to penetrate that market with other products or in some other way. Moreover, the former licensee may well be a viable partner who has already been tested.

There are disadvantages to licensing. A licensee may become a competitor when the agreement expires, or it may seek to market aggressively outside its territory through direct sales or sublicenses. Alternatively, the licensee may not care to maintain product quality or may adopt marketing programs that lower the perception among target customers of the product's desirability. Another disadvantage is that royalties are often restricted by LDCs to 5%, and in some countries they are subject to tax deductions. However, considered overall and in many circumstances, licensing has proven a useful way to enter a foreign market at low risk and with net benefits. Firms both big and small have used licensing to earn from technologies that have outlived their usefulness in the home markets.

Franchising: International Expansion

The burgeoning field of international franchising includes a host of products. An advantage of franchising is that the franchisee buys an established marketing package without the risks of product acceptance, market location, and managerial false starts. The franchisor gets foreign market entry at minimum cost, plus a local entrepreneur. Franchising is "a form of marketing or distribution in which a parent company customarily grants an individual or relatively small company the right or privilege to do business (for a consideration) as a franchisee in a prescribed manner over certain periods of time in a specific place."[40] The privilege may be the right to sell the parent company's product, to use its name, to adopt its methods, or to copy its symbols, trademarks, and architecture. Today there are well over 200 American firms operating through thousands of franchisee outlets abroad. Currently U.S. franchise systems are largest in Canada and Western Europe. A recent survey indicated that although the larger franchisors do currently dominate in total outlets abroad, large size is not a prerequisite for global involvement.[41]

The most frequently used entry strategy in international franchising is 100% franchisee ownership. Over 47% of the firms responding to the survey used this ownership method. Some 21% used the master or area franchise and 17% used a company-owned policy. Food retailers, business services, and fast-food systems frequently adopted this last ownership form. Several firms noted that new markets are tested with company-owned outlets prior to beginning major franchising efforts. Joint venture ownership is the most commonly used ownership tactic among the hotel and motel systems. It should be noted that ownership strategies are often chosen because of legal limitations imposed by the host country. In Brazil, for instance, profits and royalty payments may be remitted only on capital brought into the country or on reinvestment of profits derived from such capital. Thus, franchisors often institute company-owned and joint venture operations in order to repatriate profits.

Many franchise systems have successfully penetrated foreign markets with little alteration of their domestic marketing strategy. The soft drink, business services, and automotive product groups are the strongest adopters of the standardized approach, whereas the more visible retailers are likely to use an adaptation strategy. But some fast-food groups significantly alter certain product offerings in operations outside the U.S. McDonald's, for example, serves beer in West Germany and often uses a heavy wood decor in those northern European nations where wood furnishings are traditional. The franchisors currently involved in international markets are highly optimistic. They are planning further expansion, particularly as other economies adopt Western lifestyles and as their discretionary incomes rise.

Exporting

Exporting can be very profitable. Some 35% of world exports are intra-MNC, but exporting can also be a profitable strategy for many small firms. Although competition in international markets is generally keen, small firms may encounter less competition abroad because they are serving market niches not served by larger corporations.[42] For larger exporters of capital goods, government export credit schemes are generally available.

A firm can export directly or indirectly. If it elects to go direct, it may set up a foreign sales subsidiary in the foreign country, or a foreign branch, or export from a third country location, or sell via joint venture organizations. Also, it can send out salespeople from the head office. Another alternative is overseas distribution channels, either foreign agents or foreign distributors. Direct export can also be conducted through an export consortium.

Indirect Exporting

If a firm has little knowledge of exporting to a foreign market or does not wish to commit resources, it may export indirectly through an export trading company or an export house. The export house buys on its own account, stores, and markets goods overseas. Another indirect method is for a firm to piggyback by asking another company to market its product through their overseas marketing channels. A third alternative is to engage an export management company (EMC), also known as a combination export manager firm (CEM). When choosing this last alternative, a firm should obtain references from other manufacturers and banks.

The most powerful trading companies in terms of volume are the Japanese *sogoshoshas*. The nine largest sogoshoshas do about half of Japan's international trade. They have offices in many countries and also do trade for non-Japanese firms into third countries. Sumitomo, for example, supplies Brazilian shoe manufacturers with designs for fashionable shoes popular in American cities, and then helps the shoe manufacturers compete with Italian shoes in the U.S. The nine leading sogoshoshas are among the largest corporations in the world. They have a combined total of more than 1,200 manufacturing and natural resource development operations, hotel, and other service projects abroad. In addition, there are smaller but major trading companies in Brazil, South Korea, and the West, mostly based in Europe. Most of the Western companies have existed since colonial empire days. The famous Danish trader, the East Asiatic Company, is also a major player.

Under the U.S. Export Trading Company Act of October 8, 1982, bank holding companies and bankers' banks may own 100% of the equity of an export trading company. As banks generally do not have international business expertise in most goods and services, it is likely that they will buy into or team up with existing export management companies to form export trading companies. The new act makes provision for obtaining prior exemption from antitrust suits for the certified export conduct. It also is symptomatic of a changing American attitude. The Department of Commerce was authorized to promote U.S. export trading companies and to set up a service to facilitate contact between producers of exportable goods and services and firms offering export services. For a small fee a producer and/or manufacturer, an export trading company, a provider of export services, or an export management company can register in the contract facilitation file which is available to anyone requesting a search.

It is possible that many small- and medium-sized U.S. manufacturers will be exporting through U.S. export trading companies in the future. A number of major U.S. corporations already have export trading companies and are expected to enlarge their activities with the flexibility provided under the new act. Some of these are

Philbro-Salomon Inc., General Electric, Sears Roebuck, General Motors, Rockwell International, and Control Data.[43]

AREAS OF CONFLICT AND CONFLICT RESOLUTION

The objectives of international businessmen and the governments of the host countries with whom they do business obviously cannot be identical, although the international businessman who wishes to be welcomed on a long-term basis must necessarily try to conform as much as possible. The general pattern is then overlap and conformity in many sectors but differences in some. Differences that arise and their resolution through diminished conflict are discussed below.

1. *Direction of industrial growth.* This often happens with centrally planned economies that wish to allocate resources into particular economic sectors. Foreign direct investment may have entered for certain types of industries and the governments may later have new plans. This has often been the case in those countries that previously were colonies of Western empires, and also is the case for the Soviet bloc and China. The answer for international businessmen is to try and offer their expertise in the new areas. One way to do this is not to repatriate earnings but to leave them for new area investment while charging for new services and new technology.

A similar type of conflict arises from national government control of key sectors of the economy. The answer for international businessmen is again to relinquish a confrontational stance and instead to joint venture with the host government and/or cooperate by selling them services of different kinds.

2. *Credit and pricing policies of international businessmen.* Conflict does not usually arise when exporting to countries, except when the exporter is pricing products so as to violate GATT "dumping" criteria. These criteria are defined as:

1. exporting at a price below the exporter's shipment price in the country of origin, and
2. because of the above, causing material injury to the industry in the importing country.

However, most international businessmen are cognizant of dumping and only dump as a deliberate choice with knowledge of its attendant penalties.

The credit and pricing conflict usually arises with MNCs that may be adjusting credit terms when supplying products from their global system to their subsidiaries/joint ventures in host countries. Host governments often suspect that the adjustment as to timing and length of credit is made when MNCs think the host country currency valuation is going to change. Credit is lowered when there is a possibility of devaluation and raised on expectations of revaluation. But the host government would like to have credit raised in order to help avoid a devaluation and vice versa. In the matter of pricing policies, host governments suspect MNCs of taking advantage of taxation differences by manipulating prices of equipment and/or materials they supply their subsidiary/joint venture so that they may repatriate more from the high tax country. This lowers the taxable profit and consequently corporate taxes within the high tax country, and creates a foreign exchange drain. The answer for MNCs is probably to maintain stable pricing as far as possible, with well documented justification for any changes.

3. *Transfer of technology and the extent of R & D done in host countries by MNCs.* The transfer of technology sector will always remain a conflict area. One of a firm's basic advantages is its technology: hardware, software, and/or human skills. The firm is prepared to transfer only some of its technology, never all of it. Further a profit-seeking firm must want to be paid for the part of technology it is prepared to transfer. The payment may be low but can never be zero, if only because of the transfer costs.

Every international businessman has to decide what price to charge, but technology is the Ace of Spades in the pack given the fact that technology provides the best way to achieve greater productivity in every field. In today's world this fact is well understood by every government and businessman. An answer of accommodation is to negotiate responsibly, provide adequate information, and where suitable conduct R & D in host nations.

4. *Human resource development policies.* Host governments want MNCs who enter their countries to adopt progressive human resource development policies for their nationals. The skill level

arising from this is transferable to other local enterprises if the employees leave their original firm. Most enlightened MNCs encourage human resource development in host countries because of the high cost of posting a home country employee abroad. Many MNCs have reached a point of maturity where operations in various host countries abroad are run almost wholly by host country nationals. A few global MNCs have even achieved the higher level of taking host country nationals into MNC corporate headquarters. These MNCs, IBM, GE, and Alcan, for instance, think in terms of a world executive group who may have members from many host country subsidiaries/joint ventures and from the home country. This group is then transferable to other countries. Moreover, the synergistic learning effect of such a multicultural world executive group is very beneficial to corporate strategy and implementation.

5. *Subsidiary/joint venture not develop their own export markets because of the global policies of its parent*. There is no real answer to this problem. If nothing was promised initially by the MNC, then it becomes a matter of the balance of power. If promises were made, then attempts should be made to keep them.

Governments in advanced countries gradually are rationalizing the environment for MNC growth by tending toward a greater degree of international harmony of policies in such fields as company law, patent law, company taxation in relation to overseas earnings, merger and monopoly regulations, and capital movements. This should help reduce confrontation. Furthermore, the rapid growth of an international web of cross-investments among countries limits to some degree the actions rich countries may take against MNCs from other countries. Can France, which has companies with American affiliates such as Renault with American Motors and Peugeot with Chrysler, whose success in turn depend in some part on the goodwill of the U.S. government, customers, and companies, afford to be too restrictive against U.S. MNCs in France?

Resolution of Deep Conflicts

At times conflicts between national governments and international businessmen are deep and can extend to negative acts such as expropriations. In such cases, international businessmen can adopt a number of tactics. First, one could request helpful intervention from the home government through its embassies or directly. This type of official government to government diplomatic intervention is often successful. The U.S. MNCs Standard Oil of New Jersey, W.R. Grace, Heinz, and General Mills, all had trouble with their operations in Peru in the late 1960s and early 1970s. In consequence the U.S. Government withheld its support of World Bank and U.S. Export-Import Bank loans to Peru. Finally an agreeable settlement was reached.[44] A second tactic is to have done professional independent valuation of the assets involved, and then to propose a compromise based on the price for the assets, plus additional service contracts for a fee. Third, an MNC could offer to help exports of the output from the plant in the host country if feasible. Fourth, if there is still no resolution, an arbitration can be proposed. If possible, the arbitration should be done outside the host country.

INTERNATIONAL BUSINESS STRATEGY AND PLANNING

Strategy operates within an environment that was described in preceeding sections of this chapter. What does the environment tell the international businessman? Basic truths include the following:

— National economies are of different sizes, and at different economic and technological levels.
— Some national economies are market economies, others are centrally planned. All those centrally planned control foreign entry and foreign exchange. Many market economies have generalized rules governing foreign entry but specifically control very few key economic activity sectors. A number of LDC market economies have foreign exchange controls.
— National philosophies vary from positive encouragement of foreign investment entry like Canada's to complete discouragement of such entry like Albania's.
— Foreign exchange rates are volatile.
— Extended credit is a feature of international business.
— A global shopping center has emerged in the Western world and is emerging elsewhere.

— The world economy is advancing through rapid improvements in technology.
— The international marketplace is 20% of the world economy.
— Three-quarters of the international marketplace is dominated by large firms: MNCs, trading companies and state owned enterprises, plus government to government sales.
— The international marketplace is intensely competitive.

Given the above, what are the major decision areas and strategic options that emerge? A firm has to recognize that it is essential to go international in order to gain from the experience curve effects and thereby be more competitive toward fellow domestic firms and international foreign firms in its product markets. A local firm in England, for instance, is disadvantaged when competing against another local firm that has a plant abroad. The competitor could possibly lower costs by importing from its foreign plant and is certainly gaining from the experience curve as its total volume, domestic plus international, grows. A firm must also realize that a long-term commitment is necessary for success in the international marketplace. It takes time to build market share abroad where one is operating with distributors/agents and customers from a foreign culture and one is a new entrant. Another crucial point is choosing the correct product-market fit. Country selection is of utmost importance and the product-market fit is the major key to success. This involves studying the foreign market scope through analysis of customers and their needs, market segments, and the products and technology required to satisfy those needs. The firm also must distinguish between its global and its domestic products.

The market stage must be studied. At what stage of the product life cycle is the market? This stage will indicate the competitive structure. The next point to be decided is the performance expectations of the firm. What constitutes international business success? Is it to be measured by increased exports and/or foreign sales, market share, return on investment, net income to headquarters, or other measures? Now the firm must decide its overall strategy. Is it going for a foreign market concentration strategy or for a foreign market dispersion strategy? Concentration means resource concentration in a few markets and then gradual expansion into new ones. In contrast, dispersion implies fast penetration into many foreign markets simultaneously and thus diffusion of efforts among them.

A strategy of market diversification is characterized by a fast rate of expansion in a number of foreign markets served. This is usually accomplished by devoting only limited resources and time to a careful study of each foreign market prior to entry. The firm is therefore likely to make some mistakes and may have to drop out of some unprofitable markets later. Given fixed resources, the level allocated to each foreign market in a strategy of diversification will always be lower than with concentration. The lower level of marketing effort implies less promotional expenditures, more reliance on commission agents, and a stronger tendency for a skimming approach to pricing. A strategy of concentration, on the other hand, involves investment in market share. This implies heavy promotional outlays, stronger control of the distribution channel, and, in some cases, penetration pricing.

The selection of market expansion strategy is influenced by characteristics of the product, of the market, and the decision criteria of the firm. Once the concentration or dispersion route is decided on and the markets selected, then a strategy can be developed based on market domination or market development. The domination alternative usually requires a mature market and is often open only to the large firm that has commensurate resources. Seiko Watch, the Japanese MNC, is one example of a firm following a concentration strategy of market domination in the U.S. Most firms with no differential advantage, and most smaller firms, must follow a market development strategy. With either alternative the next stage of strategy development is choosing whether to multiple target or to selectively target.

Another point that a larger multiproduct firm has to keep in mind is global product portfolio management. Products that are cash cows must be retained for their cash flow which is necessary to feed the growth of question mark products. Star products that are leaders in rapidly growing markets must be encouraged for themselves and because they will become future cash cows. Dog products must be retained if necessary to sustain the firm's overall image of a wide and deep product line.

The major question for the international businessman is whether the firm has a differential advantage. If yes, how does one exploit it in the international marketplace? Increasingly firms are looking at a global strategy where a product can be positioned relatively similarly in a global segment that crosses many national markets. This gives synergistic efficiencies in international business programming. The small firms can do somewhat the same globalization if their product is in a marketing niche. In today's world this is the way for the small firm to achieve large international business success. The all-important subjects of global strategy, global marketing, and global trends will be taken up in the final chapter of this book, as will the future growth of international business through countertrade. The chapters in between are specific to different countries/regions. They outline information and discuss what is necessary and useful for international businessmen to achieve success in their respective areas.

SUMMARY AND CONCLUSIONS

The base on which large sections of the world marketplace rest is geopolitical. International businessmen have to be cognizant and sensitive to geopolitics in order to understand the risks and to gauge the probabilities of their investments' success in business efforts abroad. Countries change alliances at times. To succeed, the international business manager must understand the philosophic value systems, the history, the reasons for alliances, and the changing trends in political alignments. Modern international businessmen operate in an interdependent and interconnected world. The oil crisis is a dramatic example. It first affected the business managements of petrochemicals, automobiles, and tourist services, but by the early 1980s every segment of the world economy had become deeply involved.

For international businessmen, a major dimension of the world economy is the difference in affluence of the regional economies, specifically the difference between the OECD countries and the oil-deficit LDCs. In purchasing power and real product terms, the gap is relatively less wide, especially after taking the unrecorded parallel economy into account. Many LDCs are entering the manufacturing age. The rich countries will have to be willing to allow access to manufactured exports from the LDCs. In response, the rich will be steadily restructuring their economies toward more capital-intensive industries, requiring an increasingly skilled workforce. They will be entering the postindustrial service economy age. The world marketplace will continue to expand at a relatively rapid pace as the rich trade service products, including technology, for LDC primary products and manufactures. Services such as transportation are tied to the involvement of goods whereas tourism, technology transfer, and international banking are more independent. The latter have evidenced faster patterns of growth than merchandise trade and are likely to continue to do so.

MNCs will continue to grow but many will change their approach and strategies toward becoming global companies supplying world-class products to global marketing segments that transcend national boundaries. As the decade unfolds it is likely that the low-technology MNC will retreat, while nation states will have to accommodate to the foreign corporations with high technology and those that have vertically integrated or energy-related systems. Moreover, state owned enterprises from centrally planned economies will continue, and the Japanese sogoshoshas will continue to grow.

Religions and the technical and material cultures are different. They also have profound effects on the beliefs and attitudes of the population. International businessmen who are thoroughly conversant with the different cultural backgrounds can better plan their product-market strategies, manufacturing locations, and negotiations with foreigners. The chapter also alerted international businessmen to the political and legal environment in the world marketplace, and suggested how to assess political risk. Further, it discussed the rationale and types of control on international trade, and explained how to look for international business opportunities. The sources of available information were described.

Entry and Strategy

The methods of entry to be used in foreign markets were shown to be determined partly by the external environment and partly by the organization's resources, characteristics, and differential advantages. However, many of the methods of entry are alternatives. The organization often has a choice between whether foreign investment should be wholly owned or a joint venture. It may also select other contractual arrangements that are more beneficial. The additional alternatives of licensing, franchising, or exporting should be investigated. In each entry method, there is also a choice of substrategies to follow.

The primary components of international business are the decisions about which products to go with and to what foreign markets. The choice has to be based on the differential advantage of the organization, market desirability criteria, and the position of products in their life cycle. The overall product-market selection is a guide to whether the organization should follow a strategy of market diversification or market concentration. Further, it indicates whether there should be foreign investment or one should export into the markets. Formulation of the final international business strategy must involve consideration of a product market portfolio approach so that a competitive lead can be maintained. Such a competitive lead necessitates selective increase in market share and volume, with the consequent greater generation of internal resources. If the international business strategy is to be successful, the organization must carefully analyze the advantages and disadvantages of a global approach and different entry methods before proceeding on implementation.

REFERENCE NOTES

1. Kirpalani, V.H. (1985), *International Marketing*, New York: Random House Inc., pp. 296-297.

2. The World's Traders Ply the Pacific (1985, May 4), *The Economist*, p. 73.

3. Hunkering Down for the Long Haul (1985, October 11), *The Economist*, p. 24.

4. Bradbury, Frank R. (1978), *Technology Transfer Practices in International Firms*, Leiden, Netherlands: Sigthoff and Hoordhoff, p. 73; and Benson, Soffer (1978, November), Patent Activity and International Competitiveness, *Research Management*, pp. 34-37.

5. The IMF and Latin America (1982, December 11), *The Economist*, pp. 69-76.

6. Henry, Gordon M. (1985, September 23), A Red Star Rises on the High Seas, *Time*, p. 61.

7. Kahn, Herman and Phelps, John B. (1979, June), The Economic Present and Future: A Chartbook for the Decades Ahead, *The Futurist*, pp. 202-222.

8. American Tax Evasion: Welcome to the Black Economy (1979, September 29), *The Economist*, p. 84.

9. Ghosts, Moonlighters and Shadows (1986, October 18), *The Economist*, p. 63.

10. Friedman, Irving S. (1975, May), The New World of the Rich-Poor and the Poor-Rich, *Fortune*, pp. 244-252.

11. Henderson, Nancy (1979, December 3), The Problem of Cultural Differences, *Business America*, pp. 8-9.

12. Van Zandt, Howard F. (1970), How to Negotiate in Japan, *Harvard Business Review* (November-December), 48 (6), pp. 45-56.

13. Hall, Edward T. (1960) The Silent Language of Overseas Business, *Harvard Business Review* (May-June), 15 (3), pp. 87-96.

14. Almaney, Aduan (1974), Intercultural Communication and the MNC Executive, *Columbia Journal of World Business* (Winter), pp. 23-27; and Lee, James A. (1966), Cultural Analysis in Overseas Operations, *Harvard Business Review* (March-April), 21, (2), pp. 106-114.

15. Big Profits in Big Bribery (1981, March 16), *Time*, pp. 44-47.

16. Berkman, Harold W. (1976). Corporate Ethics: Who Cares? In Harold W. Berkman and Ivan R. Vernon (Eds.), *Contemporary Perspectives in International Business* (pp. 254-263), Chicago: Rand McNally College Publishing Company; and Casuistry: the Ethics of Social Responsibility (1981, September 14), *Forbes*, pp. 162-166.

17. The Unfolding of a Torturous Affair (1976, March 15), *Forbes*, pp. 27-28.

18. Waldman, Joseph M. (1978), Corruption and Overseas Business in Southeast Asia. In Richard N. Farmer and John V. Lombardi (Eds.), *Readings in International Business* (pp. 84-87), Bloomington, Ind.: Cedarwood Press.

19. Landauer, Jerry (1978, June 28), Boeing Company's Friends in Some Arab States Helped in Plane Sales, *Wall Street Journal*, pp. 1ff.

20. Kim, Suk N. and Barone, Saun (1981), Is the Foreign Corrupt Practices Act a Success or Failure? *Journal of International Business Studies* (Winter), pp. 123-128.

21. Farmer, Richard M. and Richman, Barry M. (1974), *International Business*, 2nd ed., pp. 153-172, Bloomington, Ind.: Cedarwood Press.

22. Ryan, John K., Jr., Shanklin, William L. and Wills, James R., Jr. (1982), Beware of Restrictive Business Practices Worldwide, (2) *Journal of International Marketing*, pp. 81-99.

23. Hawkins, Robert G., Mintz, Norman and Provissiero, Michael (1976), Government Takeovers of U.S. Foreign Affiliates (Spring), *Journal of International Business Studies*, pp. 3-16; Bradley, David G. (1977), Managing Against Expropriation, *Harvard Business Review* (July-August), pp. 75-83, and Mario, Lewis, (1979), Does Political Instability in Developing Countries Affect Foreign Investment Flow, *Management International Review*, 19, pp. 59-68.

24. Knudsen, Harold (1974), Explaining the National Propensity to Expropriate: An Ecological Approach, *Journal of International Studies* (Spring), pp. 51-69; Rummel, R.J. and Heenan, David A. (1978), How Multinationals Analyze Political Risk, *Harvard Business Review* (January-February) pp. 67-76; and Kobrin, Stephen J.; Basck, John; Blank, Stephen and La Palombara, Joseph (1980), The Assessment and Evaluation of Noneconomic Environments by American Firms: A Preliminary Report, *Journal of International Business Studies* (Spring-Summer) pp. 32-47.

25. Bennett, Peter D. and Green, Robert T. (1972), Political Instability as a Determinant of Direct Foreign Investment in Marketing, *Journal of Marketing Research* (May), pp. 182-186; Robock, Stefan H. (1971), Political Risks Identification and Assessment, *Columbia Journal of World Business* (July-August), pp. 6-20; Jain, Subhash and Bavisli, Vinod (1979), Strategies for Doing Business with LDCs, *Management International Review*, 19, pp. 69-76; Boddewyn, Jean J. (1979), Foreign Divestment: Magnitude and Factors, *Journal of International Business Studies* (Spring-Summer), pp. 21-27; Bradley, David G. (1977), Managing Against Expropriation, *Harvard Business Review*, (July-August), pp. 75-83; and Nehemkis, Petr (1979), Expropriation Has a Silver Lining, *California Management Review* (Fall), pp. 15-22.

26. Shapiro, Alan C. (1981), Managing Political Risk: A Policy Approach, *Columbia Journal of World Business* (Fall), pp. 63-70; Doz, Yves L. and Prahalad, C.K. (1980), How MNCs Cope with Host Government Intervention, *Harvard Business Review* (March-April), pp. 149-157; and Boddewyn, Jean J. and Cracco, Etienne F. (1972), The Political Game in World Business, *Columbia Journal of World Business* (January-February), pp. 45-56.

27. The Tricks of the Trade (1985, October 7), *Time*, p. 50.

28. Ryans, John K., Jr., and Ryans, Cynthia C. (1981), Northeast Ohio "International' Firms" Evaluation of Select Foreign Market Information Sources, *Akron Business and Economic Review* (Winter) pp. 19-22.

29. Brophy, Hugh (1983), The International Statistical Data Bases of the United Nations. In V.H. Kirpalani (Ed.), *International Marketing: Managerial Issues, Research and Opportunities*, Chicago: American Marketing Association.

30. Townsend, James B. (1979), Forms of International Involvement. In Berkman, Harold W. and Vernon, Ivan R. (Eds.), *Contemporary Perspectives in International Business* (pp. 151-161), Chicago: Rand McNally College Publishing Company.

31. Dunning, John H. (1980), Toward an Eclectic Theory of International Production: Some Empirical Tests, *Journal of International Business Studies* (Spring-Summer), pp. 9-31; and Rugman, Alan M. (1979), *International Diversification and the Multinational Enterprise*, Lexington, Mass.: D.C. Heath and Co.

32. McMillan, Carl H. (1981), Trends in East-West Industrial Cooperation, *Journal of International Business Studies* (Fall) pp. 53-67; Hill, R. Malcolm (1980), International Industrial Marketing into Eastern Europe, *European Journal of Marketing* (3), pp. 139-164.

33. Killing, J. Peter (1982), How to Make a Global Joint Venture Work, *Harvard Business Review* (May-June), pp. 120-127.

34. Gullander, Stafan (1976), Joint Ventures and Corporate Strategy, *Columbia Journal of World Business* (Spring) pp. 104-114.

35. Volvo Tar Over DAF (1974, September 18), *Svenska Dagbladet*, p. 11.

36. Hayashi, Kichiro (1978), Japanese Management of Multinational Operations: Sources and Means of Joint Venture Control, *Management International Review* (4), pp. 47-57; and Milosh, E.J. (1973), Imaginative Marketing in Eastern Europe, *Columbia Journal of World Business* (Winter) pp. 69-72.

37. Harvt, Andrew (1981, March 16), China's Turnaround Hurts Business, *The Gazette*, p. F-1.

38. Wright, Richard W. and Russell, Colin S. (1975), Joint Ventures in Developing Countries: Realities, and Responses, *Columbia Journal of World Business* (Summer), pp. 74-80.

39. Recent Experience in Establishing Joint Ventures (1971), *Business International*, New York: Business International.

40. Vaughn, Charles L. (1974), *Franchising*, pp. 3-11, Lexington, Mass: D.C. Heath and Co.

41. Hackett, Donald W. (1976), The International Expansion of U.S. Franchise Systems: Status and Strategies, *Journal of International Business Studies*, (Spring), pp. 65-75.

42. Daniels, John D. and Robles, Fernando (1982), The Choice of Technology and the Export Commitment: The Peruvian Textile Industry, *Journal of International Business Studies* (Spring-Summer), pp. 67-87; Jackson, Graham I. (1981), Exporting from the Importers' Viewpoint, *European Journal of Marketing* (3), pp. 3-25; Michell, Paul (1979), Infrastructures and International Marketing Effectiveness, *Columbia Journal of World Business*, (Spring), pp. 91-101.

43. Scouton, William (1982, October 18), Export Trading Companies: A New Tool for American Business, *Business America*, pp. 3-15; and Baldridge, Malcolm (1982, May 3), The Need for Export Trading Company Legislation, *Business America*, p. 1.

44. Carrying a Small Stick (1971, January 21), *Time*, pp. 72-73.

Part 2

Doing International Business:
Countries/Regions

Chapter 2

Doing Business in the Andean Countries

Robert Grosse

This chapter focuses not on a country but on a region which constitutes about one quarter of Latin America in population and economic activity. The six Andean countries — Bolivia, Chile, Colombia, Ecuador, Peru, and Venezuela — are situated along the Andes mountain range in western South America. They all currently have elected, democratic governments; all except Chile are members of the Andean Common Market; and all are former colonies of Spain. The following 15 sections discuss many of the relevant concerns of foreign business people seeking to operate in the Andean countries.

1. International Influences

International business is extremely important to all of these countries, substantially because domestic transportation between urban areas in each country is so poor that commerce with outside trading partners via ocean or air routes is simply more efficient. Virtually all of the important cities are located on either the Pacific Ocean or the Caribbean Sea. (The main exceptions are La Paz, Bolivia, and Bogota, Colombia.) This logistical aspect of the Andean nations continues to foster international business (and hinder domestic business) throughout the region, regardless of the political currents of any particular moment.

A. International Trade. The general trade picture can be seen in Table 1, which shows aggregate exports from each country to the others and to the rest of the world.

The international trade situation is striking in several ways. First, the level of intraregion trade is dwarfed by trade with the United States and with the rest of the industrial countries. Second, most of the Andean countries are running trade surpluses with the United States and with the rest of the world — exactly the opposite of what one normally would expect for less developed countries, but in keeping with Latin America's need to generate foreign exchange to help pay the massive foreign debt.[1] Third, the amount of Andean trade is very small compared with the size of total world trade; this is true also within Latin America (though not shown here), where Argentina, Brazil, and Mexico have greater international activity.

B. International Financial Flows. Other international business

TABLE 1. Exports to and from the Andean Countries, 1985

(In millions of current U.S. dollars)

from \ to	Bol.	Chile	Col.	Ec.	Peru	Ven.	U.S.	Europe	total world
Bolivia	...	3.7	4.8	0.1	10.6	0.2	92.2	84.8	673.0
Chile	14.2	...	44.9	29.8	45.6	31.7	849.8	1260.2	3797.3
Colombia	1.3	20.7	...	40.1	18.6	77.3	1323.8	1109.5	3334.2
Ecuador	0.1	44.6	54.0	...	7.8	2.3	1636.5	132.5	3017.2
Peru	9.9	39.2	76.0	24.6	...	34.0	1047.3	655.9	2966.4
Venezuela	0.4	233	317	2	21	...	6209	2624	15,116
U.S.A.	120	682	1468	591	496	3399	...	46,461	213,144
European Community	85.9	627	868	405	382	1721	69650	...	629,112
total world	597	2743	4113	1606	1624	6866	361627	636463	...

Sources: International Monetary Fund, *Direction of Trade Yearbook* (1986); and *International Financial Statistics Yearbook* (1986).

activities in the region tend to follow the same distribution as trade flows. (The industry-by-industry content of business in the region is discussed in Section 2 below.) Incoming foreign direct investment is greatest in Venezuela and least in Bolivia, distributed according to the size of the market in each country. The flows have dropped dramatically since 1980, when the Latin American debt crisis began to appear. Table 2 shows U.S. foreign direct investment, which constitutes about half of the total, into the region.

As far as foreign portfolio investment is concerned, most takes place through bank loans. (Very few international bonds have been issued by borrowers in Latin America during the 1980s.) In fact, it is widely believed that very little new voluntary lending is taking place into these countries from foreign banks; the banks are simply trying to protect their already large portfolios of loans to public and private sector borrowers in the region. Table 3 shows the level of foreign bank lending to each Andean country.

C. International Agreements. The Andean countries have actively participated in efforts to integrate their economies and stimulate economic growth. The Latin American Free Trade Area, founded in 1960 (and today known as ALADI), represents one unsuccessful effort to reduce barriers to Latin American international trade in which these nations participate. The Interamerican Devel-

TABLE 2. Foreign Direct Investment in Andean Countries, 1985

(in millions of current U.S. dollars)

host | source |	Bol.	Chile	Col.	Ec.	Peru	Ven.	all Latin America
U.S. firms stock of FDI	n.a.	71	2142	406	1684	1548	29,479
U.S. firms flow of FDI	n.a.	25	-125	35	-219	-214	4,250
all sources flow of FDI	10.0	66.4	729.0	60.0	-54.0	106.0	4011.0

Sources: U.S. Department of Commerce, Survey of Current Business (August 1986); and Interamerican Development Bank, Economic and Social Progress in Latin America (1986).

opment Bank, established in 1959, is another Latin American institution in which the Andean countries participate, and which plays a minor role in business among them.

The Andean Pact, or ANCOM, was formed in 1969 among these countries and still continues today. This regional bloc (that since 1976 has not included Chile) historically has taken positions antagonistic toward foreign multinational firms, largely codified in the Pact's Decision 24 in 1971. That rule required foreign investors to sell majority ownership to local investors in each country over a period of time, and it also limited profit remittances and technology transfer. During its entire life, Decision 24 was implemented unevenly by the member nations, and many exceptions existed to its restrictive rules.[2] In May of 1987, the Pact formally replaced Decision 24 with a new, less restrictive policy as prescribed in Decision 220. This rule calls for most of the restrictive conditions to be placed only on those foreign firms wishing to take advantage of the ANCOM tariff preferences on trade between member countries. In the case of foreign multinational enterprises (MNEs) seeking to serve only the given host country, the new rule calls for essentially equal treatment of local and foreign firms.

TABLE 3. Foreign Commercial Bank Loans Outstanding to Andean Countries

(In millions of U.S. dollars at yearend 1985)

borrower lender	Bol.	Chile	Col.	Ec.	Peru	Ven.	all Latin America
all industrial countries' commercial banks	644	14,258	6397	5043	4685	27,105	235,540
United States commercial banks #	102	6536	2192	2148	1470	9716	80,035

* These figures include both public- and private-sector borrowers.
# These data on U.S. bank lending are updated to June, 1986.

Sources: Bank for International Settlements, "Semi-annual International Lending Survey" (June 1986); and Federal Financial Institutions Examination Council, "Country Lending Exposure Survey" (October 1986).

2. National Economic and Physical Environment

A. Economic Structure. These six economies are largely agriculturally based, though population centers are very large and industrial in each one. Table 4 gives an idea of the main types of economic activity in each country.

Note that manufacturing has become the leading sector in four of the countries, although agriculture generally remains very substantial in all of them. The most industrialized countries in the group are Chile and Venezuela, whereas Bolivia and Colombia remain most agricultural.

B. Income Distribution. Income distribution in the Andean countries presents perhaps the largest, most intractable problem constraining economic development there. Historically, the indigenous Indian populations of the countries have lived near subsistence lev-

TABLE 4. Economic Activity in the Andean Countries, 1985

country aggregate	Bolivia	Chile	Colombia	Ecuador	Peru	Venezuela	Total
population (millions of people)	6.4	12.1	26.5	9.4	19.7	17.4	91.5
% rural	52.3	16.4	30.1	48.0	32.7	19.7	...
GDP ($ billion)	5.4	21.9	33.0	12.5	20.8	42.5	136.1
per capita GDP ($ per person/year)	840	1817	1243	1222	1055	2451	...
Sectoral Activity ($ billion)							
agriculture	1.1	2.1	7.3	1.6	3.2	3.2	18.5
mining	0.9	1.9	0.7	1.7	2.1	2.9	10.2
manufacturing	0.6	4.5	7.0	2.2	4.5	8.9	27.7
wholesale and retail trade	0.6	3.7	4.1	1.8	2.8	3.9	16.9
government	0.7	1.1	2.7	1.1	1.7	6.3	13.6

Source: Interamerican Development Bank, Economic And Social Progress In Latin America (1986).

els, while the European immigrants and their descendents have gained in wealth and economic power relative to them (though not relative to industrial countries). Political power in each nation lies substantially with the descendents of European immigrants, and large populations of indigenous Indians still exist outside of the mainstream of national economic and political life.

C. *Physical Resources.* Adequacy of physical resources is *not* one of the major problems of Andean nations. From oil to copper to forests to fish and finally to arable land, these countries are endowed with a wide array of valuable natural resources. The most important natural resources for each country are:

- Bolivia: tin, natural gas, silver
- Chile: copper, iron ore, molybdenum, fish
- Colombia: coal, coffee, oil, natural gas, gold
- Ecuador: oil, fish, bananas, coffee, cocoa
- Peru: copper, fish, oil, silver, cotton
- Venezuela: oil, natural gas, iron ore

D. *Logistics and Physical Distribution.* This is the main problem in stimulating intraregional trade and also in stimulating intracountry commerce within the six nations. Each country possesses hundreds of thousands of square miles of land, populated sparsely by inhabitants except in the urban areas. The Andes mountains create huge natural barriers to roads and other transportation, and few navigable rivers offer an alternative. The Pacific Ocean and the Caribbean Sea provide the main form of intercity transport, followed by air shipment. In sum, due to geographical constraints, physical distribution in these countries tends to be limited to ocean and air transport, both of which are relatively expensive. The logical (and actual) implication of this situation is that much commerce beyond each urban area is international, most often involving the United States, but also Europe and major South American partners such as Argentina and Brazil.

Comparative transportation costs within and among the Andean countries (except Chile) can be obtained from the Junta del Acuerdo de Cartagena (the Secretariat of the Andean Pact) in Lima, Peru (at Esquina Avs. Paseo de la Republica y Andres Aramburu, Casilla

3237, Lima, Peru or telephone 40-5500.) Additional country-specific data is available from each country's Ministry of Transportation.

3. Socio-cultural Environment

A. Cross-Cultural Differences. Although the six countries certainly possess substantial cultural differences, they can be characterized within Latin America as being relatively similar. In each nation, Spanish is the official language, though Indian dialects are widespread. Much of what is now the Andean region belonged to the Inca empire (11th to 16th century, A.D.) and local language, art, music, etc., are much more similar within the region than compared with those of Brazil, Argentina, or Central America.

Similarities notwithstanding, nationalism is quite fervent in each country, and border wars as well as less deadly disagreements frequently occur. Ecuador and Peru appeared near military conflict when the Ecuadoran president was killed in a mysterious plane crash near the Peruvian border in 1981; within a few months a leading Peruvian general died in a comparable situation. Bolivia and Chile have fought repeatedly (mostly through diplomatic channels) over landlocked Bolivia's demand for a "road to the sea" through Chilean territory. These disagreements are indicative of the conflicts that have arisen continually since the independence of the region from Spain in the early 1800s.

B. Consumer Behavior. Because of the highly dichotomized economies in every case, the "consumer" relevant to foreign firms tends to be the urban white- or blue-collar worker. That is, a large part of each country's population are rural, usually Indian, inhabitants who live outside of the modern, semi-industrial economy. This "periphery" is largely ignored by most foreign firms, due to its lack of purchasing power, inaccessibility to physical distribution, and dissimilarity of demands from those of the industrial countries.

The relevant consumers, then, tend to have preferences for many of the kinds of products popular in industrial countries, though their purchasing power on average is much lower. Shopping centers and modern household goods are quite common throughout the region. Personal computers have been available in the large cities since about 1983. Volkswagens are much more common than Cadillacs, but cars, trucks, and buses are very numerous in all urban areas.

C. Business Behavior. In terms of business practices, Latin American countries tend to follow the U.S. model, with adaptations to deal with the special environmental differences that exist. Beyond any doubt, the net result is a less-efficient, more chaotic business environment in Latin America; but the principles of business management are largely derived from those of the U.S. (and often learned through college education in the U.S.).

The clearest difference to U.S.-style free-market capitalism is the very substantial govermental participation in business in Latin America, and specifically in the Andean region. Each country has its own state-owned national oil company, national mining companies, national banks, and state-owned utilities. Many more examples of government ownership and control of business activities exist in each country. Nonetheless, there is a clear recognition of the benefits of private-sector enterprise, and many foreign MNEs operate in each Andean nation.

4. Political and Legal Systems

A. Basic Political and Business Values. At this time, all of the Andean governments are freely elected. All of them have been nondemocratic at some time(s) during the period since World War II, usually under military control. Given the fact that the rate and level of economic development remain unsatisfactory in the eyes of many, political instability does play a significant part in national politics, and it would not be wholly surprising to see a military coup in a country such as Bolivia (though it is highly unlikely in a country such as Venezuela today).

All six countries give free enterprise a high priority in national development strategies. This situation is not likely to change in the near future, though some firms that ally themselves with particular governments could find important backlash effects if new governments succeed in taking power. This is especially true in Chile, where an end to military power could easily lead to negative reaction against firms that currently support General Pinochet.

B. Powers of Constituencies. Important political actors in each country include political parties, the military, and labor unions. Table 5 lists the main political parties and other key actors in each country.

C. Political Stability. Political instability has not dramatically affected business conditions in the Andean nations since the early 1970s. Although many governments have changed hands and in Bolivia many military coups have occurred, the business climate

TABLE 5. Political Actors in the Andean Countries

country	political parties	key unions	military
Bolivia	Movimiento Nacionalista Revolucionario Historico - right/center led by President Victor Paz E. Accion Democratica Nac. - right Union Popular Democratica - left	Confederacion Boliviana de Trabajadores (communist-led union)	civil-military alliance is a key political force
Chile	Alianza Democratica - 5 opposition parties Democrato Cristiano - center Partido Comunista - communist	Central Democratico de Trabajadores (goverment opposition)	currently in power; led by President Pinochet
Colombia	Liberal - center/left party led by President Virgilio Barco Conservador - center/right party led by Alvaro Gomez	Confed. de Trabajadores Colombianos (Liberal) Union de Traba. Colom. (Conserv.)	under civilian control, but still powerful
Ecuador	Partido Social Cristiano - center led by Pres. Leon Febres Cordero Izquierda Democratica - left	Confed. de Traba. Ecuad. (communist)	under civilian control nominally, but remains powerful
Peru	APRA - center/left party led by President Alan Garcia; Accion Popular - center/right Izquierda Unida - coalition of leftist parties including communists	Confed. de Tra. de la Rep. del Peru (communist) Confed. de Tra. del Peru	last gave up power in 1980; very strong political force
Venezuela	Accion Democratica - center party led by President Jaime Lusinchi COPEI - center/right party Union Republicana Democratica - center party	Federacion de Trabajadores	under civilian control; less a force than elsewhere

has not altered radically in the region since 1973. This general view has its variations in each nation, to be sure.

Bolivia has experienced more unscheduled government changes than any other country in the world since World War II. On average a coup or other change in the ruling group has occurred more than once a year in that period. This fantastic instability belies a business environment that shows much greater stability, subject mainly to economic factors such as changes in the world tin price and in the vast, relatively unmeasured cocaine business. Given that Bolivia has been the weakest of the six economies during this century, economic rather than political factors probably should be the focus of a foreign firm's attention. The frequent changes in government have not been followed with major changes in business legislation or in interpretation of the rules.

Chile contrasts directly with Bolivia and presents certainly the most politically risky environment in the region. The Pinochet military government has been in power since the overthrow of leftist Salvador Allende in 1973. No regime changes have occurred during this period. However, discontent with the Pinochet regime has risen to extremely high levels in the 1980s, and some kind of unplanned government change appears quite possible in the next few years. The right-wing military dictatorship espouses free-market capitalism, but its successor could very well oppose firms and people who have supported Pinochet. On the other hand, Pinochet himself could easily remain in power for another decade, and is very likely to continue following open market economic policies.

Colombia falls at the highly stable end of the spectrum of political risk in the Andean region. Despite guerilla movements (such as M-19) and high levels of urban crime that both threaten individuals and organizations, the national government appears to be firmly entrenched in power and within a process of orderly transition through regular elections. The liberal party, which won election over the previous conservative government in 1986, shows no signs of disturbing the status quo of government/business relations. Probably the largest political risk today in Colombia is the anarchic impact of the guerilla movements and of the cocaine traffickers.

Ecuador's government has gone through regular elections during the past two decades, and appears fairly stable at present. The largest threat to continuing democratic rule is the economic crisis that began with the debt crisis in 1982 and has continued with the oil price decline in the mid-1980s. Since the vast majority of Ecuador's export earnings come from petroleum and derivatives, the halving of world oil prices has dramatically cut export revenues and national income. IMF support programs have helped in dealing with the immediate crisis, and the political environment in general remains quite unthreatening, but the continuing economic difficulties may lead to greater social unrest as in Peru.

Peru rivals Chile as the candidate most likely to face unexpected regime change in the near future. In Peru's case this is not because of a military government, but rather due to the continuing economic crisis of the 1980s. Not only has the debt crisis profoundly affected Peru, but domestic growth has been stifled because of depressed copper prices, disastrous harvests in several recent years, and lack of a major successful export product (such as oil in Venezuela and Ecuador or coal and coffee in Colombia). Added to this weak environment, the Sendero Luminoso guerilla group has terrorized people in both rural and urban areas for the past five years, and caused many millions of dollars in property damage. The last military government gave up power to an elected regime in 1980, but it is quite possible that a coup will occur in the next few years, failing any major economic improvement.

Venezuela falls near Colombia at the stable end of the political spectrum in the Andean region. In fact, because Venezuela lacks the intense guerilla and drug problems that afflict Colombia, this country probably ranks as most stable in the group (and in all of Latin America) today. Despite the oil price decline since 1984 and the debt crisis since 1982, Venezuela has demonstrated an ability to avoid the worst difficulties of its neighbors during this decade. The current Lusinchi (Accion Democratica) government took power in 1984 and shows no signs of failing to complete its five-year term of office. Indeed, the major political risk to speak of is the possibility of major improvement in rules toward business that could shift from Decision 24-type restrictiveness to a much more pro-business framework.

D. Laws and Regulations Affecting Business. Table 6 summa-

TABLE 6. Selected Andean Rules Affecting Foreign Business

rule country	ownership	profit remittance	technology transfer	exchange controls	local content	price controls
Bolivia	Decision 220	Decision 220	Decision 220	2-tiered exchange market	n.a.	on some products
Chile	unrestricted	unlimited	royalties up to 5% of sales	very open	n.a.	
Colombia	Decision 220	Decision 220	Decision 220	2-tiered exchange market	required in autos	on 30 categories of of products
Ecuador	"	"	"	fairly free	required in autos	on drugs & some foods
Peru	"	"	"	2-tiered exchange rate	25-50% in many sectors	on all products
Venezuela	"	"	"	3-tiered exchange rate	required in many sectors	on 150 categories of products

Decision 220 of the Andean Pact requires fade-out of foreign ownership in foreign direct investment projects to a maximum of 49% over a 30 year period. Also, payments for technology transfer from parent to subsidiary firm are specifically limited -- all for direct investments that propose to utilize the Andean internal tariff preferences for exports to other member countries. Ownership limits do not apply to firms serving only the country in which the subsidiary is established.

rizes major rules in the Andean countries that relate to foreign business operating in the region.

5. Technology Environment

A. Material Culture. The large and successful private firms in each country, whether domestic or multinational, use up-to-date industrial technology and follow modern management practices. Although it is true that none of these economies functions overall at the same level of efficiency as, say, France or Canada, still the leading firms tend to be more similar technologically to their industrial-country counterparts than to traditional, very low-tech local firms. The two reasons for this situation are that: (1) hundreds of foreign firms operate locally in each country, bringing in some of their parent company knowledge and skills; and (2) thousands of company and government managers received their undergraduate and/or graduate school training in the U.S. or in Europe, thus obtaining directly industrial-country knowledge. Thus, the technology base in Andean countries is best characterized as disparate, i.e., some firms operate as in industrial countries and others follow very traditional, low-tech practices common in less developed countries in general.

B. Human Resource Skills and Availability. The reverse side of the coin from the commentary in the last paragraph is that even though some firms and people are quite up-to-date and skillful with current technology, most still are not. For every firm that does use a personal computer, there are thousands that do not. There is no lack of intelligent people in the region, but there is a huge, fundamental lack of resources to pay for their university and graduate educations. Business and engineering schools do exist, but highly qualified (e.g., Ph.D.) instructors are rare.

The rest of this section notes leading sources of trained managerial and technical people in each country.

In Bolivia, the leading business school and engineering school are in the Universidad Catolica de La Paz in La Paz. The scarcity of local expertise is most pressing in the key mining industries, but it is general throughout the economy.

In Chile the leading business schools are those of the Universidad de Chile (in Santiago) and the Universidad Santa Maria (in Valparaiso); very good engineering programs exist at both the Universidad de Chile and the Universidad Catolica (both in Santiago).

In Colombia, the leading business schools include those of the Universidad de los Andes and Externado Nacional, both in Bogota. In engineering, the leading institutions are the Universidad de Santander (in Bucaramanga) and the Universidad de Antioquia in Bogota.

In Ecuador the leading business school is in the Universidad Catolica and the leading engineering school is the Escuela Polytecnica, both in Quito.

In Peru, the leading business schools are ESAN and the Universidad del Pacifico, which graduate a total of about 100 MBAs and 80 undergraduates per year. The leading engineering school is the Universidad Nacional de Ingenieria. All of these institutions are in Lima.

In Venezuela the leading business school is IESA in Caracas, which graduates about 100 MBAs per year. The leading engineering school is at the Universidad Simon Bolivar, also in Caracas.

In sum, there are some local sources of skilled human resources in each Andean nation, but the numbers of graduates remain quite low, and much of the managerial and technical skill is imported from abroad, especially from the U.S.

6. Organizational Culture

A. Organizational Forms. The limited-liability corporation (usually called Sociedad Anonima) is the standard corporate form in Latin America, as in the U.S. Shareholding generally is far more centralized in this region, with family-owned and government-owned firms being the rule. National stock markets are extremely undeveloped, and few shares are widely traded. The specific rules governing corporations, partnerships, and other legal forms are readily available from local corporate law firms in each country and from information vendors such as Business International Corporation and the Big Eight accounting firms in the U.S. (References are given in Section 9 below.) For U.S. firms entering the local market, most competition tends to come from the largest local firms and from other multinational firms there, almost all of which are Sociedades Anonimas.

A major difference in organizational form that does exist is the ownership pattern, even beyond the predominance of family-owned companies and government firms. Since the advent of the Andean Pact, foreign investors have been required (except in Chile) to sell majority ownership to local investors, so joint ventures are numerous. Many, many exceptions exist—and firms that entered Andean countries before 1971 were exempted from the requirement—but still a large number of foreign/local joint ventures do operate in the region. The impact of this ownership structure is difficult to appraise, though joint ventures in general have been studied widely in the past few years.

B. Decision-Making Patterns. Since the main organizational forms follow the U.S. model (except state-owned firms), decision-making also tends to follow this path. Perhaps the major noticeable difference is the time frame typically involved. The *mañana* culture of Latin America pervades the business system, thus slowing down the process of decision-making. In addition, the bureaucratic nature of government relations and the widespread presence of government in the economy tend to slow down business implementation (when permissions or approvals are needed).

7. National Control of International Trade

A. Trade Policy. Trade policy throughout the region is highly restrictive. Balance of payments deficits in every country have led to severe protectionism against imports and limits on access to foreign exchange. Import restrictions in most cases include the requirement of a license permitting importation of the specific products in any shipment and the prior deposit of some percentage of the import value with the Central Bank for a period of time such as 180 days. A sketch of these policies appears in Table 7.

Since detailed commentary on relevant rules in each country would require too much space here, reference is made in Section 9 to useful sources.

B. Free Trade Zones. Four of the Andean nations operate at least one free trade zone. The zones are located in Punta Arenas and Iquique (Chile); Baranquilla and Cartagena (Colombia); San Lorenzo (Ecuador); and Isla Margarita (Venezuela). Basically, the free zones allow duty-free importation of products into the zone and tariff only on the imported content of products manufactured there and sold domestically.

8. Business Opportunities

A. National Plans. National planning occurs in every Andean nation, and published plans do provide opportunities for foreign suppliers. Since the plans differ widely from one country to another, it is not useful to generalize about the kinds of products or services that may be most desirable. Instead, it can be noted that a national ministry (usually the Ministry of Planning) creates and im-

TABLE 7. Import Restrictions in Andean Countries, 1986

sector country	manufacturing	mining	services	government
Bolivia	depressed due to hyperinflation	depressed	improving	major budget cutbacks
Chile	improving due to privatization	depressed	improving	major budget cutbacks
Colombia	improving due to coffee,oil, and coal bonanzas	growing rapidly	improving	fairly stable spending
Ecuador	depressed due to oil price fall	depressed	depressed	major budget cutbacks
Peru	very depressed due to low copper price, external debt, etc.	depressed	depressed	slight budget increases
Venezuela	improving versus 1985	oil sector very depressed	weak	slight budget decreases

Sources: Inter-american Development Bank, Economic and Social Progress in Latin America. (1986); Business International Corporation, Investing, Licensing, and Trading Conditions (1986 edition).

plements a national plan with a five-year horizon in each country. Annual reviews and adjustments normally take place, so that a potential supplier should be able to obtain indications of market potential for some products (especially those sold directly to the government) through this Ministry.

B. *Industry Trends.* All six of the Andean countries face the problem of large external debt. This problem greatly limits the likelihood of any of them attracting major quantities of new foreign investment, portfolio or direct. Domestically, each one possesses a growing economy, recovering from the economic crisis of 1982-84. Broad trends can be sketched for each nation, and they are summarized in Table 8.

By far the most important industry in Bolivia in the 1980s is cocaine. This industry is estimated to generate up to half of Bolivia's total exports and a substantial portion of domestic employment. Because the industry operates illegally, it is impossible to obtain exact data on its size and importance.

TABLE 8. Sectoral Trends in Andean Economies, 1986

country	policy tariffs	non-tariff barriers	other
Bolivia	n.a.	n.a.	n.a.
Chile	10% uniform tariff ad valorem	Import payment must be made after 120 days after shipment; license required on all imports	used cars may not be imported
Colombia	maximum 80% ad val.	license required on 33% of products imported; quotas on raw materials	prior deposit required for import license
Ecuador	range of 0-200% ad valorem	license required for most imports; 180-day prior deposit required	
Peru	average 57% on mfg, 25% on raw material ad valorem	300 products prohibited; license required on all imports; no prior deposit	
Venezuela	range from 0-500% ad valorem	license required for many products; coffee, salt, some clothing are prohibited	

Sources: Business International Corporation, *Investing, Licensing, and Trading Conditions*. Price-Waterhouse, *Guide to Doing Business in Bolivia, Chile*. current editions.

Second in importance is mining, which will remain a very important sector into the 21st century. At present, world tin prices are extremely depressed, so that production and revenues in that sector are likely to remain historically low and tin will continue to be in a severe recession.

Manufacturing and agriculture appear unlikely to improve substantially in 1987 due to depressed domestic demand and low prices for agricultural products.

In Chile, the copper industry continues to suffer from extremely low international prices, hence it is greatly depressed. The local economy generally has not recovered from the severe recession of the first part of the 1980s. Manufacturing and agriculture are weak, with no major improvements forecasted for the near future.

The economic policies of the "Chicago Boys," which began in 1973 and were accompanied by rapid growth, have failed to cope with the debt crisis and low raw materials prices worldwide. These problems cross all industries, and they (along with the political risk) make Chile relatively unattractive as a market for foreign firms.

In Colombia, the 1986 "bonanzas" of coffee, coal, and oil sales, along with a relatively small foreign debt problem, have combined to put the economy into very positive real growth. The coal industry, following the opening of the Cerrejon project, is booming. Coffee, long a staple export product, benefited from a 1985 Brazilian production shortfall, and prices and volumes remain high even two years later. Additional oil deposits have added greater income to that sector as well.

Both agriculture and manufacturing have been pulled along with these raw materials successes. Although neither industry's growth is spectacular, both are improving compared to the first half of the decade.

In Ecuador, the oil industry has kept the rest of the economy in recession in the mid-1980s, after the initial crisis of foreign debt in the early-1980s. Industrial production is expected to decline or remain stagnant for 1987.

The agriculture industry offers a somewhat better picture. Coffee exports have boomed, similar to Colombia's situation, during the past two years. Banana and shrimp exports are forecasted to rise greatly in 1987 due to increased output, despite depressed prices of these commodities.

In Peru, the economy has stabilized somewhat since the onset of the debt crisis, but real income has not recovered to its late-1970s level. Major natural resources such as copper and oil, whose prices are still depressed compared to the 1970s, have failed to restimulate growth. Government spending has been forced to follow suit.

Perhaps the main bright spot for Peruvian industry is agriculture, where production of sugar, cotton (and, very importantly, cocaine), and other commodities is increasing. After disastrous weather conditions in the early 1980s, Peruvian crops have returned to normal and included production for export. Although price controls and severe restrictions on funds transferred out of the country make new foreign investment generally unattractive, agriculture will be a growth sector for at least the next few years.

In Venezuela, the major devaluation of the bolivar in December of 1986 (along with low world oil prices) will lead to depressed gross domestic product (GDP) in 1987. The oil sector plays such a dominant role in the Venezuelan economy that the forecast for any future time parallels the forecast for the price of oil. Given an expected $U.S. 15-20 per barrel price for 1987-88, Venezuela's economy will not grow rapidly. Likewise, government spending must remain limited due to low tax receipts on oil income.

Industries that have improved in a major way recently include agriculture. Venezuela once again produces most of its own food supply, rather than importing many products at relatively low bolivar prices. Crops such as corn and wheat are again being produced at a surplus over domestic needs.

Manufacturing does not show strong growth, but it is attracting more foreign direct investment as the dollar cost of investing falls and the market remains the third largest in Latin America.

C. Market Trends. Beyond the brief sketches offered above, the best sources of information on national market trends are listed in the next section. Generally speaking for U.S. firms, national market trends can be obtained from local U.S. embassies in each country. The U.S. Department of Commerce publishes periodic surveys of national market trends that cover some of these countries (most often Venezuela), but more current information is available from commercial attaches in the embassies. Other sources are as listed.

Sources of Information

A. Foreign Sources. The most up-to-date information is available from companies that supply this service on a fee basis. For example, Business International Corporation in New York publishes extensive information on government regulations, business conditions, financial markets, and company anecdotes that relate to U.S. companies doing business in each of the Andean countries. In addition, the company carries out specific research as requested by clients. More specific information is provided for greater fees, as would be expected. The *London Financial Times* publishes a biweekly newsletter on Latin America (viz., *Latin American Markets*) that gives additional insights into government policies and company experiences in these countries (and elsewhere in Latin America). And finally, an independent British newsletter organization called Latin American Monitor, Ltd., publishes a monthly regional report, the *Andean Group Monitor,* as well as a newsletter on all of Latin America.

The U.S. government publishes a wealth of information about economic and political conditions, market trends, and individual company trade leads in various formats. The best way to become familiar with these services is to visit a Department of Commerce field office near your firm, the main office in Washington, or the commercial section in a U.S. embassy overseas. The Commerce Department publishes *Overseas Business Reports* periodically on individual countries around the world. Similarly, this agency publishes *Global Market Surveys* focusing on individual industries around the world. Trade leads for specific products are compiled by each embassy and made available through the Department's international computer network. In all, the Department of Commerce is an important source of business information on the Andean countries (and the rest of the world). A key difference between this service and those of the private information companies is that the Commerce Department tends to be much less up-to-date, and inversely much less expensive.

Selected published sources of business information about the Andean countries,[3] which originate outside of the countries, are listed in Table 9.

B. Local Sources. Local information sources in each country are fairly numerous and virtually only available in Spanish. The information should be sought through a local law firm, commercial bank, or accounting firm. In each country aggregate economic data is available from the Central Bank, which publishes a monthly bulletin of domestic and international financial statistics. In addition, the local agency responsible for Andean Pact relations (except in Chile, which is no longer a member) usually is able to offer information about current rules relevant to foreign investors seeking entry into that country. Due to restrictive policies in each country, information about export requirements (i.e., rules for importing into the Andean country) are needed from several different sources, including the Central Bank, the Ministry of Economy, and another agency responsible for import licenses. For this reason, and the fact that responsibility for the policies changes from time to time, it is best to consult with a local intermediary such as a commercial bank to obtain the latest rules and information.

TABLE 9. Non-Local Sources of Information on Andean Countries

country	sources
All Andean Nations	Business International Corporation, Investing, Licensing, and Trading Conditions (updated by country yearly); Financing Foreign Operations (updated annually by country).
	*Price-Waterhouse, Doing Business In ..., for each country (updated every 3 or 4 years).
	*similar publications from other Big Eight accounting firms.
	*U.S. Department of Commerce, various publications; computerized listing of trade opportunities for U.S. exporters.
	*International Monetary Fund, International Financial Statistics for macroeconomic data on each country (updated monthly).
	*Inter-american Development Bank, Economic and Social Progress In Latin America (annual edition) for economic data and brief country analyses each year.
	*Oceana Publications, Digest of Commercial Laws of the World (annual edition) for information on contract law, commercial procedures, business associations, and more for most countries.
	*United Nations Economic Commission for Latin America, Economic Survey of Latin America (annual issue) for macroeconomic data and forecasts on each country.
	*Frost & Sullivan, World Political Risk Forecasts (updated monthly) for forecasts of political conditions relevant to business.

10. Methods of Entry into National Business

There are no *de facto* limits on the range of entry methods in Andean countries, except that some activities such as telephone and mail service and electric power provision are reserved to the government. Andean Pact rules *de jure* restrict some forms of doing business, but these rules are widely broken. For example, there are many wholly owned foreign manufacturing plants in each Andean nation, despite the fact that the Andean Pact's Decision 24 required 51% ownership to be sold to local investors over 15 years (until 1987, when this restriction was dropped). All of the major forms of international business that apply in the industrial countries are used in the Andean region: exporting, wholly owned direct investment, partially owned direct investment, portfolio investment, licensing, franchising, turnkey projects, and other contractual ventures.

11. Areas of Conflict

A. Direction of Industrial Growth. There is no question that a major factor hindering foreign firms in the Andean region is the divergence of interests between profit-making firms and social welfare-seeking host governments. Even when their interests coincide (which is often), governments often feel obliged to criticize foreign multinational firms as scapegoats for the countries' general economic and social ills. The concept of dependency in international politics grew out of the economic dependence of Latin American governments on the activities of U.S.-based firms that supplied industrial machinery and finished goods, bought mining and agricultural exports, and even financed much of this business after World War II. This dependency (or better stated, inter-dependency) has not faded away over the years, and resentment of foreign investors and lenders remains.[4]

A fundamental and intractable problem is that multinational firms almost always deal with the most industrialized sectors of the Andean economies. These sectors are the ones that use industrial equipment and/or services, buy internationally traded consumer goods, sell to foreign customers, and generally form the "center" (or most wealthy, educated, and politically powerful part) of the host economy. The "periphery" of the host economy — the primarily rural, uneducated, and very poor people — tend to be ignored by the multinationals because of their very low purchasing power and failure to produce outputs used by those firms. Host governments tend to serve mainly the centers of their own economies, and fail to deal adequately with the periphery. Given this situation, there is little the MNEs can do to resolve the center/periphery problem, but these firms are quite easily targeted scapegoats for pressure groups seeking improved income distribution and faster development. This serves as a warning to foreign firms about a continuing social problem; unfortunately, no easy solution can be presented.

B. National Control of Key Sectors. Government/business conflict in this area primarily occurs when foreign firms seek to enter or expand in Andean markets, and they are blocked by local government-owned companies. Conflicts tend not to be terminal (expropriations and nationalizations are few, especially since 1975), but foreign firms do come up against barriers that preclude some business activities. A simple example is the nationalization of the oil industry in Venezuela in 1975. Foreign firms (e.g., EXXON, Texaco, and Gulf) were forced to sell their oil producing and refining affiliates in Venezuela to the government oil company, PDVSA.

Since then, the foreign oil firms are limited to selling their technical services in Venezuela, buying PDVSA's oil and derivatives, and operating in other businesses (such as chemicals). Similar situations have occurred throughout the region in many raw materials industries and in public utilities. Foreign firms in manufacturing or in service sectors have not encountered such severe problems, and there is no sign that such inward-looking policy will arise in the future. Most of the state-owned firms are in utilities and raw materials areas, and the current trend is toward denationalization (i.e., "privatization") of businesses to improve efficiency.

C. Credit and Pricing Policies. Credit tends to be restricted for foreign firms, often through simple bans on foreign entities from use of local long-term capital markets. Governments are trying to force these firms to seek financing from retained earnings and from foreign sources, to maintain liquidity in local financial markets. Because the situation changes rapidly and frequently, it is not useful to list current credit terms available to foreign firms; the references in Section 9 should provide the necessary information.[5]

D. Research and Development. R & D is a topic of continuing frustration for less developed country governments. Regardless of incentives or threats toward MNEs, it has proven impossible to attract basic scientific research to Third World host countries. The companies find it unacceptably expensive and risky to site R & D activities in politically risky nations with relatively small domestic markets. The vast majority of industrial R & D takes place in the industrial nations of North America, Western Europe, and Japan. Foreign direct investors often do find a place for product adaptation in their Andean activities. This task of changing typically minor product characteristics such as electric power requirements, packaging, and promotion, may be considered product development. But moving beyond such rudimentary R & D has thus far not occurred, despite the repeated efforts of governments to attract such activities.

For a multinational firm to pay for technology imported from the home office to an Andean subsidiary is quite difficult. The Andean Pact rules forbid payment of any royalties to a parent firm. Aggregate data on royalty payments from Andean subsidiaries to U.S. parent firms amount to millions of dollars annually,[6] so exceptions to the rule are being made in every country. (Of course, this limit does not exist in Chile.) Patent protection is usually available for most products and processes, though rules on pharmaceuticals tend to provide much less protection than in industrial countries.

E. Human Resource Policies.[7] In every country there are highly restrictive local labor requirements. This limitation in practice is not often important, since virtually all firms employ local workers and "import" only a very small number of expatriate managers and technical staff. Nonetheless, permission is needed to bring in nonlocal personnel, and bureaucratic delays are typical.

Worker benefits including wages and job protection are mandated by the national governments, and it is not easy to fire workers regardless of their performance on the job. Labor relations can be conflictive, and strikes are much more common than in the U.S. Since labor unions are affiliated with national political parties in each country, the economics of wage and benefit bargaining become mixed with the politics of government regulation.

F. Taxation. Corporate taxes follow similar progressive bracket-based schemes as in the U.S. Table 10 shows the corporate tax rates in effect in 1986 in each country.

12. Resolution of Conflicts

The main types of conflicts encountered by foreign companies in Andean countries are commercial disputes, which must be settled in local courts. Since the ITT attempt to interfere in Chilean politics in the early 1970s, the U.S. government has made a consistent effort to avoid involvement in commercial problems of U.S companies in the region. This means that local disputes leave U.S. firms with no recourse to outside mediation or arbitration. None of the Andean nations belongs to the World Bank's International Court for the Settlement of Investment Disputes, so that avenue of appeal is not available.

An important additional form of business dispute that has become quite important in the 1980s involves payment of foreign debt by both public and private borrowers. Borrowers in every Andean country have encountered difficulty meeting interest and principal payments during the 1980s, due not to simple commercial problems

TABLE 10. Corporate Taxes in the Andean Countries

tax country	corporate * income	dividend withholding	royalty withholding	interest withholding
Bolivia	30%	30%	30%	30%
Chile	37%	40%	40%	none
Colombia	40%	40%	52%	20%
Ecuador	39%	40%	15%	8-10%
Peru	40%	30%	55%	55%
Venezuela	50%	20%	18-50%	18-50%

* highest marginal corporate income tax rate

Sources: Business International Corporation, *Investing, Licensing, and Trading Conditions* (1986 edition); Price Waterhouse, *Information Guides for Doing Business in Chile, Bolivia* (1986 editions).

but rather to the generalized debt crisis which has made access to foreign exchange much more difficult throughout Latin America. Colombian borrowers have faced the least critical shortage of dollars, whereas the crises in Peru and Bolivia have been most severe. Commercial bank loans to government borrowers in the other five nations have been repeatedly rescheduled in negotiations involving hundreds of U.S. and European banks. The real importance of this problem is that it continues today and affects credit availability in every country of the region.

13. Corporate Strategy for Foreign Firms

A. Strategic Options. The basic strategy for a foreign multinational (or even a small) corporation looking to operate in an Andean country is to seek commercially viable projects and then create hedges to avoid the country and currency risks that plague the region. Hedges can be viewed under four headings: risk avoidance, risk adaptation, risk transfer, and diversification. Risk avoidance implies simply avoiding investment in extremely risky countries (such as Nicaragua or Iran in 1987), and requiring a higher projected return on investment in countries such as the Andeans to offset the higher-than-usual country risks. Risk adaptation involves structuring projects to balance local assets and liabilities (or at least local currency assets and liabilities, wherever they may be booked), e.g., buying inputs or products locally to balance local accounts receivable; borrowing locally to offset local assets; seeking forward or futures contracts to protect futures payables and receivables; and/ or producing only part of the product(s) locally to reduce the attractiveness of the project to local government interference. Risk transfer involves purchase of insurance or guarantees where possible to transfer political, currency (or even commercial) risks to an outside agency (such as the U.S. government agency, OPIC, or an insurance company). And finally, diversification simply implies doing business in a portfolio of countries to reduce the potential negative impact that a problem in the Andean country would have on the total company.

B. Financial Options. Financial hedging can be accomplished through local borrowing (to increase local-currency liabilities) and by placing local deposits into dollar-denominated instruments that generally exist (thus reducing local-currency assets). Neither of these alternatives provides total protection against exchange rate risk—nor against interest rate risk or risk of price controls—but each tends to reduce the net asset exposure that is typical of foreign firms operating in Andean countries.

Exporters to Andean countries often can price their sales in U.S. dollars, or they may be able to obtain letters of credit that can be discounted in order to eliminate exchange risk. No organized forward or futures markets exist for these countries' currencies, though in principle many U.S. banks could offer such contracts, if negotiated by the firm.

Countertrade is a financing technique that has gained wide acceptance by governments in the region. Since countertrade usually involves payment for some product(s) with other products, it is unappealing to most firms. Given real constraints on dollar availability in the Andean region at present, this technique may be a viable alternative to doing no business at all (or falling victim to a Central Bank's inability to provide dollars for local currency sales).

Foreign investors face numerous restrictions on access to dollars (e.g., unfavorable official exchange rates, unavailability of dollars, complex procedures to buy foreign exchange, etc.) in most Andean countries. Methods to transfer funds abroad include dividend remittances, loan repayments, intra-company shipments of goods or services, and a variety of other alternatives.[8] By transferring funds out of an Andean country, obviously exchange rate risk and political risk are reduced.

C. Recent Examples. Foreign company strategies in all of Latin America during the 1980s have tended to try to avoid new capital infusions and to obtain payments from subsidiaries in dollars as they come due. Neither has been very easy to accomplish. In fact, foreign direct investment flows have mostly been limited to reinvestment of earnings that are difficult to repatriate, rather than new funding, during the decade. Often when a foreign firm does seek to expand its operations in an Andean country, the funding can be obtained partially or wholly from another multinational firm locally which has a surplus of funds from its activities. (The parent firms of these subsidiaries then lend funds between themselves in the reverse direction, creating a "parallel loan.")

Another interesting financial strategy that has developed during the debt crisis is the debt/equity swap. One version of this kind of swap involves a foreign multinational firm that buys a dollar loan from a foreign bank lender to some Andean client, say the Central Bank of Chile. The firm pays 75% of dollar face value for the loan, thus implying that the bank loses 25% of face value, but is able to get the loan off its books. The firm next sells the loan back to the Chilean Central Bank for 85% of face value in pesos, thus saving the Central Bank 15% of the value and escaping any need to pay in dollars. Finally, the firm invests its discounted pesos in the local subsidiary for desired expansion that instigated the whole process. The firm is swapping dollars for pesos, and the banks are liquidating a problem loan. In 1986, it is estimated that Chile's government carried out over $2 billion of such transactions to reduce the foreign debt.

14. Corporate Organization and Control of Foreign Firms

This issue has been treated in Sections 6, 10, and 14, and needs no additional explanation here. A couple of examples are offered to demonstrate what some companies have done recently in this area.

Although joint ventures have been heralded as the investment strategy of the late 1980s, and the Andean Pact rules still call for fade-out of foreign ownership in Andean foreign direct investment (FDI) projects that seek regional tariff preferences, such ventures are not replacing wholly owned ventures to any major degree. The percentage of FDI that occurs in joint venture projects rather than wholly owned ones has risen over the past two decades, but there is no evidence that they are replacing 100% foreign-owned subsidiaries. Similarly, licensing and management contracts have come into widespread use in extractive industries and public utilities, but some foreign ownership does exist at least in equipment production in all of the countries, and it appears likely to remain.

A strategy that has been used widely in the pharmaceuticals industry to avoid creation of large excess capacity in the small Andean markets is tolling. This technique requires one firm to invest in a final assembly (formulating) plant. Then several other firms, plus the investor, produce their pills, liquids, tablets, etc. in the plant. The noninvesting firms pay a fee to the investor for processing their products (i.e., tolling), and all of the participants are able to meet local production rules in the host country. Proprietary chemical ingredients are generally imported from parent countries.

15. Future Business Opportunities and Scenarios

These issues were discussed in Sections 4 and 8 above. Annual country forecasts are available from services such as Business International Corporation (in *Business Latin America*), Frost & Sullivan, and Wharton Econometrics.

NOTES

1. For information on the Latin American debt crisis, see William Cline, *International Debt*. Washington, D.C.: Institute for International Economics, 1984.

2. An analysis of Decision 24 appears in Robert Grosse, "The Andean Foreign Investment Code's Impact on Multinational Enterprises," *Journal of International Business Studies* (Winter 1983).

3. For many additional references see, Donald Shea et al., *Reference Manual on Doing Business in Latin America*. Milwaukee, WI: University of Wisconsin, 1979.

4. The dependency view, initiated by economist Raul Prebisch after World War II, is presented in some detail in Fernando Henrique Cardoso and Enzo Fal-

letto, *Dependencia and Development in Latin America*. Berkeley, CA: University of California Press, 1979.

5. Business International Corporation's *Financing Foreign Operations* is a particularly current and useful source of price/credit control information.

6. The U.S. Department of Commerce's *Survey of Current Business* (August issue) presents data on royalty payments to parent U.S. firms.

7. A useful reference on this issue is Spalding, Hobart, *Organized Labor in Latin America*. New York: New York University Press, 1977.

8. A recent discussion of fund transfer methods appears in Grosse, Robert, "Financial Transfers in the MNE: the Latin American Case," *Management International Review* (1986).

Chapter 3

International Influences Affecting Great Britain

Ronald Savitt

EXPORTS AND IMPORTS

Great Britain remains one of the world's most important industrial nations and an active participant in world trade. External trade for the United Kingdom (Great Britain and United Kingdom are used interchangeably) for 1986 is shown in Table 1. The distribution of trade in export markets in descending order are the United States, West Germany, France, the Netherlands, Ireland, Belgium-Luxembourg, Sweden, Italy, Saudi Arabia, and Switzerland. For 1986, export proportions for major trade areas are as follows: the United States, 14.2%, the European Economic Community (EEC) including Ireland, 48.0%; The Commonwealth excluding Canada, 8.8%; Canada, 2.3%; the Middle East, 6.9%; and Soviet Eastern Europe, 1.6%. Through the postwar period, British exports have moved away from the Commonwealth nations toward European markets, especially as a result of British entry in the EEC. In the past 28 years, the British share of world exports of manufactures has declined from 18.2% in 1958 to 7.6% in 1986. This shift is the result of new and more aggressive competitors such as Japan and internally because of low investment, high production costs, and less than aggressive management.

TABLE 1. United Kingdom External Trade, 1986

SITC CODE1	IMPORTS(cif)2 (1 million)	%	EXPORTS(fob)3 (1 million)	%
Total	86,066.6	100	73,009.0	100
Food and live animals	8,719.0	10.1	3,740.0	5.1
Beverages and tobacco	1,347.0	1.6	1,737.9	2.4
Crude materials, inedible except fuels	4,622.7	5.4	1,904.9	2.6
Minerals fuels, lubricants, etc.	6,294.1	7.3	8,683.4	11.9
Animal and vegetable oils and fats	365.1	0.4	105.3	0.14
Chemicals	7,345.7	8.5	9,691.8	13.3
Manufactured goods, classified by materials	15,327.9	17.8	10,979.0	15.0
Machinery and transport equipment	28,769.2	33.4	25,348.9	34.7
Miscellaneous manufactured articles	11,391.0	13.2	8,575.5	11.7
Other commodities and transactions	1,884.0	2.2	2,206.2	3.0

1   Standard International Trade Classification
2   cost, insurance and freight
3   free-on board

Source: *The Economist Newspaper*, 1987.

IMPACT OF INTERNATIONAL AGREEMENTS

The most important international economic arrangement that affects Great Britain is the Common Custom Tariff of the European Economic Community. Under this arrangement duties are charged on a wide range of basic and processed agricultural products, raw materials, and semiprocessed and manufactured goods imported into the United Kingdom from outside of the Community. Such duties are collected for the Community and hence any such goods may pass freely into the rest of the EEC. Under this agreement, goods manufactured in the UK can be exported to all countries of the EEC without further duty. Similar though not as widespread tariff agreements exist between the UK and the European Free Trade Association (Austria, Finland, Iceland, Norway, Portugal, Sweden, and Switzerland) through the reciprocal agreements by the EEC. As a result of Britain's membership in the EEC, loans to aid development in the Community are available to foreign investors intending to invest in the UK. The institutions that extend these loans are the European Investment Bank, the European Coal and Steel Community, and the New Community Instrument. In order to facilitate industry's taking advantage of such loans in the UK, an exchange risk guarantee program has been established in which the borrower takes only a slight liability and the government takes the remainder of the exchange rate risk. The UK is also a signature to the General Agreement on Trade and Tariffs (GATT) which provides a mechanism for facilitating reciprocal reduction of tariffs and other trade barriers, the standardization of trade formalities, and the resolution of trade disputes. Most favored nation (MFN) status is guaranteed to all members except for common markets and other bilateral agreements among GATT members. The impact of these and other such agreements is to place and maintain the UK as one of the keystone trading nations in the world. Membership in the EEC means that firms located in the UK have substantial advantages in finding investment funds and operating freely in an important market area second only to the domestic American market. The UK no longer accords preferential treatment to Canada, South Africa, New Zealand, and Australia under Commonwealth arrangements. For other members of the Commonwealth, with some exceptions, preferential treatment is found with trade agreements through the EEC.

INTERNATIONAL CAPITAL TERMS

Over the past five years, the current balance of all visible trade, service, transfers, and investment earnings has been in decline. In 1981, the current balance was 6,929 million pounds, slipping to 3,135 million pounds in 1983, increasing to 2,946 in 1985, and turning down to a negative (1,100) in 1986. The visible trade account for the 1981 to 1986 period is as follows:

	1981	1982	1983	1984	1985	1986
Imports	47,617	53,510	61,941	74,751	80,289	81,096
Exports	50,977	55,565	60,776	70,367	78,111	72,842
Visible Trade Balance	3,360	2,055	–1,165	–4,384	–2,178	–8,254

The deterioration in the trade balance stems from a number of factors, including the lack of competitiveness of British firms, changes in exchange rates, increased consumer expenditures with a strong preference for imported goods, and imports of capital goods aimed at increasing domestic productivity. Terms of trade will most likely continue in this fashion and at the same time increases in service accounts, even with sustained growth rates, will not be able to offset trade balances.

MAJOR BRITISH MULTINATIONAL FIRMS

British multinational firms are among the most important in world trade; they operate in just about every country in the world. They include interests ranging from raw material development to consumer goods and services. Some of the most powerful are: British Petroleum, BAT Industries (tobacco, retailing, paper and packaging), P & O Steam Navigation, Grand Metropolitan (hotels, dairy products, brewing), Rio Tinto-Zinc Corporation, George Weston Holdings (food manufacturers and distributors), S & W Berisford (wholesale merchants, commodity traders), Allied Lyons (hotels, brewers, food), Rothmans International (tobacco), Marks and Spencer Ltd, (retailing), Saatchi and Saatchi (advertising), and United Biscuits Ltd (food products and fast-foods).

NATIONALIZED INDUSTRIES

As a result of the Labour Party's domination of British politics for most of the postwar period, a significant part of British industry was nationalized. In the UK, public enterprise accounts for more than 75% of the ownership in telecommunications, electricity, gas, coal, railways, and shipbuilding. Oil production is 25%; airlines, 75%; automobiles, 50%, and steel, 75%. In contrast, the US public enterprise accounts for only 25% of electricity production and 25% of rail services. The Conservative Party under the leadership of Margaret Thatcher returned to power in 1979 with a strong platform based on "privitization" – the sale of state-owned industries to the private sector. Their premise was: "The British people strongly oppose Labour's plans to nationalize more firms and industries such as building, banking, insurance, pharmaceuticals and road haulage. More nationalization would further undermine our freedom." The program has had four major parts: (a) sell to private ownership the recently nationalized aerospace and shipbuilding industries; (b) "achieve substantial private investment" in the National Freight Corporation; (c) relax regulations in rural bus transportation (not deregulation in the American sense); and (d) make the National Enterprise Board sell off its shares in public markets. Further, the government pursued the sale of public housing to tenants.

To date there has been some change in the balance of British ownership to private ownership. More than 400,000 jobs have moved from the public sector to the private sector since 1979. These have been found primarily in transportation, oil production, and communication. Included are British Aerospace in 1981 and 1985, Associated British Ports in 1984, BritOil in 1982, and British Telecom in 1984. The last major national firm sold was British Airways.

There are mixed results to date and it is probably too early to draw any conclusions. The government has been able to use proceeds to finance public spending projects and could conceivably use proceeds to reduce taxes. Private managers are excited by the prospect of the new freedoms of more open markets. The whole success of privitization hangs on the question: "Does being in the private sector inspire companies to better?" (*The Economist*, October 19, 1985, pp. 70-71.)

NATIONAL ECONOMIC AND PHYSICAL ENVIRONMENT

Economic Sector

The economy of the UK is a generally open market in which there is a significant combination of national firms, large and small firms, and private and public firms. The economy is composed of the traditional assortment of energy, manufacturing, distributive, financial, and agricultural sectors, each with the traditional subsegments. The UK is almost self-sufficient in many of these areas, such as many aspects of agriculture, and is highly sufficient in others, such as energy when atomic, coal, and petroleum resources are examined.

The British economy, like many others, is moving across all sectors from being manufacturing-based to service-based. Since 1951 manufacturing employment has dropped from 39% to 19% of total employment in 1986, while for the same period service employment has increased from approximately 43% in 1951 to 66% 1986. Within the service sector, banking has shown the largest increase in employment in this period with an increase of 150%. Hidden in this evaluation of employment data is the increase of employment in the government portion of the service sector, namely in education, health, public administration, and defense.

For many countries the service sector is viewed as the market of the future; however, the UK may have difficulties here. In 1986, Britain earned a surplus of 5.3 billion pounds on services, second only to the US. The two major components are financial services and civil aviation. These increases have not been able to overcome the substantial increasing deficits in the manufacturing sector, however. Tradable services are subject to the same competitive pressures as manufacturing and the longer run trend may be difficult to reverse. Britain's share of world export of services has fallen from 18% in 1958 to 7% in 1963 at about the same rate as the decline in its share of manufacturing trade.

Of all the Western economies, the British is going through the greatest change. Like other industrial nations, Britain has moved away from its traditional manufacturing base and has moved toward services in the broadest sense. This transition as well as the movement toward increases in productivity and greater private sector ownership and management in the UK has not been cost-free in human terms. The new investment has been more efficient than that of the past, but it has put pressures on the business community and labor. There has been a significant reduction in the number of firms and retrenching of a number of major industries in both the public and private sectors. A net result has been dramatic increases in unemployment. Up to 1979, the unemployment rate in the UK was under 4%. After 1976 the rate climbed dramatically from 5.4% to 6.7% by 1980, then to 10.2% in 1981, to 12.7% in 1983, and eventually to 12.9% in 1986. Since then there has been a dramatic reduction in the unemployment rate to 9.4% in late 1987.

Since 1981 the rate of inflation in the United Kingdom has fallen from 11.4% to 8.7% in 1982, 5.4% in 1985, a twelve-year low of 3.7% in 1986. Price increases across industry groups for the 1980-1986 period have varied. Increases, using 1980 as 100 for the period for selected sectors, are: general index of retail prices, 46%; food, 34%; housing, 71%; clothing, 23%; and consumer durables, 20%.

Gross fixed capital investment as expressed in 1980 prices have gone from 40,070 million in 1970 to ± 41,774 million pounds in 1980 and then increased significantly to ± 46,602 million pounds in 1986. Within that period, however, the percent going to investment has declined (1980 prices) from 20% in 1970, to 16% in 1980, to 12% in 1986. The only sector to show dramatic growth has been financial and business services, which increased threefold from 6% in 1970 to 18% in 1986. Petroleum and natural gas extraction increased dramatically from 1% in 1970 to 6% in 1980 but has now begun to drop (4% in 1986) as a result of rapid expansion and now completion of the exploitation of North Sea oil.

Problems in productivity result from the poor investment performance of the UK; it has had the lowest proportion of gross domestic product of the UK's major competitors. For example, in the manufacturing sector American output is three times that of the UK, yet the US invests less per unit of output. American productivity advantages come from both better trained employers and better (higher quality investments) in equipment. In general, the rate of return on fixed capital has been lower in the UK than in other major industrial countries though the current recovery which was initiated by the policies of the Thatcher government including tax reform has begun to show important results. Additional readjustments in tax rates as part of the 1987 budget has further propelled the economic recovery well into 1988. The current recovery in the UK has stretched over the past seven years and with the exception of the coal miner's strike in 1984/85, has been gaining strength.

It is difficult, if not impossible, to describe what the structure of the economy will be in 10 years as a result of the strategies pursued by the Thatcher government. It will be different; high unemployment rates will be associated with lower inflation rates. Some new investments will move the economy toward higher productivity in manufacturing but with lower employment. Reduced tax rates, national insurance contributions, and increased investment incentives will affect labor costs and decrease employment, as the productivity advances will be at the cost of jobs over the next several years. On the other hand, there have been signs of a wealthy middle-class developing as a result of the Thatcher government's tax program. It was recently noted: "It will again be possible to get rich by working. This simple change may prove to be the most revolutionary part of Margaret Thatcher's social engineering" (*The Economist*, April 9, 1988, pp. 13-14).

The challenge for the British government regardless of political stripe is to pursue policies that ensure greater competition among firms in domestic and foreign markets, especially in anticipation of the time when production of North Sea oil and gas decline. The decline of oil revenues as a result of the world oil surplus will also affect the economy. Selling off nationalized industries, opening the British market to foreign competition by encouraging foreign investment, pressuring labor to accept meager wage increases, and introducing higher-productivity technology may bring the economy out of the doldrums. Within all of this there will be opportunities for foreign firms to do business in the UK.

Income Distribution

For the most recent reporting period (1983-84) British distribution of income on a pretax basis was: £ 2,499 and below, 12.4%; £ 2,500 to £ 4,999, 45.3%; £ 5,000 to £ 9,999, 35.5%; £ 10,000 to £ 49,999, 6.4%; and £ 50,000 and over, 04%. Also important are representative wages or earnings for various occupational classes; these amounts represent midpoint estimates in pounds sterling for 1987: airline pilot (captain), 34,335; doctor (general practitioner), 25,960; university professor, 26,585; graduate school master (high school), 10,050; accountant (age 30), 17,500; factory worker, 9,950; miner, 12,150; bank clerk, 8,900; bus driver, 10,244; and shop assistant, 4,480.

When examining income statistics in Great Britain, several considerations must be kept in mind. First, as a result of the National Health Program most medical expenditures are not the individual's responsibility; exceptions are dentistry and eye care. Second, for about 50% of the population there are subsidies for housing. Third, bus and rail transportation are highly subsidized. Direct comparisons with the distribution of income and expenditure patterns elsewhere are difficult. Purchasing power has not increased dramatically over the past six years though it went up by 7% in 1985 and by 3% in 1987 after no increases in the previous two years.

Physical Resources

Britain's natural resources include agriculture, energy, mineral, and sea fishing. Agriculture production in a number of areas has increased substantially over the past several years. Among the important products are wheat, barley, oats, potatoes, sugar, and repeseed oil; also significant are meat, dairy products, and wool. In many areas the UK is self-sufficient and has established export markets, though the UK faces the same problems of agriculture experienced everywhere in the developed world. British agriculture has been greatly harmed by the agriculture policy of the EEC whose extensive price support system has led to higher prices and lower prospect for export markets.

The most important sector is energy in which the UK is self-sufficient. For over a decade it has been a net exporter of oil and relatively high levels of production will continue for the next several decades. There is an important coal industry and estimated reserves are sufficient for about 300 years at current extraction rates. On the continental shelf there are substantial reserves of natural gas. The country also has pursued atomic energy which already supplies nearly 20% of electricity requirements.

Fishing has been a major natural resource for the UK. At one point not more than 20 years ago, the UK was not only self-sufficient but a major exporter of fish and fish products. With the influx of Eastern European, Spanish, and Icelandic fleets, British production has declined.

Logistics and Physical Distribution

Great Britain should be viewed as a market composed of 10 regions, as shown in Figure 1. These regions reflect historical events, present administrative units, and correspond to a variety of government incentive programs. Two of the regions, Northern Ireland and Scotland, are very different from the remaining eight in terms of legal systems and administrative operations. They also represent areas where different types of governmental assistance programs are available. Scotland has its own legal system and many business practices, especially those dealing with real estate and land, are different from England and Wales. Wales, though fully integrated,

FIGURE 1. Regions of the United Kingdom

has an important Welsh-speaking population (it has its own Welsh language television network). Northern Ireland has its own administrative procedures, some of which are in line with the new agreement with the Republic of Ireland and the British Government.

Each of the regions has its unique combination of human and physical resources including educational facilities, raw materials, industrial specialization, and the like. Scotland, for example, has developed a "silicon glen" based on computer technology and university research establishment. Edinburgh has become one of the major financial centers in Europe competing in importance with London for certain types of transactions. Heavy machinery has long been produced in the Midlands, and the business and commercial center is found in the Southeast, better known as "the home counties," which includes London. Northwest England, which includes the major cities of Liverpool and Manchester, includes centers for chemical production, vehicle manufacture, and electronics.

Each of the regions are linked with one another by sophisticated communications and transportation systems. Most of the regions are also connected with Europe and North America by sea, rail, and air services. Internally, most goods are moved by road though rail still plays an important role in commodities for steel production. There is continuation of the freeway (motorway) development plans and these connect major industrial areas; there are about 2,800 kilometers of motorways. There are vast numbers of motor transport companies, some of whom serve Europe and the Middle East by ferry service (roll-on/roll-off). Rail passenger service is excellent by American standards, with high speed trains between London and most major cities on an hourly schedule.

London represents the world's hub for both passenger and air freight traffic with Heathrow and Gatwick airports. There are other major terminals with services to North America in Manchester, Birmingham, Glasgow, and Belfast. These terminals also provide direct service to major European cities as well as to the Far East with over-the-pole flights to Tokyo. There is increasing development of internal air services within the UK with shuttles between London and Scotland, London and Belfast, and other points. These services are primarily directed toward passenger service though airfreight is also carried. The UK has a series of ports whose traffic goes throughout the world. Among the most important are London, Milford Haven, Hull, Harwich, and Southampton.

British postal services are efficient and reliable. The post office claims that it delivers approximately 90% of first-class mail to UK destinations in one day of mailing. It has developed several services that are valuable for business, including: *Datapost*, a door-to-door service for urgent goods and documents in Europe and North America; *Intel post*, facsimile transmission; and *Electronic post*, priority bulk mailings. British Telecom, which has recently separated from the Post Office, offers a wide variety of standard electronic communication services including *Prestel*, which is the world's first public view data service. It allows home and office subscribers to view information ranging from weather and transport schedules to goods for sale.

SOCIAL-CULTURAL ENVIRONMENT

Cross-Cultural Differences

Britain is the the world's oldest democracy and has been the wellspring of many of the economic values which have driven the Western world. In the recent past, there has been a serious decline of the British economy. Economically, the UK has not kept pace with the rest of western Europe. Italy, which has always been viewed the poor cousin of Europe, has begun to surpass Britain in many economic and social areas. With the election of Margaret Thatcher and her administration in 1979, there has been some turnaround in the health of the British economy. There are bright signs in certain areas of technology, energy, and industrial development, though there are serious social and economic problems stemming from many years of neglect.

The social class system still exists in the UK despite many years of work toward elimination. It may even have grown in importance as a result of policies of a series of Labour Governments since the end of World War II. For many Americans the British social classes are not important, but they still remain a factor influencing the direction of economic activities. Unlike what might be expected, the upper classes in the UK have a strong and traditional antibusiness attitude. Business and commerce have not been professions that the scions of the upper classes seek. Much of the commerce in Great Britain has been undertaken by Armenians, Greeks, Jews, and Scots. More recently, these minorities have been replaced by Indians and Pakistanis.

Within the past 10 years, analysis of the class system has focused on those who are employed and those who are known as the "underclass." The latter refers to the large number of Britons, some estimates of which are as high as 4 million out of 55 million, who may never hold a job in their lives. This class is composed of people who have been displaced or "made redundant" as a result of the economy's decline, as well as a number of individuals who are immigrants from Commonwealth countries. These people are primarily located in major metropolitan areas, though there are significant collections in rural areas in Northern Ireland, Scotland, and Wales. In spite of job opportunities, they have limited mobility because of educational deficiencies and because of the nature of public housing which does not encourage people to move from one region to another. Although there are major job training programs and some relaxation of the housing restrictions, which provide the ability to move though not necessarily the quality of housing, these people are generally unprepared for the "new" jobs.

In recent years there have been explosive situations in many of the urban areas that are linked to the unemployment, an overly bureaucratic welfare system, racism, and other urban problems. It is expected that this segment of the population will continue to grow unless new jobs can be created in Britain. Given the concern for increasing labor productivity, great leaps in the number of new jobs are not likely to happen. How any government deals with this segment of society will have great implications for the total growth potential. The immediate implications are found in the clear distinctions between those holding jobs and those who are not. At the same time there appears to be a similar division within employment groups. There are disproportionate rates of income growth. Those in professions, accountants, barristers, some doctors, many civil servants, and so on have an average higher income and higher income growth rates than factory workers, nurses, school teachers, and many service workers. In this context there may well develop three very disparate classes built around income.

Culture-Conditioned Consumer Behavior

The UK consumer market is conservative in spite of the major changes in economic and social life. There are some exceptions such as the high per capita ownership of home computers used primarily for entertainment, and the important trend of meals (fast-food) consumed outside of the home. Stock ownership is not yet widespread, but with the sale of nationalized industries this is becoming an important prospect. Many factors including lagging wage rates, inflation, and energy costs affect consumer purchases. Aggregate consumption patterns in the UK are similar to those in western economies. The British have similar inventories of durable goods and purchase nondurable goods in about the same proportion as their neighbors in the EEC though quantities and qualities are somewhat lower. Even if the British economy were performing at very high levels, it is doubtful that the consumption of some of these items would increase greatly and match the levels of EEC consumers.

The point that needs to be made is that the British consumer is not an active risk taker, changes in consumption patterns for a great many individuals come slowly, and older processes, methods of accomplishing tasks, and even "hardships" are valued as virtues. This is in direct contrast to American instant gratification, French esthetics, and German efficiency.

These conservative circumstances provide challenges for the firm interested in doing business in Great Britain in so far as the ability to market "state of the art" products from North America may not work. In fact, what is marketable in the UK may be one step behind acceptable levels in the rest of the EEC. There is consumer rigidity; the UK has remained with right-hand drive (recall Sweden changed) and has made only small advances toward the metric system. A "pint remains a pint."

Business Behavior

In perhaps no segment of society has there been more change in the last decade in the UK than in industry or business. British business has been multinational as part of the long process of colonization but with that at an end and the general demise of the Empire, business was the first to react. The most important political decision bringing even greater impact has been the decision of the UK to join the EEC. Membership in the EEC has provided in part the challenges of a more competitive environment which business lacked for many years. Although the characterization of Britain as a "nation of shopkeepers" still has some truth, internal industries are extremely large, markets are highly concentrated, and business philosophies generally avoid the rigors of competition. And, of course, some major parts of the British economy were nationalized. While liberal economic doctrines of free trade and open markets were developed in Great Britain, they have generally been observed in their breach.

The new sticks of competition have brought both recognition and action to British industry. An important element in this process has been Thatcher's government policy of "privitization" of public firms. Another element has been the great influx of European dollars and general respect for sterling and hard currencies as a result of increased oil incomes in the Middle East, and the entry into the EEC with its associated advantage of firms choosing the UK as a place to manage European operations. There has been some development of an entrepreneurial class, though compared to the almost fad-like pursuit of entrepreneurial activities in the US, the UK falls far short.

There is a strong antibusiness bias in the UK which has been depicted on BBC television viewed in America. The stereotypes are often unfair but they remain strong. Although the old hierarchy of church, agriculture, education, and civil service has been replaced, there is still enough of it to prevent full-blown competitive activities from taking place. Seeking employment in a commercial field or banking, except at the top or in the retail or distributive trades, is not fully accepted for middle-class individuals in the same way that it is elsewhere in Europe or in North America.

POLITICAL AND LEGAL SYSTEM

The UK is a monarchy in form, but a parliamentary democracy in practice. The sovereign, Queen Elizabeth II, is the head of state and as such is the head of the legislature, the executive, and the judiciary, commander-in-chief of the armed forces, and temporal head of · the Church of England. Presently, the situation is that the sovereign's powers are expressed through Parliament: "the sovereign reigns but not rules." The UK is governed by a body of ministers in the name of the crown. These ministers come from the political party that has been voted into power by the public at large. Parliament itself has supreme legislative authority. It consists of the sovereign, the House of Lords, and the House of Commons. The sovereign formally summons and dissolves Parliament. The House of Lords is composed of peers of the realm including natural hereditary peers, life peers, and spiritual peers. Over the years the powers of the house have been greatly reduced and the main purpose is to supervise the law making process.

The Parliament (House of Commons) must be elected every five years, though elections may be held more frequently. Each Parliament may during its lifetime make or unmake any law. Executive power is vested in the prime minister, who, though nominally appointed by the sovereign, is traditionally the leader of the majority party in Parliament. The most senior ministers represent the cabinet which meets regularly to decide policy on major issues. Ministers are responsible for the running of a variety of governmental departments ranging from domestic affairs to foreign relations to the armed forces. There are more ministries or departments in the British government than there are cabinet positions in the United States. Directly under the ministers are a wide number of civil service positions whose responsibility and tenure are not dissimilar to the situation in the United States.

The United Kingdom does not have a single body of law applicable throughout the realm. Scotland has its own distinctive legal system and courts; some parts of the law in Northern Ireland differ greatly from Scotland and England and Wales. However, a feature common to all UK legal systems – and one that distinguishes them from many continental systems – is the absence of a complete legal code. Legislation and common law are the key parts of the system; unlike the US, there is no written constitution. Final adjudication of matters rests in the hands of the Law Lords.

There is a strong system of local government throughout the various areas of the UK. These are created and their limits defined by acts of Parliament. In England local governments are supervised by the Department of the Environment; in Wales, by the Welsh Office; in Scotland, by the Scottish Office; and in Northern Ireland, by the Department of Environment for Northern Ireland. The "local councils" provide numerous social, sanitary, educational, and police services; they often get involved in business development programs. Depending on legislation, some councils are responsible for levying and collecting local property taxes, known as rates.

There are two major political parties and several smaller parties. The Conservative and Labour Party represent the major political forces, though in the past several years the Liberal/Social Democratic Alliance has become an important minority force in national politics. From time to time other parties, including the Communist Party and the Scottish Nationalist Party, have had influence on political affairs. All of the British parties including the Conservative Party are generally to the left of American political parties in terms of state direction and participation in economic matters. The Conservative party headed by Prime Minister Margaret Thatcher has tended to parallel a number of economic policies from the Reagan administration in the US, especially in regard to monetary matters and foreign trade. However, they still represent practices and policies in domestic affairs that more closely approach Democratic Party goals.

Major parliamentary elections are waged between the Conservative and Labour parties with direct confrontation over government involvement in the economy. The Labour Party is closely aligned with much of the union movement through the Trade Union Conference, which is similar to the AFL-CIO in terms of serving as a central focal point for union presence. The Labour Party has been directly supported by the individual unions though changes in these practices are taking place. Within the Labour Party there are several views about the role of government in the economy and there have been serious disagreements between the unions and Labour governments. The Labour Party favors government ownership and control over business practices, supports social reforms, and encourages job preservation at all costs in the public and private sectors. Another issue between these parties is foreign policy, especially related to international defense and alignments. In spite of strong general differences, both parties supported the Falkland's War.

The Liberal/Social Democratic Alliance represents a loose confederation of the Liberal Party and the Social Democratic Party to find an intermediate way to solve UK problems. They do not accept the significant changes in the economic structure of the Conservative Party and yet are unaccepting of the excesses of the Labour Party especially with regard to the lack of union democracy. It is not clear whether they can provide a middle force in British politics. The Scottish National Party attempted to bring devaluation and complete local government to Scotland in 1979, but has failed in that effort though its small presence has created awareness and some solutions for problems of Scotland. Similar parties and forces have brought a clearer recognition of Welsh problems, too.

Northern Ireland presents the most controversial and difficult political and economic problems in the UK. The strong Protestant majority led by the Reverend Ian Paisley is intent on keeping Northern Ireland an integral part of the UK. The Catholic minority would prefer integration with the Republic of Ireland. For a number of reasons, including political strife, Northern Ireland represents one of the most economically depressed areas in the UK. In November 1985, the British government and the government of the Republic of Ireland attempted to provide the basis of maintaining internal integrity between Ulster and Erie and allowing an Irish solution, whatever that might be.

Laws and Regulations Affecting Business

The UK has as wide a set of laws and regulations affecting business operations as is found in the US; most of these are at the national level, though some represent regional and local areas. For example, the British Health and Safety Executive has the responsibility of overseeing industrial health and safety as much as the Office of Safety and Health Administration in the US. Statutes exist for copyrights, trademarks, and intellectual property, and the UK participates in international agreements in these areas. There is an extensive system of retail planning in the UK which originated in the 1948 Town and Country Planning Act and was amended in 1974. While similar to land planning and zoning activities in the US, the UK approach constitutes comprehensive planning of location and form of building, size of facilities and access, historical preservation and architecture, and use of promotional devices. The retail planning process has greatly affected the shape of traditional retailing and the development of shopping centers.

The UK has an active monopolies policy. Even though antitrust policies have been shifting in recent years, the Monopolies Commission plays an important role in takeovers and mergers. Officially, the UK law permits the Monopolies and Mergers Commission to investigate, and hence delay or block any proposed merger that may be against the public interest (which is not fully defined). Though a deterrent to quick takeovers, the investigative process takes less time than the investigative or litigative processes in the US. And as everywhere, politics often creeps in. Lonrho PLC was blocked from acquiring the House of Fraser, PLC (Harrod's Department Store and other retailing interests) in part because Lonrho Chairman Roland "Tiney" Rowland was an unpopular outsider in British business circles. Yet in 1985, the government permitted the takeover of the House of Fraser by an Egyptian family.

More regulation and regulatory agencies are in the offing as the UK moves toward more public and open markets. The British government is currently viewing legislation that would protect investors as the nation's financial markets are deregulated. Other such activities may well develop as additional sectors such as communications and transportation become deregulated. Such types of activities are natural outcomes of the transformation of British industry from government control or tight private ownership to more open markets and wider public ownership. Such activities really mirror the era of regulation that was fashionable in the early part of this century in the US where the solution to market imperfections and potentially abusive behavior was handled by legislation and regulation rather than by nationalization.

As a member of the EEC, Britain is also subject to its various laws and regulations. The most important of these is Article 85 of the Treaty of Rome which is substantially the "antitrust law" for the EEC. Article 85 in the broadest sense is equivalent to Section 1 of the Sherman Act. Article 86 is similar to Section 2 of the Sherman Act. The EEC also imposes a wide set of regulations on British firms and industries in the market.

TECHNOLOGICAL ENVIRONMENT

The UK has a history rich in the development of new products and processes. The industrial revolution began in Britain and many advances in basic technologies and their application in production processes began here. Many of these have disappeared, others are slowly disappearing, and others are re-emerging in new forms. During much of this decade much hope was raised in regard to developments in the computer and information technology industries. There has been a contraction of this industry in the past several years as a result of aggressive American and Japanese competition. Two major domestic firms, Acorn and Sinclair, have had to take drastic measures including Acorn's merger with Olivetti and Sinclair's limited production as a reflection of the liquidity crisis. The public company was sold to Thorn in the private sector and the new venture may not survive. What is taking place is a restructuring of the industry, the process itself should not be regarded as a lack of opportunity or absence of potential.

British industry has been working in the development of new technologies in the area of off-shore production of petroleum products, fiber optics, robotics, and opto-electronic components. It is home to the greatest concentration of semiconductor manufacturers in Europe and uses more semiconductors than any other European country. The underpinning of achievements in this area has been support for basic research and development activities carried out by private firms, government research facilities, and universities. The UK has a strong higher education system which contains universities and polytechnical institutes. These institutions share the responsibilities for higher education and research across all disciplines as well as provide support and direct services for training programs in a number of occupational categories.

One of the most important resources in Great Britain is the sophisticated financial institution often affectionately called "The City." The City of London has long been one of the major financial centers of the world. They are the entire set of banking, financial, and insurance services required for doing business anywhere in the world. The banks in the UK are linked directly with banks throughout the world and they provide not only access to funds but also information about business opportunities in a number of countries. The London Stock Exchange remains one of the most important financial institutions and should become more important as ownership of British firms becomes wider.

One of the most important parts of the technical resources is found in the National Engineering Laboratory, founded in 1947. The facility does basic and applied research in a great number of areas for governmental agencies and private firms. Among some of the areas that it engages are manufacturing technology, materials technology, fluid power and control engineering, flow measurement, marine operations, component and structural assessment, and engineering metrology. It has also developed expertise in marketing technical products and services. The Laboratory is located in East Kilbride, Scotland near Glasgow.

The British working population was 27,790,000 in 1986, of which 3,329,000 or approximately 11.6% are unemployed. Agriculture, forestry, fishing, coal, and oil and gas and electricity and water generation employ about 4%; manufacturing and processing including construction employs another 27%; transportation and communications, 5.4%. The remainder are in service areas under both private and public management.

The education system has begun to make significant studies to better train and educate people for new employment opportunities. Although there has been much concern about the government's attitudes toward university education, annual enrollment has slowly increased to 310,287 students recently. The government supports a variety of programs that provide incentives to firms for training and retraining and has instituted training programs for "school leavers" and the unemployed. Some schools are actively engaged in programs to integrate industrial needs into curricula of all sorts. The major problem in the UK, as elsewhere, is that skill requirements are changing so quickly that they outpace the education system's ability to provide well-trained individuals. The problem in Britain is especially acute since unemployment is increasing at the same time the shortages of skilled workers is increasing.

There are great numbers of individuals who have basic literary and numerical'skills, but these are often insufficient to qualify for technological occupations and to adapt to change. Several proposals have been made to keep children in school for two more years (to age 18, as in the US), in order to provide additional educational opportunities.

One of the most interesting trends in the labor force is the significant increase in self-employment in the past few years. It has increased by over 13% in the 1980-1986 period and reflects business opportunities primarily in service areas.

ORGANIZATIONAL CULTURE

Business and government organizations in the UK are generally larger in size than similar organizations in the US. Large size stems from the paternalistic role that organizations played, especially in the public sector where they were a means of dealing with unemployment. Most organizations have a strong hierarchical structure with a predominantly downward flow of communication. Organizational structure and individual roles are clearly defined. Entry into the organization is often dictated by place in society rather than by ability, though there have been dramatic changes in the past 10 years. Given this pattern there is a great deal of horizontal mobility between and among organizations and between sectors. Individuals who have excelled in private management often move laterally into public sector positions; in large part this reflects the organizational form but is also related to the extensive degree to which nationalized firms dominate certain sectors that would be private enterprise in the US.

Upward mobility from lower ranks to middle and upper management takes place, though not to the same degree as in North America. Educational achievement is not viewed as the key to the door to business or organizational success as it sometimes is in the United States. Among the three most important economic organizations — the business community, the government, and the labor unions — there are strange organizational relations. At the highest of all levels there is almost mutuality of interest. The CBI, Confederation of Business Industry, is an old boys' club where members generally see their vested interests as the same; this, of course, differs at lower levels of the organizational structure where confrontations take place between and among business, labor, and government.

Organizations tend to be paternalistic when handling employees. Benefits are extended across the board but little effort is given to specific problems of the workplace. Management and unions often easily come to agreements about working hours as a general principle, but often disagree on the application to specific situations. In the UK, laying-off employees and making people redundant is relatively arbitrary and dramatic with no more than a day's notice. Individuals often exhibit loyalty to organizations but cannot be certain that it will be reciprocated. Marks & Spencer, one of Britain's foremost retailers, has become a major exception to the rule by promoting human relations and motivation among its employees, though some would contest this assessment.

Paternalistic behavior has created and maintained adverse conditions between organizations and their employees. Unions that exercise some of their power through the Labour Party attempt to diminish the power of employers in arbitrary ways without considering improvement in the industrial relations system. Many British unions are strident and would not negotiate agreements to reduce salaries as a means of saving jobs — they would prefer plant closure. These behaviors are tied to complex historical issues stemming back to the Luddite movement of the early nineteenth century which saw machinery and technology as evil. And, of course, there is some belief that confrontation will bring capitalism to its knees so a Socialist society can be built. There has been some change in these behaviors as a result of high levels of unemployment, the change of government, and more aggressive activities of some business managers. Also, with more influx of new firms, changes in the above have been seen and will probably come along. Worker participation in management actions associated with worker ownership of stock may also affect management/labor relations.

Decision-making is highly centralized and orders and mandates are passed from higher to lower echelons with high degrees of rigidity. Although policy decisions are executed through all levels of organizational hierarchy, there is little room for discretion low in the structure. For instance, several large retailers require that floor supervisors review change made from 10 pound notes (in current exchange rates, about $16.85) and approve credit cards and checks. As the importance of an issue increases, the matter must go further and further up the hierarchy before a decision is reached.

British boardrooms and management decision-making processes have not been as closely examined by business academics or journalists in the same way that they have been in the United States. Government reporting requirements are much less stringent, and the clubbiness of executives tends to keep activities behind doors except when pushed out into the open by rebels. There is a tradition of business history, but it is not the same thing as the efforts of academics and journalists to keep the business in the spotlight. In spite of attempts to bring business and governmental decision-making out of the boardroom, there is little success except at the time of a scandal. Although *The Economist* is an excellent newspaper, it does not report on the coming and goings of business leaders, business practices, and behavior as does *Business Week* or *Fortune*. There is a general view that such decisions are best handled without public interference and criticism. As a result, there are few media idols like the US's Lee Iaccoca or Carl Ichan.

Although research dominates the technical side of similar industries in the UK and in the US, managerial research and especially marketing research is much less prominent in the UK. This is in part a reflection of attitudes against prying, a certain disregard to the seamier side of business operations, and a reluctance to believe that valuable information can be found beyond the collective wisdom of management. Not all firms ignore the role of marketing research, but it has not been a driving force in market development for British firms as it has for entrants into their market. Market research firms do exist in Britain though many are branches or departments of major advertising agencies. Aggressive use of marketing research can provide an immediate, significant advantage for the entering firm over the home firm.

It is generally fair to suggest that British management has been less aggressive on a number of fronts than firms elsewhere in Europe, North America, and the Far East. There are significant exceptions such as Marks & Spencer, Ltd., STC Ltd., Beecham Group PLC, ICI, House of Fraser, and firms in the oil industry. Management has strong linkages among individuals to families and tradition, and the British business establishment is the origin of the "old boys club." Entry into management at middle and especially upper levels has been related to family, that is, "the right families," rather than entrepreneurial or managerial skills. Therefore not only is it untrue, but patently unfair to blame the British decline solely on recalcitrant unions. Much of the blame must fall directly on management, whose heritage is not aggressive. Within organizations the structure is relatively paternalistic, with clear demarcations between ownership, management, and staff. Only now, for example, as privitization of national industries takes place do average Britons have the opportunity to become shareholders in corporate enterprise. The development of a professional management class is relatively new; in the past many managers received their appointment as a result of family connections or military service. Management structures are isolated from top to bottom as well and are defined around occupational specialties that have their own degrees of hierarchy and status. Even at the same level of the organization and when working on the same project, engineers are isolated from marketing people; the engineers have higher credentials, those in the marketing have less.

Many British manufacturing firms can be viewed as a series of internal adversarial relationships, top to bottom and side to side. Such a system does not encourage the mutual goals of owners, manager, and employees to be reached but creates conditions in which there are incompatible subgoals, few of which ever are achieved. There is often a lack of cadence and various functions are in conflict rather than in general harmony with one another. Marketing divisions attempting to develop new products are thwarted because of the conflict among units of the same firm. These conditions may be generally unknown in Japan and they appear in American firms where there are attempts to rationalize operation, but they are fairly widespread in British firms.

The evaluation of managers in the American sense is a relatively new concept for the British and is making great strides. "Attaching a stick to the carrot" has only recently become acceptable. In those cases where individuals are relieved of their duties another suitable position is still found for them, however. Managers move freely among business, government, and the nationalized industries and move in with relative ease from the military. "Sacking" or making managers "redundant" was rare until relatively recently. A recent incident points toward change in this area. Lord Keith of Castlecase who is Chairman of two of Britain's largest corporations, STL PIC and Beecham Group PLC, has carried out mass purges; his view is "Now, investors demand performance. Pressure is all around, and I think it's a good thing" (*Wall Street Journal*, November 22, 1985, p. 34).

NATIONAL CONTROL OF INTERNATIONAL TRADE

The national control of international trade is minimal. The major restrictions come from EEC regulations and other agreements. The UK has pursued policies of free access to its markets and minimal control over UK firms and foreign firms operating in the UK. The UK is probably the freest environment in which international firms can operate. From time to time there have been restrictions on currency, trade embargoes, and production controls, but these are the exceptions.

Foreign Trade Policy

The Government of Britain seriously supports the development of businesses in the UK whose major intent is the exportation of goods and services produced in the UK. The policy in the vast majority of cases treats foreign firms who maintain operations in the UK the same as native UK firms. Investment is welcomed and foreign-owned firms are eligible for the same benefits as British companies.

The UK belongs to the General Agreement on Tariffs and Trade

(GATT) which is the forum through which international trade policies are liberalized. These policies include: (a) nondiscrimination in trade regulations among member states; (b) a commitment to abide by negotiated trade relations among members; (c) prohibitions against quantification restrictions on exports and imports; and, (d) special activities to promote trade with LDC's. GATT is quickly moving toward a general reduction of tariffs.

The UK also belongs to the European Economic Community (EEC), which has as it goals the creation of a common market in which no custom duties would be established or trade restricted within the market. It has uniform external customs duties. The EEC also created the basis for free movement of the citizens among the various countries primarily for seeking employment. Membership would entitle any country's firm to operate in any one of the other countries. Overall, membership in the EEC has been beneficial for the UK in so far as it has opened up the large European market to British firms. Because of domestic financial problems, however, the UK has not been able to share as greatly in the technical progress of the EEC.

A major issue in the EEC has been the Common Agricultural Policy (CAP), which really was an attempt by the French to protect inefficient agriculture. Within the EEC there are nontariff problems relating to agricultural goods including "lamb wars, wine wars," and for the UK "whiskey wars." Subsidies, though not permitted, taxes, and issues of freshness have affected the free movement of agricultural goods within the EEC.

Free Trade Zones

There are several varieties of free trade zones, each of which offers different opportunities. A freeport is an enclosed zone within or adjacent to a seaport or airport, inside which goods treated for customs duty and agricultural review are payable only when goods are consumed within the zone, or when they cross the border of the freeport into the UK or into the EEC. Relief from customs duties for goods destined for re-export is already widely available through the UK. There are six freeports: Belfast, Birmingham, Cardiff, Liverpool, Glasgow-Prestwick and Southampton.

There are 25 enterprise zones in the UK. Their purpose is to promote industrial and commercial activity in a designated area by removing administrative and financial burdens for firms moving there. Among the incentives are 100% capital allowances and exemptions from local property taxes (known as rates) which last for 10 years from the origin of the zone. Development within the zones is also exempt from some parts of planning control.

New zones are scattered throughout the UK. They offer sites ready for development, with space for expansion and readily available housing for employees. In many, office development is encouraged.

BUSINESS OPPORTUNITIES

The general plan for the UK is the redevelopment of industry, increasing productivity, increasing levels of employment, expanding research and development activities, and expanding exports. The "plan" is part of the Conservative Government's platform and activities since they took power in 1979 and is being executed through a number of measures. The plans that most directly affect firms willing to locate in the UK are those related to incentives for innovation, research and development support, and job creation in the so-called "assisted areas." These programs are composed of direct financial incentives, tax relief, and financial aid.

The Department of Trade and Industry offers selective financial support for approved research and development projects for any British firm (foreign firms operating and managing local operations in the UK are treated as such) engaged in projects that improve the technological base of UK industry. The aid also extends to helping companies get new or significantly improved products and processes onto the market more quickly and effectively. Grants are made for collaborative projects, two or more firms or firms with research facilities or with universities, and greatest emphasis is given in selected key areas. Among those technological areas that have been selected are microelectronic applications, software products, fiber optics and opto-electronics. Those firms who wish to carry out research and development work in the UK have opportunities for several types of help. Among these are tax allowances, regional development grants for the creation of new jobs created by the work, selective assistance grants which are given to safeguard jobs in assisted areas, and support for innovation programs. These are under some scrutiny and changes may be forthcoming, however, they are favorable as compared with others in Europe.

The British Technological Group (BTG) is an independent public corporation whose primary function is to assist the transfer of technology from the laboratory to the market. It provides financial assistance to support companies on commercial terms if a proposed project is based on a new invention or contains a significant technical innovation. All sectors of industry and the subsidiaries of foreign-owned companies are eligible for BTG grants, provided that the resulting business will be located in the UK. Finally, specific assistance for research and development in Northern Ireland is available. This covers the costs of basic research, related design work, prototype testing, final design, and production development costs.

Three of the EEC's institutions provide finances for firms in the UK, including foreign-owned firms who intend to invest in the UK. The three are the European Investment Bank, the European Coal and Steel Community, and the New Community Instrument; they all make loans at low rates of interest to aid development in the EEC. The loans are made in various currencies but guarantees against exchange losses can be made available under the Exchange Risk Guarantee Scheme. The Investment Bank loans are intended to finance industrial projects that aid regional development, usually for seven to eight years. The loans from the European Coal and Steel Community are for the modernization of coal and steel industries and for any sector of industry that provides new employment opportunities for ex-coal or steel workers.

An important part of the aid to firms in the UK is in the Regional Development Grants. A number of areas of the UK have been designated "assisted areas" which means that firms meeting certain criteria, usually the ability to create and maintain jobs, will receive some type of support. There are three categories of assisted areas: they range from Northern Ireland, which has the full range of incentives including some with higher benefits, to development areas and intermediate areas. These assisted areas are to be found in all 10 regions except the Southeast. In general, the applicant firm must be able to demonstrate a good prospect for viability both for the business in general and for the specific project.

In order to tempt business to come to the UK both enterprise zones and freeports have been established in a number of areas. These provide breaks for companies who do work there and export to other countries; they also provide other types of support for investing firms. Many of these zones and freeports are associated with major transportation centers and facilities.

METHODS OF ENTRY INTO NATIONAL BUSINESS

Setting up a business in the UK is as easy as it is in the US. The most popular method of setting up in the UK is the private limited company (PLC), which is nearly the equivalent to the closely held corporation in the US and the branch office. Most foreign firms choose this form since the formalities are few and they can usually be completed within several weeks. Although the opening of a branch office demands fewer formalities, it carries the same requirements as to disclosure of information and therefore offers no real advantage over forming a PLC. Depending on the nature of an operation partnerships or joint ventures with UK firms are also reasonable choices.

Market entry for American firms in the UK will vary with the firm's size, product line, production and/or marketing orientation, and familiarity of foreign markets. Those firms who are unsure about the prospects of the UK are best advised to engage an exclusive distributor to cover the entire country until sales patterns merge, then regional distributors can be used. In such cases many American firms maintain a sales organization in the UK to provide help to their distributors as well as to monitor trends and market potentials. If there are long range goals for producing in the UK or establishing European operations, the sales office is a must. If threshold levels are reached, then the American firm needs to consider direct investment, joint venture, licensing, and other arrangements.

The choice of a marketing representative for the UK is flexible. The same assortment of agents, brokers, commission merchants, and distributors exist there as in the US. Many of the large retail firms have buying offices that search out new products as well. The trade consulates at the British Consulates throughout the US as well as trade officers attached to the US Embassy in London have up-to-date information about these institutions.

The UK has no laws designed to discriminate between national and foreigners in the formation and operation of British companies. American corporations establishing a UK subsidiary have no restrictions regarding the nationality requirements for directors and shareholders. Further, there are no limitations on foreign acquisitions or rent of other types of property.

AREAS OF CONFLICT

The British economy is managed like most major economies, though the UK has pursued greater direct involvement by government ownership than in the US or Canada. Direct ownership is found in the basic industries, communications, energy, transportation, steel, and coal. Government ownership came about as a reaction to what were seen as the "evils" of business and governments used these sectors as a means of controlling employment levels. As with many nationalized industries, the UK prevented the establishment of technologically advanced facilities, bound itself to disastrous labor agreements, and prevented competitive processes from working.

The major area of conflict has been labor relations, though this is an area in which important progress is being made. Management's regard for labor, labor's demand for job security, and the Luddite Movement created a situation in which the labor market has remained rigid and generally impervious to change. Though not directly related to the labor-management issues, labor mobility has been affected by limited education requirements (children leave school at 16) and public housing. The longstanding policy of subsidized housing has decreased labor mobility. People have been literally locked into housing arrangements that do not provide options when employment shifts, so the Thatcher government has established a program of selling off public housing in an attempt to create more mobility. On top of this, pensions related to certain occupations have not been transferable. The result of these policies is that a number of unemployed are unwilling to move because of the absence of housing.

The rigidity of labor toward greater appreciation of the demands of operating in a more open economy has been attacked in several ways. The entire industrial relations system has undergone major change as a result of the Employment Acts of 1980 and 1982 and the Trade Union Act of 1984. These pieces of legislation have attempted to provide a democratic framework for the organization and behavior of unions and to safeguard the interests of employees. The result has been to reduce the power of the union, which has led to changes in work rules and practices. The effects brought by changes in union legislation are difficult to assess because they came at the same time that the UK experienced its deepest post-war recession.

The UK tax system aims to encourage and reward business. In April 1986, the tax rate became lower than in many major economies. The UK has a number of agreements with other countries, including the US, dealing with double taxation issues. There is no restriction on the repatriation of profits. For purposes of taxation, there are two types of firms: (a) resident companies—companies controlled and managed in Britain—which are taxed on all their profits, even if they arise abroad and are not remitted to Britain; and, (b) nonresident companies—companies controlled and managed abroad but conducting business through a permanent establishment in Britain—which are taxed only on the profit of their UK branch or agency.

There are also provisions for group relief. In a group of companies where both the parent company and its subsidiaries (at least 75% owned) are residents in the UK, the losses of one company in the group may be set against the profits of another group member to reduce its tax liability. This relief is available between members of a UK group even if the UK parent is itself the subsidiary of the nonresident company. There are also tax relief programs for new investment, continuous roll-over provisions, and social security contribution deduction provisions.

A significant variation from the American tax system is the value added tax (VAT). Britain, like other members of the EEC, has VAT. This tax is applied at a single rate of 15% to most goods and services supplied by individuals or companies registered as taxable. No VAT is charged on exported goods or on most services performed overseas. As VAT is a tax that is intended to be borne by consumers, registered individuals or companies may reclaim the VAT they pay on almost all supplies received by them including imports, provided that they are used in their businesses or are goods for resale. Customs duties fall under the Common Tariff of the European Community. They are charged on a range of basic and processed agricultural products, raw materials, and manufactured goods imported to the UK from outside the Community. These duties, ranging from 2%-24% on the value of goods, are collected for the Community, not the British government. Goods on which duty has been paid on entry into any member state of the EEC are free to circulate within the EEC without further payment of customs duty. Goods produced in the UK can be exported to all other countries in the EEC without payment of customs duty. Preferential treatment, and often complete exemption from duty, is also given to a large number of goods manufactured in the UK when they are imported into countries such as the members of the European Free Trade Association (EFTA) with which the EEC has reciprocal agreements.

The only local taxes in the UK are "rates." They are similar to property taxes in the US and they are collected by local authorities. The rates applied are based on location, size, amount of investment, and similar factors. They are often negotiated away in whole or part as a result of local policies to attract new industry.

RESOLUTION OF CONFLICTS

There are several indirect means by which conflicts can be resolved as well as direct appeal to the legal system and internal action within firms. There are three important organizations to be considered. The Confederation of Business Industry (CBI) represents over 300,000 British firms. It is the largest employers' organization in the UK and it makes presentations to the government about economic, financial, industrial, and trade issues. Services to members include legal advice about trade unions and labor relations. The Advisory, Conciliations and Arbitration (ACAS) funded by the government provides arbitration services in industrial disputes; it also provides consulting on all aspects of industrial relations and personnel management. Its services are free.

In recent years with only one major exception, there has been a general turnabout in the industrial relations situation in Great Britain. There has been a steady decline in the number of strikes per year from 2,922 in 1974 to 1,983 in 1986. At the same time there has been a dramatic decline in the thousands of working days lost in such strikes. There were 14,750 days lost in 1974 and only 3,754,000 in 1983 and to 1,852,000 in 1986. The year 1984 was an exception with a long and bitter strike against the National Coal Board (26,564,000 days were lost in 1984 as a result of this strike). Given the new Trade Union Act, the decline in the formation of new employment, the problems of high unemployment, and new attitudes, the notion of a country with poor labor relations is no longer true.

Union leaders have generally realized it is in their best interests and the best interests of their members to work toward new policies in labor relations. Unlike unions in the US and elsewhere, they still see themselves as adversaries in the economic process. Although it is unfair to brand the British labor movement "socialistic," it does have strong ties with the Labour Party. The perspective which British unions bring to the negotiating process is different from what American unions bring. Long-lasting and responsible labor agreements are part of the scene in the UK. The path to them is significantly different.

There is a well-established court system with effective means of adjusting conflicts between private parties and between private parties and government agencies. It is strongly based on a system of common law which has developed over hundreds of years. In general, conflict resolution in the legal arena is not substantially different from in the US. The same is true in the political arena where government agencies provide hearings and government officials and legislators are open to public lobbying on major issues, though in the latter case the scale befits the British environment.

CORPORATE STRATEGY AND PLANNING

Strategic options for foreign firms in Great Britain are as wide as they are in the US and certainly greater than in most developed countries. The major elements influencing the choice of Great Britain are found in the commonality of culture and the position of the UK in the European Community.

How an American firm approaches the British market is basically related to the size of the firm, its goals for market expansion in Britain and/or the European Economic Community, and the amount of resources that can be committed. There is basically no one best approach and the process should be approached in the same way that strategies about American internal markets are determined. Only Canada is more similar in formulation strategy.

At the most general level, the basic issues are: (a) How much control does the firm desire to have?; (b) How extensive a market does the firm wish to serve?; (c) How much capital does the firm need to extend?; and (d) How much further development possibilities does the new market offer.

Since marketing issues often represent the greatest challenges to doing business in a foreign country including the UK, this discussion will focus on them. Regardless of whether the firm engages in exporting, limited investment, joint venture, or total investment, these issues need to be addressed. Product and service offerings need some modification in the UK for several reasons:

1. There are language differences and the British often view us "as a group of peoples divided by a common language." These differences are significant at the national level as well as at the regional level, such as between England and Scotland.

2. Great Britain has embarked on a program to move toward the metric system. Although many goods are still measured on the English basis with exact transformation to the metric, there is some effort to define many items in liters, grams, and meters.
3. For electrical goods, there is need to adapt to the British system which is different not only in wattage but also in instrumentation.
4. Differences in income between the United States and Great Britain mean that some product simplification is required to market in mass markets. This includes attention to size, complexity, and service components.

Channels of distribution vary distinctly from those found in the US. Wholesale intermediaries are generally weaker in the variety of alternatives they offer and their levels of performance. More effort must be expended on the direct development of promotion to retailers and to ultimate consumer markets than in the US. There are many large retail chains or groups in each of the various lines of trade in Great Britain, not all of whom can be regarded as national. In many ways they mix merchandise more highly so that Marks & Spencers, Woolworth's (not related to F.W. Woolworth in the United States) and Littlewoods' all carry food items, from full to limited lines, in "groceterias."

British retailers are moving through a dynamic period in which they are adapting many American managerial practices to European values. The hypermarket has taken hold throughout the UK and has greatly affected the marketing of a wide variety of goods and services. In scope of operation, ASDA and TESCO, for example, have moved well past similar American firms. The UK may be traditionally viewed as a "nation of shopkeepers," but large-scale operators dominate most lines of trade. Boots in pharmaceuticals, British Home Stores in soft goods, and Marks & Spencer in general merchandise, clothing, and some grocery items, as well as others, dominate retail markets.

Market entry for consumer goods producers requires an understanding of the size and importance of these retailers, many of whom provide directions to suppliers in terms of design, quality, and production. British retailing has become very sophisticated in the past several years as a result of the recognition by the financial community of their cash flows and ownership of prime real estate. Many companies have merged and now under new ownership are becoming active competitors.

CORPORATE ORGANIZATION AND CONTROL FOR FOREIGN FIRMS

Organizational Options

American firms have a full range of organizational options in the UK. The major factors affecting choice are: (a) The scope of the UK operation, that is, is it for the domestic market and the EEC or is it wider? (b) The basis of the arrangement, that is, is it a new operation, a joint venture with a UK firm, or a takeover of a UK firm? (c) The degree of integration, that is, is the firm fully integrated to customers from production or are there intermediaries? Generally, American firms are organized around products and structured vertically whereas a great number of British firms are organized around functional divisions. The difference in form can be exceedingly important in terms of working through relatively simple operating systems, particularly in the area of communications within the organizational types. In the case of joint ventures and takeovers by American firms, there are often significant difficulties in making what appear to be similar if not exact operations work, especially if American management is brought in.

The variety of options creates difficulties in so far as subtle differences are not often recognized. This is found in the titles and ranks given to both line and staff in the British organization. The comparison of organization charts does not give much help when attempting to understand corporate organization. As a generalization it is fair to suggest that the levels used for making decisions vary greatly between American and UK firms. In UK firms there is less discretion at lower levels in the organization and many simple decisions that are given to the discretion of the retail sales force in the US require consultation at higher levels in the UK firm. It is often difficult for British management to restructure organizations to move decision-making authority down the organization. All of these issues stem from the hierarchical structure that permeates British organizations.

Control Systems

Control systems in British firms are different from those in similar American firms; although they serve the environment that operate in, they are not always compatible with practice in US firms. The evaluation of control systems is critical; there are three factors to be considered:

1. The familiarity of a "common language" often leads American managers to believe that such systems exist when indeed the same words are used to describe different concepts.
2. Control systems in the UK follow the top-down structure; the word "control" does not assume the same amount or quality of feedback from operations as seen in the US.
3. Those firms that do have control systems with a two-way flow of quantitative and qualitative information are often less sophisticated than in the US; they often are historical reports of events which have taken place rather than the monitoring of ongoing events whose results can be influenced by change in procedures.

Three areas in which data for control of operations are generally lacking in the UK, in contrast to the US, are current sales reports, the development of bottom-up forecasts, and the monitoring of physical distribution activities. Often sales reports in the UK simply list what has been sold rather than evaluate what might have been, what was not sold, and what competitors are doing. The use of the sales force in acquiring the data to develop sales forecast information is present but the use of this source of information is neither as extensive nor as well understood as in the US as a check for top-down forecasts. Control of the logistic system in the UK is only beginning to appear in the way that it has in the US in the past five years. It is perhaps a reflection of geography that control of inventory, storage, and transportation costs have not received as much attention as they should.

FUTURE MARKET OPPORTUNITIES

The purpose of this section is to describe potential areas for business activities in the UK. These have been selected to reflect those areas which have been of highest interest to American firms in the past, and opportunities that are likely to develop.

Electrical components have been important products for both export and domestic production. The government is providing a great deal of support in this area but American technology is still widely regarded as the "leading edge" by UK manufacturers. American firms have had great success in this area. With easing dollar/pound exchanges rates, the market for American electrical components should improve substantially over the next several years.

Computing and information processing equipment and technology still represent areas where demand for American products will remain high. Included here are the entire collection of hardware and software elements as well as the transmission equipment and services. IBM and Wang have made substantial investments in the UK. In spite of the success of home-grown firms in the small computer market (primarily sold as games), the major market appears to be in applied computing systems for small business. These systems will most likely have to be tied to personal computers, networks, software, and consulting services, in contrast to the more loosely marketed "systems" in the US. With the increase in small business activity in the UK, this area appears to be particularly important.

The *fast-food service industry* is one in which significant business opportunities are developing. There is increased urgency to upgrade and expand touristic facilities to match standards in Europe and in North America. Within the UK there is a critical need to update food preparation methods at retail, that is, in hotels, pubs, and restaurants of all sizes. There are large demands for all types of food processing, handling, and storing equipment. Some of these may extend up the marketing channel to wholesalers and the food industry itself. Included at retail are such items as beverage dispensers, ovens, mixers, and similar kitchen equipment.

With changed employment patterns and lifestyles, more and more Britons are eating their meals outside of the home. It is a trend that will continue, though the proportion of meals eaten out in the

UK may not reach that in North America. Many major American fast-food operations, including McDonald's, Burger King, and Wendy's are already present, and variants of UK taste patterns also have the chance of success. Pizzaland and Wimpey's, operated by United Biscuit Ltd., are examples of "home-grown" fast-food.

Convenience operations have begun to develop in the UK. In spite of the great numbers of independents that have proliferated on the landscape, companies such as "7-11" have begun to seriously enter the UK. The market saturation point of these changes is not yet clear, but considering their operational efficiencies and skills, they can have a competitive advantage over the independent grocery.

Medical supplies and health care represent a large potential for business in the UK. The National Health Service (NHS), is under great pressure to deliver better health care while at the same time increasing operating efficiencies. The NHS is also under competitive pressures because of growth in the private health care system. Some firms and individuals, in small but important numbers, are moving toward private health care. It is probably premature to speculate about the privatization of the British health care system, but it is not premature to examine it as an area that future governments will want to improve. The areas for consideration include equipment, supplies, and management systems.

Telecommunications equipment is an area worth considering over the next five years. British Telecom has moved from public to private ownership. With the greater pressures on management to perform and a lessening of some regulatory constraints, new suppliers may have great access to this market. There is a 10-year history in the industry between the predecessor of British Telecom and American firms working together as buyers and sellers, respectively, which will be important in setting specifications. Management and technicians on both sides have become accustomed with working with one another.

Transportation equipment and services will be an important growth area in the UK. The major development in the next 10 years will be the completion of one of several proposals for linking the UK with Europe; this linkage will come in the form of a tunnel, tunnel and bridge, and other variations with regard to rail or automobile. The project has been referred to as the "chunnel." Though it is viewed as an Anglo-French project, there is no doubt that a wide variety of elements and services will be put out to bid to a number of countries throughout the world. The project is well into the design stage and test holes have been drilled.

SOURCES OF INFORMATION

British Technology Group (National Research Development Corporation), 101 Newington Causeway, London SE1 6BU

National Engineering Laboratory, East Kilbride (Glasgow) 675 QU, Scotland/Tel East Kilbride (03552) 20222, Telex: 777 888NE-LEK

Scottish Enterprise Foundation, University of Scotland, Stirling, FK9 4LA Scotland, Tel (0786) 73171

National Economic Development Office, Millbank Tower, Millban, London SWIP 4QK, Tel 01-211 3000

Business International, 12-14 Chemin Rieu, Geneva, 757 Third Avenue, New York

Invest in Britain Bureau, British Consulate-General, 845 Third Avenue, New York, NY 10022

The Economist Newspaper Limited, 25 St. James Street, London, England SW1A 1HG

Embassy to the United States of America, 3100 Massachusetts Avenue NW, Washington, D.C. 20008

United States Embassy to Great Britain, 24 Grosvenor Square, London, W1A 1AE

Organization for Economic Co-Operation and Development, Economic Surveys 1984/1985, *United Kingdom*, January 1985

The Financial Times

Marketing Week, Centaur Limited, St. Giles House, 50 Poland Street, London WI1 4AX 01-439 4222 The OEECD Observer

The OECD Observer

OEECD Publications and Information Center, Suite 1207, 1750 Pennsylvania, N.W., Washington, D.C. 20006-4582, tel. (202) 724-1857

The Institute of Economic Affairs, 2 Lord North Street, Westminster, London SWIP 3LB

Young & Rubicam Ltd., Greater London House, Hampstead Road, London, NW1 7QA England

Arthur Young Rolls House, 7 Rolls Building, Letter Lane, London EEC4A 1NH, England

USA Exports, ITA Publications, Room 1617, International Trade Administration, U.S. Department of Commerce, Washington, D.C. 20230

British Trade Development Office, 150 East 58th Street, 19/20th Floors, New York, NY 10155, tel. (212) 593-2258

Invest in Britain Bureau, Department of Trade and Industry, Kingsgate House, 66-74 Victoria Street, SW1E 6SJ; phone: 01-212-0994

REFERENCES

All Change in the City (1985, November 7). *The Economist.*
Both Sides of Britain's Multinational Coin (1985, December 7), *The Economist*, p. 77.
Britain: A View from the Outside (1987, February 21), *The Economist*, Special report.
Davies, R.L. (ed.) (1979). *Retail Planning in the European Community*, Westmead, England: Saxon House.
Dawson, J.A. and Lord, J.D. (eds.) (1985). *Shopping Center Development*, London: Croom Helm.
Growing Rich Again (1988, April 8), *The Economist.*

Howells, D. (1981). Marks & Spencer and the Civil Service: A Comparison of Culture and Methods, *Public Administration* (Autumn).

Ingrassia, L. and Winkler, M. (1985, December 17). With British Megamergers Blumming, Some call for More Government Review, *The Wall Street Journal*, 36.

Privatisation: Everybody's Doing it, Differently (1985, December 21). *The Economist*, p. 71.

Sampson, A. (1982). *The Changing Anatomy of Britain*, New York: Random House.

Serving the Economy (1985, November 30), *The Economist*, 62-63.

Stacey, N.A.H. and Wilson, A. (1965). *The Changing Pattern of Distribution*, London: Pergamon Press.

Stopford, J.M. and L. Turner (1985). *Britain and the Multinationals*, New York: John Wiley & Sons.

Tse, K.K. (1985). *Marks & Spencer*, London: Pergamon Press.

Wills, G. and Rushton, A. (1982). UK Progress in PDM, *International Journal of Physical Distribution*, Vol. 12, 6.

Winkler, M. (1985, December 20). Britain Unveils Bill to Protect Its Investors, *The Wall Street Journal*, p. 29.

Chapter 4

Central America

James Makens

INTRODUCTION

The area known as Central America geographically comprises seven nations: Guatemala, Honduras, El Salvador, Nicaragua, Costa Rica, Panama, and Belize. Belize is seldom mentioned in a discussion of "Central America" and some Panamanians also deny being a member. In both cases, denial of inclusion is the result of historical and cultural rather than geographic considerations.

Belize is basically a black, English-speaking nation and is technically claimed by Guatemala as its territory. This dispute is symbolically witnessed by the presence of British antiaircraft bunkers manned by Englishmen on the Belize airport perimeters. Many Panamanians consider themselves to be Caribbean or even South American due to the historic ties with Colombia.

This nation also has a heavy percentage of blacks although Caucasians, Indian Americans, Indian immigrants, Chinese immigrants, and others are also Panamanian citizens. Although the language of Panama is Spanish, many are fluent in English as a result of decades of close affiliation with the United States. The strength of these ties is perhaps most pronounced in the national Panamanian currency, the United States dollar.

Differences may be most pronounced in Belize and Panama but it would be an error to view the remaining five nations of Central America as homogeneous. In fact, the primary element of similarity is the Spanish language. Politically these neighbors range from a model effective democracy to a Marxist-Communist state.

The geographical proximity of Central America to Mexico and

the United States creates economic and political importance for the region. Mexico with 80 million people is sometimes viewed as the industrial power to the north. Guatemala in particular feels the political and economic presence of both the United States and Mexico.

Central America cannot be separated from Mexico by other than political barriers. Highway transportation to United States markets must pass through Mexico. Culturally, the two areas have many similarities except for Belize. Mexican and United States television programs vie for the attention of Central America. Historically, events in Mexico and Central America have often been interrelated. Today, Mexico is a refuge for many who fled Central America and is a passageway for thousands headed to the United States.

Many observers fear a spillover of Marxism from Nicaragua to Mexico. A future common market of Mexico and Central America with over 100 million population would be a market that no industrialized nation could ignore.

POPULATION

Population growth rates and projections for Central America are among the highest in Latin America. The percent of population growth for 1980-90 of the U.S. is projected to be .7.

By contrast, projections for Central America follow (Table 1):

TABLE 1

Population Projection for Central America

	Population Growth Rate
Costa Rica	2.3
El Salvador	3.3
Guatemala	3.0
Honduras	3.5
Nicaragua	3.5
Panama	2.2

TABLE 2

Population Estimates - Central America

	Population	Land (Sq. Miles)
Belize	127,200	8,866
Costa Rica	1,993,800	19,730
Guatemala	5,211,929	2,042
El Salvador	4,255,000	8,124
Honduras	2,998,700	43,277
Nicaragua	2,451,418	50,193
Panama	1,830,175	29,762
Total	18,868,022	210,994

LITERACY

Central America has a high rate of adult illiteracy (Table 3). Belize and Costa Rica have better illiteracy rates; education expenditures are considerably higher in these nations and literacy is much higher than the surrounding area.

TABLE 3

Percent of Illiteracy - Central America

	% Illiterate Adults
Belize	8.8
Costa Rica	11.6
El Salvador	38.0
Guatemala	54.0
Honduras	43.1
Nicaragua	42.5
Panama	12.9

INTERNATIONAL INFLUENCE

Central American has become a stage for world press attention. This region of roughly 200,000 square miles is smaller than the state of Texas (262,015 square miles), yet its population of

21,000,000 is twice that of Texas. The importance of population to this region may be better understood by comparing Central America with two other areas (Table 4).

Central America has long experienced international tension among the member nations caused in part by rapid population growth. El Salvador, roughly the size of New Jersey, supports a population of 5 million, yet Honduras has over five times the land area and a population of less than 4 million. Settlers from El Salvador have crossed the Honduras border for decades in search of land or employment. Resulting tensions exploded in the famous "Soccer War" of 1969 between the two nations.

Cultural differences have also created the basis for tension. Costa Rica is a model for democracy. This largely Caucasian nation is culturally akin to Europe and the United States. Nicaragua with its different population is culturally more akin to the Caribbean. This nation has lived under the Somoza dictatorship and currently the Marxist Sandanista regime. It would be difficult to find two neighbor nations more dissimilar anywhere in the Americas.

The influences of European colonization and American political-economic and cultural influence remain strong factors in the political problems facing these nations. Mexico, Spain, Great Britain, and the United States have each exerted a role in shaping the current political structure of the region.

During the early to mid-1970s, unification of the area seemed hopeful. President Kennedy's administration had earlier taken an interest in Central America and a program known as The Alliance for Progress was enacted. A central part of this program was the establishment of a Central American Common Market and educational and social progress.

The program in fact showed signs of working. Barriers to trade

TABLE 4

Comparison of Central America to Other Land Masses

	Square Miles	Population
Central America	3,200,000	21,000,000
Australia-New Zealand	3,071,792	18,835,000
Canada	3,381,033	25,100,000

began to disappear. A Central American graduate management program leading to an MBA was established in Managua and a Central American Common Market with headquarters in Honduras was formed. Belize remained separate but the other six nations began to cooperate.

One of the early fissures in the program occurred as a result of the Honduras-El Salvador Soccer War. This was being remedied when a key nation experienced revolution. Nicaragua, geographically situated in the center with the largest land mass of all and rich in natural resources, suddenly moved from obscurity to world attention. New players had entered the scene. Cuba, the Soviet Union, and its European satellite states were now involved in Central America.

NATIONAL ECONOMIC ENVIRONMENT

The seven nations of Central America are basically agricultural economies with a small manufacturing sector. This consists primarily of small consumer manufacturing firms who produce for domestic consumption or export within Central America. Few industrial firms exist and consumer products generally do not meet world quality or price standards to permit international competition outside the region. A limited amount of manufacturing for export exists, notably in a free zone of Panama and within textile plants in several countries. El Salvador had begun to develop a semiconductor business with Texas Instruments, Inc., but this was badly disrupted due to political upheaval.

Social welfare programs officially exist in each nation but Costa Rica has a history of proven medical, education, and retirement programs.

PRINCIPAL TRADING PARTNERS

The United States is the dominant trading partner in terms of imports and exports for each nation but Nicaragua. This was formerly true of Nicaragua until Communist bloc nations replaced the United States. The sum of trading with other Central American nations generally represents the second most important trading partner. This is no longer true with Nicaragua. Belize has historically traded very little with its Central American neighbors and instead trades with the United States, Great Britain, the Netherlands, Japan, Mexico, and Caribbean nations.

The remaining countries of Central America trade principally with the following nations (Table 5).

The top trading partners for each nation are the U.S. and other Central American nations. Other trading partners vary by nation. For example, a principal import country for Guatemala is Mexico. Costa Rica imports comparatively little from Mexico. Honduras has developed a good export base in Belgium. Panama has developed trade relations with Colombia, Ecuador, Norway, and Sweden.

It is apparent that trading relationships must be developed on a

TABLE 5

Principal Trading Partners with Central America
(Excluding Nicaragua and Belize)

Primary

U.S.A.
Other Central American Nations
Venezuela
Mexico
West Germany
Japan
Netherlands

Secondary

France
Spain
Caribbean Nations
United Kingdom
Italy
Taiwan
Belgium
Colombia
Ecuador
Sweden
Norway

nation by nation basis rather than by using a regional market strategy. (See Table 6.)

Each of the countries of Central America has been incurring trade deficits during the 1980s. This is in large measure due to the nature of the items purchased and sold in international markets. Exports consist principally of commodities (see Table 7). Coffee, bananas, cotton, livestock, shrimp and fish, lumber, sugar, and petroleum are primary export items. These economies remain in the early developmental stage relative to manufacturing. Clothing and textiles represent the primary manufactured goods.

The majority of the commodity items produced in Central America are highly sensitive to price fluctuations. Very few of the commodity items are further processed in Central America, with the exception of sugar which is processed into molasses and rum. None of the nations have achieved consumer brand recognition for agricultural products processed there such as is the case of Kona Coffee or Macadamia Nuts of Hawaii or Dak Meat Products of Denmark.

IMPORTS

The countries of Central America share an import commonality. Machinery, chemicals, fertilizers, paper, building materials, petroleum, and miscellaneous industrial equipment represent major import items. Consumer goods are relatively more important as import items in Costa Rica where the citizens enjoy a higher standard of

TABLE 6

Imports/Exports - Central America

Trade Deficit - 1986

Belize	Yes
Costa Rica	Yes
El Salvador	Yes
Guatemala	Yes
Honduras	Yes
Nicaragua	Yes
Panama	Yes

TABLE 7

Principal Exports from Central America

	Belize	Costa Rica	El Salvador	Guatemala	Honduras	Nicaragua	Panama
Bananas	5	2			1		1
Cardamom				5		7	
Chemicals						4	
Clothing - Textiles	2		7				
Coffee		1	2	1	2	2	4
Cotton			5	3		5	
Foodstuffs							
- Cattle	4	3	1	6&7	5	1	
Fresh Shrimp							
- Shellfish	3		6		4		2
Miscellaneous							
- Mfr.			3				
Petroleum Products			8	4			
Raw Materials			4		6	3	
Sugar	1	4		2		6	3
Tobacco					7		
Wood	6				3		

148

living than other nations in the region. In recent years the importation of armaments has become increasingly important, particularly in Nicaragua.

Important foodstuff imports include wheat and other cereals, dairy products, and other products not commonly produced in the tropics including fruits such as apples and grapes. The New Zealand Dairy Promotion Board has long recognized the value of dairy imports to the region and operates an office in Guatemala.

COST-PRICE SQUEEZE

Like many other "Third World" nations, those of Central America are generally caught in a cost-price squeeze. They have witnessed the world price for their commodities decline as the prices for processed consumer goods and industrial products have risen.

NATIONAL BUDGETS

Virtually all the nations of Central America have operated with both a trade deficit and a national budget deficit into the 1990s. These have been created by:

1. cost-price squeeze in imports-exports;
2. armaments;
3. border wars, guerilla insurrection;
4. consumer imports, principally Costa Rica;
5. low levels of productivity in manufacturing sectors;
6. social programs;
7. subsidization of some sectors
8. flight of capital; and
9. low level industrial investment.

The problems of capital flight has been particularly severe for Central America. Hundreds of millions of dollars have been placed in foreign banks in Europe and the United States.

UNEMPLOYMENT

The level of unemployment is high throughout most of Central America. Costa Rica is the exception (Table 8).

Care should be exercised in using available statistics, including unemployment data, from the region. There is often wide variance in the measurement process.

RESOURCES

As a region, Central America is relatively resource rich in forest, aquatic, and agricultural resources. Limited mineral supplies are also available in gold and petroleum.

The area faces severe pressure on much of its resource base from poor management practices, war destruction, pollution, overgrazing, overcutting, burning and general population growth.

Tourism opportunities abound throughout Central America and an infrastructure was developing in Guatemala and El Salvador prior to the onslaught of terrorism, kidnapping, and armed insurgencies. A tourism resource base exists in pre-Colombian and colonial-era historic sites, diverse cultures, islands, beaches, and volcanoes. The relative nearness to major markets of Europe, North America, and South America combined with the resources have made this area a "natural" for tourism development, provided, there is a stable political environment.

TABLE 8

Unemployment Percentages in Central America - 1984

	Unemployment - 1984
Belize	13.6%
Costa Rica	9.4%
El Salvador	30.0%
Guatemala	44.0%
Honduras	24.0%
Nicaragua	24.0%
Panama	---

Costa Rica, Panama, and Belize have continued to enjoy a visitor industry despite political and economic regional problems. Guatemala and Honduras actively promote tourism and could build a strong industry if political tensions lessen (Table 9).

POLITICAL AND LEGAL ENVIRONMENT

With the exception of Costa Rica, Central America has been subject to frequent political upheavals and endemic corruption. Costa Rica is highly regarded as a model of democracy in which more has been spent for education than for police or military. Nicaragua appears to be fairly entrenched as a Marxist state. The nations of Panama, Honduras, El Salvador, and Guatemala are quite unpredictable in terms of political problems. As of this writing it appears that democracy may be taking root, but El Salvador and Honduras are both heavily supported by United States military assistance and the situation could change at any time in the near future. Belize has been fairly stable, although it has been threatened by Guatemala who claims it as territory.

Laws affecting business development vary by each nation. More importantly, they are generally subject to change. Again Costa Rica offers comparative stability, but it is subject to serious labor union problems. For example, in 1984 banana plantation workers in Costa Rica went on strike for 72 days. This created an estimated loss of $500 million to the banana companies. As a result, The United Brands subsidiary closed its operations in Costa Rica.

TABLE 9

Visitors to Central America - 1984

Tourism	Number of Visitors in 1984
Belize	8,731,511 (No. of Tourist Nights)
Costa Rica	273,901
El Salvador	---
Guatemala	191,934
Honduras	144,232
Nicaragua	---
Panama	347,826

There is a wide variance in the form of governments within Central America. These range from a Marxist Regime to a model of democracy:

Belize. The system of government may be described as a combination of British Colonial and United States Congress. Belize became independent in 1981; however, executive authority is vested in the British Monarch and exercised by a Governor General who appoints a Prime Minister. The leader of opposition is also appointed by the Governor General. An elected legislature exists with a Senate and House of Representatives.

Costa Rica. Costa Rica has a long and successful history as a democracy. A president is elected for a four-year term. Also elected is a unicameral legislature.

El Salvador. El Salvador accepted a new constitution in 1983. The country is now officially a democracy but is going through very difficult political times.

Guatemala. This country has experienced a history of military coups. A new constitution was enacted in 1986. This provides for a republican representative democratic system with an elected president and a congress.

Honduras. The country has been ruled by dictatorships and a combination of military strongmen. Military rule officially ended in 1980. The country is now a democracy with a constitution, elected president, and elected National Assembly.

The nation is going through a difficult period made even more troubling by the threat of war with Nicaragua.

Nicaragua. Nicaragua has a constitution of 1979 that supposedly provides for a "Statute of Rights." In fact, the nation has increasingly drifted closer to the Communist Block and is regarded by many as a Communist state.

Panama. Panama has a constitution, amended in 1983. It officially is a democracy with an elected president and Legislative Assembly. In reality, the nation continues to operate with a military strongman.

Central America is in the process of political change. All nations including Nicaragua are officially democracies, but only Costa Rica has a long period of stability as a democracy.

TECHNOLOGICAL ENVIRONMENT

Agriculture. The level of technology in certain areas of agriculture within the region has been commendable. Productivity in the production of bananas is high and in some areas cotton, coffee, and cardamom productivity is excellent. Del Monte has opened vast acreage in Costa Rica to pineapple production using the latest technology. Modern agricultural programs in Macadamia nuts and horticultural products have also been established.

Finance. Panama has developed as an international finance center. Services provided 75.5% of that country's gross domestic products in 1985 and banking is an increasingly important element. Many foreign banks have established branches in Panama. These represent the United States, United Kingdom, Japan, Colombia, Brazil, Spain, Venezuela, Switzerland, West Germany, Argentina, France, and the Bahamas.

Panama has an opportunity to build on international banking expertise and technology and become a "Switzerland of the Americas."

Other areas. No other sectors demonstrate a strong technological base although occasional companies demonstrate unusual innovation and creativity, such as the Hilalsal Towel Company of El Salvador. Manufacturing technology is generally behind the United States, Europe, and Japan. Import restrictions and capital flight have tended to generally worsen this situation.

ORGANIZATIONAL CULTURE

In structure the corporate organization forms tend to reflect those within the United States. In fact, the true organizational form often tends to more accurately reflect the cultural and historic background of these nations.

Costa Rica tends to closely mirror the United States in its private and public organizational culture. Throughout Central America, several factors continue to exert a dominant force in many public and private organizations including: paternalism, macho thinking and behavior, family decision-making, lack of trust in subordinates, power plays, acceptance of corruption, reciprocity, and other cultural factors. In extreme cases, particularly in rural areas, personal and family vendettas play a role. Organizational structures are changing throughout Central America. This may be attributed to the following influences:

1. United States and European companies who own, control, or work closely with Central American companies. The same influence is apparent in some government departments.
2. A growing number of graduates from MBA programs such as INCAE (Harvard Business School Affiliate) in Costa Rica and Universidad Francisco Marroquin in Guatemala.
3. Increased exposure by members of management to management practices elsewhere.
4. War, terrorism, and other political problems. Particularly in El Salvador, many owners have been forced to place management control in the hands of subordinates since the owners moved to other nations, principally the United States, to avoid personal harm.
5. The United States Military and State Department who have exerted pressure for change.

NATIONAL CONTROL OF INTERNATIONAL TRADE

International trade is highly regulated within Central America. The central governments have a direct role in imports and exports. Throughout Central America, primary export crops are controlled through a central marketing board. The federal government, through the central bank, also generally has direct authority over imports by limiting the availability of hard currency.

Tariffs are common on products produced outside Central America. These vary by nations but reach 50% or more of the value of the imported item.

BUSINESS OPPORTUNITIES

Business opportunities for foreign entrepreneurs and corporations are generally limited and are often adversely affected by political disturbances, government restrictions, union activity, and in some cases Marxist philosophies on the part of influential parties. Repatriation of earnings can be a problem.

In spite of obstacles, opportunities exist within each of these nations, excepting Nicaragua, for entrepreneurs. Examples exist in each nation of successful enterprises owned and managed by expatriots from the United States, Canada, Europe, India, the Middle East, and other nations. These tend to be small firms and generally require residence by individuals who are willing to invest in the long run and who are also willing to live with limited capital repatriation.

Unfortunately, conflicts between the private and public sector exist even in nations with an industrial-service base such as Panama and Costa Rica.

Multinational foreign companies have developed manufacturing plants in Central America but these are primarily small manufacturing companies of consumer goods such as cosmetics, cigarettes, and pharmaceuticals. A few small textile/clothing plants have been established throughout the region to take advantage of less expensive labor and nearby markets. These have failed to reach the potential demonstrated in other nations such as Taiwan due to the government restrictions and conflicts between the private and public sectors.

The existence of a few large and powerful companies owned by nationals has also sometimes been viewed as a factor inhibiting competition and economic development. Although there may be truth in this sentiment, the effect has not been carefully studied and care should be exercised in directing accusations. In Nicaragua, the Somoza regime owned all or part of many local companies. In other Central American nations government and military officials sometimes gain partial or total ownership of companies and appear to exert influence through political power.

SOURCES OF INFORMATION

Primary sources of information concerning Central American nations are: International Banks, the United States Department of Commerce, the United States Foreign Agricultural Service (U.S.D.A.). Each nation (including Nicaragua) has a Chamber of Commerce; a list follows (Table 10).

OTHER SOURCES

Conditions are subject to rapid change in Central America. Hence, there is no substitute for a personal investigation of each nation. The following is a list of inquiries to make during this visit. If the representative from your organization is not fluent in Spanish, professional interpreters are available in each nation. Many government and industry leaders in each nation speak English.

Suggested itinerary:

1. Visit embassy of your nation in the respective nation and speak with commercial and political officers.
2. Visit foreign banks located in the nation.
3. Visit Chamber of Commerce and other industry associations.
4. Visit factory or office of noncompeting company from your nation.
5. Visit related wholesalers, large retailers, distributors, brokers, etc.
6. Visit appropriate departments or ministries of the host government.

Allow ample time for this investigation. Remember, the custom in most Central American nations is a period of mid-day shutdown. Local and international holidays usually prevent any meaningful commerce. It is often necessary to allocate 3-7 days per nation to conduct even a superficial investigation.

TABLE 10

Sources of Information - Central America

Belize
                Belize Chamber of Commerce
                P.O. Box 291, Belize City
                Belize

Costa Rica
                Camara de Comercio de Costa Rica: Barrio
                Tournon, Apdo 1.114
                San Jose, Costa Rica

                Camara de Industrias de Costa Rica
                Calles 13-15
                Anda 6, Apdo 10.003
                San Jose, Costa Rica

El Salvador
                Camara de Comercio y
                Industria de El Salvador
                9 Ave. Norte y 5 Calle
                Poniente, Apdo 1640
                San Salvador, El Salvador

Guatemala
                Camara de Comercio de Guatemala,
                10 Calle 3-80, Zona 1
                Guatemala City, Guatemala

Honduras
                Camara de Comercio y
                Industrias de Cortes, 17 Avda
                10 y 12 Calle
                Apdo 14
                San Pedro Sula, Honduras

Nicaragua
                Camara de Comercio de Nicaragua,
                Plaza de Ferias
                Col. Centroamerica
                Apdo 135
                Managua, Nicaragua

Panama
                Camara de Comercio, Industrias
                y Agricultura de Panama
                Avda Cuba 33-18
                Apdo 74
                Panama, Panama

METHODS OF ENTRY INTO BUSINESS

Prior to the Sandanista regime in Nicaragua and political disturbances in El Salvador and Guatemala, foreign businesses established wholly owned subsidiaries in these nations. A limited number of wholly owned subsidiaries remain in Central American
nations. However, many foreign companies such as Sears Roebuck
and Glidden Paint have sold their assets in the region. A limited
number of United States and European companies continue to operate in Nicaragua including the Esso (Exxon) Oil Company, IBM,
and Tropigas.

Interest in contract manufacturing is limited to a few of the nations perceived to be stable, such as Costa Rica, and is limited to a
few items. These are principally in the agricultural, forestry, fish-
ery, and textile/clothing areas. The area has not achieved its potential for contract manufacturing due to political instability, unfavorable or changing laws, and low labor productivity. However,
examples do exist of relatively good labor productivity in some limited industries. A paint brush manufacturer in Guatemala claims
excellent labor productivity and a good work ethic among its female
workforce. In other nations, including Costa Rica, employees complain of problems created by unions, a poor work ethic, too many
holiday interruptions, import restrictions, and other work-inhibiting
factors.

Joint ventures appear to have decreased in popularity for the
same reasons that have created a lack of interest in wholly owned
subsidiaries. However, it should be recognized that there are always
exceptions.

Central America is a land of contrast and this extends to the success or failure of enterprises. Some joint ventures and wholly
owned subsidiaries continue to successfully operate where others
fail. This extends even to the action of revolutionary mobs in areas
such as Nicaragua. Certain factories were burned to the ground
while others were untouched. Reportedly, the employees of a ciga-
rette plant distributed free cartons of cigarettes to vandals as they
burned and looted factories. Whatever the validity of the story, the
factory was untouched.

Franchising and licensing remain popular vehicles for entry into

Central America. McDonald's and Pizza Hut have long been established in the area.

CORPORATE STRATEGY AND PLANNING
FOR FOREIGN FIRMS

"Management in Crisis" is the name of a popular seminar offered by INCAE, a Central American management school. This exemplifies conditions in Central America prevailing during the '80s.

Within Costa Rica, long-range strategies can be designed and implemented. Long-range planning is far less certain within other Central American nations. Guatemala is the largest market in the region and can serve as a stimulus for growth if political stability can be assured.

There is evidence of optimism and strategic planning on the part of private industry in Guatemala, Costa Rica, and Panama. This is particularly true in the retail sector and the visitor industry. Retail stores, hotels, and others have made capital investments indicating a positive outlook for the future. Guatemala hosts several very successful retail chains such as "Paiz." This chain has rapidly expanded under the leadership of the Paiz brothers. These gentlemen have excellent academic credentials including one who has a PhD from the Harvard Business School.

The company Pinturas Centroamerica of Guatemala offers further proof of successful strategic planning. This company is now a major producer of paint in Central America. It purchased the manufacturing plant of Glidden Paint (U.S.) and has continued to experience increased market share throughout Central America. Again, management exemplifies the emergence of a new educated managerial group in Central America. The owner-president holds an engineering degree from the United States and an MBA from Universidad Francisco Marroquin in Guatemala.

Central America is a land of contrast. Sears Roebuck and Glidden Paint left Central America, yet a generation of highly educated and strongly motivated local owner-managers have achieved remarkable success in the industries abandoned by United States companies.

Financial options for indigenous companies in Central America include the private banking system, limited equity financing, and in some cases indirect or direct assistance by an international agency. There are several examples of firms who have located international funds through development organizations from a variety of nations. These include but are by no means limited to the United States. Companies have found assistance through organizations in the United Kingdom, West Germany, Spain, Canada and other nations, as well as international organizations.

Investment options for locally owned companies are generally restricted and they often tend to bet on the long range. Foreign companies have a much wider range of international investment options than local companies and tend to rank Central America opportunities lower than in other nations.

FUTURE BUSINESS OPPORTUNITIES AND SCENARIOS

Scenario 1

Regional communism. The worst possible scenario would be a spread of communism from Cuba and Nicaragua through the entire region and into Mexico. This would have disastrous consequences but is unlikely to occur due to the military presence of the United States and relative success in El Salvador and Guatemala quelling guerilla insurgency.

Scenario 2

Elimination of all Marxist influence including that in Nicaragua. It is doubtful that the United States Congress and world opinion would permit an invasion of Nicaragua by the United States and Central American allies such as Honduras.

Scenario 3

Continuation of regional political instability with Nicaragua as a "Cuban style" nation in the center. This scenario appears most likely with intensified efforts by the United States to strengthen the economic structure of surrounding nations including those in the Caribbean. It is also likely that a strong United States military pressure will continue in Central America as a deterrent to possible expansion by Cuba and Nicaragua. This situation could give rise to the development of several relatively strong neighbors such as Guatemala, Costa Rica, and possibly El Salvador and Honduras. Thus, the area would function much like South Korea or West Berlin despite the presence of an armed communist neighbor.

Central America is too close for the United States to ignore. It is likely that future administration, whether Republican or Democrat, will be forced to fund Marshall-type aid plans for the region, similar to those used in Western Europe after World War II. This will create opportunities for the private sector. A strong Marshall-type program could elicit support from several nations in the form of intensified investments and in social programs such as health and education.

As production costs increase in Asian countries, Central America will become more desirable as a source of international contract manufacturing. The Japanese have financial interests in Costa Rica and other nations. For example, in Costa Rica the Japanese own and manage a chain of supermarkets. Other nations outside North America have demonstrated a continuing interest in Central America. These include Spain, France, the United Kingdom, Venezuela, the Netherlands, and West Germany.

Currently, investment opportunities in Central America should be viewed as speculative with long-range payback possibilities. Nevertheless, the region is likely to become more important to the United States and to other neighbors such as Venezuela. Consequently, a presence in Central America is desirable as it can only enhance the experience base of a company, and it promises future opportunities for market participation and economic payback.

The nation for investment must be carefully selected. Currently and historically, Costa Rica must be rated as superior to others based on its political stability. Panama is an exception for financial services. Guatemala remains the largest consumer market in Central America with a fairly well-developed infrastructure. If political stability holds in Guatemala, it should be considered a likely investment area.

Any investor in Central America will be faced with the need for "Crisis Management" in the foreseeable future. It is hoped that this will be followed by long-term growth in an area close to major markets in North and South America and Europe. This area rich in natural resources and with a growing population should not be overlooked for inclusion in the long-run investment portfolio of a company.

REFERENCES

The Europe Year Book, 1986, Vols. 1 and 2, Europe Publications, Ltd., 18 Bedford Square, London WC1B 3JN, England.

Statistical Yearbook, Department of International Economic and Social Affairs, The United Nations, New York, 1985.

Wilkie, James W., *Statistical Abstract of Latin America*, UCLA, Latin America Center Publications, University of California, Los Angeles, California.

EDITOR'S NOTE (as preface to Chapter 5)

As we go to press, China is undergoing internal conflict. In the mid 1980s the Chinese Government introduced significant changes in the country's economic structure and development strategy, resulting in its Open Door policy becoming an inseparable part of its economic development. The economy and the amount of incoming foreign investments grew at well over 10% a year, but this has caused internal political tensions.

A few weeks ago an open fratricidal struggle for power between the entrenched Communist Party members, led by the paramount leader Deng Xiaoping, Chairman of the Central Military Committee of the Party, and the Prime Minister Li Peng, and the new freedom/change proponents in China broke out. Student leaders massed in Beijing's famous Tiananmen Square. On the night of June 3rd-4th, for the first time since the Communists took power 40 years ago, a unit of the Peoples Liberation Army turned on the people themselves and cleared Tiananmen Square. The struggle within China is ferocious, but the majority of the army generals in command reportedly favor Deng Xiaoping and his chief ally, President Yang Shangkun.

Although condemnation for the Beijing assault has mounted, the Western response has been measured. For example, the U.S. has banned military sales to China. France, Holland, and Sweden have frozen diplomatic relations. The U.K. has cancelled ministerial visits and suspended military contacts. But nobody has banned commercial sales. Today's China is much more involved with the West. Its foreign loans are well over $30 billion. For most of the 1970s China's foreign trade only amounted to some $9 billion annually. In 1988 it was over $100 billion, almost one-third of China's national income. Roughly one-third of China's foreign trade is with Hong Kong, Japan is the next largest partner, and substantial amounts occur with the U.S. and EEC. Many Western firms are involved in joint ventures although the average investment is still small. Hongkongers have demonstrated but are traditionally pragmatic. Hong Kong businesses employ some 3 million workers in China's neighboring Guangdong province, which so far is unaffected by the political disturbances.

My prognosis for the future is that China will not attempt to change its Open Door policy. Internal pressures for more democracy will persist, although probably at a dampened pace. The economic growth rate stipulated in the Chinese Government Plans is about 7% annually to the year 2000. This necessitates a continuing change in the economic organization from rigid central planning to a combination of central coordination and market regulation. However, the political system will remain unstable and will not easily accommodate economic reforms. It is likely that China will move toward a more market-oriented structure, but probably in a point-counterpoint sequence. The West and Japan will be more cautious in extending foreign loans. Their firms will more carefully evaluate political risk in doing business with China. But global competition among foreign business firms will force most of them to continue to be interested. The lure of China's market size will always tempt.

V.H. (Manek) Kirpalani

Chapter 5

China

Joseph Eastlack
Susan Kraemer Watkins

INTRODUCTION

President Richard M. Nixon's historic trip to the People's Republic of China (PRC) in 1972 established a relationship between the United States of America (USA) and the PRC when President Nixon signed the Shanghai Communiqué. This treaty proclaimed China's willingness to accept foreign investment and its movement toward becoming a more "open door" nation. With the normalization of full diplomatic relations between the USA and the PRC in 1978, USA investments in the PRC have gained momentum along with the interest of world marketers in the consumer potential of the PRC. Today there is intense interest in the potential of the PRC market among USA consumer goods manufacturers of both consumer durables and nondurables. USA consumer goods companies are starting to produce their products for and in China.

But the 10 years since political normalization is only a split second in Chinese time. And the "New Economic Plan," which seems to open up so much more of the economy to free market forces, dates only from October 1984. Furthermore, we must remember the dramatic and unpredictable swings of political power and policy since the end of the Qing Dynasty in 1911. This period includes the Republic, the Warlord Period, Japanese occupation, Guomindang versus Communist Civil War, and the People's Republic, which has had at least one dozen, often violent, changes in direction since 1949, as shown in Table 1.

Shortly after the "New Economic Plan" was approved in Octo-

TABLE 1

BRIEF CHRONOLOGY OF TWENTIETH CENTURY CHINA

Fall of the last Dynasty (Qing)	1911
The Republic of China (Guomingang)	1911-1949
. Warlord Period	1916-1926
. Communist Party Founded	1921
. Civil War	1945-1949
The People's Republic of China (Communist Party)	1949-
. Liberation	1949
. Consolidation and Land Reform	1949-1951
. First Five Year Plan	1953-1958
. "Campaign Against Counter-Revolutionaries"	1955-1956
. "Hundred Flowers"	1957
. "Anti-Rightist Campaign"	1957-1958
. "Great Leap Forward"	1958-1959
. "Cultural Revolution"	1966-1976
. "Counterattack the Right Deviationist Wind"	1976
. Mao Zedong Dies	Sept. 1976
. Fall of the Gang of Four	Oct. 1976
. Deng Xiaoping Consoldiates Power	1978
. Democracy Wall	Nov. 78-Dec. 79
. "Four Modernizations"	1979-
. Joint Venture Law	1979
. Four Special Economic Zones Established	1979-1980
. New Constitution	1980
. Fourteen Additional Open Cities Established	June 1984
. New Economic Plan Approved	Oct. 1984
. National Party Conference	Sept. 1985

*   Party Campaigns noted by quotation marks.

ber 1984, the *People's Daily* even "repositioned" Marx. This official Communist party newspaper now says that Marxism-Leninism is irrelevant to much of what is now happening in the PRC. "We cannot expect the works of Marx and Lenin in their day to solve all the problems of today," the official party organ stated.[1]

This quotation from *People's Daily* received a great deal of play in the Western press because it, plus the use of the word "irrelevant," had such shock value. Probably of greater importance to understanding the pragmatists now in charge of the PRC is a definition that received less notice in the West. Chinese socialism is now defined as "seeking truth from facts." This statement comes far closer to explaining recent economic policy with its broad-based experimentation and willingness to learn from (and rectify) temporary mistakes in the pursuit of the Four Modernizations.

Capitalism is, however, still not fully present in the PRC. "For all the government's intent to change, China remains a poor socialist economy that is tough and expensive to break."[2] Although we see a movement away from Marxism now, no one can be definite how long the current policies of Premier Deng Xiaoping will remain. The PRC in the twentieth century has been known for sudden ideological swings. Deng Xiaoping is well over 80 and his choice of successor is by no means clear, although he has maneuvered younger officials of his own more pragmatic economic persuasion into positions of power. In September 1985, the National Conference of the Communist party replaced 10 of 22 members of the ruling Politburo with younger, nonmilitary, more technically oriented leaders.

Many USA companies — led by heavy industry — seem to believe that the time has come to invest in the PRC. There are certainly many years of pent-up demand for consumer goods in the PRC due to conscious transfer of priorities from agriculture and consumer goods to heavy industry beginning in 1949 until recently.

NATIONAL, ECONOMIC, AND PHYSICAL ENVIRONMENT

The PRC, the third largest country in the world, has an area of 3,692 million square miles. Having the largest population in the world, the PRC has 1,035 million people (51.5% male, 48.5% female), about 22% of the world's population. Thirty-five percent of China's population is under the age of 15. Eighty percent of the population live in rural areas.

KEY POPULATION INDICES FOR THE PRC VERSUS SELECTED COUNTRIES

(1986 WORLD ALMANAC REPORTING 1984 STATISTICS)

	(Rank)	Size (MM Sq. Miles)	(Rank)	Population (MM)	Population Density Per Sq. Mi.	Percent Urban
PRC	(3)	3.692	(1)	1,035	290	20
India	(6)	1.269	(2)	746	582	22
U.S.S.R.	(1)	8.649	(3)	273	31	64
USA	(4)	3.619	(4)	236	65	80
Canada	(2)	3.850	(6)	25	6	76
Brazil	(5)	3.286	(5)	134	41	56

PRC's population is unevenly distributed. The population is concentrated mainly in the eastern half of the country (90%) with an average density approaching 600 people per square mile. The birth rate in the PRC is among the highest in the world. The official goal in the PRC is planned control of the birth rate at 1.3% per year, but population growth is probably closer to 1.5% per year because of families with more than one child, encouraged growth of minority populations, and steady increases in longevity.

Stringent birth control measures are encouraged by the government through various economic and social incentives as well as sanctions. Outdoor posters everywhere extol the virtues of the official "one child family" policy. However, many young Chinese hope this policy will be relaxed soon. Minority populations have recently been exempt from the "one child family" policy. It is projected that the minorities will comprise 9% of the then-current population by year 2000, compared with today's 5%; this translates to more than a fourfold growth in 15 years.

The most populated cities in the PRC are:

	POPULATION (MILLION)
Shangai	12.5
Beijing (Peking)	9.2
Tianjin(Tientsin)	7.8
Chongqing (Chungking)	6.0
Guangzhou (Canton)	5.0
Senyang	5.0
Wuhan	3.5
Nanjing (Nanking)	3.0

SOCIOCULTURAL ENVIRONMENT

The dominant ethnic group is the Han, after which the Han Dynasty was named (202 B.C.-A.D. 220). The Han comprise about 95% of the population of China. Most overseas Chinese are also Han. The several minority ethnic groups are concentrated in relatively remote areas, so are seldom encountered by foreigners.

North China is the original home of the Han. They constitute a homogeneous block and speak the same Mandarin of Beijing dialect. The situation in Southern China is different, however; the Han moved southward over the first thousand years A.D and absorbed numerous "non-Chinese" elements. The language spoken in the south varies markedly from that of the north, the main southern dialect being Cantonese.

The Southwest and West are largely occupied by the original inhabitants, the Minorities. Altogether the Minorities occupy 50 to 60% of the surface area of China, although they are only 5% of the population. The Han are, above all, plains dwellers dependent on agriculture, whereas the Minorities have settled in the mountains, on the steppe, and in the deserts.

The written Chinese language is hieroglyphic, as opposed to alphabetic, and can be understood throughout China. However, the spoken language and dialects are Cantonese, Shanghanese, Fukienese, Hakka, and Mandarin. The government has decided, as a matter of policy, that Mandarin—the northern Chinese language—will be the national language for the whole of China.

Written language is uniform, but simplified characters are used which differ from traditional characters used in Chinese communities overseas. There are several alternative spellings for place names in China. In 1958, the State Council for the PRC adopted the Chinese Phonetic Alphabet system (Pinyin) for romanizing Chinese names and places. Beginning on January 1, 1979, all translated texts of Chinese diplomatic documents and Chinese magazines published in foreign languages have used the new Pinyin system of spelling Chinese names and places. It is an important change which replaces various and different spelling systems, including the Wade-Giles (English) and Lessing (German) systems, and will end the confusion that has existed for a long time in romanizing Chinese. Essentially, the system reflects the Beijing (Peking) dialect in pronunciation. As a result, spellings for many names changed, e.g., Peking became Beijing, Hong Kong became Xianggang and Canton became Guangzhou.

The literacy level has improved substantially since 1977, but it is still low by Western standards. Nearly 30% of the population has had no formal education and only 0.6% received postsecondary education.

The following statistics show the educational levels in the PRC for persons aged 9 and above.

No formal schooling	28.3%
Primary	35.5%
Junior secondary	17.8%
Senior secondary	6.7%
Post secondary	0.6%

In 1978, there were approximately 600 universities, colleges, and other institutes of higher education offering courses to 850,000 full-time students. There were 160,000 secondary schools with 65 million pupils, and 950,000 primary schools with 146 million pupils. All primary and secondary education is free.

GOVERNMENT POLICY ON EDUCATION

There have been many changes in the government's policy on education in the recent past. During the cultural revolution, students were judged not on academic merit, but on political loyalty and activity. With the recent changes in government, the policy has been to select students for higher education more on their academic merit than on their political background. Moreover, universities are now taking part in the international academic exchanges, and foreign scholars and specialists have been invited to deliver lectures. In institutes of higher education, research and teaching emphasize scientific and technological disciplines, especially those relating to computers and engineering.

One continuous obstacle that faces economic restructuring in China is the lack of trained personnel. For the first time, the 1984 Economic Plan addresses this issue. The PRC expects to graduate 8 million students from technical schools and 26 million university students during the seventh Five-Year Plan. These figures represent a 70% increase over the sixth Five-Year Plan.[3]

POLITICAL AND LEGAL ENVIRONMENT

The Chinese Communist Party (CCP) is the guiding force behind the PRC. Until very recently, the Politburo of the CCP Central Committee was the actual governing body of the country. Since 1978, however, there has been a vigorous campaign to reduce the Party's participation in technical, managerial, and administrative decisions and to confine its role to overseeing the political welfare of the people.

The PRC is a socialist state. Although there is no official head of state, the General Secretary (a post created in September 1982 to substitute for that of the Party Chairman) performs most ceremonial functions.

The basis of governmental structure at all levels is in the People's Congress. The highest organ of state power is the National People's Congress (NPC), which is composed of elected deputies from all over the PRC. The NPC meets once a year; during the period when it is not in session, decisions are implemented by the NPC standing committee.

The country is governed by a State Council, under a premier and two vice-premiers, whose members are appointed by the NPC.

The Central Committee is the seat of state power in the PRC and is composed of 210 members plus 138 alternates. An annual session of the Central Committee examines and approves important matters, such as the national economic plan, the state budget and the final state accounts. The 25-member Politburo formulates policy and has a six-member standing Committee.

The Party Secretariat, the highest executive organ of state administration, is headed by the General Secretary. It includes nine secretaries, three alternate secretaries, a five-member Military Commission, and another five-member Advisory Commission.

Each of the 21 Provinces in the PRC is administered by a local congress with standing committees similar to those of the National People's Congress (NPC).

CURRENCY

The PRC has a dual-currency system — Renminbi (RMB) for local Chinese and Foreign Exchange Certificates for foreigners, including overseas Chinese. The basic unit is yuan (dollar) and the subsidiary units are jiao (10 cents) and fen (cent). One yuan is about 27 U.S. cents.

RMB banknotes are not permitted to be brought into or taken out of the country. RMB deposits held by foreign banks may be transferred abroad by being converted into foreign currencies if so agreed by both parties. Exchange rates of RMB to foreign currencies are published by the General Administration of Exchange Control (GAEC). Since April 1, 1980, foreign visitors to China may use only foreign exchange certificates, which are equivalent to various denominations of RMB.

TECHNOLOGICAL ENVIRONMENT

During the 1950s and 1960s the PRC focused on the heavy industrial segment and placed little emphasis on advancing the technology of its food industry. Food processing is the third largest industry in the PRC and the need for modernization of this industry has recently been recognized. The recent production surpluses of crops in the PRC have created the need for advanced food technology to reduce the spoilage problem and to increase sales (and exports) of food stuffs.

Farmers experience substantial crop spoilage. Farming is decentralized and therefore it is difficult for farmers to distribute their crops to the food processing factories. Research conducted by Dr. David M. Lampton of Ohio State University concluded that from 25 to 50% of the fruit and tomato crops studied spoiled before reaching the consumer. It has been estimated by the State Economic Commission that only 8% of China's fruit crop is processed. This Commission has set a goal to reduce the spoilage level to only 5% by the year 2000. Improved canned food facilities are being developed to decrease the spoilage problem. The canned products could be sold for both domestic consumption and export.

Historically food processing facilities have been located in the urban areas since the processed food demand is highest there. However, this practice has created a great demand on the inadequate transportation systems available to transport the produce from the farm areas to the cities. Transportation bottlenecks that many times result in the spoilage of their products are common. Erecting the new food processing centers in the countryside rather than in the cities will help to alleviate this transportation burden. The government has asked the cities' food processing centers to establish field locations in the countryside.

DOING BUSINESS IN CHINA

Although joint ventures are the most frequent method by which USA companies have chosen to enter China, this mode of organization is by no means universal. A brief review of methods of business organization for marketing in the PRC follows.

EXPORTS TO CHINA

Within the constraints of limited hard currency exchange, several major USA companies have chosen this initial market entry method. Notable examples are Johnson & Johnson for baby care products and Nestlé for a widely distributed range of products including Nescafé regular and Classic brands of instant coffee, Nespray powdered milk, Krematop powdered creamer, Milo tonic food drink, and Cerelac baby food. Nestlé is reported to be actively negotiating for joint ventures for the production of a range of instant coffee brands, powdered milk products, tapioca products, and other instant foods. R.J. Reynolds' Del Monte range of canned fruits and vegetables enjoy substantial distribution, principally in Guangzhou Province, for products reportedly manufactured in the Philippines. Imported Parker brand writing instruments are featured prominently beside Chinese-made pens and pencils in friendship stores (which cater to foreigners and where purchases can only be made with Foreign Exchange Certificate) and department stores. Unilever's Lux soap brand has good distribution in major cities. Perhaps the most unique example of a prelocal manufacturing strategy is that being employed by Procter & Gamble. P&G is advertising on Chinese television for four of its brands, all included in the same commercial, which are not as yet in retail distribution in China. The featured brands are Ivory soap (available in some friendship stores), Ivory shampoo, Crest toothpaste, and Tide detergent powder.

JOINT VENTURES WITH CHINESE COMPANY OR GOVERNMENTAL AGENCY

There are generally two types of joint ventures referred to in China: equity and contractual. An equity joint venture involves Chinese and foreign partners in a limited liability corporation including joint investment and operation, and mutual sharing of risks, profits, and losses in proportion to the equity shares of each party. Contractual joint ventures cover a variety of other types of cooperative projects that may or may not involve setting up a separate corporation. The partners bring readily available resources that do not necessarily include cash. The foreign partner often provides technology and equipment while Chinese contribute land, labor, and other resources. Profits are distributed according to a formula specified in the contract, rather than determined by equity shares, and payment is usually geared to provide a relatively rapid payback to the foreign partner.

It appears that most USA consumer goods companies have either chosen the equity joint venture mode of market entry or are actively negotiating equity relationships.

JOINT VENTURE ESTABLISHMENT

Establishment of a joint venture in China is subject to examination and approval by the Ministry of Foreign Economic Relations and Trade. It is this Ministry that entrusts the various provinces with the power to analyze and approve the proposed joint venture provided that certain requirements are met. First, the amount of the investment must be within the limit set by the state council and the source of capital of the Chinese participants must be ascertained. Second, it must be determined that no additional quantity of raw material would be required and that those raw materials do not affect the national balance of fuel, power, transportation, and foreign trade export quotas.

To establish a joint venture, the Chinese participants submit a preliminary feasibility study of the joint venture being proposed to the department in charge of joint ventures. Once the department in charge has examined the preliminary feasibility study it is then submitted for review and final approval to the Ministry. At that time parties to the joint venture will negotiate and sign the joint venture agreements, contracts, and articles of association. Submission of the following documents is required by the Chinese participant on applying for approval of the joint venture:

1. Application for the establishment of a joint venture.
2. Feasibility study report jointly prepared by the parties to the venture.
3. Joint venture agreement, contract, and articles of association signed by representative authorized by the parties to the venture.
4. List of candidates for the joint venture board of directors for chairman, vice-chairman, and directors appointed by the parties to the venture.
5. Written opinion from both the department in charge and the respective government of the province.[4]

All referenced documents are to be written in Chinese. Items 2, 3, and 4 may be written simultaneously in a foreign language agreed upon by the parties to the joint venture. Both versions are considered to be legally and equally authentic.

A decision will be made within three months by the approval authority once all required documents have been received. If the approval authority believes that an inappropriate item is contained in the documents, then an amendment will be demanded and is to be submitted within a limited time period. No approval will be given without the amendment.

Once approval of the joint venture has been received, the applicant must register with an administration bureau of industry and commerce for the respective province of the Chinese-Foreign Joint Venture. The date on the business license represents the official date of the formal establishment of the joint venture.

LENGTH OF JOINT VENTURES

China's state council revised Article 100 of the joint venture regulation extending the duration of joint ventures from 10-30 years to 50 years, and in special cases it can be longer. Expanding the length of the joint venture may be one method to increase foreign capital. Expansion allows more opportunity for the foreign investors to recoup their investments.

Some USA companies have been reluctant to enter into the joint ventures because under most of the current laws, most of the plant and equipment reverts to the Chinese upon completion of the joint venture. According to one Chinese official, there are approximately 20 laws that are currently being deliberated concerning Western business practices. Some of these statutes include bankruptcy, customs, cooperative ventures, and ventures totally financed by foreign funds.

NATIONAL CONTROL OF INTERNATIONAL TRADE

China will continue to place pressure upon certain companies to transfer their technology to the Chinese plants during the seventh Five-Year Plan. Those industries include chemicals, electronics, food processing, machinery, and any other energy-efficient "know-how" technology. Measures will be enacted by the Chinese to regulate technology aimed at ending purchases of duplicate technology.

Over the course of the next five years, China's leaders will be restructuring the economy by placing less emphasis on planning and more on market forces and managerial initiative. Should all go well with the plan, China will grow at a market rate and become more market driven.

Controlling growth, importing only essential goods, and increasing exports to bring foreign currency into China are some of the goals of the seventh Five-Year Plan. Imports will focus on high technology and equipment. China's campaign to attract foreign investors will continue. However, energy and infrastructure inadequacies are also anticipated to continue, while imports will be subjected to tighter controls.

The plan anticipates an annual growth rate of approximately 7%, which is a 3% decrease from Deng's policies in the 1981-1985 plan. Additionally, the plan is off sharply from the 23% industrial growth that was achieved during the first 6 months of 1985. It was necessary to slow the growth rate, which had caused a number of problems including a drain on hard currency reserves. Deng's program suffered difficulty during 1985 that resulted in a huge borrowing spree and widespread corruption that led to a fall in the foreign exchange reserves. It was Deng's decision to grant wider autonomy to approximately 400,000 state and collective enterprises, leading to a "free-for-all" that created the crisis by 1985.

As a result of the 1985 crisis, there has been a shift in attitude toward the decentralization of economic decision-making. The government has now reinstituted tighter controls on loans, foreign exchange, and other matters that used to be left to the local authorities for each province.

As China's foreign trade remains in deficit the renminbi (China's currency) will continue to depreciate. Exchange rate adjustments will be implemented by the Chinese financial authorities in an attempt to balance the current account and to increase the linkage between domestic and international prices.

Western businesses should be aware of the planned decrease in foreign trade growth. The economic plans projection of 9 to 10% is down from the 20.5% that was achieved during 1981-1984. China's large trade deficit implies that imports will decrease and that export growth will increase. Western technology is needed to help China achieve its export goals.

BUSINESS OPPORTUNITIES

Chinese law governs the joint venture contract including its validity, interpretation, execution, and the settlement of disputes. The law of the PRC on joint ventures using Chinese and foreign investment is referred to as the Law on Chinese-Foreign Joint Ventures. Those joint ventures using foreign investment established within China's territory are Chinese "legal persons" and are subject to the jurisdictions and protection of Chinese law. The joint ventures have been established to strengthen China's economy in addition to raising the level of technology. The types of joint ventures that are being permitted into China fall into the following categories:

1. Foodstuffs
2. Energy development
3. Machine manufacturing
4. Electronics, computer, and communications industries
5. Light, textile, and packing industries
6. Medicine and medical apparatus
7. Agriculture, animal husbandry
8. Tourism and service trades[5]

On applying for joint venture the applicant is to stress economic results. In addition, the applicant should adhere to at least one of four following requirements.

1. Adopt advanced technical equipment as to ensure the increase of quality and output plus saving energy.
2. Provide technical renovation of industry that will result in less investment, quicker returns, and bigger profits.
3. Expand production to meet the needs of export demand so that China can enjoy an increase in foreign currency.
4. Provide the training of technical and managerial personnel.[6]

No applicant will be granted approval if the anticipated profit would be detrimental to China's sovereignty or a violation of Chinese law. In addition, any obvious inequity in the agreements, contracts, or articles of association that would impair the rights and interests of one party would be prohibited. The applicant must remain within China's guidelines concerning the development of its national economy.

AREAS OF CONFLICT – JOINT VENTURE TAXATION

Lui Zhicheng, consultant to the General Tax Bureau of China's Ministry of Finance, states that tax regulations have been established in order to implement China's open door policy. China's objective is to create a favorable investment environment and provide favorable conditions for the business operations in order to promote economic cooperation with foreign countries.[7]

Joint ventures may apply for a reduction or exemption from income tax if they are equipped with state-of-the-art technology. A restitution of income taxes paid may be obtained by the foreign participants if they reinvest any portion of their net income within the Chinese territory. The overall tax rate is 33% for USA companies establishing an equity joint venture. Should the foreign investor repatriate its earnings, it is subjected to a withholding tax of 10% of the amount remitted from China.[8]

Taxes on foreign enterprises (other than joint ventures) such as the cooperative ventures and branch offices can range from 20% to

40% in addition to the fixed local tax of 10%. China is attempting to establish itself as a low tax country. The 14 coastal cities as well as the four special economic zones offer various tax incentives. All of these areas offer a 15% tax rate in addition to other tax waivers and tax holdings for businesses with contracts to 10 years or longer. According to the 1984 Chinese government figures, foreign investment of approximately USA $8 billion has been absorbed by China since 1979.

Tax legislation is relatively new in China for it was not until 1980 that taxation on foreign investment in that country began. A tax treaty was developed and agreed upon by the USA and China in 1984 that would eliminate double taxation and avoid tax evasion. As a result of the tax treaty, USA businesses are better equipped to plan their investments knowing what their taxes will be. There are favorable provisions in the tax treaty for Western businesses. For example, there is a 20% withholding tax that China levies on investment income. Those rates are reduced to 10% on royalty, interest, and dividends due to the tax treaty.

A controversial tax area is the 15% tax on income for consulting services that China made retroactive to January 1985. The consulting offices representing the USA companies' joint ventures are affected by the tax rate. However, according to Michael D. Cannon, partner with Price Waterhouse, the tax effect will be approximately 6% of gross income. If the representative office is merely providing information to a parent company and is not generating any income, the office will not be taxed.[9]

BUSINESS ISSUES IN CHINA

Trading in China is becoming a more intense challenge as the market expands. "Besides not knowing whom to deal with, experts say, foreign businessmen stumble over such things as advance preparation, attempts at humor, language and the use of interpreters. Moreover, foreign companies sometimes bungle agreements or hamstring themselves when it comes to setting prices with the Chinese, experts say."[10]

Time could be saved if Western companies would contact the

correct authority from the start. Dealing with the correct Chinese partners can also make the difference between being in negotiations for 2 years resulting in no deal, or approval in just a few weeks. One must realize that the Chinese are familiar with the foreign market. It is recommended not to start with unrealistic prices. "It does not help, because the Chinese think that you have tried to rip them off, says John Burke, manager of Star Offshore Services (HK) Ltd."[11] However, the company dealing with China should feel comfortable with the first price quoted, "The Chinese accept the concessionary price as a benchmark, rather than acknowledging world market prices and effects of inflation."[12]

When determining who should be chosen partner, "most USA companies hope for one with Guanzi (pronounced gwanshi) which roughly translates as 'connections,' who can at least ensure an adequate supply of raw materials."[13] The Chinese have been known to bring no money to joint ventures. Real estate is their contribution to the deal.

It is also important to bring your own interpreter to the negotiations, to help make certain of the proper translation of crucial information. There seems to be no consensus as to which language works best for negotiations. It does not matter what sex the negotiators are, because sexism is not an issue in China. One thing is certain: patience is a must. "What takes 2 hours in London may take a week in China. One reason the Chinese do not hurry is because they need to show their superiors what shrewd bargainers they are, experts say."[14]

DISTRIBUTION

Second only to the problems of negotiating a venture in the PRC is the problem of physical distribution of products within China. However, there is one big difference between these two major problem areas. Most USA companies that are considering entering the Chinese market will by now have heard all about the pitfalls of negotiating a joint venture in the PRC. Most will probably have a carefully prepared strategy of which agency to contact and how to do it. But most companies probably will not even think about distribution. They are likely to take it for granted for two reasons. First, USA companies are used to the ease of mass distribution in their home markets or even in the developed economies in which they do business overseas. Second, they assume that their prospective joint venture partner knows how to handle distribution and will "take care of" that part of the business. These assumptions can lead to some painful surprises because there simply is no infrastructure for mass distribution of consumer goods in China. Physical distribution is often only provincial or even local.

The PRC is really a series of large markets, each usually dominated by a large coastal city, rather than a homogeneous market. Although coastal Chinese cities represent the most highly developed consumer economies, exceptions include Beijing and Nanjing as well as some inland manufacturing centers with large, though isolated, populations. This clustering of consumer marketing centers, rather than one integrated marketplace, results from the current status of transportation facilities within China. Of course, there are national scale transportation facilities, but they are not geared to the distribution of consumer goods.

The national airline is a passenger, not cargo, operation. Furthermore, it is fully booked by government demands including the China International Travel Service. It is unlikely that a traveler will see an empty seat on the national airline (CAAC).

The other two national transportation systems are geared to bulk transportation. Coal for the railroads and bulk food and other commodities, such as building materials, are moved via the extensive system of river and canal transport.

There is no system of mass distribution by motor truck because there is no highway system to compare with "interstate" or inter-city roads. The highway network consists of roads leading out from the major cities to the surrounding countryside so that locally grown food can be brought to the cities.

Chinese seaports are notoriously congested. This is a major problem as the PRC attempts to expand its foreign trade. Port congestion results from inadequate cargo handling capabilities, insufficient warehousing, and from the problems with moving goods away from the ports to population centers as discussed above. "In fact, (China) as a whole has fewer (seaport) berths than the single port of (either) Rotterdam, or New York."[15]

PROFITS

Companies have found that profits cannot be easily taken out of the PRC. They do not actually see a return until exporting from China brings in foreign exchange.[16] As yet, there is no national clearing on foreign exchange credits, nor may a foreign company balance foreign exchange credits among several joint ventures. Any sales made for local currency (RMB) are effectively frozen because no rules for translating RMB profits to foreign exchange have been established.

Furthermore, total foreign exchange earning exports from China are decreasing for 1985.[17] Economic changes adopted in October 1984 have permitted factories to become more flexible in determining what they produce. For this reason, a drop in export growth can be seen because less is being produced for export in the face of growing demand for consumer products.[18]

"Generally in China, economic performance is poor, financial control is weak and financial and economic discipline is lax," Auditor General Yu Mingtou was quoted saying.[19]

CONSUMER CREDIT

Deng Xiaoping has realized the necessity to stimulate the Chinese economy by "energetically promoting consumer and service industries."[20] The *China Daily* quoted the Ministry of Commerce saying, "More flexible ways of selling goods will be adopted, such as allowing sales on credit or by installment payments and encouraging advance orders for durable goods including color television sets, refrigerators, washing machines, cameras, and motorcycles."[21]

Credit sales were at one time common, but then banished when so many became indebted. This is the first time credit purchases may be made since the Communist takeover in 1949.[22]

EXPENSE OF DOING BUSINESS IN CHINA

"China represents an excellent opportunity for the USA investor," declares Alexander Trowbridge, president of the National Association of Manufacturers.[23] Many companies agree, then the shock hits when they soon recognize that China "is among the world's most expensive business centers."[24] Although China is a low-wage nation, to adequately "maintain a manager in Peking, $250,000 is needed, roughly 40 percent more than it costs in London."[25]

Foreigners are charged outrageous prices. Scarce apartments rent for $6,000 monthly and the rent has to be paid a year in advance. When they travel in China, foreigners pay more than twice as much as Chinese for plane tickets. There is not much to do after work or on weekends at any price. Quite a few expatriates spend their free time drinking in each other's homes while griping about conditions.[26]

BUSINESS MANAGEMENT SKILLS

China will soon have its first American-run MBA program. In the spring of 1985, the State University of New York at Buffalo was granted permission to help develop such a managerial class. "With all the pressure of new joint ventures," said Joseph Alutto, dean of SUNY's Buffalo business school, "the Chinese do not have a core of high-level managers to deal with American managers."[27]

The University of International Business and Economics (UIBE) in Beijing will soon be graduating its first undergraduate fourth-year class. UIBE also has a graduate business curriculum with marketing and economics concentrations. Advertising was added to the courses available for study with the 1985-1986 school year.

ADVERTISING

There had been limited advertising in China up to the Cultural Revolution in 1966. During the Cultural Revolution, however, advertising was ideologically unacceptable, and it was only after the change in government policy that advertising began again for domestic foreign advertisers in early 1979.

Interpublic-Jardine advertising agency believes that advertising is now very positively perceived by most key officials and the government in China. Domestically it is seen primarily as an efficient means to give or receive information about products.

The major traditional western mass media are available for advertising foreign products in China — TV, radio, newspapers, and magazines. Lesser media such as cinemas, transportation advertising, and billboards are also important though billboards have recently been downplayed, particularly in Beijing. Even where media have previously not accepted advertising, it is often possible to negotiate a rate and advertise. In effect, all media are commercial, and can accept advertising.

There is as yet no media representative organization within the country that represents all the media, and no single source of media rates and information.

Foreign companies must pay for advertising in hard currency. Local corporations pay in local currency and enjoy lower rates from media. For joint ventures' advertising in China, there is no established procedure and the media rates which apply and the currency used must be negotiated on a case-by-case basis.

In China, the three municipalities of Beijing, Shanghai, and Tianjin and all the major provinces have advertising corporations affiliated to the Ministry of Foreign Economic Relations and Trade, and they are a major channel for foreign advertising in China. They are not full-service advertising agencies in the western sense, but rather act as media representatives for the media in their area. As such, they work with all recognized foreign advertising agencies and advertisers on a nonexclusive basis, and are accountable in foreign currency.

There is a parallel network of advertising corporations which operates independently, handling domestic advertisers' requirements.

They are accountable in the local currency (RMB). Their national association is the China United Advertising Corporation which was established under the auspices of the State Administration for Industry and Commerce.

MEDIA OVERVIEW

Virtually all media are commercial but rates are often arbitrarily fixed and bear little relation to audience delivery. Audience and readership data are limited. No national media surveys have been conducted, although ad hoc surveys have been carried out in the most important cities.

At the end of 1984, there were around 45 million TV sets in the country reaching 300 million Chinese via the national channel (CCTV). The medium is experiencing very rapid growth with domestic production amounting to just under 10 million sets in the year, with sales of color sets reported at 1 million.

There are also 55 local TV stations in addition to CCTV. TV campaigns can be executed nationally, regionally, or locally. Sponsored programs are very popular since usually they have better program content and quality. Major cities are served by two or three channels.

Television is just opening up as a medium of advertising in China. Perhaps 20% of the population owns a TV set. However, the effective audience can be far higher, perhaps as high as 60% due to TV sets in public places. A favorite subject in advertisements — more out of national pride than desire to sell products — is heavy industrial goods. One of the most popular ads in China now is for ball bearings.[28]

There are over 300 national and local newspapers. All newspapers, except the *China Daily*, are in Chinese. Circulations are not audited. Major newspapers in cities are also displayed on the street for people to read. The *People's Daily* has the largest circulation by far at 5 million, but as noted above, there is a much higher (but unknown) readership.

There are over 1,200 magazines circulating in China. Most of them circulate nationwide through subscription. In some of the magazines, the number and position of pages for advertising is restricted. Both technical and general interest magazines are popular and carry a major portion of advertising expenditures.

Radio has the highest potential coverage, especially in rural areas. Virtually all households own at least one radio. The CCPBS national network is said to reach 650 million and the Beijing station, 450 million. In addition to the national network, there are 122 local radio stations.

At a seminar conducted by Cadwell Davis Partners, a Chinese participant asked, "If you compare two products, aren't you disgracing one of them?"[29] Comparative advertising is not yet used in China, although there has been print advertising comparing Texas Instrument's PC with the IBM PC.

FUTURE BUSINESS OPPORTUNITIES

A major drawback to any country contemplating a joint venture with China is the cultural differences. The USA multinational companies have been successful with their ventures in Western Europe; however, doing business with China is different. Only very recently has China begun to establish business ties with the Western world. The Chinese are not accustomed to signing a contract that includes all the details of the joint venture. It takes time for the Chinese to sign a contract, and Western business people should not anticipate rushing through the process. Western business people should allow themselves the time for the formal sessions, elaborate dinners, and walks through their scenic park areas. The Chinese business leaders place great emphasis on knowing their American partners' customs and behavior.

Any company pursuing a joint venture with China should be aware that the written contract is only secondary to the verbal agreement. A major *Fortune* 100 executive believes that the Chinese are very committed to their verbal agreements but place less priority on their business written contracts. Coca-Cola encountered that type of situation when PepsiCo entered the Chinese market in 1984. Coke believed that they had the exclusive right to sell their beverage in China in accordance with their contract with the central government trading company in 1978. Coke was informed by the Chinese government on Pepsi's arrival in China that they do not have the exclusive right for all of China. Rather, Coke has priority right to sell their beverage only in the province in which they are operating.

The key issues in doing business in consumer and industrial products in the PRC seem, by consensus, to fall into the following frustration order. They all can and are being resolved through patience and an expanding economic base, but it pays to know what they are "going in."

1. Negotiating the joint venture or other package including slowly evolving commercial law under the new economic policies.
2. Physical distribution of the goods produced. How fast can even a national urban distribution system be developed?
3. Repatriation of profits from export-earned foreign exchange credits and, eventually, from local currency.
4. Who will manage the labor force?
5. Negotiation of favorable (local) advertising rates.
6. High, often arbitrary, expenses for foreign nationals doing business in the PRC.

Even though the most avid China watchers have had plenty of surprises over the years, the consensus is that Deng's open-door policy will continue. Although the door may swing back and forth from time to time, largely dependent on how quickly and firmly his successors are able to grasp power, most observers believe that once open, it will be very difficult to retreat into a closed economy. The Chinese people are far better off than they were five or even three years ago. This is true most obviously in the countryside where the responsibility system first took hold. But it is true for the cities, too. Today's access to Western influences, whether expressed in disco dancing, Western music, colorful clothing, or color TVs, will be very hard to reverse. It is not that these influences, often expressed in trivial ways, are particularly significant in the big picture. The fact is that the largely young population of urban China enjoy them. As long as the most popular musical group in China features soft rock, Chinese versions of American songs, it will be difficult for any future regime to gain support for a return to the drab existence of the 1960s. Peoples' lives as measured in food and material goods are better today. The young people, particularly, like the limited social freedom and better economic outlook for the future.

Deng and his pragmatists are embarking on a fast track. So far, they seem to have done a lot more right than wrong. Many USA consumer and industrial goods companies believe that their business commitments in China are sure to grow at an accelerating pace.

NOTES

1. Jones, Dorothy E. and Dorinda Elliot, Edith Terry, Carla Anne Robbins, Charles Gaffney and Bruce Nussbaum, (1985, January 14), Capitalism in China, *Businessweek*, p. 54.

2. Kraar, Louis (1985, February 18), Open for Business? *Fortune*, p. 29.

3. China's Five-Year Economic Plan Seeks to Control Growth, Spending (1985, September 23), *The Wall Street Journal*, p. 35.

4. 1984 Almanac of China's Foreign Economic Relations and Trade (1984) Beijing, China: Hsiang-Kang: Hua Jun Mao 1 Tzu Itsu Yu Hfei Kung Fssu.

5. *Ibid.*

6. *Ibid.*

7. China's Tax Rules Favor Business (1985, June 4), *The Journal of Commerce*, p. 3A.

8. *Ibid.*

9. *Ibid.*

10. Fung, Vigor, As Chinese Markets Open, Foreign Businessmen Learn the Special Tricks of Making a Deal There (1985, August 1), *Wall Street Journal*, p. 20.

11. *Ibid.*

12. *Ibid.*

13. Gilbert, Nick, The China Guanxi (1985, July 29), *Fortune*, p. 104.

14. *Op. cit.*, As Chinese Markets Open, Foreign Businessmen Learn the Special Tricks of Making a Deal There, p. 20.

15. China's Economy and Foreign Trade 1981-85 (1984), Washington D.C.: U.S. Department of Commerce, International Trade Administration, p. 7.

16. *Op. cit.*, Open for Business?, p. 32.

17. China's Exports Seen To Be On the Decline (1985, July 2), *Wall Street Journal*, p. 1.

18. Bangsberg, P.T. (1985, May 10), China Makes Plea For Foreign Investment, Journal of Commerce, p. 3A.

19. Audit in China Finds $299 Million in Errors (1984, September 4), *Wall Street Journal*, p. 1.

20. China To Remove Ban on Credit Sale of Goods (1985, February 14), *Wall Street Journal*, p. 1.
21. *Ibid.*
22. *Ibid.*
23. *Op. cit.*, Open for Business? p. 29.
24. *Ibid.*, p. 32.
25. *Ibid.*
26. *Ibid.*
27. China's So-called Capitalism (1984, May 28), *Fortune*, p. 24.
28. *Ibid.*
29. *Ibid.*

Chapter 6:

Egypt:
International Business Perspectives

Gillian Rice
Essam Mahmoud

INTRODUCTION

Arab countries can be divided into two groups: the capital surplus group (such as Saudi Arabia, Kuwait, Libya, and Iraq) and the capital importing group. The second group is described as capital importing because of its large domestic investment possibilities and the lack of internal financial resources (Ghattas, 1984). Outstanding in this group are countries such as Egypt (with a population of 51 million), Morocco (20.65 million), Sudan (18.90 million), Syria (9.31 million), and Tunisia (16.51 million), which possess vast investment opportunities in agriculture, industry, mining, and services (Ghattas, 1984; EIU Annual Supplement, 1985).

The focus of this chapter is Egypt. The analysis of Egypt from an international business perspective is divided into three main parts: environmental analysis, business opportunities analysis, and business strategy analysis. The environmental analysis begins by examining Egypt in its regional context, paying particular attention to politics and trade. Next, discussions of the economy, human resources, infrastructure, sociocultural factors, Egypt's foreign trade and investment policy, and the political environment are presented from the viewpoint of an international manager. The section on business opportunities examines the development plan, specific industry trends, and the growing banking sector. Also, a discussion of business information sources includes a description of a new marketing information system called National Information for Egyptian Development. The business strategy analysis comprises sections dealing with market entry, managing conflict and controlling operations, strategic planning, and organization. The chapter concludes with a brief examination of future business scenarios in Egypt.

ENVIRONMENTAL ANALYSIS OF EGYPT

The Regional Context: Politics and Trade

Following the peace-making process with Israel in the late 1970s, Egypt has become the second largest recipient of U.S. foreign aid. The Economist Intelligence Unit (EIU) (Annual Supplement, 1985) reports that in 1983/84, Egypt received $1.3 billion in military aid, $75 million in economic support funds and $240 million in commodity aid. Although the U.S. is Egypt's chief ally, cooling relations between Egypt and Israel in the past few years has meant a gradual reconciliation between some other Arab countries and Egypt. Most Arab nations have restored diplomatic relations with Egypt. Also, as a result of Moroccan pressure, Egypt was invited to return to the Islamic Conference Organization (ICO), without preconditions, early in 1984 at the ICO's Casablanca summit.

Egypt's main trading partners are shown in Table 1. Egypt has an association agreement with the European Economic Community (EEC) which entitles the country to certain preferences within the EEC. Egypt, Syria, and Iraq form a free trade zone. In November 1985, Egypt's annual trade agreement with Iraq was doubled to $200 million (*Middle East Economic Digest [MEED]*, November 9, 1985). A $250 million trade agreement between Egypt and Jordan has also been signed (*South*, March 1986).

In the Middle East, Egypt is a large importer of U.S. goods, second only to Saudi Arabia. In the years 1981, 1982, and 1983, Egypt accounted for 12.8%, 15.4%, and 17.7%, respectively, of U.S. goods sold in the region (Al-Dabbagh, 1985). U.S. exports to Egypt totaled over $2.7 billion in 1984 (*Business America*, September 16, 1985). As the price of oil has fallen, the imports by Arab oil-exporting countries have also fallen considerably, whereas the imports by non-oil Arab countries have fallen only slightly. Al-

Table 1
Main Trading Partners

Main Destinations of Egypt's Exports 1985		Main Origins of Egypt's Imports 1985	
	(% of total)		(%of total)
Italy	30.7	USA	18.9
Japan	10.5	West Germany	8.8
West Germany	9.9	France	8.2
France	7.9	Italy	7.9
Romania	5.2	Japan	6.0
UK	3.5	UK	5.0
USSR	3.3	Spain	3.5

Source: Economist Intelligence Unit, *Quarterly Review of Egypt*, No. 4, London:
The Economist Publications Ltd., 1986.

Dabbagh (1985) explains that this is related to the fact that a large percentage of the major oil countries' imports comprises "compressible imports" of consumer and durable goods. Therefore, the response of these countries to reduced oil exports would be expected to be more significant than the response of countries such as Egypt, whose imports are noncompressible items like food and industrial development goods.

Arab investors from capital surplus Arab countries have tended to regard the Arab region as the natural sphere for the utilization of their funds. In addition to political and cultural ties, the return on capital invested in capital importing Arab nations like Egypt tends to be higher than that in more advanced Western economies because of the scarcity of capital and the ample investment opportunities (Ghattas, 1984). The need to protect Arab investments from political risks led to the formation of the Inter-Arab Investment Guarantee Corporation (IAIGC) which began operating in 1975. IAIGC is a regional organization with over 20 member nations from the Middle East and North Africa. One of its objectives is to further develop Arab economic relations and to design new trade and investment agreements. Ghattas (1984) provides full details on IAIGC. He notes one interesting development: IAIGC and COFACE (Compagnie Française d'Assurance pour le Commerce Exterieur) shared risks on two contracts of a joint Arab-French bank, the former covering political risks and the latter commercial and natural disaster risks.

The Economy

Egypt's economy is burdened by a large trade deficit (over $5 billion in 1985/86) and a chronic foreign exchange shortage. Egypt has four main sources of hard currency: crude oil sales, money sent home by migrant workers in oil-exporting countries, tourism, and Suez Canal dues. The first three have fallen recently (*Wall Street Journal*, February 27, 1986). Egypt's oil revenues of approximately $2 billion in 1985/86 are expected to shrink to $800 million in 1986/87 (*MEED*, February 14, 1987). Also, as a result of the falling price of oil, there has been a drop in overseas work opportunities as recession squeezes the economies of the Arab region's major oil producers (*South*, December 1985a). Many Egyptian emigrants have had large pay cuts, and openings for would-be emigrants are sparse. Income from tourism has fallen because Westerners are staying away from Egypt in the wake of increased terrorism in the region. Even before the February 1986 riots in Egypt, tourism income was expected to drop 30% in the fiscal year ending in June 1986.

In 1984, Egypt moved toward establishing a unified market exchange rate by adopting, in principle, an adjustable peg system. The objective is to divert more money traditionally traded in the black market into the banking system, and thereby ease shortages in the Central Bank's pool of foreign exchange (*Business America*, August 20, 1984). In May 1987 Egypt reached agreement with the International Monetary Fund (IMF) on an economic adjustment program and a standby credit of $300 million. The agreement involves reforms of Egypt's heavily subsidized, centrally planned economy (*South*, April 1987; *The Economist*, January 23, 1988). The most radical reform is a three-stage reduction in the external value of the local currency over 18 months and rationalizing the current multitier exchange rate system.

With a few exceptions (for example, Lebanon and Jordan), in the Arab economies the public sector is either the primary or the dominant sector in terms of influence or investment behavior (Makdisi, 1985). The Arab private sector is active and growing, however, especially in the fields of trade and banking. The dominance of the public sector in Egypt is reflected in the Five Year Plans (see below, "Business Opportunities Analysis"); for example, in 1982/87 76.7% of the total planned investment was public sector investment. This does, however, show a considerable drop from the public sector's 94.1% share in 1973/74 before the "Open-Door Policy" (see below, "Egypt's Foreign Trade and Investment Policy") was implemented (EIU Annual Supplement, 1985). The Egyptian government is concentrating on the growth of the relatively more productive private sector by maintaining tax incentives for private sector firms, facilitating their acquisition of operating licenses, and encouraging joint ventures between local or foreign private investors and Egypt's numerous private sector firms (*Wall Street Journal*, October 9, 1985).

Egypt's principal nonhuman resource is its land. Only 3.5% of Egypt's surface is inhabited, although 15.5% has been designated as currently habitable (Waterburg, 1983). The main crops cultivated in the summer are millet, maize, sorghum, rice, and cotton, with winter crops of berseem (clover), wheat, and pulses. Fruits, vegetables, and sugar cane are grown year-round. Cotton remains Egypt's main agricultural export. Food processing and spinning and weaving are the most important branches of industry, with each contributing about a sixth of the total value of manufacturing output (EIU Annual Supplement, 1985).

Per capita income in Egypt is about U.S. $720 (The World Bank, 1984), which puts Egypt in the middle range of the developing countries. This figure reflects Egypt's large population (see below), but living standards are poor for the majority of the nation's inhabitants. From an international business perspective, it is important to examine the spread of wealth and the general level of discretionary income which influences major shifts in the demand from different groups of consumers for products and services (Michell, 1979). A dual society has emerged in many developing countries; an elitist segment demands the products of the industrialized economies, while the vast majority continue their present subsistence economy. For Egypt, a Business International (1980) survey reports a sharp widening of the disparities in both rural and urban income distribution since 1974. For example, in rural areas the top 10% take approximately 25% of available income and the lowest 40% take about 20% of that income. The disparity is slightly greater in urban areas.

Human Resources

The population in Egypt is growing at 2.7% annually. In 1987 it was estimated to reach 51 million (*Insight*, 1987). Population density in nondesert areas is high and the urban population is increasing rapidly as the limited agricultural area fails to absorb the mounting population. Greater Cairo's population in 1980 was estimated at over 9 million, compared with 7 million in 1976 (EIU Annual Supplement, 1985). Housing investment is the largest single construction sector activity in Egypt.

Foreign businesses contracting in Egypt are not expected to bring in labor to Egypt, with the exception of a few experts and management personnel. Egypt has a large and diversified labor force which represents one of the country's most valuable resources for long-term development. Though high wages in some of its Arab neighbors have caused a shortage of skilled workers such as electricians, plumbers, and carpenters, there is an adequate supply of workers with other skills and plenty of unskilled and semiskilled labor (U.S. Department of Commerce, 1984). The number of Egyptians working abroad is shown in Table 2. As the price of oil falls, however, so do the opportunities for Egyptian workers in the oil-rich nations, as noted earlier.

Egypt has the largest trade union movement in the Arab and African countries. All Egyptian workers have the right to belong to a labor union, and Egypt's general trade unions belong to the government-affiliated Egyptian Trade Union Federation (ETUF). The Ministry of Manpower and Vocational Training enforces labor laws, including those on labor standards and trade unions; administers the public employment service; and carries out labor inspec-

Table 2
Egyptians Working Abroad

Location	Number (millions)
Iraq	1.25
Saudi Arabia	0.80
Libya	0.30
Kuwait	0.20
United Arab Emirates	0.15
Other Middle East	0.16
Total Middle East	2.86
North America	0.25
European Community	0.12
Australia	0.05
Total Abroad	3.28

Source: Economist Intelligence Unit Annual Supplement (1985).

tion, vocational training, and planning functions (U.S. Department of Commerce, 1981).

A major manpower problem in Egypt is low productivity. Many factories have been overstaffed in an effort to absorb unemployment (the rate of unemployment is about 10-15% and is a social and economic burden). The government's policy of guaranteeing a job to all graduates of higher educational institutions exacerbated the problem. Many who might, in a more competitive environment, have become artisans, chose to obtain degrees that would lead to an assured white collar job at higher pay. This policy contributed to the simultaneous shortage of skilled workers and overstaffed government bureaucracy. The government recently discontinued the policy.

The Infrastructure in Egypt

Egypt's physical infrastructure suffered substantial deterioration due to lack of adequate investment and slow project implementation (U.S. Department of Commerce, 1981). Although most of Egypt's major centers are linked by roads, in many cases they are inadequate to handle traffic because of their condition. More recently, however, the infrastructure has improved (*The Economist*, August 2, 1986). Traffic in Cairo is less of a crawl than it was a few years ago, partly thanks to new flyovers. Progress is being made on the Cairo metro system under construction by French firms. The concentration of Egypt's population along the Nile and the flat topography there have meant the development of the railroad as the backbone of Egypt's freight hauling system. Egypt's system of inland waterways is also an important means of freight transportation.

The Alexandria Port Authority handles most of Egypt's cargo (about 80%) and there are various projects to improve facilities there. Port Said and Suez City, the terminals of the Suez Canal, are able to handle much less cargo because of war-related damage and smaller facilities. Cairo is among the most active air centers in the Near East and is served by many international airlines.

The telecommunications network in Egypt has become inadequate for the needs of the economy. In 1982 Egypt had one telephone per 82.4 inhabitants (EIU Annual Supplement, 1985). Perhaps in no other sphere as in telecommunications, however, has there been such a marked improvement in services over the last several years. When direct dialing to Egypt became available in 1984 it became much easier to dial locations outside Cairo. The long-term goal of Arento (the telephone organization) is to provide a fully comprehensive telephone system by the turn of the century. However, many logistical problems remain. The telephone directory is available in Arabic only, except in some embassies.

The media are entirely state-controlled in Egypt and function as organs of the state information department. Nevertheless, Cairo is the largest publishing center in the Middle East and the media capital of the Arab world. Foreign businesses can advertise in newspapers and magazines and on radio, television, cinema, and posters through the government-owned advertising agency. In 1983 there was one radio receiver per 5.5 persons and one television for 11.5 persons in Egypt (EIU Annual Supplement, 1985). In 1974 there were 239 cinemas in the country and movie attendance was 70 million (Kurian, 1982). Even in the advanced sector of developing countries in the Middle East such as Egypt, modern advertising is relatively new. Media selection is constrained by the reach of media vehicles and low literacy rates (Kaikati, 1979). Egypt has a relatively low literacy rate despite increased emphasis on education which admittedly led to an improvement in the literacy rate from 26% in the 1960s to 54.3% in 1980. Foreign businesses must advertise using appropriate media such as billboards, which are widely available and provide a useful medium of communication. The cultural adaptation of advertising messages and brand names is very important. The sociocultural influences on doing business in Egypt are discussed next.

The Sociocultural Environment in Egypt

Cultural and social considerations are perhaps the most constraining variables when doing business in a foreign country. For example, the marketing implications of cultural differences may be seen in terms of a number of activities within the overall marketing function such as marketing research, understanding consumer behavior, organizational behavior and salesman activity, and marketing strategy formulation (Redding, 1982). Ways of doing business in a Middle Eastern nation cannot be understood by reference to Western models.

Egypt is a predominantly Moslem country; over 80% of the population follows the Islamic faith. An important feature of the sociocultural environment which may have implications for the success of Western-oriented products and advertising, is Islamic revivalism. People unhappy with rapid social change and the spread of Western values are finding solace in Islam. Some observers believe that social conservatism has grown in Egypt as a consequence of increasing contact with the oil-exporting states (Ikram, 1980). Products and services conceived and/or manufactured in the West are seen as symbols of a new "imperialism of values" (Eilts, 1982).

Culture-Conditioned Consumer Behavior

Reliance on purely economic or demographic indicators can foster misconceptions about the size of a market and consumer behavior if an in-depth understanding of Egyptian culture is missing. This can be illustrated by an examination of consumer decision-making.

Because of prevailing natality and mortality conditions, the populations of developing countries are relatively young. Consequently much of the potential market, even for established products, consists of new buyers without strong preferences for specific brands or products (Leff and Farley, 1980), This does not take into account the family structure in Egypt, however, which is heavily influenced by the Islamic tradition. Consumer decision-making depends partly on the fact that the father, according to Islam, protects and provides for the entire family. The family members, in return, are to respect all the father's wishes and remain psychologically under his control. Obligations toward parents are sacred. From a marketing standpoint questions may be raised as to the real amount of a teenager's discretionary income. The tradition of deference to parental wishes is likely to affect buying patterns in clothing and leisure expenditure, especially in view of the fact that it is normal to live at home until marriage. The image of functional products could be enhanced by advertisements stressing parental advice or approval; even with children's products there should be less emphasis on children as decision-makers (Luqmani, Quraeshi, and Delene, 1980). Furthermore, advertising appeals based on Western values of youthful looks and energy are likely to be less successful in Egypt where the older generation tends to be much more respected. Pezeshkpur (1978) suggests that signs of old age may be helpful; grey hair, for example, can represent wisdom through experience.

Egyptian society has emphasized the domestic roles of women. Improved educational opportunities have increased their social and occupational mobility in recent years and women now constitute about a third of total enrollment in universities. The Islamic influence, however, includes an obligation to conform to codes of sexual conduct and social interaction, which implies modest dress for women in public. More colorful clothing and accessories are worn by women at home, so promotion of products for use in private homes could be more intimate – such audiences could be reached effectively through women's magazines (Luqmani et al., 1980). The use of magazines as a communications medium would necessarily be confined to educated and more wealthy women. A further implication of the Islamic moral code is that communications with customers should avoid use of immodest exposure and sexual connotations in public settings.

Business Customs

The Egyptian culture is characterized by a much slower pace of life. What takes one day to accomplish in North America or Europe may take a week in Egypt. Attitudes toward doing business emphasize the importance of personal relationships and in communications, social position and power are ever present factors (Badawy, 1980). Arbose (1982) attributed the success of Japanese salesmen in Egypt to their appreciation of the local attitudes toward doing business. For example, the Japanese are more polite, patient, efficient, flexible, alert, neat, and generous than their Western counterparts. The Japanese salesmen wait patiently and know the different attitudes Middle Easterners have about time. They are prepared to talk for one or two hours before mentioning business. An article in *Business America* (1982) advises that such a patient style of market development usually leads to successful business dealings in Egypt.

Badawy (1980) explains that typical managerial styles in the Middle East and North Africa involve highly bureaucratic, overcentralized organizations with power and authority at the top. The chain of command is followed rigidly and in leadership there is a highly authoritarian tone. Relationships are vague and the organizational environment is ambiguous and unpredictable. Planning is often ad hoc with decisions made at the highest level of management. Generally, management methods are old and outmoded. Day-to-day survival or tactical responses to emergencies is the way of doing business. Managers of foreign firms therefore have to make incremental decisions (El-Ansary, 1986).

Negotiating, according to El-Ansary (1986) is a way of life in countries like Egypt. He emphasizes that it is the first and most difficult step in establishing international business relations. Negotiating is time-consuming and continuous. Government officials and businessmen in Egypt, looking for good deals, may even haggle over prices and terms after draft agreements have been signed by the parties involved. Although American businessmen strongly believe in establishing business relations on a contractual basis, the Egyptians are more likely to seek foundations of mutual trust to strengthen these relationships (El-Ansary, 1986). Hence the mere presence of lawyers in the early stages of negotiations can create an atmosphere of mistrust among the Egyptians.

For further information and a succinct analysis of the differences in American and Middle Eastern managerial styles, the reader is referred to El-Ansary (1986).

Organizational Forms in Egypt: Dealing with Bureaucracy

In Middle Eastern nations like Egypt, foreign executives often must work with the government because of the dominance of the public sector and the types of business projects — frequently large-scale and government-sponsored (El-Ansary, 1986). Inevitably, this means coping with bureaucracy. Ayubi (1982) notes that for a variety of organizational and political reasons, the performance of the Egyptian bureaucracy is declining sharply in quality, when the desire to encourage foreign investment is actually calling for a more innovative, flexible, and efficient bureaucracy. Part of the problem may be attributable to the massive state bureaucracy established in the mid-1960s (Gillespie, 1984).

The principal criticism made by investors is the lack of coordination between various government agencies and their apparent inability to honor important undertakings (Business International, 1980). For example, a customs exemption from the investment authority (the General Authority for Investment and Free Zones, or GAIFZ) does not automatically mean the customs service will abide by it.

The Cairo metro project was due for completion in November 1985, but work did not start to progress smoothly until early 1984. A report on the metro project (*MEED*, November 1985) notes that the main problems have been bureaucratic. For example, the Governor of Cairo would not allow sections of the road to be closed off to enable work to commence, the ministries concerned failed to give adequate support to the project, and the powers of the authority in charge of the metro were not clearly defined. These administrative problems were eventually solved in 1983 by the formation of the National Authority for Tunnels, which was given power to make the necessary decisions for progress of the project.

In response to international marketers' complaints that they have been deterred by bureaucratic obstacles, Egypt is making efforts to clarify the investment situation and to speed up and centralize the investment approval process so as to attract new investors into priority sectors (*Middle East and African Economist*, 1982). Business International (1980) reports that GAIFZ is improving its promotion effort through trade missions abroad and through its own promotions department in Cairo, where it has set up a special informations center. The government also is now making regular visits to the free zone area at Cairo Airport to ensure the speed of transactions and to eliminate unnecessary obstacles (*Arab Youth*, March 1987).

Egypt's Foreign Trade and Investment Policy

Egypt has a fairly liberal trade and investment policy. The broad framework of a fundamental change toward a more open and market-oriented economy was enunciated a decade ago in April 1974 by President Anwar Sadat. The "open-door" investment policy of "El-Infitah" (the opening) was implemented with the passing in 1974 of Law 43, "Concerning the Investment of Arab and Foreign Funds and the Free Zones." As the name implies, the law outlines the conditions under which foreign investment can be undertaken within Egypt, either inland or within designated free zones. The policy was more than just the encouragement of foreign investment. In a larger sense it involved the dismantling of import controls, the development of the private sector, and the relaxation of restrictions on the possession and use of foreign currency (Davies, 1984). Law 43 was amended by Law 32 in 1977, which further liberalized Egypt's trade and investment policy. Amendments were made in the area of exchange control and Law 32 set out the projects covered by Law 43 in more detail. The incentives provided were clarified and in some respects extended.

Law 43 covers five areas with respect to benefits and privileges for foreign investors. These are: (a) taxation; (b) customs duties and import/export regulations; (c) expropriation; (d) exchange control; and (e) business and labor law. Davies (1984) stresses that the open-door policy of Egypt does not refer only to Egypt's foreign investment program, but also to the general liberalization of the economy and measures to encourage the development of the private sector.

Foreign investment is welcome in the form of joint ventures with the private and/or public sectors. All such ventures are free from public sector controls. Priority is given to those projects designed to generate exports, encourage tourism, or reduce the need to import basic commodities, as well as to projects that require advanced technical expertise or make use of patents or trademarks and therefore promote technology transfer. Investments are judged on a case-by-case basis and the General Authority for Investment and Free Zones is the "control" mechanism or investment-licensing agency (Gillespie, 1984). Full details of Law 43 are provided by Davies (1984). More than 1,600 Law 43 projects had been approved by mid-1982. The total investment involved was just under 10 billion Egyptian pounds, 15% of which was destined for the free zones.

The Free Zones

According to the 1977 amendment to Law 43, free zone projects do not require any local participation. Also, firms may be granted export processing zone (EPZ) status wherever they are located, and four commercial EPZs (Alexandria, Cairo, Port Said, and Suez) are permitted to include industrial activities. Firms granted EPZ status are entitled to customs-free import and export status of all goods including spare parts. Firms receive exemptions from Egyptian income tax and other taxes for an unlimited period. Salaries and wages of expatriate employees are exempt from Egyptian income tax. Firms may export to the Egyptian market at 50% tariff reduction if at least 40% of value (including labor) is added locally.

At the end of 1982, 361 projects had been approved with a total investment value of $2,450 million, almost all from foreign sources. Two hundred and fifty firms with a total investment value of $250 million were actually in operation. Most of the activity is concentrated in storage and communications; of the 215 firms established at the end of 1981 only 50 were in manufacturing. Of these, eleven were in spinning and weaving, ten in the chemical industry, six in the food industry and five each in metals, pharmaceuticals and petroleum (EIU, Special Report No. 190, 1985). The investors are mostly European firms with some Middle Eastern and American firms. Two percent of the investments are local and 98 percent foreign. Table 3 illustrates some firms approved and in operation.

Table 3
Free Zones: Some Firms in Operation and Approved

Name of Company	Origin	Main Products/Services
Suez Zone		
Cardboard Boxes Manufacture	Saudi Arabia	Cardboard boxes
Sapesco, Sahara Petroleum Services Co.ª	USA	Oilfield service & equipment
Cairo Zone		
Fiberglass Mediterranean Co.ª	Egypt/France	Refrigerated containers, insulated partitions, bungalows
Economic Industrial Development Company California Overseas	USA	Readymade clothers
Alexandria Zone		
Misroject Co.	Egypt/Kuwait/ W. Germany	Plastic injections
Ramses American Computer	Egypt/USA	Computer systems & software
Port Said		
Arab American Contracting Co.ª	Egypt/USA	Cement manufacture
Memphis Industrial & Trading Co.ᵇ	Netherlands	Steel production for ship building, petro-chemical tanks; pipes

ªApproved; all others in production
ᵇUnder construction

Source: Economist Intelligence Unit, Export Processing Zones in the 1980s Special Report No. 1980, London: Economist Publications Ltd., 1985.

Risks of Policy Reversals

For the multinational enterprise the problems with respect to Egypt's trade and investment policy lie in the risk of policy reversals. In addition, the managed manufacture sector, with multiple exchange rates and consequent bureaucratic delays, has been cited as a factor hindering development (EIU Special Report No. 190, 1985). Policy reversals may occur for a variety of reasons, and some may be the result of the liberalization process itself. Unless carefully and gradually implemented, liberalization often creates social and political tensions that can force a government to abandon or change policy drastically. For example, early in 1982 the Egyptian government placed a high priority on intermediate and capital goods rather than luxury and nonessential imports (*Middle East and African Economist*, 1982). This new emphasis on the productive sector rather than on the consumer sector resulted both from the decrease in available foreign exchange and President Hosni Mubarak's desire for a more equitable distribution of Egypt's financial resources.

More recently, a *MEED* Special Report on Egypt (November 1985) reported that the Economy and Trade ministry was drawing up a list of goods with a view to announcing a four-level tariff system. The aim is to control imports by price mechanisms, cutting out luxuries and protecting local industries. According to *MEED*, Cairo business people support the proposed tariff system in principle, but are doubtful about how effectively it will be administered. It is also questionable how far the import bill can be reduced without sharply cutting back on food imports, which account for more than 25 percent of the total and constitute the largest single category.

The Political Environment in Egypt

Economic policies and business opportunities in Egypt must be evaluated within the context of political stability in the country and the surrounding region. As a result of Egypt's large and increasing foreign debt, projected to be over $38 billion in 1986/87 (*South*, December 1985a), Britain's export credit agency downgraded Egypt to its worst risk category. The West German "Hermes" agency requires a priority certificate issued by the Egyptian government before agreeing to back export orders. Credit agencies in Belgium, the U.S., Japan, Italy, and Spain, according to *South* (December 1985a), are showing similar caution.

Deepening economic difficulties threaten the stability of Egypt's regime. The falling revenues from oil, workers' remittances, and other sources of hard currency are stretching the government's ability to meet basic popular needs and are aggravating social problems left unsolved during the more prosperous 1970s (*South*, December 1985b). Gillespie (1984) identifies four major interest groups that have a stake in the economic opening and privatization of the economy in Egypt. These groups or constituencies are Egypt's poor; the managements and defenders of Egypt's public companies who believe that the economic opening is not revitalizing these companies but is destroying them; organized labor, because many jobs are threatened by increasing economic efficiency (The General Confederation of Egyptian Trade Unions stated its hostility to *El-Infitah*); and political opposition in parliament and the press.

The majority of the population in Egypt has remained poor since the economic opening, while a few people have grown conspicuously rich (Jabber, 1986). There is a severe housing shortage, especially in Greater Cairo. Inflation as measured by the official Consumer Price Index dropped from 18.7% in 1980 to 9.6% in 1981 (*Middle East and African Economist*, 1982). *South* (December, 1985a) reported inflation to be 30% in 1985, however. Direct control of prices of basic commodities to protect the poor is a legacy from Nasser's time, but the cost then was small. In 1981/82 subsidies on basic commodities were budgeted to reach $2.9 billion, or 17.5% of the government's expenditure budget. Previous attempts to remove subsidies resulted in food riots in 1975 and 1977 (Gillespie, 1984). Nevertheless, the government of President Hosni Mubarak is focusing on reducing price subsidies on items such as agricultural commodities, electricity, water, gasoline, and cigarettes (*Business America*, March 17, 1986). There is a powerful lobby for the removal of subsidies, but popular sentiment remains in favor of their retention, and subsidies in general may remain for some time (The EIU Annual Supplement, 1985). This may indeed occur, despite the recent agreement with the IMF involving some restructuring of the Egyptian economy.

As the economy has worsened the appeal of a return to the Islamic faith in Egypt has grown significantly. Nevertheless, the amorphous "threat" that Islamic resurgence was deemed to pose to Egypt's secular regime has failed to materialize (*South*, April 1987). One vital reason for this has been the lack of a charismatic leader for the Islamic movement. It is therefore important for business managers to monitor any growth in the power of the Islamic militants.

Summary

Although Egypt is a developing country in the Middle East region with economic and political difficulties, it still represents opportunities for the international business firm. Egypt's large population and the government's liberal trade and investment policy suggest present and future potential. A thorough understanding of Egypt's environment will enable a foreign manager to take advantage of the industrial development opportunities in the country. The following section considers what these opportunities are and provides details on where to obtain information about the Egyptian market.

BUSINESS OPPORTUNITIES ANALYSIS

This section provides details of business opportunities in Egypt and useful sources of information for the foreign business executive. A good place to start evaluating business opportunities in a developing country like Egypt is the development plan. It is important to become familiar with the government's planning activities and resulting plans. It is also necessary to appraise the degree of commitment to planning and to the plans that actually exist. The problem for the multinational enterprise is that its own sales forecasts and strategic plans may depend to a certain degree on the government's economic plans. In Egypt, for a variety of reasons, government actions may not follow published plans. For example, ministerial changes cause instability in planning and this affects the continuity of existing projects (Mahmoud and Rice, 1984). An extreme case is the construction project to build the "Cairo International Market" (where the annual Cairo Fair is held), which took almost 12 years to complete due to the changing policies and priorities of the different ministers in office (Mahmoud, 1973).

The Development Plan

Egypt achieved 8.5% per annum growth in gross domestic product (GDP) over the period of the 1977-82 development plan, with an actual investment of 18,038.0 million Egyptian pounds. The 1982-87 development plan included projected total investment of 35,500 million Egyptian pounds and GDP annual growth of 8.6%. Table 4 shows the sectoral allocations of the development plan (1982-87). The main objectives of the plan included continuation of the "open-door" policy to encourage foreign and private investment; an increase in productivity, especially in agriculture, energy, and industry; enhancing export ability and self-reliance; and im-

Table 4
Egypt's Development Plan 1982-87; Sectoral Allocations (in millions of Egyptian pounds)

	Projected Investment	% of total Investment	Projected Growth Rate
Social Services	10104.8	28.5	8.1
Industry and Mining	8617.6	24.3	10.3
Transportation	5779.1	16.3	9.7
Agriculture/Irrigation	3739.7	10.5	3.7
Electricity	2903.9	8.2	10.7
Oil and Oil Products	1336.7	3.8	12.2
Contracts	941.7	2.7	--
Trade	461.1	1.3	6.8
Restaurants & Hotels	352.5	1.0	7.0
Suez Canal	335.0	0.9	5.4
Finance & Insurance	219.2	0.6	6.9

Total Investment: 35,500 million Egyptian pounds (of which private sector investments amount to 23.3 percent of the total).

Source: South, January 1986a

proving standards of living and achieving a fairer distribution of income (*South*, January 1986b).

Industry Trends

It is useful to consider investment and trade opportunities in Egypt according to industry categories. For example, good prospects exist in the agribusiness, health, computer and data processing, telecommunications and petroleum equipment sectors. There are also opportunities to establish firms in the service sector, such as support services, tourism, and maintenance and repair. An article in *Business America* (May 28, 1984) discusses opportunities in construction, agribusiness, and computer and data processing equipment. Sales of construction machinery are forecast to grow by 10 to 15% per annum over the next several years. Egypt imported about $1.5 billion in building materials and services in 1983. One of the most acute problems for Egypt is lack of low-cost housing. The demand for new units is about 200,000 per year, while no more than 80,000 units are constructed. There is also a large demand for road rehabilitation and network expansion, and water and sewage facilities.

Egypt is a strong market for a range of agriculture and agribusiness products. The mechanization program in Egypt is considered primarily in terms of seven basic crops which constitute the typical crop rotation and comprise 7.5% of all crops grown in the country. These are cotton, wheat, rice, sugar cane, clover (berseem), corn, and potatoes (*Business America*, January 20, 1986). Irrigation system equipment is important; the Egyptian government continues to encourage the reclamation of vast areas of desert. There is demand for equipment for use in the production of sugar cane, cotton, and rice. Poultry and egg production equipment, fisheries, and dairy industries also have good growth potential. Increased exports of fresh, off-season horticultural produce from Egypt to Middle Eastern and European markets mean increased demand for packing stations and containerized transportation. Egypt faces intense competition in the citrus export markets. Egyptian fruit often arrives in poor condition because of careless packaging. If Egypt is to take advantage of citrus market opportunities in the European Community, such deficiencies will have to be overcome (Wilson, 1984). There are opportunities for foreign firms to help Egyptian firms in this regard. Finally, with respect to agribusiness opportunities, *Business America* (May 28, 1984) points out that a continuing and careful analysis of local agrarian conditions and cultural practices is important in determining the best sales prospects. Many farmers along the Nile delta still use traditional cultivating techniques.

In 1983, Egypt imported about $90 million in business and computer equipment. This sector is relatively new in the Egyptian economy, but the market has grown quickly since the private sector was first permitted to operate in this field in 1977. Major users of computer equipment are banks and the tourist industry.

Demand for electricity has grown rapidly in Egypt in recent years, increasing from about 1,000 megawatts in 1969 to more than 4,000 megawatts in 1983 (*Business America*, January 20, 1986). The recent annual growth rate of about 15% per year was expected to continue through 1985 and then to taper off gradually to about 5% by the late 1990s. At this pace, Egypt's consumption of electric energy will exceed 20% of its total energy consumption by the year 2000. This ratio is about twice the current ratio of industrial countries, and is considerably higher than that for most developing countries. Expansion and upgrading of telecommunications is also one of the most important infrastructure needs in Egypt.

Current and projected improvements in existing hospitals and new hospitals in Cairo, Alexandria and the new cities (for example, Tenth of Ramadan City) offer opportunities in the sales of medical equipment and related items.

For consumer goods, the real opportunities for international marketers frequently lie in regional and cultural segments rather than a broad, national market opportunity. For example, the market for most consumer and durable goods is concentrated in Cairo and Alexandria, where a large demand for foreign goods exists. Market opportunities also extend to Port Said and other cities around the Suez Canal.

The environmental analysis implied that although Egypt had the potential to industrialize and had a growing population, economic difficulties have created considerable financial risk for the foreign firm. Hence firms should investigate opportunities through their various countries' aid programs. Egypt receives aid from a number of sources: Japan, France, Italy, Canada, West Germany, U.K., Spain, The World Bank, The African Development Bank, Arab Industrial Development Organizations, and especially from the U.S. Firms of all sizes can take part in aid-funded projects as contractors, consultants, and subcontractors and can thereby reduce their financial risks.

Business Information Sources

Marketing Information Systems in Egypt

Access to marketing information in Egypt can be obtained from sources such as the Department of Commerce or the Department of Trade, and from private consultants or market research firms. The following provides some detail on possible sources.

The Central Agency for Public Mobilisation and Statistics is one of the most reliable sources of information; it is a well-established organization and has been collecting information on the Egyptian economy in general for a number of years. This agency administers the population census in Egypt and regularly obtains information on different sectors such as industry, energy, trade, and more. Public sector organizations are required to provide the agency with financial reports and data about manpower and products. Private sector organizations provide this information voluntarily.

The Agency for Importing and Exporting collects information on Egyptian imports and exports pertaining to goods, prices, regulations, taxation, and customs duties. El-Ahram Information Center, run by the government newspaper El-Ahram, provides various kinds of information. At several universities in Egypt there are professors who were educated overseas and who can provide marketing research services as private consultants. Owen's World Trade Middle East and Mediterranean Business Directory (1984/85) lists banks; financial institutions; insurance firms; real estate firms; courier services; shipping and freight forwarding organizations; port; warehousing, and transportation services; advertising agencies; manufacturing and wholesale firms; and manufacturers' representatives in Egypt. The Cairo International Fair is an important annual trade event in Egypt and is a good way for foreign firms to introduce themselves to or expand in the Egyptian market (*Business America*, September 16, 1985). Trade missions with the U.S. Department of Commerce for industries such as food processing and packaging equipment, construction and building materials, and water resources are an excellent way for a company to meet potential customers and business partners, both in the Egyptian government and the private sector. According to *Business America* (September 16, 1985), some firms have made immediate sales on these missions. The American Chamber of Commerce in Egypt, established in 1983, holds monthly luncheons and as of 1984 had a membership of nearly 300 companies. Table 5 lists some useful addresses for the American businessman. Similar organizations exist in Canada, Western Europe, and Japan for international executives based in those areas.

National Information for Egyptian Development

From the standpoint of the international executive, information sources in Egypt are improving considerably. Egypt has realized that it can no longer afford to have the country's most vital resources and professional and managerial manpower function below their potential because of a lack of awareness and poor use of information. The Egyptian Academy of Scientific Research and Technology (ASRT) therefore has embarked on an ambitious program to establish a nationwide system for scientific and technical information services intended to support Egypt's socioeconomic development.

The program is a bilateral agreement between ASRT and the U.S. Agency for International Development, USAID (The Academy of Scientific Research and Technology, undated) and has been called National Information for Egyptian Development (NIED). Development of the program has taken five years and implementation was scheduled to start by 1986 in five sectors (agriculture, energy, industry and natural resources, medicine and health care, and science and engineering) that constitute priority areas for Egypt's socioeconomic development. Figure 1 describes the NIED

Table 5
Useful Information for the American Businessman

Free Zones

Under Sec. of State for Free Zones
General Authority for Investment
  and Free Zones of Egypt
8 Adly Street
P.O. Box 1007
Cairo, Egypt

**Projects Competed for by
International Tender**

U.S. Embassy
Commercial Section
5 Sharia Latin America
Cairo, Egypt

U.S. Department of Commerce
Office of Major Projects
Room 2007
Washington, D. C. 20230
(202) 377-5225

Trade Missions

U.S. Department of Commerce
Export Development Office
Washington, D. C. 20230
(202) 377-1209

Trade and Investment

U.S. Department of Commerce
Senior Egypt Specialist
Room 2039
Washington, D.C. 20230
(202) 377-4652

U.S. Department of Commerce
Commercial Office
Alexandria, Egypt

Egyptian-American
Chamber of Commerce
New York, NY
(212) 466-1866

Insurance and Financing

Export-Import Bank of the U.S.
811 Vermont Avenue, N.W.
Washington, D. C. 20571
(202) 566-8990

Agency for International Development
Washington, D. C. 20523
(202) 632-1850

The World Bank
1818 H Street, N.W.
Washington, D. C. 20433

Overseas Private Investment Corp.
1129 20th Street N.W.
Washington, D. C. 20527
(202) 632-1804

network through which users will have access to information via specialized nodes in the national information system. The service nodes will use minicomputers or supermicros to handle their basic informational functions. Through suitable telecommunications the nodes will be interconnected to form an open-ended, undirected

FIGURE 1. National Information Network

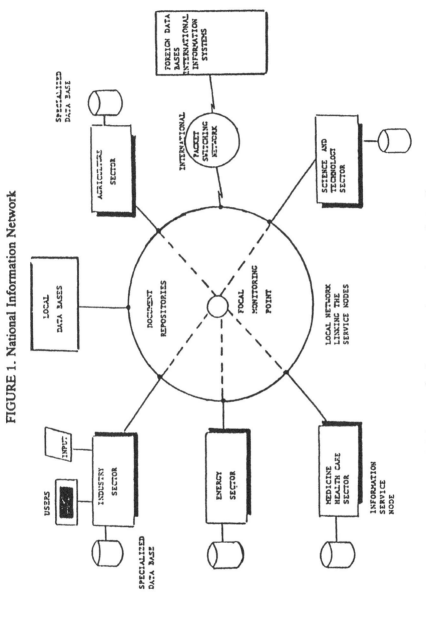

Source: National Information for Egyptian Development Project (undated),
Cairo: The Academy of Scientific Research and Technology

215

network allowing eligible users to communicate directly with any information service and document repository. Through the system-distributed ring network, the authorized user will be able to access any of its service nodes and repositories to obtain answers for queries or copies of original documents. Through public packet-switching networks such as TELENET or TYMNET, users will have access to databases abroad. Users will also have access to document repositories. The system provides users with a variety of numeric and textual data bases representing a diversified range of information sources. These include books and monographs, trade magazines, product catalogs, patents, and bibliographic data bases. The system gives users bilingual Arabic/English capability through bilingual computer terminals and modification of database management software to store and retrieve bilingual information. The system is intended to serve scientists, engineers, managers, and applied researchers. Among many other trained professionals, the system includes full-time marketing specialists.

The Banking Sector in Egypt

Banks and other financial service institutions are often useful sources of information for international businessmen. There are approximately 100 banks now in Egypt either as joint venture banks or branches of representative offices (Owen's World Trade, 1984/85). They include British, American, European, and Asian banks. Four main Eygptian banks — National Bank of Egypt, Banque Misr, Banque du Caire and Bank of Alexandria — account for about 80% of commercial banking activity and are government-owned.

The two most important classes of banks to reemerge in Egypt after the open-door policy was initiated in 1974 were the joint ventures and the private local banks. Public Law 43 of 1974 amended by Law 32 of 1977 extended the benefits to Egyptian citizens investing from abroad. Several very competitive and successful new banks have taken advantage of these changes and have been established in Cairo. Joint venture banks include a minimum of 51% local control. These banks are free to pursue all types of local business as well as financing foreign trade. Table 6 lists some major joint venture banks.

Table 6
Major Joint Venture Banks, 1984

	Principal Egyptian Partner	Principal Foreign Partner
Alexandria Kuwait International Bank	Bank of Alexandria	Kuwaiti interests
Banque du Caire Barclays International	Banque du Caire	Barclays Bank
Banque du Caire et de Paris	Banque du Caire	Banque Nationale de Paris
Egyptian American Bank	Bank of Alexandria	American Express
Misr International Bank	Banque Misr	First Chicago

Source: Arab Banking Systems, ABC, 1984, quoted in Economist Intelligence Unit, Quarterly Economic Review of Egypt, Annual Supplement, 1985, London: The Economist Publications Ltd.

Among the most significant of the "local Law 43 banks" are the Nile Bank, Mohandes Bank, Delta International Bank, Pyramids Bank, Al Watany Bank of Egypt, and Suez Canal Bank. It is also important to note the recent growth in the Islamic banking sector in Egypt. For example, Faisal Islamic Bank of Egypt (FIBE) was established in 1977 and engages in financial and investment activities in foreign trade, manufacturing and industrialization, housing and contracting, hospitals and pharmaceuticals, animal and farm production, food processing and packing, and land reclamation (*Arabia*, November 1985).

Two new institutions in Egypt's financial sector are the Egyptian Investment Finance Corporation (EIFC) and the Export Development Bank of Egypt (EDBE). EIFC is a merchant bank that will offer a wide range of services geared mainly toward boosting Egypt's weak securities market. Its shareholders are eight local concerns, two South Korean institutions, and the World Bank's International Finance Corporation. EDBE's shareholders are the National Investment Bank and the four state-owned banks. EDBE, which has been pledged $125 million from the World Bank, will provide a range of services for exporters, including supplier and buyer credits and export credit guarantees (*MEED* Special Report, November 1985).

The final section considers business strategy analysis for the Eyptian market.

BUSINESS STRATEGY ANALYSIS

Given an understanding of the Egyptian business environment and knowledge of market opportunities and information sources, the next step for the international firm is formulating a business strategy. The strategy includes a mode of entry, operational control, planning, and organization. These issues are discussed below, placing the emphasis on joint ventures and using the example of General Motors Corporation.

Entering the Egyptian Market

Root (1982) distinguishes between three foreign market entry modes: export entry modes; contractual entry modes (including licensing, franchising, service contracts, management contracts, turnkey contracts, and contract manufacture); and investment entry modes (sole ventures or various kinds of joint ventures). The selection of an entry mode will require the multinational firm to make decisions on the following issues:

1. The target product and the target market in Egypt.
2. The firm's objectives and goals in Egypt.
3. The marketing plan to penetrate the target market in Egypt.
4. The control system to monitor performance in Egypt.

Specific factors to be considered are market factors (such as sales potential, competition, and distribution channels); production factors (such as the quality, quantity, availability, and cost of inputs for local production); and political, economic, and sociocultural factors. Internal company factors affecting entry decisions in the Egyptian market include product factors (such as pre- and postpurchase services, technological intensity, and the need for adaptation), and resource/commitment factors (such as resources in management, capital technology, and functional skills, and the willingness to commit them to foreign markets).

In this section two common modes of entry to the Egyptian markets are discussed: contract manufacturing and joint ventures. To illustrate firms using these methods of entry, a listing of some recent business deals in Egypt is included in Table 7.

Contract Manufacturing

As mentioned earlier, state organizations play a major role in the Egyptian economy. Most large industrial firms, transport companies, and even some retail outlets, as well as many foreign trade and wholesale firms, are in the public sector. Hence the major projects are generally in the public sector. The government usually requests separate contracts for the consulting, design and engineering, and construction phases of its projects. Foreign firms are invited to bid for consulting services and for the detailed engineering on projects which require technical capabilities beyond those available from Egyptian companies. Civil engineering and construction is often done by local contractors, unless special requirements dictate the use of foreign expertise (U.S. Department of Commerce, 1984).

International calls for tender may be announced in local newspapers and disseminated by Egyptian embassies overseas. In some cases, the calls for tender are issued to a limited number of companies who have prequalified by making their capabilities known to the Egyptian organization undertaking the project. Bids are reviewed by a technical committee which generally chooses the two or three lowest price proposals meeting the specifications and begins negotiating with these firms. During negotiations the Egyptians may show the bids to the competing firms in an attempt to get better terms and prices. Even the firm submitting the lowest bid can expect demands for significant concessions before the contract is signed (U.S. Department of Commerce, 1984).

The Egyptian government normally requires foreign contractors

Table 7
Examples of Recent Business Deals in Egypt

Firm(s) Involved	Type of Contract	Approximate Value of Contract	Financing Arrangements
Consortium of Japanese firms, led by NEC	Contract to supply electrical control system to monitor power supplies between Cairo and Aswan	$34.2 million	Japan's Overseas Economic Cooperation Fund ($27.5 million
Alfa-Laval (Sweden)	Contract to build a dairy complex south of Alexandria	$26 million	NA[1]
Fives Cail Babcock (France)	Negotiation of contract with Helwan Portland Cement Co. to build a white cement works in Minya	$100 million	European Investment Bank (Approx. 25% of project cost)
European Consortium led by W. Ger. SMS Schloemann Siemag	Wire rod mill contract at the Dikheila Steel Complex	$29 million	NA
Krebs et Compagnie & Chemiean Lagen (French-E. German)	Equipment contract for Misr Chemical Industr. Co's sodium carbonate factory at Alexandria	$50 million	NA

Table 7 cont'd.

Company	Description	Value	French protocols signed 1984 ($184m) 1985 ($66m)
Group of French companies led by Alsthom	Contract to supply rolling stock for Cairo's metro; 96 power coaches to be built in France (delivery 1987); 48 trailer coaches to be made locally by the General Egyptian Co. for Railway Equip. (Semaf), w/ assistance from French Consortium	$102 million	French protocols signed 1984 ($184m) 1985 ($66m)
Westinghouse Elec. Corp. (US) & Benha Electronic Indust. Co.	Supply of 34 TPS-63 radars for the Air Defense Command	$190 million	NA
Pavan (Italy)	Turnkey construction of 3 pasta factories with total daily cap. of 45 tonnes	$10 million	NA
Daimler-Benz (West Germany)	Supply of 600 mini bus	$12.4 million	NA
Babcock Contractors,w/British Mining Consultants (UK)	Overseeing reopening of Maghara Coal Mine in Sinai, including the design, procurement & management of the supply of equipment, plus training of local staff	$55.7 million	NA

Table 7 (cont'd.)

Hudsons Freight Services (UK)	Arranging worldwide supplies & shipments for Petrogaz	$1.7 million	NA
Irish Livestock & Meat Board	3-yr protocol for the annual supply of 30,000-50,000 tonnes of beef, plus live cattle	$102 million/year	NA
NFK Kabel (Netherlands)	Supply of 69 kilometers of 66-kV oil-filled cable, plus supervision of installation & staff training	$5.3 million	NA
Inland general Motors (US) and Husam Abou el-futeh Establishment (Egypt)	Building a factory to make car seat covers, as part of a scheme to set up an integrated local car industry.	$7 million	NA

'NA. Information not available.

Sources: EIU Quarterly Economic Review of Egypt, No. 3, 1985; MEED Special Report Egypt, Vol 29. No. 46, November, 1985; MEED Vol. 30, No. 2, 11-17 January, 1986, MEED Vol. 30, No. 3, 18-24 January, 1986.

to put up both bid and performance bonds and stipulates fixed price bids for contracts of two years duration or less. Although there are no strict language requirements, English is preferred to all languages except Arabic.

Joint Ventures

Kirpalani (1985) distinguishes between three different joint venture strategies: the spider's web, go-together split, and successive integration. A spider's web strategy is when a firm has joint ventures with many other firms. This means that the firm obtains economies of scale but avoids the dangers of excessive dependence on any individual partner. A more dynamic joint venture strategy which is common in Egypt for large projects is the go-together split. This refers to a strategy where two or more firms cooperate over a certain period of time and then separate. An example is Interinfra-Arabco. a consortium of 17 French firms led by SGE-TPI and two local concerns headed by Arab Contractors (Osman Ahmed Osman and Company). In 1981 this consortium was awarded the contract for the tunnels and stations for the Cairo metro project. The third kind of joint venture strategy is the successive integration strategy which begins with weak interfirm linkages and then develops toward more interdependence, perhaps resulting in a takeover or merger. The following example of a planned joint venture in Egypt may include elements of the successive integration strategy in the relationships between the General Misr Car Company and the auto-parts makers.

Example: General Motors in Egypt.* In early 1986 the Egyptian government accepted a General Motors Corporation proposal to assemble cars in Egypt and to bring 22 auto-part plants to the country. General Motors won the bid over the chief rival, Fiat S.P.A of Italy, which is losing its place as the major car assembler in Egypt. Nissan Motor Co. of Japan and Peugeot S.A. of France also made offers.

---

*The sources for this section are: *Wall Street Journal*, "General Motors to Assemble Cars in Egypt," March 6, 1986; Economist Intelligence Unit, *Quarterly Economic Review of Egypt, No. 4*, London: The Economist Publications Ltd., 1985; *MEED*, 7 February 1987.

The proposal involves the reorganization and expansion of the Egyptian passenger car industry in an assembly operation with El-Nasr Automotive Manufacturing Company, an Egyptian public sector company. The new joint venture company would be called General Misr Car Company. Its target would be to achieve 50 to 80% local content after five years. The 22 auto-parts makers who plan to locate in Egypt to supply both the Egyptian plant and overseas markets include TRW Inc., to make steering components; Allied Signal Inc., brake fluids and friction materials; Roth-Technic (West Germany), exhaust systems; Awab (Sweden), clamps; Valeo (France), radiators; and Di Avia (Italy), air conditioners.

A joint venture can be analyzed in terms of the benefits to each party. For GM, the 22 car-parts plants would provide a source of inexpensive parts for GM's European operations. As part of the plan, GM is promising to buy approximately 60% of the parts produced in Egypt for shipment to Europe. These parts are expected to be attractively priced because of Egypt's low wages. GM, like all other auto makers, is looking for alternate, cheaper sources of auto parts throughout the world. Cheaper Egyptian parts could help European operations reduce some costs. There is no plan to export cars from Egypt. GM would take advantage of Egypt's large demand for cars: local production up to now has been less than half of the estimated demand of 50,000 to 60,000 cars a year.

For Egypt, the GM transaction is needed to boost the country's weak economy. The venture would not immediately earn a hard-currency profit for Egypt, but it would be expected immediately to reduce the need for car imports. It would also stem losses by the state-owned car company, which were estimated at $45 million in 1985. Furthermore, Egypt would benefit from at least 5,000 new jobs, technology transfer, and enhanced credibility among investors. At the time of writing, however, negotiations for the joint venture have not yet been concluded. Reasons for the delay include a reorganization at GM and the legal and technical formalities of Egypt's complex investment code.

GM is also involved in a truck operation in Egypt. General Motors Egypt is owned by GM (31%), Isuzu (20%), and various Egyptian, Saudi, and Kuwaiti interests. The company assembles trucks at a plant in 6 October City, with a target output of 18,000 trucks per year and 40% local content. To extend its operations in Egypt, GM is also examining the bus market.

Joint ventures in Egypt have been encouraged by the Law 43 open-door policy for investors which provides considerable tax and other incentives. Among the American firms that have set up joint ventures with Egyptians under Law 43 are Colgate-Palmolive, Xerox, Borg-Warner, Pfizer, Squibb and Union Carbide, American Standard, Proctor and Gamble, and R.P. Sherer.

Conflict and Control Issues for Foreign Firms in Egypt

The nature of the Egyptian environment for business explained in the first section of this chapter implies that there will be areas of conflict and issues of control for the foreign firm.

Political issues in Egypt and the surrounding region are likely to remain a major concern. The February 1986 riots are clearly symptomatic of a deepening crisis in Egyptian society (*MEED*, March 8, 1986). The crisis includes bureaucracy, price subsidies, industrial inefficiency, inflation, external debt, the poor, contempt for Egypt in the Arab world because of Sadat's treaty with Israel, and the growing dependence on the U.S. Egypt's foremost commentator, Mohamed Hassanein Haikal, recently wrote, "Perhaps I may suggest that we are on the brink of a dangerous situation because our problems – in particular inflation, reflected in the galloping rise of prices – have started to afflict the middle class, which is still the backbone of Egyptian society. . . . Egypt is getting by – but for how long?" (quoted in *MEED*, March 8, 1986). International business diplomacy, in the light of Egypt's sensitive political situation, is important. Czinkota (1985) explains that U.S. businesses, for example, have four alternatives to consider. These are:

1. to live with the concerns and try to do business as usual;
2. to attempt to alter the concerns;
3. to try to alter the foreign environment that causes the concerns; or
4. to try to alter the home country or domestic environment that causes the concerns.

Foreign business must also cope with some more immediate issues of control, such as in the areas of distribution and pricing.

The organization of the retail trade in Egypt, as in other Middle Eastern nations, may cause marketing control problems. Egypt's retail trade is dominated by a large number of small privately owned shops and vendors (Kaynak, 1981). Customer service at the retail level is poor (Saddik, 1973) and pre- and after-sales service are provided at a level far below that given in developed countries. The wholesale and distribution operations tend to be carried out by vertically integrated merchants or public sector trading companies. The generally small size of firms and limited market opportunities (because of low levels of consumer expenditure, for example) often lead to local competition and long channels of distribution. The latter effect gives the distributor a predominant role (Hibbert, 1979). Regardless of the method of entry into the Egyptian market (exporting or sales subsidiary, for example) and despite possible reduction of central marketing control, it is advisable to have an Egyptian partner. Multinational firms which sell directly in other overseas markets find local partners indispensable in the Middle East (Dunn, 1979). Indeed, in Egypt, the law generally requires that a foreign firm doing business have an Egyptian agent. This requirement does not apply in the case of transactions or projects involving U.S. Agency for International Development (AID) financing. Both private and public firms act as agents. However, the appropriate public sector firm may represent several companies with conflicting interests. In this case, a private firm may be more aggressive in looking after the foreign firm's interests. A foreign firm may establish a branch office in Egypt but most prefer to form a joint venture with an Egyptian company. The loss of control is compensated for by the local firm's knowledge of the market and ability to deal with problems concerning quotations, import regulations, and collections, for example.

Price controls are implemented by the Egyptian government on most goods, limiting a foreign firm's freedom to control prices. For example, consumers purchasing more nonsubsidized and especially imported goods face higher rates of inflation; luxury commodities in particular tend to attract indirect taxes, sometimes referred to in Egypt as "price differences" (Ikram, 1980). The government, however, has been decontrolling the prices of some products by removing subsidies in order to help alleviate the burden on the budget and to encourage more efficient resource allocation.

Strategy, Planning, and Organization for Foreign Firms

For the international firm, Egypt can be viewed strategically as a point of entry to other Middle Eastern nations and the countries of North Africa, the Eastern Mediterranean, and Africa. In the General Motors example, it was seen how firms associated with the planned Egyptian joint venture could provide a point of low-cost supply to Europe for GM. Egypt's central location is enhanced by its excellent transportation links by ship via the Mediterranean and the Suez Canal and by air. Given its population's educational skill levels, Egypt has a large potential to industrialize (Kirpalani, 1985). The opportunities for the sale of technology, skills, and consulting in the building and improvement of Egypt's industrial infrastructure provide market diversification options for many foreign firms. As discussed above, one way that firms can take advantage of these opportunities is by using aid financing options for development projects such as those offered by U.S. AID, the Canadian International Development Agency (CIDA), and the World Bank.

The main organization consideration for the foreign firm's Egyptian operations is the degree of centralization or decentralization. Whether the firm's management is ethnocentric (home-oriented), polycentric (host-nation-oriented), or geocentric (internationally oriented), it must be remembered that the correct type of organizational structure is vital for the successful implementation of the chosen strategy. In addition to managerial attitudes, Kirpalani (1985) notes some of the internal strategy-related factors that affect how a firm organizes. These are the firm's product line, the number of foreign markets in which it operates, the number of businesses in which it is engaged, and technological change in the firm's industry. Organizational options are also influenced by external factors including governments, regulatory agencies, and the various publics of a firm. In this context, an important consideration in Egypt is Law 43 and the encouragement of joint venture operations.

CONCLUSION:
FUTURE BUSINESS SCENARIOS IN EGYPT

This chapter has evaluated the Egyptian environment from an international business perspective, described business opportunities in Egypt, and analyzed some strategic alternatives. The implication for the international executive is that he or she should develop sensitivity to local conditions and be creative in coping with financial and economic risks. The executive's success will be measured by his or her abilities to appreciate environmental similarities and differences and to formulate strategies accordingly. It is also important to have an understanding of possible future developments. For example, the following elements are likely to characterize the future business environment (the next 10-20 years) in Egypt:

1. The continued growth of the private sector with more efficient and productive operations in industry, agriculture, retailing, and other services.
2. Egypt's large and growing population means that the absorptive capacity of Egypt is much greater than that of its neighbors and continued market growth will mean continuing investment possibilities especially in agriculture, land use, transportation, housing construction, electricity, telecommunications, computerization, health care, and other services. Continued population growth, improved literacy, and increased travel and communications will result in more sophisticated consumers and broader demand for consumer and durable goods, especially foreign goods.
3. The continuing spread and growth of the Islamic faith will heighten the importance to foreign businessmen of understanding what this means in socioeconomic terms: culture and consumer behavior, and Islamic banking and finance. Leadership of the Islamic movement will determine its strength and the power of its implications for business.
4. Intensified competition as the number of foreign investors in Egypt increases with further opening of the economy. Competition from the Far East and particularly from newly industrializing countries such as Brazil and Korea will grow.

5. The industrial development of Egypt will mean continued use of technology to rationalize industry and develop the land.

REFERENCES

Al-Dabbagh, A.T. (1985). The Influence of Oil Revenues on U.S.-Arab Trade: Possible Changes in Arab Imports. In M. Czinkota and S. Marciel (Eds.), *U.S.-Arab Economic Relations: A Time of Transition* (pp. 269-297). New York: Praeger Publishers.

An Introduction to Contract Procedures in the Near East and North Africa. (1984, November). Washington D.C.: U.S. Department of Commerce.

Arab Youth (published in Arabic) (1987, March). Cairo: Egypt.

Arabia: The Islamic World Review (1985, November). Faisal Islamic Bank of Egypt: An Assessment, pp. 63-64.

Arbose, J. (1982, May) Wise Men From the East Bearing Gifts, *International Management*, pp. 67-68.

Ayubi, N.M. (1982). Bureaucratic Inflation and Administrative Inefficiency: The Deadlock in Egyptian Administration, *Middle Eastern Studies*, 18 (3), 186-229.

Badawy, M.K. (1980). Styles of Mideastern Managers, *California Management Review*, (Spring), 22 (2), 51-58.

Business America (1982, November 15) Egypt: Adequate Market Research and Financial Support Should Result in Successful Ventures for U.S. Firms, pp. 28-30.

Business America (1984, May 28) Egypt: Economy Is Still Robust As Government Prepares to Deal With Problems That Threaten Future Growth, pp. 30-32.

Business America (1984, August 20) Egypt: U.S. Traders and Investors Will Find a Strong Market, p. 50.

Business America (1985, September 16) Egypt: U.S. Exports Maintain High Levels During 1985, pp. 31-32.

Business America (1986, January 20) Worldwide Business Opportunities, p. 21.

Business America (1986, March 17) Egypt: U.S. Exports of Selected Commodities Continue Strong, pp. 33-34.

Business International (1980, July) *Egypt Opportunities for Suppliers and Investors.*

Czinkota, M.R. (1985). Current Problems and Future Prospects of U.S.-Arab Economic Relations. In M. Czinkota and S. Marciel (Eds.), *U.S.-Arab Economic Relations: A Time of Transition* (pp. 304-8). New York: Praeger Publishers.

Davies, M.H. (1984). *Business Law in Egypt*, Deventer, Netherlands: Kluwer Law and Tax Publishers.

Dunn, D.T. Jr. (1979). Agents and Distributors in the Middle East, *Business Horizons*, (October), 22 (5), 69-78.

Economist Intelligence Unit (1985) *Export Processing Zones in the 1980s* Special Report No. 190, London: The Economist Publications Ltd.

Economist Intelligence Unit (1985) *Quarterly Economic Review of Egypt No. 3*, London: The Economist Publications Ltd., pp. 21-22.

Economist Intelligence Unit (1985) *Quarterly Review of Egypt No. 4*, London: The Economist Publications Ltd.

Economist Intelligence Unit (1986) *Quarterly Review of Egypt No. 4*, London: The Economist Publications Ltd.

Economist Intelligence Unit (1985) *Quarterly Economic Review of Egypt Annual Supplement*, London: The Economist Publications Ltd.

Egypt's top priority is beefing up private sector, Prime Minister says (1985, October 9). *Wall Street Journal*.

Eilts, H.F. (1982). Islamic Resurgence and American Business in the Middle East. In M. Winchester (Ed.), *The International Essays for Business Decision Makers* (pp. 241-252). Dallas: The Center for International Business.

El-Ansary, A.T. (1986). Managerial Gap Analysis: A Frame of Reference for Improving International Business Relations with the Middle East. In E. Kaynak (Ed.), *International Business in the Middle East* (pp. 43-56). New York: Walter de Gruyter.

General Motors to assemble cars in Egypt (1986, March 6). *Wall Street Journal*.

Ghattas, E. (1984). The Arab Investment Guarantee System: A Model for Regional Cooperation, *Studies in Comparative International Development*, (Fall), XIX (3), 60-92.

Gillespie, K. (1984). *The Tripartite Relationship Government, Foreign Investors, and Local Investors During Egypt's Economic Opening*, New York: Praeger Publishers.

Hibbert, E.P. (1979, January) The cultural dimension of marketing and the impact of industrialization, *European Research*, pp. 41-47.

Ikram, H. (1980). *Egypt Economic Management in a Period of Transition*, Baltimore: The Johns Hopkins University Press.

Insight (1987, January 12) Egypt's Economy: The New Sphinx, pp. 8-14.

Jabber, P. (1986). Egypt's Crisis, America's Dilemma, *Foreign Affairs*, (Spring-Summer), 64 (4-5), 961-980.

Kaikati, J.G. (1979). Marketing Prices in Iran vis-à-vis Saudi Arabia, *Management International Review*, 19 (4), 31-37.

Kaynak, E. (1981). Food Distribution Systems: Evolution in Latin America and the Middle East, *Food Policy*, (May), 78-90.

Kirpalani, V.H. (1985). *International Marketing*, New York: Random House, Inc.

Kurian, G.T. (1982). *Encyclopedia of the Third World*, Revised Edition, Facts on File, Inc.

Leff, N.H. and Farley, J.V. (1980). Advertising Expenditures in the Developing World, *Journal of International Business Studies*, (Fall), XI (2), 64-79.

Luqmani, M., Quraeshi, Z.A., and Delene, L. (1980). Marketing in Islamic Countries: A Viewpoint, *MSU Business Topics* (Summer), 28, 17-25.

Mahmoud, E. (1973). The Development of Labour Productivity in the Construction Industry, unpublished MBA thesis, Ains Shams University, Cairo.

Mahmoud, E. and Rice, G. (1984). Marketing Problems in LDCs: The Case of Egypt. In G.S. Kindra (Ed.), *Marketing in Developing Countries*. London: Croon Helm.

Makdisi, S.A. (1985). Observations on Investment Behavior of the Arab Countries. In M. Czinkota and S. Marciel (Eds.), *U.S.-Arab Economic Relations A Time of Transition* (pp. 183-190). New York: Praeger Publishers.

Marketing in Egypt, Overseas Business Reports 21-31. (1981, December). Washington D.C.: Department of Commerce.

Michell, P. (1979). Infrastructures and International Marketing Effectiveness, *Columbia Journal of World Business*, (Spring), 91-101.

Middle East and African Economist. (1982). 36 (7/8), 43.

Middle East Economic Digest. (1985). Egypt Special Report, (November), 29 (46).

Middle East Economic Digest. (1985). Egypt, (November 9), 29 (45), 16-17.

Middle East Economic Digest. (1986). Egypt, (January 11-17), 30 (2), 4.

Middle East Economic Digest. (1986). Egypt, (January 18-24), 30 (3), 3-4.

Middle East Economic Digest. (1986). Egypt: Mubarak's debt to the army, (March 8-14), 30 (10), 4-5.

Middle East Economic Digest. (1987). (February 7), 8-9.

Middle East Economic Digest. (1987). (February 14), 11.

National Information for Egyptian Development Project (undated). Cairo: Academy of Scientific Research and Technology.

Owen's World Trade Middle East and Mediterranean Business Directory, (1984-85), 32nd edition.

Pezeshkpur, C. (1978). Challenges to Management in the Arab World, *Business Horizons*, (August), 47-55.

Redding, S.G. (1982). Cultural Effects on the Marketing Process in Southeast Asia, *Journal of the Market Research Society*, (April), 24 (2), 98-115.

Rioting by Egyptian police underscores fragility of President Mubarak's position (1986, February 27). *Wall Street Journal*.

Root, F.R. (1982). Entering International Markets. In I. Walter and T. Murray (Eds.), *Handbook of International Business*. New York: John Wiley and Sons.

Saddik, S.M. (1973). An Analysis of the Status of Marketing in Egypt, *European Journal of Marketing*, (Summer), 77-81.

South. (1985a, December) Mubarak on shifting sands, p. 33.

South. (1985b, December) The day of reckoning, pp. 33-34.

South. (1986a, January) Mubarak takes extreme remedies, p. 13.

South. (1986b, January) Development Plans, p. 72.

South. (1986, March) Signed and Sealed Countertrade, p. 82.

South. (1987, April) Between a rock and a hard place, pp. 35-36.

Statistical Digest. (1981). Paris: UNESCO.

The Economist. (1986, August 2) Egypt a people wandering into the wilderness, pp. 31-35.

The Economist. (1988, January 23) Egypt a beggar with influence, p. 34.

Waterburg, J. (1983). *The Egypt of Nasser and Sadat*, New Jersey: Princeton University Press.

Wilson, R. (1983). Egypt's Export Diversification: Benefits and Constraints, *The Developing Economies*, (March), XXII (1), pp. 86-101.

World Development Report 1984 (1984). Washington D.C.: The World Bank.

Chapter 7

West Germany

Peter Zurn

HISTORICAL AND GEOGRAPHICAL BACKGROUND

The German people look back on a long cultural past as a "germanic" nation from the days of Vercingetorix as opposed to the memory of Rome and the Romans. In the days of Charlemagne in Franconia in the 8th century — long before the aspirations of another great Charles (de Gaulle of France) — the German peoples were first united in the so-called "Holy Roman Empire of the German Nation," the memory of which is still kept alive in the stonework of the coronation cathedral in Aachen (Aix-la-Chapelle). This empire lasted with varying boundaries for nearly 1,000 years until the days of Napoleon; portraits of the succession of emperors line the walls of the "Emperors Hall" in the Frankfurt City Hall.

However Germany as a state, comprising one territory, one language, one government, in spite of the long historical and cultural tradition, is a very young and short-time national experience dating from the days of Bismarck, first and former iron chancellor and his victory over France in 1870/71, leading to the German "Reich" which was proclaimed in the palace of Versailles. Here Frederick the Great of Prussia had admired the French spirit and language in his discussions with Voltaire, and Louis XIV had long been a figure of admiration for all the European aristocracy, especially in Germany where his castle was often imitated in style and luxury, as for instance in Ludwigsburg near Stuttgart.

All this royal and aristocratic German past must be kept in mind when looking at the now 40-year-old Republic of Bonn, founded on the failures of monarchy, the first Weimar Republic, and Hitler's despotism. It is good to recall the "golden twenties" in Germany with the nightmares of World War I over and all Europe blooming, until the unfortunate economic crisis in Wall Street in the dark days of 1929.

Situated in the middle of Europe as a land with neither natural frontiers nor a classic history as a state, compared for instance to France or the United Kingdom, Germany has had to struggle for its identity as a nation throughout the centuries. As a part of this process, Germany lost two world wars in the course of one generation. It was the end of World War II in 1945 which marked the historic moment in its development at the end of the National Socialist Policy nightmare which had drawn Europe and its population into disaster. Unfortunately, this moment also divided the German territories along the Iron Curtain into East and West.

When speaking of Germany today and in the framework of this book, we mean Western Germany, or the Federal Republic of Germany, founded with the constitution of the "Basic Law" (Grundgesetz) in 1949. With its preamble, this constitution is still seen as provisional, awaiting the reunification of Germany as a whole and its approval of a constitution in free elections. But as Napoleon states: "C'est le provisoire qui dure," and today we have two states within the boundaries of one country. Although the Eastern "German Democratic Republic" with its population of 17 million could be of interest in a European context, especially in regard to the inter-German trade which represents half of East Germany's non-communist transactions, the following pages refer solely to West Germany and West Berlin.

Although West Berlin with its 2 million inhabitants – still under allied control – is not correctly speaking a territory of the Federal Republic, most of the Federal laws have been adopted by a vote of the city council, subject to the approval of the occupying powers, France, United Kingdom, and United States of America. Free access to Berlin along the road, rail, and air corridors is guaranteed, but much to the chagrin of the German airline Lufthansa, only British Airways, Pan Am, and Air France are permitted to fly the air corridors regularly.

The city of Berlin, the radiant capital of Germany in the early years of the century, has become a symbolic island in the sea of communism, divided in two by the Wall, built in August 1961 to hinder immigration from East Berlin. With Herbert von Karajan's Philharmonic Orchestra, the German Opera and other theaters, historic and contemporary museums, leading high schools and universities, and important designers in the fashion business, the city has partly kept its leading position in the world of fine arts and culture.

On the other hand, Schering, Siemens, BMW, Axel Springer, and other great names of German industry remain and invest in West Berlin, supported by the federal government and the will for freedom of the Western world, expressed in J.F. Kennedy's famous confession: "Ich bin ein Berliner" (I am a Berliner). This statement marked the end of his speech before hundreds of thousands gathered in the free part of Berlin whence he came after his meeting with Khrushchev in Vienna — and only months before his assassination in Dallas in November 1963.

The Federal Republic of Germany consists of 10 states ("Länder"). From north to south with their capitals they are:

— Schleswig-Holstein (Kiel)
— Hamburg
— Bremen
— Lower Saxony (Hannover)
— North Rhine Westphalia (Düsseldorf, with the Ruhr industrial area, Cologne, and Bonn, the federal capital)
— Hesse (Wiesbaden, and the Rhine/Main area around Frankfurt)
— Rhineland Palatinate (Mainz, and the conurbation of Mannheim/Ludwigshafen and famous Rhine valley vineyards)
— Saarland (Saarbrücken, center of coal mining and steel foundries)
— Baden Württemberg (Stuttgart, home town of Robert Bosch and Daimler)
— Bavaria (Munich, German high-tech center of today and home country of the famous German beers)

Germany covers an area of approximately 248,600 square kilometers with a population of around 62 million, including 4.5 million foreign nationals.

Germany is one of the most important trading nations of the world. Its export trade centers on capital goods (all forms of industrial machinery) and consumer durables, motor vehicles in particular. "Made in Germany" symbolizes high quality and reliability rather than the land of origin.

The major industrial areas of the country correspond to the centers of population listed above. As a basis for its industry, Germany has large resources of anthracite and brown coal, iron, and some natural gas. Large areas are still devoted to agriculture and forestry; as a general rule the flat lands of the north are intensively cultivated whereas the hills and mountains of the south are forested.

As a consequence of the decentralized urbanization, considerable industrial and commercial development has taken place in many areas, differing locally with types of investment and economy. This is encouraged by an extensive network of road, rail, and waterways between the major cities and neighboring countries. The most important international airport — even in European terms — is Frankfurt Rhein/Main, followed by Hamburg, Munich, and Düsseldorf with almost hourly Lufthansa connections. Seaports are located on the North Sea coast in Hamburg, Bremen, and Bremerhaven, and Rotterdam in Holland is becoming more and more important for the Ruhr industrial area, where Duisburg-Ruhrort is the biggest European port for river traffic.

Germany's network of communications covering the three branches of goods traffic, passenger transportation, and transmission of news and information is one of the densest in Europe and permits direct-dialing to all major centers of the civilized world. The long distance road network of the federal "Autobahn" is one of the most powerful inner European links which still has the advantage of being toll-free and has few speed limitations. Consequently motor car traffic has become the most important means of transport, and 90% of all households own a car. Proportionally, rail traffic continues to diminish with the exception of special goods and express trains such as the "intercity" network.

The European dimension is often decisive for this rather small country right in the heart of the old continent where Spain and Portugal have recently joined the European Economic Community. The main objective of the Treaty of Rome, the founding document of the EEC, is to secure and enforce free trade and competition and to harmonize certain national laws which is becoming increasingly difficult to achieve. As far as the Federal Republic is concerned, its constitution states it "wishes to serve the peace of the world as an equal partner in a united Europe," which means that by appropriate legislation national sovereignty can be transferred to international institutions.

CONSTITUTION AND LEGAL BASIS

In general terms, the constitution emphasizes the guarantee of human and fundamental rights, based on the rule of law and protected by law and jurisdiction. Recourse to law is open to all whose rights might be infringed by executive authority — the liberty of the individual overrides the power of the state which is clearly a hopeful and positive reaction after 12 years' abuse of power by the Nazi Reich. On the basis of this constitutional orientation there has been a lively development of the law throughout the years through international treaties, domestic legislation, in the courts, and by voluntary arrangements within the world of business. The emphasis is, and continues to be, more on protection of the private consumer and of labor under the otherwise maintained principles of the market economy.

"Social market economy" is the banner under which the continuous progress of West Germany's economy has taken place and which has been named the "miracle of economy" after World War II. It combines freedom of private enterprise and ownership with social ties on the basis of competition.

Fair competition among businesses is governed by several statutes and a great deal of case law. Under the Act against Unfair Competition (*Gesetz gegen den unlauteren Wettbewerb*), any competitive business action which violates "good morals" as defined by the ethics of reasonable and honest businessmen may be stopped. Application of this general principle to specific situations (misrepresentation, comparative advertising, gifts, etc.) is governed by case law.

Cartels and other associations for restricting competition are essentially prohibited. Agreements establishing retail price maintenance are also prohibited in general, except in cases involving publishers' products and branded goods for which price competition with similar goods exists. The Act against Restriction of Competition (*Gesetz gegen Wettbewerbs-beschränkungen*) is administered by the Federal Cartel Board (*Bundeskartellamt*) in Berlin. The Board may grant permission for the creation of cartels in certain circumstances, e.g., within industries in a state of depression, to promote production efficiency, or to promote exports. The Federal Cartel Board is also active in the field of takeovers and mergers. It fulfills a watchdog function to prevent misuse of power by firms in a monopoly or oligopoly situation. The Board will usually prohibit any merger which results in or emphasizes a situation of market domination. This apparently does not apply to the recent takeovers of Daimler Benz (MTU, Dornier, and AEG).

As a general rule of German law and administration, German nationals and foreigners receive the same legal treatment. Nationals of member states of the EEC enjoy free mobility including the right to employment. German economic and social policy favors the free international movement of capital goods and labor, particularly within the EEC, but also with other countries by bilateral agreement, including the United States since 1954.

German law is as detailed, voluminous, and complex as the body of law in any other civilized and industrialized community. Legal terminology and regulatory techniques are highly developed and as uniform and abstract as possible. Though a so-called civil law country — since the main body of its laws has been adapted from Roman law — Germany has established modern business and commercial law. The major codes are in the field of civil law, *Bürgerliches Gesetzbuch* (BGB), and commercial law, *Handelsgesetzbuch* (HGB), followed by many others and specialized codifications.

Most German law is federal law. State law is practically limited to special fields of public law, the foundations of private law, and the constitution of state banks (*Landesbanken*), the latter being subject again to federal banking law (*Bundesbank*). In addition, state law supplements certain federal statutes, whereas federal law, always prevails over state regulations (*Bundesrecht bricht Landesrecht*).

Federal and state legislation is published in official gazettes

(*Bundesgesetzblatt, Bundesanzeiger*). The latter is also prescribed for official financial and other company notices. Most important is the Commercial Register (*Handelsregister*) which records data of merchants and commercial enterprises. In some cases, entry in this register has a constitutional effect: a corporation becomes a legal entity only on registration. The appointment of corporate officers, on the other hand, is effective with the appointment and is not dependent on the subsequent registration. The second court register of general importance is the Title Register, *Grundbuch*, which indicates rights and encumbrances of real estate. Titles to real estate, mortgages, and land charges become effective only on entry into the register.

Legislation as well as the correct application and interpretation of the law is assured by the local courts for civil, commercial, and criminal matters whose impartiality is guaranteed by professional judges appointed for life. In addition to these courts of general jurisdiction, there are special courts to deal with administrative, tax, labor, and social insurance matters (*Verwaltungs-, Finanz-, Arbeits- und Sozialgericht*). Both the regular and the special courts are separate national courts with no concurrent competence of federal and state courts. The state and federal constitutional courts (*Bundesverfassungsgericht* in Karlsruhe) are the supreme guardians of the application of law and constitution.

To ensure the uniformity of decisions of the various supreme courts, a joint senate of these courts has been established.

As a whole, German law and behavior of people is more codification-oriented than the Anglo-Saxon system of case law. There is a tendency toward regulations for everything — and believing in the rules and laws more often than in one's own capability. For instance, driving a car often appears very dangerous on the roads of the Federal Republic since everyone relies wholly on his given "right of way," not caring for the poor foreigner or others not used to the system.

Foreign law may govern business relations in Germany where such law applies as a consequence of the German rules of conflict of laws, and if its application is not contrary to German public policy. The Federal Republic has ratified the European Convention of 1968 on Information on Foreign Law, which obligates the ratifying countries to provide information to courts in pending cases.

CONTRACT AND TORT

The right to the personal freedom of man in a free society is also the right to private property ownership and the freedom of contract. Under German law a contract exists when an offer has been made and accepted by both parties agreeing on the subject matter. Consideration is not a legal requirement for the validity of a contract. There is complete freedom of contract subject to certain statutory prohibitions and moral obligation. The parties may agree on any matter and in any manner desired. Contracts require no specific form unless expressly prescribed by statutory provision.

Any oral agreement therefore may be as valid and enforceable in court as a written document, provided there is proof of such an agreement. In former times many business deals were confirmed with a handshake as was the case with royal merchants (*königliche Kaufleute*). This tradition is still common today when both parties keep their word.

On the other hand, a written form of agreement is required for leases on real estate exceeding one year and a still higher degree of formality — attestation by a qualified notary public — is required to buy or sell real estate and for certain corporate transactions, e.g., the assignment of shares in a limited liability company.

Interpretation of contracts is based upon the expressed or implied intention of the contracting parties. Good will, with due regard to common custom, is a rule of interpretation. There are elaborate provisions in codes and statutes designed to construe party declarations in case of error, dissent, and their consequences and to supplement points on which the true intention of the parties cannot be ascertained. If a part of a contract is void, the remainder is also void — unless it may be assumed that the contract would have been accepted even without the void clauses.

The supreme law of contract, however, remains the expressed or implied intention of the parties at the time of agreement. The courts have developed a remedy in cases of deviation from the originally intended purpose of the contract. If one party can prove that the jointly understood essential basis of the contract (*Geschäfts-grundlage*) did not in fact exist or no longer exists due to intervening circumstances, it may demand an equitable adaption of the mutual rights and duties to the new situation.

General business conditions will only be recognized if they are expressly or tacitly accepted by the other party and they may constitute trade agreements between merchants, as previously mentioned. Parties are mutually obliged to a measure of trust in their negotiations, leading to the fulfillment of a contract which includes liability at an early stage (*culpa in contrahendo*).

Tort is defined in the Civil Code as the intentional or negligent violation — by action or omission to act — of life, body, health, freedom, property, or other personal rights. Such personal rights include the lawful exercising of an existing business ("eingerichteter und ausgeübter Gewerbebetrieb") as well as protective statutes (*Schutzgesetze*) which may not be violated.

An enterprise may also be liable if an officer, employee, servant, or agent commits a tort in the execution of his duties or assignments, particularly if he is a legal representative ("Organ") of a corporation. In cases where no priority of contract exists, product liability has been established by Supreme Court decisions when the manufacturer concerned is unable to supply proof that he is not at fault.

CONSUMER PROTECTION

Supply and demand are the determining factors in the market economy as practiced in Germany. Apart from the freedom to produce and offer for sale, and to buy or ignore on the side of the potential consumer, the latter are in the weaker position because of incomplete or insufficient information.

Although advertising is expected to provide serious information, its main purpose is to influence the consumer to buy. Unlike the American system of suing any producer possibly responsible for consumer damage, Germany has tried to develop a legal and practical preventive consumer protection system in line with the corrective social components included in the basically free and liberal market economy system.

For potential participants in the German marketplace it is good to know about the "Comparative Testing Foundation" (*Stiftung Warentest*) established in West Berlin in 1964. This foundation examines and evaluates all kinds of consumer goods from the ballpoint pen to the prefabricated house according to quality and money-for-value criteria. The foundation publishes the monthly magazine *Test*, where findings are made available to the interested consumer. This publication has gained wide acceptance because of its competence and objectivity.

Consumer protection legislation was necessary in various fields: Installment Payments Act/1970, revised General Conditions of Sale/1977 (*Allgemeine Geschäftsbedingungen*), Food Stuffs Legislation/1975, and Pharmaceuticals Act/1978 (*Arzneimittelgesetz*) are examples.

Generally speaking there is a growing awareness of the weak consumer position and unfair business practices. This is the background to the private "Association of Consumers" (*Arbeitsgemeinschaft der Verbraucher*, AVG) which runs more than 150 local advisory centers with some financial support from the state. They answer, free of charge, all possible consumer queries concerning quality and prices of goods and thus help to keep the market transparent. These state and private institutions have helped to make consumer protection more comprehensive in Germany and have laid the ground to deal with this new field of social policy which can affect every producer or service business within the federal frontiers.

WORKS CONSTITUTION ACT AND CO-DETERMINATION

In the field of employer/employee relationships, there is another basic regulation in Germany in the form of the Works Constitution Act from 1956, amended in 1972 (*Betriebsverfassungsgesetz*). This act, providing for co-determination at shop level, applies to all employers, natural persons, or legal entities with a permanent staff of five or more employees from whom a Works Council (*Betriebsrat*) has to be elected. The Works Council is afforded a diversity of rights allowing an active role in management decision-making.

In all instances in which the Works Council has equal rights, the employer is obliged to provide all information necessary for the fulfillment of its duties in due time. There are various tasks and obligations of a more general nature requiring Works Council participation, whereas other areas of management such as those affecting the "social status" classificatory titles (e.g., "supervisor") and promotions — require Works Council consent prior to any implementation.

Works Council and management also have equal rights in the field of so-called "personnel matters of general significance," such as systematic planning of personnel, personnel evaluations, wage and salary systems, hiring, transfer, dismissal, etc.

The basic idea of the Works Constitution Act as expressed in §2 is cooperation between employer and Works Council on the basis of mutual confidence in order to guarantee the welfare of both employees and the company, thus ascertaining profitability and humaneness, two principles necessary to run a business in the framework of the "social market economy."

This statutory arrangement, instituted with the express consent of both labor and management, should be regarded as a vital component of the social system in the German business world of today. The idea of co-determination, as expressed in the Co-determination Act of 1976 for larger companies at board level, has been developed in West Germany after World War II to a greater extent than in any other western industrialized country (with the exception of Switzerland and its *Friedensabkommen* of 1937, excluding the right to strike and any other union combative measures). With the historic burden of the Nazi Reich and its 12 years of absolute dictatorship and legal darkness, Germany has opted for political freedom and social self-government within and without the firms. Employees today are no longer prepared to be slaves; they want to become industrial citizens, seeking a demanding partnership in their places of business and employment, rather than just performing a job.

Although the right to personal property and inheritance is guaranteed by the constitution, which thus encourages private enterprise, this right is modified by law to consider the rights of others and the responsibility of ownership (*Sozialbindung des Eigentums*), providing the basis for the social market economy.

Unlike the trade unions operating nationwide, the Works Councils are representatives of and within their respective companies, where they are elected by all employees (top management excluded) among the workforce following a complicated statutory system of voting.

WORK ETHICS AND FORMALITY

In this country one expects a high degree of perfection, not only in goods and materials, but also in people, in oneself, and in others. Commitment, dedication, trustworthiness, and confidence are ruling principles in the world of work and business, more than command and control. With a high level of standard education in school and university it is taken for granted that men and women who work in business offices are able to communicate following the codes and rules of behavior that are often more strict and formal than in other countries.

Despite two world wars and the ensuing economic and social upheaval and change which has taken place in Germany, particularly after 1945, there are still remnants of a type of class system, even if it is not as clearly noticeable as in the United Kingdom, France, or Italy where money tends to be recognized only in or after the third generation. The old German aristocracy is still a class to be reckoned with, particularly in business life. One obvious vestige of this system is the continuing emphasis on good manners. Educated, responsible people are expected to display perfect manners at all times, and the same is expected from their partners in social or business negotiations. There are many underlying do's and don'ts that can easily aid or hinder business in Germany in this subcultural context.

The Anglo-Saxon in particular, whose tradition is the quick and easy personal contact on a first name basis, should keep a more formal attitude in mind when establishing business relations in Germany. Within the German tradition, first names are confined to personal relationships; it is an honor, and indication of trust, to be awarded or won over a period of time.

There are always a few exceptions, especially following the 13 years of social democratic rule and the ensuing "social state," but there is a tradition and a tendency toward hard work and discipline in the population and economy. This is particularly valid in managerial positions where 50 to 60 hours a week is much more common than the official 37.5 hour week, with continuing pressure from trade unions for a further reduction in weekly working hours. It is true that the younger generation in Germany, like in many other countries of the world, having grown up in a flourishing economy seem less interested in working hard than their parents who suffered from the postwar trauma.

Even if "Care parcels" and the Marshall Plan laid the grounds for resurrection and survival, there was a great reservoir of hidden values and potential strengths that enabled Germany to create the *Wirtschaftswunder* (economic miracle) admired and envied at the time by European neighbors and transatlantic teachers.

One thing the American business world must note when dealing with their former disciples from the early years after World War II: the Germans are now used to living their own lives as adults, are proud of their achievements and their share in world business, and should no longer be considered occupied country. Although Germany with its population of 65 million is literally half of Japan and one-third of the United States, some industry names such as Zeiss, Leitz, or Siemens, as well as the car companies already noted, rate at the top of the scale in the world market. It will certainly pay to deal with them on equal terms, knowing that it is a German virtue to stick to what has been said and agreed. Personal credibility is often held in still higher esteem than product or service quality and a salesman may have to spend years cultivating his clients, building up long-term relationships based on reliability, which are then more important than short-term profitability.

To really understand each other, it will certainly be a key to speak the other's language: this means German in Germany, although people here tend to speak foreign languages, English being the most common. However, to participate in the German economy and marketplace—not only today but tomorrow—it will be necessary to communicate in German. This will be particularly appreciated as proof of good will, even if it is not perfect right from the start.

Germans appreciate—and in fact demand—fine workmanship,

excellent design, and high quality materials. Knowing that they can rely on the solidity of their own products, particularly in the field of engineering and machinery, they will seek the same high standard in imported goods. After two (lost) world wars, waste was considered a sin, whether of consumer products, energy, space, or long-lasting goods. German houses are built to last; Mercedes, BMW, and Volkswagen produce cars that can be driven for hours at top speed on the motorways and remain roadworthy, reliable vehicles after 10 years or more. Cars and other long-lasting goods are kept and maintained meticulously and it is only in recent years that the "disposable" attitude has developed after a few decades of welfare. This attitude is perhaps more typical of the American society with its sense of "using" things rather than "owning" them.

Owning things often is still more important in Germany than using them. For sure, Germans also drive their fast cars just for fun — which has led to the BMW advertising slogan, *Aus Freude am Fahren* ("for the fun of driving"). On the other hand, cars of a certain class are status symbols in society, viewed by the neighbors who judge the available income by the size and class of the car, the lady's fur, or her sparkling jewels. This also means that cars are extremely well looked after: no middle-class German will miss the opportunity to wash and polish his car every weekend. He is extremely sensitive while driving and parking his car; the slightest scratch on his bumper bar can end in a court case of "hit and run" if the contrahent does not exchange personal data and insurance details. Some people have called the car the most sensitive part of a German's body!

EMPLOYMENT, TRADE UNIONS, AND LABOR REGULATIONS

Of the approximately 25.7 million actively working people in Germany, 2.2 million are self-employed and 22.5 million are in dependent employment as wage and salary earners, public servants, or trainees — "employees" (*Arbeitnehmer*) as opposed to "employers" (*Arbeitsgeber*).

Employers and employees apparently have common and contrasting interests at the same time which lead to co-operation and sometimes confrontation. Contractive or social partners for the collective bargaining of general working conditions in the Federal Republic are the trade unions and the employers' associations, autonomous parties for whom the state only sets down the general conditions by legislation.

Trade unions in Germany are few, but large. The biggest labor organization is the German Trade Union Federation (*Deutscher Gewerkschafts-Bund*, DGB) with close to 8 million members in 17 unions. Characteristic of the DGB union is the principle, "one union—one industry." As a rule, therefore, the employers of a given industrial branch negotiate with only one labor organization. The trade unions in the Federal Republic are supposed to be party-politically neutral and independent, but they operate with open sympathy for the Social Democratic Party—now in opposition—where they nominated several ministers during their legislation. In addition, the DGB acts as employer and entrepreneur itself in several fields. In recent times the DGB ran into trouble in management and financing of its own housing and public utilities construction company, *Neue Heimat*, which is still not definitely saved from bankruptcy.

Employers, on the other hand, are organized in several hundred associations organized both regionally and according to the type of industry in a joint organization, "The Federation of German Employers Associations" (*Bundesvereinigung der Deutschen Arbeitgeberverbände*, BDA). The BDA, like the DGB, does not enter into collective agreements itself, but works as a coordinating organ on fundamental questions.

Under the act of Tariff Contract ("Tarifvertragsgesetz") of 1949 both parties are granted the greatest latitude by state and federal governments. A collective agreement, tariff contract or *Tarifvertrag*, applies in the first instance to both sides. In practice, however, it covers all workers in the industry concerned whether they are union-organized or not. Frequently tariff contracts are also declared as generally binding by the federal labor minister and then apply to the entire branch of industry concerned.

A distinction is made between two types of collective agreements. The "wage and salaries tariff" regulates pay, i.e., wages and salaries and their yearly increases, and is usually agreed on for a year at a time. The "frame or general tariff" (*Manteltarifvertrag*) regulates general issues such as working hours, dismissal notice periods, overtime rates, bonus, etc. and often extends for several years. The terms of employer/labor agreements are as binding as law on both sides. On the other hand, there is the principle of contractual freedom prevailing in the whole of civil, commercial, and labor law which means that deviations from a tariff contract are possible, but only to the advantage of the employee. Such deviations are indeed not infrequent since in many cases actual wage, salary, and other payments to individuals are considerably above those agreed on in the general contract framework.

If labor and employer negotiations cannot reach agreement, industrial action including strikes may occur. There are several safeguards to prevent this happening too easily and too often. The usual process is to bring in an impartial arbitrator to reach a solution. Even if the arbitrator fails, strike is not necessarily inevitable. Within the trade union concerned, several bodies have to approve of the strike action. A vote must then be taken among union rank and file. Only if 75% of the members vote in favor can a strike take place.

In the Federal Republic the workers' right to strike is countered by the employers' right to lock out, i.e., temporarily close down plants during industrial disputes. Although expressly confirmed by Federal Labor Court judgment, the lock out right is highly controversial in public opinion. Since the state remains neutral in labor disputes, neither strikers nor locked out workers receive unemployment benefits from the state labor funds as compensation.

There has been an important public campaign recently about §116 of the 1962 Labor Promotion Act (*Arbeitsförderungsgesetz*) which with corrected wording will partly change means of action in this field. However, one can say that in Germany strikes are not very popular, and compared to other countries like the UK, France, or Italy, there have been very few strikes. One of the saddest and most famous strikes since the end of the War was started by workers in Eastern Germany and East Berlin in 1951 which led to a revolutionary movement, only to be stopped by Soviet arms and tanks. This event lives on as a day of national commemoration in the "Day of National Unification" on June 17th.

In 1980, 128.000 working days were lost due to strikes; in 1982 only 15.000 and 34.505 in 1985 were lost.

The weekly working hours were subject to strike during 1985 following the trade unions' demand of a 35 hour week. The compromise finally reached was a package around 37.5 hours with 30 days of annual leave guaranteed for every employee, compared to 44 hours and 17 days leave in 1962 and 48 hours and 14 days' leave in 1950. The working week and leave are a continual subject in German sociopolitical discussion, as is retirement age which is still officially 65 for men and 60 for women, though there is a strong movement to lower it. Thus, in recent years, several companies have offered special preretirement pension schemes to employees between 58 and 63. These company plans are presently optional within the framework of the state pension regulations.

Compared to other countries such as the United States or Japan, the German federal holiday law appears very generous. Unlike Japanese employees who frequently do not even take the 10 days vacation allocated, Germans take advantage of all statutory and local holidays. They like to travel abroad where they undoubtedly head the international statistics with more than 30 million people traveling, 60% to foreign countries where they spent more than 40 billion Deutsche Mark in foreign currencies in 1985.

Besides trade unions and employer associations, labor market policy is determined by the Federal Institute of Labor Exchange and Unemployment Insurance (*Nürnberger Bundesanstalt*). Its self-government is guaranteed under an arrangement whereby equal numbers of employers, employees, and public authorities are represented. On a lower level are the Labor Offices (*Arbeitsamt*) in every town and country district. Besides giving professional advice and courses of instruction, their task is to match open positions with available labor—an enormous task today with unemployment running at a rate of close to 10% of the working population.

Federal, state, and local labor offices have more or less a complete monopoly on the placement of employed people. Private employment agencies are therefore not permitted to place personnel as in other countries; they may, however, handle part-time jobs or contracts on a limited time basis under certain conditions. In such cases the companies employing pay all costs involved. Management consultants may assist companies in recruiting for vacant managerial positions by search or advertisement, but a consultant may never work for or accept payment from an individual looking for a job. Another type of service with a growing need and scope, particularly with the high level of unemployment and general tendency toward early retirement, is the so-called "outplacement," where consultants help companies to get rid of people otherwise protected by law against sudden termination of employment.

Although contracts of employment follow the general law of contract, there are numerous mandatory rules affording special protection for employees (i.e., disabled persons, expectant mothers, minors, members of works councils). Generally speaking and according to the *Kündigungsschutzgesetz*, a person employed by the same firm for more than six months can only be given notice if the dismissal is "socially justified." In cases of conflict this has to be proven by the employer in a special Labor Court (*Arbeitsgericht*). The minimum length of the lawful notice period is six weeks prior to the end of a calendar quarter. Many employees have a notice period of three months which is extended up to six months after 10 years of employment, and may not be reduced in advance by private contract.

All in all it must be kept in mind that employment and dismissal in the German business world is a far cry from the rather easy "hire and fire" system which is common practice in the United States.

There are several reasons for the present high rate of unemployment. The major one is certainly the international economic crisis. Inflation, as in all western industrial countries, was accelerated by the explosion of petroleum and other raw material prices since 1973. It will be interesting to note the consequences of the recent price drop for oil and petrol in early 1986. This had already led to an inflation rate close to zero in Germany and has helped to sustain economic expansion through 1988. Since then oil prices have started to rise and unemployment is relatively high.

The increasing automation of work procedures, made possible by microelectronics above all, has destroyed many industrial and clerical jobs, and created some in other fields. The population development also plays a role; there is a general population decrease while the number of elderly and retired people is rising proportionately. It will be interesting to see how the Germans solve this problem of changing generations which is typical for every industrial country with a high standard of living and a rising life expectancy (today 69 for men and 74 for women).

CHAMBER OF COMMERCE

Other important regional organs in the economic self-government of industrial enterprise are the Chambers of Commerce (*Industrieund Handelskammer*). They represent the local associations of people in trade and business and are expected to look after the general interest of the world of commerce as a whole, acting as statutory corporations with compulsory membership. Dating back to 1802 (Mayence) and 1803 (Cologne) when the first chambers were founded in Germany, there are more than 80 in the Republic today, associated at federal level in the German Industry and Trade Convention (*Deutscher Industrie- und Handelstag*, DIHT) which looks after the interests of more than 30 German and International Chambers of Foreign Trade (*Aussenhandelskammern*) which form a kind of diplomatic or foreign service of the federal DIHT in most of the industrial countries of the world.

In addition, the German Chambers of Commerce play an important role in professional education in the apprenticeship system: 2-3 years of practical training and education of young people after leaving school within companies where specialized employers (master tradesmen) are responsible for their development, accompanied by part-time vocational schooling. At the end of this apprenticeship young men and women take a written and oral examination under the supervision of the local Chamber and are awarded a type of diploma (e.g., *Kaufmannsgehilfenbrief*), opening doors to their sector of employment and the possibility of rising to managerial positions.

Whereas other countries of the Western world rely on specialized high school or university programs for the education of their business managers, apprenticeship is a unique system of practically oriented business education that broadens the access to careers and secures a guaranteed level of competence for commercial employees. For instance, Hermann Josef Strenger, Chairman of the Board of the Bayer Aktiengesellschaft, has neither an MBA nor a doctorate in chemistry. He started his career with Bayer in 1952 when he passed his final apprenticeship exams as one of 25 apprentices taken in by Bayer every year — an apparently highly qualifying training!

Other companies like Siemens or the Deutsche Bank are equally renowned for their apprentice training, which is often the basis for a successful career. Only exceptional scholars are accepted after entrance tests of up to several days' duration. This type of education is reminiscent in some respects of the Japanese system, only there companies take in the best students after university examination. The usual Japanese life-long fidelity of employees to their company is equaled in some German companies, whereas the professional mobility in the USA is characterized by frequent moves and changes from company to company. It is a natural consequence that a service business such as Executive Search first developed in the States before crossing the Atlantic and the Channel to Europe. Although now a commonly accepted practice, a consultant calling a typically German manager can still hear the reaction, "I don't want to be poached."

Another typically German phenomena in the labor market is newspaper advertising on a much larger scale than in Europe or America. It is a time-consuming task to read through the weekend editions of the *Frankfurter Allgemeine Zeitung*, for instance, which has become the leading paper in this respect with up to 100 pages of job advertisements for positions ranging up to the highest paid senior management posts and board memberships.

BANKING AND FINANCE

Besides consulting and advertising in national daily newspapers, recruitment at the top level of banking and finance is often directed by the supervisory boards of companies where bankers hold important offices.

Public, cooperative, and private credit institutions operate in Germany. According to the 1982 figures, there were 240 lending banks, 12 giro clearing banks, 6,000 saving banks, 9 cooperative central banks, 2,266 larger credit cooperatives, 38 mortgage institutions and public mortgage banks, 16 banks with special functions, and 128 installment credit institutions.

The city of Frankfurt am Main is the most important banking center in the Western world after New York and Tokyo, hosting more than 380 banks.

The Deutsche Bank, Dresdner Bank, and Commerzbank are the three largest private and by far the most important banks in Germany, the Deutsche Bank having recently acquired the 5 billion DM industrial imperium of Friedrich Karl Flick for replacement. Flick ran into trouble following political affairs concerning tax exemption and party donations.

The private commercial banks and state banks which act as central clearinghouses for the local savings banks (*Sparkassen*) provide short-term and long-term credits and loans for private enterprise. They are all subject to the provisions of the Banking Act (*Kreditwesengesetz*) and to the supervision of the Federal Banking Supervisory Authority (*Bundesaufsichtsamt für das Kreditwesen*). The Federal Bank (*Deutsche Bundesbank*) is the state-owned central bank with headquarters in Frankfurt am Main. In each of the 11 states (including West Berlin), the *Bundesbank* is represented by the state central banks (*Landeszentralbanken*) which again are represented by 230 branches and offices throughout the country. The Central Bank Council (*Zentralbankrat*) controls the monetary and credit policy of the country by means of regulation of interest rates, establishment of minimum reserve policies, etc. The Federal Bank issues the country's bank notes. The Deutsche Mark has become one of the most stable currencies in the world, after being introduced in 1948 by Professor Ludwig Erhard's *Währungsreform* with a per capita quota of 60 marks. Since 1958 the Deutsche Mark is freely convertible, with free currency trading in the Federal Republic since the Foreign Trade and Payments Act in 1961.

Although independent of the federal government, the *Bundesbank* exercises a supervisory function over the banking system as a whole. The federal and state governments provide low-cost investment loans out of public funds or act as guarantor for other loans to promote underdeveloped areas and the establishment of small businesses. Even large firms running into financial difficulties are eligible for public assistance to avoid additional unemployment in the area concerned. A recent example is Arbed-Saarstahl after the near-crash of AEG a few years ago, now safely in the port of the Daimler Benz imperium.

In general there are no exchange control restrictions on the borrowing of funds by nonresident individuals or companies wishing to establish a business enterprise in Germany, nor is there any limit imposed by law on the extent to which an individual or company may borrow funds. On the other hand, individuals or business enterprises resident in Germany who wish to invest abroad may under specific conditions take advantage of certain tax incentives. The conditions and benefits are set out in the Foreign Investment Act (*Auslandsinvestitionsgesetz*) and in the Developing Countries Tax Act (*Entwicklungsländer-Steuergesetz*). Special depreciation allowances and tax advantages are applicable for West Berlin as well as areas directly bordering the German Democratic Republic (*Zonen-Rand-Gebiet*) in order to support and strengthen the local economy.

The export of merchandise from Germany is normally unrestricted, although restrictions may be imposed to safeguard internal supplies or for other reasons of national interest or security. To import into Germany nonresidents must have a permit; German residents require none. The inward and outward transfer of profits, dividends, interest, fees, and royalties is currently free from exchange controls. Nonresidents wishing to invest in Germany must comply with certain formalities and must report the following transactions to the Federal Bank:

— Establishment or acquisition of a business undertaking, whether independent or a subsidiary
— Acquisition of shares or securities
— Granting of loans or other assets
— Disposal of an investment

REGISTRATION AND LEGAL FORMS OF BUSINESS ENTERPRISE

Apart from the above-mentioned and with the exception of certain trades, i.e., banking and insurance which are subject to government license control, no special permission is necessary to commence business in Germany. Certain registration requirements must be fulfilled with the trade office (*Gewerbeamt*), the tax authorities (*Finanzamt*), and the commercial register (*Handelregister*) in the town or district concerned. The name of the company or partnership must be registered with the local Chamber of Commerce, where every business is subject to compulsory membership and is required to pay annual subscriptions, a variable fee based on annual business income, subject to municipal trade tax (*Gewerbesteuer*).

The common legal forms of business enterprise in Germany are:

1. Companies with limited liability:
   - Stock corporation (*Aktiengesellschaft*, AG)
   - Limited liability company (*Gesellschaft mit beschränkter Haftung*, GmbH)
   - Partnership partly limited by shares (*Kommanditgesellschaft auf Akten*, KGaA)
2. Partnerships
   - General partnership (*Offene Handelsgesellschaft*, oHG)
   - Limited partnership (*Kommanditgesellschaft*, KG)
   - Limited partnership where the unlimited partner is a GmbH, Gmbh & Co. KG
3. Sole trader (Einselfirma)
   A foreign business enterprise may also conduct its business in Germany through a
4. Branch (*Zweigniederlassung*) or
5. Office.

In the specific case of a branch being established by a foreign company or partnership, the application for registration must be signed by all authorized members of the Board of Directors and accompanied by a notarized copy of the company's articles or statutes together with a certified German translation and a certificate of incorporation. If a foreign company, resident in a country outside the EEC, wishes to establish a branch in Germany, it must obtain permission from the Ministry of Commerce in the state where the branch is to be opened.

A branch is not an independent legal entity. Third parties have a right of legal regress against the business enterprise to which the branch belongs and liability is therefore governed by the legal form of that enterprise, which may also be foreign.

TAXES AND FEDERAL BUDGET

Since 1972 a specific law (*Aussensteuergesetz*) exists regarding foreign business interests and financial interests of German nationals abroad. On the other hand, the question of unlimited or limited tax liability in Germany depends on "residence" or "customary abode." Broadly speaking, "residence" is a question of whether or not the taxpayer has a permanent residential address in the country. The condition establishing "customary abode" is an uninterrupted stay in Germany for a period of six months in any year; after six months foreigners automatically become subject to unlimited liability to tax.

For both individuals (*Einkommensteuer*) and corporations (*Körperschaftsteuer*), the income tax is the most relevant contribution to the state household. It is calculated as part of the yearly income and deducted monthly from the payable income of individuals or paid in advance on the expected company income in quarterly installments.

With a progressive tax rate of up to 56%, Germans today are probably amongst the most heavily taxed people of the western world. The zone of the progressions for individuals varies from 22 to 56% (18.000 to 130.000 DM income per annum for singles and 30.000 to 260.000 DM for marrieds) and is relevant for 13 million of 22 million taxpaying citizens.

The taxation yield since 1950 has grown more rapidly than the gross national product, which has led to a public sector spending rate of 50% in 1982 compared to 25% in the early 1950s and 38% in 1970. Although this quota rose continuously under social-democratic government from 1969 until 1982, the trend was stopped in 1983 and the public spending rate is 48% today, with a diminishing tendency.

Amounting to 35%, or 92 billion DM, income tax from individuals and companies constitutes the largest part of the state income of 260 billion DM in 1985, followed by another 25%, or 64 billion DM, for value added tax (VAT). This tax which is calculated on the sales value of goods or services delivered or performed within Germany and in accordance with the EEC, currently runs at 14%. A reduced rate of 7% applies to food, agricultural products, and printed materials, as well as services supplied by persons exercising independent occupations or professions. Although VAT is collected from producers or traders at an early stage when the "value is added" to goods or services, it is effectively borne only by the final consumer and thus in the end operates as a kind of sales tax.

Another changing trend within the field of public expenditure is the debt service, currently 30 billion DM and more than 10% of the total federal budget, but now kept stable and under control by the federal government.

The greater part of the state budget relates to social expenditure, amounting to 32%, or 83 billion DM. Since social expenses are not only part of the federal budget, but also the responsibility of the states, municipalities, and local communities, together they show a budget of 540 billion DM, a sum double the federal budget. This sum has doubled within 15 years, reflecting the trend toward more welfare from public sources. However, there is evident danger in continually rising government and social expenses, taking from some by taxation and giving to others where need is apparent.

Although free enterprise and competition are still the basis of West Germany's success and society, there has been a notable movement toward a collectivist or socialist society. As Milton Friedmann said about the future of capitalism, it appears easy at first to do good with other people's money, which he rightly defines as the philosophical basis of the welfare state. It is becoming more and more difficult to fulfill the growing needs of those who feel encouraged to rely on public welfare rather than their own efficiency and productiveness. He is therefore probably right in saying that it is not possible for a politically free society to exist unless the major part of its economic resources are operated under a free, i.e., capitalist, private enterprise system.

The social system in the Federal Republic should therefore continue to be embodied in personal responsibility; only in cases where the individual appears virtually incapable of functioning productively should the state step in.

INCOME AND PRICING

West German incomes derive from a wide range of sources, primarily wages and salaries from dependent employment. In addition, there are shareholder dividends, properties and assets, state transfer payments such as child endowment, unemployment benefits, and pensions of various kinds. The disposable income of private households in Germany after deduction of taxes and social insurance contributions has risen in total from 207,000 million DM in 1960 to 970,000 million DM in 1981. This has enabled the population to spend an increasing share of their incomes on higher-valued goods and services, i.e., luxuries such as motor cars, household appliances, more comfortable furniture, leisure pursuits, recreation, and holidays.

Private household savings have also risen continuously parallel to consumption. Savings deposits of 205 million DM in 1970 rose to 524 million DM in 1982, more than half of these deposits being placed with public saving banks and giro clearing banks. After the devastating experience of two complete currency devaluations within one generation (in 1920 and 1948), it is a comforting sign that the Germans of today place trust in money and value, accompanied by the general wish to save part of their income for unforeseen events. Generally speaking, the ordinary family's financial scope has widened considerably throughout the years.

Since the standard of living depends not only on income but also on prices, the consumer price development is one of the major issues of domestic politics. Public opinion surveys have consistently shown that the main thing people expect of the government is to keep prices stable. This is certainly understandable considering the two devaluations, both of which both followed enormous inflation and resulted in the total collapse of the currency and sweeping destruction of financial assets. On the whole the German authorities have been able to constrain price increases better than in other countries, with still better results in the first half of 1986. Whereas the price increase rate occasionally rose above 6% until 1982, it has floated since then around 3% and is now down almost to zero, following the continuous breakdown of oil prices which are now close to the standards of 1973.

FOREIGN TRADE

Situated in the middle of Europe without traditional frontiers, West Germany is highly dependent on external relations. From the outset of its existence the Federal Republic opted for integration into the world economy and committed itself to free markets and to the principle of international division of labor. This stance is in line with a liberal foreign trade policy which has always been and continues to be directed toward dismantling tariffs and other trade barriers.

The total value of the Federal Republic's imports and exports rose from 20.000 million DM in 1950 to 805.000 million DM in 1982, placing Germany second after the United States in world trade. It is a very remarkable feature of German foreign trade that since 1952 exports have exceeded imports, despite considerable DM revaluations. The export surplus rose year after year from 700 million DM in 1952 to 50.000 million DM in 1974. Because of the higher cost of imported oil, it then dropped substantially but in 1982 rose again to 51.000 million DM.

The large export surplus was often criticized abroad, as today the figures and tendencies of the Japanese market are criticized even from within Japan's own borders. On the other hand the surplus was necessary to counterbalance the 40.000 million DM spent abroad by German tourists, (the number one travelers in the world), the 6.600 million DM remissions from foreign workers in the Republic to their relatives in the home countries, and for the surplus of 5.000 million DM more paid into the European Community fund than received from it.

As a result of the European Community, Germany's trade with the other EC states by far exceeds that with other countries. In 1982 48% of Germany's imports came from EC states, while 48% of the German exports also went to EC trading partners, with France and the Netherlands on top of the list. Exports out of Germany comprise all sorts of machinery, motor vehicles, electrical engineering, and chemical products. The major items imported are food, beverages, tobacco, petroleum, and natural gas. This is typical of a densely populated industrial country with few raw material resources, but with a high standard of technology, a highly skilled work force, and an efficient productive sector.

Another component of external economic relations is foreign investment, whose importance to Germany's economy is growing. Securing and widening export markets is one of the main motives for investing abroad but also cost advantages in producing and avoidance of trade barriers play a part in deciding whether and where to invest abroad. Of the 58.000 million DM German foreign investments in 1980, 82% were made in Western industrial countries and some 18% in developing countries.

Foreign direct investment in Germany is also constantly growing because of attractive and apparently secure conditions and promising rates of possible profits. In 1980 some 94.000 million DM were invested from abroad in German states, with 95% coming from Europe and America and a growing minority, coming from the Middle Eastern petroleum countries. So, for instance, Kuwaiti Sheikhs have been elected onto the supervisory boards of such traditional German companies as the Hoechst AG and the Metallgesellschaft.

As a consequence of the stability and reliability of Germany as a trading partner and the government trend toward a policy of relaxing tensions toward countries in Eastern Europe, there will certainly be more scope for foreign money and business in the country. This may even be an advantage to the so-called "intra-German trade" between West and East. The formal basis for this trade between the two states of the same nationality is an agreement concluded in Berlin in 1951, long before the more recent activities at government level. Payments within the framework of this trade agreement are accounted for through the federal *Deutsche Bundesbank* and the GDR State Bank in units of account, more or less similar to one DM. The GDR has been conceded an interest-free credit line with the *Bundesbank*, known as the "swing" and currently equivalent to 1,000 million units.

In economic terms, intra-German trade is much more important to Eastern Germany than to the Federal Republic. The value of 6.500 million units in the West is equal to about 2% of the West German foreign trade volume, whereas trade with the Federal Republic represents about 10% of East German trade. It is therefore accepted by East Germany because of its economic advantages, although it practically represents an open door in the otherwise hermetically sealed wall to the West.

The GRD or DDR (*Deutsche Demokratische Republik*) as the eastern part of former Germany is by far the most important trading partner of Soviet Russia and occupies the number two position within the framework of the Warsaw Treaty which unifies the eastern countries opposite the NATO in the west. Of all the socialist countries, the GDR is an unequaled second behind the USSR in political, military, and economic terms. However, Erich Honecker, who could be called Mikhail Gorbachev's master disciple in East Berlin, has still not been allowed by his Soviet masters to visit the Federal Republic of Germany, a visit which has been officially announced and expected for some time.

The existing economic power and technological know-how of East Germany, based on names like Zeiss and others, is usurped by the Soviet Union and its continuing need for high tech and other goods and values, even if they are often only second class compared to the free world standards. It is interesting, however, to see that within the limits of a restrictive political system the "red prussians" as heirs of a common German tradition and history are developing to take a position in the eastern socialist world similar to West Germany's place behind the United States in the free Western world.

WELFARE AND SOCIAL SECURITY

"The Federal Republic of Germany is a democratic and social federal state" — so stipulates the Basic Law of 1949. To achieve the aim of social justice and a dignified life for all its inhabitants, the state has evolved a wide framework of social welfare legislation, ranging from sickness, accident, old age, and child support, to rent subsidy and the promotion of vocational training.

The Social Insurance (*Sozialversicherung*) dates back to the famous laws of the late 1880s initiated by Chancellor Bismarck, which were very progressive at the time of rapid industrial development and today are still the basis of the German welfare system. Social insurance covers sickness, unemployment, and pensions on a contributory basis, with the employer and the employee each contributing one-half of the premium in relation to gross earnings, subject to a maximum earning level. Pensions and unemployment insurance are obligatory for all employees including legal representatives and officers of corporations, with the exception of Board Members of an *Aktiengesellschaft* (stock corporation). Sickness insurance is obligatory only for employees up to a specified yearly income, but the employer is nevertheless obliged to contribute 50% of the employee's payment to a qualified private health insurance fund (up to the amount of the employer contribution to the compulsory scheme).

In the case of the absence through sickness, an employee is entitled to receive wage or salary payments from the employer up to a period of six weeks. Thereafter the health insurance pays sickness benefits up to 78 weeks which can be as much as 85% of the regular income.

The statutory pension scheme — one of the central pillars of social security in Germany — takes effect at the pension age of 65 for men and 60 for women, with certain possibilities of payment two years earlier under the so-called "flexible retirement age" provision. The pension payment depends on the duration of insurance (working years) and the amount of income from employment and is thus performance oriented and not subject to a means test. In addition, the index-linked pensions principle (introduced in 1957) ensures that the pensions are included in general income growth. Although there is an ongoing public debate as to the correct index system, there is at least a certain guarantee of social justice attached to the actual "generations treaty."

Foreign nationals employed in Germany are in general obliged to pay the same social security contributions as Germans, with the right to the same benefits. However, there are certain regulations within in EEC and agreements with social insurance conventions in other countries, often on a reciprocal basis.

In addition to the state pension scheme, many German companies give their employees additional retirement benefits. Such company pension grants are quite common and represent a valuable supplement to the statutory scheme and are therefore encouraged for taxation advantages by the companies. These pensions are secured by mandatory law and rest on voluntary agreements, individual contracts, or company awards. They become vested rights when the employee reaches the age of 35 and 10 years of service with the company, even if he leaves the company before reaching retirement age. Such schemes are also protected against insolvency of the employer by a pension insurance fund established for this purpose.

Protection and support after accidents at work or in the case of illness and disease arising from particular vocations are provided by special employers' liability insurance associations (*Berufsgenossenschaften*), for which the funds are raised by dues (for compulsory membership) paid only by employers.

Altogether the German social security system is highly developed and effective and has often been copied in part by other countries. On the other hand, in recent years it has also been criticized as being too generous and efforts are continuing to reduce costs, particularly in the field of health care (*Kostendämpfungsgesetz*).

Since the high costs of social services have to be recovered somewhere, this system has led to very high social security contributions. This means that for every single Deutsch Mark paid out as wage or salary, at least 30% (for the compulsory charges) or as much as 80% (depending on the range of voluntary fringe benefits) must be added for social charges. In terms of international competition, this makes Germany a high labor-cost country, a matter which must also be taken into consideration when deciding if and how to do business with or in Germany.

USEFUL ADDRESSES AND PUBLICATIONS

Addresses

Presse- und Informationsamt der Bundesregierung
(Press and Information Office of the Federal Government)
Weickerstrasse 11, D 5300 Bonn, Germany

Canadian Embassy/Trade Commission
Friedrich-Wilhelm-Strasse 18, D 5300 Bonn 1, Germany

United States Embassy/Trade Commission
Deichmanns-Aue 29, D 5300 Bonn 2, Germany

British Embassy
Friedrich-Ebert-Allee 77, D 5300 Bonn 1, Germany

Canadian German Chamber of Industry and Commerce
2015 Peel Street, Suite 1110, Montreal, Quebec, Canada

German American Chamber of Commerce, Inc.
666 5th Avenue, New York, NY 10103, U.S.A.

American Chamber of Commerce in Germany
Rossmarkt 12, D 6000 Frankfurt am Main 1, Germany

British Chamber of Commerce in Germany
Heumarkt 14, D 5000 Cologne 1, Germany

Kommission der Europäischen Gemeinschaften, Presse- und
    Informationsbüro
(Press and Information Office of the EEC)
Zitelmannstrasse 22, D 5300 Bonn 1, Germany

Deutscher Industrie- und Handelstage
(German Industry and Trade Convention)
Adenauerallee 148, D 5300 Bonn 1, Germany

Bundesstelle für Aussenhandelsinformation
(Federal Office for Foreign Trade Information)
Blaubach 13, D 5000 Köln 1, Germany

Bundesverband des Deutschen Gross- und Aussenhandels
(Wholesale and Foreign Trade Association)
Kaiser-Friedrich-Strasse 13, D 5300 Bonn 1, Germany

Bundesverband der Deutschen Industrie
(Federation of Industry)
Gustav-Heinemann-Ufer 84, D 5000 Köln 51, Germany

Ausstellungs- und Messe-Ausschuss der Deutschen Wirtschaft
(Trade Fairs Council)
Lindenstrasse 8, D 5000 Köln 1, Germany

Bundesvereinigung der Deutschen Arbeitgeberverbände
(Confederation of Employers Associations)
Gustav-Heinemann-Ufer 72, D 5000 Köln 51, Germany

Deutscher Gewerkschaftsbund
(German Trade Union Federation)
Hans-Böckler-Strasse 39, D 4000 Düsseldorf 30, Germany

Publications

Facts about Germany.
Bertelsmann Lexikothek Verlag GmbH, Gütersloh, 1984
Democracy in Germany.
Press and Information Office of the Federal Government, Bonn,
1985
Statistical Compass 1984.
Federal Statistical Office, Wiesbaden, 1984
Hidden Differences—How to Communicate with the Germans.
Gruner + Jahr AG, Hamburg, 1983
Verbände, Behörden und Organisationen der Wirtschaft.
(Assocations, Administration and Organizations of Industry)
Verlag Hoppenstedt & Co., Darmstadt, 1985

Chapter 8

New Perspectives in East-West Business: The Case of Hungary

Jozsef Beracs
Nicolas Papadopoulos

From a Western perspective, Eastern European markets are often seen as an unknown and uniform mass operating under a rigid central planning system. This does not reflect the fact that although sharing many common characteristics, socialist markets also differ from one another in many significant respects. Perhaps more importantly, it does not take into account the economic and other reforms of the past two decades in Eastern Europe, which have resulted in the adoption of economic management models that rely increasingly on market forces. Although media coverage of the Soviet Union's *glasnost* policy since 1986 has attracted attention to changing conditions in Eastern Europe, detailed and systematic information is still scant and the policy itself is often viewed with suspicion.

Change may or may not accelerate under the *glasnost* policy, and the policy itself may or may not succeed in all respects. Yet the underlying impetus to a greater reliance on market forces will likely continue. The following statement, reading as it does like conventional "Western" marketing thinking but made by an executive of a major Hungarian textile company, is indicative of emerging conditions in Eastern Europe:

> Having studied possibilities of streamlining [marketing and other activities] we decided to concentrate our forces on turning out saleable, profitable products by using existing materials and capacities. . . . Advertising forms of course an organic

part of the company's marketing activity. . . . we branded some groups of our products and launched advertising campaigns on the domestic market. . . . Lately we opened our own retail shop which is the best way to measure buyers' reactions and developed our own marketing network. (Honti, 1984)

Just as Eastern markets are moving away from "pure" centrally planned economic models, the degree of government regulation and market intervention in the West has tended to increase over the long term. These simultaneous shifts suggest a certain convergence of the two systems. However, it would be a mistake to believe that this also signifies a convergence in ideology and the political sphere. East European countries remain socialist and Western countries remain capitalist (Samli and Jermacowicz, 1983). Simply put, Eastern socialist countries aim at different national goals than those of the West (e.g., in terms of income distribution) while recognizing the need to enhance the role of the market as a means of achieving those goals.

Hungary is perhaps the best known and most successful example of a country charting a course toward a marketplace-focused economy coupled with socialist political thinking. In fact, certain recent developments in the Soviet Union, such as a new law about cooperatives in agriculture, are patterned after Hungary's experiments in the 1970s. To Western businesses, Hungary today represents a major area of opportunity both because of its internal market and because of its potential role as a gateway to other Eastern socialist countries. Expanding into Hungary and beyond, however, presupposes a good understanding of the unique elements which make that country so similar to, and yet so different from, traditional conceptions about both East and West.

This chapter discusses Hungary as a potential market for Western firms. Since reforms are still in progress and since they affect a broad spectrum of economic activity, any discussion of technical details about trade with and investment in Hungary would quickly become dated. (Technical information on trading with, or investing in, Hungary is available in several publications which are referred to later.) Therefore, the chapter emphasizes a conceptual understanding of the market and the factors that affect it. To this end, this chapter (a) examines recent developments with a view to explaining both the background and potential future direction of Hungary's economic, political, and social systems; (b) suggests areas where potential opportunities for business cooperation exist, especially in the context of the general directions of East-West trade; and (c) discusses various approaches by which these opportunities can be capitalized upon.

BACKGROUND

Hungary lies in the Carpathian Basin in Middle Europe. It has an area of 93,000 square kilometers (about 36,000 square miles). Of its 10.7 million people (1984), almost 20% (2.1 million) live in Budapest. An additional 36.7% live in 108 other cities and towns of which the largest, Miskolc, is about one-tenth the size of Budapest (population: 212,000). The remaining 44% live in 2,957 villages. The country is divided administratively into 19 counties (*megye*) and the city of Budapest.[1]

As a Central European power, Hungary has been involved in, and has suffered from, many wars during its 1,100-year history. In the aftermath of the First World War, the country lost two-thirds of its territory. As a result, almost one-third of the native Hungarian-speaking population now live in neighboring (mainly socialist) countries. The consequences of that loss were felt in all aspects of life as the entire political, economic, and social structure of the country had to change following the disintegration of the Austro-Hungarian Empire.

After World War II Hungary became a Republic (1946) and then a People's Republic (1949). In spite of significant economic and social progress in the early postwar years, the transformation of the political and socioeconomic systems also brought about tension and eventually unrest which culminated in the tragic events of 1956 when Russian troops quelled what the U.S.S.R. officially termed, "the Hungarian Counterrevolution." These caused severe material and personal losses to the population and influenced the nature of subsequent developments.

The change in political power following the events of 1956 resulted in the evolution of new perspectives on and approaches to managing the country. The Hungarian Laborers Party (Communist party) was replaced by the Hungarian Socialist Workers Party (HSWP) which, under the leadership of Janos Kadar, began a reform process that continues to this day. For the purposes of this discussion, it is necessary to highlight three key elements in the conceptual background that have had a significant impact on the changing character of economic management in Hungary.

First, the country's leadership decided to depart from the Communist society model as proposed by the classics of Marxism, concentrating instead on the construction of a "socialist society" which is considered to be an attainable goal within the foreseeable future. The "communist" model places emphasis on such elements as state ownership of the means of production and trade, central planning, and common ownership accompanied by centrally determined distribution of goods. By contrast, "socialism" accepts the concept of private ownership except in certain essential sectors, and permits the functioning of market forces — albeit within the context of national planning with the objective of achieving overall social justice. The adoption of the socialist model was formalized during the 1972 amendments to Hungary's constitution of 1949.

Second, under socialism, commodity, monetary, and market forces are recognized as important and as having a decisive role to play in economic activity. This emphasis makes it necessary to reexamine many of the earlier hypotheses on the basis of which economic leadership was exercised. The principal task of economic science and of practical economic leadership is now seen as determining the appropriate *market* mechanisms and tools which fit the socialist society model.

Finally, it is recognized that economic and political life are interrelated. Therefore, changes in the political sphere may be necessary in order to enhance industrial innovation and creativity and to ensure the effective and efficient functioning of the marketplace.

Many of the elements of this emerging philosophy were incorporated in the "New Economic Mechanism" (NEM), a comprehensive reform program proclaimed in 1968. Both political and economic leaders in Hungary recognize that only initial steps have been taken in the desired direction since that time, and that compromises have been and will continue to be made in order to maintain social stability and to avoid disruptive swings in the economy. Caution is necessary especially since the period 1968-1988 was characterized by three- to five-year cycles of economic success and economic difficulty, reflecting international economic conditions as well as policy changes and experimentation in the domestic market.

Nonetheless, the overall direction has been one of progress. A series of new goals and methods, proclaimed since 1984, go well beyond those established in the reform program of 1968. These sketch out the main items on the government's agenda until the end of the 1980s and into the next decade. Although the relevant aspects of this program will be referred to in more detail later in this chapter, it seems useful to summarize its main objectives here. These include reform in banking, establishing company interests in capital formation, introducing a uniform and general personal taxation system, encouraging the independence of firms, and establishing the preconditions for converting the Forint, Hungary's national currency, into a ''hard'' currency. (U.S. $1 = approximately 50 Ft.)

INTERNATIONAL INFLUENCES AFFECTING HUNGARY

A de facto open economy and membership in the Council of Mutual Economic Assistance (CMEA, see Table 3) are the two key international influences that have affected Hungary's economic progress in the post-World War II period. The country's small size in terms of land area and population, its geographic position, a relative shortage in raw materials, and other factors combine to give foreign trade a decisive and increasing role. At the same time, membership in the CMEA defines or affects both internal policies as well as Hungary's trade relations with Western countries.

External Trade

Unlike the policy direction toward autarky and self-sufficiency which characterized the period to the 1950s, the importance of foreign trade in the economy has been increasing since the 1960s. Exports now account for more than 40% of Gross Domestic Product (GDP), a figure comparable to those of many West European countries (the EC average is 25%). Table 1 shows Hungary's export, import, and GDP growth for the period 1970-1985. The relatively even growth of exports in current prices since 1975 has been significantly exceeded by the growth of exports in real terms, as shown in the same table. The discrepancy is due to the deterioration in the Terms of Trade (changes in export vs. import prices), because of which Hungary "lost" roughly the equivalent of one year's GDP between 1974 and 1984.

Significant change can also be observed in the commodity structure of foreign trade. This is shown in Table 2. Over the past 50 years, the share of machinery, manufactured consumer goods, and raw and semifinished products in exports has increased while the relative importance of food products has decreased dramatically. A similar shift, albeit less pronounced, is observed in regard to imports. These shifts in external trade occurred in parallel with a high volume of domestic food production. In a nutshell, Hungary has moved from a backward, primarily agrarian country to an industrialized country at a medium level of development.

The U.S.S.R. and other CMEA members are Hungary's primary foreign trade partners. Traditionally, trade between Hungary and the U.S.S.R. has been concentrated heavily in a handful of sectors.

Table 1
GDP, Exports, and Imports, 1970-1984

Year	GDP (bFt)	Exports Value (bFt)	Exports Volume Index	Imports Value (mFt)	Imports Volume Index	Exports -to-GDP (%)
1970	332.5	100.2	100	N.A.	100	30.1
1975	481.5	198.4	157	N.A.	142	41.2
1980	718.5	281.0	220	299.9	172	39.1
1981	774.2	299.4	226	314.3	173	38.7
1982	847.9	324.5	243	324.8	173	38.3
1983	896.3	374.1	266	365.0	180	41.7
1984	978.7	414.0	281	390.0	180	42.3

Legend: bFt - billion Forints (U.S. $1 = approx. 50 Ft)

Source: Statistical Pocket Book of Hungary

Table 2
Commodity Structure of Foreign Trade

Sector	Imports		Exports	
	1938	1984	1938	1984
Materials, energy	72	67	21	38
Machinery	11	16	9	25
Manufactured consumer goods	9	10	10	14
Food	8	7	60	23
Total	100	100	100	100

Source: Statistical Pocket Book of Hungary

Almost half of Hungary's exports to the U.S.S.R. consist of only 20 commodities, and one-fourth of the total is accounted for by the top-five product groups (buses, spare automobile parts, medicines, apples, and women's shoes). On the other hand, and in spite of some decreases in recent years, imports from the U.S.S.R. are heavily concentrated in mining and energy products and building materials, which account for about 60% of the total.

The share of industrialized and developing capitalist countries in Hungary's foreign trade is increasing. As shown in Table 3, the socialist countries' share decreased from about 65% in the 1970s to 53% by 1984. The origins of this shift can be traced back to Hungary's geographic position and to its traditionally close economic links with West Germany. The Federal Republic of Germany is Hungary's second most important trade partner, a position occupied by the German Democratic Republic (GDR) in 1970. The data in Table 3 suggest Hungary's efforts to establish balanced economic relations with a variety of regions in both East and West.

A good example of this is the growth of trade with the ASEAN group and Hong Kong. Although comprising less than 1% of Hungary's external trade in absolute terms, trade with that group of countries more than doubled in the period 1976-1983 alone (Hungarian exports grew from 402 to 983 million Ft., and imports from 1 to 2.2 billion Ft.). Another example is trade with the United States, a country which, despite the great distance involved, is seen

Table 3
Import and Export Share of Main Trade Partners, 1984

Countries (1)	Imports from -		%	Exports to -	
	1970	1984		1970	1984
Ranked by "exports to - 1984"					
U.S.S.R.	*33.2	29.1		34.1	30.1
Federal Republic of Germany	5.3	10.7		6.0	7.4
German Democratic Republic	*10.4	6.4		9.7	5.9
Austria	3.3	5.1		2.8	5.3
Czechoslovakia	*7.9	5.0		8.7	5.2
Poland	*5.8	4.4		6.0	4.2
Yugoslavia	*2.3	3.9		2.5	3.4
Italy	3.8	2.4		5.7	3.3
United States	1.5	2.5		0.4	2.7
Switzerland & Lichtenstein	1.1	2.0		2.8	2.2
France	2.0	1.7		1.1	1.7
Algeria	0.1	0.7		0.1	1.7
Romaina	*2.8	1.8		2.3	1.5
United Kingdom	2.2	1.8		1.1	1.5
Bulgaria	*2.0	1.4		1.2	1.4
Iraq	0.1	0.1		0.3	1.4
The Netherlands	1.3	1.3		1.1	1.1
Iran	0.6	2.2		0.5	1.0
Libya	0.0	2.7		0.2	1.0
Cuba	*0.2	0.2		0.4	0.9
People's Republic of China	0.7	0.6		0.8	0.8
Sweden	0.9	1.0		0.9	0.7
Brazil	0.8	3.1		0.4	0.5
Belgium & Luxembourg	0.9	1.0		0.0	0.5
Finland	0.5	0.7		0.4	0.5
Japan	0.6	1.1		0.1	0.4
India	1.0	0.3		1.0	0.3
CMEA Total (2)	64.6	52.2		64.9	52.6

Notes: (1) The table shows only the main countries in Hungary's external trade. In 1984 Hungary imported from 103 and exported to 142 countries.

(2) The Council for Mutual Economic Assistance (CMEA) includes the Soviety Union, Bulgaria, Czechoslovakia, the German Democratic Republic (East Germany), Hungary, Poland, Romania, Cuba, Mongolia, and Vietnam. Yugoslavia is a special-status member. Finland, Mexico, Iraq, Angola, Ethiopia, North Korea, Afganistan, and Laos hold observer status or are otherwise contractually linked with the Council. The sum of Hungary's trade with the CMEA includes only those countries that are marked with an asterisk, above.

Source: Statistical Pocket Book of Hungary

as offering great trade potential for Hungary. Trade expansion was made possible when the U.S. granted Hungary "most favored nation" status in the late 1970s. This was followed by measures reinforcing confidence between the two countries, such as the strengthening of cultural ties and exchanges, the return by the U.S. of the Hungarian coronation jewels to Budapest in 1978, and the issuing by Hungary of commemorative stamps following the Challenger space shuttle disaster in January, 1986.

Influences on Economic and Trade Growth

Hungary has participated in the General Agreement on Tariffs and Trade (GATT) since 1975. The GATT provides for "most favored nation" status and reciprocal tariff concessions in trade among its members. However, Hungary's simultaneous membership in the CMEA means that trading with the West is often subject to general restrictions addressed to socialist countries. These range from the availability of credit to trade in high technology products, and often act as significant barriers to further trade growth. When added to other trade obstacles, such as the European Community's (EC) external import barriers or the current wave of protectionism in the U.S., these restrictions engender a frustration which echoes similar feelings that are frequently encountered in the West. For example, Tibor Melega, Hungary's Deputy Minister of Foreign Trade, has said,

> We think that our participation in the work of GATT has been useful, though . . . our most important Western partner, the European Community, has lagged much behind [our] expectations. . . . Based on political considerations, several countries curb the export of certain high technologies to the CMEA countries. [Hungarian] delegates in the EC grasp every opportunity to point out that [these] are harmful, senseless and besides, they cause nervousness and unnecessary tensions. (Benedek, 1986)

Furthermore, since imports are heavily concentrated in raw materials and energy resources, the international energy price increases between the early 1970s and early 1980s have had a particularly serious negative effect on Hungary's economy. The continuous deterioration in the Terms of Trade since 1975 made it necessary to increase real exports in order to balance the higher price of the same volume of imports. As this was not sufficient to keep the economy in balance, Hungary's economic policy during the 1970s followed the approach chosen by many other countries: it tried to fill the gap with external loans.

By 1988, however, the debt burden had increased to an extent (U.S. $16 billion) that made economic policy changes necessary. Besides unfavorable world market conditions, which were made even worse by the second oil price explosion of the late 1970s, domestic economic growth and the rising need for imports were not accompanied by the necessary advances in the structure of domestic industry. In addition, the "cooling" in East-West political relations at the beginning of the 1980s (e.g., Poland, Afghanistan) resulted in freezing the channels of credit for Hungary. As only a small part of the capital flowing into the country was working capital as the rest had to be used to balance the trade deficit, it became increasingly necessary to restrict imports and commence an offensive in exports.

This new economic policy had to be supported by a variety of measures. Among other initiatives, in 1982 Hungary sought and obtained membership in the International Monetary Fund (IMF) and the World Bank. Of special importance was the association with the World Bank, which was seen as one way of partially compensating for the shortage of direct credit. This association was followed by an intense (and successful) bidding activity by Hungarian enterprises which, because of their capital shortage, would have been unable to compete in some markets, especially in developing countries (Huszti, 1984). For example, Hungary participated in seven World Bank projects in 1985 alone; this resulted in direct loans of U.S. $668 million from the bank itself, and an additional U.S. $1.1 billion in long-term credit from international commercial banks. This intensive involvement in international projects reduced the need to impose more drastic restrictions on imports which would likely inflict the concomitant hardship on the population that other countries had to experience (e.g., Turkey, Rumania).

POLITICAL AND LEGAL SYSTEMS

The political tendencies toward overcentralization during the 1950s affected all aspects of life and resulted in hindering economic and political reform. This was perhaps inevitable, since the transition to a new system that would replace capitalism involved a sudden liquidation of the old political structure coupled with a naturally gradual evolution of the new one.

In orthodox (or dogmatic) Marxism, the acceptability of ideas, concepts, and policies is evaluated in absolute terms against the texts of Marxist classics. Orthodox Marxism still numbers several supporters in Hungary, which reflects the reality of philosophical debate that is both understandable and necessary when one considers that socialism is one of the major enterprises of mankind. Generally, however, following 40 years of experience with socialism, the prevailing thought is that effective economic management can evolve only if socialist goals are viewed in the context of prevailing socioeconomic conditions and of scientific or technological know-how. Stated differently, the earlier system is not viewed as unchangeable or eternal. An increasing number of Hungarians are taking the proverb, *de omnibus dubitandum* ("everything should be doubted"), allegedly written on Marx's own desk, more and more seriously.

As a result, long-term goals, such as the primary role of social ownership of the means of production and the reasonable limitation of personal ownership, are seen in the context of undesirable extremes. Just as the exaggerated leveling of incomes can limit the constructive intellectual forces of society, so can the exaggerated differentiation of incomes lead to the unequal acquisition of goods, inducing such tensions that would require the intervention of the political system.

Political and Social Institutions

Unlike some other socialist countries such as the GDR or Poland, there has been only one political party in Hungary since 1948; this is the Hungarian Socialist Workers' Party (HSWP), with over 850,000 members. However, parallel with the national consolidation process marked by the advent of Janos Kadar in 1956, and with the overall hegemony of the party, the role of other institutions has been increasing since 1956. Two political and two social organizations, which act as the pivot points around which Hungarian political, economic, and social life revolves, should be mentioned here.

The political organizations are the Hungarian Communist Youth Union (HCYU) and the Patriotic Front. The HCYU represents the interests of young people to state organs and educates them in regard to national goals and ideology. Although the number of active HCYU members, at almost 800,000, is still large, it has tended to decline in recent years partly because of the rise of new groups (such as university students' associations) that appeal more directly to their members' interests. As a result, the decisive and in some ways monopolistic role of the HCYU has been changing. The Patriotic Front is the mass political movement which aims to unite and mobilize all Hungarian citizens toward attaining national goals. It is the main vehicle through which nonparty members can become active in political life.

The trade union and the Chamber of Business (roughly equivalent to Chambers of Commerce in the West) are the two main socioeconomic institutions. The union is organized on sectoral and regional levels and serves the interests of workers at the workplace and in political life. Measures affecting workers cannot be taken without the trade union's approval. While being organizationally independent, the union's mandate is such that it must follow the political and ideological instructions of HSWP. With about 5 million members who comprise almost all wage and salary earners in Hungary, the union is the largest organization in terms of membership. The Hungarian Chamber of Commerce is an official and independent economic organ, empowered to coordinate and represent the interests of its members. Membership in the Chamber is voluntary and comprises about 1,100 companies from all sectors. The Chamber's operations and activities are financed exclusively by membership fees.

Legislative Developments

Hungary lives in a constitutional order. Citizens have equal rights regardless of party affiliation, religion, nationality, or race. Except for functions within the HSWP itself, any position can be filled by nonparty members. Although Parliament plays a less important role in socialist than in capitalist countries, a new electoral law in Hungary has brought changes to this field as well. According to the new law, used for the first time in 1985, a minimum of two candidates must be put up (officially by the Patriotic Front) in every electoral district. Candidates are expected to campaign for themselves, presenting their program for the voters at electoral meetings during which participants can also propose new candidates.

Rivalry among candidates is expected to increase the Parliament's authority. Efforts toward this end have been undertaken since the 1970s. For the time being, the legal system is dominated by low-level legal statutes (decisions of Ministers or Deputy Ministers). To counterbalance this situation, Parliament has taken the initiative to pass a number of important new laws, such as the company act, the commercial act (which includes provisions on consumer protection), and the press act.

Still, the majority of legislation affecting economic life is outdated. Some acts from the 1920s and 1930s, or even dating back to the end of the last century, are still technically in force. Although many of these acts have become de facto invalid with the advent of the socialist economy, they have not been repudiated by law. For example, there can be no bankruptcy in socialist enterprises, yet Hungary still has a bankruptcy act. This has left a void in some important areas of marketplace regulation, since de facto invalid legislation has not been replaced with new legislation.

An example of this void occurred in 1985, when a foreign trade company, Transelektro, had to double its capital base as a result of a newly received license to operate as a trading house. New capital was not available from the central organs or the banks. Transelektro elected to change the firm into a share company, a move which met with substantial difficulties in the short run since the establishment and operation of share companies is regulated by the outdated commercial act of 1875. Formulating a new commercial act has been delayed by the unsolved economic and conceptual problems concerning the operation of shares and of the stock market under the socialist model. There already are some enterprises operating as share companies, and their functioning has been made possible by individual decrees whose provisions do not extend to other firms.

NATIONAL ECONOMIC ENVIRONMENT AND THE STRUCTURE OF INDUSTRY

The reforms of 1968 emphasized enterprise independence, abolished the system of central plan directives, and made profit the main goal of companies. National plans now play only an orienting role in the planning process of the firm. These changes can be understood better if seen as being part of the global shift away from the polar "laissez-faire" versus "state-controlled" forms of national economic management that characterized earlier periods in the development of Western and Eastern countries, respectively.

Researchers suggest that these early models can be defined in terms of economies relying exclusively on either "vertical linkages" between the state and its enterprises, or "horizontal linkages" among firms. Five major economic models have been identified at various points of the continuum defined by these tw·ʼ\ extremes (Samli and Jermacowicz, 1983; also Kornai, 1971).

1. *Authoritative* model: the entire national economy is one enterprise; all aspects of business management are centrally planned and controlled.
2. *Directive* model: reliance on central decision making continues but a small degree of flexibility in inter-firm linkages is allowed.
3. *Mixed-middle* model: plans are still made centrally, but they are now based on input from individual enterprises and other elements of the market.
4. *Integrative* model: the enterprise is the focal point; individual firms make their own plans so long as these reflect the goals and constraints of a national development plan.
5. *Laissez-faire* model: this model relies exclusively on the competitive forces of the marketplace.

Western economies, such as those of the U.S., Canada, Japan, or France, have tended to move from a laissez-faire to an integrative system as governments increasingly see the need to intervene and control market forces through regulation or the development of national industrial policies. Eastern economies also are moving toward the integrative model through reform policies aimed at correcting the inefficiencies of centrally controlled economic systems. In the above continuum, East Germany and Czechoslovakia have been placed between the "directive" and "mixed-middle" systems, while Poland, Hungary, and Yugoslavia (in ascending order) are hypothesized to be closer to the "integrative" model (Samli and Jermacowicz, 1983). This approach is a useful basis as a background to the remainder of this discussion.

The National Economy

Hungary is relatively poor in raw materials. The country has significant ore reserves only in bauxite. Aluminum production, however, covers only a small part of domestic demand. Thus, Hungary relies heavily on imports for its resource needs, of which a large proportion is supplied by the Soviet Union. According to the pricing formula used in trade transactions among CMEA countries (the so-called Bucarest Principle), prices are set in relation to world market rates over the preceding five years, rather than in relation to current costs. Among other factors, this formula resulted in temporarily shielding Hungary from the price fluctuations that rocked the world market during the 1970s. Once these started to be felt, however, they served to highlight some of the country's internal economic weaknesses.

As a result of these forces, economic debate in Hungary currently focuses on the dilemma of pursuing short-term economic stability versus accepting some instability in view of the need to achieve larger social goals. Key goals include, for example, reducing the importance of energy- and materials-intensive products in the domestic economy, reforming the underlying structure of industry, and improving productivity and efficiency in manufacturing. To achieve these goals, it is recognized that the natural regulating role of the market has to be strengthened, and that production methods which are out of step with modern technologies must be phased out.

Notwithstanding temporary fluctuations, the production of national income is continuously expanding. As shown in Table 4, manufacturing plays a major and increasingly important role in generating national income. Although the agricultural sector continues to be significant, future development will clearly be determined by the extent of advancement and progress in manufacturing. The 7th Five-Year Plan, covering the period 1986-1990, includes clear provisions to increase the share of industrial production in national income.

As with every ranking of national priorities, it must be noted that this emphasis on industrial development is also a source of debate. The forced development of industry, and especially of heavy industry, which characterized the early period of socialist development, had several beneficial effects but also caused disproportions and inconsistencies in the development of the national economy. For example, much of the destruction suffered by Hungary in World War II, during which the country lost some 40% of its national wealth, was concentrated on communication and transportation systems. In spite of this, investments in infrastructure have lagged behind others. This has led to chronic shortages and problems in certain key sectors, such as the telephone and telecom systems, which now often act as impediments to modern business activity. Rebuilding or modernizing these systems is now a key goal in Hungary.

Table 4
Sectoral Shares In Production of National Income

Sector	1975	1980 (%)	1983
Manufacturing	41.6	44.2	46.6
Construction	11.5	12.4	12.0
Agriculture and Forrestry	21.1	18.6	18.2
Transport, Post, Telecomm.	9.6	9.4	9.0
Trade	15.2	14.3	13.2
Water Works and Supplies	0.6	0.7	0.4
Other Materials Activity	0.3	0.4	0.6
Total	100.0	100.0	100.0

Source: Statistical Pocketbook of Hungary

Industrial Structure

In line with the integrative model described above, reforms in Hungary rest on the premise that socialist economic goals can be reached through indirect economic regulators (e.g., price, credit, currency, interest, wage policy, etc.), not much unlike the policy bases of the West. However, the need for stability also resulted in a time lag between marketplace and institutional reform. Ensuring a smooth transition from central planning to indirect economic management necessitated the continuing presence, at least in the short term, of highly centralized (and therefore powerful) institutions. Thus, for example, the Ministries of Light Industry, Heavy Industry, and Metallurgy and Machine Industry were merged into one, and their combined staff was reduced by one-half only in the early 1980s — or about one-and-a-half decades after the economic reforms were first proclaimed. The new Ministry of Industry is better able to formulate industrial policies in the context of the principle of company independence.

Another manifestation of the need for stability was the fact that several companies were encouraged or directed to merge, on the assumption that larger economic units would be easier to control in the early phases of the transition to company independence. Along with the continuing influence of the old system of central planning, and in spite of the spirit of the 1968 reforms which emphasized decentralization, this resulted in a wave of mergers during the 1960s and 1970s. Given that industry was highly centralized to begin with, the share of large companies thus reached very high levels.

The number of state industrial companies and industrial cooperatives in Hungary declined from 1,633 in 1970 to 1,360 in 1980. These organizations form the "socialist sector" of the economy, which accounts for the vast majority of industrial activity. Although concentration can result in both ease of control and economies of scale, it eventually came to be seen as a factor that was hindering the development of a market orientation in companies and their managers. In recognition of this potential problem, new legislation was passed in the 1980s making it possible to establish new enterprises and to break up some large companies into smaller units. As a result, almost 600 new companies have been formed since 1980.

Of these, 400 are independent and the remaining 200 are subsidiaries of preexisting concerns. This decentralization resulted in strengthening the role of medium-sized companies with 800 to 1,500 employees. Still, in the socialist sector 30% of all companies employ more than 2,000 workers. The largest producer's share (in terms of output) in each of 460 main commodity groups is at least 51%. In all but a few sectors, the two largest producers account for about 75% of output (Csillag, 1986).

Competition and the Emerging Organizational Culture

In addition to addressing questions of industrial concentration, the new legislation included measures aimed at enhancing competition and the independence of firms. Hungarian companies fall in three categories: state-owned companies (involved mainly in manufacturing), cooperatives (found mostly in agriculture), and private enterprises (active mostly in retailing, catering, and certain intermediate manufacturing sectors).

At this time, and in spite of a growing trend in this direction, only 5% of national income originates from the private sector. However, in certain branches of the economy, the private sector plays a determining role. For example, the number of private retail dealers doubled from 10,229 in 1970 to 19,293 in 1983. Most of this increase represented significant growth in the number of catering establishments and clothing outlets (by 491 and 494%, respectively, during the same period). The emergence of two new forms of private enterprise during the 1980s, the Economic Working Communities (EWC) and Enterprise Economic Working Communities (EEWC), should also be noted here. These are groups of 2 to 30 people who either operate within an existing company and engage in manufacturing by renting equipment from it (EWCs), or operate as completely independent enterprises. By 1988, there were almost 10,000 EWCs and 20,000 EEWCs.

Changes in the structure of industry play an important role in promoting competition, but the newly introduced forms of decentralized decision-making are just as important, if not more so. According to reforms implemented in 1985, management decisions are now made at the company level by "Enterprise Councils" in the case of large and medium-sized enterprises, and by "General Assemblies" in small ones. (An exception to this system is the management of "enterprises under public administration control"; these are public utilities and companies in other sectors of special importance, such as energy.) Enterprise Councils consist of representatives from the management and worker groups, whereas General Assemblies consist of all persons working in the company. The authority of these management groups extends over most of the strategic and operational decision-making spectrum, including mergers, loans, human resource management (including dismissals), investment plans, and foreign trade.

The main driving force behind this change is the imperative of transferring the locus of decision-making to the point where both the necessary information and the decision-maker's interests coincide. Although this system of management may still appear cumbersome by Western standards, it represents a major departure from past practices in the socialist context. Functions such as those mentioned above were previously in the hands of the supervising ministry. In practice, the operation of "self-governing" companies represents a transfer of decision-making authority from the company's owner (i.e., the state) to its management. To further enhance the positive effects of decentralization on competition, the new system also contains provisions for the establishment of bonus plans for managers and profit-sharing plans for workers. A good indication of the emerging emphasis on authority and responsibility at the individual manager's level is the publication in 1986, for the first time in Hungary, of a "Who's Who"-type roster of Hungarian business managers.

SCIENCE AND TECHNOLOGY

The effective use of human resources is a decisive factor of development, especially in a country that is poor in raw materials. Hungary possesses an adequate pool of technical and professional knowledge and expertise, especially when this is viewed in relation to the country's medium level of industrial development.

In several sectors, Hungarian products are at or near world levels of technological advancement. In the international trade of intellectual products there are sectors where Hungary is a net exporter. This is the case, for example, in the pharmaceutical industry, where more than half of domestic production is exported. In addition to exports of original products ranging from medicines to toiletries and cosmetics, the capabilities of Hungarian companies are reflected in the growth of contract research work on behalf of Western firms. For example, Nattermann of West Germany commissions part of its phytopathological and herbological research to Hungary through LICENCIA, a Hungarian company specializing in innovation management and the commercial exploitation of inventions (Licencia, 1985). Along similar lines, there is a growing participation of Hungarian consulting engineers and workers in international engineering. Firms such as UVATERV are involved in large-scale turnkey projects such as Calcutta's underground railway system or bridge-building in Egypt ("Among the first . . .," 1985).

A significant part of Hungarian production is accounted for by so-called "commission work," which became widespread in the 1970s and involves cooperation between mainly West European and Hungarian companies in the clothing, textiles, and related sectors. In the early years, this form of subcontracting took mostly the form of clothes manufacturing by Hungarian companies from precut fabrics, accessories, and designs provided by the foreign partner.

With time, commission work often resulted in technology transfer and a larger involvement on the part of Hungarian firms. (An example of this, involving a Hungarian plastics company and a West German manufacturer of suitcases, is detailed by Kovats, 1984.)

Technology is supported by high expenditures on scientific and applied research, which stand at about 3% of national income. Research efforts are coordinated by the Hungarian Academy of Sciences, the National Committee for Technical Development, and various special-purpose institutes. In an effort to increase the share of applied research and make the overall research and development effort more responsive to market needs, there is a trend toward turning the research institutes into independent enterprises and encouraging them to commercialize their findings as soon as possible.

Although there is progress in technology, the ability to manage innovation effectively is lagging behind. An obvious example of the results of this discrepancy is Rubik's Cube. The product itself became a symbol of Hungarian intellectual innovation, but the management of the process (from production to distribution and trademark protection), following the invention itself, showed many defects. The lack of indigenous marketing know-how is shown by the fact that a significant part of the profit was realized by producers in the Far East. According to one estimate, over one-half of the 100 million cubes sold by 1982 were unauthorized editions. To avoid a recurrence, worldwide distribution rights for "Rubik's Magic" (Erno Rubik's new puzzle which appeared in 1986) were assigned to an experienced international marketer, Matchbox International Ltd. Matchbox took several steps to discourage pirated versions including global patenting, extensive licensing to well-established companies, and the identification of each puzzle with Rubik's own signature.

As a side note, Erno Rubik provides a good example of present trends in Hungary, a country which adheres to socialism but also encourages entrepreneurship. According to a Canadian magazine, Rubik went from a $200/month salary as a teacher in Budapest to becoming a millionnaire who ". . . owns three cars [and a] large home [with] a basement swimming pool and sauna . . . [and who can] keep one third of his income in convertible currency that can be spent abroad" (Mclean's, 1986).

A variety of approaches are being utilized to counteract the relative absence of marketing skills. In addition to encouraging creativity and innovation through decentralization in company management, these approaches can be classified in two broad categories: cooperation with foreign firms, and the domestication of selected market functions.

Perhaps the best illustration of the first of these approaches in action is the international success of Ikarus buses, which can be found in 50 countries ranging from the Soviet Union and Czechoslovakia to the U.S., Canada, China, Sweden, Greece, Turkey, and several countries in the Third World. Ikarus Body and Coach Building Works, the largest manufacturer of its kind in Europe, designs and assembles or produces buses both domestically and abroad. Its international cooperative agreements cover such areas as marketing, postpurchase service, the supply of component parts, or local assembly at the destination point. Foreign partners include Volvo of Sweden, Crown Coach in Los Angeles, and Turk Otomotiv Industrileri of Turkey. Partly because of this extensive international network, Ikarus has been able to penetrate various foreign markets and to develop and maintain technological leadership in bus design and manufacturing. Fully 90% of its production in Hungary is exported. Its highly successful articulated buses account for about one-third of total production (about 4,000 of 13,000 units per annum), but emphasis is also placed in manufacturing specialized buses that are in high demand around the world. These include, for example, the "mobile grocery," the "X-ray bus," an opthalmological laboratory (which includes a mobile eye-surgery unit), and the "conference bus."

It is interesting to note that these buses were developed in response to unique demand conditions in various countries. For example, mobile medical units are sold mainly where standard hospital facilities, especially in rural areas, are inadequate. By contrast, the conference bus is for customers in developed countries. In addition to standard features such as air-conditioning and a washroom, it is equipped with a conference table, swivel chairs with writing boards, table lamps, audiovisual recording and playback facilities, a bar, and a pantry with serving table ("Design . . .," 1985; "Conference . . .," 1985).

The effort to domesticate market functions revolves around programs which encourage Hungarian companies to become more closely involved in industrial design and the management of innovation. This thrust is supported, for example, by:

- the Design Center of the Hungarian Chamber of Business, which, among a variety of educational and other activities, operates a retail store that functions as a test market for designed consumer goods;
- Licencia, the above-mentioned company whose mandate was expanded from a "patent registry" to innovation management; and,
- the spreading use of computers in business applications. Between 1980-1984, the number of mainframe installations grew

from 684 to 1,210; of these, 58% were domestically produced, 18% were imported from socialist countries, and 24% were imported from the West. Perhaps more significantly, during the same five-year period the number of mini- and microcomputers in operation grew from 588 to 10,236. In contrast to the origin of distribution of mainframe installations, domestic production represented only 21% of this total and imports from socialist countries were only 16%, whereas imports from nonsocialist countries accounted for 63%. (*Statistical Pocket Book of Hungary*)

SOCIAL AND CULTURAL ENVIRONMENT

Before World War I, Hungary was essentially a multiethnic society. The population shifts and changes in Hungary's land after World War I resulted in what is today a practically homogeneous population where the proportion of citizens of non-Hungarian ethnicity stands at only 3 to 4%. The country's unique culture is dominated by the fact that the Hungarian language is fundamentally different from the major language families of Europe, having some resemblance only to Finnish (with which it is grouped into the Finno-Ungric group of languages).

The relative literary and communicative isolation engendered by the uniqueness of the language has not resulted in a narrow-minded culture. The most talented politicians, artists, scientists, and poets have always kept a close eye on, and sensitively reacted to, international changes (which meant, more often than not, developments in Western Europe), and writers and poets have traditionally played a significant role in progressive movements.

The knowledge of foreign languages has played and continues to play a decisive role in both cultural and economic life. Latin, and later German, was the official language of Hungary for centuries. At the present time Russian is compulsory throughout the 12-year school system, and an additional foreign language is compulsory in the four years of secondary schooling. Due to the traditional German-Austrian-Hungarian ties, German is the most common foreign language learned after Russian, although the use of English is becoming more widespread among the younger generations. French, Italian, and Spanish are also commonly found.

The importance of foreign languages is growing not only because of Hungary's growing international economic ties, but also because of the growth of international tourism since the 1960s. The Hungarian government has traditionally emphasized that political tensions should not be allowed to affect East-West economic and cultural relations, and has in fact expressed its aspiration to strengthen such relations. The data in Table 5 reflect this policy. The international economic recession and political tensions of the late 1970s and early 1980s had a dampening effect on the growth of tourism, resulting in a decline in the number of visitors to Hungary from its peak of 17 million in 1978. However, this decline was accounted for by visits to and from socialist countries, while the number of visitors from nonsocialist countries to Hungary, and of Hungarians to nonsocialist countries, continued growing.

As a consequence of programs undertaken after World War II, 98% of the population is literate. Education is practically free from primary school to university. The number of undergraduate students attending university grew from 80,500 in 1970 to 99,900 in 1983 but growth in individual disciplines is uneven. Table 6 shows that enrollment growth has occurred mainly in service professions, such as teaching and law. Enrollment in economics and medicine has increased, but in direct proportion with overall growth in university attendance. Interest in engineering, agriculture, and the natural sciences has declined. Finally, it is interesting to note that enrollment in night and correspondence courses has increased faster than full-time attendance, suggesting a rising interest in continuing education.

These data reflect a variety of factors which affect the preferences of young people in Hungary, thereby providing an indication of the prevailing value hierarchy in the social environment. Referring to Table 6, such factors, and the fields of study they affect, are the present economic environment (e.g., economics, law), a growing standard of living (e.g., law, teaching), a shift in emphasis from production to marketing (e.g., natural sciences, engineering, economics), and prevailing social and political values (e.g., arts and philosophy, fine arts). Remuneration levels also play a major influ-

Table 5
International Tourism

	1975	1980	1983	1984
1. Foreign travelers to Hungary		Number of visits		
Total	9,404	13,996	10,463	13,429
From socialist countries	8,238	12,053	7,521	9,910
From non-socialist countries	1,166	1,944	2,942	3,519
Tourists	4,995	9,413	6,764	8,731
From socialist countries	4,064	8,189	5,221	6,904
From non-socialist countries	931	1,224	1,543	1,827
		Change index: 1975 = 100		
Total	100	149	111	143
From socialist countries	100	146	91	120
From non-socialist countries	100	167	252	302
2. Hungarians travelling abroad		Number of visits		
Total	3,477	5,164	4,754	5,380
To socialist countries	3,225	4,694	4,196	4,755
To non-socialist countries	255	470	558	625
Tourists	3,153	4,975	3,922	4,602
To socialist countries	2,938	4,549	3,447	4,032
To non-socialist countries	215	426	478	570
		change index: 1975 = 100		
Total	100	149	137	155
To socialist countries	100	146	130	147
To non-socialist countries	100	184	219	245

Source: Statistical Pocket Book of Hungary

encing role; engineering is one example of a field of study where, partly due to ideological and political influences, remuneration levels are comparatively low and are seen as nonsatisfactory.

Rising education levels and the increasing interaction between Hungary and other nations through trade, tourism, and the spreading of foreign languages have played a key role in bringing about

Table 6
Undergraduates in Higher Education (Universities & Colleges)

Subjects	Students				
(Ranked by 1983/1970 Growth Index)	Number		Percentage		Index 1983/1970
	1970	1983	1970	1983	
Teaching	13,988	27,268	17	27	195
Law	3,544	6,357	4	6	179
Medicine & Related	7,378	11,212	9	11	152
Economics	8,290	11,335	10	11	137
Arts & Philosophy	4,250	5,595	5	6	132
Veterinary Science	452	559	1	1	124
Natural Sciences	4,569	4,468	6	4	98
Engineering	29,464	25,673	37	26	87
Agriculture	7,319	5,381	9	5	74
Fine Arts	1,292	2,017	2	2	56
Total	80,536	99,865	100	100	124
Of which, Day:	53,821	62,944	67	63	117
Evening & Correspondence:	26,715	36,921	33	37	138

Source: Statistical Pocket Book of Hungary

changes in consumer behavior. Interestingly, these changes started occurring in the 1960s — that is, at a time when Western economists, marketing experts, politicians, and the youth were highly critical of aspects of Western life such as materialism, corporate social responsibility, advertising, and product obsolescence. At exactly the same point in time, Hungary's leaders were preparing to begin the reform process which placed greater emphasis on the forces of the marketplace. Naturally, there was serious debate in Hungary about the possible detrimental effects of Western approaches to economic management, of which the West itself was critical.

Notwithstanding the potential dangers, and with some hesitation, the economic leadership accepted the view that growing consumer expectations could become a healthy driving force for the economy. As a result, domestic production of manufactured consumer products grew substantially, and the share of consumer goods in imports from the West increased. Western products which are available in the Hungarian market, whether through imports or local manufacturing under license, are representative of such companies as Nestlé, Pepsi-Cola, Shweppes, Fiat, Siemens, and AEG. An increasing amount of Western consumer goods is imported by Hungarians returning from tourist trips abroad, as well.[2] The increasing availability of and ability to purchase consumer products, are shown by the varying rates of growth in certain key consumption categories. Using 1960 as a base year (100), per capita consumption in 1983, in constant prices, was 147 for foodstuffs, 258 for beverages and tobacco, 269 for manufactured goods, and 266 for services. One in three Hungarian households owns a car, and there are high saturation levels in such products as radios, television sets, and refrigerators. Table 7 provides selected statistics on consumption, together with a range of statistics on cultural and social life in Hungary.

AREAS AND RESOLUTION OF CONFLICTS

Since 1957 the internal political situation in Hungary has been stable. Nonetheless, some conflict between goals and means was inevitable in light of the ambitious economic growth objectives envisaged in the reform package of 1968. In essence, Hungary attempted a market-based experiment within a socialist ideological context. As with any experiment, this resulted in a number of mistaken decisions. A particularly important set of decisions had to be made in 1973, when growing public expectations for expansion had to be balanced against the worsening international economic climate. Although some support for a downward revision of expansion goals was present, Hungary opted for continuing with a growth strategy since it was felt that the majority would not have supported policies resulting in the stagnation or even reduction of public consumption.

By the late 1970s, however, the need for austerity could not be avoided any more and new strategies were developed for the 1980s. By that time, the populace was becoming aware of the fact that development cannot occur without conflict, but also that it is better to make conflict public rather than leave the necessary decisions for its resolution to a small privileged group. In other words, a social

Table 7
Selected Household and Cultural Statistics, 1982

1. Household (h/h) Expenditures

Type of h/h[1]:	Working Class	Farmers	Two-Income h/h	Non-Maunal Workers	Inactive
a. Number h/h observed	3,841	1,097	761	1,454	1,365
b. Members per h/h	3.3	3.3	3.9	3.0	1.7
c. Personal expenditure	Monthly average				
Total forints per h/h	9,442	9,158	10,302	11,267	4,457
Total forints Per capita	2,844	2,750	2,657	3,781	2,685
d. Per capita personal	Percentage Expenditure				
Foodstuffs	33.2	34.6	34.5	26.5	41.5
Beverages & tobacco	9.9	10.5	10.6	7.2	10.4
Clothing	10.0	9.8	11.2	10.1	7.5
Real Estate[2]	17.5	19.9	16.6	17.1	16.5
Furnishings h/h equip.	8.3	8.1	8.6	9.3	8.3
Health, physical, culture	2.3	1.8	1.8	2.9	3.4
Transport, health, telecom.	8.8	8.2	8.5	13.0	4.3
Culture, recreation, enter.	6.8	4.8	5.0	10.7	5.3
Other	3.2	2.3	3.2	3.0	2.8
Total	100.0	100.0	100.0	100.0	100.0
e. Stock per 100 h/h	Number				
Refrigerators	96	91	93	106	82
Washing machines	96	97	100	100	81
Vacuum cleaners	86	74	77	101	60
Passanger cars	33	27	31	54	6
Motorcycles	25	41	45	18	8
Radios	156	135	148	194	124
Televisions	111	103	109	121	89

2. Culture Statistics (000s)	1970	1980	1982
Library subscribers			
– local council libraries	1,583	1,601	1,605
– trade union libraries	642	621	610
Museum visitors	n.a.	16,217	17,717
Cinema admissions	80,000	61,000	70,000
Theatre admissions	5,591	5,635	6,133
Concert admissions	828	1,205	1,234
TV license holders	1,769	2,766	2,838
Members of sports clubs	1,115	1,172	1,205

Notes: [1] The terms used in Hungary for the household categories are "annual laborers", "co-operative peasantry", "households with dual income", "intellectuals", and "inactive", depending on the principal wage earner.
[2] Includes maintenance, purchase, construction.
Source: Statistical Pocket Book of Hungary

consensus has emerged that the attainment of national goals necessitates input from, and interaction among, the various participants in public life, politics, and the workplace. This emerging view explains in large part the tendencies toward decentralization of decision-making in both the economic and political spheres.

The continuing adjustments to various aspects of life in Hungary, made necessary by the quest for a rather unique economic model, can be illustrated best through a brief discussion of four key problem areas.

Material incentives and private ownership. There is growing acceptance of the views that, (a) material incentives are important in worker motivation and cannot be easily substituted by other approaches to motivation; (b) at least in several trade and service sectors, large enterprises are not necessarily the best solution; and (c) socialist ownership should not mean state ownership exclusively.

These views manifest themselves through political, economic, and cultural measures, as well as in legislation. The independent operation of household plots in agriculture, of the economic working partnerships in services, and of the private sector in commerce suggest the presence of room for flexibility within the socialist system. Generally, the prevailing philosophy seems to be that what is good for the workers cannot be alien to the system. Yet, as might be expected, reform advocates believe that changes are not fast enough, while critics feel that the country has gone "too far" (another way of saying that too many tools and approaches are being borrowed from the West). Along with the 1986 declaration of the Soviet Party Congress concerning the need for "radical reforms," the new policies proclaimed by Soviet First Secretary Mikhail Gorbachev are expected to weaken the arguments of those who oppose reforms in Hungary and to help accelerate the reform process.

The "shortage effect." The relationship between the state and its enterprises under socialism is often characterized by so-called "state paternalism." This condition, coupled with the inefficiencies of central planning, is a main factor leading to the phenomenon of chronic and systemic shortages in the economy. State paternalism suggests that a firm which experiences difficulties, no matter their seriousness, can always expect to get a helping hand from the state. Research has shown that this is a main reason behind the relative lack of sensitivity of socialist enterprises to costs and to the need for improved productivity and modern management practices (Kornai, 1980; Papadopoulos and Beracs, 1985). Conversely, in many cases dynamic and innovative firms do not receive enough support. A significant part of company income is taken away in the form of transfer payments, which can have the effect of penalizing high performers and benefiting weaker ones. In 1983, 56% of the state's revenues came from payments by enterprises and co-operatives, and its budget accounted for 60% of Hungary's GDP. In light of this, the companies rightly complain that this system of transfers dampens innovativeness, initiative, and risk-taking. A variety of new measures, including the decentralization in decision-making and the introduction of the personal income tax, are seen as key steps toward improvements in this area.

Pricing. Since 1980, domestic prices are adjusted by taking into account corresponding price levels in Western markets. For firms that export to the West, this means that profitability is calculated on the basis of what they would have obtained "under realistic (Western) market conditions." This principle appears rational on the surface, as an attempt at making domestic industry more responsive to world market conditions. In practice, it is a source of tension and profitability calculations are often "adjusted" through negotiation (and occasionally favoritism) with state organs. This artificial adjustment process has become subject to considerable criticism and several analysts are calling for a "real market system" to replace it.

Furthermore, when it was proclaimed in 1980 this pricing principle reflected government's tendency to change the regulatory system itself whenever the need arises in order to meet social demands or to adapt to changes in external markets. Company managers are critical of this approach since it effectively results in changing the "rules of the game" rather frequently and therefore prevents them from developing effective and consistent long-term plans.

Another price-related area where the potential for conflict exists is in those sectors where prices are set freely by marketplace processes (mainly the vegetable and fruit markets). Prices in such markets often rise to unrealistically high levels, generate unusually high income levels for entrepreneurs, and draw widespread criticism among the populace and in the press. The government has traditionally tried to avoid interfering in these free markets, regulating them, where it can, only through indirect measures.

A good example of conflict resolution in this area, as well as of the increasing emphasis on market forces in Hungary today, is the so-called "tomato war" of 1986. This was "fought" by SKALA, an agro-industrial cooperative organization which is Hungary's second-largest retail department store chain. The price of domestic tomatoes sold by private fruit and vegetable growers had risen to artificially high levels (about 400 Ft./kilo, or $8/kgr, $3.60/lb; this was 40 times higher than the summer price and five to seven times higher than the winter price in West Germany and Austria). Rather than inviting government action, SKALA used its hard currency reserves and imported tomatoes in order to force down their price. While rival domestic producers protested against this action, it was received very favorably by the public and the media (an interesting and detailed case study of SKALA can be found in Naor, 1988).

Labor and capital markets. When the market concept started making inroads in the regulation of the economy in the 1960s, this extended only to product markets. However, economic research and the failure of several practices that were tried out in the 1970s and early 1980s led to the realization that a real "market" cannot operate without labor and capital markets.

Concerning labor, the pace of economic reforms creates the potential of dislocations. This became the subject of intense criticism which resulted in hindering the reform process itself. Lay-offs, resulting from the liquidation of loss-producing companies, are not accepted without hesitation by a society that is used to, and would like to adhere to, a full-employment status. Unemployment is still relatively unknown, as are its related institutions (e.g., job opportunity offices). Therefore, efforts are being made to adjust this area to the overall direction of the reform process. These include the development of plans aimed at increasing worker mobility through such means as retraining, human resource requirements planning, and the establishment of employment offices.

The process of developing a full capital market, albeit for some undetermined future point in time, has also begun. A significant step in this direction was the reform of the institutional system of credit. Until recently, the National Bank of Hungary (NBH) was essentially the only source of credit for Hungarian enterprises. In addition to the NBH, the entire banking system comprised only three other institutions, each with a specific and specialized mandate: the State Development Bank (infrastructure development), the National Savings Bank (mainly retail services to the public), and the Foreign Trade Bank. Companies could not grant credit to each other on merchandise transactions, and outstanding debts were subject to centrally mandated penalties. Because of the conflicting pressure of having to pursue growth while also having to transfer a large part of their revenues to the government, companies were frequently forced to request loans from NBH. Since the bank also is a state authority, it granted only a limited sum of credits and often did so with little regard to the merit of individual applications. Consequently, many companies were in a perpetual cash-short position.

The credit monopoly of NBH has now been abolished. The function of granting credits was separated from that of a central issuing bank where, naturally, NBH maintained its monopoly and will continue to use monetary policy to regulate the business cycle. In addition to general banks, a number of new specialized banks have been established since 1985. These grant commercial loans and provide venture capital in support of innovations aimed at technological development.

Credit among enterprises has also been allowed. To facilitate credit transactions, the bill of exchange has reappeared in Hungary (these bills are rediscounted by NBH). Capital can also be raised by issuing bonds, although this option is now available only to certain types of companies or for financing community investments; purchasing bonds is open to the public, and interest income from them is tax-free.

In all, Hungary now has eight general banks in addition to the NBH; seven specialized banks; six representative offices of banks from Austria, Italy, France, Yugoslavia, and the U.S.; and several savings cooperatives. In addition, two new banks have been established on a joint venture basis. The Central-European International Bank Ltd. (CIB), with the participation of seven banks from Italy, Austria, West Germany, Japan, France, and Hungary, is an internationally active offshore bank working in convertible currencies around the world (including Hungary itself). Citibank Budapest is an 80-20% joint venture between Citibank and the Central Bank of Exchange and Credit Ltd., a NBH subsidiary. (See Timar, 1985 for a discussion providing useful insights into the key aspects of the new legislation on banking and credit.)

NATIONAL CONTROL OF INTERNATIONAL TRADE

After the nationalizations of 1948-49, foreign trade became a state monopoly. The license to trade was transferred to export-import enterprises whose mandate was strictly defined in sectoral terms. Since each product was expressly assigned to one company, smaller firms could only trade through their licensed, and considerably larger, counterparts. Thus, competition was virtually nonexistent and smaller producers did not always receive the attention and help they needed or deserved.

Only 35 companies held a foreign trade license up to 1956. That number increased slowly after that time to only 136 by 1980, as some manufacturing enterprises were given the right to trade on their respective product groups. Following a large foreign trade deficit in 1978, government policies in the 1980s have been influenced by efforts to balance imports and exports, while remaining within the general spirit of the GATT. Several new measures, including a renewed effort to get more companies involved in exporting, resulted in a surplus trade position since 1982. By 1985, the number of companies involved in imports and exports had risen to 272.

Nonetheless, the original principles of a state monopoly on trade and of "one product, one company" remained in force until 1985. A new regulating system was introduced in 1986. Except for a small number of product groups, the new laws make it possible for every company to obtain the right of individual exports and imports with nonsocialist countries. This represents a major change in the modus operandi of individual firms. In effect, the new legal background introduces to foreign trade the principle of "free choice of partners," which has been in force in domestic commerce since the reforms of 1968. The main purpose of the new legislation is to integrate foreign trade with other forms of economic activity and to enhance competition, in line with the integrative model of economic management.

BUSINESS OPPORTUNITIES

As previously mentioned, starting with the NEM in 1968 Hungary chose a radically new path by abolishing the system of central plan directives. Today, the government's task is using indirect economic measures through the National Plan to focus enterprise activity toward general socioeconomic goals. Thus, the National Planning Office fulfills most of the tasks that are carried out by public economic research institutes in the West. This office includes various "theme" groups that work with scientists and university-based specialists in the appropriate subjects. The groups' task is to point out trends in technology and market development, and to determine the fields where steps should be taken to enhance the country's potential or to avoid falling behind its international competitors.

Thus, although the plan does not direct economic activity in the traditional sense of central planning, it does provide a good measure of the business opportunities that are likely to arise as a result of overall national economic policies. Following an analysis of favorable, neutral, and unfavorable scenaria in the international environment, the 7th Five-Year Plan for 1986-1990, took a modest view of medium-term growth. Against a 15 to 17% growth target for national income, and in light of the dual goals of a favorable balance in foreign trade and a reduction of foreign indebtedness, private consumption is forecasted to expand by 8 to 10% during the plan's five-year horizon.

The plan rests on the belief that development must be fueled primarily by industry. Attention is focused on the need to counterbalance the relative shortage in energy and raw materials, to keep pace with international scientific research and technological development, and to further enhance growth in those sectors where Hungary is already strong. Addressing these broad areas of need was operationalized in the form of six economic development programs for the period starting in 1986:

1. Rationalization of energy management.
2. Increased efficiency in raw material usage and technological modernization.

3. Effective recycling and use of waste and secondary raw materials.
4. Increased applications and spreading of microelectronics.
5. Development of a microelectronics component and spare parts industry.
6. Development of industries such as pharmaceuticals, insecticides, and pesticides, which are seen as the "locomotives" of the national economy, and of intermediate production through the creation of favorable growth conditions and the supply of necessary capital. (The detailed list of specific sectors which have been declared "spheres of outstanding importance" is found in "Economic associations . . ." [1985/86]. It includes such sectors as packaging technology, motor vehicle parts, agricultural and food machinery, textile and clothing manufacturing technology, robotics, and tool production.)

Although these areas represent focal points in the national planning process, they are not an exhaustive list of business opportunities. Three other areas should be mentioned here. First, any type of industrial cooperation which has the potential of eventually leading to exports, regardless of sector, is likely to be seen favorably and supported. A variety of options for cooperative arrangements exist (see below). The 1986 legislation, which enables most Hungarian companies to negotiate freely with their chosen foreign partners, is likely to reduce the time and effort necessary to conclude such agreements. Although large multinational companies, ranging from Eli Lilly, Volvo, and Siemens to Corning, Renault, and Bayer, have been cooperating with Hungarian enterprises for several years, the new laws have introduced new flexibility into the system and thus make it possible for smaller firms to also enter the Hungarian market.

Second, the very fact that the Hungarian economic system is becoming decentralized creates a variety of opportunities beyond the areas which constitute national priority in Hungary. A case in point is opportunities created by the introduction of new methods of retailing, and a typical example of capitalizing upon them is provided by a compensatory trade agreement reached in 1985 between Quelle, a West German mail-order house, and Hungarotex, a Hungarian export trading company. Quelle's catalogs carry about 40,000 different products, from fashion accessories to small appliances. The agreement provides for the establishment of a network of catalog outlets by Hungarotex in several Hungarian cities. These outlets will initially operate with Quelle catalogs supplemented with a Hungarian translation. Plans for a separate Hungarian issue, which will include domestic goods, are in progress. In return, Quelle has agreed to include a series of Hungarian goods in its catalogs for West German consumers (Hungarotex-Quelle, 1985).

Third, Hungary can be seen as a gateway to other markets in Eastern Europe and other regions. In this respect, Hungary plays a similar role to that of Yugoslavia. Artisien and Buckley (1985) have shown that one-third of market-driven Western firms investing into that country did so in order to take advantage of opportunities beyond Yugoslavia itself, mainly in Eastern Europe but also in the Middle East. As a result of its more advanced stage of industrialization and a faster pace of reforms, Hungary constitutes a good familiarization ground for Western firms wishing to expand into other socialist countries. This approach is made especially possible by the establishment in Hungary of customs-free zones, which are especially designed to encourage the importation of materials and parts for domestic production and reexport (see below).

The presence of business opportunities in Hungary must be viewed in relation to some typical concerns of Western businesses about trading with Eastern socialist countries. According to a recent study, there are four major concerns: difficulties in financing trade agreements; the effort required of senior management to develop cooperative arrangements; the fear of default in light of the socialist countries' foreign debt burden; and the possibility of infringement of western copyrights and patents (Hisrich and Peters, 1983).

Although it would be wrong to assume that such problems are totally nonexistent in Hungary, the preceding discussion suggests that steps have been and are being taken to correct them. The gradual evolution of capital markets, the new legislation which liberalized the foreign trade structure, and the national plan's modest expansion goals for the next few years address the first three of the above problem areas. Regarding patents and copyrights, there seems to be no more reason for concern in Hungary than in other

countries at an intermediate stage of development. Hungary sub-
scribes to all major international treaties in this area, including the
Universal Copyright Convention, the Berne Union, and the Lisbon
and Madrid Conventions. In addition, Hungarian law prohibits the
registration of trademarks that are in use abroad, even if these have
not been registered in Hungary. (Patent and copyright protection
provisions in Hungary are explained in detail in "How to Trade
With Hungary" [1984].)

Ultimately, however, perhaps the best testament to the presence
of opportunities and the relative absence of risk in Hungary, in addition to the large number of Western businesses that are active
there, is the renewed interest in that market following the thaw in
international political tensions in the mid-1980s. This is exemplified by (a) the growing number of meetings, such as the 1985 conference on "Trade and Investment Opportunities in Hungary,"
which was attended by over 200 industrialists from Western Europe, the U.S., and Canada; (b) the emergence of new, specialized
publications, such as a special bulletin on Hungarian-U.S. trade
issued by the chambers of commerce of the two countries; (c) the
creation of the Hungarian Management Center, a management
training institute sponsored financially by a variety of Hungarian,
West European, and North American public and private institutions; and, of course, (d) the growing number of applications for
various cooperative agreements on the part of Western firms. (A
complete discussion of advantages arising from joint ventures between Western and Hungarian companies appears in Toldy-Osz,
1979; if anything, these advantages have been enhanced since that
time.)

METHODS OF ENTRY AND CORPORATE STRATEGY FOR FOREIGN FIRMS

Generally, Hungary does not impose high customs duties and
tariffs on imports. Those restrictions that are in effect have been
placed mostly in order to protect the country's balance of payments
position, especially after the worldwide recession of the late 1970s
and early 1980s. Because imports are subject to the availability of
hard currency needed to pay for them, those Western business part-

ners who are familiar with compensatory, barter, and countertrade practices often find themselves in a more advantageous position (Kirpalani, 1985).

Hungary's external economic policy generally aims at making its market attractive to foreign investors and encourages long-term rather than short-term commitments to the market. In this context, several market entry methods are available. The principal ones are highlighted below.

Commission work. This can cover a broad range of activities, ranging from the production of finished or semifinished goods from component parts or raw materials (whether these are supplied domestically or by the foreign partner), to scientific or applied research. As a rule, these subcontracting agreements tend to be long-term and involve varying degrees of technology and knowledge transfer.

Leasing. Another form of cooperative venture that has been spreading recently is machinery leasing. Leasing essentially enables Hungarian companies to manufacture products which might otherwise be impossible due to capital shortages or a lack of technological know-how. Since such products normally are within the sphere of interest of the Western lessor, leasing may in fact be a first step toward eventual closer cooperation.

Joint ventures. Together with Yugoslavia and Rumania, Hungary was one of the first socialist countries that made it possible for foreign firms to establish joint ventures in their territory. The provisions for establishing joint ventures under the original laws of 1972 were rather strict, and foreign participation was limited to a maximum of 49%. Thus, the joint ventures that had been formed by 1985 played only a minor role in foreign trade and were rather few in number, at about 50 (by comparison, about 200 such ventures were formed in Yugoslavia between 1968 and 1980). New regulations that came into effect on January 1, 1986 aim at stimulating the inflow of foreign capital and encouraging Hungarian enterprises to participate in joint ventures. They provide for special tax reductions, simplified administrative procedures for establishment, and increased flexibility of accounting procedures. Majority foreign participation in the joint venture's capital (but not wholly owned subsidiaries) is possible if this is deemed to be advantageous to the national economy. Further, joint ventures are possible in certain new sectors, such as advertising and banking (see above).

Customs-free zones. Growth in international trade and joint production possibilities between capitalist and domestic firms are served also by the customs-free zones of Hungary. As is the case with free trade zones in other countries, their major advantage is that certain requirements and regulations are waived for companies operating within the zones (for a more complete discussion on this subject, see Papadopoulos, 1987). In the case of Hungary, fewer or no restrictions apply to zone-based companies in such areas as accounting in convertible currency, foreign exchange laws, remuneration levels for foreign and domestic employees, and foreign trade transactions. It should also be noted that Hungary is one of only a handful of countries (e.g., U.S., Belgium) that permit any individual plant to be designated as a free zone, whether or not it is located inside an industrial park set aside for this purpose. These advantages are of particular interest to investors who plan to reexport a significant part of domestic production. One example of such an operation is the economic partnership between Hungary's SKALA cooperative and the U.K.'s Mape Agency Ltd., for the production of knitwear in a customs-free zone. SKALA entered this association with the objective of acquiring manufacturing and marketing know-how in this sector, while Mape's objective was to establish a source of supply for its own and other markets. Of the total output, 80% is taken over by Mape and exported. Profits are distributed 50-50 between the two partners, which equals their capital contribution to the joint venture.

Other forms of entry. Other forms of foreign business participation include the establishment of independent representative offices, arrangements for sales representation through state-owned or cooperative companies, and franchising. This last option is particularly prevalent in the catering industry. For example, the growing number of Western visitors to Hungary made it necessary to build new hotels, and franchising was seen as the best way to secure a steady flow of visitors by becoming part of the franchisors' international network. As a result, various international chains now have member hotels in Hungary (mainly in Budapest), including Hilton, Intercontinental, Forum, Novotel, and Atrium-Hyatt.

Corporate Organization and Control of Foreign Firms

Hungarian law provides for six main forms of economic association between foreign and domestic firms: partnership, joint stock company, limited company, joint enterprise, limited partnership, and economic association in a free zone. Partially because they are very similar to the type of joint ventures with which Western companies are most familiar, *joint enterprises* are the most widespread. Unlike the question of ownership, which is generally subject to approval by the Ministry of Finance, the internal organizational system of the company depends on the mutual agreement of the parties concerned.

The national tax rate is 40% of gross company profit, which is determined after the normal deductions from total revenue for direct and overhead costs (including a social security surcharge of 40% on workers' wages). The new laws of January, 1986 contain a number of provisions aimed at making foreign investment even more attractive than before. For major investments (over 25 million Ft.) involving a substantial degree of foreign participation (over 30%), a tax holiday amounting to one-half the normal tax rate is granted for the first five years of the investment. If the investment is made in one of the priority sectors established in the National Plan (see above), a complete tax exemption is given for the first five years and this is followed by taxation at one-half the normal rate, or 20%, from the sixth year on. Furthermore, Western businesses are free to take home or reinvest their net profits in Hungary after the above deductions. Reinvested profits benefit from a further tax deduction which can be as high as 75% of the total, depending on the size and nature of the investment.

Invested capital and profits can be repatriated in the convertible currency specified in the partnership contract. Along the same lines, foreign employees may transfer up to 50% of their earnings abroad in convertible currency. Other than these provisions, the same rules apply to joint ventures as to purely domestic Hungarian companies (e.g., in terms of accounting for foreign currency, or the conditions under which credit may be granted). "Foreign Investment . . ." (1986) and Creditanstalt Bank (1986) provide more information on conditions about and controls of foreign investments.

COMMERCIAL INFRASTRUCTURE

A number of comments have already been made above regarding the overall environment for business in Hungary (e.g., concerning banking and the nature of competition). It is necessary to make two additional points here, however, concerning the commercial infrastructure of Hungary.

Marketing Services

In addition to credit institutions, patent protection, and other aspects of the business environment, of special importance to Western businesses is the infrastructure of advertising and marketing research agencies, mass media, and the like. In Hungary, such facilities are available, albeit mostly state-owned. Various forms of promotion are possible, including mass media advertising and trade fairs, but several restrictions apply to the promotion of imported products. Promotion is handled by a handful of full-service advertising agencies and several smaller, specialized creative or media bureaus; marketing research is carried out by two major and several smaller market research institutes, university-based researchers, or the advertising agencies.

Information Sources

The international organizations of which Hungary is a member (e.g., CMEA, IMF, World Bank, GATT, U.N.) produce a variety of data about the country and its economy. Two particularly useful surveys of current conditions were published by the IMF (de Fontaney, 1983) and Austria's Creditanstalt Bank (1986). Hungary's Central Statistical Office produces a wealth of statistics on demography, social conditions, foreign trade, and the economy. In addition to the main Hungarian editions, its most important publications are also published in English, Russian, and German. The Hungarian Chamber of Commerce, the NBH, several major companies and banks, and many research institutes and professional associations also produce a variety of ad hoc or periodic publications on topics such as investment regulations and opportunities, credit conditions, and the overall business environment. Generally, the amount and quality of information that is available on Hungary, whether generated domestically or by international organizations, roughly parallels that which one would expect to find in most Western industrialized countries at an intermediate level of development.

SUMMARY AND CONCLUSION

The preceding discussion portrays a country which is attempting to build a market-focused economy within a socialist political context. Hungary today shares many common characteristics with its CMEA partners but also with Western developed economies and with some newly industrialized countries. Perhaps better than any other East European nation, it reflects the opportunities and difficulties involved in the process of decentralizing economic management within the general framework of East-West relations: industrial and technological development, a growing domestic economy, increasing trade both overall and particularly with Western countries – but also occasional political tension, a substantial amount of foreign indebtedness, and the presence of conflicts resulting from the effort to bridge marketplace and socialist thinking.

In this chapter, recent developments were placed in a historical context while emphasizing those current trends that are likely to have a major influence on Hungary's future. From a Western business perspective, the most important trends are the growing emphasis on entrepreneurship, the strengthening of market mechanisms, and the increasingly important role of competition and foreign trade (especially with Western countries). A new three-year "redirection" program, launched recently for the 1988-1990 period, aims at reducing some of the most significant weaknesses of the Hungarian economy, such as growing foreign indebtedness and inefficiencies in the sectoral structure of industry. Following the HSWP's extraordinary Congress of 1988 and the replacement of Janos Kadar with Karoly Grosz, there is a greater emphasis on the need to reform various aspects of life, including the political system, in order to enhance the probability of success of the reforms in the marketplace.

The reform process which was initiated with the NEM in 1968 and continues with renewed strength in the 1980s has resulted in an environment in which Western businesses should find comfortable to operate. Barring any unforeseen developments in the general international environment, the economic and business conditions outlined above are likely to provide ample occasion for cooperation between Western and Hungarian companies.

ENDNOTES

1. Unless otherwise noted, in this and the following sections basic facts and statistics on Hungary are taken from: *Statistical Pocket Book of Hungary, Direction of Trade Statistics, Basic Statistics of the Community, Hungary* (Creditanstalt Bank, 1986), and a variety of publications from the Hungarian, U.S. and Canadian Chambers of Commerce.

2. Hungarian citizens can travel to any part of the world. Unlike earlier times and some other East European countries where passports are issued for specific trips, as of January, 1988, Hungarian citizens are issued standard 5-year passports. A condition is that travelers must have the foreign currency needed for subsistence while abroad. The central bank grants an amount equivalent to three-months' wages each year for travel to the "rouble zone," and the same amount once every three years for travel elsewhere. Citizens can have their own currency account if they can verify its source (e.g., employment abroad, author's rights, presents, savings from other travel allowances). Amounts in currency accounts can be used freely for traveling abroad and for buying foreign goods while there.

REFERENCES

"Among the first two hundred" (1985). *New Hungarian Exporter*, Vol. 35, No. 3 (March), 13-14.

Artisien, P.F.R. and P.J. Buckley (1985). "Joint Ventures in Yugoslavia: Opportunities and Constraints," *Journal of International Business Studies* (Spring), 111-135.

Basic Statistics of the Community (annual), European Community.

Benedek, G.I. (1986). "Hungary and the International Economic Organizations," *New Hungarian Exporter*, Vol. 36, No. 3 (March), 8-9.

"Conference on the Road" (1985). *New Hungarian Exporter*, Vol. 35, No. 3 (March), 23.

Creditanstalt Bank (1986). *Hungary* (Vienna).

Csillag I., (1986, November 19). "Only the Market is Missing—Organization Development of Companies," in *Figyelo* (*Observer*) in Hungarian, p. 3.

De Fontaney, P. et al. (1983). *Hungary: An Economic Survey* (Washington, D.C.: International Monetary Fund).

"Design: There is always 'new' from Ikarus" (1985). *New Hungarian Exporter*, Vol. 36, No. 9 (September), 13-14.

Direction of Trade Statistics (annual), International Monetary Fund.

Economic Associations in Hungary with Foreign Participation (1985/86 Amendment). Hungarian Foreign Trade Bank, Budapest.

"Foreign Investment in Hungary" (1986). *Hungaro Press Economic Information*, No. 4, 3-5.

Hisrich, R.D. and M.P. Peters (1983). "East-West Trade: An Assessment by U.S. Manufacturers," *Columbia Journal of World Business* (Winter).

Honti, L., Deputy General Manager, Buda-Flax Hungarian Linen Works (1984), "Marketing Strategy as a Means of Improving Competitiveness," *Marketing in Hungary*, No. 3, 15-18.

Hungarian Chamber of Business (1984). *How to Trade With Hungary* (Budapest).

Hungarian Yearbook of Foreign Trade Statistics (annual), Budapest.

"Hungarotex-Quelle co-operation agreement" (1985). *New Hungarian Exporter*, Vol. 36, No. 9 (September), 20.

Huszti, D. (1984). "Hungary's Membership in the World Bank," *Marketing in Hungary*, No. 4, 19-21.

Kirpalani, V. (1985). *International Marketing* (New York: Random House).

Kornai, J. (1971). *Anti-Equilibrium on Economic Systems Theory and the Tasks of Research* (Amsterdam: North-Holland).

———, (1980). *Economics of Shortage* (Amsterdam: North-Holland).

Kovats, K. (1984). "Timely Issues of East-West Co-operation," *Marketing in Hungary*, No. 1, 30-32.

"Licencia, getting involved in managing" (1985). *New Hungarian Exporter*, Vol. 36, No. 9 (September), 6.

Mclean's, October 6, 1986

Naor, J. (1988). "Innovative Retailing in Hungary: A Case Study in Innovation," in E. Kaynak, ed., *Transnational Retailing* (New York: Walter de Gruyter), 227-238.

Papadopoulos, N.G. and J. Beracs (1985). "Expanding the Geographic Scope of Research to Eastern European Shortage Economies," *Broadening the Uses of Research* (Wiesbaden, FRG: 38th Congress, European Society for Opinion and Marketing Research, September), 1-21.

———, (1987). "The Role of Free Zones in International Strategy," European Management Journal, Vol. 5, No. 2 (Summer), 112-120.

Samli, A.C. and W. Jermacowicz (1983). "The Stages of Marketing Evolution in East European Countries," *European Journal of Marketing*, Vol. 17, No. 2, 26-33.

Statistical Pocket Book of Hungary (annual), Budapest.

Timar, M. (1985). In "Changing banking system," *New Hungarian Exporter*, Vol. 35, No. 3 (March), 7-9.

Toldy-Osz, I. (1979). "Possibilities for Western Companies to Participate in Joint Ventures," *Marketing in Hungary*, No. 1, 20-25.

Chapter 9

Israel

Samuel Rabino
Jehiel Zif

CHARACTERISTICS

Area and Population

Israel is situated on the eastern Mediterranean Sea coast, and has a common border with four countries: Lebanon, Syria, Jordan, and Egypt. Israel's area (inclusive of the new areas that were added during the 1967 and 1973 wars), is 21.501 km. Its total population is 4.4 million, with roughly 83% Jews and 17% Arabs and Druse. As an immigrant's country Israel has a relatively high proportion of nonnative citizens. Only 55% of the Jewish population was born in Israel. Hebrew is the language used by 83% of the Jews, and Arabic is used by 95% of the non-Jewish population. However, English is taught at all schools from elementary through high school as well as the universities, and English-speaking people can use English for the conduct of their business and other needs.

The three largest and major cities in Israel are: (a) Jerusalem, 428,700 people; (b) Tel-Aviv, 327,300 people; and (c) Haifa, 225,800 people.

The population in Israel resides as follows:

- In urban localities: 84.6% (3,508,000)
- In rural localities: 12.8% (530,000) including:
  Moshavim & Collectives: 150,000 (3.6% of total)
  Kibbuzim: 116,000 (2.8% of total)

Climate

For about seven months, April through October, Israel enjoys a warm season of temperatures ranging from 25°C to 30°C. The rainy and cold season lasts from November to March, when the temperatures range from 4°C to 15°C. However, one of the characteristics of the Israeli weather is the big difference in climate among Israel's different regions, the Galilee, Sharon, Jerusalem mountains, and the desert.

Government

The State of Israel was established on May 14, 1948. Israel is a secular, parliamentary, democratic republic. Elections to the Knesset (Israel's one-chamber parliament) are open to every citizen over 18 years old, countrywide, confidential, and proportional. The Cabinet (Government) headed by the Prime Minister is the main policy-making body of the state.

The Knesset, the supreme legislative body of the State of Israel, is a unicameral house of 120 members. Its members are elected every four years in a general election. The Knesset may dissolve itself and call new elections in less than the four-year period. Members are elected from party rosters. Succession, in the event of death or resignation, is drawn from these same rosters.

The cabinet takes office for a four-year term after a vote of confidence, but the term may be shortened if the Prime Minister resigns or dies or the Knesset withdraws its vote. If a Prime Minister resigns, he may, subject to the Knesset confirmation, co-opt for a replacement.

The government is collectively responsible to the Knesset, which must approve its composition and programs. Only the Prime Minister is required to be a member of the Knesset. In practice most ministers are also members of the Knesset. There is no limit to the number of ministers whom the Prime Minister might appoint. Once the cabinet gains the confidence of the Knesset and majority support, it might develop foreign, defense, internal, and economic polices, bringing each before the house for its acceptance. It holds its regular sessions in Jerusalem every Sunday. The bulk of legislation is initiated by the cabinet, but there is provision for private members' bills. In the main, bills are drafted by the Ministry of Justice, and presented by the Minister responsible.

The president is elected for a five-year term. His duties are ceremonial in nature. After the elections, the president assigns the head of the party that got the majority of the votes to negotiate with several parties in order to set up a new cabinet. The structure of the Israeli system and the parties' makeup make it almost impossible for one party to get a simple majority, and most governments consist, therefore, of a coalition of several parties. However, two parties, Labor and Likud, are the largest and most influential. They have headed the government since the establishment of Israel: the Labor Party from 1948 through 1977 and the Likud from 1977 through 1984. Since 1984 a rotation arrangement has been established between the two parties.

The juristic authority is headed by the Supreme Court, and is divided into a system of three levels of courts.

Religion

The Ministry of Religion is one of the government's offices. It is responsible to supply and serve the religious needs of the four major religions in the state: Judism, Islam, Christianity, and Druse. Israel's public services and offices are closed on Saturdays and Jewish holidays. The non-Jewish population is free to observe its own holidays.

International Influences Affecting Israel

Import-Export

	Imports ($ Mil.)				Exports ($ Mil.)			
	1984	%	1985	%	1984	%	1985	%
European Common Market	2,810	37	2,801	38.5	1,674	36.5	1,731	35.5
USA	1,756	23	1,675	23	1,061	23	1,348	28
Other	3,029	40	2,804	38.5	1,861	40.5	1,774	36.5
Totals	7,595	100	7,280	100	4,596	100	4,853	100

A general trend of increasing deficits in the trade balance is indicated here.[1] Israel exports about 39% of its local industrial and manufacturing products.[2] However, Israel needs to import 59% of basic material for the local production.[3] Israel is one of the 10 largest export countries in the world, which is another indication of the country's dependence on foreign trade.

Due to the unique situation of a small country surrounded by hostile neighbors, three international agreements are especially important to Israel: 1975 and 1976, the free trade zone agreement with the Common Market; and 1985: Agreement to establish a free trade zone with the U.S.

The Arab boycott on trade with Israel is another factor in Israeli international trade[4] which has economic as well as political implications. Israel is trying to offset the Arab boycott efforts more for political reasons than for real damages it has been causing to the Israeli economy. The real cost of this boycott to Israel is not quite clear, nor is the cost to Arab countries themselves. In the U.S., two antiboycott bills have been introduced (1976, 1977). The European Economic Community also cooperates with Israel in efforts to make the boycott less effective.

NATIONAL ECONOMIC
AND PHYSICAL ENVIRONMENT

Israel's economy suffers from three principal problems: a trade deficit, a large foreign debt, and accelerating inflation.

Though export-intensive, export earnings still only account for some 60% of import expenses. As a result, Israel currently runs a civilian trade deficit of $3.5 billion. Furthermore, defense imports add another $1.5 billion, so that the annual trade deficit is about $5 billion. Half of this deficit is covered by contributions from nations and private individuals; the other half has to be borrowed from abroad.

As a result, Israel has accumulated a foreign debt of about $22 billion. Although Israel maintains considerable foreign currency assets and most of the loans are long-term and to friendly lenders, the cost of maintaining the national debt is burdensome.

About 25% of Israel's gross national product (GNP) is derived from manufacturing. It employs 30% of the work force in the country. Agriculture contributes only 5% to the GNP.

The Israeli economy is composed of three main sectors: the private sector, which consists of 95% of the employers; the public sector (mainly the government); and the general labor union, *Hista-*

drut. Its membership amounts to 66% of the working force, and they are organized in about 40 different specific unions.

The Histardrut controls a large portion of economic activity in Israel. It owns directly or has a partnership in large segments of industry, construction, banking, publishing, insurance, and other activities. Its main industrial arm, Koor Industries, employs over 40,000 workers and has branches worldwide. The Histadrut also has direct influence over other segments of the economy that are governed as cooperatives. These include the largest transportation companies, the largest distributor of goods, supermarket chains, printing houses, hotels, agricultural production, and other activities.

The economic public sector in Israel can be divided into state-owned enterprises (SOEs) and special boards or authorities. According to Ahroni (1979) the SOEs in Israel account for only 5% of the GNP. This percentage is lower than in most European countries. The best known SOEs in Israel are El-Al Israeli Airlines, Israel Aviation Industries, The Electrical Company, Israel Chemicals, Israel Shipbuilding, Bezek-Israel Telephone Company, and Shekem (the large retail chain for the military and defense employees). Only about half of the SOEs are business firms with a profit motive. Many SOEs perform a service function as an extension of the government.

The second group in the public sector includes agricultural marketing and production boards as well as special institutes and authorities. The agricultural boards are cooperative bodies of the government ministries, farmers, distributors, and consumer representatives. They are designed to supervise the orderly production and marketing of agricultural goods in order to guarantee adequate supply at "reasonable" prices. Their boards operate under statutory law.

The other institutes or special authorities, such as the Israel Institute of Standards, are designed under special law to coordinate or regulate some social or economic activity.

It is important to note that the SOE is only one instrument to control or influence economic activity. The Government of Israel, like most governments, has a major influence on the economic activity through a variety of policies and regulations other than the direct control of business enterprises.[5]

Israeli industry is highly concentrated; a small number of companies control large assets, resources, and power. This phenomenon is not considered to be desirable because it stifles competition. The advantages are in the economies of scale that can be achieved in production as well as in the purchasing of sophisticated new equipment, high investment in research and development, and maintaining and supporting skilled professional staff. These factors give Israel a competitive advantage in its dealings with the foreign markets.

Over the years, Israel has shifted focus from labor-intensive to increasingly capital high-tech-intensive industries. Israel's economy is also increasingly trade-intensive, where a high proportion of its industrial production is exported. The main advantage of the Israeli industrial export is its high level of innovation.

Israel's sophisticated agricultural sector is noted for its high productivity. Except for beef, wheat, coffee, and oil-producing grains, Israel is virtually self-sufficient in food. In addition to citrus products, Israel today exports fresh and processed foods as well as agricultural know-how.

NET INDUSTRIAL EXPORTS 1983

($ millions)

Mining and quarrying	276
Food, drink and tobacco	316
Textiles	97
Clothing	243
Leather and leather products	3
Wood and wooden products	21
Paper and paper products	6
Printing and publishing	23
Rubber and plastics	118
Chemicals	664
Non-metallic minerals	15
Alkaline metals	35
Metal product	440
Machinery	99
Electric and electronic equipment	539
Transport vehicles	282
Others	260
Total, without diamonds	3,357
Diamonds, net	1,001
Total industrial exports	4,358

In July 1985 a "new economic program" was declared by the government. This was an austerity program intended to reduce the government's budget, impose new taxes, and freeze wages and prices. The 1986 budget contains provisions to:

1. Continue to stabilize prices;
2. Improve the balance of payment, especially the trade balance;
3. Increase export;
4. Improve productivity; and
5. Encourage savings.

Future economic growth depends on the implementation of some major changes in the structure of the Israeli economy:

1. Transfer of basic industries that are owned by the government to the more efficient and productive private sector;
2. Improved control over the public sector's purchases;
3. Relaxation of the tax burden; and
4. A gradual withdrawal of the government's control over the money market.

Natural Resources

Most of Israel's natural resources are found in the Negev Desert and the Dead Sea. They include minerals like potash, bromine, magnesium, and others. Israel is the world's largest exporter of bromine. Israel's energy sources are limited and consist primarily of natural gas, and a small amount of oil which meets only 2% of the country's yearly needs. Most of Israel's oil is imported from Egypt, Brazil, and the European Common Market. The government is investing in the development of additional energy resources: hydroelectric power, nuclear energy (in planning stages only), and increased use of coal to replace some of the oil consumption.

LEGAL SYSTEM

Laws to Encourage Foreign Investments

(a) *The law to stimulate capital investment (5719, 1959).*[6] This law was designed to attract capital to Israel and to enhance economic initiative (foreign as well as local) in order to expand the economy's production capabilities utilizing local resources and skills. The objective is to improve the trade balance. Another benefit of this law is to help increase population dispersion by the government's selective encouragement of new enterprises in different regions. A company which gets the "approved" status is eligible for different government grants and loans. An approved company does not pay income taxes and will pay only up to 30% of the "corporate tax" during the first seven years of profitable operations. In addition, the company might also get a five-year accelerated depreciation on equipment. Those privileges are contingent upon meeting certain production or export quotas.

(b) *The law to stimulate industry investment* (*1969*). A company with at least 90% of its income generated via local production is entitled to pay 20% income tax instead of 35%, and a 40% corporate tax.

TECHNOLOGICAL ENVIRONMENT

Manpower and Employment

Human resource is Israel's most important resource. The country enjoys a high percentage of professional manpower — about 28% attained a college or other technical degree. Fifty percent of the work force have had at least 11 years of elementary to secondary education, and 12% have a four-year college education. About 40% of the students major in math, physics, and the medical fields. Manpower in the manufacturing sector is highly skilled: 9 out of 1,000 employed are engineers and researchers. This number increases yearly by a factor of .16. The *civil* work force had 1,440,000 employees in 1984, which was an increase of 3% from 1983. The percentage of work force in the manufacturing sector has leveled off during the last few years, with a growth rate of only .6%. A more meaningful growth has been realized in the electric, electronic, metal, printing, and food production sectors. The construction field has been frozen since 1973. Contributing factors to "soft" employment in construction are improvements in workers' productivity and improved efficiency due to modernization and automatization. The weekly average number of employees was 1,390,000 in 1984, a growth of 1.5% from 1983. The job market was hit hard in 1985; as a result, productivity and production have been somewhat negatively affected.

Israel's Population Change and Unemployment'

	1981	1982	1983	1984	1985
Emigration	25,900	11,300	9,200	11,300	17,500
Immigration	14,500	16,100	19,100	21,700	12,500
Net Effect	(11,400)	4,800	14,400	10,400	(5,000)
Unemployment%	5.1	5.0	4.5	5.9	6.7

Wages and Social Benefits

Wages are usually set by agreements between the government, the employer, and the Histadrut (labor union). The base wage is set in general by adjustments linked to the cost of living index, and is calculated according to the price index. The total cost of the benefit package for the employer is about 35-50% of the total direct pay to the employee. The benefit package consists of the following:

1. *Compensation and retirement.* Any person who has been laid off or who has retired is entitled to one month's pay for every year he has worked for the company. A daily waged employee will get two weeks per year. In most cases this arrangement works also for employees who leave in order to work for another company. This sum is tax deductible up to a certain amount. The employers usually save the amount needed for the compensation benefit in a special fund. This savings is tax deductible.

2. *Savings.* Employees can save from their salary a certain percentage and get the same amount from their employer added to his savings. The employers can deduct those amounts as expenses. Employees may also transfer their savings from one company to another, in case they move to work for another company.

3. *Life insurance.* Managers usually can participate in a life insurance program offered by the employers. This program incorporates a compensation, pension, and savings plans.

4. *Vacation.* Two to four weeks of vacation is the general rule, depending on the number of years with the company.

5. *National Insurance.* All self-employed people pay according

to preset guidelines. Employers pay 18.5% of an employee's wage. The employee's share is 4.2% of his wage, which is deducted from the pay check and transferred directly to the National Insurance. Accidents and pensions are covered by the National Insurance. Often the employers arrange for a more comprehensive coverage than the National Insurance so that in case the employee is out on sick leave, the employer is covered for the wage payments.

6. *Work and Rest Law.* According to a 1951 law, a 47-hour work week is the maximum allowed by law. Some companies offer a 42 to 45 hour work week.

7. *Breaktime.* Saturday is the official rest day. Most companies have a 7-day work schedule. Some companies are moving now to a 5-day work week. Employees are entitled to 10 days per year of paid holiday.

8. *Sick pay.* Each company is setting its own guidelines on the number of paid sick days.

9. *Hospitalization.* Employers payment to the National Insurance includes a hospitalization insurance. Hospitalization is, therefore, free to all employees.

10. *Additional benefits.* Some employers pay travel expenses to and from work. These payments are taxable. Professional books, tuition, and seminars are also usually paid, under certain conditions, by the employers.

Wage scales in Israel are generally lower then in other developed countries. Engineers and other professionals earn on the average 80% of the same level professional pay scale in the U.S. or Europe, and industrial workers earn about 60% of the pay in developed countries. Since 1984 real wages have gone down.[8] This has been part of the government's efforts to strengthen the Israeli economy. In addition, the government has now decided that no compensation will be given for price increases, which was a common practice up to now, unless prices rise by at least 6%.

ORGANIZATION CULTURE

Organizational Forms

1. *Public companies.* Managers are elected by shareholders. Minimum number of shareholders is seven, with no upper limit on

the number of shareholders. The company cannot repurchase its shares and it needs court approval to reduce its capital. The company must present public reports at least once in two years, and they have to be controlled by an independent, licensed CPA. The company is also required to provide a financial forecast report before a new share issue is offered to the public.

2. *Private company*. The company needs to have at least two owners and cannot have more than 50 owners. This number does not include current and past employees. As a private company, it cannot sell its shares to the public. Less than 40% of the companies in 1984 were private companies, and this number continues to decrease.

3. *Other organizations*. There are also other kinds of organizations such as consortiums and hybrids of joint ownership from public and private sources but they are attracting foreign investors.

4. *Israeli subsidiaries of foreign companies*. In order to open a local Israeli branch, a foreign company must supply the following:

— Documents showing the company's registration abroad;
— A list of the company's directors;
— Names and addresses of people that reside in Israel and can represent the company; and
— A notary document that permits an Israeli resident to act on behalf of the company.

Decision-Making Patterns

With Israel's inflationary economy, the tax laws have a great influence on the business decision-making process. Profits do not reflect real capital gains. On the other hand, financing via loans is especially popular in inflationary conditions. In addition, the full deduction of interest (on loans) has a strong effect on taxes paid by the company. Another way of dealing with inflationary conditions is to invest in capital equipment. The Israeli economy is very sensitive to upturn and downturn in the economies of industrial countries. Import- and export-related decisions are particularly influenced by this factor. The Israeli economy is also quite volatile due to internal political conditions which affect government's decisions. There is a strong emphasis by the government on stimulating export. Export increased by 27% in 1982 as a result of the govern-

ment's policies and the internal economics crisis thereafter. The
security situation is yet another factor that influences business decisions. In war times local production is drastically reduced due to the
fact that most male employees are enlisted in active military service.

NATIONAL CONTROL OF INTERNATIONAL TRADE

Foreign Trade Policy

Israel imports most of its production materials, including oil and
military equipment. Israel exports most of its products and services.
Export to the U.S. has been increased during the last decade, while
exports to Europe have been reduced as depicted in the next table.

	1975	1984
Europe	45.5%	35.6%
U.S.	22.9%	34.0%

Another trend in export is the increase of industrial export and the
decrease of agriculture export:

	1970	1985
Agriculture	16.6%	7.8%
Industrial	82.0%	91.0%

There are also changes in the makeup of the industrial export:

	1970	1985
Textile & leather	15.8%	6.5%
Metal, machinery, electronics	10.0%	33.2%

Chemical and diamond sales account for 14% and 25% of the
export volume, respectively.

International Trade Agreements

The development of a high-tech sector since the late 1960s, the open trade zone agreement with the common market in 1975, the generalized system of preferences (GSP) arrangement with the U.S. in 1976, and the signing of the free trade zone with the U.S. are some of the more important developments in Israel's foreign trade. Some developments are described below:

1. *A free trade agreement with the Common Market, July 1975.* The agreement includes the following:

— Economic cooperation;
— Free trade zone for industrial products;
— Substantial tariff discounts on agricultural products; and
— A gradual reduction of Israel's tariffs on import from the common market, and gradual reduction of all quotas on trade between the countries by 1989.

2. *A free trade zone agreement with the U.S., September 1985.* All trade restrictions between the countries will be removed by 1995. The GSP agreement is still in effect, and the exporting company can choose between the two agreements. This agreement opens new opportunities for the Israeli export, because it covers products that were not included in the GSP and GATT agreements like electronics, metal, medical equipment, optical and measurement devices, rubber, plastic, and jewelry.

3. *Special arrangement with developing countries.* These agreements give Israel a competitive advantage over developed countries and enables it to penetrate selected markets in those countries.

4. *Single tariff agreements with various countries.* Those countries are: Japan, Australia, New Zealand, Sweden, Switzerland, and Canada.

5. *Agreements with developing countries, February 1973.* Tariff agreements on special discounts with 16 developing countries, including: Brazil, Chile, Greece, South Africa, South Korea, Mexico, Philippines, Spain, Turkey, Egypt, India, Yugoslavia, and others.

Trade Control Through Tariffs and Other Requirements

Three different import and export laws (1978, 1979, 1981) specify who might deal with foreign countries and the requirements for doing so. These laws specify the products that are permitted to be imported and the appropriate procedures to be followed. Several taxes are imposed on import products in order to protect local manufacturers:

1. Value added tax of 15% on total amount of the product value, including taxes and tariffs.
2. Import tax.
3. Deposit requirement, in addition to the import tax. For certain products the importer must pay also a deposit which is returned after 12 months.
4. Port taxes of 2% of the C.I.F. value of the products.

In order to stimulate export from Israel, a 1961 law specifies the conditions under which a company can get a property tax waiver on the spare parts and equipment it is exporting.

SOURCES OF INFORMATION

International Sources

Information about foreign companies is available from Dunn & Bradstreet at 105 Hachashmonaim Street, Tel-Aviv.

Government Sources

1. *Investment Authority.* It coordinates between the public agencies and the government to promote foreign investment in Israel. This agency belongs to the Ministry of Treasury, and has offices in the main Israeli consulates abroad.
2. *The Investment Center* at the Commerce Department. This center processes all applications that are submitted to the investment authority.
3. *The Center for Documentation and Market Research* operated by the Commerce Department. The center supplies updated information on various markets and organizes symposiums for manufac-

turers and exporters. It works in coordination with the Center for International Trade.

4. *The Commerce Department Regional Marketing Unit.* The unit collects information on Israel's foreign economic activities in cooperation with the economic attaché. The Unit also participates in negotiations for international trade agreements.

5. *The commercial attaché* at the Israeli consulates abroad.

6. *The Israeli Export Institute.* The Institute promotes export by getting exporters involved with its various export-related activities. It also serves as an information resource for exporters.

7. *The Israeli Standards Institute.* The Institute determines product standards (42 Hauniversity Street, Tel-Aviv).

8. *The Institute for Production and Productivity.* The Institute provides manufacturers with consultation on productivity and efficiency issues, economic research, and human development and training (4 Henrieta Soldz Street, Tel-Aviv).

Industry Sources

1. The Israeli Manufacturing Union (29 Hamered Street, Tel-Aviv).

2. The coordinating Chamber of the Economic Organizations (31 Karlibch, Tel-Aviv).

3. The Israeli General Merchants Union (6 Wilson Street, Tel-Aviv).

4. The Commerce Chamber (84 Hachashmonaim Street, Tel-Aviv).

5. The Small Manufacturers Union (16 Mercas Bahalay Melacha, Tel-Aviv).

6. Other organizations: importers, exporters, and distributors.

Information regarding these organizations can be obtained from business directories like the Yellow Pages. A summation of the various companies that deal with international trade appears in the Appendix.

Service Sector Sources

1. Commercial and mortgage banks;
2. Financial and investment institutes;
3. Maintenance, insurance, CPA's and consulting firms.

AREAS OF CONFLICT AND CONFLICT RESOLUTION

Control of Economic Growth

The state budget serves as a stabilizer of the economic system. This is especially important in Israel's volatile economic environment. The government's 1984 Package Deal failed to stabilize the market. As a result, the government developed a new plan (June 1985) which was an "Emergency Program to Stabilize the Market." The program attempts to decrease government's involvement with the money market. The savings institutes are no longer required to invest in treasury bills. The idea is to encourage investments in manufacturing, tourism, and agricultural industries in order to speed up market recovery. The government's Development Loans were abolished. It is hoped that less government involvement in the market will enable the market to regulate itself. National production is expected to be in 1986 as low as in 1985 (2%). However, consumers' consumption is expected to decrease by 2.5% and export to increase by 7% over the 1985 figure. Investments in the industry are expected to increase in all sectors except residential construction.

Credit and Prices Policy

In November 1984 the Package Deal between the government, Histadrut, and the employers' organizations went into effect. This deal focuses on the partial abolishment of government subsidies and price control while imposing full freeze on wages and prices for a specific period. The first component of the package deal achieved partial success in slowing the rate of inflation, but the second component has not achieved its objective. This program was replaced on July 1, 1985 with the "Emergency Program to Stabilize the Market." A one time 18.8% devaluation was imposed. The shekel-dollar exchange rate was stabilized at around 1.5 Shekel per 1 dollar. Most products and services changed by 17% as a result of this program, while subsidized produce rose by up to 100%.

Inflation control was achieved as a result of several factors: frozen exchange rates, wages, eroded wages, and decreased consumer demand. Steps taken included a reduction in the government's budget deficit and a slowdown in the growth of financial assets and credit. In addition, the interest rate has been drastically increased in real terms since 1984.

The monetary policy focused during 1985 on controlling banks' short-term credit via high interest rates on loans. The policy caused a 40% increase in credit costs compared to 1984. The objective of the high interest policy has been to stabilize prices and reduce foreign exchange hoarding in order to improve the trade balance. A negative outcome has been a slackening economic activity since local companies rely on credit for ongoing operations and not all companies can afford the new high interest on commercial loans. In fact a sluggish demand coupled with a build-up of inventory and expensive debt financing has driven many companies into difficulties.

RESEARCH AND DEVELOPMENT

The Israeli economy depends to a large extent on the high-tech sector, which requires in turn large investments in R & D. Research institutions attached to universities work in cooperation with different industries and serve as catalysts for the innovations and modernization of the Israeli industry. Various funds and agreements have been established to promote and support the sophisticated industry:

1. BIRD—fund for industrial R & D, U.S.
2. BARD—fund for agricultural R & D, U.S.
3. Governmental funds for Israel, South Africa R & D
4. Governmental funds for Israel, Canada R & D
5. R & D fund between Israel and Holland
6. R & D cooperation between Israel and other countries now being negotiated.

R & D Grants

The government funds various R & D projects with up to 50% financing of the total investment. These funds are expected to be returned if and when the implementation of the R & D effort is successful, in yearly payments of no more than 2% of sales. Only

25% of the original fund is expected to be returned to the government.

In some cases loans are offered instead of funds. The loans can amount to 54% of the project's cost. This arrangement is attractive since R & D expenses in Israel are tax deductible to U.S. investors.

HUMAN RESOURCE DEVELOPMENT POLICY

The Israeli economy is characterized by a high level of advance technology utilization, a process which will continue and even increase in the coming years. Israel must, therefore, adjust its educational system to a higher level of manpower training so that it can cope with the challenges of a changing economy. Today, the formal educational system is composed of elementary and secondary schools. Universities and other educational institutes fall under the responsibility of the Ministry of Labor. The informal system included the Open University. Only 34% of the high education students chose science and math, and only 38% of that group were females.

The Ministry of Labor is in charge of professional training, technical high school, and adult vocational schools. In addition, the Ministry is in charge of training problem youth, unskilled adults, disabled individuals, and immigrants.

Previously most courses were developed for labor-intensive industries, but new courses are now being developed for the high-tech industries of electronics and plastic, as well as the integration of automation and computers into the industry. Construction, management, and tourism are additional fields that are being developed.

TAXATION

The state's principal source of income is tax revenue. The tax system includes direct and indirect, permanent and temporary taxes. The most important taxes are:

- Income tax (on all kinds of income, according to applicable tables)
- Corporate tax (on all taxable income)
- Capital gains tax (on sale of any real property)
- Property tax (this tax is applied to all properties other than agriculture lands since 1981)
- Stamp tax (on documents)
- Value added tax (15% of purchase price of products and services)
- National insurance
- Health payments (deducted from the paycheck)
- Import deposit (returned after a year, without interest)
- Vehicle tax (3% on all vehicles)
- Employers tax
- Travel tax
- Different import taxes
- Local municipalities tax

It should be pointed out here that in order to stimulate market growth and attract foreign investment, a reduction in the tax burden is imperative.

ADVANTAGES OF INVESTMENTS IN ISRAEL

A foreign investor can realize several advantages that are unique to the Israeli market:[9]

1. Skilled worker manpower with relatively low wages;
2. Diverse R & D opportunities;
3. Convenient geographical location;
4. Availability of a sophisticated infrastructure;
5. A familiar and comfortable cultural background of a Western society;
6. A free trade zone with the U.S.;
7. Trade agreements with different countries;
8. Minimum government supervision of international foreign exchange;
9. Agreements to prevent double taxation;

10. Contacts with many foreign companies already operating in Israel; and
11. Government aid and support in: grants, low interest loans, participation in R & D efforts, tax benefits, support of employees' training, and insurance coverage for damages in war or hostile activities.

There are a few hundred foreign companies that operate today in Israel. The most common and successful modes of involvement in Israel include:

1. *Wholly owned subsidiaries*. Some of these subsidiaries (e.g., IBM, Motorola, Intel) started as planning and R & D centers, and later expanded into production.

2. *Joint ventures between foreign and Israeli firms*. This facilitates, for example, the establishment of R & D activities in Israel.

3. *Foreign investment as minority ownership of Israeli firms*. A mode of involvement that is less popular and involves a technology transfer in exchange for a partial partnership with the Israeli company, while letting the foreign company control its area of expertise.

4. *Investment firms with foreign ownership or involvement – A "silent ownership."* This mode typically involves a bank or other investment institute that assists in locating venture capital in order to finance special projects.

5. *Foreign investment projects in industry, tourism, and real estate*. This kind of investment is more active than the preceding one. Usually the group appoints at least one of its own people to be in charge of the local daily operations.

6. *Israel securities offered for sale on foreign stock exchange*. Stock of Israeli companies is sold and traded abroad. Many Israeli high-tech companies like Elscint, Elron, Elbit, Scitex, and others use this strategy in order to finance their growth strategies.

7. *Joint R & D investment*. About 35 Israeli companies are involved with American and European companies in conducting R & D projects in Israel.

8. *Venture capital*. A special legislation – "Elscint Law" – facilitates tax benefits to individuals and companies that invest in the industrial sector, especially in the high-tech industries.

9. *Limited partnership*. This enables a limited risk while allow-

ing the investor to realize capital growth. However, the investor cannot become an active participant in daily operations of the firm.

10. *Establishment or acquisition of foreign firms by Israeli companies*. This is a useful way of expanding operations into foreign markets by Israeli companies which have already penetrated the foreign market. The Israeli company can produce its products and improve its distribution within a target country. This also enables the Israeli company to market its products abroad in cases of import restrictions.

11. *Israeli experts in planning, agriculture, and industry who work in foreign countries*. Depending on the specific situation (e.g., the priority assigned to any given country) different tax benefits and incentives can be realized by the company.

FORECASTING THE FUTURE

One of the objectives of the new economic program is to achieve a better and advanced infrastructure for future growth. Growth attracts investment, and a lot of effort is currently being made by the state of Israel in order to encourage foreign investments in the country. This includes incentives offered to both individual investors and business firms that have been increased during the last year.

At present there are plans to open special offices for foreign investors in order to assist and reduce the considerable red tape they face while conducting business in Israel. The government also established the New Company for Investments in Israel, with the initial investment of 100 million dollars. All this is an indication of Israel's need for increasing foreign investments. Toward this end Israel is willing to offer attractive incentives to foreign investors, including export channels to both the U.S. and Europe.

ENDNOTES

1. The Central Chamber of Statistics, *International Trade Statistical*, Quarterly, Vol. 4, Oct.-Dec. 1985, Jerusalem, pp. 42-44 and 45-47.
2. The Ministry of Commerce and Industry, Planning and Economics, the *Center for Industrial Planning, Export from Israel — Target Countries and Industries*, 1984, p. 48.

3. *Ibid*. p. 49.
4. Prittie, T., "The Arab Boycott of Israel," *Focust*, Condon, Dec. 1985.
5. Based on Yair Aharoni, *State-Owned Enterprise in Israel and Abroad*, Cherikover Press, 1979.
6. *The Encouragement of Capital Investment Law*, 1953-1957, Oct. 1984.
7. *Yediot Achronot*, Your Schekel, June 10, 1986, p. 9.
8. *Yediot Achronot*, Financing, June 24, 1986, p. 1.
9. Investing in Israel, Investment Authority, Jerusalem.

REFERENCES

"The FTA Directory," A Guide to the Free Trade Agreement with the U.S., American-Israel Chamber of Commerce & Industry, Inc., 500 Fifth Ave., New York, N.Y. 10110.

Handbook of Israel High Technology, Arnold Sherman and Paul Hirchom, The Israel Economist, 1986.

Income Tax Ordinance, A.G. Publication, P.O. Box 7422, Haifa, 31070, Israel.

"Israel Business," Israel Communications, Inc., 350 Fifth Ave., New York, N.Y. 10118 or A.G. Publications Ltd., P.O. Box 7422, Haifa 31070, Israel.

Israel Defense Sales Directors, The Israel Economist, 1986.

The Israel Economic & Business Review, Annual Publication, The Israel Economist, 1986.

"The Israel Economist," P.O. Box 7052, Jerusalem 91070, Israel.

"The Israel Tax Law Letter," A.G. Publications Ltd.

Statistical Abstract of Israel, Annual Publications, Central Bureau of Statistics.

"Who is Who is Israel," Bronfman & Cohen Publishers, P.O. Box 1109, Tel-Aviv, 66181, Israel.

Chapter 10

Japan

William Lazer
Midori Rynn

INTERNATIONAL INFLUENCES AFFECTING THE NATION

Exports and Imports

Japan has long been acutely aware of its vulnerability because of the relatively small size of the nation, the lack of natural resources, a geographic location next to the powerful neighbor China, the opening of Japan under duress with the threat of Western colonialism and aggression, and the industrialization and technological advancement that followed. As a consequence, Japan has become very sensitive to its surroundings and the impact, actual and potential, of developments in the rest of the world.

Modern Japan always placed great emphasis on exports because of their critical importance for survival. The well-accepted economic theme of the 1950s was "export or perish." Both the Japanese government and business became well attuned to export opportunities, they excelled, and by 1986 Japan accumulated very large trade surpluses. It became the world's largest creditor nation with foreign assets of $180.4 billion. Conversely, the U.S., which was formerly the world's largest creditor nation, became the largest debtor nation. The result has been a dramatic shift in the position and status of Japan, now a major economic power.

Japan's current and future economic influence is far greater than Japanese tend to think it is. Japan is in a period of transition, reassessing its economic strength, restructuring its successful economy, reevaluating its important position in the international arena, and undertaking a far-reaching five-year plan. Currently Japan's main trading concerns are how to maintain harmonious relationships with primary trading partners by helping them redress their trade deficits, opening up Japanese markets to them, moving toward an expansion of domestic rather than foreign markets, while at the same time maintaining its own economic growth.

Japan's posture is one of freer trade worldwide so that all countries may benefit. Its markets are more open now than they have ever been. It desires harmonious trade relations, reduced trade friction, and the utilization of trade surpluses to help developed nations. Japan's stated goals are to expand domestic demand, open the Japanese market further, and contribute to the development of the world's economy.

The U.S. and Japan represent the most important political/economic relationship in the world. Together they have over 40% of the world's GNP. Economically they are the number one and two countries of the free world. The U.S. continues to be the largest exporter to Japan, but it imports far more than it exports. Japan is the largest supplier of products to the U.S., the largest purchaser of agricultural commodities, and the largest investor in American securities. Thirty percent of Japan's food imports are from the U.S., while the U.S. is the largest purchaser of Japanese manufactured goods. Japan's direct investment in 1988 totaled over 50 billion dollars, a large part of it in the U.S. The two economies are economically intertwined—what happens in one impacts on the other and indeed on the rest of the world.

Japan's trade surplus in 1987 was over $100 billion, up from $93 billion dollars in 1986 and $56 billion in 1985. But with the rapid appreciation of the yen versus other currencies, particularly the dollar, the trade surplus is being reduced reflecting an increase in industrial product imports from the U.S. and Europe. The principle of free trade is respected in Japan although its imports are controlled in a very limited way. Except for the items subject to import quotas, imports of most products need only follow custom clearance formalities and submit import reports to an authorized foreign exchange bank. The Japanese government is exerting even greater effort to open its market wider by reducing both tariff and nontariff barriers.

International Capital Flows

In recent years, the investment in Japan by foreign corporations has been increasing. Investments in chemical, pharmaceutical, and other high-tech areas by the U.S. and European companies have increased considerably. This is due to the high economic growth rate of Asia in general, and Japan in particular, making the area attractive to European and American investments. Among foreign direct investors, the U.S. is by far the largest, representing over one-half of the direct investments. Others by the volume of investment are Switzerland, England, West Germany, Canada, France, and the Netherlands. The U.S. and seven European nations account for 74% of the total foreign direct investment in Japan.

Japan's direct overseas investments have also increased substantially, though they are still relatively small compared to the U.S.'s. There has been a substantial growth in recent years spurred by the increase in value of the yen. The rapid growth is due mostly to a surge in securities investment. The trend is expected to continue, with the major investment regions being North America followed by Asia, Latin America, Europe, and Oceania.

Impact of International Agreements

At this time, Japan does not belong to any active regional international group. It has, however, actively supported ASEAN and other countries in their economic development efforts, particularly in Asia. The Japanese government budgets a sizable sum for that purpose each year.

With regard to regional integration, unlike Europe the Asian and Pacific nations include both advanced and less developed countries. It becomes rather difficult to reach agreement and achieve regional integration because country objectives and needs are too diverse. However, there have been ongoing discussions on the subject and a number of agreements and organizations have been established, some under Japan's leadership. None is operative yet.

Business and industry groups from five Pacific countries, Australia, Canada, Japan, New Zealand, and the United States have formed the Pacific Basin Economic Cooperation Organization to support private enterprise and establish international institutions for the overall economic development of the Pacific Basin.

To provide a comprehensive organizational framework, the Asian and Pacific Council (ASPAC) was formed recently. Its members include Australia, New Zealand, Korea, Japan, Taiwan, Malaysia, Thailand, and the Philippines, with a total population of about 290 million. Membership is open to other countries of the region, and perhaps Burma, Indonesia, and Singapore will eventually join. ASPAC is supposed to work toward an Asian common market. To achieve this, preparatory studies and negotiations have been going on for some time on both government and nongovernment levels.

At this juncture in Asia, international business relations are more accurately characterized as international cooperation rather than integration. However, there is a great need for integration in the Asia-Pacific region. The Japan-Australia Axis emphasizing the special interests of both might be an interesting future development.

Active MNCs/State Owned Enterprises/Trading Companies

The Japanese sector that has been most active internationally for many decades is the import/export business. Of the many trading companies among the top 500 foreign companies listed by *Forbes* in 1987, 19 of the top 10 were Japanese trading companies. These companies are called *sogo shosha*, and they can handle a complete line of products anywhere in the world. Mitsui, Mitsubishi, and Sumitomo were founded with *zaibatsu** money nearly 100 years ago under the far-sighted Meiji leaders, who knew that trade was most crucial for Japan's well-being if not for its very survival. Japan's lack of natural resources and large, concentrated population makes it dependent on foreign source for necessary raw materials and food.

More recently, many other successful trading companies were founded independent of zaibatsu money. Some stem from the pre-World War II trade with China and are also among the world's largest multinational corporations. The trading companies are credited for selling the bulk of Japan's manufactured goods to all parts of the world.

---

*Very large Japanese industrialists combine with a financial and banking core.

There are also numerous trading companies that are specialized either by commodity or by geographic regions. They range in size from medium to small and have contributed greatly toward Japan's successful trade and favorable trade balance. Other multinational corporations cover various industries such as petroleum, banks and securities, cameras, electronics, automobiles, textiles, and other manufactured products, all of which expanded internationally in the recent decades.

Although the Japanese economy is driven by private business firms, it also includes a number of public corporations. *Kosha* refers to nationalized industries and represents one such type of public corporation. Examples are the Japan Tobacco and Salt Public Corporation, the Nippon Telegraph and Telephone Public Corporation, and the Japanese National Railways. *Kodan* refers to business organizations wholly capitalized by the government, such as the Japan Highway Public Corporation. *Jigyodan* cover a broad spectrum of agencies such as the Japan International Corporation Agency, the National Space Development Agency of Japan, and the Environmental Pollution Control Service Corporation. In addition, there are a number of government financial organizations, such as the Overseas Economic Cooperation Fund, the Export-Import Bank of Japan, the Japan Development Bank, and the Smaller Business Finance Corporation.

The trend for some time has been steadily away from government corporations to the privatization of all industries. Even the famous National Railroads is currently preparing to be turned over to the private sector. Many enterprises that were started by government funds and were government managed, like Japan Airlines, have long been privatized.

NATIONAL ECONOMIC AND PHYSICAL ENVIRONMENT

Economic Structure

Japan's economic policies, as a rule, are set by the cabinet. The government offices chiefly responsible for economic matters are the Ministries of Finance, International Trade and Industry, Transport, Agriculture/Forestry, Fisheries, and the Economic Planning

Agency. The Ministry of Finance controls the budget and is considered the most influential ministry. Each of the ministries is responsible for specific economic and business activities in the private sector.

In terms of GNP, Japan is second only to the U.S. among the economies of the free world. Japan's per capita GNP is now comparable to the per capita GNPs of the industrial economies of Western Europe. Yet, housing quality and leisure time use are not up to the levels of the economically advanced countries of the West. The Japanese government, therefore, has started to pursue methods of increasing both. The domestic economy is being developed, public works projects are being pursued, and the quality of life of Japanese consumers is being enhanced.

Current unemployment figures for Japan in recent years are about 2.5 to 2.7%, which is much higher than before the oil shock of the 1970s. While the large corporations in Japan are superefficient and highly productive and their workers enjoy much higher income, as a whole, the large number of small and medium-size establishments comprise Japan's backbone. According to a labor-force survey conducted by the Prime Minister's Office in March 1983, of the nation's 56.3 million employed workers, 9.1 million were self-employed, 5.4 million were working in a family operated business, and 41.7 million were employees (of whom 37.6 million had regular jobs). By sex, 34.3 million were male and 22.0 million were female, of whom less than half had regular jobs.

In retailing, for example, stores with four or less workers accounted for 86% of all establishments, but only about 30% of the total sales in the trade. Stores employing 100 workers or more account for only 0.1 of all retail stores by number but the bulk of the sales. Similarly, in wholesaling, small and medium-size wholesale outlets are predominant. In 1986 340,000 outlets employed 3.5 million persons. The fact that the gross annual sales of wholesalers are four times those of retailers indicates the multilevel structure and intricate division of Japan's distribution system. Sometimes there are as many as seven or eight layers of wholesalers involved before a product reaches consumers.

Income Distribution

The statistics for 1984 show that only 0.7% of the population was at the lowest family income category (below 1 million yen), with 5.8% for the next lowest (1-2 million yen). The next four categories (2-6 million yen) are the four largest categories, containing 67.2% of the population. The categories of 6-8 million yen comprised 15.3% of the population.

Income has steadily increased because of rapid growth in industrial activities. Not only do most Japanese consider themselves middle-class, but their lifestyle has much improved in the past two decades or so. Income distribution is becoming more concentrated in recent years. The high-income bracket shoulders a higher portion of the burden of income tax and other taxes, and income is being redistributed.

According to the Economic Planning Agency's 1985 White Paper, the average monthly family net income of those who identified themselves as middle-class (84.3% of male and 89.2% of female sample population) was 293,000 yen, with a disposable income of 253,000 yen. The middle-class families, as they were perceived by those reporting, have annual incomes of 2.25 to 6.25 million yen. Of those who identified themselves as upper-class (4.5% of both the male and female sample population), average monthly net family income was 511,000 yen, with disposable income of 422,000 yen. Of this, 85% was spent for consumption. Those who identified their families as lower-class (11.2% male and 6.3% of female sample population) had an average monthly net family income of 145,000 yen with a disposable income of 135,000 yen.

An interesting fact here is the unique Japanese sense of identifying oneself in a given social ranking. The Japanese usually consider their education, type of work, and position of the head of household, and do not place so much emphasis on income alone. Also others who have things that they do not are considered the upper class, and those who cannot have things they have must be the lower class. At any rate, their spending patterns emphasize slightly more differentiation. Those with higher incomes tend to choose more active leisure activities, and to purchase more luxury items and higher quality things than others do.

Incomes of workers at the larger, more efficient corporations are about 50% more than those at the smaller companies (less than 100 workers). This difference is primarily due not to wage differentials, but to the larger semiannual bonuses received in the summer and winter by those in the larger firms. Consideration of income alone can be misleading, however, for Japanese companies offer substantial nonmandatory fringe benefits, in addition to legally mandated fringes such as social security payments. Japanese companies commonly subsidize the meals eaten during work hours, give additional pay to cover commuting expenses, pay for workers' recreation trips, and construct recreation facilities.

According to a 1981 survey taken by Nikkeiren (Japan Federation of Employers' Association), the monthly corporate payment per worker of legally mandated social security contributions amounted to Y29,632, compared with nonmandatory welfare expenditures of Y18,017. These payments combined amounted to 14% of the monthly cash wage.

Physical Resources

Japan consists of four main islands—Hokkaido, Honshu, Shikoku, and Kyushu—and literally thousands of adjacent smaller islands. The total land area, which is about 4% that of the United States accounts for less than 0.3% of the earth's total area. Japan is primarily mountainous, containing 10% of the world's active volcanoes; and many natural hot springs.

Japan is located in the temperate zone, and the primary agricultural activity has been to grow rice with yields that have steadily increased because of technological developments virtually eliminating the influence of weather. The rice supply now exceeds demand despite government efforts to maintain a balance. About two-thirds of the nation's 377,700 square kilometers are forests, but Japan is not self-sufficient in lumber and relies on increasing amounts of imports from North America, the Soviet Union, Southeast Asia, and New Zealand.

Fish are a major source of protein and fishing has always been a very important activity. The worldwide adoption of 200 nautical-mile economic zones that began in 1975 caused difficult fishing problems for Japan, which has now become a net importer of fish. More recently, aquaculture has been used successfully for the production of such items as shrimp, yellowtail, scallops, and oysters.

Japan feels vulnerable because due to the limited amount of arable land it cannot produce enough food to feed its population. It is lacking most of the required natural resources. Japan depends on overseas supply to meet its basic needs. A 1982 White Paper on International Trade pointed out the following proportion of imports highlighting its vulnerability: aluminum, nickel, wool, raw cotton, and corn: 100%; oil, iron ore, copper, tin, and soybeans: over 95%; natural gas: 90%; lead, wheat: 85%; coal: 80%; and zinc and lumber: 64%.

Logistics and Physical Distribution

Japan is a small country with a relatively large population of about 120 million. Its population density of 317 per square kilometer is among the highest in the world. About 76% of the Japanese live in cities, with nearly 60% of the urban population living in Japan's four largest metropolitan areas: Tokyo, Osaka, Nagoya, and Kitakyushu. By necessity, Japan's public transportation system is highly developed to move its large working population from the growing number of bedroom communities to their workplaces. Rail, subways, truck, and air transport play a significant part. Air transport has been increasing in significance as Japan ranked third in passenger miles among the 150 members of the International Civil Aviation Organization in 1982. Being an island nation, Japan depends on maritime transport, has 953 ports, and has the world's second largest merchant fleet, after Liberia. Yet, Japan's merchant fleet can hardly keep up with the rapid expansion of the country's foreign trade, and its ships handle but a small portion of its exports and imports.

Japan has adapted to the advancing technology in information and communications. Japan's videotext system, CAPTAIN (Character and Pattern Telephone Access Information Network) has been in commercial operation since late 1984. A new development, the Nippon Telegraph and Telephone Public Corporation's Information Network System, is targeted to be in operation by the year 2000. It will connect telephones, facsimile devices, cable TV, and other communications media through a nationwide network of optical fiber cables. Japan is rapidly progressing on both the information and communications hardware and software fronts.

SOCIOCULTURAL ENVIRONMENT

Cross-Cultural Differences

Historically Japan has developed a very strong central government. The highly selected career civil service elite are people of integrity, extremely competent, and committed to the well-being of the nation. Traditional Japanese norms dictate that anyone in a responsible position must take it most seriously and much is expected of them.

Contemporary Japan is an overwhelmingly middle-class society with a totally literate population. While its population is homogenous, Japan's culture may be described as "historically heterogeneous." It is a society on which some cultural elements of the historical past are readily mixed with the present. This can be seen in music, theatre, food, clothing, and other aspects of the Japanese way of life. At the same time, Japan is also a mixture of the West and East in many phases of its lifestyle, such as housing, furniture, sports, entertainment, dress, and so on.

Japanese employment practices are characterized by so-called lifetime employment and seniority-based wages. Wages and salaries, however, are also based on education. Not all employees are covered by lifetime employment. These features may become less prominent in the future, yet even in a recession, layoffs rarely occur in Japan. Rather, top management cut their own salaries rather than lay off workers, which reveals the basic employer-employee relationship. Both labor and management tend to regard the entire company as one big family. It is rather natural, therefore, for workers to develop loyalty to the company, and for management to adopt a paternalistic posture toward its workers.

The Japanese are said to be lacking in class consciousness, but to be "proper" with each other is very much required and expected. This necessitates awareness of a given relationship and an evaluation of one's proper place in it, e.g., *senpai* and *kohai* (senior and junior, or those before and those following oneself), *dohai* (colleague who started the same year), and so on. Each person is expected to show a proper degree of deference depending on the role in the relationship. The proper amount of respect is also shown by the use of language with its various levels of honorifics, which makes the Japanese language among the most complex. One must always place oneself in a humble position, at the proper level, in relation to those with whom one is interacting.

An interesting consequence of language is the impact on mobility. It is much easier for men to master proper language usage than it is for women. Women have an almost impossible task of mastering the proper and correct style of speech used by the upper echelons unless a woman is born and brought up in an upper-level family. However, with the increased entry of women into the managerial work force and the impact of industry on "commonizing" the Japanese language, the language factor is no longer a barrier for the advancement of women in the workplace. Although, on the social scale, it is still easier for men to be upwardly mobile than it is for women.

The accomplished Japanese have a tendency for understatement, paralleling a tendency among some Americans for overstatement. Most competent Japanese everywhere typically understate both difficulties encountered in completing tasks and their own accomplishments. Since Japanese tend to adapt the behavior patterns of those just above themselves, a widespread preference exists for understatement. This is harmonious with the traditional dislike for conspicuous spending, which is attributable to the nouveau riche, who are deemed vulgar people who do not know any better. Tradition is appreciated and valued in Japan, while new items, particularly material things, are accepted though not necessarily considered valuable.

Somewhat related to the preference for understatement is the Japanese sense of privacy. Since Japanese must live and work in very limited spaces, they have a special need for and tradition of respecting the privacy of others. They have a strong desire to keep their home and private lives nonpublic. At school or work, no one is expected to reveal family background because private affairs are not perceived as relevant to others. This special respect for privacy is an extremely important consideration that is often overlooked by Western observers. Many social rituals exist to protect privacy, and one need not answer any personal questions if he/she does not wish to. Asking a personal question is very uncouth. The smile often perceived of as an expression of Oriental inscrutability, may actually be meant to convey the thought, "You are embarrassing me by asking me that question. Please back off so I don't have to get angry at you." Embarrassing someone is considered extremely rude and unacceptable behavior.

Japan, has recently been moving toward becoming a meritocracy. Upward mobility for competent men was long readily attainable by graduating from one of the best universities. Graduation from Tokyo University, for example, places one in an exclusive clique, almost guaranteeing a promising future. Similarly, graduating from the best private universities, such as Keio University, opens opportunities. Universities are ranked, and the better the university, the better the chances for its graduates. What has changed is the opportunity for almost anyone who can pass the appropriate examinations to earn a degree, which has in turn opened up opportunities. Thus, the Japanese society as a whole is currently undergoing considerable change.

Culturally Determined Consumer Behavior

Japanese consumers are characterized as being discriminating and demanding, particularly about quality. Low price is not a substitute for unacceptable quality. Since those at the top echelons were used to custom-made products, they did not readily accept lower-quality, mass-produced items. Since Japanese consumers tend to follow the example of those above them in status, the desire for quality trickles down.

Japanese consumers generally have a desire for differentiating and individualizing product purchases. They seek wide selections to choose from, with many product options, in different price categories. In durable goods they prefer well-known, branded items.

Gift giving is an important Japanese activity. Japanese spend freely and generously on gifts, selecting them with great care, and usually buying something of higher quality than they would use themselves. This is especially the case when a gift is for someone to whom they feel an obligation, or who is important, or for whom they truly care. The most important thing is not the money spent, but to be dutiful and proper.

A wide variety and assortment of retail stores service Japanese customers. The Japanese government has recognized that smaller retailers cannot possibly compete with large, well-established department stores, and adopted specific regulations to aid neighborhood stores. The regulations control large stores' practices, standards, store locations, and have included strict conditions for special sales and price discounting. This makes it a little easier for small retailers to compete and enjoy the advantage of serving their local neighborhoods.

In addition to neighborhood stores, some of the smaller retailers are specialty stores, often located in fashionable areas, serving their exclusive clientele by carrying selections of higher quality and unique items, as well as their own renowned brands. The stores known as *shinise* are old, well-established specialty stores, some of which have existed for several generations, and are household words in Japan. They are patronized by the most discriminating clientele, and are often the source of gift items.

Research reports have indicated repeatedly that Japanese consumers are interested in and willing to pay for quality. At the same time they seek value for their money. Extensive retail competition assures them of this.

Traditionally, Japanese consumers have considered installment purchases and general credit purchases suitable practices for only the poorer and lower classes. They prefer to save money each month till they can afford large-scale purchases such as durable goods, education, and weddings. Other than home mortgages, Japanese consumers have purchased with cash or on a monthly store charge basis. It was the store charge that resulted in the use of credit cards becoming an acceptable practice.

Japanese consumers seem to inherently dislike borrowing money. They are savers, putting aside around 20 to 25% of the paycheck. They tend to feel uncomfortable with debt and frequently pay off all indebtedness at the end of each year, prior to the New Year, a long-established custom. In recent years, some of the salaried people got into trouble by borrowing too much, but this is an atypical problem.

For business, the saving habit is a two-edged sword: it has created large sums of relatively low cost capital that is available for investment which has given Japanese businesses an advantage over other nations, it does, however, limit customer purchases.

The role of women, especially wives, as household purchasing agents is most significant. Wives are in control of most of the families' finances. Japanese husbands give their entire salary to their wives, or have the salaries directly deposited to bank accounts controlled by wives. The wives are responsible for the bulk of the purchasing decisions. They do the day-to-day shopping and exercise a strong influence over the larger, more expensive items, such as automobiles and furniture. Young single women comprise an important market segment. Their salary is the equivalent of their male counterparts at the job entry level. They still live at home with their parents and work until they get married. Their salaries are basically discretionary income available for their own use. They have been described as very astute shoppers who know prices and values, and they are also willing to pay for quality.

In the past, products made in the West, particularly in the U.S., were perceived as high quality, luxury items. Products such as watches, cameras, and fountain pens were among the imported items identified as exclusive possessions of the upper classes and were admired by the masses. That situation has changed, however, as consumer preferences have shifted to many Japanese products. In many instances, both American and European items have lost market share to Japanese products that have earned reputations for high quality and superior value.

In recent years, at the very time that Japanese middle- and working-class discretionary income increased and markets have expanded, the attractiveness of many Western-made products has declined. But the Japanese still have a preference for certain popular imported products such as ornamental and artistic items, furs, chocolate, crystal vases, paintings, fountain pens, leather goods, some food products, perfumes, and luxury cars. A recent survey indicates that Japanese women prefer Renault autos, whereas men prefer the

Mercedes Benz and BMW. The same survey also found that Japanese women like dresses imported from the West because of their good design. The point is that Japanese consumers readily accept quality items from the West and do not purposely set out to buy Japanese to the exclusion of imported items.

Business Behavior

A characteristic of Japanese business is the very large number of small business establishments that play such an important economic and social role. Regardless of their large numbers, most of them are not very profitable. It seems that the owners' objectives are to produce enough income to support their families, rather than to maximize profits or economic efficiency. Competition is very keen but at the same time, small businesses recognize that they must coexist with each other. This tends to encourage the establishments' search for uniqueness, and a competitive thrust that is tempered by the need to be fair with each other.

Many of the small enterprises, such as those in retailing or wholesaling, were established as a result of the traditional practice *noren-wake*, whereby an apprentice is given a branch store by his master, as the master gives up a share of his own business. The intricate Japanese wholesaler/retailer relationships and structures are due, in part, to this custom. Retailers served by the same wholesaler may be related to each other in this manner and are, naturally, friendly competitors, even though they may later change affiliations and methods of operation. As was noted, those serviced by the same wholesaler engage in friendly rather than predatory or hostile competition among themselves. They comprise a separate, identifiable, friendly, competitive group within the retail industry.

Many small business establishments have a special parent-child relationship with a larger corporate structure, referred to as *oya-gaisha* (parent company) and *ko-gaisha* (child company). The latter companies function as special feeder plants, or special suppliers that manufacture parts exclusively for the parent company. In such cases, the costs of maintaining large inventories for *kanban*, or the just-in-time methods of inventory control, are shouldered primarily by the suppliers, rather than the parent companies. Similarly, the cost of overproduction arising from the overestimation of demand, or economic declines are absorbed by *ko-gaisha*. *Ko-gaisha* are not the equivalent of American subsidiaries in either function or operation, but they are uniquely Japanese organizations. As a group of enterprises they serve as economic shock absorbers during hard times.

Larger Japanese companies have more formal structures that are similar in many ways to government organizations. They recruit from among the new graduate classes of high schools, colleges, and universities. The attribute most often sought in the selection of new management candidates is the capability of becoming a fine contributing member of the company, rather than one's special knowledge or skills. Traditionally, companies look for generalists rather than specialists. The Japanese company will train new recruits to fit its system and style of operation. Harmonious group relationships are expected, and any dissonant, abrasive personalities are not welcomed. Character is important, with attention paid to trustworthiness and the willingness to work hard.

Japanese companies avoid customer confrontations and hostilities, particularly public disputes. They tend to settle disagreements quietly, even if a complaining customer is totally wrong. Their dislike of adversarial publicity should not be interpreted as a sign of weakness or an admission of guilt. Rather, it simply represents a traditional way of handling customer relations. If in the future Japan becomes a litigious society like the U.S., this custom will have to yield to a more defensive business posture to protect the company. At this juncture, however, there seems to be no such trend in sight.

"The customer is always right," and "employees are there to serve," are the basic philosophies of Japanese businesses, and employees take special care not to appear arrogant, intimidating, rude, or offensive to customers. In this regard the common use of uniforms serves a special purpose, in addition to promoting group identity. Uniforms render management indistinguishable from other staff members to all outsiders including customers. Management by their attire cannot dominate customers, as is often the case in other countries. Psychologically, this tends to create an atmosphere in which customers feel more important than the staff around them which may induce customers to spend more. Also, complaints from customers on the floor about an employee or policy can be heard firsthand by management. Arrogant staff behavior in turn is likely to turn away Japanese customers for good, because it is interpreted as being the fault of managers signaling an inept business establishment. Management, therefore, tends to be careful in selecting, training, and supervising staff.

Japanese consumers put their trust in the retailers and brands that they select and tend to be loyal. Given the existence of keen competition, manufacturers recognize the importance of developing ever improved branded items. Customer dissatisfaction can do long-term harm to a company. Also, new businesses must be patient and very careful in developing new clientele, which because of brand loyalty can be a very slow process. Japanese businesses generally adopt a long-run approach to their operations, and seem to be much more patient than their U.S. counterparts for a host of reasons, both economic and cultural. As part of the long-term perspective, top management takes very seriously and personally their responsibilities and trust of looking after the well-being of the company and its employees. Top management is very attuned to developments around the world that will impact on their companies and continuously seek new ideas from many sources and levels, both inside and outside the firm. Japanese management is basically very adaptive to change — it has had to be — and it stands ready to adjust to major trends and changes in a positive manner.

Cooperation, harmony, and a group orientation, all marks of Japanese management, are merely ways of increasing a group's productivity. Avoiding dissonant relationships stems from the fact that such relationships can be very damaging to the group. Generally, the norms are the basic quality of hard work and the maintenance of integrity. Although work is separated from personal situations and interests, management does take care of subordinates' personal problems when consulted. And, significantly, as expected, disputes with outsiders are settled with nonconfrontational postures and attitudes.

There are many behavioral tendencies of Japanese executives that might confuse non-Japanese in normal business dealings. An example is the serious listening posture of closed eyes so not a single word of a conversation is missed. This may be interpreted as a lack of interest, boredom, or even an insult, because the executive seems to be sleeping. Then there are the confusing signs given by the Japanese "Yes" and "No," *hai* and *iie*. Hai does not translate precisely into the English "yes" but refers more accurately to "that is correct," and iie is simply "not so." The possibilities for confusion are great.

Also, foreign businessmen doing business in Japan must be careful in interpreting the apparent modernity of Japan. It often misleads them to expect more cosmopolitan behavioral patterns from Japanese executives than is realistic. And many Westerners, in their attempts to be considerate and utilize Japanese ways, try to adopt well-intended manners and gestures, imitating what they perceive to be Japanese ways. This can create serious misunderstanding because the Japanese assume that the behavior, which is unfamiliar and puzzling to them, must be some unknown American or Western custom. Well-intended thoughtfulness results in a breakdown of communication. This points up the value of the services of a competent bicultural person to assist with cross-cultural business negotiations.

POLITICAL AND LEGAL SYSTEMS

Basic Political and Business Values

Political System

Japan was the first Asian country to introduce parliamentary procedures; it did so in 1890. Then after World War II, the Japanese Imperial Diet was changed to the current Diet system, the supreme organ of the government, the sole legislative organ of the state. The Diet is made up of elected officials and consists of the House of Representatives and the House of Councillors. The latter includes representatives from both the national and prefectural constituencies.

Executive power is vested in the Cabinet, the Prime Minister, and some 20 Ministers of State which is collectively responsible to the Diet. The Prime Minister, who must be a member of the Diet, is designated by the Diet, and a majority of the Ministers of State are also chosen from among the members of the Diet. The Prime Minister has the power to appoint and dismiss the Ministers of State, all of whom must be civilians.

Judicial functions are exercised by the Supreme Court and other inferior courts. There are 8 High Courts, 50 District Courts, 50 Family Courts, and 575 Summary Courts. Judges and public prosecutors are career civil service officials. They enter the Ministry of Justice by passing the ministry examination on graduating from universities and their practices are free of party politics. The same is true for other civil servants. Thus, they can avoid political influence from local or national groups and are able to maintain neutrality as is expected of people with high public responsibility.

While the national government is in charge of such national functions as defense, foreign policy, and justice that are the inherent responsibility of the state, matters such as land preservation and development, disaster prevention, pollution control, labor, education, social welfare, health, and the like are dealt with almost entirely by local government bodies in cities, towns, and villages.

Political Philosophy and Business Norms

Japan's multiparty system results in the freedom of expression of various political philosophies from the far right to the far left. However, the political-economic-social orientations of the vast majority of Japanese lie in the middle. In reality, the extreme groups have very little influence, except in the sense of keeping the leading political party in check. The fact that the Japanese are a well-educated population makes it very difficult for extreme political ideologies to flourish.

Japan is a middle-class society where about 90% of the people identify themselves as middle class (and 4.5% identify themselves as upper class). Moreover, surveys indicate that the vast majority feel they are doing much better than average. This self-perception is the backbone of Japan's, being a meritocratic society where people feel their children have just as much of a chance as anyone – anyone at all, including the children of those at the top, if they work hard and are successful in competitive situations, such as entrance examinations.

Japanese labor unions in the post-WWII period moved away from trade unionism to form enterprise unions, within a company, in cooperation with other company groups. The result is not a company union as is understood in the U.S., because Japanese enterprise unions are not company-controlled. They negotiate furiously and very shrewdly with the management. At the same time, they are aware of the fact that if they act to harm their company they will be losing jobs, their lifetime jobs. In a society where the bulk of the workers feel secure in their jobs as long as the company lasts, and where workers do not change jobs, for unions to act to hurt their company is senseless. It not only hurts management but also the workers and unions. They do not wish to lose their lifelong positions and join the unemployed whose job opportunities are limited to temporary employment.

Japanese companies are generally quite democratic in their operations, but often view Western democracy with its egalitarianism as neglecting important considerations such as different employee situations, age, education, and seniority, and other important personal factors. Following the social norms, one treats each person properly depending on the specific relationship with the person, giving due respect to those above and affording all the appropriate degree of deference. This concern contributes greatly to the maintenance of Japan's social order and generates harmonious interpersonal relationships among organizations.

At the same time, this custom maintains the traditional role expectation of those at the top toward those below in an organization, resulting in a form of paternalism. Even though one's subordinates do not stand in a consanguineous relationship, superordinates are to assume the responsibility of looking after subordinates as if they are one's own family members, like the previously noted analogy of parents and children. For that reason, the latter will not be exploited by the former: subordinates can expect the superordinates to protect them. In turn, subordinates are to respect and be loyal to their superiors, resulting in a very special kind of mutual relationship. Those who fail to live up to the norms are deemed to be unworthy of the respect of others.

This strong concern for proper behavior is also reflected in the complexity of the Japanese language, as was noted. The use of proper language indicates not only one's proper upbringing, but the specific relationship between the two interactants.

Japanese businessmen view their democratic business approach of allowing subordinates to express their opinions and participate actively in decisions as simply acting in an appropriate manner toward subordinates, respecting their special knowledge, and treating them as a member of the group. The executives are simply being very practical by allowing everyone to contribute based on their expertise and insights, regardless of their position, so the whole organization benefits.

Since everyone in a company is "a member of the group" representing the whole business, businesses all are expected to conduct themselves properly: to be trustworthy, fair, responsible, respectful, and punctual for appointments. Being tardy causes others inconvenience and is interpreted as a sign of disrespect, a lack of concern for the matters under consideration, a failure indicating the lack of quality and trustworthiness of the company, and an action that puts the company in an awkward or compromising position.

In Japanese companies it is very important to be a team player and, therefore, acting in a manner that harms the group or that is selfish and egotistical is not tolerated. The norm is to have harmonious and proper attitude toward others, avoiding open confrontation, controlling unpleasant emotions, and being polite and civil to those one does not like. Business disputes and problems are settled by negotiation and compromise rather than by adversarial approaches that are designed "to win." Litigation is not the proper approach to settlement because it ends by clearly defining one party as right and the other party as wrong. Japanese do not believe that situations are black or white for very seldom is one party is all guilty and the other totally flawless.

Japanese businesses generally treat complaining customers with special care, even when they believe that the company is not at fault. The preference is to settle amicably, *enman-ni*, literally "without corners." Often a mediator whose opinions and judgment are respected by both parties is trusted to settle a dispute, thereby avoiding legal battles. The relatively small number of lawyers in all of Japan, fewer than exist in many states, indicates the preference for finding a less confrontational manner of handling discord.

In business, as in other relationships, to cause others to lose face or to embarrass them is not acceptable behavior. Politeness and modesty are desirable qualities, particularly for business leaders. Modesty and unassuming behavior are interpreted as indications of an accomplished individual, a person of depth and culture. Loudness, an example of lower-class behavior, is unacceptable for educated people.

Political Stability

Japan has a multiparty system of parliamentary representation. The Liberal Democratic Party is the leading party and is conservative. There are several major opposition parties, including the Japan Communist Party, represented in the Diet. In spite of the fact that the average duration of a cabinet has been rather short, Japan enjoys remarkable political stability. Japan's political stability is supported by the strong career civil service elite who are the core of the government and actually carry out the administration of the affairs of state. They are not only able but are also very proud of their responsibilities. Adding to their importance is the fact that the duration of office for Prime Minister has also been rather short and Cabinet members barely have enough time to get thoroughly familiar with the office of their ministry, let alone gain power over the ministry. In fact, drafts of legislation are prepared by those career civil service officers who work under an Administrative Vice-Minister who heads each group. Then they are presented by the Cabinet to the Diet. Because of this strength of the career civil service elite, government planning tends to be quite consistent, long-term, and unaffected by the change of Prime Minister.

Laws and Regulations Affecting Business

Japan's legal system reflects the civil law tradition, and was patterned after the French legal system when Japan revised its legal system at the Meiji Restoration about 100 years ago. The general legal system, therefore, resembles that of other European nations, as does the way government regulations are enacted and enforced.

Since the Cabinet has the executive power vested on it, the ministries with their career civil service officers are given the power to enact their regulations and administer them. In doing so the civil service officials are not affiliated with any political parties and do not owe their positions to them.

In comparison with the government regulations of the U.S., those in Japan are generally more practical and realistically attainable, and enforceable. That is, unlike some of the American business regulations that can be "technology forcing," the technology necessary to comply with any Japanese regulation is already available. For that reason, government officials may well meet with representatives of business sectors as well as the leading authority on the pertinent subject from academia, when drafting a regulation. Cost-effectiveness practicality, social impact, and other important factors are all carefully considered. If new technology is necessary, the government may solicit the cooperation of business and organize a special joint research and development project.

Aside from formal regulations, there are many administrative guidelines that ministries may issue. Voluntary compliance is usually expected although some companies may ignore ministerial guidelines. Such behavior, however, may be negatively sanctioned in a subtle manner.

Basically the government and the business sector are in a cooperative relationship, but not in the manner that the term "Japan, Inc." might suggest. Government policy may be rejected by business occasionally. For example, in the case of automobile industry, the Ministry of International Trade and Industry (MITI) was not keen about expanding that industry because of Japan's population density and congestion in the cities. Greater use of private automobiles was not deemed necessary given the extent of public transportation and the environmental conditions. The automobile industry, however, had other thoughts and developed the industry, resulting in a great export commodity.

Usually, however, the government exercises a strong leadership over business, although they are certainly not confrontational. Government is in the position of giving advice to various business sectors, because it has vast stores of information on hand from the excellent research facilities at their disposal. Also, the civil service elite are highly selected and able people whose concern is primarily for the well-being of the whole society. Many of them move into top positions in the private business sector after retiring from their public offices, creating a certain degree of comingling at the top levels. In addition, university cliques, such as the graduates of the University of Tokyo, may be found in both sectors' leadership ranks, which creates friendly communications between the sectors. All this certainly makes it easier for the business leaders to accept government recommendations and to cooperate with the government.

With regard to labor, the management must have an in-depth awareness of laws such as the Labor Standards Law, the Labor Union Law, the Labor Relations Adjustment Law, the Working Youths' Welfare Law, the Working Women's Welfare Law, the Physically Handicapped Persons' Employment Promotion Law, the Minimum Wage Law, and the Law Concerning Special Measures for Employment Promotion for Middle-Aged and Older Workers.

TECHNOLOGICAL ENVIRONMENT

Due to the language barrier, much of the scientific work done in Japan is not widely shared by scientists outside of Japan. Yet, the level of research and the development of technology is recognized as world class, despite the short history of applied and practical science in Japan. Accomplishments are attributable to a fine educational system and numerous, well-equipped research facilities in both the public and private sectors. Japan invests a great deal of money on science, has world renowned scientists, and is a leader in many scientific areas. Government and private scientific and technological research expenditures are estimated to be the third largest in the world, after the U.S. and the Soviet Union. Some of Japan's applied research has resulted in breakthroughs and in the development of legendary new products.

As of 1982, there were some 18,000 experimental and research bodies in Japan, representing an increase of 3,500 since 1976. About 1,030 are public institutes, with approximately 650 belonging to public and private universities and colleges. Most of the remaining 16,000 belong to private companies. Together they have a combined staff of 330,000 (an increase of 70,000 since 1976), and this sector is still growing.

The application of some of the results of Japan's stepped up efforts in scientific and technological research in the recent years has impacted and influenced industrial sectors such as the Shinkansen super express (the bullet train), electron microscopes, steel making, shipbuilding, motor vehicles, cameras, radio and television receivers, synthetic fibers, fertilizers, seasonings, antibiotics, fish breeding, pearl culture, and the improvement of rice, barley, and fruit strains.

Material Culture

The Japanese standard of living has been improving steadily. Due to the shortage of land, living spaces are very limited and affordable housing is a real need. Yet, according to the national surveys, overwhelming proportions of Japanese feel that they are doing quite well and are content with their lifestyles and living arrangements.

Japanese manufacturers, particularly of durable goods, compete vigorously among themselves. They place a strong emphasis on developing new and better products. They claim that domestic competition is keener than overseas competition, and that domestic competitors prepare Japanese companies well for their international challenges. Manufacturers also face expanding markets for a broad spectrum of products that were formerly deemed to be luxury items enjoyed only by the upper classes such as air conditioners, video recorders, stereo sets, computers, color TV, and so on. Very affluent markets have sprung up in Japan, the demand for luxury items is high, and Japanese manufacturers are poised to cultivate them.

Japanese consumers are moving more and more toward Western lifestyles and products. This can be seen in their kitchens and dining rooms, furniture, tastes in music, entertainment, sports, and purchases. This does not mean that Japanese are abandoning their traditional way of life for a new Western one — they are not. What usually occurs among Japanese consumers is a blending of both the traditional Japanese and Western styles of living in a unique way that best suits Japanese. Western products and ideas are embraced, changed, and adapted to suit the needs of the Japanese culture.

Automobile ownership is often used as an indicator of consumer affluence and well-being. According to the Economic Planning

Agency's 1984 survey, about 40% of the families owned automobiles. However, this figure may be misleading as an indicator of Japanese affluence because it is customary to furnish upper echelon people with chauffeur-driven limousines as a normal part of their professional perks. It is also national policy to control and restrict the number of individually owned automobiles in use. Policies such as prohibiting any private automobiles from entering a city during business hours, limited street parking, and requiring that cars be garaged at night have a dampening effect on increasing automobile ownership. (Such approaches are possible because almost all of Japan is served by reliable, efficient networks of commuting trains.) Automobile ownership, therefore, does not necessarily reflect a given Japanese family's socioeconomic status.

Human Resource Skills and Availability

Japan has a well educated population (almost 100% literacy) that can support the diversity of industrial needs. Schooling, which is provided free of charge, is compulsory. The state partially subsidizes the operating expenses of private colleges and universities, recently accounting for about 25% of the budget, and this amount is expected to rise gradually and eventually reach 50%. The quality of Japanese education is evidenced by the exceptional performance of Japanese students on international achievement tests, particularly in mathematics.

Japan produces a large number of scientists and engineers which augurs well for its future. Among university students in 1982, 681,046 specialized in social sciences, 388,575 in science and engineering, 239,486 in humanities, 133,724 in education, 114,457 in health including 73,401 in medical and dental faculties, 59,072 in agriculture, 44,183 in arts, 31,453 in home economics, and 23,444 in other disciplines. The scientific areas in which Japan has made notable progress and achieved outstanding results include theoretical physics, astronomy, seismology, pathology, mathematics, genetics, high polymer chemistry, microbiology, metallurgy, agronomy, fisheries, molecular biology, and telecommunications.

ORGANIZATIONAL CULTURE

Organizational Forms

A typical Japanese corporation is headed by a *shacho* (president). The position of *kaicho* (chairman) is sometimes, but not commonly, used and usually refers to a more ceremonial position for a semiretired president or founder. There are some companies, however, in which the kaicho is the top decision-maker. Under the *Shacho* is the position of *fuku-shacho* (vice-president), followed by *senmu* and *jomu*, senior executive vice-president and junior executive vice-president, respectively. At the next level are functional departments, *bu*, headed by *bucho*. Each *bu* is divided into several sections, *ka*, headed by *kacho*.

The term *juyaku*, which literally means "double-office-holders," refers to the top management group, including the president, vice-president, senmu, jomu, and some department heads. All of them have the designation of *torishimari-yaku,* in addition to their primary title, which literally means "those who control," and is the rough equivalent of directors.

The traditional retirement age for workers in Japan is 55, but that is now being extended to 65 in most companies because of the impact of the rapid aging and greying of society.

Because most Japanese corporations operate with bank loans, the role of the stockholders is not as significant as it is in the U.S. and other Western countries. Thus, some pressures on the company's officers are minimized, particularly the achievement of short-run results and the payment of dividends. (There are exceptions when a company is owned by a small number of stockholders and is not public.) Company officers have more power and freedom than is the case in the Western companies, since they are involved with day to day company operations.

Japanese manufacturing organizations are well-known for their joint responsibility and quality circles, which is the term given to team work and consultation at all levels for common problems. Increasingly, however, many plants are applying robotic technologies and the operator is often the only person involved, and indeed checks his/her own production. Advancement usually follows the rule of seniority, with a flexible rank order existing among those who begin serving the company in the same year.

The *doryo* relationship, which refers to colleagues who started in the company in the same year and have the same ranking, is very important. Those who started the year before, or earlier, are called *senpai*, senior members, while those beginning afterward are *kohai*, junior members. They are not exactly colleagues in the Japanese sense of the *doryo*, who are considered equals, resembling a class in a school system.

Decision-Making Process

If a company does not have a kaicho with power, the company's president, shacho, is the top decision-maker. The power of the board of directors is very different from that of Western businesses because all Japanese directors are usually corporate officers. Although the stock of most large Japanese corporations is widely held, stockholder impact on corporate policies, decisions, and actions is almost nonexistent. This enables Japanese management to focus on long-term opportunities without regard to short-term performance considerations.

Decisions regarding a company's future direction are primarily made by the chief executive officer, shacho, in consultation with other members of the management team. As to the implementation of specific plans, top management shares their ideas with subordinates, who in turn discuss them with their subordinates, and so on. At each stage, consensus is gained, and at the same time any foreseeable and possible problems are identified and solved. Discussions are held about how the operations involved can be carried out. When top management chooses a plan and implementation begins, there should be no hitches and the proposed course of action proceeds smoothly. The idea is that those who will actually be involved have been fully apprised, will have thought about implementation, and once a decision is made they can proceed with confidence and efficiency. In Japan the planning and discussions involved in decision-making take much time, while implementation becomes a relatively quick, smooth process, just the reverse of many U.S. decision situations.

Japanese managers pay attention to constructive suggestions from anyone in the organization, those in operating as well as in management positions. Company magazines usually feature ideas that have proven successful, and contributors are recognized and rewarded further, thereby encouraging employees.

The Japanese consensus-building style of decision-making generates a sense of personal involvement, creating a psychological advantage. Studies indicate that the time-consuming deliberations involved in decision-making are compensated for by the actual time saved in implementation, with the result that the total time from beginning to implementation is about the same in the U.S. and in Japan.

Large Corporate Groups

The enormously powerful *zaibatsu* of the pre-WWII period (the large horizontally and vertically integrated industrial giants) were disbanded by the Allied Powers during the Occupation. With the rapid economic expansion from the time of the Korean Conflict, however, new types of large-scale conglomerates have emerged. We shall distinguish three different types. The first primarily comprises the old *zaibatsu* groups, such as Mitsui, Mitsubishi, Sumitomo, and all their affiliates. The second is the bank groups in which the conglomerate is made up of corporations that are business affiliates of a major bank, such as the Fuji Bank, Sanwa Bank, and Daiichi-Kangyo Bank. The third type consists of independent corporate groups, such as the Hitachi group, the Shin Nittetsu group (Nippon Steel Company), and the Toyota Group. Each consists of a giant corporation in the center and its surrounding subsidiary and satellite member companies.

The first and second types both have very large enterprises among their members, including a banking and financial institution, and *sogo-shosha* (a large, complete-line trading company). They are usually linked by mutual stock interdependence, and may also have special arrangements for member presidents such as regular conferences, exclusive clubs, and social gatherings.

The third type, by contrast has different characteristics. Each group has a definite focal point, the giant company. The other members are its subsidiaries and satellite companies, the *ko-gaisha*. The core corporation owns stock in each of the other member companies. It dispatches directors to them, and renders technological and financial assistance. Thus, a very close working relationship exists between the core company and each of the ko-gaisha.

In recent years, however, this large corporate grouping trend seems to be diminishing and even reversing itself. Stimuli are the weakened position of some banks stemming from the slowing economy as well as the changing personalities and methods of operation of business leaders and the high-tech revolution. More and more, an increasing number of corporate projects, encouraged by the high-tech revolution and recent technological innovations, are being conducted outside of the large group confines.

NATIONAL CONTROL OF INTERNATIONAL TRADE

Foreign Trade Policy

Japan is the third largest trading country in the world, following the U.S. and West Germany. Being poor in natural resources, Japan imports raw materials and energy to manufacture products for export. Consequently, supplies of industrial materials account for two-thirds of Japan's imports, with manufactured industrial imports accounting for about 25% them. Japanese exports consist almost entirely of manufactured industrial products. Developing countries absorb about one-half of the exports and supply about one-half of the imports. Import figures from 1984 show that industrial countries accounted for 36.7%, developing countries supplied 57.7%, and the Communist bloc 5.6%.

Japan is a member of GATT (General Agreement on Tariffs and Trade), and following the beginning of the Tokyo round has cooperated with the multinational trade negotiation efforts by significantly reducing tariffs, eliminating many nontariff barriers, and adopting measures to open Japanese markets further. Yet, trade friction with the European Economic Community and the U.S. has became even more intensified. This has been exacerbated by the relatively weak yen, and the deteriorating trade position of many of Japan's trading partners. Japan's basic policy is that of striving to preserve a free trade system. The removal of the troublesome trade restrictions on beef and citrus products were announced at the June 1988 summit meeting. In 1988 Japan's tariff rates were lower than those of the European Community or the U.S. The government is also moving in the direction of the continuing reduction of procedural problems and other nontariff barriers. Japan plans to become more actively involved in industrial cooperation in a wide range of fields with other industrialized countries.

To cooperate with the economic development efforts of developing countries, Japan applies preferential duties to imports from over 100 countries and 25 regions. Since 1978 Japan has applied the "cumulative rules of origin" system of imports from the five countries of the Association of Southeast Asian Nations (ASEAN), thereby expanding the scope of preferential duty application to imports from a country other than the country of origin. Special attention and economic cooperation is given to ASEAN countries because of their close relationships with Japan.

Many recent measures and decisions are paving the way for greater participation by foreign companies in Japan's growing economy. Included are: easing foreign currency exchange controls, removing most restrictions on foreign banking institutions, opening Tokyo Stock Exchange membership to American and other foreign countries, opening the construction of Kansai Airport to foreign bidders, and the like. Foreign lawyers are now permitted to practice in Japan, though they are not yet allowed to represent a client in the courts.

Japan has been steadily and drastically reducing most of its tariffs and is now among the lowest tariff nations in the free industrialized world. As in every nation, a few import restrictions still covered selected items, such as some farm products and a few industrial products. Japan has no free trade zones and enforces a rigid restriction of weapons export.

Nontariff Methods of Trade Control

This situation is changing very greatly with the rapid removal of barriers to trade and the renewed emphasis on freer trade. The general trend in nontariff barriers and tariff barriers alike is to remove them. The stated policy of Japan is "free trade as the rule with restriction as exceptions." The same policy also applies to currency exchange, which in the past was an effective means of controlling imports and building trade surpluses. That has now been completely removed. Certain items still have a ceiling on the quantity that may be imported per year, but even such restrictions are being gradually removed. Safety requirements for imports are the same as those for domestically produced items. Inspection processes, which formerly constituted nontariff barriers have been greatly liberalized, substituting a self-reporting process in most cases.

BUSINESS OPPORTUNITIES

Japan liberalized direct foreign investment in wholesaling and retailing businesses in 1975. Since that time foreign capital has been making active inroads. Currently, with the continuing trend in open Japanese markets, foreign portfolio investment is increasing. The opening of Tokyo Stock Exchange memberships to non-Japanese brokerage firms heralds a new era of foreign financial activities. American and European brokerage firms and financial institutions are expected to continue to extend their financial inroads rapidly.

Many American corporations and others from foreign countries have established successful businesses in Japan, far more than is often recognized. Included are IBM, Credit Suisse, Coca Cola, Nestle, and scores of others. They represent companies who carefully studied Japanese markets, and adjusted their methods of operation and marketing mixes to Japanese needs and desires. Many of the most successful have Japanese executives holding top positions. Some of them are joint ventures that utilize the knowledge, contacts, and marketing networks of the Japanese partners.

National Plans

The seven-year plan that the government published in July 1983 covering the period of 1984-1990, described the economic prospects and policies for that period. The aims included the construction of a creatively stable society based on the premise of the advent of a high-level information society. Economic targets were described as achieving full employment with adequate growth, stabilized prices, and maintained external equilibrium. The goals are an annual growth rate in real GNP of 4%, an increase in prices of 3%, and a jobless rate in the final year of the plan of 2%.

Since that time, because of rapidly changing economic conditions, the increasing value of the yen, and changes in Japan's status and importance worldwide, Japan has reassessed economic situations and issued other important economic reports. The latest published report released in the spring of 1988, "Economic Management Within a Global Context," directed by Hiraiwa, presents a far-reaching program of economic reforms that are designed to deal with the restructuring of the Japanese economies well into the 1990s. It addresses economic problems such as trade imbalances, market access, quality of life, expansion of domestic markets, distribution systems, and a broad variety of complaints from foreign critics. The Hiraiwa report specifically recognizes Japan's responsibility to the international community and its role in promoting international economic well-being.

Japan recognizes that the world economy is now in the throes of a major transformation, as is the economy of Japan. Reference is made to the Endaka revolution, the very high value of the yen that is changing the economies of the world, and of Japan. Above all, Japan recognizes that it must adjust to the new economic realities and it is in the process of doing so.

Industrial Trends

One of the main Japanese industrial trends reflects the development of "soft industries" such as computer software, the information industry, high-tech developments for "thinner-smaller-shorter-and-lighter" products, investment in R & D projects, the biotech industries, bioengineering, and the like. It reflects a scientific and engineering trend that is well attuned to the output of Japan's education sector. This contrasts with the previous emphasis on heavy industries and the manufacturing of consumer durables such as automobiles, television sets, and electronic equipment.

Japan's investment in R & D is increasing very rapidly, particularly by the business sector. The share of the total expenditures for R & D by business has been expanding, while that for colleges, universities, and research institutions dropped. Japan is now fast becoming a technology-providing country instead of the technology-purchasing country it was previously. For example, Japan now leads the world in optical communication technology.

Starting in the mid-1960s there was a rapid growth of research- and development-oriented small-scale companies, which was referred to as the "venture business boom." These businesses developed around large cities. The growth trend slowed for a while, but regained its momentum in the 1980s. Many highly specialized ventures have found business niches neglected by giant enterprises. The venture groups have been developing new technologies in such avant-garde areas as "mechatronics" and biotechnics. At the same time, the usual marginal small businesses have seen increasingly high levels of bankruptcy.

Direct investments abroad by Japan increased notably in the 1970s, and again in the 1980s. The most recent increase was spurred by the strong rise in the value of the yen. In the past the majority of Japanese investments abroad were made in developing countries, but Japan has shifted production to countries with abundant natural resources in compliance with host country wishes to industrialize.

More recently, however, an increasing number and proportion of investments have been made in industrialized countries with the purpose of moving production facilities from Japan to other countries for ready access to local markets. The sudden surge in U.S. investments in the past few years has resulted in large-scale borrowing by Japanese investors from foreign banks; they have become the world's largest foreign bank borrowers.

Japan is under great international pressure to contribute to the expansion of the world economy by improving access to Japanese markets, expanding domestic markets, extending economic cooperation to other countries, reducing trade surpluses, and investing overseas. Such actions will affect domestic economic activities in the years to come.

Those companies who wish to gain a market share in Japan might consider a variety of arrangements with Japanese import/export firms. They have well-established distribution systems at their disposal, and have excellent market knowledge and know-how. Many excellent middle-sized trading companies exist that are well-attuned to Japanese consumer preferences, changing tastes, business trends, effective methods of operation, and government regulations. They can provide a fine vehicle for market entry.

SOURCES OF INFORMATION

International Sources

A rich variety of sources of information now exists about every aspect of business operations in Japan. Much of the literature has been translated into other languages. Various world organizations and government agencies publish useful information in both monographs and journals. International sources include the yearbooks and surveys published by the United Nations and its affiliates, including the International Monetary Fund and the World Bank. Excellent information is also published by banks: The Chase Manhattan Bank, Exim Bank, Federal Reserve Bank of Chicago, Manufacturers Hanover Trust Company, and Swiss Bank Corporation. Top Japanese sources are the National Government Ministries and Jetro (Japanese Trade Organization), New York. Additional important sources are the 450 Japanese Chambers of Commerce, and business and trade group associations.

The Japan Federation of Economic Organizations (*Keidanren*) is usually considered the most important Japanese trade group. It resembles the National Association of Manufacturers in the U.S. Its officials maintain very friendly relationships with foreign business leaders.

The Federation of Employers' Associations (*Nikkeiren*) represents management in matters relating to labor. It is known as a helpful resource for American businessmen who want to acquire information and advice about Japanese labor practices, labor-management relations, and labor trends.

Service Sources:
Banks, Legal Firms, Major Accounting Firms

Foreign businessmen, especially Americans, often find the Japanese way of doing business rather annoying because it is so very different. A particular point of annoyance is the lack of available, qualified consultants for U.S. companies similar to those available to Japanese companies in the U.S. The reason stems primarily from Japanese employment practices. The very best from the graduating classes have a choice of companies, and once they choose, they intend to stay with the company until they retire. The companies preferred are the most able, successful, and secure, and can promise extra bonuses.

As has been mentioned, the "cream of the crop" among the new college graduates also choose to enter the service of the national government and they too do not leave their civil service career in mid-stream. Hence, the most reliable and competent consultants a foreign businessman may find in Japan may be from another elite group, i.e., college professor, especially those of some renown. Because of their high status and prestige, they have excellent opportunities to mingle with the most successful business and government executives, and they may be the best source of consulting assistance. But it is likely that they too are employed by a competing firm and are not available. Some trade associations provide excellent consulting services, and a number of governmental offices such as MITI are often helpful.

As discussed, because of Japan's general orientation to conflict avoidance, the Japanese attitudes toward lawyers is unique. There is no such thing as a tax lawyer; all accounting matters are handled by a certified accountant, and tax matters are handled by certified tax accountants. Bringing a lawyer to a negotiating table would likely generate a feeling of distrust, if not confrontation, making the others very uncomfortable. Although foreign lawyers are now permitted to practice in Japan, the use of lawyers requires very careful consideration.

Similarly, the role of accounting firms is very different in Japan. Their use is also much more restricted. When negotiating with a government official or making an inquiry about tax negotiations, there is no need to take along a lawyer; an in-house tax accountant is the one who should accompany the chief executive officer or his representatives. After all, in Japan one does not go to a government office to confront officials but to seek advice, to explain matters, or to get information.

Japan's banks play a very active role in promoting businesses. They not only lend money but provide assistance and participate in business. For example, when a borrower seems to be failing, they may send a director to a business to help it along and protect the bank's interests. Since the top management of large security companies and large commercial banks are acquainted with many influential leaders of the business world, they can be of tremendous help to foreign companies. They are very knowledgeable and can often act as a go-between in finding suitable partners for joint ventures or other business arrangements.

REFERENCES

Aida, Yuji (1984), *Rekishi o Kaeta Ketsudan no Shunkan* (The Moments that Changed the History), Tokyo: Kadokawa Shoten, Chapter 1, pp. 9-38.

Alden, Vernon R. (1987), "Who Says you Can't Crack Japanese Markets?" *Harvard Business Review*, (January-February), No. 1, pp. 52-56.

Anderson, Charles A. (1984), "From the Boardroom: Corporate Directors in Japan," *Harvard Business Review*, May-June 1984, pp. 30-38.

"A Yen for Fun," (1988), *Forbes*, July 11, pp. 38-40.

Baranson, Jack (1981), *The Japanese Challenge to U.S. Industry*, Lexington, MA: Lexington Books.

Christopher, Robert (1986), *Second to None: American Companies in Japan*, New York: Crown.

Courdy, Jean C. (1984), *The Japanese: Everyday Life in the Empire of the Rising Sun*, New York: Harper.

Davidson, William H. (1983), *The Amazing Race: Winning the Technorivalry with Japan*, New York: Wiley.

Destler, I. M. and Hideo Sato (Eds.) (1982), *Coping with U.S.-Japanese Economic Conflicts*, Lexington, MA: Lexington Books.

Economic Planning Association and Economic Planning Agency Monthly, (1985), The Economic Planning Agency's White Paper on Japanese Life, November, No. 163.

The Economist, (1985), "Japan: A Survey," December, p. 7.

Fields, George (1984), *From Bonsais to Levis*, New York: Free Press.

Forbes, April 20, 1987, "Dokushin Kizoku," pp. 46-48.

Hall, Edward T. and Mildred Reed (1987), *Hidden Differences: Doing Business with the Japanese*, New York: Doubleday.

Imamura, Ann E. (1987), *Urban Japanese Housewives: At Home and in the Community*, Honolulu: University of Hawaii Press.

Japan Handbook: JETRO's Desktop Economic Encyclopedia, (1985), The Japan External Trade Organization.

Japan Economic Institute (1988), *Japan: Exploring New Paths*, Washington, D.C.: Japan Economic Institute.

Joel, James (1988), "Interpreting Japan," *Speaking for Japan*, January, pp. 6-13.

Lazer, William (1984), "Comparative Insights into Japanese Marketing: Myths and Realities," *Comparative Marketing Systems*, E. Kaynak and R. Savitt, eds., New York: Praeger.

Lazer, William (1985), "Different Perceptions of Japanese Marketing," *International Marketing Review*, 2, No. 3, Autumn, pp. 31-38.

Lazer, William and Rynn, Midori (1986), "Japanese Competitive Strategies: Some Issues and Cultural Roots," *Emerging International Strategic Frontiers*, V. H. Kirpalani, ed., (Proceedings of the American Marketing Association's International Marketing Conference), Singapore, 1986.

Mainichi Daily News (1985), Cracking the Japanese Mark, Tokyo.

Mansfield, Mike (1988), "Promises to Keep," *Speaking of Japan*, April, pp. 1-6.

Mine, Manabu (1982), "Quality of Working Life in Japan: Trends and Characteristics, *Labour and Society*, Vol. 7, No. 3, July-September.

Mitsubishi Corporation (1988), *Tatemae & Honne*, New York: The Free Press.

Miyazawa, Kiichi (1987), "Preparing for the Asia-Pacific Century, *Speaking of Japan*, September, pp. 1-3.

Morishima, Michio (1982), *Why Has Japan Succeeded: Western Technology and the Japanese Ethos*, New York: Cambridge University Press.

Morita, Akio (1986), *Made in Japan*, New York: Dutton.

Moroi, Ken and Itami, Hiroyuki (1987), "Changing Japan's Corporate Behavior," *Economic Eye*, September, pp. 18-22.

Nakane, Chie (1970), *Japanese Society*, Berkeley: University of California Press.

Nihon Keizai Seisaku Gakkai, com. (1986), *Nihon Keizai ni Okeru Seifu no Yakuwari*, (The role of the government in Japan's economy). Kobe: Kobe University, Bureau of Japan Economic Policy Association, published by Keiso Shobo.

Norbury, Paul and Bownas, Geoffrey (eds.), (1980), *Business in Japan: A Guide to Japanese Business Practice and Procedure*, Boulder, CO: Westview Press.

Norman, E. H. (1975), *Origins of the Modern Japanese State: Selected Writings of E. Norman*, John W. Dower, ed., New York: Pantheon Books.

Ouchi, William G. (1981), *Theory Z: How American Business Can Meet the Japanese Challenge*, Reading, MA: Addison-Wesley.

Ozawa, Terutomo (1979), *Multinationalism, Japanese Style: The Political Economy of Outward Dependency*, Princeton, NJ: Princeton University Press.

Pascale, Richard T. and Athos, Anthony G. (1981), *The Art of Japanese Management*, New York: Simon & Schuster.

Patrick, Hugh, ed. (1977), *Policy Making in Contemporary Japan*, Ithaca: Cornell University Press.

Pempel, T. J. (1982), *Policy and Politics in Japan: Creative Conservatism*, Philadelphia: Temple University Press.

Richardson, Bradley M. and Ueda, Taizo, eds., (1981), *Business and Society in Japan: Fundamentals for Businessmen*, New York: Praeger.

Rischauer, Edwin O. (1977), *The Japanese*, Cambridge, MA: Harvard University Press.

Rohlen, Thomas P. (1974), *For Harmony and Strength*, Berkeley: University of California Press.

Sato, Hideo (1988), "The New Reality," *Speaking of Japan*, March, pp. 1-6.

Sato, Kaquo, ed., (1980), *Industry and Business in Japan*, London: Croom Helm.

Shimaguchi, Mitsuaki and Lazer, William (1979), "Japanese Distribution Channels Invisible Barriers to Market Entry," *MSU Business Topics*, Winter, pp. 49-62.

Shiratori, Rei, ed., (1982), *Japan in the 1980s: Papers from a Symposium on Contemporary Japan Held at Sheffield University, England, September 11-13, 1980*, New York: Kodansha.

Suzuki, Yoshio, ed., (1987), *The Japanese Financial System*, Oxford: Clarendon Press.

Committee for Economic Development (1987), *United States-Japan Trade Relations: A Critical Juncture*, New York, October.

Vogel, Ezra F., ed. (1975), *Modern Japanese Organization and Decision Making*, Berkeley: University of California Press.

Vogel, Ezra F. (1979), *Japan as Number One: Lessons for America*, Cambridge, MA: Harvard University Press.

Vogel, Ezra F. (1971), *Japan's New Middle Class: The Salary Man and His Family in a Tokyo Suburb*, Berkeley: University of California Press.

Whitehead, Sir John (1987), "Japan's Emerging Role, *Speaking of Japan*, November, pp. 25-32.

Who's Who in Japanese Government, 1988/89, Tokyo: International Cultural Association, Japan, Co.

Yamamura, Koza (1974), *A Study of Samurai Income and Entrepreneurship*, Cambridge: Harvard University Press.

Yoshino, M. Y. (1971), *The Japanese Marketing System*, Cambridge M.I.T. Press.

Chapter 11

Marketing Opportunities in the Middle East

M.R. Haque

From high mountains in the north the great land mass of Southwest Asia (commonly known as The Middle East) sprawls for 6,492,500 km. Along its northern edge are the Black Sea, the Caucasus Mountains, and the Caspian Sea. Its western shores are washed by the Mediterranean and Red Seas, its eastern and southern shores by the Arabian Sea. This region has been occupied for a long time, and by many peoples. Civilization had one beginning here. Sumerians, Babylonians, Hittites, and Assyrians successively held sway over the cities of the region. Later Persians, followed by Greeks, Romans, Arabs, Mongols, and Turks, ruled the region.

And from this part of the world have also come ideas that changed human living. In medieval times when Europe was still ignorant of scientific knowledge, Damascus and Baghdad were centers for mathematics, medicine, philosophy, and law.

Today, Southwest Asia contains a curious mixture of nations. Bahrain, Qatar, and Lebanon are tiny in area, whereas Saudi Arabia is enormous. The average income in Iraq, Jordan, Syria, and Yemen is less that $600 a year, while in Kuwait and the United Arab Emirates it is over $10,000.

Southwest Asia has witnessed a tremendous amount of human history. Here, "today" is lived alongside an enduring "yesterday." Three great faiths, the only religions to worship one God,

The research assistance of Anne Creery and the secretarial assistance of Susanne Patterson in the completion of the paper are gratefully acknowledged.

arose in this part of the world. Here, Jehovah made his great covenant with Abraham, and Judaism had its beginnings. Here, Christ was born, and from here Christianity spread to encircle the globe. Here, Muhammed, the prophet of Allah and founder of Islam ("submission to God"), inspired his followers.

There can be no doubt that the nations of Saudi Arabia, Kuwait, Iraq, Qatar, Bahrain, Oman, and the United Arab Emirates have a mighty grip on the world oil market today. Clustered around the Persian Gulf, these members of the Organization of Arab Petroleum Exporting Countries (OAPEC) control approximately 60% of the world's known oil reserves.

Little of the oil produced by the countries of Southwest Asia is used in the region. Seventy-five percent of western Europe's oil requirements are today supplied by the countries of Southwest Asia.

Today, Southwest Asia is very much in the news. It is notable as a hotbed of conflict between the Jewish state of Israel and Arab nations. And due to modern demands for energy, its oil-rich countries have what amounts to a stranglehold on the economy of the Western world. As a result, the countries of the region also have unparalleled growth in national and per capita income and historically unprecedented potential for consumption of products and services of the Western technology and industry.

INTRODUCTION

This chapter deals with marketing opportunities in the Middle East. Although from a technical standpoint the term "West Asia" or "Arabian Peninsula" is more appropriate, the world usually uses the name "Middle East" more than anything else. However, it is necessary to emphasize here that this chapter examines marketing opportunities only in the Arab countries of the Arabian Peninsula and that it excludes Egypt and Iran. The following countries will be examined:

Bahrain	Saudi Arabia
Iraq	Syria
Jordan	The United Arab Emirates

Kuwait	North Yemen
Oman	South Yemen
Qatar	Lebanon

Egypt and Iran have been excluded from the analysis for the following reasons.

1. As the thrust of the analysis is on emerging marketing opportunities as a result of the sudden richness in buying power caused by oil, Egypt is obviously ruled out because it has no comparable oil resource. Also, it is not a part of the Arabian Peninsula.
2. The recent political problems in Iran and the fact that it is a non-Arab country has led the writer to exclude Iran from this analysis.

The intention here is to examine the forces affecting marketing in the Middle East (as defined above) and the opportunities that are available. In the past North Americans have shied away from this region, partly due to the Iranian hostage-taking incident. It basically reaffirmed Westerners' fears of political instability in the region, but it is time for business firms to seriously consider entering this lucrative market.

A very useful source of information and basic facts on all these countries is the *Quarterly Economic Review* published by The Economist Intelligence Unit of London, England. Readers may want to consult recent issues of this valuable publication for detailed information on each country of the region.

EXTERNAL INFLUENCES AFFECTING INTERNATIONAL MARKETING

International Influences Affecting Nations

Exports/Imports

On the whole, the countries making up the Arabian Peninsula mainly export oil and import food and manufactured goods. However, this is only a generalization. More specific exports and imports of each country are provided below.

Bahrain is an "entrepôt, mainly re-exporting to Saudi Arabia." Thus, its main import is minerals and fuels, with machinery and transport equipment following in second place.[1]

Since the 1950s, oil has been the key element in trade for Iraq. Thus, fluctuations in the oil market have accounted for fluctuations in their economy. A total ban on the import of luxury goods was instituted in 1982. This can be enforced since all trade is handled by state agencies and government purchasing boards.[2]

Jordan's main export is phosphate and its main imports are capital equipment and oil. They mainly deal with other Arab countries in the region.[3]

Kuwait's main exports are crude oil and refined products. These products accounted for about 86% of their exports in 1983. However, "the biggest share of Kuwait's non-oil exports are accounted for by transit trade, mainly to neighbouring states (i.e., fertilizers)."[4]

There is little data, let alone reliable data, available from Lebanon. However, it is known that they mainly reexport to other Arab countries.

Oil accounts for 99% of Oman's exports. Some non-oil exports are: dry limes, copper, fish, flour, dates, and fruit which mostly are sent to the United Arab Emirates (UAE). By far their largest import is machinery and transport equipment.[5]

Qatar's main exports are oil, steel, and reexports. They mainly import capital goods, foodstuffs, and live animals. Japan is their major trading partner.[6]

Without a doubt, crude oil is Saudi Arabia's main export. But they depend on imports for almost all of their manufactures and most of their foodstuffs. Even though capital goods have been the major import in the past, consumer goods are rapidly becoming more important.[7]

When the Ba'athists took over in Syria, they imposed tough trade and exchange controls to protect their dwindling foreign exchange reserves. As a result, over 75% of all imports and exports are handled by state-owned trading organizations. Moreover, many policies have been formulated to restrict the import of items that are domestically produced.[8]

The UAE's imports are composed of consumer goods (49%), capital goods (37.6%), and intermediary goods (12.9%). As its other neighbors, the UAE's main export is oil.[9]

In the case of North Yemen, half of the import total is foodstuffs, although development has led to a rapid rise in the imports of capital goods. Strangely enough, their largest export is biscuits.[10]

Finally, there is South Yemen, a small country on the Indian Ocean and geographically close to their neighbors' oil. They depend on everyone else's oil to run their petroleum refinery. Oil pretty well accounts for the bulk of their imports and refined oil products for their exports.[11]

Impact of Agreements

The most publicized agreement in this area is the Organization of Petroleum Exporting Countries (OPEC). It is a producer cartel which is "a unilateral agreement among producers of a commodity, or suppliers of a natural resource, to deal collectively as a group with the buyers for the purposes of trading the commodity."[12] The 13 member countries are: Saudi Arabia, Kuwait, Iran, Iraq, UAE, Qatar, Algeria, Ecuador, Gabon, Indonesia, Libya, Nigeria, and Venezeula. This agreement has had the most far-reaching affects on this region. Established in 1960, the power of this group was not felt until 1975 when the price of oil soared. However, OPEC is presently facing strong competition from non-OPEC countries, and is losing market share. They have recently announced that it is their intention to defend their share of the market, regardless of the cost (i.e., lowered prices).

An offshoot of OPEC is the Organization of Arab Petroleum Exporting Countries (OAPEC). Its members include Iraq, Kuwait, Qatar, Saudi Arabia, the United Arab Emirates, and also Algeria and Libya from outside the region.

The Arab Common Market (ACM) is an example of a regional group. "It was formed in 1964 with Egypt, Iraq, Kuwait, Jordan and Syria as the members." This group plans to achieve free internal trade and regularize external tariffs.[13]

The Gulf Cooperation Council (GCC) was formed in 1980 with the intention of promoting all forms of cooperation between Saudi Arabia, Kuwait, Bahrain, Qatar, UAE, and Oman.[14] Another aim is to ensure Persian Gulf security and economic integration. Objectives of the council are: the abolition of customs tariffs on locally produced goods, bulk purchases of imported foodstuffs, and the standardization of the costs and fees for electricity, water, telex, telephones, oil products, and gas.[15]

A final group which has significantly affected this region is the League of Arab Nations. "Headquartered in Cairo, it has several specialized organs which deal with the specialized problems of telecommunications, inland and ocean transport, civil aviation and the economic boycott of Israel. The Arab League is not a sovereign entity, but effectively espouses the Arab consensus on various issues."[16]

National Economic and Physical Environment

Economic Structure

The economies of the Middle East are predominantly based on oil production. Thus, many of these countries have been suffering due to falling oil prices. A quick synopsis of each country should give an adequate picture of the state of the economy.[17] See Exhibit 1.

Bahrain's economic development depends heavily on political stability in the Gulf region and the financial involvement of neighboring countries. Their economy is based on oil, but more specifically on the processing and reexporting of oil.

The Iraqi economic picture is difficult to describe in view of the prolonged war with Iran. However, a cease-fire has taken place recently. In Iraq, work is presently in progress on two major pipelines. The non-oil component of the economy is based on industry and agriculture.

The economy of Jordan grew at an average real rate of over 11% per year from 1975-81 and is now adjusting to slower rates of growth. The growth rate for 1984 is estimated at 3.8%. The manufacturing and mining sectors have been the largest contributors to the GDP. This has ousted the agricultural sector from its number one spot.

EXHIBIT 1. Classification of Countries for Locating Future Business Opportunities

INDUSTRIAL BASE

RESOURCES	RELATIVELY STRONG	RELATIVELY WEAK
	Group I: Iraq, Saudi Arabia, Kuwait	Group II: Qatar, UAE

Rich	- already have basic infra-structure in place, now want technology and management skills
	
	- thus main opportunities
	A) INDUSTRIAL
	  - computers
	  - telecommunications
	  - medical equipment & services
	  - downstream petro-chemicals
	
	B) CONSUMER
	  - foodstuffs
	  - Furniture & home furnishings
	  - sports & leisure goods
		- must build up the indigenous base
		
		- main opportunities
		A) INDUSTRIAL
		  - oil field services & supplies
		  - water desalination
		  - power generation tech. & equipment
		  - light industries
		  - project mgmt & design services
		B) CONSUMER
		  - foodstuffs
		  - clothing

Potentially Rich	NONE	Group III: North Yemen - new resources, no base - main opportunities: A) Industrial Capital Goods B) Consumer -foodstuffs

Poor	Group IV: Lebanon, Syria, Jordan, Bahrain
	
	- strong base, but large populations negate any productive gains, need appropriate technology
	
	- main opportunities
	A) INDUSTRIAL
	  - mining & industrial equipment
	  - transport equipment
	B) CONSUMER
	  - foodstuffs
		Group V: Oman, South Yemen
		
		- small to no oil production, encouraging firms to establish industrial projects
		
		- main opportunities
		A) INDUSTRIAL
		  - construction
		  - telecommunications
		  - water power generation
		  - irrigation systems
		B) CONSUMER
		  - foodstuffs

Source: Author compiled based on model presented in: Luqmani et. al. "Marketing in Islamic Countries: A View Point." MSU Business Topics 28 (Summer 1980).

Kuwait's economy is currently in a recession. Until the economy turns around, the Kuwaiti market will remain protective, conservative, and highly competitive. Kuwait's wealth is based on oil and natural gas (70% of GDP). A bright spot is that their 60 billion-plus barrel reserves should last for over 100 years at the current production levels.

The Lebanese economy rests on commerce rather than industry. The light industries that they do have produce consumer goods, and only comprise 17% of the GNP. A small agricultural sector is also present which produces fruit and vegetables and accounts for 9% of the GNP.

By international standards, Oman is a minor oil producer. However, oil and gas revenues account for a major portion of their earnings. Thus, like other oil-exporting countries, it has seen its revenue suffer due to the fall in oil prices. Attempts are now being made to diversify the economy as their reserves are predicted to last only until the end of the century.

Qatar's economy has witnessed a noticeable improvement during the past year. As a result of increased production, revenue from petroleum exports (main export) rose by one-third in 1984 to about $4 billion. Another bright spot is the upcoming exploitation of the Northwest Dome, an offshore gas field that could prove to be the world's largest.

Saudi Arabia is in a recession which is likely to continue for several more years. Total GDP probably fell in 1984-85, even though the non-oil component of GDP may have grown by 2-3%. GDP dropped from $150 billion in 1981-82 to $110 billion in 1983-84 at current prices. Nonetheless, Saudi Arabia has the largest proven oil reserves in the world and is one of the largest oil exporters, second only to the USSR.

Syria's economy is based on agriculture, although industrialization is rapidly increasing. The growth rate of GDP at the end of the 1970s was 3-5%, with a GDP of $7.3 billion in 1978. The following is the breakdown of contribution to GDP: industry, 26%; agriculture, 18%; trade, 17%; government, 16%; and other services, 20%.

"Revenue from exports of crude petroleum, which accounts for a large share (90%) of the UAE's GDP, has fallen sharply in recent years, dropping from $19.5 billion in 1981 to an estimated $13 billion last year." This has had disastrous effects on UAE's economy and the government is in the midst of consolidating to help level out the economy.

North Yemen has a unique economic profile in that it has no export industry to speak of. "Forty percent of the GDP is derived from an estimated $1.4 billion in remittances sent home by yemenis working outside of the country." The other 60% of the government revenues come from import duties as well as donations from foreign countries, which amount to well over $1 billion yearly. "Economic growth during 1985 is expected to continue at a sluggish pace as the government struggles to solve a number of serious problems. However, a bright spot for the economy may be a recent oil discovery."

Income Distribution and Physical Resources

As a rule, this region has very high per capita incomes due to oil wealth. However, this is not the case for all countries, as can be seen in the per capita income range of over $30,000 in Qatar down to $350 in South Yemen.

Logistics and Physical Distribution

In consumer goods, foreign suppliers normally sell to local importer/wholesalers who sometimes resell to others, but more often retail the imported goods only in their own outlets. This is an illustration of a typical Arab trading firm which is an organization that combines the functions of importer, wholesaler, exclusive distributor, and retailer. In most Arab countries a local citizen agent is required as a partner. Kuwait is an example of such a country with its Commercial Companies Law, which states that a foreign firm must have an agent or distributor who is a Kuwaiti national or a company with at least 51% Kuwaiti ownership. Moreover, an agent is required when dealing with governments.[18]

Retailing is still conducted in the traditional bazaars, but due to the growth of suburbs, many supermarkets, shopping centers, and showrooms with Western merchandising techniques have been popping up more frequently. Shopping plazas allow for faster and more coherent product distribution and display methods; provide clean and pleasant surroundings (in contrast to traditional suqs or bazaars), making it more conducive for wives and families to shop; and by being located in outlying suburbs, they ease the problem of traffic congestion in the central cities. Also, shopping malls, by attracting large numbers of regular customers, can be important aids in product promotion efforts.

Socio-cultural Environment

Cross-Cultural Differences

In order to formulate and implement effective marketing strategies in the Middle East, it is necessary to understand the differences between the North American and the Middle Eastern environments. These cultures will be compared at the individual and group levels.

Individual level. Historically, the Middle Easterners have been very religious. They may even appear to the uninformed to be fatalistic. The phrase *Insha Allah* — if God is willing — often precedes action-oriented statements. However, the North American religious orientation is tempered by other values. Situations are not evaluated solely on the basis of religious values, but rather, they are categorized according to the differing circumstances.

Arabs are more emotional. Many items can be sold based on an appeal to their emotions. Although North Americans are not emotionless, demonstrating emotion is appropriate at different times. Simply, they exhibit a more rational behavior from a Western perspective.

Finally, individual status in the Arab world is determined primarily by family position and social contacts. Moreover, status is sought more than wealth. The terms status and walth are not synonomous. Although status in North America is also affected by family position and social contacts, it is further affected by education, leadership qualities, levels of expertise, and achievement.

Group level. The most important thing to recognize is the importance of the Arab family. According to Islam, the father protects and provides for the entire family. This family quite often includes more than just the immediate members. In return, the members of the family respect the father's wishes.

On the other hand, families in Western societies are much

smaller and wield much less influence. The American extended family was more close-knit in past generations, but as the family activities of education, religion, and recreation have been taken over by the school, the church, and social organizations, respectively, family members have had less contact with each other. Also, the increased mobility of North Americans due to the burgeoning growth of industries and cities has led to the nuclear family's becoming the primary social unit. Thus, the typical Western person is less dependent on his family and is more dependent on groups outside of the family.

Luqmani, Quraeshi, and Delene provide an excellent outline of how religion is reflected in the mainly Islamic culture of countries of the region.

Consumer Behavior

We are all familiar with the tales of the rich Arab spending exorbitently. There is a story of a Saudi "who bought 16 cars for cash, one for each of his 15 sons and one for himself. Is this story true or false? It might be true but it is not a typical consumer purchase. More than likely the man was an exceptionally rich Saudi who had a desire to impress his sons after years of being poor," explains Antoine Tadros, research director, Saudi Research and Marketing Company. Further, he states that although little is really known about specific Arab consumer habits, we do know that the "real consumer is shrewd and understands competition, value, price and availability."[19] It can be further surmised that since the family plays such an important role, the family leaders and respected members are the opinion leaders.

With the influx of money, a rapidly growing middle class, and a relatively large number of people returning home with Western educations, there has been a growing demand for nontraditional consumer products. "Not so long ago the area of Jeddah was mostly desert. Now the streets are paved with asphalt. Three years ago a Saudi did not think about air conditioners. Now most stores and many homes and cars have them."[20] In a growing trend American products are preferred, even in more traditional product categories such as foodstuffs and apparel. Luqmani et al. provide a list of some current consumer products and some products which will have a potential demand in Islamic markets.

Business Behavior

Arabs "are essentially oral people; they do not like to negotiate by paper. They want to feel out — to talk, to assess, to bargain — and to take their time, without pressure."[21] They also pay close attention to body language. Typically, Arabs sit close together when making deals. They establish eye contact, as much can be read from the eyes, including interest or disinterest. Frequent touching as well as thermal, olfactory, and kinesthetic cues will help them to decide how they feel about a person.[22] The integrity of a person is often more important than the fine points of a deal.

The following are some characteristics that Arabs value highly, and which the North American marketer may want to keep in mind.

1. *Quiet, secure strength*. Arabs look for clear, honest facts; their sense of logic operates on an unambiguous, right/wrong or yes/no basis.
2. *Patience*. Arabs do not follow the North American maxim of time is money. Business is transacted leisurely and courtesy calls are very important.
3. *Politeness*.
4. *Friendship*. Arabs have historically been traders who have emphasized reputation and personal relationships when doing business. Luqmani et al. outline the major implications for marketing of some of the fundamental Islamic concepts fairly prevalent in the countries of the region.

Political and Legal Systems

Basic Political and Business Values

The main aim of all of these Arab governments is to develop an infrastructure in their country so they can diversify their economy. Most of these countries depend mostly on their oil reserves to pay the bills, however, they realize that some day the well is going to run dry. Thus, they are using the revenues from the oil industry and the capital and technology of foreigners to develop as quickly as possible.

Powers of Constituencies

The countries of the Arabian Peninsula exhibit basically five different forms of government. Qatar and the UAE are Sheikdoms. There are also several monarchies: Kuwait, Jordan, Bahrain, and Saudi Arabia. North Yemen is the only military regime at this point. Iraq, Syria, and South Yemen all are party governments, while Oman is the only Sultanate. Then we have Lebanon, which is a political mess. One Beirut newspaper described the plight of Lebanon thusly: "here we are with 3 armies, 2 police forces, 22 militias, 42 parties, 9 Palestinian organizations, 4 radio stations and 2 t.v. stations and much destruction."[23] *Quarterly Economic Review* (a publication of The Economist Intelligence Unit) provides periodic reports on the goverments of the countries of the region.

Political Stability

"Following the Iranian revolution, foreign corporations operating in the Middle East took an increased interest in 'political risk' forecasting. Political risk can be defined as the probability that a given political event will result in strategic financial or personnel losses to the firm."[24]

A number of symptoms indicate instability of a government: public unrest, government crises, armed attacks by one group of people on another or from a neighboring country, guerilla warfare, politically motivated assassinations, coups d'etat, and irregular change in top government leaders. The countries that fall into at least one of these categories are: Iraq, Lebanon, Jordan, Syria, and the Yemens to some extent. Marketers will probably find it advantageous to avoid these countries until more stability develops.

Laws and Regulations Affecting Business

The administration of foreign direct investment regulations are mainly handled on a case-by-case basis. The main screening criterion is the functional contribution of the investment.

If the company is allowed to enter the market, joint ventures are required 9 out of 10 times. However, there are few limitations on repatriation of profits. Several other investment incentives are prevalent, such as five-year tax holidays and free trade zones.

There are no controls on technology transfer as this is what the host nations are hoping to develop. But there are local quotas for the work force.

A foreign company looking to enter this market must make a careful analysis of all laws. One must also make sure that the information is up-to-date, as the laws change quite often, though in some cases not often enough. Not surprisingly, the legal system has not evolved at the same pace as the modernization process.[25]

Technological Environment

Material life refers to economics, that is, what people do to derive their livelihood. The two essential components of material life are knowledge and economics. The material culture of this region is rapidly evolving. The importance of agriculture in the economy will be the measure by which we will assess each country.

As Bahrain has continued to develop, farming has declined in social status and many agricultural workers have been attracted to higher income in industry. Therefore, only about 25% of the population is among the agricultural labor force, and the standard of living is rising.

Jordan, Kuwait, Lebanon, Qatar, UAE, and the Yemens all employ less than 25% of their labor force in agriculture. This is due to the shift from agriculturally based economies to industrial economies. One other variable also comes into play: not all of these countries are able to support crops in their desert climate. As a result, these countries have had to find other ways to support themselves.

On the other hand, several countries are still highly dependent on agriculture. For example, 53% of Iraq's labor force, 48% of Oman's labor force, 30% of Saudi Arabia's labor force, and 50% of Syria's labor force are all still employed in agriculture.

Oman and Saudi Arabia, even with their high percentage of agricultural workers, still have some of the highest per capita incomes in the world; per capita income in Saudi Arabia was estimated at $13,750 in 1980.[26]

Therefore, the Arab market has enormous opportunities due to the generally high disposable incomes in this region. As a matter of fact, "there are several products in the Middle East — fragrances and soft drinks are two examples — where per capita consumption is the highest in the world. Because of this potential, the marketplace is highly competitive."[27]

Human Resource Skills and Availability

Assessments of the labor situation in the Middle East usually conclude that productive labor is insufficient.[28] One major problem is the relatively small and scattered populations. Many people are uneducated and illiterate, which renders them unqualified for the specialized or technologically sophisticated industries. Rather than allow their relatively sparse populations to be further overwhelmed by expatriates, most of the countries of the Arabian Peninsula require contractors to import expatriate labour in large groups, to provide their housing, food and entertainment for the duration of the project, and to see that they leave when the project is completed.

Furthermore, another large portion of the population is immediately eliminated on the basis of sex, because women are barred from almost all jobs, except for those in teaching and medicine where they are needed to train or treat other women.

In answer to these labor problems, the various governments have included clauses in their development plans to aid in the training of the indigenous labor force.

INTERNAL INFLUENCES AFFECTING MARKETING

Organizational Culture

Special Facets

Before analyzing the organizational climate of the Middle East, the major influences of Islam on business operations should be recalled: emphasis on high ethical standards, the principle of egalitarianism, and the Muslim's belief in God's control over personal events of one's life.

Organizational Forms

There are two basic forms of organizations in the Middle East: the indigenous organizational form and the Western organizational form.[29]

Generally, small Arab companies emphasize substance over form in organizing a company. This is done by building flexibility into positions. Thus, the organizational structure will be more horizontal than vertical in nature, and will reflect the notion of egalitarianism which facilitates decision-making by consultation and consensus. This results in an organization that is relatively flat with a broad span of control.

In contrast, since large Arab businesses usually engage in international operations, the adoption of systematic Western management methods is required. Therefore, a triangular organizational structure with a clearly defined hierarchy and a narrow span of control is present.

There is one more organizational form that is developing at this time. It is found mostly in medium-sized companies formed as joint ventures between Arab businessmen and foreign companies and is characterized by a cross between Western and indigenous organizations. "It appears that an integration rather than adoption of Western management techniques will be the means by which Middle Eastern companies can further develop their management practices."[30]

Decision-Making Patterns

It is clear that in the large companies with a hierarchical structure, the majority of the decision-making power will rest at the top.

As a general rule, the small Arab companies tend to have centralized decision-making authority. These companies tend to be patriarchal, as they are owned and operated by a select group of male family members. Decision-making authority is vested in those managers who have earned the trust and respect of the extended family. Furthermore, the process of developing a consensus before making a final decision creates an atmosphere of open communication, but it also slows down the decision-making process.

The joint venture is an opportunity to grow middle management skills from within. Fahad M. Saja, managing director of Saudi Basic Metal Industries, Ltd., has called this "indigenization."[31] In other words, it is the practice of sharing the business of decision-making with those at the plant level (and) subjecting their own staff to similar processes of evaluation, motivation, and job control so that all of those involved in the business move toward equal contribution.

Corporate Organization and Control of Foreign Firms

Organizational Options

The structure of an international organization is mainly determined by the following environmental factors: quality of local management, diversity of product lines, size of the firm, location of the subsidiaries, and economic regions.

As a result of the interaction of these factors, four types of organizational structures are prevalent: (a) international division structure, (b) geographic structure, (c) product structure, and (d) matrix structure.[32]

The organizational structure that a firm chooses should be based on several criteria: emphasis on foreign versus domestic markets; evolution of the parent corporate structure; nature of the business and the related strategy; management's orientation toward overseas business; and the availability of qualified managers. However, it must also be noted that "there is no real standard model—the structure must be tailored to the unique situation and needs of the individual firm."[33]

AREAS OF CONFLICT

Direction of Industrial Growth

It is the goal of the Arab countries to become more industrialized and diversified in order to become less dependent on their oil wealth. However, with industrialization comes modernization, and these countries must be able to reconcile it with their traditional culture. A brief summary of the direction of industrial growth for each country is presented below (see Frank Bair[34]).

Bahrain has been developing a very large aluminum smelting operation over the past few years. Manufacturing in the areas of mechanical engineering, food processing, building materials, and electrical equipment has also been rapidly expanding.

Iraq is still highly dependent on petroleum refining, but they have been recently diversifying their efforts into areas such as textiles, food processing, cement, petrochemicals, paper, glass, vehicle assembly, iron, and steel, as well as various light manufacturing projects.

Jordan's industry is mainly based on the mineral industry. Thus mining such things as phosphates, the production of cement, and oil refining are all offshoots of the mineral industry.

Kuwait has not been doing much to diversify its economy. Anything to do with the oil industry will still be the object of their focused industrial sector.

Lebanon's industry has not been growing or changing over the last few years due to the political turmoil of the country.

Oman and Qatar are following the same direction as Kuwait, as they are still actively developing their oil- and mineral-related industries.

Saudi Arabia has thus far put forth the greatest effort to diversify its economy. The industries presently being developed are the hydrocarbon-based industries, solar power, water resources, mining, and others.

Syria's oil refining industry is still growing, as are the cement, sugar refining, and phosphate industries.

Since the UAE is intent on further developing their present petroleum and gas-based economy, they have been hard at work developing Ruwais (an industrial city complex) and Jebel Ali (an artificial industrial port) to give the petroleum industry an extra competitive edge.

Finally, in North Yemen industrial growth will be accounted for mainly in the development of an infrastructure, the production of basic building materials, and unsophisticated consumer goods.

National Control of Key Sectors

Most of the Arab countries participate heavily in the industrial sectors and to a lesser degree in the commercial sectors. The main reason is that an adequate infrastructure must be built so that additional industries and commercial enterprises may be able to open and operate. Saudi Arabia is an excellent example of this phenomena. Now that the majority of infrastructure is in place, the government has been slowly handing over control to the private sector and is only remaining active in the sectors which individuals cannot yet handle.

Credit and Pricing Policies

The Arab countries, especially the oil rich ones, have been known for many years as a strictly cash society.[35] However, as more and more Arabs begin traveling more frequently and extensively, they are exposed to methods of payment other than cash – namely, the credit cared. The Islamic faith embraced by almost all Arabs prohibits usury, so the Western-style credit card with its revolving credit facility is a foreign concept. Nonetheless, more and more Arab establishments are honoring cards.

In Arab countries, careful pricing is extremely necessary. Pricing policy is made more difficult by two contradictory philosophies held concurrently: (a) the cheaper the better, and (b) quality at any price. Cost becomes the dominant factor in government tenders. Quite often the laws state that the lowest bid must be accepted. However, quality is a more dominant factor when an individual is purchasing for private use or when status is important.[36]

Human Resource Development Policies

A major problem which has been encountered time after time is the lack of a skilled or even semiskilled labor force. Over the years the majority of the labor force in the Arab countries has been largely expatriate. However, many countries are finally recognizing this problem and references to training and education are appearing in many of the development plans. Many of the Persian Gulf states including Bahrain, Kuwait, Qatar, Oman, and Saudi Arabia are setting up specialized technical training schools for the larger population.

Saudi Arabia, in particular, has taken this issue quite seriously. Almost every project being tendered will now have a training component. So, while expatriate managers will still be charged with getting the project running, they will eventually be accountable for getting it running with Saudi manpower. A project starting from scratch these days will have approximately 15% of its budget committed to training.[37]

Taxation

The taxation laws vary from country to country. They range from the tax haven of Bahrain to the unusual system in Saudi Arabia which taxes only non-Saudi firms and foreign partners in a business enterprise. Exhibit 2 offers a quick overview of some selected tax laws.

SETTING UP A BUSINESS

National Control of International Trade

Foreign Trade Policy

Foreign trade policy in this region has generally been quite liberal. Most of the countries even have a free enterprise orientation, which is a definite plus for the foreign marketer. However, a few countries with socialists in power (such as Iraq, Syria, and South Yemen) do not espouse as liberal a trade policy. These countries tend to have state organizations do the bulk of the import purchasing.

Even though many Arab countries are fairly liberal now, it is only because they are seeking the technology and products of foreign industrialized countries. As some of these countries become more industrialized themselves (e.g., Saudi Arabia), more and more trade restrictions are being instituted in order to protect domestic industries. This is something a marketer who is considering entering this market should monitor very closely, as it may adversely affect any future profit potential. *Quarterly Economic Re-*

EXHIBIT 2. An Overview of Selected Middle Eastern Countries' Tax Laws

1. Bahrain
   Tax is only levied on the profits of corporate bodies in the extraction and production of oil. Otherwise, Bahrain may be considered a tax haven.

2. Kuwait
   Tax is only levied on such income as is earned in Kuwait from a trade or business carried on by a corporate entity. All types of income are subject to the same rates. The rates are as follows:

Taxable Income		Tax Rate %
Over	Not Over	
-	KD 5,250	Nil
KD 5,250	18,750	5
18,750	37,500	10
37,500	56,250	15
56,250	75,000	20
75,000	112,500	25
112,500	150,000	30
150,000	225,000	35
225,000	300,000	40
300,000	375,000	45
375,000	---	50

3. Lebanon
   Taxes are levied on four sources of income:
   a) Profits of industrial, commercial & noncommercial occupations or professions.
   b) Salaries, wages & pensions.
   c) Income derived from movable capital assets.
   d) Income earned by nonresidents.
   The following is the tax scale:

Rates		Commercial Occupations %,	Non-Commercial Occupations %
First 5,000 of taxable income		5	4
Next 10,000	-do-	7	5
" 10,000	-do-	9	7
" 10,000	-do-	13	10
" 15,000	-do-	17	13
" 25,000	-do-	22	17
" 25,000	-do-	27	22
" 150,000	-do-	32	27
" 500,000	-do-	37	32
portion over 750,000 -do-		42	37

4. Oman
   The only tax in Oman is the tax on "trade for business". There is no personal income tax on salaries or earnings, no estate or gift tax, no capital gains tax, no tax on interest or dividends and no tax on sales or transactions. The following is the tax scale:

Income (OR)	%	Income (OR)	%
0 - 5,000	Nil	100,000-200,000	30
5,000-18,000	5	200,000-300,000	35
18,000-35,000	10	300,000-400,000	40
35,000-55,000	15	400,000-500,000	45
55,000-75,000	20	500,000 plus	50
75,000-100,000	25		

EXHIBIT 2 (continued)

5. Qatar
   Qatari income tax is levied on all corporate bodies, wheresoever incorporated, that are carrying on trade or business in Qatar at any time during the taxable year. In practice now, only the profits of foreign participants in corporations are taxed. It is possible to have a specific tax exemption written into certain contracts. However, this only occurs with prestigious projects or ones dealing with national interest. The tax rates in 1982 are as follows:

Taxable Income		Tax rate %
Over	Not Over	
0	QR 70,000	0
QR 70,000	250,000	5
250,000	500,000	10
500,000	750,000	15
750,000	1,000,000	20
1,000,000	1,500,000	25
1,500,000	2,000,000	30
2,000,000	3,000,000	35
3,000,000	4,000,000	40
4,000,000	5,000,000	45
5,000,000 +		50

Income derived from the production and export of oil from Qatar is taxed at a rate of 85%.

6. UNITED ARAB EMIRATES
   Income tax laws exist in Abu Dhabi and Dubai, but only apply to oil companies.

Taxable Income		%
Over	Not Over	
	UD 1,000,000	0
UD 1,000,000	2,000,000	10
2,000,000	3,000,000	20
3,000,000	4,000,000	30
4,000,000	5,000,000	40
5,000,000		50

There are no tax laws in the other Emirates.

7. North Yemen
   Business is taxed on net profits. The following is the tax scale:

Rates		%
First	YR 7,500	7
Second	7,500	10
Third	7,500	15
Fourth	7,500	20
All over	30,000	25

8. Saudi Arabia
   Non-Saudi companies operating in the Kingdom must pay taxes on income derived from operations within Saudi Arabia. A graduated income tax scale applies only to Non-Saudi firms

EXHIBIT 2 (continued)

and to foreign partners in a business enterprise.   The
applicable rates on business income are:

Income (SR)	Marginal Rate %
0-100,000	25
100,001-500,000	35
500,001-1,000,000	40
1,000,000 plus	45

Sources: Author compiled based on information presented in Price
Waterhouse Information Guides.   Doing Business In: Bahrain,
Kuwait, Oman, Qatar, UAE & Lebanon and

Frank Bair, International Marketing Handbook, 3 vols. (Detroit:
Gale Research Co., 1981).

view provides periodic summaries of governmental control on international trade in the region.

Tariffs and Nontariff Methods of Trade Control

Tariffs in this region are basically worked out *ad valorem*, that is, a tax based on a percentage of the value of the item. There is an emerging trend in this region. With the increasing number of regional agreements, the tariffs imposed on foreign goods are all becoming semistandardized.

Nontariff barriers are various ways in which a country can impede trade. Some of the methods used are state trading, entry procedures, health and safety regulations, product standards, exchange controls, import restraints, and licensing.

Free Trade Zones

There are presently nine different free trade zones in the Middle East. Jordan has two—Zarga and Agaba. Syria has established three in Damascus and one each in Aleppo, Tartous, and Latakia. The most recent addition is the Jebel Ali zone in the UAE, which was established on January 9, 1985.

All of these free trade zones essentially operate in the same manner. The principle advantages of these zones to foreign businesses are:

1. Retention of 100% foreign ownership.
2. Total transfer of profit for at least 15 years.
3. 100% repatriation of profit for at least 15 years.
4. General customs exemptions.
5. No need for import licenses to bring in raw materials.
6. Red tape cut out at customs.

In addition to these, the Zarga Free Zone also offers:

1. Finished goods and raw materials that may be exported tax-exempt for the first 12 years of production, with fees levied only if the finished product is for the domestic market.
2. No building licenses, nor land or building tax.
3. Exemption from plot rent for 2-3 years, depending on the type of structure.[38]

These free trade zones provide excellent opportunities for international businessmen to get their foot in the Middle Eastern market without incurring any more costs than necessary.

Methods of Entry

Exporting

Exporting is a way in which a company can minimize the risk of dealing internationally. Only minimal capital is required, and it is a very easy way to gain international experience. Export is the most common entry method into international markets.

Every country examined does participate heavily in this type of trade. The only real difference between the various countries is that some require that the foreign firm have a local agent or deal directly with a government agency. Exhibit 3 outlines the methods of entry for the countries of the region.

Wholly Owned Subsidiary

This is an entry method in which a foreign company has contributed 100% of the investment and holds 100% ownership. As a rule, this method is very rare among the Arab countries. Lebanon is the only country that will allow 100% foreign ownership, because they

EXHIBIT 3. A Brief Look at the Methods of Entry into the Middle Eastern Market

COUNTRY	EXPORT	WHOLLY OWNED SUBSID.	JOINT VENTURE
Bahrain	Yes, agent recommended	No	Yes, onshore - must have 51% local ownership; off-shore - no local participation req'd
Iraq	Yes, must sell to state organization	No	No foreign equity investment not desired
Jordan	Yes	Yes	Yes, general partnership, limited partnership, limited liability
Lebanon	Yes	Yes	Yes
Oman	Yes	No	Yes, general partnership, limited partnership, limited liability
Qatar	Yes	Yes, under special circumstances	Yes
Saudi Arabia	Yes, agent required	No	Yes, need a licence from FCIC; limited liability, 49% foreign ownership
Syria	Yes, sell to public agencies	No	
UAE	Yes, local agent required	No	Yes, joint venture partnership, limited liability company
North Yemen	Yes, local agent required	No	
South Yemen	?	?	?
Kuwait	Yes, must have a local agent	No	Yes, general partnership, limited partnership, etc.

Source: Author compiled based on information from Frank Bair, *International Marketing Handbook*, 3 vols. (Detroit: Gale Research Co., 1981).

need the foreign capital to rebuild what the war has destroyed. Surprisingly, Qatar will also allow 100% foreign ownership. However, this can only happen under *special* circumstances.[39]

Joint Venture

A joint venture is a business agreement entered into by a foreign company and a local person, group, or existing company. It is the second most common type of entry strategy utilized in this region. In fact, it is the most commonly required entry strategy, if the foreign firm is going to invest money. In the past, the only requirement was that the local participant have at least 25% ownership. However, in most countries of the region a minimum of 51% local ownership is now required, so the Middle Eastern countries can learn to stand on their own two feet. For example, in Saudi Arabia, the government "actively seeks and supports foreign investment in joint ventures as the preferred means of technology transfer. In addition, a range of investment incentives is offered by the government, including official credit facilities, subsidized utility rates and in some cases, tariff protection."[40] Several laws have been drawn up by the various countries (for example, the Foreign Capital Investment Regulation in Saudi Arabia and the Federal Companies Law in the UAE) to implement, monitor, and control the foreign investment.

The only country in which a joint venture, or any foreign equity investment at all, is not desired is Iraq.

Licensing

Several types of licensing agreements are allowed in each of the countries.

One type of foreign commercial representation is the "liaison" (or representative) office. "A liaison office is a branch or representative office of a foreign company having contracts with a ministry or public agency." A liaison office is considered a licensing agreement since a license must be obtained from the government before the office may be opened. In Saudi Arabia these offices are used mostly by oil companies and some defense contractors, hence the government involvement in the licensing.[41]

Another way to enter the market is to license a productive process or give technical assistance to a local enterprise. Such an involvement will allow a foreign company to study the day-to-day business operations of the local company with which it is cooperating. Through this contact the foreign company will be able to assess whether a more detailed and committed involvement in financial, manufacturing, staffing, and other terms will in fact work commercially.

Contracting

This was a major mode of entry during the initial construction period. Companies would submit fixed price bids to the various governments, and if awarded the job, complete it and leave. However, this type of contracting is no longer possible for foreign companies since many of the governments (e.g., Saudi Arabia) will only award such contracts to 100% locally owned firms.

Management contracts are one of the oldest vehicles that foreign contracting, service, and manufacturing companies have sought to use. Under this type of contract, the foreign company essentially manages the business while the local partner stands back. This is another entry method used as a hedge to test the waters. It can be considered an experiment in working with the local partner to assess whether the more committed cooperation required by a joint venture, such as financing and staff, would be worthwhile.

The majority of these entry modes appear to be the prelude to the permanent business relationship—the joint venture. Thus, a marketer looking to enter this market must carefully examine the laws and regulations in force at that time concerning setting up and operating a joint venture.

PRESENT AND FUTURE BUSINESS OPPORTUNITIES

Business Opportunities

National Plans (Development Plans)

Due to the influx of oil wealth, each of these countries has now had the opportunity to develop its own economy and infrastructure.

To aid them in this pursuit, development plans have been formulated, outlining the objectives of the respective governments for a specified period of time. Each plan will now be briefly examined.

Bahrain is planning to launch a large new development program in 1986 as part of an expansionary two-year budget. As a result a total expenditure of $3.2 billion is expected between 1986 and 1991 on capital projects. Priority is being given to the construction of 3,000 new housing units and to health and educational services. Bahrain offers the following inducements and facilities for foreign investors: (a) absence of income/profit taxes, and (b) no restriction on the repatriation of funds.[42]

Although Iraq has engaged in development planning since the 1950s, they have been unable to follow their own plans. In 1982, the government finally recognized that the state was underequipped to support a war and a program for economic development. By 1984, they only "maintained the elements of the investment program that either directly contributed to the war effort or which were financed by foreign credits."[43]

The current development plan of Jordan (1981-85) envisages rapid expansion of the economy with a targeted growth rate of real GDP of 11% per annum. "Maintenance of a strong private sector and a basically free enterprise economy remain a priority, the role of the public sector being to create the basic infrastructure for private business and to promote the larger scale productive projects."[44]

The new 1985/86-1989/90 developmental plan of Kuwait focuses on rationalization of public expenditure, with priority given to productive investments and projects of social importance (i.e., housing, electricity, water, health, education, and security).[45]

Oman will be embarking on its third five-year plan in 1985. Diversification into the non-oil sectors of agriculture and fisheries, and natural water resources and industry are the main priorities. If a project is considered developmental, then Oman offers a five-year tax holiday as an investment incentive.[46]

Qatar published its new budget in late April 1985. The government hopes to stimulate economic activity by pumping money into the economy. Major new projects in the works are road building and water and public works.[47]

The objectives of Saudi Arabia's third development plan (1980-85) are to: (i) assure the defense and internal security of the Kingdom; (ii) maintain a high rate of economic growth; (iii) reduce dependence on oil; (iv) develop human resources; (v) raise the standard of living; (vi) develop the physical infrastructure (i.e., water, electricity, communications); (vii) restraint on growth of expatriate labour force; and (viii) increased emphasis on agriculture, industry and mining. It is also intended that private capital will play a greater role in achieving some of the national economic goals, especially in the productive sectors. Thus, the expenditure budgeted for this plan was scheduled to total \$235.8 billion (defense spending not included).[48]

The basic objective of Syria's fifth five-year development plan is the continuation or completion of those projects started under previous plans. Their ultimate goal is self-sufficiency in agriculture.[49]

Aims of the UAE's development plan for 1981-85 are: (a) contain population growth; (b) strengthening of the agricultural sector in a way conducive to improving food security; (c) development of local education and training to put more UAE nationals into skilled jobs, and (d) continued investment in housing and health to meet the growing demand.[50]

A second five-year plan was published for North Yemen in 1982. However, problems with the first plan and an earthquake in 1982 disrupted the objective of the plans: (i) help out textiles, food processing and building materials to deter import substitution and (ii) continue support of agriculture, transport and communications.[51]

The start of South Yemen's ambitious second five-year plan (1979-83) was delayed until 1981-85 due to the war with North Yemen and financing problems. Overall expenditure was set at YK558 million (\$191 million) with foreign financing expected to pay for 70% of the total cost. The slated project areas are: (a) industry, agriculture and fisheries; (b) irrigation schemes; (c) oil exploration; (d) social services; and (e) improved electricity capacity, road and port expansion, improved telephone and postal services, and airport expansion.[52]

Industry Trends

In most countries there is still a trend to the development of an infrastructure. This still leaves open many opportunities for construction firms, machinery manufacturers, and others. However, in Saudi Arabia this is not the case. Now that the basic infrastructure is in place, a trend called "Saudiization" has developed. "This includes changes in tender laws (i.e., 100% national firms), the agency laws, the investment regulations and, most important, in the way in which business is done."[53] Basically, the government is trying to become less dependent on foreign firms and to give its own national firms a chance to stand on their own two feet.

Corporate Strategy and Planning for Foreign Firms

Strategic Options

The two factors underlying strategic market planning are markets and competition. When analyzing these two factors, the North American marketer must also consider how the sociocultural, technological, political, legal, and economic factors affect the marketplace.

In addition, a company must set up a grid of broad short- and long-term options, considering that innovation and market maintenance are the keys to success, as "firms that cannot adapt to the new economic, political and competitive realities of this sprawling, fragmented and viciously competitive region will risk losing out on many new opportunities—in second-tier industrialization projects, operations and management contracts, technical manpower training, environmental control, technology transfer and defense contracts."[54]

A firm may cope with these problems by entering into a joint venture with a Third World multinational corporation (MNC) as the former often enjoy the advantages of: lower labour and management costs, lower input costs, a more appropriate technology supplied without strings and a greater familiarity with the business and working environment.[55]

However, these same MNCs often lack capital, are subject to exchange controls in their own country, and lack a flow of up-to-date and improved technologies in manufacturing. It is these resources that a foreign firm can provide in addition to management and marketing skills. Such assets may prove to be the difference between success or failure for both the foreign firm and/or the Third World firm.

Planning Framework

Before a firm decides to enter a market, there are five essential steps to perform. The first is a *preliminary survey* of the potential significance of the market before investing heavily in the research and analysis necessary to make the business decision. Second, if the preliminary survey proves promising, then a more detailed analysis of the *competitive situation* must be conducted. This includes answering the following questions: (a) How much demand exists? (b) What technical standards must you meet? and (c) How well entrenched is the competition? Third, a *profit potential assessment* should be conducted. That is, "given the high fixed costs of setting up a business, will sales volume generate sufficient contributions for the break-even to be exceeded?" Fourth, the *distribution options* should be evaluated as this will directly affect profit potential. Finally, an explicit and comprehensive *marketing plan* must be prepared. This plan will "document the decisions reached in the previous four steps, set out contingency steps in case changes to the plan become necessary and define the milestones to help determine whether or not implementation is on track."[56]

FUTURE BUSINESS OPPORTUNITIES

The time has passed when a foreign firm would participate in any venture desired, as many of these countries have become more and more industrialized. Several years ago, a typical foreign company would be involved in some sort of construction project related to the development of the respective infrastructures. However, there are not too many of these projects left, and what is left must be carried out by a national firm (100%). However, many other opportunities are arising which are much better suited to the capabilities of North American businesses. These opportunities will be examined on the basis of two variables: (a) natural resource wealth, and (b) present indigenous development base.

Classification of the various Middle Eastern countries will make the assessment of marketing opportunities much easier by providing segments of the market. While different approaches for that purpose exist in marketing literature (e.g., Kaynak[57]), it appears that Luqmani et al.[58] provide the best approach for segmentation of the Arab countries of the Middle East from an international marketing perspective. Exhibit 1 illustrates the model using the variables of resources and industrial base.

Group I countries consist of Iraq, Kuwait, and Saudi Arabia. There are few opportunities in the construction sector as the basic infrastructure is already in place and whatever is left to be completed is put out for tender, and can only be bid on by national firms. Instead, these countries are more interested in foreign technology and managerial skills. North American firms may not be as interested in selling out their technical advancements, since valuable bargaining power would then be lost. However, if they can enter into joint ventures with national firms in the various countries, their interests may be protected in the high-tech market. North American firms may also offer their technically advanced products through one of the many available export opportunities.

However, an increasingly affluent population is developing in the Group I countries. Disposable incomes and the standard of living of average families have been steadily increasing over the past few years. The cities are rapidly expanding and with this increasing urbanization, the development of urban sprawl is evident. From urban sprawl comes the development of suburbs, where shopping malls are now beginning to appear. As a result, a large market for consumer goods has been evolving. Durable goods and some items such as clothing are a few examples of North American products which are considered superior in quality or status symbols.

An important point to note is that the globalization of products theory will not "hold water" in this area. At the grass roots level, all people have the same basic innate needs. But when variables such as culture, environment, history, etc. are added in, we find many differences. It is clear that it will be necessary to adapt most products (especially consumer durable goods) to the needs and tastes of these countries in order to be successful.

More specifically, Iraq offers opportunities in the following areas: agriculture, medical apparatus and supplies, irrigation equip-

ment and services, water treatment equipment and services, petroleum development and exploration equipment and services, and
computers and electronic equipment.[59] In the agricultural sector,
they are particularly concerned about new food processing equipment and techniques. One other field gaining a lot of attention is
computer technology. "Iraq is firmly committed to the use and application of computers and have shown an interest in robotics."[60]

Kuwait is a highly competitive market, so a Canadian marketer
(for example) must be careful that the price is right. Kuwait has
shown an interest in oil field equipment and services, electric power
generation/distribution equipment, telecommunications, safety and
security equipment and systems, medical equipment, and alternative energy expertise and equipment. Products such as foodstuffs
and apparel (especially North American) will also always have the
potential for future sales, if priced competitively.[61]

Saudi Arabia is looking mainly for technology, training, and
management. Foreign investment is being looked on favorably in
these areas.[62] Of course many of the traditional opportunities are
still open as well, such as light manufacturing, supplies for down-
stream petrochemical plants (i.e., plastics), avionics, and agricultural equipment and chemicals.[63]

In general, excellent opportunities exist for marketers in the
Group I countries, primarily in the consumer goods and high-tech
areas. However, a firm may want to think twice about entering Iraq
at this point. Even though many opportunities are available there,
foreign investment is regarded with suspicion and they are usually a
war zone. This is not to say that Iraq should be discounted totally,
but one may want to monitor the situation for awhile before making
a firm decision to enter the market.

Group II consists of Qatar and the UAE. The major problem
these countries must overcome is their weak indigenous base. This
can be accomplished through massive technical assistance from the
West. Foreign firms can take advantage of the infrastructure projects available there, which are not available in the Group I countries. The private sector plays a very large role in the industrial
development of Qatar, and they will accept investment in their various light and medium industries through joint ventures.[64] Furthermore, a foreign firm is presently allowed to open a wholly owned

subsidiary in Qatar, a definite incentive for a marketer who requires complete control.

However, in the UAE "emphasis is shifting toward operations, maintenance and services. Significant business opportunities are developing in oil field services and supplies, water desalination, power generation, office machinery, and project design and management services."[65]

This group offers the second best opportunities for foreign firms as they offer the basic infrastructure and ground floor projects in a relatively more politically stable area.

Group III consists of North Yemen. Presently they have a weak indigenous industrial base, but they have discovered what could be a major oil field. Future business opportunities could include oil extraction, port expansion, computers, water resource technology, and even solar energy.[66] There are still plenty of opportunities in food and consumer products as well as the traditional capital goods of cement, steel, machinery, and transport equipment. As tempting as all of this may seem, a marketer must remain wary of this market. Yemen is a country which recently has been plunged into a revolution. There would be no guarantees as to the safety of an investment. Again, this is another good market to monitor, but to avoid at this time.

Group IV consists of Lebanon, Syria, Jordan, and Bahrain. These countries can all boast of a strong indigenous base, but they are resource poor. In Syria agriculture remains a major industry, thus there is a market for tractors, combines, pickers, and irrigation equipment. However, the other countries are much more industrialized and have a need for mining and industrial equipment, avionics equipment, transport equipment, irrigation systems, electric power generation equipment, health care equipment, and more.[67] Again, it appears unwise to attempt entry into most of these markets due to political instability. But Bahrain is fairly stable and offers not only the industrial opportunities, but also many offshore financial opportunities. These quite often include the option for 100% foreign ownership as well as freedom from many of the constraints of onshore laws.

Finally, the fifth group consists of Oman and South Yemen, who have minor to no oil production. They have been encouraging firms to establish industrial projects so they can build up their indigenous base. Opportunities are arising in construction, telecommunications, water generation, irrigation systems, and agricultural equipment.[68] In fact, Oman has set up Rusail Industrial Estate, which is the cornerstone of their current industrial plan. Rusail will accommodate businesses such as piping, glass, fiber, and building materials. Thus, Oman provide the third best opportunities for marketers since the incentives are attractive and the government is relatively stable. Again, although South Yemen offers some attractive opportunities, a marketer is well-advised to avoid this country until a more stable government is reinstated.

In conclusion, the Arab countries of the Middle East provide many opportunities for the ambitious marketer, whether it be in consumer goods in the Group I countries or in industrial goods in the remaining country groups. However, one must be willing to give these countries of the Middle East a chance. In order to successfully exploit the potential and opportunities existing in these countries, a smart marketer must be willing to wait out or hedge against the present economic crisis caused by falling oil prices, as many more unfathomed opportunities in the second-tier industrialization phase will undoubtedly present themselves.

NOTES

1. "Bahrain, Qatar, Oman, North Yemen and South Yemen," *Quarterly Economic Review* (Annual Supplement 1984):15.

2. "Iraq," *Quarterly Economic Review* (Annual Supplement 1984):17.

3. "Syria and Jordan," *Quarterly Economic Review* (Annual Supplement 1984):44.

4. "Kuwait," Quarterly Economic Review (Annual Supplement 1984):19.

5. "Bahrain, Qatar, Oman, North Yemen and South Yemen," *Quarterly Economic Review* (Annual Supplement 1984):44.

6. *Ibid.*, p. 27.

7. "Saudi Arabia," *Quarterly Economic Review* (Annual Supplement 1984):22.

8. "Jordan & Syria." *Quarterly Economic Review* (Annual Supplement 1984):24.

9. "United Arab Emirates (UAE)," *Quarterly Economic Review* (Annual Supplement 1984):17.

10. "Bahrain, Qatar, Oman, North Yemen and South Yemen," *Quarterly Economic Review* (Annual Supplement 1984):58.

11. *Ibid.*

12. Subhash Jain, *International Marketing Management* Boston, Massachusetts: Kent Publishing Company, 1984.

13. *Ibid.* p. 138.

14. "Saudi Arabia," *Quarterly Economic Review* (Annual Supplement 1984):5.

15. "Kuwait," *Quarterly Economic Review* (Annual Supplement 1984):4.

16. Ragaei El Mallakh, *Kuwait: Trade & Investment* Boulder, Colorado: Westview Press, 1979.

17. Frank Bair, *International Marketing Handbook*, 3 vols. (Detroit: Gale Research Company, 1981), p. 590.

18. *Ibid.* p. 1355.

19. George Young, "Research and Understanding Are the Keys," *Advertising Age* (July 11, 1977).

20. M. Luqmani, Zahir Quraeshi, and L. Delene, "Marketing in Islamic Countries: A Viewpoint," *MSU Business Topics* 28 (Summer 1980):21.

21. A. Lanier, "Chinese, The Arabs: What Makes Them Buy?" *Sales and Marketing Management* 122 (March 1979):39.

22. E. Hall, "Learning the Arab's Silent Language," *Psychology Today* (August 1979):54.

23. R. Kilmarx, *Business and the Middle East: Threats & Prospects*, (New York: Pergamon Press, 1982), 52.

24. C. Kennedy, "Forecasting & Managing Political Risks in the Gulf," *Middle East Executive Reports* (June 1985):8.

25. J. Saba, "Saudi Arabia Investment Climate: Its Risks and Returns," *Middle East Executive Reports* (October 1985):19.

26. Frank Bair, *International Marketing Handbook*, 3 vols. (Detroit: Gale Research Company, 1981), p. 177.

27. P. Whitaker, "Marketing in the Arab World: Understanding the Consumer," *Middle East Executive Reports* (September 1985):9.

28. "Pitfalls in Mideast Trade: Myth or Reality?" *Commerce America* (August 28, 1978):5.

29. D. Anastos, A. Bedos, and B. Seaman, "The Development of Modern Management Practices in Saudi Arabia," *Columbia Journal of World Business* (Summer 1980):81.

30. *Ibid.*

31. *Ibid.*, p. 90.

32. Subhash Jain, *International Marketing Management*, (Boston, Massachusetts: Kent Publishing Company, 1984), p. 629.

33. Vern Terpstra, *International Marketing*, (Chicago: Dryden Press, 1983), p. 601.

34. Frank Bair, *International Marketing Handbook*, 3 vols. (Detroit: Gale Research Company, 1981), p. 180.

35. C. Acker. "Saudi Arabia: Credit Cards in The Kingdom," *Middle East Executive Reports* (November 1982):4.

36. L. Jensen, "Widespread Affluence Makes the Arabian Peninsula A Prime Market for U.S. Home & Leisure Products," *Business America* (April 4, 1983):20.

37. C. E. Acker, "Meeting the Demand for a Trained Saudi Work Force," *Middle East Executive Reports* (April 1984):15.

38. P. Robins, "Zarga Free Zone a Local Success — But Where Are the Foreigners?" *Middle East Executive Reports* (October 1983):13.

39. Frank Bair, *International Marketing Handbook*, 3 vols. (Detroit: Gale Research Company, 1981), p. 934.

40. T. Sams, "Saudi Arabia: U.S. Services Exporters Report Sustained Sales," *Business America* (September 16, 1985):32.

41. A. McNair, "Liaison & Technological Offices," *Middle East Executive Reports* (April 1985):9.

42. "Bahrain, Qatar, Oman, North Yemen & South Yemen," *Quarterly Economic Review*, (Annual Supplement 1984):17.

43. "Iraq," *Quarterly Economic Review* (Annual Supplement 1985):8.

44. "Syria & Jordan," *Quarterly Economic Review* (Annual Supplement 1984):32.

45. "Kuwait," *Quarterly Economic Review* (Annual Supplement 1984):7.

46. "Bahrain, Qatar, Oman, North Yemen, & South Yemen," *Quarterly Economic Review* (#3 1985):19.

47. *Ibid.* p. 17.

48. "Saudi Arabia," *Quarterly Economic Review* (Annual Supplement 1984):9.

49. "Syria & Jordan," *Quarterly Economic Review* (Annual Supplement 1984):10.

50. "UAE," *Quarterly Economic Review* (Annual Supplement 1984):15.

51. "Bahrain, Qatar, Oman, North Yemen, & South Yemen," *Quarterly Economic Review* (Annual Supplement 1984):51.

52. *Ibid.*, p. 64.

53. "Saudiization: The Emerging Trends," *Middle East Executive Reports* (June 1984):16.

54. "Tactics & Strategies for the Middle East," *Business International* (April 6, 1984):105.

55. S. Connolly, "Joint Ventures With Third World MNC's: A New Form of Entry to International Markets," *Columbia Journal of World Business* (Summer 1984):18.

56. Kevin Corcoran, *Saudi Arabia: Keys to Business Success*. (London: McGraw Hill Book Company, 1981), p. 31.

57. Erdener Kaynak, ed. *International Business in the Middle East*, New York: de Gruyter 1986.

58. M. Luqmani et al. "Marketing in Islamic Countries: A Viewpoint," *Michigan State Business Topics* (Summer 1980):23.

59. M. Roth, "Iraq: Market Improving, But Financing Key to Sales," *Business America* (March 4, 1985):52.

60. "Economic Slowdown Persists in Near East/North Africa/South Asia," *Business America* (September 16, 1985):30.

61. V. Eicher, "Kuwait: Price Remains Key Factor in Competitive Market," *Business America* (March 4, 1985):54.

62. J. Saba, "Saudi Arabia Investment Climate: Its Risks and Returns," *Middle East Executive Reports* (October 1985):19.

63. E. Kleinwaks, "Saudi Arabia: Some Markets Shrink as New Opportunities Develop," *Business America* (March 4, 1985):50.

64. "Qatar: A Guide to Sales Opportunities in Near East/North Africa Region," *Business America* (October 19, 1981):9.

65. UAE: U.S. Exports Fall in Line With Lower Oil Prices," *Business America* (March 4, 1985):53.

66. "Yemen Arab Republic: Though Sluggish, Economy Contains Some Good Prospects for U.S. Firms," *Business America* (January 31, 1985):37.

67. V. Eicher, "Jordan: Competition is Tough, But Market Worth the Effort," *Business America* (March 4, 1985):55.

68. "Oman: Economic Outlook," *Middle East Executive Reports* (February 1985):19.

BIBLIOGRAPHY

JOURNALS

Acker, C.F. and Whittingham, K. (1984). Manpower Training in the Arabian Peninsula, *Middle East Executive Reports* (April), 15.

Acker, C.F. (1982). The Switch to 'Plastics': Credit Cards in Saudi Arabia, *Middle East Executive Reports*, (November), 4.

Ackes, C. (1984). Meeting the Demand for a Trained Saudi Work Force, *Middle East Executive Reports*, (April), 17.

Advertising Age, 57 (January 30, 1986), pp. 9-16. Five short articles on marketing to the Arab world.

Alganhim, K. (1976). How to do Business in the Middle East, *Management Review*, (August), 65, 19-28.

Anastos, D., Bedos, A., and Seaman, B. (1980). The Development of Modern Management Practices in Saudi Arabia, *Columbia Journal of World Business* (Summer), 81-92.

Angus, C. (1985). UAE: Joint Ventures Today, *Middle East Executive Reports*, (February), 8.

Apgar, M. (1977). Succeeding in Saudi Arabia, *Harvard Business Review*, (January), 55, 14-16ff.

Bahrain, Qatar, Oman, North Yemen & South Yemen (1984, 1985). *Quarterly Economic Review*.

Business Outlook Abroad: Jordan (October 14, 1985). *Business America*, pp. 26-27.

Business Outlook Abroad: UAE (May 31, 1982). *Business America*, p. 22.

Business Outlook Abroad: Yemen Arab Republic (January 21, 1985). *Business America*, pp. 37-38.

Campbell, D.I. (1982). Canada's Natural Advantage in Saudi Arabia, *Canadian Business Review*, (Autumn), 25-28.

Clement, C. (1984). Near East/North Africa/South Asia Hampered by Lower Oil Prices, *Business America*, (March 4), 16-17.

Clement, C. (1984). Regional Integration Strengthens Gulf Economics, *Business America*, (June 25), 16-17.

Clement, C. (1985). UAE: U.S. Exports Fall in Line With Lower Oil Prices, *Business America*, (March 4), 53.

Connan, B. (1983). Pricing is Major Factor in Competitive Market, *Business America*, (August 22), 42.

Connolly, S.G. (1984). Joint Ventures With Third World MNC's: A New Form of Entry Into International Markets, *Columbia Journal of World Business*, (Summer), 18-22.

Counsell, A. (1985). Jordan: New Government, New Optimism, *Middle East Executive Reports*, (May), 8.

Economic Slowdown Continues in Near East/North Africa/South Asia (September 16, 1985). *Business America*, pp. 30-34.

Edwards, R.S. (1985). U.S. Apparel Makes Strong Showing in Mid-East Markets, *Business America*, (January 7), 38-39.

Eicher, Vicky. (1985). Kuwait: Price Remains Key Factor in Competitive Market, *Business America*, (March 4), 54.

Guide to Sales Opportunities in Near East-North Africa Region (October 19, 1981). *Business America*, 4, pp. 3-11.

Gulf Economies in Transition (March 1985). *Middle East Executive Reports*, pp. 10-13.

Hall, E. (1979). Learning the Arab's Silent Language, *Psychology Today* (August), 54.

Iraq (1984, 1985). *Quarterly Economic Review*.

Jebel Ali Free Zone Invites Foreign Business (August 1985). *Middle East Executive Reports*, p. 8.

Jensen, L. (1983). Widespread Affluence Makes the Arabian Peninsula A Prime Market for U.S. Home and Leisure Products, *Business America*, (April 4), 7, 20.

Joint Venture Guidelines in Saudi Arabia (June 10, 1983). *Business International*, p. 181.

Jordan: Additional U.S. Assistance May Spur Export Sales (October 14, 1985). *Business America*, p. 26.

Kalin, M. (1985). Saudi Arabia: The Kingdom's Lucrative Telecommunications Market, *Middle East Executive Reports*, (August), 14.

Keeling, N. (1985). UAE—What are the Best Options for Setting Up a Business in the UAE?, *Middle East Executive Reports*, (September), 9.

Kennedy, C. (1985). Forecasting & Managing Political Risks in the Gulf, *Middle East Executive Reports*, (June), 8.

Kleinwaks, E. (1985). Saudi Arabia: Some Markets Shrink as New Opportunities Develop, *Business America*, (March 4), 50.

Kuwait (1984, 1985). *Quarterly Economic Review.*

Kuwait, Information Technology: Who's Buying What (April 1985). *Middle East Executive Reports*, p. 20.

Lanier, A.R. (1979). Chinese, The Arabs: What Makes Them Buy? *Sales and Marketing Management*, (March), 122, 39-41, 91.

Lebanon (1984, 1985). *Quarterly Economic Review.*

Luqmani et al. (1980). Marketing in Islamic Countries: A Viewpoint, *Michigan State University Business Topics*, (Summer), 28, 17-25.

McCarthy, J. (1978). Recruiting & Training for Joint Ventures, *Middle East Executive Reports*, (March), 47-55.

McNair, A. (1985). Entering the Saudi Market: Management and Licensing Requirements, *Middle East Executive Reports*, (June), 18.

McNair, A. (1985). Liaison & Technical Offices, *Middle East Executive Reports*, (April), 9.

Pezeshkpur, C. (1978). Challenges to Management in the Arab World, *Business Horizons*, (August), 47-55.

Pitfalls in the Mid East Trade: Myth or Reality? (August 28, 1978). *Commerce America*, 3, pp. 4-5.

Robins, P. (1983). Zarga Free Zone a Local Success—But Where Are the Foreigners?, *Middle East Executive Reports*, (October), 6, 13-14.

Roth, M. (1985). Iraq: Market Improving, But Financing Key to Sales, *Business America*, (March 4), 52.

Saba, J. (1985). Saudi Arabia Investment Climate: Its Risks & Returns, *Middle East Executive Reports*, (October), 19.

Samman, N. (1985). Lower Oil Revenues, More High Technology Contracting, *Middle East Executive Reports*, (April), 9.

Samman, N. (1985). Oman: Economic Outlook, *Middle East Executive Reports*, (February), 19-21.

Sams, T. (1983). Saudi Arabia Provides A Dynamic Market for Medical Equipment & Services, *Business America*, (July 11), 6, 10-13.

Sams, T. (1985). Saudi Arabia: U.S. Services Exporters Report Sustained Sales, *Business America*, (September 16), 32.

Saudi Arabia (1984, 1985). *Quarterly Economic Review.*

Saudi Arabian Survey: A Changing Market (April 1985). *Middle East Executive Reports*, pp. 9-17.

Saudiization: The Emerging Trends (June 1984). *Middle East Executive Reports*, p. 16.

Shilling, N. (1976). Arab Gulf Countries Present Unique Market Opportunities—To Exporters With Savvy, *Industrial Marketing*, (April), 61, 88-90.

Synder, J. (1975). Selling in the Mid East: A Sizzling Market Unveiled, *Sales Management*, (May 5), 114, 41-7.

Syria & Jordan (1984, 1985). *Quarterly Economic Review*.

Tactics & Strategies for the Middle East (April 6, 1984). *Business International*, p. 105.

The Islamic Development Bank: Operation, Organization, Goals (May 1985). *Middle East Executive Reports*, p. 18.

UAE (1984, 1985). *Quarterly Economic Review*.

UAE: Jebel Ali Free Zone Invites Foreign Business (August 1985). *Middle East Executive Reports*, p. 8.

Walker, R. (1985). Selecting Distributors & Agents in the Arab World, *Middle East Executive Reports*, (November), 8.

Whitaker, P. (1985). Marketing in the Arab World: Understanding The Consumer, *Middle East Executive Reports*, (September), 9.

Whittingham, K. (1985). Qatar: New Foreign Investment Law, Little Effect of Major Projects, *Middle East Executive Reports*, (May), 18.

Wright, P. (1981). Organizational Behavior in Islamic Firms, *Management International Review*, 2, 87.

Yemen Arab Republic: Though Sluggish, Economy Contains Some Good Prospects for U.S. Firms (January 21, 1985). *Business America*, p. 37.

Young, G. (1976). Look at Problems & Opportunities for U.S. Marketers in Middle East Market, (interview with H.M. Hyde), *Industrial Marketing*, (April), 61, 98ff.

BOOKS

Abu Naba'a, A. (1984). *Marketing in Saudi Arabia*, New York: Praeger Press.

Bair, F. (1981). *International Marketing Handbook*, 3 vols., Detroit: Gale Research Company.

Business International (1981). *Saudi Arabia: Issues for Growth*, New York: Business International Inc.

Corcoran, K. (1981). *Saudi Arabia: Keys to Business Success*, London: McGraw Hill Publishing Co. Ltd.

El Mallakh, R. (1979). *The Economic Development of the UAE*, New York: St. Martin's Press.

El Mallakh, R. (1979). *Kuwait: Trade & Investment*. Boulder, Colorado: Westview Press.

El Mallakh, R. (1982). *Saudi Arabia: Rush to Development*, London: Croom Helm Ltd.

Kilmarx, R. (1982). *Business and the Middle East: Threats & Prospects*, New York: Permagon Press.

Jain, S. (1984). *International Marketing Management*, (Boston, Massachusetts: Kent Publishing Co.

Jureidini, P. and McLaurin, R. Jordan (1984). *The Impact of Social Change on the Role of the Tribes*, Washington: Praeger Publishers.

Kaynak, Erdener (1986). *International Business in the Middle East*, New York: de Gruyter.

Looney, R. (1982). *Saudi Arabia's Development Potential*, Lexington, Massachusetts: D.C. Heath & Co.

Mallakh, R. (1981). *The Economic Development of the United Arab Emirates*, New York: St. Martin's Press.

Metra Consulting Group (1975). *Saudi Arabia: Business Opportunities*, London; New York: Financial Times.

Moliver, D. and Abbondante, P. (1980). *The Economy of Saudi Arabia*, New York: Praeger Publishers.

Price Waterhouse Information Guide (1984). *Doing Business in Bahrain*, (June).

Price Waterhouse Information Guide (1985). *Doing Business in Kuwait.*

Price Waterhouse Information Guide (1986). *Doing Business in Oman*, (January).

Price Waterhouse Information Guide (1983). *Doing Business in Qatar*, (July).

Price Waterhouse Information Guide (1979). *Doing Business in Saudi Arabia.*

Price Waterhouse Information Guide. *Doing Business in UAE.*

Schwartz, E. Brantley (1977). *Marketing in the Middle East*, CMC Monograph 8, Princeton, N.J.

Terpstra, V. (1983). *International Marketing*, (Chicago: Dryden Press.

Weeks, Richard V. (ed.) (1978). *Muslim Peoples, A World Ethnographic Survey*. Westport, Conn.: Greenwood Press.

Chapter 12

Poland

Leon Zurawicki

INTERNATIONAL INFLUENCES AFFECTING THE NATION

In recent years Poland has been the subject of much publicity focused on the economic problems and social and political unrest. The economic situation of the country has international ramifications, the most significant being the foreign debt.

In April of 1986 Poland's debt to the West amounted to $31.0 billion whereas the debt to the COMECON countries (mainly USSR) reached 5 bn roubles. Poland's proposals for rescheduling the debt in mid-1983 called for repayment to be spread over a 20-year period, with 8 years' grace. In 1984 and 1985 agreements with both the foreign governments and private banks were reached and the payment of past due principal and some interest postponed.

Poland's Hard Currency Debt Structure ($ bn)

| Creditor | Debt maturing in | | | |
	1983	1984	1985	1986
Western sources				
Government guaranteed	1.8	1.5	0.7	0.7
Bank guaranteed	1.1	0.6	0.7	0.8
Comecon	0.6	0.2	0.2	0.1
Brazil	0.5	0.3	0.1	0.1

Other	0.2	0.3	0.1	0.1
Supplier credits	0.6	0.4	0.2	0.1
Total	4.8	3.2	1.9	1.8

Source: Bank Handlowy

Notwithstanding the seriousness of the problem, signs of improvement in the economic situation are visible. In 1982 Poland recorded its first hard currency trade surplus since 1971, and in 1983 and 1984 these results were repeated. However, this was achieved only following a disruptively large reduction of imports which more than offset a fall in exports. In 1985 the value of Polish exports was still below 1980 level, while imports represented merely 55% of the 1975 purchases. The devaluation of the zloty in mid-1985 and 1986 has contributed to a moderate expansion of exports in the late 1980s. The country badly needs exports in view of the current very high debt service ratio, amounting to 25%. As far as Poland's current hard currency account deficit is concerned, it has been narrowed considerably from $3.1 billion in 1981 to an estimated $0.9 billion in 1984. Over the same period, in spite of the continued deterioration of the terms of trade, the hard currency balance of trade has shifted from a $0.8 billion deficit to an estimated $1.4 billion surplus.

In the short term, any further lending to Poland will entail efforts to assist Poland in refinancing current debt and paying for imports destined to export-oriented industries. In 1986 Poland gained access to financial assistance from the International Monetary Fund and the World Bank. This creates the opportunity for additional loans up to roughly $1 billion, better chances for new investment credits tied to specific projects, and it requires a more rigorous feasibility analysis of undertakings to be financed. World Bank membership would also allow Poland to bid on Third World projects, thus providing a potential boost to hard currency revenues. More important, the World Bank may be able to provide guidance as to which unfinished projects in the export sector have the potential for generating net hard currency earnings. It is clear, however, that without export expansion the usefulness of drawing new loans is problematic. Similarly, any increase in interest rates in international money markets would adversely affect Poland's trade links with the West. It is difficult to say whether a reduction in the interest rates would have the entirely opposite effect but it might result in accelerating the repayment of outstanding debt.

Exports and Imports

Compared to a number of countries of her size and level of development, foreign trade plays a relatively minor role in Poland. In 1985 the estimated value of exports was $17.50 bn, whereas imports amounted to $15.60 bn. Per capita exports and imports are below $500. Nevertheless, with respect to specific products, Poland's share in international markets is significant. Table 1 reflects the commodity structure of Polish foreign trade in 1984.

The more processed manufactures made in Poland are sold mainly to other COMECON and developing countries, whereas exports to the developed Western countries consist mainly of raw materials and produce (for example, apples, onions, preserves, and concentrates).

Materials, semiproducts and spare parts constitute altogether 70% of the import total. These supplies are still insufficient for full utilization of existing industrial capacities in Poland. In particular, imports from developed market economies were dominated by production supplies, chemicals in particular. Imports of capital equipment account for 7.5% of Poland's hard currency imports.

With respect to geographic structure of foreign trade, in exports

Table 1. Commodity structure of Polish foreign trade in 1984.

Exports % of total	Type of Products	Imports % of total
17.5	Fuels and energy	23.1
9.2	Metallurgical products	9.5
39.3	Machinery and equipment	30.4
9.8	Chemical products	13.3
0.9	Products of mineral industry	1.4
2.0	Timber and paper products	2.0
5.3	Textiles	5.9
6.3	Processed food products	7.2
2.8	Farm products	5.5
0.6	Forestry products	0.2

the share of the COMECON countries is close to 54%. USSR alone accounts for 30%. Exports to the developed Western countries represent about one-third of the total whereas the developing countries purchase the remaining 13%.

In imports, the CMEA countries supply 63% of the total (USSR, 30%), the developed Western countries account for 29.5%, and the developing countries for 7%. (See Tables 2 and 3.) The major foreign trade partners of Poland are: the USSR, West Germany, Czechoslovakia, German Democratic Republic, Great Britain, Hungary, Yugoslavia, Romania, Bulgaria, Austria, France, Italy, Switzerland, and the USA. Poland is currently a limited market for the West due to the suspension of credits by all NATO countries after martial law was declared. Even though some of the economic sanctions were lifted in 1984 by the United States, that does not yet

Table 2
Geographical Structure of Polish Foreign Trade by Groups of Countries In 1984

Exports (cif)		
Total	100.0	
Socialists Countries	53.1	
– USSR		29.6
– Other CMEA coutries		19.3
– Other socialists countries		4.2
Capitalist countries	46.9	
– Developed		34.5
– Developing		12.4
Imports (fob)		
Total	100.0	
Socialists Countries	62.9	
– USSR		36.4
– Other CMEA coutries		21.6
– Other socialists countries		4.9
Capitalist countries	37.1	
– Developed		29.5
– Developing		7.6

Source: National Statistics

Table 3
Poland's Foreign Trade by Country In 1984 (unit: billion zlotys at current prices)

Imports from:		Exports to:	
USSR	439.7	USSR	395.4
West Germany	89.1	West Germany	113.8
East Germany	76.7	Czechoslovakia	75.3
Czechoslovakia	74.3	East Germany	61.9
United Kingdom	44.2	United Kingdom	54.9
Yugoslavia	42.7	Hungary	43.2
Hungary	41.0	Yugoslavia	39.2
Switzerland	38.0	Romania	37.2
Romania	36.6	France	33.5
Austria	29.0	Italy	32.5
Bulgaria	26.0	USA	29.2
Italy	22.5	Austria	28.6
USA	19.8	Libya	26.1
The Netherlands	19.8	Sweden	24.4
Brazil	18.2	The Netherlands	21.8
Japan	9.1	Finland	21.2

Source: The official statement of the Central Statistical Office,
Statistical Yearbook – 1984

represent full return to normal trading conditions between the two countries, and the volume of Polish trade with the USA is still low compared to the level of 10 years ago.

Polish hard currency exports of manufactures typically go to less developed countries which had to slash imports themselves due to their own debt problems. Given the financial constraints facing Poland, the country will have to be highly selective in its imports of goods other than those necessary to feed ongoing production (chemicals and spare parts should feature strongly).

Impact of International Agreements

Poland is a member of the Warsaw Pact and Council for Mutual Economic Aid. These two affiliations have a paramount impact on the economic policy of the country as Poland is bound by a number of development and specialization programs linking its industries to their counterparts in the Soviet Union and other Eastern European states. Consequently, the future of key industrial sectors in Poland is determined by its role within the COMECON and by its assigned specialization areas in particular. Also, Poland is a member of a loose grouping of Baltic Sea countries including the Soviet Union, Finland, Sweden, Denmark, and East Germany, whose mission is to deal with ecological problems, fishing, transportation, and maritime industries.

Following the amnesty for political prisoners in 1984, Poland's relations with the Western countries improved significantly and her diplomatic contacts with the West gained momentum.

Active State Trading Organizations

In Poland, all the large enterprises, including the foreign trade organizations (FTOs), are state owned. Some of the FTOs were established long ago, even before World War II, and have earned certain recognition by developing brands. Among the better known names are: METALEXPORT, CIECH, ANIMEX, AGROS, and TEXTILIMPEX.

NATIONAL ECONOMIC
AND PHYSICAL ENVIRONMENT

Poland is the largest country of Eastern Europe (excluding the USSR) in terms of its area — 312,683 square kilometers — and the seventh largest in Europe. Administratively, Poland is divided into 49 provinces and 2,365 rural communities. The main towns are:

TOWN	POPULATION (end of 1981)
Warsaw (capital city)	1,611,600
Lodz	843,000
Krakow	722,900 (metropolitan area, 900,000)
Wroclaw	621,900
Poznan	558,000
Gdansk	458,000 (metropolitan area, 700,000)

| Szczecin | 389,900 |
| Katowice | 363,500 (agglomeration, 1,250,000) |

The population of Poland totaled 36.7 million in October 1983. It is expanding rapidly and is expected to grow by an additional 2.3 million people by the year 1990. The share of the urban population is growing continuously, 57.5% of the population live in towns and cities, 42.5% are registered as rural. In 1982, of the total population there were 51.4% women and 48.6% men. Both the population and the workforce are young. At the end of 1981 half of the Polish people were less than 30 years old. Fifty-nine percent of the population were of working age (18-64 for men, 18-59 for women).

Structure of Economy

Before World War II, Poland had a narrow industrial base in the textile, machinery, iron, and steel and chemical industries. It was also an important coal producer. Today, the development of the Polish economy continues in these directions. In addition, however, new specialized industries like petrochemical and fertilizer industries, machine tools, electronics, and shipbuilding have gained in importance. Poland has also begun to exploit newly discovered resources like sulfur, copper, and natural gas, and has developed the aluminum industry based on the supplies of bauxite from Hungary. Table 4 illustrates the output of basic products in Poland. In general, however, a low degree of innovativeness in Poland increases the demand for imported technology.

Poland's economy has been declining rapidly since the late 1970s as a result of earlier expansionist policies that failed to produce the desired growth. For the Communist bloc the decline has been unprecedented. In 1985, Poland's national income was estimated at $5,510 per capita. Following the 24% drop in real national product (net material product) during 1979-1982, output partially recovered by 5.8% in 1983 and 5% in 1984. Growth was led by industrial production, up 6.7% and 5.3%, respectively. Also, coal output recovered after having slumped to only 163 million tons in 1981.

Table 4
Output of Major Products by the State Owned Sector in 1984

Hard coal *(thousand tons)*	191,600
Brown coal *(thousand tons)*	50,400
Coke from hard coal *(thousand tons)*	16,620
Processed crude oil *(thousand tons)*	13,646
Crude steel *(thousand tons)*	16,533
Rolled steel products *(thousand tons)*	12,196
Electrolytic copper *(thousand tons)*	372
Zinc *(thousand tons)*	176
Lead *(thousand tons)*	83
Aluminium *(thousand tons)*	46
Sulphur (100%) *(thousand tons)*	4,990
Nitrogeneous fertilizer *(thousand tons)*	1,369
Phosphorous fertilizers *(thousand tons)*	869
Plastic *(thousand tons)*	593
Chemical fibres *(thousand tons)*	238
Washing agents *(thousand tons)*	265
Cement *(thousand tons)*	16,660
Paper *(thousand tons)*	1,042
Meats and fats *(thousand tons)*	1,565
Sugar *(thousand tons)*	1,740
Washing machines and driers *(thousand pieces)*	730
Refrigerators and freezers *(thousand pieces)*	537
Passanger cars *(thousand pieces)*	279
Trucks and tractors *(thousand pieces)*	47
Universal agricultural tractors *(thousand pieces)*	59
Acid storage batteries *(thousand pieces)*	2,807
Radio receivers *(thousand pieces)*	2,416
TV sets *(thousand pieces)*	587
Tires *(thousand pieces)*	8,104
Natural gas *(cubic metres)*	6,072 million
Electric power *(kilowatts)*	134,787 million
Sea-going vessels over100 dead weight tons *(thousand dead weight tons)*	485
Footware *(million pairs)*	147

Source: Data supplied by the Central Statistical Office of Poland

However, in 1985 with inflation curtailed to 15%, the growth rate dropped to 3%.

Poland's agricultural yields are lower than those of other East European countries due to the short growing season, mediocre soil, and inadequate fertilizer utilization. Another major problem is lack of machinery. Of the total 3.5 million private farms supplying altogether 80% of agricultural products, only very few own a tractor; the rest rely on horse power. The agricultural sector has for years been unable to meet the country's requirements for food, feed grains, and vegetable oils. Despite that, Poland is one of the leading European producers of rye, oats, potatoes, and sugarbeets. Agricultural production increased by 3.6% in 1983 and 4.5% in 1984. Good harvests contributed also to a modest improvement in livestock production, which is still well below pre-1981 levels. The increases of crops and livestock did not immediately translate into increased meat output.

In the mid-1980s negative phenomena such as disequilibrium in the domestic market and high inflation still prevailed. The changes in the structure of domestic production in favor of consumer goods did not fully materialize. Generally the manufacturing output remained far below the 1978 level. The difficulties are compounded by the fact that Poland's industries are energy-intensive. For every $1,000 of net industrial output, Poland uses 2.5 times more fuel than Western capitalist countries. Further, there are some negative trends regarding the quality standards of the manufactures made in Poland. The number of items of international quality (mark "Q") sharply dropped from 30,483 in 1980 to 19,373 in 1983.

One of the areas targeted for future growth is the machinery and equipment industry. Specifically, Polish manufacturers of coal-mining equipment have achieved world status. Although Poland has the capability to produce the construction machinery of a quality similar to that made in the developed countries, it does not offer a full range of product support systems.

Shipbuilding can also be singled out as world-class, with the shipyards of Gdansk, Gydnia, and Szczecin constructing the most technically complex vessels, like chemical carriers, gas tankers, and container vessels. Poland has also attained a high degree of specialization in building fishing vessels, both small and trawler-factory size. It also builds sailing yachts, most of which are delivered to Western customers.

Income Distribution

Official Polish information suggests a fairly even income distribution among the population. However, indirect evidence points to significant discrepancies among different groups of society as far as the standard of living is concerned. The representatives of free professions, individual farmers, and small businessmen earn much above the average level. Focusing on the family situation, one realizes that roughly 20% of all the households enjoyed a monthly income of 14,000 zloty per capita, whereas the same percentage of the households had a monthly income per capita of less than 6,000 zlotys in 1983.

Also, the geographical distribution of income reveals that the Eastern part of the country is lagging behind the central and Western regions.

Natural Resources

Coal is one of the basic resources of Polish economy. Its mining is highly automated, with 97% of output produced by mechanical means. Lignite (brown coal) mining is also important. Reserves are estimated at 900 million tonnes. The output of lignite mining was planned to rise 13% to 42.9 million tonnes in 1983, to 80 million tonnes per year by 1990, to 120 million tonnes per year by the year 2000. Poland is believed to have Europe's largest copper deposits, estimated at 2.8 billion tonnes, located mainly in the Legnica-Glogow region. A long-term expansion program will raise the output of copper ore to 44.5 million tonnes in 1990.

Oil production is insignificant. USSR supplies 95% of imports. Natural gas reserves amount to 730 billion cubic meters. Domestic output, around 6 billion cubic meters per year, meets 50% of domestic consumption. Other minerals include salt, and sulfur.

Logistics and Physical Distribution

In terms of logistics, Poland enjoys a convenient geographic position in Central Europe. This facilitates the transit of merchandise through her territory from Northern to Southern Europe and from Eastern to Western Europe (and vice versa). Poland and its well-developed ports—Szczecin, Gdynia, and Gdansk—serve as gateways for the neighboring countries, as well. The rail and road network of Poland is underdeveloped by Western standards and in view of the current economic situation and the development priorities, this situation is not going to change in the immediate future.

Further, the number of trucks, locomotives, railroad cars, and containers is limited and on the verge of obsolescence. The lack of adequate storage facilities adds to the problem. Also, the inland waterways are not adequately utilized for transportation purposes. As far as air cargo transportation is concerned, its share is minimal. Consequently, the speed and timeliness of local deliveries are adversely affected and the risk of damage and waste of the merchandise is substantial. On the other hand, the distances to cover in Poland seldom exceed 300 miles radius and the country's capital is centrally located. Except for the Southern region, the terrain is relatively flat, has a pretty regular shape, and enjoys a rather mild climate.

Poland's telecommunication network is outdated, phone availability is limited, and the whole system is incapable of permanently securing reliable long-distance and international communications.

SOCIOCULTURAL ENVIRONMENT

Cross-Cultural Differences

The Polish people are very sensitive to the issue of Polish independence and feel hostile to foreign interference. Should the foreign creditors or any other business partners try to interfere in day-to-day management, that might create considerable political consequences. The Poles are religious people (90% are Roman Catholics) who are serious about their devotion.

Polish society is fairly well educated. Approximately 6% of the population have a college degree. Among foreign languages spoken, Russian is fairly well known, and one can also communicate in English. Traditionally, Poland has been linked to Western Europe and today it still shares common European heritage. Owing to the flow of information, cultural exchange, individual travel and, compared to other Eastern European countries, lesser censorship, Poles are well vested in Western trends regarding patterns of consumption and fashion.

Consumer Behavior

The Polish economic system has not been able to satisfy all the needs of the consumers. Many products are in short supply and the price increases have placed numerous items, even some rationed products, beyond the reach of the average household.

Polish consumers spend easily but, to a greater extent than in the West, expect their purchases to last. They tend to be more practical and less given to impulse. Foreign-made goods enjoy a certain patronage enhanced by their scarcity in the marketplace.

There is a great demand for fashion products of consistent quality. Most of the apparel supplied to Poland by the Western companies have a relatively high retail price, hence the consumer more often faces a greater risk when buying. This is further compounded by the fact that consumer credit is hardly available. Also, the buyer's decision-making is longer and more complex in view of the inadequate personal assistance by salespeople. One way to overcome the problem is through establishment of "factory outlets," company-sponsored stores.

Customers in Poland are relatively insensitive to advertising for basically two reasons. First, the advertising intensity has traditionally been very low. Second, in an economy marked by continuous shortages, advertising has been used as an instrument for promoting sales of slow-moving or unwanted products and therefore provoked a negative attitude.

Business Behavior

Polish institutional buyers have a tendency to look for the cheapest sources of supply, on occasion at the sacrifice of quality. Also, they are trained to turn to local suppliers before considering foreign sources. In a somewhat uncertain environment, Polish enterprises tend to hedge against the future risks by hoarding the stocks of key production materials, components, and spare parts. This leads to frequent "overbuying" and less regular purchases in the future.

As far as FTOs are concerned, they tend to provide low to medium quality items. Ends of the line, irregulars, and even fake products posing for genuine find their way to Polish markets. Fighting piracy constitutes a problem. When the purchasing decision has been made and it comes to choice of the supplier, previous experience weighs heavily. Though the industrial companies play an increasing role in buying decisions regarding smaller items, it is important to note that even here the final say belongs to the FTOs, which are more concerned about the financial and delivery terms.

POLITICAL AND LEGAL SYSTEMS

Basic Political and Business Values

Poland is a socialist country led by Marxist ideology. Planned development of the country should enhance the quality of life of the population. The development priorities are determined by the government and the appropriate allocation of resources is assured through the state ownership of productive capacities. Even though the private ownership of means of production is allowed in some sectors of the economy (agriculture, small-scale manufacturing, services), it is considered an exception from the systematic ground rules. Consequently, profit is not the objective of business activities, but rather is applied as a gauge of efficient production management. Production is deemed much more important than the distribution, and is evaluated by the degree of its agreement with the plan. Hence, the manager's attention focuses on meeting the production quota rather than on making profit. The more so, that the prices are to a great degree controlled by the state and not by the manager. Also, the upper echelon executives often assume various responsibilities within the party apparatus and/or government administration throughout their careers. As a result, the managers are sensitized to the nation's goals and realize the subordinate role of their respective organizations. Also, the manager's promotion prospects are not necessarily tied to one specific enterprise. Promotion is based on the executives' skills and involvement in the management process.

Powers and Constituencies

Poland's 460 member parliament, the Sejm, is the supreme organ of the state. Its deputies, elected from officially approved lists of candidates, serve for four-year terms.

The Sejm elects a 17 member Council of State that exercises limited legislative and executive functions. Sejm also elects the Council of Ministers (government). In terms of actual power, all major decisions are made by the Polish United Workers' Party and its executive bodies, the Central Committee and the Political Bureau, and the government implements those decisions. The Roman Catholic Church has a strong following. It is independent of the State and it has considerable status. It plays an important role in Poland's life, and often mediates in social and political problems.

The official trade unions play a limited political role and concentrate predominately on social issues. Apart from the central government, mention should be made of the local governments in 49 voivodships (administrative districts). Their authority extends over regional social and economic issues.

Political Stability

Poland's past and present political problems are the direct consequences of its economy. The material well-being of the population is still below the level of the mid-1970s. Following the imposition of martial law (which has subsequently been lifted) and disbanding of the Solidarity movement, the military-like style of administration gave the government a firm command over the political and economic developments.

Poland's economy is centrally planned and controlled and the state-owned sector dominates the country's economic life. All major enterprises (factories or groups of factories) are directly controlled and administered by the government. Annual and five-year plans are issued (the latter approved by Parliament) setting the rate of growth, the level and direction of investment, and sectoral priorities. In 1982, Poland initiated the Economic Reform Program aimed at an increase of the self-dependence, self-government, and self-financing of the individual enterprises. One of its radical measures was granting the foreign trade rights to productive enterprises, greater latitude for existing FTOs, and a provision for the operation of the foreign-owned companies in Poland. The chaotic state of the domestic economy, and particularly the price movements, rule out the Hungarian type of profit-related incentive schemes through direct linkage of domestic and foreign trade prices.

Also, the bank credit and attractive forms of financing will be used by the government to promote the export-oriented investments with a short payoff period. The state combines (large groups of enterprises) are being disbanded and individual enterprises can now form voluntary associations for the conduct of their business and foreign trade operations. Even though the large-scale operations prevail, medium and small enterprises in the light industry are important in Poland, and already this type of firm accounts for 38% of clothing output, 14.5% of chemicals, and 18.2% of wood products manufacture.

Laws and Regulations Affecting Business

Only the central level of government has the sole responsibility for balances in basic raw materials, fuels, and energy sources; construction materials; basic food supplies; and other strategic materials of fundamental importance for the present and future functioning of the system. The issues involved are presumably too complex to be appraised according to the profitability criteria of any industrial organization. At the central level, macro-economic decisions are made to establish the direction of national economic development. In particular, the share of consumption (and investments) in the national income is determined as well as the level of consumption of the most important products and services. Also, the most important tasks in the area of technological development are set forth at that level including the objectives of economic, scientific, and technological cooperation with other countries. When the overall economic situation is good and fulfillment of the socioeconomic development plan is secured, some drift toward decentralization of the decision-making process takes place with more autonomy left to the lower level decision-making centers. In turn, the lower level managers then feel less inhibited to take the burden of responsibility.

The Central Planning Commission is subordinate to the Council of Ministers, and is charged to plan the implementation of decisions already reached by the government. In practice, the Commission has considerable latitude in interpreting those decisions. In particular, the planners responsible for the coordination of foreign trade activities with other segments of the plan are vested with the authority to modify any request concerning foreign trade in view of the balance-of-payments considerations. They are also expected to ensure the fulfillment of the commitments resulting from the trade and cooperation agreements.

Following the economic reform, the functional ministries (especially the Ministries of Finance, Prices, Foreign Trade and Labor, Wages, and Social Affairs) assume a much greater role in implementing economic policy, whereas the branch ministries will have less authority to intervene in the operations of enterprises under their jurisdiction.

In particular, the Price Ministry defines the list of commodities to be exchanged under freely determined market prices and another list of commodities to be traded at prices determined by the Ministry. The latter are officially set for rationed foods or are regulated based on strict rules regarding profit markups. Goods subject to fixed prices include consumer goods and services of basic significance for the population's subsistence — industrial equipment and means of production — and agricultural produce purchased by other industrialized units of the socialized economy and by consumers.

TECHNOLOGICAL ENVIRONMENT

Material Culture

Locally manufactured automobiles, TV sets, refrigerators, and smaller household appliances are common goods in Poland. Less abundant are more advanced high-tech consumer durables like microwave ovens, video recorders, personal computers, or items like photocopy machines.

Three basic areas are clearly underdeveloped: housing, health care, and communications. Clear shortages and poor quality of products/services available in these sectors adversely affect the quality of life. Inefficient public transportation adds to everyday difficulties.

Poland has mastered complex production processes and manufactures fairly advanced industrial and consumer products. Also, it has relatively modern production facilities—more than 50% of all equipment is less than 10 years old. However, in some sectors of the economy (energy, transportation, construction) the equipment has been used beyond its booklife. This increases the susceptibility of the economy to bad weather and other unforeseeable disturbances.

Human Resource Skills

Poland is one of the better educated countries in Europe and has a large number of employed citizens with college degrees. Among them the number of engineers is quite substantial. The management training institutes are less prevalent and the techniques of efficient business administration are not commonly known. There is a shortage of well-prepared and qualified middle-level specialists, such as technicians. This is due to the weaknesses of vocational training programs as well as to job fluctuations. Since the level of employment is high, human resources are pretty well tapped and the lack of better trained work force can be a barrier to expansion of certain industries.

ORGANIZATIONAL CULTURE

Organizational Forms and Decision-Making Patterns

Apart from a smaller number of cooperatives and small companies, a typical business unit in Poland is a state-owned enterprise which is further grouped into an association of similar units and subordinated to the respective ministry in charge of a specific industry. A production enterprise may consist of more than one plant/workshop. The management of the latter is charged merely to control the productive task. The organizational system is rigid and decisions flow from the top down. The only flexibility allowed is when the plan objectives are negotiated between the enterprise and the higher administrative levels.

An essential method of controlling the range of goods produced are the governmental orders for materials and products. The list of such products is a part of the annual plan. The orders cover important export products, among others. The selection of the enterprise to be trusted with a government order follows the tender of bids which are evaluated by comparisons of cost, prices, and import contents.

Government has the right to found and dissolve enterprises, authorize them to conduct activities other than those defined in their foundation act, and the right to appoint the top managers. A state organ may impose upon an enterprise the obligation to introduce the specific task into its plan or set forth a task outside the plan. The self-sufficiency principle gives the enterprise the right to make the decisions regarding its activities on the basis of economic calculation. Self-financing means that the enterprise pays its expenses from the obtained income. This does not mean, however, that the subsidies have been eliminated completely. Motivation toward economic progress is ensured through subtle profit orientation and linking the wages with productive results.

Managers of the Polish plants which simultaneously manufacture different products are fighting for scarce elements (ingredients, space, equipment). That might affect the quality of the licensed products and the efficiency of the production processes based upon licensed technology. The top-level political and executive bodies are frequently enormously overloaded with the details of day-to-day management. Also, continuous troubleshooting and crisis management-type situations put a lot of pressure on executives.

NATIONAL CONTROL OF INTERNATIONAL TRADE

Foreign Trade Policy

Foreign trade has been a state monopoly of the Ministry of Foreign Trade (MFT) which was established to implement the foreign trade plans. The Ministry is directly subordinate to the Council of Ministers. Other constraints are placed on it by the Ministry of Foreign Affairs, the Ministry of Finance, the State Committee for Supply, the State Committee for Science and Technology, and other organizations. The Ministry of Foreign Trade formulates trade policy and coordinates the work of all the individual organizations involved in foreign trade. Directly subordinate to the MFT are foreign trade organizations (FTOs), specialized by the product lines. Following the economic reform, several of the official foreign trade enterprises have become joint stock liability companies. The Ministry of Foreign Trade has a 51% share in the company's stock, while the remaining 49% is held by the producers from the state and cooperative sectors. For example, 21 electronics equipment producers now hold 49% of the capital of the FTO Unitra. A series of foreign trade enterprises have up to now been the only entities authorized to conclude contracts with foreign companies. They acted as intermediaries between foreign suppliers and Polish firms. As of 1984, individual Polish enterprises have been given the right to undertake their own foreign trade dealings, and it is expected that this will lead to a greater development of trade. As far as trade in technology is concerned, in 1986 Poland issued new regulations on licenses. Accordingly, the Committee for Science and Technological Progress of the Polish Council of Ministers has the authority to make recommendations both with respect to export and import of technology, and approve the plans in that area. Licenses purchased abroad are supposed to meet the requirements of the national socioeconomic plan. The prospective buyer is expected to submit an application describing the characteristics of a specific license, its costs and benefits, and the prospects of linking the purchase of the technology with the countertrade arrangements. An estimate of imports (materials, components, additional licenses) accompanying the main license should be presented. As a principle, the accompanying imports should not exceed 25% of the value of all materials and components necessary for licensed production.

Poland has resorted to compensation as the main method of countertrade — a reflection of the cash shortages. The present debt also affects the nature of the industrial cooperation agreements. Self-liquidating projects represent the preferred formula and an increased emphasis is being placed on buy-back commitments. The debt can affect the choice of business relationships if the Polish authorities start selecting partners from the countries with which Polish payments are approximately in balance.

With virtually no new credit opportunities from the West, the mixed capital ventures offer another solution. Poland's contribution will consist of idle productive capacities and unfinished projects, whereas the Western partner will supply additional equipment, operational capital, and possibly the marketing expertise. Involvement in the countertrade requires a lot of creativity. For example, in the 1970s PEPSICO, Inc. initiated manufacturing chairs in Poland to be delivered to their pizza restaurants in the USA. However, on occasion Western companies discover that it is easier to sell to than to buy from Poland. Lack of prompt reaction, inability to offer quick quotations, and uncertain deliveries are cited as major obstacles.

Methods of Trade Control

Poland applies customs duties on most items imported to the country. The average level of tariffs is high. As far as transactions by the individuals are concerned, exports are taxed as well. The tariffs have only a secondary impact on the volume of foreign trade, however, since the most powerful instrument tends to be the economic plan itself. Almost by definition Poland does not import beyond the targeted plan quotas and special authorization from financial and foreign trade authorities is needed for additional deliveries. In the future, the customs duties can be assigned a more active role if the hard currency quotas left with individual Polish exporters to be spent on items of their choice are to increase.

Overall, the financial issues play a crucial role and are used as control instruments. It is not unusual for Polish foreign trade organizations to make a purchase contract contingent on the Bank of Commerce (bank of foreign trade) securing "competitive financing" from foreign banks. The introduction of the so-called hard currency retention accounts represents a slight relaxation of this provision. The accounts serve the purpose of both rationalizing the allocation of convertible currency for imports and providing an incentive to export. The size of the quota allocated varies from industry to industry and depends on the import content of the exports — the maximum that can be retained is 50% of export earnings, but the average allocation is 19% of export earnings. Over 1300 enterprises now have access to these retention accounts. In 1982, $358 million flowed into these accounts. The funds can be passed on by the account holding enterprises to nonexporting Polish producers that provide supplies. This provision widens the number of enterprises to benefit from retention accounts.

Further, the Polish zloty (current exchange rate 1 US $ = 270zl) is still overvalued and that constitutes a barrier to the growth of exports and at the same time impedes a more rational selection of imports. Any change in that regard would necessitate a major shake-up of domestic prices, however.

There are no free trade zones in Poland yet. However, customs duty postponement provisions and waivers are applied to supplies imported in the framework of industrial cooperation agreements whenever the processed products are being re-exported.

BUSINESS OPPORTUNITIES

National Plans

Information about opportunities to do business with Poland can be derived from the goals quoted in the national economic plans. For example, the plan for 1986-1990 points optimistically to an annual growth target of 3% including a 5.7% rise in industrial production and 1.5% growth in agriculture. Investment is to rise 9% per annum, and is to be aimed largely at the completion of numerous projects started before 1981. Other priorities are to produce enough food for the population to avoid large-scale imports, to increase output of consumer goods to curb inflation, and to produce large quantities of high-quality goods to earn export revenues.

With respect to foreign trade, the national economic plan consists of two parts. Part A encompasses the deliveries of basic commodities, minimum amounts of exports, and the foreign exchange limits on imports for investment purposes. This part is administered centrally by the Ministry of Foreign Trade. Part B is decentralized and subject to the parametric system. The central plan does not attempt to solve the question of full specification of exports and imports for particular organizations. It is the job of the latter to find the best ways to respond to external demand. There are presently wider possibilities for the domestic trade firms to use exports and imports to enrich the supplies in the consumer market.

Another way of exploring business opportunities is to refer to the input-output tables of the whole economy and check the balances between various industries in order to estimate the outputs and demands. Also, the official reports on the fullfilment of one-year plans (for example quoting less predictable figures, like crops) are instructive as to the future course of events. However, the published data indicate only general trends and lack specificity as far as foreign trade and consumption objectives are concerned. With a constrained economic environment, the extrapolations based on past production, consumption, and foreign trade data (whenever available) are usually inaccurate.

Industry Trends

Poland continues to develop modern industries such as electronics and chemicals and is definitely a market for technology transfer in these areas. Also, for years it has unsuccessfully tried to shift its economy into a more'consumer-oriented production structure. The continuation of this trend will translate into a greater emphasis on manufacturing fertilizers, plastics, paints, consumer durables, clothing, and processed foods. Still, one has to remember that in the near future the more expensive investment projects will have to be postponed.

Rather, the economic strategy is to increase the efficiency of the existing production apparatus by supplying larger quantities of various semiproducts and components. The Polish packaging industry as a whole represents another sector requiring attention as its under-development affects both the quality and the distribution of many products.

As a general rule, one is advised to check which industries are major buyers/users of specific product lines. This information coupled with the analysis of the industry trends can help in developing a marketer's program focused on the most promising segments.

Market Trends

There is a substantial shortage in Poland of a large variety of products ranging from medical instruments, pharmaceuticals, and personal hygiene items to furniture, clothing, foods, and certain consumer durables. In the inflationary environment, growing demand for consumer goods can hardly be satisfied. On the other hand, a (rather unlikely) redirection into the domestic market of products currently exported by Poland can help to ease the problem. Still, with low propensity to save, Polish consumers can theoretically absorb a number of goods provided that disposable income is available.

SOURCES OF INFORMATION

International Sources

Except for very general information, there is little published data available from international sources on the import needs of Poland. In view of the countertrade stipulations, one is advised to contact the companies specializing in that sort of deal, many of whom are located in Vienna. The offices of Polish trade representatives abroad are active in disseminating hints as to the needs of various sectors of the Polish economy. A similar function is also performed by the foreign branches of the FTOs. Further, it is customary that during the official visits abroad the representatives of the Polish government bring along the list of products in which the country is particularly interested.

National Government Sources

The government sources include a variety of publications sponsored by different ministries and the Polish Chamber of Foreign Trade. On occasion, a very detailed list of the product assortments and services that are in short supply is prepared by individual ministries for consideration by prospective foreign investors. It also contains names and addresses of Polish companies looking for partners. This catalog is published by Omnipress Publishers, Warsaw. Major transactions are reported in the weekly *"Rynki Zagraniczne"* ("Foreign Markets"). Business leads appear also in the form of paid advertisements in the monthly *"Handel Zagraniczny"* ("Foreign Trade") and foreign language editions of the monthly *Poland*.

Except for the still-limited number of manufacturing companies conducting export/import transactions on their own, the bulk of the operations is carried on by the FTOs specializing in specific product areas. The inquiries should be addressed to them. One should observe, however, that the latter usually prefer to continue previous business relationships than to establish new ones.

Polish Chamber of Foreign Trade performs important functions regarding promotion of exports and imports. First of all, its subordinate office organizes the Poznan International Fair, one of East Europe's major tradeshows. There is an annual exhibition in June of each year, covering industrial and consumer goods. There are also specialized shows in October and April. Traditionally, trade shows have been a very efficient instrument for getting in touch with Polish customers. In addition, two new trade and industry fairs have been operating since 1984. One is Simmex, an international exhibition covering mining energy and metallurgy, held in the steel making center Katowice. The other is "Kooperacja," held in Poznan and catering to smaller companies. Also, the International Book Fair organized annually by the FTO Ars Polona is an important event in that it also encompasses educational and scientific materials and is important to the whole of Eastern Europe.

The Polish Chamber of Foreign Trade offers market research and legal services, including the expertise of its patent attorneys. Finally, since the word of mouth is an important element of business information in Poland, contacts between the administration and one's own direct representation are of great help to the Western company.

METHODS OF ENTRY INTO NATIONAL BUSINESS

Exports to Poland

Traditionally, export has been the main form of marketing foreign products in Poland. Straight sales are easy to handle for Western exporters and Polish FTOs and therefore are preferred by both. However, exports to Poland develop less dynamically compared to other forms of international business in view of the hard currency shortages the country experiences.

Direct Foreign Investments

Poland alone among the CMEA countries allows subsidiaries of non-Polish companies to do business in Poland — there are 600 foreign-owned units currently operating. Direct foreign investment in Poland is currently confined to small business. According to the law of July 1982, the Western investor puts down a deposit of $10,000 to 50,000 and receives a license to conduct business for 20 years or more. Enterprises enjoy a three-year corporate tax holiday. The foreign investor can transfer abroad 10% annually of the original investment contribution in convertible currency, and 50% of the annual net export surplus over imports available after the initial 50% of the export revenues have been exchanged into zlotys. However, after the three year grace period, apart from the turnover tax, the increased rate of corporate profit tax applies. These taxes prove to be quite steep, especially after their rates were increased in 1984 and only slightly eased in 1986. Most of the foreigners that have taken advantage of these opportunities have been of Polish descent but there is nothing to stop others from doing the same. Activity is predominately in the textiles and leather goods sectors, followed by production of plastics, various wood-based products, and cosmetics. The Polish authorities are keen to see new companies involved in food processing and manufacturing consumer goods which are in short supply, such as footwear. Opportunities so exist in farming, production of construction materials, paints and varnishes, musical instruments, and phonograph records.

As of mid-1986 the new Polish law on joint ventures with foreign capital was still in the making. It is expected that the law will provide ample opportunities for this type of major undertaking while offering the foreign investors the provision of the majority share as well. At the same time the implementation of the law will be an accurate test of the government's willingness to allow the foreign capital participation on a larger scale.

Following the period of large spendings on license acquisitions in the 1970s, Poland will be much more selective in future purchases and will apply more stringent criteria. Nonetheless, foreign licenses and know-how seem to be one of the more promising techniques for entering the Polish market, as they are considered to be the stimulants of technological progress and help to overcome the development barriers. Also, provided the problems of quality control are taken care of, the industrial cooperation and contract manufacturing agreements are worth pursuing. For some time already, the ongoing cooperation projects in the machine, electronics, and textile industries have demonstrated success. These agreements involved International Harvester, Honeywell, Grundig, Sulzer, and the West German department stores, among others.

AREAS OF CONFLICT

Direction of Industrial Growth

The economic system in Poland allows the ruling Communist party and the government a tight control of the development goals. On the other hand, the difficulties experienced force Polish authorities to change the priorities and attitudes in search of new solutions. Hence, in relations with foreign partners the major risk can be the lack of stability. Also, the drive for self-sufficiency means that once a particular objective is accomplished (for example, the satisfaction of local demand for modern tape recorders with domestic production), there is no more need to deal with a foreign supplier. With respect to exports, the cyclical developments may then often take place whereby foreign firms will not purchase from Poland, especially when the deliveries to Poland are coupled with the transfer of technology.

The price controls exercised by the government make it difficult for a Western partner to pursue an active price policy in the Polish market. This issue might prove relevant in the case of joint ventures. The same problem arises with the exports of the licensed products from Poland to other countries. The geographic delineation of the marketing areas for the supplier of the original technology and the Polish partner occasionally creates tension and the clout of the Polish government affects the balance of negotiating power. Typically, in an industrial cooperation agreement, the Polish party is allowed to compete with the Western counterpart in marketing the finished product to the developing countries, while the partners retain exclusive rights to serve Eastern European and developed markets.

In view of the technology gap, Poland tries whenever possible to include in the purchase agreements a provision for the transfer of know-how and employee training. Unfortunately, due to the substantial turnover of personnel, much of the effort and money is wasted and additional programs have to be initiated. And further, from the perspective of the Western supplier, the undesirable spillover effects often take place through information sharing not only between Polish recipients, but also between Poland and other Eastern European countries.

Taxation

Poland has limited experience with the active implementation of the tax policy applied to business enterprises since other instruments of guidance and control (notably the plan itself) have proven quite effective. Poland is experimenting with schemes which would entice foreign businesses and at the same time maximize the revenues for the Treasury. In practice, this approach leads in the longer run to squeezing most out of the investors and in turn invites a "hit and run" strategy on their part. Thus the investors are made to think in terms of how fast they can extract their principal and a good return rather than building up their Polish venture to yield greater profits over time.

RESOLUTION OF CONFLICTS

Parties to Conflict

The individual state-owned enterprises in Poland have an independent legal status. Hence, in case of a dispute, they are solely responsible for their obligations. In practice, however, the situation looks somewhat different. At first, the state has an obvious interest in backing up its own enterprises and intervening on their behalf. But because several parties can be involved in a business agreement, including for example the user of imported products/technology, the FTO, Bank of Commerce, and shipping and forwarding companies, the delineation of responsibilities does not always prove easy.

Types of Conflict

A general source of conflict might have origins in contract negotiation and interpretation. On the Polish side no commitment is final until signed by the FTO and on occasion approved at the supervisory level. Even then, however, the agreement can be suspended indefinitely or even made void by unilateral decision. Such developments, although rare, can be very frustrating as exemplified by the General Motors light truck licensing project. In case of a dispute it is a common practice by Polish companies to apply a broadening interpretation of contract provisions.

One of the most serious problems encountered by the exporters to Poland is the delays in payments for the deliveries. Considering the general economic situation of the country, this does not come as a surprise.

Another set of problems pertains to warranties on the products sold, and the performance guarantees regarding the equipment installed. Following the bargain-hunter attitude of Polish FTOs, the imported products are not always purchased from the original source or transported or stored in the proper way. In case of counter deliveries or buy-back agreements, the Polish side often tends to be in default as far as the quality of the supplied products and the timely shipment thereof are concerned.

International Business Diplomacy and Conflict Resolution

The climate of business relations depends heavily on past experience and previous favors rendered (for example, providing the partner outside the framework of the agreement with small items/appliances to keep the production running). Leniency and the promise of further assistance can help a lot in mitigating the problem.

It should be remembered that although in the contract negotiation stage time is usually not a very important factor for Polish companies, when it comes to a conflict related to the execution of the agreement, time is of essence. Since so much depends on the smooth production runs or fulfillment of export goals, the Polish side is frequently inclined to settle for a quick solution. To limit the up-front legal fees, mediation and arbitration are preferred to litigation as a method of conflict resolution. The Court of Arbitration acting under the aegis of the Polish Chamber of Foreign Trade is competent to consider cases brought forward by interested parties. It can and often does use the services of international experts. Also, Polish FTOs are willing to accept the jurisdiction of arbitration as well as regular courts in some neutral countries like Switzerland or Sweden. Since the Polish commercial law does not address specifically numerous business situations, it is appropriate in case of a dispute to refer to more elaborate legal systems of Western countries.

CORPORATE STRATEGY AND PLANNING FOR FOREIGN FIRMS

Strategic Options

Poland is a difficult market for foreign products in view of both the limited purchasing power and the import restrictions. Consequently, in terms of strategy foreign firms should consider two major issues:

1. Identification of the products which are on the top of Poland's buying list.
2. Methods of doing business that tentatively reduce the financial pressure on Poland.

The first task seems to be easier as some hints are available and the list of necessities is not too difficult to ascertain. However, Poland plans in the long run to attain self-sufficiency and this must be remembered when considering whether an investment in market development is worth it.

Regarding the second issue, one should ideally assist Poland in expanding her export markets. In that context, the role of Poland as gateway to Eastern European markets is worth stressing. On the one hand, success in Poland can be instrumental in opening up other CMEA markets for foreign firms. On the other hand, by helping Poland to develop her areas of specialization within the Communist bloc, the foreign company can also prospectively secure a portion of Poland's future dealings with the USSR and other Eastern European countries. Along similar lines, another option would be the off-shore projects in the developing countries through cooperation with Polish companies.

A lot of creativity is required to design the international business techniques capable of alleviating Poland's financial hardships, the more so because Polish executives have become more averse to risk. Granting credits is no longer adequate, since after the bad experience of the 1970s Poland is very sensitive about overborrowing. What is desired then, is a scheme for the projects that would more certainly than in the past generate sufficient hard currency to quickly repay the initial outlays. As a second best option, one might look at the possibilities of enabling Poland to save on foreign purchases. This can be achieved by either offering less expensive substitutes for current imports or by "unpackaging" the products and shifting part of the manufacturing processes to Poland.

Planning Frameworks

During the recovery period in Poland, it will be hard for the foreign firms to plan long ahead. Even though in the past long-term agreements were signed with companies like FIAT, International Harvester, and others, this is less probable now despite the natural predisposition of the centrally planned system. In the coming years, much will depend on meeting the debt repayment obligations and only after the encouraging results in that area will Poland open up to new commitments.

Financial Options

It is clear from previous descriptions that success of business negotiations with Polish enterprises will depend largely on the foreign partner's securing long-term financing of the transactions. Whenever an offer is made, this issue should be given a serious consideration.

CORPORATE ORGANIZATION AND CONTROL
FOR FOREIGN FIRMS

Organizational Options

Because of the specific character of business dealings with Poland, foreign firms are advised to delegate these matters to specialized departments and product managers familiar with Eastern Europe. In general, a proactive approach is recommended whereby all possible problems and contingencies are included in the contract. Whenever possible, a "hands-on" approach is advisable through direct representation in Poland and monitoring the course of events. Several Polish companies, independent of FTOs, can perform the task of representation as well.

In terms of a marketing program, the crucial task is to develop the interest of the FTOs and the end users. Foreign firms should take initiative in their own hands and a lot of attention should be devoted to details. As far as promotion is concerned, it seems that the foreign firms are better off preparing as much as possible on their own turf where they have access to a full range of supporting services.

Generally, a pro-active approach is advised. If a Western company is not well known to the Polish target audience, one can run a series of ads in connection with a forthcoming tradeshow. The rates are still a bargain. The emphasis should be on factual information. Almost all the technical publications in Poland are associated with the various state organizations of technicians and engineers. Case histories and product releases are often picked up. Reports on foreign technology represent another outlet. Hence, sending out press clippings can be a good strategy.

In Poland the ascetic style in advertising prevails. There is a number of good specialists and designers and improved graphics in advertising, but the function itself is neglected. The specialized company "Agpol" serves foreign customers and organizes exhibitions for them. Generally, the print quality (folders, brochures) is poor and it makes sense to design ads in a way that does not require extensive use of color or sophisticated techniques. In terms of promotion mix, the single most powerful and efficient element, at least in the introductory stage, is attendance at the Poznan International Fair.

FUTURE BUSINESS OPPORTUNITIES AND SCENARIOS

Eventual revival of Polish economy will depend on implementation of the country's economic reform program. In particular, without further moves toward more realistic relative prices including relative wages, real interest rates, and a realistic exchange rate, there is a risk of repeating some of the mistakes of the past. Until then, austerity measures and countertrade pressures will prevail. It is worth stressing that in the near future much of Poland's reduction in new investment involves cutbacks in machinery and equipment imports.

The paramount task is to reduce the balance of payment pressures, and to change the structure of exports and imports. In terms of opportunity, the industrial cooperation with Western firms is viewed by Poland as a strategy to achieve these objectives because it facilitates the transfer, absorption, and diffusion of technology and provides access to Western markets by helping to take advantage of the Western partner's marketing channels. In terms of threats, the government approaches very cautiously the issue of greater involvement by foreign firms in Polish economy and still prefers exports to Poland over direct investments.

Prospectively, foreign firms can identify opportunities by considering the shortages the country copes with. For example, Poland has a housing crisis. Its youthful population produces an ever-growing demand for more houses, which the construction industry cannot satisfy. People migrate to towns in large numbers, further aggravating the situation. The long-term housing program of 1972 had aimed to give every family its own home by 1990 at the latest, and 6.7 to 7.3 million dwellings were to be built over 20 years. That objective does not seem feasible now.

Among European countries, Poland has the fewest number of telephones per capita and there are more than 1.5 million subscribers waiting to be connected to the telephone system. Much of the central switching equipment is old and needs replacing.

A complementary approach consists of identifying the areas given priority in the future development plans. The development of energy supplies will be of considerable importance in the coming decade. Investment in expanding energy development, and in substitution of different types of energy supply and energy conservation measures, together with measures to improve the transportation network, will be accorded high priority in the next plan period.

Polish agriculture gets an investment priority as well. Its share in total investment is to rise to approximately one third in the late 1980s – in absolute numbers those outlays will still be less than the average in the 1976-80 period. Other priority areas include machinery, electrical equipment, chemicals, and wood processing as well as shipbuilding, all singled out as export leaders.

Finally, regardless of the difficult environment, the foreign firms can create their own opportunities. This can be achieved by researching the less exploited marketing techniques and channels. For example, an interesting marketing possibility consists of sales by local trading companies of foreign goods sold for foreign convertible currency (a lucrative niche of the market). Foods, soft and hard goods, and even pharmaceuticals are being sold through the network of "Pewex" shops. Pewex-FTO buys in relatively large quantities and is a useful channel for distributing fast-moving products.

BIBLIOGRAPHY

Crane, Keith, Foreign Trade Decisionmaking Under Balance of Payments Pressure: Poland Versus Hungary, in East European Economies: Slow Growth in the 1980's, Vol. 3: Country Studies on Eastern Europe and Yugoslavia, Selected Papers Submitted to the Joint Committee, Congress of the United States, March 28, 1986.

Fallenbuchl, Zbigniew M., The Economic Crisis in Poland and Prospects for Recovery, in East European Economies: Slow Growth in the 1980's, Vol. 3.

Foreign Economic Trends and Their Implications for the United States, POLAND, International Marketing Series, US Dept. of Commerce, Washington, December 1985.

Guidelines on the Directions of Expanding Production and Services in Small-Scale Manufacture Foreign Enterprises in the Years 1984-1986. Approved by the Government Plenipotentiary for SSMFE, Inter- Polcom 2/1985, pp. 29-32.

Kazmer, Dan, The Adjustment of the Polish Economy to Scarcities in the 1970's, in East European Economies: Slow Growth in the 1980's, Vol. 3.

Lane, David, George Kolankiewicz (eds), *Social Groups in Polish Society*, Columbia University Press, New York, 1973.

Szczepanski, Jan, *Polish Society*, Random House, New York 1970.

Zurawicki, Leon, Strategy Constraints of Polish Foreign Trade Organizations, *Journal of Business Research*, 1986.

Chapter 13

Romania:
Opportunities and Challenges

Jacob Naor

INTERNATIONAL INFLUENCES
AFFECTING THE NATION

Romania is generally regarded as one of the most ideologically orthodox members of the Eastern bloc. It occupies therefore a distinctive position among members of the COMECON trading bloc.* Given the highly conservative nature of the regime, all matters related to production and trade, both domestic and foreign, must be viewed as exemplifying "most restrictive" trade and business conditions within the East bloc (excluding the U.S.S.R. and non-European members of the COMECON). Less restrictive conditions applying to trade and business may thus be expected to be found elsewhere in the bloc. Such "bench mark" considerations impart particular significance to the Romanian data provided in this chapter. We will first present Romania's involvement in foreign trade

The author would like to acknowledge the invaluable assistance of graduate research assistant Suzanne Lynch in preparing materials for this chapter.

*The Council for Mutual Economic Assistance (COMECON or CMEA), the East-European counterpart of the Common Market, was formed in 1949. Its members are: Bulgaria, Cuba, Czechoslovakia, German Democratic Republic, Mongolia, Hungary, Poland, Romania, and the U.S.S.R. Vietnam and Yugoslavia have "observer" status.

and its membership in foreign organizations, and subsequent sections will deal with Romania's internal environment.

International Involvement — An Overview

According to Department of Commerce analyses of Romanian trade, Romania has traditionally confined its purchases from the West to technology, installations, equipment, products, and raw materials necessary to carry out the directives of its five-year plans. Romanian export efforts in the West, on the other hand, were designed to earn the hard currency needed to pay for its imports and have traditionally been directed toward machinery and equipment, fuels and lubricants, chemicals, textiles, vegetable and meat products, wood products and lumber, clothing and footwear (Overseas Business Reports, Trading and Investing in Romania, September 1978, pp. 5-6, U.S. Department of Commerce). Although the USSR is still Romania's principal trading partner, Romania has expanded commercial relations with non-COMECON countries. In 1982 trade exchanges with developing countries accounted for about 25% of foreign trade, while almost 50% of Romania's trade was with socialist countries. Romania became a contracting party to the General Agreement on Tariffs and Trade (GATT) in 1971, and joined the IMF and the World Bank in 1972. In 1979 Romania became the first CMEA member to negotiate independently with the EEC, and the first trade agreement was signed in July 1980 (*The Europa Year Book, 1984, A World Survey*, Vol. 1, p. 754).

Impact of International Agreements

It is important at this point to put recent Romanian trade experience in perspective. Already during the 1970s Romania had become a strong advocate of international and technical cooperation, changing an orientation that had previously been exclusive to COMECON relations. Thus we witness Romania's previously mentioned participation in GATT (General Agreement on Tariffs and Trade) since 1971, and Romania's membership, since 1972, in the International Monetary Fund and the World Bank.

According to an in-depth analysis of the Romanian economy prepared by the World Bank (World Bank, 1979), during the mid and late 1970s Romania's international trade efforts concentrated in particular on countries in the Middle East and Asia. Efforts included partnerships in construction of industrial units, provision of Romanian equipment and know-how (mostly in geological exploration), provision of turnkey projects, establishment of joint production and commercial ventures and technical assistance. To mention but a few, plants were set up for sulfuric acid and fertilizers (Turkey, Egypt), sodium products (Iran, Egypt), oil refining (Syria, India, Pakistan), and wood processing plants (Iran, Sri Lanka, People's Republic of the Congo).* In addition, Romania's capital participation in joint ventures abroad rose substantially between 1970 and 1975. By 1977 Romania was a shareholder in 28 production enterprises abroad, in addition to three ventures in cooperation with other socialist countries, and in 35 commercial joint ventures.** Efforts were most often geared toward developing countries to promote Romanian exports and gain access to sources of raw material. Foreign trade involvement may thus be seen to be closely linked to Romania's own development efforts, although the focus on developing countries allowed Romania access to markets that were less competitive than those of developed countries.

The following data, based on Romanian sources, will be useful to sum up Romania's foreign involvement in the postwar period. Romania had diplomatic relations with 25 states in 1947, and that number grew to 137 by 1980. At that time Romania was a member in more than 80 international governmental organizations and participated in 600 nongovernmental organizations of all kinds. International political and economic activity resulted in the conclusion of an extraordinarily large number of international agreements. The period between 1948 and 1980 saw the conclusion of 5,300 international, bilateral, or multibilateral treaties, agreements, and conventions (*Romania Yearbook*, 1981, p. 101). Similar active Romanian

---

*For a more complete listing see *Romania: The Industrialization of an Agrarian Economy under Socialist Planning*, The World Bank, Washington D.C., 1979, pp. 125-126.
**Ibid.*, p. 126.

participation in world trade and world politics may be expected to continue.

International Involvement — Exports and Imports

The more recent international involvement of Romania is best exemplified by data on exports and imports (Table 1). As the data indicate, Romanian foreign trade saw considerable and continuing growth since 1985, achieving positive Romanian trade balances each year both in total trade as well as in trade with the U.S. Romania appears thus to continue an aggressive pursuit of large trade surpluses with convertible currency countries in order to continue to reduce its foreign debt in such currencies, which stood at about $6.6 billion at the end of 1985, and at about $4 billion at the end of 1987 (*Foreign Economic Trends*, 1987, p. 2). As indicated, a trade surplus of $2.1 billion was estimated for 1987. However, Romania's

Table 1

Romanian Foreign Trade

	1985	1986	1987	1987/1986 % Change
Exports ($ million, f.o.b.)	12,167	11,660	12,250*	5.06
Imports ($ million, f.o.b.)	10,432	9,660	10,150*	5.07
Trade Balance ($ million)	1,735	2,000	2,100*	5.00

U.S.-Romanian Trade**

	1985	1986	1987	1987/1986
U.S. Exports to Romania (S$ million, F.A.S.)	208.2	251.0	200.0*	-20.3
U.S. Imports from Romania	951.1	833.9	800.0*	-4.1
Trade balance ($ million, C.I.F.)	-742.9	-582.9	-600.0*	2.9

Principal U.S. exports (1986):   soybeans, machinery, coal, cattle hides
Principal U.S. imports (1986):   petroleum products, chemicals, aluminum and steel products.

*U.S.Embassy (Bucharest) estimate/projection
**Department of Commerce data

Based on official Romanian data except as indicated otherwise.

Source: Foreign Economic Trends and their Implications for the United States, September 1987, U.S. Department of Commerce.

rapid debt repayment schedule, slated to continue unabated, may be seen to have led progressively to a curtailment of such needed capital-goods imports, without which such important Romanian development aims as "raising the level of technology" and "modernizing production sectors" may be hard to realize (*Foreign Economic Trends*, 1987, pp. 4, 7).

NATIONAL ECONOMIC
AND PHYSICAL ENVIRONMENT

The Socialist Republic of Romania lies in southeastern Europe. It borders the U.S.S.R. to the north and northeast, Hungary to the northwest, Yugoslavia to the southwest, and Bulgaria to the south. The southeast coast borders the Black Sea. The official language is Romanian, a Romance language, although minority groups speak Hungarian, German, and other languages. The dominant religion is the Romanian Orthodox Church. The capital is Bucharest (Bucuresti) (Romania, Introductory Survey, *The Europa Yearbook*, 1984, p. 753).

Traditionally based on agriculture, forestry, and petroleum production, the Romanian economy is now dominated by industrial activity (principally manufacturing), which by 1980 accounted for about 60% of net material product (NMP). The most important industries are mainly heavy: petroleum and natural gas, mining and metallurgy, mechanical engineering, chemicals, and timber processing. All of Romania's industry, mines, banks, telecommunications, transport, and external trade enterprises have been nationalized (*Ibid.*, p. 753).

Income Distribution

According to official Romanian sources, the total real incomes of Romania's population was in 1980, 34% greater than in 1975. Consequently, considerable improvements in standards of living appear to have been achieved as of 1980, continuing previous trends toward improved living conditions. Relying on Romanian sources again, by the beginning of 1981, the minimal monthly take-home pay was 1,425 lei (as compared to 1,114 lei in 1975), maintaining the officially decreed 1 : 5.5 ratio between minimum and maximum pay rates. The average monthly take-home pay was 2,238 lei in 1980 (1,028 lei in 1965, 1,289 lei in 1970, and 1,595 lei in 1975) (*Romania Yearbook*, 1981, p. 84). Table 2 presents the trend in average earnings, which indicates considerable shifts of wage earners from low to higher income earning categories. This change is particularly pronounced between 1974 and 1979.

Average nominal remuneration grew by over 40% during the 1976-1980 five-year plan and real remuneration grew by 29% during that period. The peasantry's real incomes per active person increased by 29% as well during this period.

Physical Resources

Romania is 41% arable land, 27% forests, 19% pastures and hay-fields, 3% vineyards and orchards, and 3% running waters and lakes (*Romania Yearbook*, 1981, p. 16). Romania also has some subsoil deposits: oil, natural gas, coal, salt, iron, copper, lead, gold, and uranium. Oil is found in the Sub-Carpathians, the Romanian Plain, and the Black Sea off-shore deposits; natural gas is formed in the Transylvanian Plateau. Coal deposits lie in intramontane depressions, while iron ores are found in the Banat Mountains and Poiana Rusca Mountains (*Ibid.*, p. 16). Despite its natural wealth, due to the rapid industrialization drive, Romania has found it increasingly necessary to import needed raw materials, with the notable exception of natural gas. Table 3 indicates some of Roma-

Table 2
Average monthly earnings of production workers (percent)

	March 1965	June 1970	March 1974	March 1979
Total	100.0	100.0	100.0	100.0
Under 1,300 lei	83.8	61.5	48.9	4.0
1,301 - 1,500 lei	8.0	14.1	17.7	9.2
1,501 - 1,700 lei	3.6	8.8	11.3	14.8
1,701 - 2,000 lei	2.5	7.3	10.1	26.1
2,001 - 2,500 lei	1.6	5.4	7.7	27.5
2,500 lei and over	0.5	2.9	4.3	18.4

(Romania Yearbook, 1981, p. 84)

Table 3

Resource requirement to be covered by end of 1980-1985 plan period
(percent)

Category	domestically	from foreign sources
primary energy	82	12
coal, coke, rolled goods, pipe	90-98	8-10
lead, zinc	80-90	10-20
textile yarns, fibers	80	20

(Source: Romania at a Glance, 1982, p. 15.)

nia's resource deficiencies, as projected for the end of the 1980-1985 plan period.

Logistics and Physical Distribution

In 1981 there were 11,669 km of railways and 73,364 km of national roads, of which 34,766 km had been previously modernized (*The Europa Yearbook*, 1984, p. 754). According to the same source, the state airlines of Romania, TAROM and LAR, provide daily flights between the capital and 15 towns, and international services to Europe, America, Africa, and Asia. Navigation on the River Danube is open to shipping of all nations. The chief ports of Romania are Constanta, on the Black Sea; and Galati, Braila, and Giurgiu on the Danube (*Ibid.*, p. 754).

Despite considerable advances, the road system in Romania is still poor compared to comparable Western systems. It is adequate for distribution purposes, however. The rail system serves as the major industrial supply system and has seen continued upgrading, including electrification of major trunk lines. Thus by 1979, 2,202 km of railways (about 20% of total railways) had been electrified, and further electrification of the busiest lines was planned (*Romania Yearbook*, 1981, p. 79). Plans for 1985 called for increases of 18-20% in the amounts of goods transported by rail compared to 1980, while the comparable percentages for road freight increases were 11-13% (*Ibid.*, p. 79). The primary and continuing reliance on rail transport appear evident. Romania continues to rely on rail transport as the main means of physical distribution. No change in this regard appears foreseeable for the immediate future.

SOCIOCULTURAL ENVIRONMENT

Cross-Cultural Differences

A major ingredient characterizing Romanian culture is a strong feeling of nationalism, combined with a strong emphasis on present-day Romanians' links to their ancient Roman heritage. These links, strongly and consistently emphasized by the government, date back to Roman Dacia, the colonization of that region and its Dacian people by Roman legions for 165 years (from 106-271 A.D.). These early Daco-Roman origins saw successive waves of migratory intrusions and subjugation, among which those by Slavs were the most numerous (*Romania Yearbook*, 1981, p. 25). This could explain often strongly held antislav feelings frequently encountered among Romanians. Another important cultural ingredient that affects Romanian behavior is the still strong influence of traditional rural life. As Table 4 indicates, it was not until 1980 that a predominance of urban over rural inhabitants became apparent in Romania.

We are thus witnessing a *transitional* culture, characterized by strong associations with both traditional rural values and more recent values associated with Socialist industrialization and construction. To this must be added a strong emphasis on education, both of the nonvocational and vocational kind, which again is associated with stringent governmental efforts toward rapid and comprehensive industrialization.

Table 4

Urban and Rural Population Distribution
(percent of total population)

	Urban	Rural	Number of Cities
1965	33.7	66.3	183
1975	43.2	56.8	236
1980	50.0	50.0	236
1985 (est)	54.5	45.5	505

Romania, Yearbook 1981, p. 19.

Culture Conditioned Consumer Behavior

From the preceding we are able to construct some consumer behavior patterns that reflect, at one and the same time, patterns, tastes, and habits of consumers, recently urbanized, participating increasingly in industrial life, while maintaining strong nationalistic-historic ties. To this one could add the still strong influence of the Romanian Orthodox church, whose influence is most strongly felt by older, rural, and urban population segments. One may state that current Romanian consumption patterns, particularly those of younger, urban consumers, increasingly exhibit patterns conditioned and affected by ongoing socioeconomic development efforts. Such patterns will, no doubt, increasingly approximate consumption patterns typical of other similarly developed countries in either the East or West, as industrialization continues to unfold. This can be seen from Table 5, which provides changes in consumption during the 1970s. It may be observed that rural background-based consumption is increasingly replaced by urban background, indus-

Table 5

Growth in Per-Capita Expenditures on Durable and Non-durable Commodities

(1965 = 100)

	1970	1975	1979
Consumption			
Meat and meat derivates	117	172	223
Milk and dairy products	105	126	171
Oils and fats	120	144	145
Eggs	123	186	234
Sugar and sweets	129	135	183
Cereals (flour equivalent)	94	91	83
Potatoes	82	126	93
Vegetables and derivates	115	150	181
Textiles (apparel included)	119	149	170
Footwear	133	155	171
Purchases			
Radio sets	144	167	195
TV sets	284	503	699
Refrigerators	252	488	686
Washing machines	200	297	410
Motor cars	533	11 times	21 times

Romania, Yearbook, 1981, p. 87.

trial-life-conditioned consumption, akin to consumption patterns elsewhere.

Business Behavior

The major factor that can explain Romanian business behavior is the pervasive and dominant position of the highly centralized and hierarchical national planning system. This applies to behavior in all industrial and commercial spheres. While "the plan" has long since ceased to be totally determined by "instructions" issued from above, the major policies and guiding directives are still transmitted top-down, from the apex of the political hierarchy. However, particularly since the major economic reforms of 1978, local enterprise initiative may increasingly be taken "from the bottom-up" (Naor, 1986). Decisions pertaining particularly to the *operation* of enterprises and establishments are originating increasingly from the executive levels of enterprises. Thus within boundaries set by central directives, "local" initiative is increasingly relegated and encouraged by a system of bonuses and other monetary rewards. We may thus expect increasingly more vigorous economic decision making at lower hierarchical levels. However, strong central direction may as well be expected to continue. The leadership to date has shown little inclination to decentralize the economy as to strategic decision-making, opting instead for continued strong central administration and control in order to sustain the rapid industrialization drive which remains at the heart of central national objectives.

THE POLITICAL AND LEGAL SYSTEM

On August 21, 1965, the Romanian parliament, the Grand National Assembly, adopted the present Constitution which proclaimed Romania a socialist republic. The Romanian Communist party was officially designated as the leading political force of Romanian society. According to the Constitution, Romanian citizens exercise power through the Grand National Assembly and the People's Councils elected by equal, direct, and secret ballot (*Romania Yearbook, 1981*, p. 39). But clearly, central decision-making power is vested in the party's politburo, or the "standing presidium," which has since 1965 been dominated by President Ceausescu.

State Power

The Grand National Assembly (parliament) is the supreme body of state power. It is a single-chamber legislative body, with members elected for a period of five years. A complete enumeration of its powers is provided in Appendix A.

The State Council, subordinated to the Grand National Assembly and elected from its members, for the duration of its term is the *permanent* body of supreme state power, representing the Grand National Assembly between sessions of the latter. A complete enumeration of its powers, as well as those of the Council of Ministers (government), is provided in Appendix A.

The Legal System

Under the Romanian legal system justice is administered by the following courts: the Supreme Court, county courts, local courts, and military courts. The courts try civil and penal cases, and "any other case within their competency" (*Romania Yearbook*, 1981, p. 53). Their twin aims are to "defend the socialist system and the rights of persons," aiming at reforming and reeducating the offenders and preventing the commission of new offenses (*Ibid.*, p. 53). According to the same Romanian source, in those cases specified by law and in cases brought by persons harmed in their rights by administrative acts, the courts will exercise control over decisions of administrative or public bodies. Individuals appear thus to be guaranteed protection from "unlawful" administrative acts. The Supreme Court exercises general control over the judicial activity of all the courts. Aiming to ensure uniform application of the laws in judicial activity, the Supreme Court is elected by the Grand National Assembly, and is responsible for its activity to the Grand National Assembly and, between sessions, to the State Council. Judges are elected by the county municipal and town people's councils. In their judicial activity, the judges are independent and amenable only to the law (*Ibid.*, p. 54). Judicial procedure is conducted in the Romanian language. In the territorial-administrative units inhabited also by populations of another nationality, the use of the mother tongue of that population is also ensured. Trials are held in public sessions, unless otherwise prescribed by law (*Ibid.*, p. 54).

Political Stability

Party control in Romania extends to all aspects of society and embraces educational and professional opportunities, among others. Despite rigid controls, there is some evidence that the Communist Party has met occasional difficulties in its attempts to reconcile an authoritarian system with a policy of socialist democracy aimed at encouraging public initiative and participation (*Romania, A Country Study*, 1979, p. 154). There were, it appears, cases of reported resistance to accepting job assignments in rural areas by technical school graduates trained at state expense. Other reported refusals to fulfill obligations assigned by the party involved teachers, builders, and administrative workers (*Ibid.*, p. 154). Party control therefore does not appear to be as watertight as one would suspect. It is, nevertheless, pervasive and comprehensive. Political stability appears strong, despite evidence of security-related paranoia. It must be recalled that President Ceausescu has served in the capacity of President uninterruptedly since 1967, and appears to be assured life-long tenure.

Laws and Regulations Affecting Business

Due to the centralized nature of the Romanian economic system, laws and regulations affecting business are centrally promulgated for all state bodies, local councils, and cooperative organizations. Such centralization simplifies the task of ascertaining the relevant rules applicable to particular transactions. Thus the Romanian Foreign Trade Law (1982) provides, for example, the following, in addition to a host of other laws and decrees.

- Law on Foreign Trade (Law No. 1/1971)
- Customs Code (Law No 30/1978)
- Free Port Decree (Decree No. 294/1978)
- Decree on Joint Companies (Decree No. 424/1972)

All such Romanian laws proceed from the basic premise of public (state) ownership of the means of production, whether man-made (capital) or natural (land and resources). The state, as owner (excluding cooperative ownership which is vested in its members), exercises ownership control through the Council of Ministers, which is the central administrative state body (coordinating in this capacity local councils and various cooperative bodies as well). A detailed enumeration of the powers of the Council of Ministers is provided in Appendix A. The applicable ownership pattern with regard to foreign companies wishing to operate in Romania is provided by the Decree on Joint Companies (No. 424/1972) which stipulates that the Romanian share in the registered capital of such companies shall be at least 51% (*Ibid.*, Article 4). Domestic laws thus apply to joint companies operating in Romania, however, significantly, the state guarantees, bona-fide profit repatriations, and the repatriation of proceeds of dissolution agreements (*Ibid.*, Article 7). Joint companies are thus offered protection and means of risk reduction for both domestic Romanian operations as well as joint international operations.

TECHNOLOGICAL ENVIRONMENT

Since the beginnings of Romania's industrialization drive in the early 1950s, a consistent aim of the authorities has been to bring about rapid improvements in the technological-educational level of the work force, in line with attempts to advance Romania rapidly to the level of industrialized nations. Education, both vocational and academic, was highly stressed throughout. Tables provided in Appendix B demonstrate the advances achieved in education from the mid 1960s to the early 1980s.

The far-ranging education law of 1968 extended compulsory education to 10 years and introduced changes (including more accent on practical classroom work on vocation and technical subjects and the introduction of more specialized courses) designed to relate education more closely to expanding technological and industrial needs (*Romania, A Country Study*, 1979, pp. 73-79). Romania has thus rapidly acquired the prerequisite infrastructure needed for rapid industrialization. We note in particular the accent on vocational education in the early 1970s, presumably in response to the needs of industry. Further advances are planned. According to the 1981-85 five-year plan, 1.8 million skilled workers, technical personnel, foremen, and engineers will be offered additional occupational education, upgrading technical competence in the process.

Technology Transfer

Romania has traditionally attempted to assimilate advance technologies by means of license imports from industrially developed countries (*Economic and Commercial Guide to Romania*, 1982, pp. 114-116). Thus, over the 1960-1970 span Romania purchased a great number of licenses and a large amount of technical documentation and placed orders for more than 220 industrial installations, including the pertinent engineering and manufacturing know-how, particularly in the field of mechanical engineering and chemical industry (*Ibid.*, p. 115).

According to the same Romanian source, transfer of technology from Western sources has played a key role during this period. Through cooperation and specialization in production, Romania's economy has been provided with advanced techniques and new technology in the fields of: aeronautics (helicopters and aircraft from France and England); tools from Belgium; diesel-electric locomotives from England; buses and lorries from the Federal Republic of Germany; tractors from Italy; motors and compressors from the Federal Republic of Germany; passenger cars from France; iron and steel installations (cold rolling mills and sheet iron zinc-coating) from Australia; chemical industry and building materials (fertilizers from Belgium, medical drugs from Switzerland, ceramic products and hydrated limestone from Italy); ball bearings from Japan; glass wool manufacturing technology from the Federal Republic of Germany, etc. (*Ibid.*, p. 115).

The constitution of joint production companies operating in Romania has contributed to the assimilation of the new technological advances. Worth mentioning are the advanced technologies used in the production of computing technique components (U.S.), electronic medical equipment (France), shipyard equipment (Federal Republic of Germany), synthetic proteins (Japan), top quality synthetic proteins (Italy), passenger cars (France), etc. (*Ibid.*, p. 115).

Technology transfer has not been a one-way street, however. Romania has been an important supplier of technology, particularly to developing countries. Thus cooperation in production designed to develop various projects in several countries has led to export of Romanian technology in different sectors: manufacture of tractors (Iran and Egypt); chemical industry (Turkey and Egypt); crude oil refineries (Syria and Pakistan); textile industry installations (Sudan); wood working (the People's Republic of Congo), etc.

Joint production companies set up in other countries by Romania are another means of transferring technology and management from Romania. For instance in the domains of mining (Zambia, Peru, Morocco), machine tool building (Peru), oil exploration and exploitation (Algeria, Morocco, Iraq), phosphates extraction (Tunisia, Egypt, Syria), rare metals mining (Tanzania), wood processing (Central African Republic and Nigeria), chemical industry (Ecuador), intensive agriculture (Central African Republic and Congo), etc. (*Ibid.*, p. 116).

Romania has thus made consistent efforts to upgrade the level of technology incorporated in its products, as well as to provide such technology to underdeveloped or developing countries. According to the latest five-year plan, industrial products made at "world levels" were slated to reach 95% of total industrial output by 1990, with 2 to 5% of that total slated to achieve performance indexes exceeding this level (*Era Socialista*, No. 19, October 1984, translated in Joint Publication Research Services, EEI-85-022, p. 54).

Romania's efforts to further upgrade its technology is thus seen continuing to receive highest priority by the authorities. While such efforts appear to have brought about some significant results, it appears equally true that much remains to be done in the area of technology to enable Romanian products to compete effectively on world markets.

ORGANIZATIONAL CULTURE

Basic to an understanding of Romanian organizational culture is the fact that the comprehensive national planning system, discussed previously, is at the root of all organizational structures and decision-making processes in Romania. Planning requirements are thus instrumental in determining much of the managerial form and structure of industrial organizations.

Improved central planning is perceived by the authorities as being essential, indeed indispensible, to solving Romanian economic problems and for furthering progress. This in turn requires frequent organizational changes to fit the changing needs of the planning mechanism. One is thus able to account for the duality regarding Romanian organizations, in which long-term overall stability pertaining to the *framework* is combined with frequent changes pertaining to the *components* of the framework. It is imperative, therefore, to be acquainted with both basic Romanian organizational structures, as well as details pertaining to changes, particularly as they impact decision-making. This section, due to space limitations, will deal with the basic organizational structures only, with the proviso that changes as to particulars must be expected, and should indeed be anticipated prior to undertaking commercial transactions with Romanian organizations.

The Basic Framework

Romanian industry is organized at the republican, local, and cooperative levels. Under Romania's system of centralized planning pertaining to all three organizational forms, central authorities make all major production and investment decisions, fix prices, and control the activities of the enterprises. The scope for individual decision-making in Romanian industry is thus strictly limited to achieving centrally determined targets and economic goals in a "bottom up" manner. Progress toward the achievement of these goals is monitored daily, weekly, monthly, and quarterly through a complex reporting system pertaining to fulfillment of plan goals.

The hierarchical structure is thus a central feature of the process, characterized by a highly centralized decision and control mechanism which allocates *policy* and *strategic* decisions to the center, while relegating *tactical* implementational decisions to the production and distribution units (Naor, 1986). The clear implication for foreign organizations attempting to conduct business in Romania is that contacts must be made at as high a level as possible, to permit contacts with the relevant decision-makers to take place. The determination of the precise organizational unit as well as the best level to contact are thus important ingredients for successful Romanian business transactions.

To provide greater insights into Romanian organizational structures, three such structures are provided in Appendix C: a typical industrial Ministry, a headquarters type organization (Central), and an enterprise. A close examination of these structures may provide clues as to the nature and functions of particular units as well as to significant decision-making and reporting flows that connect these units. For a more detailed description of these organizations the reader is referred to *Romania – The Industrialization of an Agrarian Economy under Socialist Planning* (1979), The World Bank, Washington, D.C., pp. 407-413.

NATIONAL CONTROL OF INTERNATIONAL TRADE

Foreign trade is a state monopoly in Romania.* Import and export operations, as well as control over all international accounts, are part of the monopoly. The monopoly encompasses foreign exchange as well, to ensure that trade activities correspond to the developmental needs of Romania. Trade policy is established by the Romanian Communist party and the government. Responsibility for implementation is delegated to the Ministry of Foreign Trade. The division of responsibilities is provided at the end of this Section.

An objective of economic and social development to the year 2000 is Romania's increasingly active participation in world trade. Adherence to this principle is apparent. Romania maintains economic relations with 150 countries, an increase from 29 in 1950. The foreign trade volume in 1953 was 39 times greater than in 1950.** The major role played by foreign trade has been to acquire resources which have been unavailable domestically and are necessary to meet development plans, as well as much needed foreign

---

*Official Bulletin of the Socialist Republic of Romania, No. 33 (3/17/71).
**Era Socialista, No. 19, (10/10/84), p. 51.

currency to meet debt obligations.

International Trade Planning

Foreign trade is planned within the overall framework of domestic activities. Targets for exports and imports for each level of organization are outlined within the five-year plan. Each economic unit prepares volumetric and financial projections of export and import needs based on foreign markets and forecast demand. The aggregate plans are formulated into the five-year plan after which the five-year plan is disaggregated and presented to each level in the form of value and volume terms of export targets and import allocations.* The targets within the five-year plan are expressed in general terms with more specific objectives outlined in the annual plans. In this fashion national control is exercised over international trade.

Foreign Trade Policy

According to Romanian sources, due to Romania's continuing financial difficulties, its efforts in international trade will center on increasing trade with Socialist countries, which accounted for 52% of total foreign trade in 1984 (*ERA Socialista*, No., 19, 10/10/84, p. 52). Collaboration with the U.S.S.R., with which trade has increased 15 times from 1950-1983, will be intensified. Trade relations with other Socialist countries will be expanded as well. Recent intensified economic, technical, and scientific collaboration within the Council of Mutual Economic Assistance (COMECON) has begun to open up new prospects for increased intra-bloc collaboration (*Ibid.*, p. 52).

However, continued expansion of trade with Western developed and developing countries is foreseen as well. In order to develop and modernize Romania's economy, economic and technical-scientific collaboration with capitalist countries will continue to expand. An indication of the importance of foreign trade is provided by the fact that the planned annual growth in trade over the 1988-1990 period (7.1 to 7.7%) was to exceed the growth planned for social

---

*World Bank, p. 115.

product as well as industrial commodity output (*Ibid.*, p. 53). Exports were expected to grow increasingly in relation to imports to create trade surpluses and thus help ensure a positive balance of payments and permit the gradual liquidation of Romania's foreign debt.

The Customs System

As with all foreign trade, the customs system is a state monopoly under the control of the Ministry of Foreign Trade.

Customs regulations are codefied in the Customs Code (Law No. 30/1978), and the Romanian free port system in the Decree of State Council (No. 294/1978) (*Economic and Commercial Guide to Romania*, 1982, p. 248). There are detailed customs provisions and procedures (Decree of State Council (No. 337/1981) and custom tariffs for goods (Decree of State Council No. 395/1976). Custom legislation may be obtained from the Romanian Chamber of Commerce, in Bucharest, Romania, and is available in English.

Custom duties are charges on the customs value of goods (*Ibid.*, p. 251). Custom duties on imports from countries with which trade exchanges are conducted on the basis of international conventions and protocols will be based on those conventions and protocols. For countries which do not give Romania most favored nation treatment, tariff duties may be increased "according to the law" (*Ibid.*, p. 201). Joint companies registered in Romania (under the Joint Companies Decree No. 42/1972) are subject to general customs regulations. Goods imported by the foreign partners as a contribution to the nominal capital of the joint companies are not dutiable (*Ibid.*, p. 252).

To summarize the issue of national control over international trade, the following is a detailed outline of the involvement of organizations and governmental units in foreign trade:

1. *Council of Ministers*: general responsibility for administering and controlling international economic relations.
2. *Ministry of Foreign Trade*: Overall responsibility for planning and implementing foreign trade activities. Joint responsibility with the State Planning Committee, Ministry of Finance, Na-

tional Bank, Bank of Foreign Trade, Ministry of Foreign Affairs.

3. *Ministry of Finance*: Responsible for foreign currency. Control international transactions in which foreign currency is involved.

4. *Bank of Foreign Trade*: Facilitates trade by organizing trade payments, obtaining domestic and foreign credits, and concluding banking arrangements required domestically and internationally.

5. *Ministries*: Each ministry is responsible for planning and implementing economic external relations to fulfill its segment of the foreign trade plan.

6. *Centrals, Foreign Trade Enterprises, Productive Enterprises*: Centrals and Production Enterprises are responsible for the development of a trade plan for integration into the annual plan developed by the Ministry. Foreign Trade Enterprises are separate legal entities with commercial responsibilities specified by law. All activities are supported through the organizations' own revenues and are operated at a profit.

7. *Other*: Other institutions involved in Romania's foreign trade include the Chamber of Commerce, Argus (office for representations and Commissions), and the Arbitration Commission. (World Bank, 1979, p. 113-114)

BUSINESS OPPORTUNITIES

National Plans

Business opportunities in Romania are tied, not surprisingly, primarily to central national annual and five-year plans that govern the rate and direction of economic development. It is imperative, therefore, to be well acquainted with the strategic goals enunciated within the framework of national five-year plans since these will provide specific indications as to development needs and priorities, which will see implementation in annual plans. Foreign firms attempting to export to Romania may, by an analysis of such goals, determine whether and to what degree their product and technology offerings meet Romanian needs. It must be clear, however, that five-year plans will provide only outlines of general needs or export capabilities, rather than product- or service-specific requirements or availabilities. These will have to be ascertained through additional sources such as those provided by the Department of Commerce (see "Sources of information" section), or direct contacts with Romanian Foreign Trade companies via the Romanian Chamber of Commerce (for a complete listing of such companies, see *Your Commercial Partners in Romania*, 1982, PUBLICOM, Bucharest, Romania).

Industry and Market Trends

An instructive example for possibilities for exports to Romania is provided by material available from Romanian sources for the 1981-1985 five-year plan (see *Romania at a Glance*, pp. 14-20). Aims listed include the following: continuing high rates of economic growth, with particular stress laid on "qualitative aspects" of development; "Intensive" (resource) use; assimilation of latest gains in science and technology; better utilization of semi-produced and raw materials; and higher efficiency and productivity "to reach world levels" (*Ibid.*, p. 14). Higher growth rates were planned for electronic, electrical, and precision engineering, machine tools, automation control devices and computers, as well as the chemical processing industries in general. Clear indications are provided here of *priority* areas for growth, modernization, and development for which, within the limitations of foreign exchange availability, well-targeted imports would appear to find considerable demand.

Similar comments may be made regarding the 1985-1990 plans, information regarding which may be gleaned as well from Romanian sources published selectively, in translated form, by the Joint Publication and Research Services (JPRS). Thus in "Strategy for Modernization of Industry Reviewed" (*Era Socialista* No. 7, April 1984, JPRS-EE1 84-0S6, pp. 47-54), we learn that goals similar to those set for the 1980-1985 plan were to be pursued. Thus priority would be assigned to "superior" utilization of raw material and energy resources, with a continuing stress on modernization, quality, and improved competitiveness of products. Priority growth will again be assigned to "branches of advanced processing, highly technical as well as low energy consuming products" (*Ibid*, p. 46). Details regarding such product types slated for priority development are provided as well (*Ibid.*, pp. 49-54).

Specific Romanian needs and availabilities are provided by Department of Commerce publications such as the annual *Foreign Economic Trends and Their Implications for the United States* (FET). The often-required stipulation to engage in barter or "buy-back" arrangements when exporting to Romania must be particularly stressed. Romania's severe financial difficulties may well continue to severely restrict imports while forcing her to maximize export opportunities to the extent possible.

SOURCES OF INFORMATION

A highly useful introduction to Romanian sources of information is provided in *Romania, A Country Study* (1979), The American University, Washington, D.C. (pp. 175-91). This source provides important background information on internal Romanian sources including the press, book publishing, libraries, etc. It is well worth consulting for a comprehensive overview of available governmental sources.

For practical business and commerce-related information, the *Romanian Chamber of Commerce and Industry* is probably the most prolific source. Indicative of the scope of activities of this organization is that its membership exceeds 800 Romanian organizations including Romanian foreign trade companies, industrial centrals (headquarters-type organizations), and numerous units of ministries and governmental departments concerned with foreign trade (*Economic and Commercial Guide to Romania*, 1982, p. 226). Following are some specialized departments of the Chamber:

The Foreign Relations Office
ROMINVENT, The Office for Foreign Patents and Trademarks

ARGUS, The Office for Representations and Commissions
ITE, The Fairs and Exhibition Company
PUBLICOM, Foreign Trade Publicity Agency
OCM, Good Control Office
International Commercial Arbitration Commission

The Chamber is thus clearly a major source for information and contacts in Romania. Specific Romanian information sources published under the sponsorship of the Chamber of Commerce by PUBLICOM include the following:

— *Economic and Commercial Guide to Romania*, yearly issues
— *Rules, Contractual Clauses and Commercial Terms Utilized in Romanian-American Economic Relations*, issued by the Romanian-American Economic Council, edited by PUBLICOM, Bucharest, Romania, 1980.
— *Romania, Yearbook* (yearly editions), Editura Stiintifica si Enciclopedia, Bucharest, Romania
— Romanian Bank for Foreign Trade, annual bulletin
— Romanian Foreign Trade Law (1982)
— *Your Commercial Partners in Romania* (1982) (lists and describes activities of foreign trade companies, as well as Chamber of Commerce Departments)
— *Romanian Industrial Centrals and Research-Design Institutes* (yearly)
— *Romanian Foreign Trade* (quarterly)

In addition, a listing and description of all domestic newspapers and periodicals is published by ILEXIM, foreign trade company, Bucharest, Romania, (yearly).

The Chamber of Commerce is also a convenient source of information for services providing organizations in Romania, including banks, of which the Romanian Bank for Foreign Trade is the central governmental organization (for details see *Economic and Commercial Guide to Romania*, 1986, pp. 123-25). Not to be overlooked is the *Romania Yearbook* series, published in Romania, which provides comprehensive annual census coverage.

INTERNATIONAL SOURCES

In addition to *Romania, A Country Study* (1979), only a few comprehensive and in-depth sources of information on Romania are available from Western sources. The most comprehensive, and in large part still current source, is the massive 1979 World Bank Study of Romania, *Romania — The Industrialization of an Agrarian-Economy Under Socialist Planning*, (A.C. Tsantis and R. Pepper, coordinating authors, The World Bank, Washington, D.C.). This volume provides the prerequisite background for an in-depth understanding of both past and present Romanian developments and institutions. For the serious student of Romanian development, it is indispensable.

For current, updated trade and development-related information, the following U.S. Department of Commerce publications are available:

- FET, *Foreign Economic Trends and Their Implications for the United States* (yearly); prepared by the American Embassy in Bucharest, Romania, International Trade Administration, Washington, D.C.
- OBR, *Overseas Business Reports — Trading and Investing in Romania* (1978) — International Marketing Information Series. Industry and Trade Administration.
- *Business America — The Magazine of International Trade* (Vol. 8, No. 5, p. 26).

It should be noted that in general Romania is one of the more difficult countries in Eastern-Europe on which to obtain data. Although this may change in the future, easier access to information, most noticeable in the case of another Eastern bloc country, Hungary, has not as yet been observed for Romania.

METHODS OF ENTRY INTO NATIONAL BUSINESS

Foreign trade activities in Romania are carried out through two basic organizational structures:

1. Authorized production/service enterprises or Centrals.
2. Specialized FTCs (Foreign trade companies).

Till 1980, foreign trading partners were required to deal with particular specialized FTCs, depending on the nature of the transaction. Since that time (pursuant to Article 48 of Law No. 12/1980), all FTCs are entitled to export any Romanian-made goods. This clearly simplifies complex transactions, particularly those involving exports of a large variety of goods. Negotiations regarding imports to Romania must apparently still be conducted with specialized FTCs or particular authorized production/service enterprises. Following are some FTCs and authorized enterprises and their areas of specialization:

Foreign Trade Companies (Selected)

ELECTRO EXPORT IMPORT (household electric appliances, motors, etc.)

ELECTRONUM (computers, radios, televisions, etc.)

INDUSTRIAL EXPORT IMPORT (cooperative ventures for installations, licenses, patents, etc.)

MASIN EXPORT IMPORT (metal-cutting machine tools; measuring instruments, etc.)

Enterprises (Central)

DE MASINE TEXTILE (light industry machinery and installations, etc.)

CONFEX (ladies and childrens' wear, etc.)

ROMSIT (light industry products, etc.)

A complete listing of authorized enterprises and FTCs is provided in the *Economic and Commercial Guide to Romania* (1982, pp. 185-194). The bulk of foreign trade activities are handled through the services of the FTCs. Production enterprises or Centrals are, however, increasingly directly involved as well. The following, based on the Romanian Foreign Trade Law (1982), will provide some illustrations as to the scope of foreign trade activities assigned to such authorized units:

- Production units work out their (own) export/import and technical cooperation plans relying on their own surveys of foreign markets (Article 17).
- Production units should seek to secure from their own activities the foreign currency needed for their imports (Article 13).
- All foreign currency resulting from foreign trade is transferred to the state through the Romanian Foreign Trade Bank. All foreign currency needed for imports is similarly obtained from the Foreign Trade Bank (Article 14).
- The Foreign Trade Bank is authorized to grant loans in foreign currency to economic units carrying on foreign trade (Article 15).
- Enterprises producing for foreign trade, either directly or through a Central or FTC, are (legally) answerable for such activities. Managers of such units are answerable for the fulfillment of export/import plans and sign contracts with foreign partners, or delegate to other executives the power to sign such contracts (Article 5).

Clearly, production units or Centrals are increasingly involved in foreign trade which has hitherto been the exclusive domain of FTCs.

The Chamber of Commerce and Industry, and in particular its Foreign Relations Office, are indispensable in providing effective access to Romanian markets, particularly for foreign companies attempting to establish initial contacts. The Foreign Relations Office maintains relations with close to 300 similar foreign organizations, as well as with all Romanian FTCs and authorized firms for the purpose of enhancing commercial negotiations and transactions. It provides domestic and foreign clients with the following (partial listing):

— Current information on foreign goods requirements and export and import information.
— Foreign technical-commercial documentation.
— Information and contact with foreign firm representatives and agencies in Romania.
— Certificates of origins, endorsed invoices, and other foreign trade documents. (*Economic and Commercial Guide to Romania* [1982], p. 230)

Based on a reciprocal agreement, there is a special U.S. section (one of 27 such sections) within the Foreign Relations Office dealing with the promotion of trade with the U.S. In addition, the Chamber of Commerce itself provides foreign firms with export/ import documentation, documentation on cooperation ventures, representation conditions in Romania, as well as current foreign trade regulations (*Ibid.*, p. 227).

As mentioned before, establishing joint companies in Romania involves reserving the state at least a 51% share of the registered capital of such companies. There is thus no possibility in Romania of establishing wholly (foreign) owned subsidiaries or joint ventures.

Nevertheless, within the last 15 years numerous cooperation agreements with Western foreign partners have been made. Thus, Romania entered into roughly 350 cooperation agreements and conventions with various countries, and numerous joint enterprises and companies have been set up, viz.: "Rom Control Data" for computation techniques (in collaboration with the U.S.); "Oltcit" for small motor cars (in collaboration with France); "ResitaRenk" for the production and marketing of reducers, toothed wheels, couplings, and other devices (in collaboration with the Federal Republic of Germany); "Rifil" for the production of synthetic fibers and yarns (in cooperation with Italy). Mention should be also made of the manufacturing in Romania of the Alouette helicopter according to the license of the French society SNIAS and of the cooperation ventures for the construction of projects in Third World markets (*Romania at a Glance* [1982], p. 30).

AREAS OF CONFLICT

Analysis of actual or potential areas of conflict could, in a large sense, be seen to apply either to the domestic national scene or to international trade. Each of these areas in turn could be subdivided into categories such as economic, political, cultural, or religious conflict areas. Space limitations will confine the discussion here to possible areas of conflict pertaining to the internal economic environment of Romania.

DIRECTION OF INDUSTRIAL GROWTH

As the preceding discussion indicates, policy and strategy decisions of national importance are made centrally in Romania by the political leadership dominated by President Ceausescu. Following traditional Soviet practices, industry (particularly heavy industry, and as of late high-technology-oriented industry) has received and continues to receive priority attention and funding. Conflicts could thus be seen to exist as to the following: interindustry (competition between priority and nonpriority segments) as to funding); intra-industry (competition among various priority components, etc); and conflicts among consumers, producers, distributors, and regulators. The planning process appears to elicit broad areas of conflicts between parties whose interests are at stake. However, much reconciliation of interest clashing does occur during the planning process. Various reconciliation and mediation mechanisms will be discussed in a following section.

NATIONAL CONTROL OF KEY SECTORS

Romanian political-governmental authorities reserve for themselves unchallenged control over industrial activities in general, whether taking place in the state sector or the cooperative sector. The small private sector, primarily small-scale agricultural production, is least controlled (involving primarily the central setting of maximum selling prices). Central control is thus pervasive and comprehensive. Such control would appear to foster conflicts at various levels of the decision-making hierarchy. Confining ourselves to the enterprise level, enterprise management interests may clearly clash with those of the bureaucratic layers above it: the Centrala (headquarter-type organization), the industrial ministry, the local and/or regional authorities, etc. However it must be kept in mind that the authority of enterprise management is generally confined to so-called tactical-operational matters, with strategic policy-related decisions made at higher levels. This demarcation of authority clearly reduces areas of actual or potential conflicts.

Credit and Pricing Policies

All "economic lever" decisions, such as credit and pricing decisions, are made centrally in Romania. The Ministry of Finance makes decisions on credits and pricing, which applies nationwide to respective categories of goods, materials, and the like. At the enterprise level again, conflicts may be seen to arise particularly as to the pricing of new products, the introduction of which is mandated for each enterprise through the specification of the numbers of new items to be produced and distributed (within the agreed upon annual plan of the enterprise). Enterprises clearly argue for higher prices, thus enabling the enterprise to earn higher profits. Since as a rule prices in Romania are set on the basis of average production and distribution costs (plus centrally determined markups on costs), enterprises must document higher costs in order to be allowed to charge higher prices. Conflicts on this basis appear to be inevitable, indeed "built-in."

As to credit rates, these are set on a national basis and allow little room for negotiations as to their level. Amounts of credit are negotiated with the Romanian Central Bank based on enterprise credit needs. The trend has been to give the bank increasing authority to withhold credit depending on the profitability of the client's operations. Pressures are thus exerted to bring about greater efficiency in production, since enterprises may no longer expect automatic subsidies or credits in cases where poor performance is judged to have occurred due to the enterprises' failings. Such pressures have intensified, particularly following the reforms of 1978 (for an in-depth description and analysis of this reform, see Naor, 1986).

Research and Development

In the Romanian context, Research and Development plans are developed jointly by enterprises, Centrals, and branch Ministries, and become central components of (binding) annual and (nonbinding) five-year plans. Pressures are clearly exerted from above on the enterprises to make consistent and substantial efforts toward modernization. Enterprises may thus be expected to press for such things as lower targets regarding the number of new products to be introduced during the forthcoming year, etc. It must be pointed out that actual Research and Development activities are often centralized at the Centrala or at attached specialized research institutions, divorced, as it were, from the production level. Since new products may require extensive retooling etc., enterprises bent on meeting output targets may be expected to resist the interruption of established protection routines. New product introductions may thus be delayed due to obstructions emanating from peculiarities of the planning process itself.

Human Resource Development

Human resource development comprises an important functional planning activity at all planning levels. With few exceptions, labor has unrestricted mobility in Romania, and workers must thus be attracted by enterprises with offers of better working or housing conditions, etc. (since wage rates are set nationally). Management is generally appointed by the Ministry, depending on the particular needs of the enterprise. Ministries act in this case as de facto owners, exercising hiring rights, rights of promotion, etc. At the university and vocational institutions the number of designated entrants and graduates is controlled through devices such as tightening or relaxing entrance exams, provisions of grants, etc. Thus national development needs will dictate the number of perspective graduates while their employment will be left to the individual's choices and preferences.

Taxation

Romania, as all other Eastern bloc nations, relies primarily on taxes levied on enterprise profits and sales taxes, with little emphasis on taxing individual's incomes. As an example, it is instructive to consider the distribution of profits of state enterprises which, while differing from year to year, appear to be as shown in Table 6.

Successful enterprises will clearly be strongly "demotivated" by the high rate of taxation due the state. Not unjustifiably, they may perceive themselves as "financing" the poorer run enterprises, lacking as it were a say in their management. Enterprise taxation is one area where considerable friction exists both between enterprises, as well as between enterprises and their supervisory and control organizations.

As stated, turnover taxes, particularly those added by producers prior to resale to wholesalers, were the most important revenue source until 1974 (*Ibid.*, p. 475). Individual income taxes were a minor source of state revenue, amounting until 1977 to only about 9% of total budget revenues. Rates were slightly progressive ranging until 1977 from 10% to 45%, (paid on incomes exceeding 910 Lei/month), averaging overall about 12% (*Ibid.*, p. 481). Due to the egalitarian income distribution (which by law adhered to the ratio of

Table 6

Approximate Profit Distribution of State Enterprises

	Percent
Paid to state budget (tax)	65
Distributed as bonuses	2
Working capital and minor investments	20
Payment of credit obligations	13

Source: World Bank, 1979, p. 474.

5.5 : 1 between highest and lowest incomes), little conflict about the taxation of individual incomes exists.

RESOLUTION OF CONFLICTS

The previous section dealt with potential areas of conflict, particularly those between Romanian firms, and between such firms and governmental units. Understanding the potential for intra-Romanian conflicts is clearly important for foreign firms attempting to negotiate with Romanian parties. This section will deal with likely avenues for conflicts resolution, including potential conflicts between Romanian and foreign firms.

Due to the hierarchical and comprehensive planning system characteristic of the Romanian economy, conflict resolution between domestic firms/agencies is apt to occur between the various stages of the planning process. Examples of such conflicts were provided, and could include conflicts of enterprise production targets (between the enterprise and its branch ministry), delivery and supply disputes (between relevant enterprises involved), disputes as to credit availability and terms (between the enterprise and the Romanian National Bank), and the like. Most disputes of this nature reach resolution through negotiations between the parties, subject to time constraints, as set forth in the various planning documents. In cases where agreement cannot be reached directly between the parties, disputes are referred to higher bodies (Centrals, Ministries, interministerial committees, etc.) for resolution. Disputes involving contractual agreements may be brought to litigation as well, although no information is available on the frequency of such occurances. It appears that most disputes are settled through mutually agreed on compromises between the parties. It must be kept in mind that under traditional Romanian sellers' market conditions, suppliers tend to hold the upper hand relative to buyers in such negotiations. However, since under prevailing monopolistic/monopsonistic conditions prevailing in Romania, suppliers are dependent in turn on a small number of buyers, such advantage may be limited, particularly in the long run. In addition, Romanian authorities have traditionally stressed the obligation and duty of enterprises to maintain "contract discipline." Frequent and continuing violations of contract terms by supply organs are not likely to be tolerated.

CONFLICT RESOLUTION BETWEEN DOMESTIC AND FOREIGN FIRMS

A host of potential conflicts may arise between host agencies and the foreign firm intending to operate, or operating, in Romania. Since all means of production are state owned, such conflicts will inevitably involve a state or quasi-state organization (Ministry, Foreign trade company, etc., or a cooperatively owned organization). Conflicts may arise concerning the actual conduct of operations of joint ventures; their financing, credit, reinvestment policies, profit distribution decisions, etc. Much will clearly depend on the desire of the parties to preserve the relationship, considering its potential long-term value. Long-term considerations may therefore be instrumental in overcoming disputes of a more tactical, short-term nature.

A frequently used means to settle disputes in international trade is arbitration. The International Commercial Arbitration Commission attached to the Romanian Chamber of Commerce arbitrates disputes arising from foreign trade, economic, technical, and scientific cooperation ventures between Romanians or between Romanian and foreign parties. It also settles disputes between joint companies operating in Romania and Romanian entities (*Economic and Commercial Guide to Romania* [1982], p. 235). Arbitration must, however, be agreed on by the parties either under the contract, or by agreement following the occurrence of the dispute. The arbitration commission itself is governed by its own rules of organization and by the Civil Law Code (*Ibid.*, p. 235).

In addition, protection of industrial property such as foreign inventions and trademarks is provided by another governmental office attached to the Chamber of Commerce, Rominvent (office for foreign patents and trade marks). Romania is a subscriber to the Paris Convention (1883) for the protection of industrial property, and has subscribed to all subsequent amendments of the convention, the last being that of Stockholm (1967). It has also subscribed to the Madrid Convention (1891) on the international registration of brands and trademarks. Foreign firms entering the Romanian market are thus assured of industrial property rights protection, as well as established means for arbitration, both of which should tend to reduce the risk of foreign companies operating within the Socialist environment of Romania.

CORPORATE STRATEGY AND PLANNING FOR FOREIGN FIRMS

Foreign firms intending to do business in Romania are well advised, as has been pointed out previously, to tie their offerings closely to Romania's development priorities as indicated by the five-year plan. Such priorities receive normally widespread elaboration in the official press. Much can be gleaned from such sources as to the various types of goods or services needed, their urgency of need, technologies desired, and the like. Sufficient lead time is thus available to the foreign firm in most cases in order to submit offers to the appropriate governmental organization (usually a specialized Foreign Trade Enterprise) and to enter into negotiations, which, depending on the financial or countertrade arrangements that can be worked out, are often likely to be protracted. If desired, foreign firms may thus tie their own corporate five-year plans to Romania's development needs for the same time-frame. In this way it appears possible to achieve long-term supply relationships in Romanian markets bent on rapid expansion and technological growth.

As indicated previously, Romanian import needs are available from U.S. sources as well. Current listings of such requirements are available from U.S. Embassy sources in Bucharest, Romania, as published in *Foreign Economic Trends and Their Implications for the United States* (FET, U.S. Department of Commerce, International Trade Administration). The following excerpt from a recent FET will serve as an example as to the type of information available to foreign firms for the current five-year plan period (1986-1990).

> The structure of investment outlined in Romania's current 5-year plan (1986-90) would suggest that the best potential for U.S. exports to Romania during the next 3 years should be found in the following areas: energy development (nuclear power generation equipment, renewable energy technology,

deep-strata oil drilling, and oil and methane gas recovery); electronics and automation (integrated circuits, electronic telephone exchanges, industrial robots, and numerically-controlled machine-tools); chemical industry (reagents, additives, catalysts, agricultural chemicals, and medical drugs); and food processing and packaging equipment and technology. The sales potential of bituminous coal and agricultural produce and other raw materials also appear to be excellent. (FET, Department of Commerce, September, 1987, p. 10)

As to the thorny question of financing Romania's imports we may once again turn to FET sources for details regarding the various countertrade arrangements that may be insisted on by Romanian foreign trade organizations. The following will underline some of the problems that may be encountered.

In an effort to remedy severe cash flow problems, Romanian foreign trade organizations (FTOs) typically demand that Western suppliers take as much as 100 percent payment in Romanian goods. Such arrangements include barter, counterpurchase, product buyback, coproduction, joint ventures, and third country cooperation. The arrangements were specifically highlighted in the 1986-90 Economic Plan, and they can be expected to continue to play a key role in Romanian foreign trade in the next years. U.S. firms willing to accept countertrade or participate in joint operations will have the best access to Romanian markets. U.S. firms making straight sales to Romania should take steps to protect themselves against payment delays. Confirmed letter-of-credit terms provide the greatest protection to the seller. Of other, less desirable arrangements, unconfirmed letter-of-credit terms are preferable to cash-against-documents or open account terms. Contracts should also stipulate interest payment if the Romanian FTO does not meet its payments on time. (FET, Department of Commerce, September, 1987, p. 11)

The ability to overcome such or similar difficulties that plague Romanian trade will however provide both sides mutually advantageous results over the long run.

CORPORATE ORGANIZATION AND CONTROL
FOR FOREIGN FIRMS

As the preceding materials indicate, foreign firms dealing with Romanian organizations are advised to look toward long-term relationships rather than short-term opportunities. Such an orientation will require appropriate organizational arrangements of a more permanent nature. Specialized export staffs within export departments or larger units such as international divisions, capable of dealing with barter and countertrade, are needed for successful negotiations which may often hinge on the willingness to work out complex payback arrangements.

Organizations lacking experience in this field may wish, at least initially, to utilize the services of specialized trading houses with experience in countertrade arrangements (such as, for example, General Electric's trading company). It is essential in such dealings to attempt to anticipate likely problems that may arise in the disposition of Romanian goods received in countertrade or barter arrangements. Top level attention and committment to the conduct of such operations, falling as they may outside the regular market activities of the firm, may be essential for long-term success. The choice of committed staffs, proper organizational arrangements, and strict control procedures appear indispensable. One approach that may be usefully applied, would be to look for long-term commitments, both to imports as well as to exports, from Romania. Such a "balanced" approach, under the control of specialized staff committed to its long-term implementation, may stand the best chance for success given the comprehensive nature of long-term development planning encountered in Romania.

FUTURE BUSINESS OPPORTUNITIES
AND SCENARIOS

Romania's socioeconomic development efforts are likely to remain in high gear for the forseeable future. The ongoing contraction of Romania's outstanding foreign debt, foreshadowing its ultimate liquidation, may be expected to continue. Romania is thus likely to remain for the forseeable future a growth market with a potentially increasing capability of financing imports, eager for Western technology and know-how.

Romania's desire for national independence, while formally remaining a member of the CMEA bloc, will undoubtably continue to dispose it to balance Eastern and Western ties. Western firms may thus continue to be assured of a "nonhostile" environment for business operations, regardless of particular ups and downs in East-West relationships. The potential for stable relationships within a growth environment appears to be an area of significant opportunity that Romania offers to foreign partners. As pointed out in the introduction to this chapter, while presenting "most restrictive" internal conditions within the Eastern bloc, due primarily to highly stringent centralized planning and control requirements, Romania's penchant for independence and closer ties with the West may well outweigh such constraints. Romania may well provide greater long-term opportunities to foreign partners than its more "liberal" neighbors within the bloc. Trade relations must, however, take Romania's needs and planning requirements strictly into account. This would argue for long-term commitments on the part of foreign partners. Joint ventures of the type previously indicated both within Romania as well as in Third World countries, appear to provide great promise as vehicles of long-term collaboration. Romania appears to emphasize and prefer such ventures, thus assuring them vital political support from the highest levels of Romania's state administration. Foreign firms are advised to carefully examine and evaluate opportunities that may be derived from such ventures. This applies both to operations within the framework of future Romanian five-year plans, and to entry into Third World markets, where Romania's expertise, Third World "affiliation," and market knowledge may represent an invaluable asset toward successful entry and operations in such markets.

BIBLIOGRAPHY

Business America, March 17, 1986, Department of Commerce.
Economic and Commercial Guide to Romania, 1982, PUBLICOM, Chamber of Commerce and Industry of the Socialist Republic of Romania, Bucharest, Romania.

Era Socialista, No. 19, October 1984, translated in Joint Publication Research Services (JPRS), EEI-85-022.

Era Socialista, No. 7, April, 1984, translated in Joint Publication Research Services (JPRS), EEI-84-056.

Foreign Economic Trends and Their Implications for the United States (yearly); prepared by the American Embassy in Bucharest, Romania, International Trade Administration, Washington, D.C.

Naor, Jacob. "Towards a Socialist Marketing Concept — The Case of Romania," *Journal of Marketing*, Vol. 50, January 1986, 28-39.

———. "Recent Changes in Enterprise Management and Marketing Practices in Romania," *European Journal of Marketing*, Vol. 20, 1986.

———. "Marketing in a Resource-Short Socialist Environment: Romania," *International Marketing Review*, Vol. 11, No. 2, 1985.

———. "Economic Reform-making in Romania — The 1978 New Economic Mechanism," Equipe de Recherche Sur La Firme Et L'Industrie, Universite de Montpellier, Montpellier, France, 1983.

Overseas Business Report, Trading and Investing in Romania, September 1978 International Marketing Information Series, Department of Commerce, Industry and Trade Administration.

Romania, A Country Study, 1979, The American University, Washington D.C.

Romania at a Glance, 1982, edited by PUBLICOM, Chamber of Commerce and Industry, Bucharest, Romania.

Romanian Bank for Foreign Trade, annual bulletin, published by PUBLICOM, Bucharest, Romania.

Romanian Foreign Trade (quarterly) published by PUBLICOM, Bucharest, Romania.

Romanian Foreign Trade Law (1982) published by PUBLICOM, Bucharest, Romania.

Romanian Industrial Centrals and Research-Design Institutes (yearly) published by PUBLICOM, Bucharest, Romania.

Romania — The Industrialization of an Agrarian Economy under Socialist Planning, 1979, A.C. Tsantis and R. Pepper, coordinating authors, The World Bank, Washington, D.C.

Romania Yearbook, 1981, Editura Stiintifica Si Enciclopedica, Bucharest, Romania, 1981.

Rules, Contractual Clauses and Commercial Terms Utilized in Romanian — American Economic Relations, Romanian — American Economic Council, edited by PUBLICOM, Bucharest, Romania, 1980.

The Europa Yearbook, 1984, A World Survey, Vol. I., Europa Publications Limited, London.

Your Commercial Partners in Romania, 1982, edited by PUBLICOM, Chamber of Commerce and Industry, Bucharest, Romania.

APPENDIX A

Powers of the Grand National Assembly:

To adopt and amend the Constitution of the Socialist Republic of Romania; to regulate the electoral system; to adopt the National Master Plan of economic and social development and the State Budget; to ratify and denounce international treaties that imply modification of laws; to organize the government; to regulate the organization of law courts and the public prosecutor's offices; to issue regulations for the organization and functioning of the people's councils; to establish the administrative division of territory; to grant amnesty; to elect and recall the President of the Socialist Republic of Romania, the State Council, and the Government; to elect and recall the president and the members of the Supreme Court and the Prosecutor General; to exercise general control over the implementation of the laws; to control the activity of the President of the Republic, the State Council, the Government, the Supreme Court, and the Public Prosecutor's Office; to establish the general foreign policy line; to proclaim the state of emergency, to declare partial or general mobilization and the state of war (*Romania Yearbook, 1981*, p. 49).

Powers of the State Council:

To set the date of elections for the Grand National Assembly and the people's councils; to organize the ministries and the other central state-bodies; to ratify and denounce international treaties with the exception of those that come within the competence of the Grand National Assembly; to establish military ranks and create decorations and titles of honor. Main attributions in between sessions of the Grand National Assembly: to issue, without amending the Constitution, enactments having the force of law; to appoint and recall the Prime Minister (and the Government if the Grand National Assembly cannot meet due to exceptional circumstances); to grant amnesty; to control the implementation of laws and enactments of the Grand National Assembly and the activity of the Government, the ministries, and the other bodies of State administration; to order, in case of emergency, partial or general mobilization and declaration of state of war (*Ibid.*, p. 49).

Powers of The Council of Ministers:

The Council of Ministers (the Government) is the supreme body of state administration. According to Constitution, the government is elected by the Grand National Assembly in its first session, for the duration of one term. The government elected by the Grand National Assembly on March 29, 1980 consists of 50 members (53 at present) who are: the Prime Minister, 3 First Deputy Prime Ministers, 9 Deputy Ministers (7 now), 18 ministers (25 now) 6 (7 now) heads of central bodies of state administration, and 13 ministers-secretaries of state and assimilated offices (10 now). The Prime Minister, the First Deputy Prime Ministers, and the Deputy Prime Ministers make up the Standing Bureau of the Council of Ministers. Main powers of the Council of Ministers: to establish general measures necessary for the implementation of the domestic and foreign policy; to decide on measures necessary for organizing and ensuring the implementation of laws; to direct, coordinate, and control the work of the ministries and other central bodies of state administration; to work out the draft national master plan of economic and social development and the draft state budget, as well as other bills and draft decrees; to establish measures for ensuring public order, defending the interests of the State, and protecting the rights of the citizens; to exercise overall direction in the field of relations with other states, and to take measures for the conclusion of international agreements (*Ibid.*, pp. 50, 51).

APPENDIX B

TABLE 1. Number of Pupils and Students per 10,000 population

	Age	1965/66	1970/71	1975/76	1979/80	1980/81
Pre-school education	3-6	186	221	382	412	419
Primary schools, gymnasiums and Lyceums	7-8	1,770	1,703	1,845	1,950	1,922
Vocational and foremen's schools	15-18	79	113	74	76	75
Higher education	18 up	69	75	77	87	86

Source: Romania, Yearbook 1981, p. 89.

TABLE 2. Higher Education Pattern (1979/80 academic year)

	Faculties	Students	Of which day courses included:
Faculties, total	134	192,456	158,089
- technical	43	85,089	75,036
- teacher-training institutes	27	22,088	14,856
- medicine and pharmacy	17	23,332	23,332
- agriculture, forestry, and veterinary medicine	15	13,142	11,298
- architecture constructions	10	18,297	16,440
- economics	9	22,371	13,549
- arts	9	2,944	1,935
- law	4	5,283	1,643

Source: Ibid., p. 89

APPENDIX C

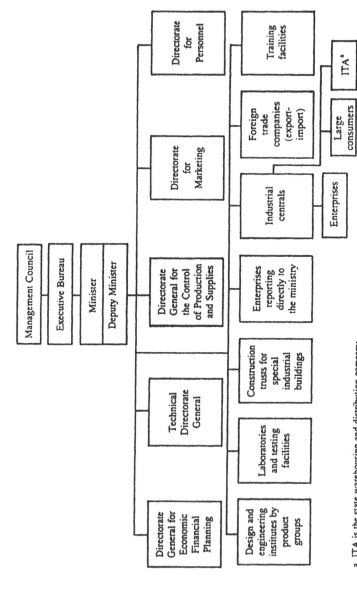

a. ITA is the state warehousing and distribution company.

Source: "Romania- The Industrialization of an Agrarian Economy under Socialist Planning," 1979, A.C. Tsantis and R. Pepper Coordinating authors, The World Bank, Washington, D.C., p. 408.

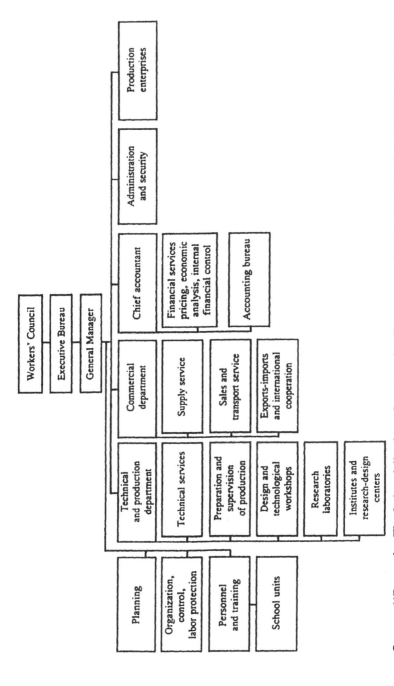

Source: "Romania- The Industrialization of an Agrarian Economy under Socialist Planning," 1979, A.C. Tsantis and R. Pepper Coordinating authors, The World Bank, Washington, D.C., p. 408.

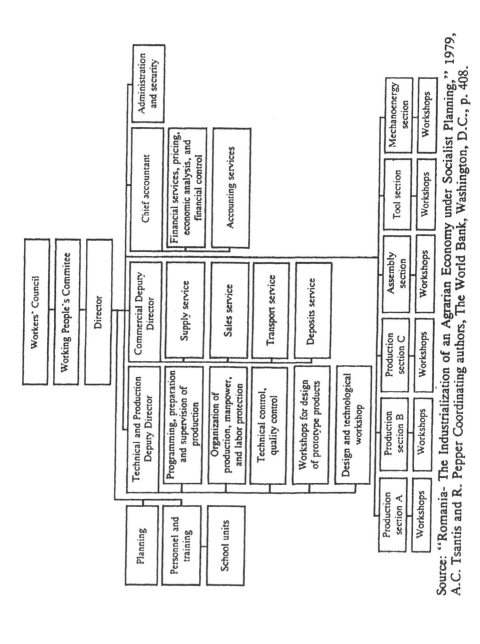

Source: "Romania- The Industrialization of an Agrarian Economy under Socialist Planning," 1979, A.C. Tsantis and R. Pepper Coordinating authors, The World Bank, Washington, D.C., p. 408.

494

Chapter 14

Singapore

Soo Jiuan Tan
Chin Tiong Tan

INTERNATIONAL INFLUENCES AFFECTING THE NATION

Exports and Imports

Unlike other Asian NICs (newly industrialized countries), the Republic of Singapore's economy is unique. Annually, as much as two-thirds of its output of goods and services are exported to overseas markets. The openness of the economy is a result of the small domestic market of 2.5 million people.

Historically, Singapore flourished as an entrepot serving the Southeast Asian region. It is thus not surprising to note the predominance of nonoil reexports over nonoil domestic exports in Singapore's export profile. Oil exports, until recently (1984-1985), have been the mainstay of Singapore's trade (see Figure 1).

The United States, which absorbs more than 20% of Singapore's exports annually, is Singapore's top export market. Major items of export comprise electrical and electronic products and electronic components. Malaysia is Singapore's second largest trading partner, importing petroleum products as well as other nonoil products. The European Community, which imports mainly items like timber, rubber, television sets, and drugs, makes up Singapore's third largest export market. Approximately 70% of exports to Japan, Singapore's fourth largest trading partner, comprise petroleum products. Japan imports annually close to S$5 billion worth of goods from Singapore.

Figure 1 Composition of Singapore Exports

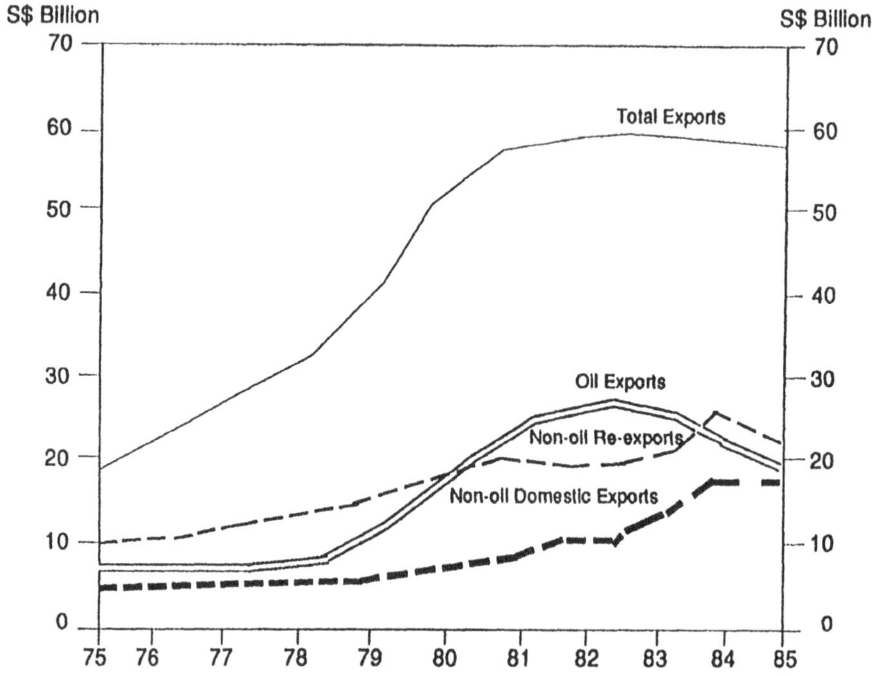

Source: Department of Statistics

Other minor but equally important export markets include Thailand, Australia, Hong Kong, and Saudi Arabia. A market receiving growing attention is China, Singapore's seventh largest trading partner. Trade between the two countries rose 54% in 1985 as Singapore refined increasing amounts of Chinese crude oil.

The Singapore economy is therefore very dependent on external demand, particularly those originating from the United States. The recent shake-up in the computer market in the United States led to lower sales of electronic products, which was responsible for the 2% decline in Singapore's exports in 1985, the first decline after nine years of continuous growth. It has been said that 1985 was a watershed year as Singapore posted a negative GNP growth, having been hit externally by the slowing down of the United States economy, increasing trade protectionism, and structural changes in the traditional industries like oil and marine-related industries. Singapore is also gradually losing its status as an entrepot trade center, and reexports declined by 3.7% to $17.6 billion in 1985, compared to an 8% increase in 1984. Many of Singapore's neighboring developing countries are beginning to deal directly with the suppliers.

Besides a high dependence on overseas demand for economic growth, Singapore is also dependent on imports to satisfy its local industrial and consumer demand for goods and services. Traditionally, Singapore's imports exceed exports, as Figure 2 shows.

Japan is the Republic's top supplier, accounting annually for more than 15% of Singapore's total imports. The other major suppliers are the United States, Malaysia, the European Community, and China. Major items of imports are food, crude materials, mineral fuels, chemicals, manufactured goods by material, machinery, and transport equipment.

International Capital Flows

Despite the perennial balance of trade deficit, Singapore is able to maintain an annual balance of payment surplus. In 1985, a surplus of S$3 billion contributed by inflows of foreign capital increased Singapore's foreign reserves to a record amount of S$27 billion. Foreign capital is thus important to Singapore's economy and the government adopts an open door policy to foreign investments.

There are very few controls on private investments except in sensitive sectors like defense and utilities. Singapore does not impose any restrictions on repatriation of profits, transfer of technology, or importation of capital, nor does it insist on domestic content re-

Figure 2 Imports & Exports of Singapore

	1981 bil. ($)	1982 bil. ($)	1983 bil. ($)	1984 bil. ($)	1985 bil. ($)
Imports	58.2	60.2	59.5	61.1	57.8
Exports	44.3	44.5	46.2	51.3	50.2

quirements for capital investments in Singapore. There are no anti-monopoly laws in Singapore and no capital gains tax. To the contrary, there is a host of fiscal incentives for foreign investors in Singapore.

In the off shore financial markets, notably the Asian Dollar Market (an offshoot of the Eurodollar Market and the Asian Dollar Bond Market), investors are free to invest in any of the instruments traded, free of exchange control restrictions. Various tax incentives such as nil withholding tax on interests paid to nonresident deposits in the Asian Dollar Market, exemption of tax on interests received on Asian Dollar Bond, and a concessionary tax rate of 10% on income received from operations in the two off-shore markets, are available to nonresident investors in Singapore. The government is in the process of considering further fiscal incentives to boost international capital inflow.

Impact of International Agreements
(Including Regional Groups)

Singapore is a member of the Association of Southeast Asia Nations (ASEAN) formed in 1967 to promote economic cooperation in the region.

The ASEAN Preferential Trading Arrangements (PTA) signed in 1977 promotes intraregional trade through tariff reduction and liberalization of nontariff measures. To date, tariff cuts (on across the board basis) have been extended to all product items with export value exceeding US $10 million a year. In fact, tariff cuts have been increased to a maximum of 50% and in all, 12,225 items form the list of products eligible for more favorable preference margins.

Trade dialogues with major industrial countries have also made great progress. In February 1985, Australia announced an additional commitment of A$3 million for the second cycle of the ASEAN-Australia Trade Investment Promotion program. Other countries like Japan, the European Countries, United States, and New Zealand have also committed themselves in various ways to promotion of trade with ASEAN.

In terms of industrial development, ASEAN industrial cooperation schemes comprise mainly the ASEAN Industrial projects (AIP) and the ASEAN Industrial Complementation Scheme (AICS). Resembling closely the United Nations "package deal"-sponsored plants with equity shared among member countries and producing mainly for the regional market, these regional projects like the urea plant in Indonesia and the proposed hepatitis vaccine plant in Singapore, receive technical and financial assistance from developed countries.[1] In May 1984, a list of four ASEAN industrial joint venture products was approved, thus paving the way for industrial joint ventures among the private sectors.

"There does not appear to be a clear cut picture of trade gains and losses among ASEAN member countries from intra-regional trade liberalization" a study of the ASEAN intraregional trade from 1978 (when PTA became effective) to 1982 revealed.[2] However, Singapore's exports to its largest regional market, ASEAN, declined by 10% (S$1.18 billion) in 1985 for the second consecutive year and indications are that they are unlikely to improve significantly in 1986. "This is because uncertainties about commodity and petroleum prices as well as relentless efforts by neighboring countries to adopt direct trade are expected to remain for some time."[3] Exports to four ASEAN countries (Malaysia, Thailand, Philippines, and Brunei) plunged by 19% from S$2.07 billion to S$1.7 billion in the first two months of 1986, according to latest trade data from the Department of Statistics. A recent report by the General Agreement on Tariffs and Trade (GATT) mentioned increased uncertainty of the countries about the course of trade policies which had discouraged trade-related investments.

Singapore's economy is complimentary to that of other ASEAN members with its comparative advantage in modern industrial skills in the region. Many multinationals have set up training centers in Singapore, and Singapore could become a center for the transfer of skills and technology for ASEAN members.

At the international level, developments in GATT and the United Nations Committee on Trade and Development (UNCTAD) receive great attention by the Singapore government. Singapore acceded to the GATT antidumping Code in 1984, which accords protection to Singapore manufacturers and exporters against frivolous antidumping charges. Only recently a Singapore exporter was cleared of United States charges of dumping heavy-walled rectangular tubing cheaply in the market. Investigations are still being carried out by the U.S. International Trade Commission on two other types of steel tubes exported by a Singapore Company.[4]

Active MNCs/State-Owned Enterprises/Trading Companies

"The rapid modernisation of Singapore in the last 15 years has been due in no small measure to the arrival of multi-national companies. Apart from helping Singapore to become an industrial and financial center, they have introduced modern techniques of management which are appropriate for running large scale enterprises."[5] The official attitude towards MNCs is that they are valuable to Singapore.

The 1985 business risk survey carried out by the Business Environment Risk Information (BERI) revealed that out of 50 countries, Singapore is rated as offering international investors the best profit opportunities in the next 5-10 years. This is despite problems such as labor shortages and declining export earnings in traditional industries, because these will be "offset by progress in the growth of operations based on advanced technology, a strong financial services industry and other efficiently managed businesses."[6] Positive features such as political stability, policies favorable to private enterprise and foreign investment, excellent infrastructure, low reliance on external borrowings, and an increasing level of economic sophistication are cited as attractions to foreign investors.

Singapore has also been picked by many MNCs to be regional headquarters. Singapore will be the nerve center of Hewlett Packard's operations in the ASEAN region;[7] Apple Computers will be investing an additional S$23 million in a new manufacturing and service plant in Singapore as part of its plans to make Singapore the Apple Manufacturing technology base from which it can expand into other locations in Asia and the Pacific Basin; Albright and Wilson, a major British manufacturer of detergents, chose to set up plant in Singapore to serve as a springboard to a new Asia-wide trading venture.

The United States is Singapore's largest investor, pumping in some S$2.7 billion in the past two years. Most of the U.S. multinationals like IBM and General Electric are already in Singapore. Europe is the second largest investor, with well known MNCs such as British Petroleum represented. Japan is the third largest with investments averaging between S$150 million and S$160 million a year in the last five to six years, with MNCs such as Hitachi and National represented.

Multinational corporations in Singapore are predominantly skill-intensive, high-technology industries such as chemicals, oil, shipbuilding and repairing, precision engineering, and electronics. The MNCs are responsible for over 50% of Singapore's exports. By and large, the MNCs are generally faring well in Singapore despite the global recession.

The Economic Development Board, the government body responsible for promoting investments in Singapore, will be sending ministerial selling missions to countries like the United States, Japan, and Europe in a bid to boost investments beyond the existing S$1.1 billion. The strategy will be to promote Singapore as an attractive center, and not just an off-shore manufacturing base for MNCs.

Besides MNCs, state-owned enterprises are playing important roles in the Singapore economy. The 500-odd government-owned companies are involved in a wide range of manufacturing and services activities including steel mills, textiles, electronics, financial services, oil refining, hotels, shipbuilding and repairing, air transport, and property development. These state-owned enterprises range from large ones like Singapore Airlines (which, went public in 1985) and Neptune Orient Lines (the national shipping line), to small ones like Jurong Bird Park and Sentosa Development Corporation. They are under government holding companies such as Temasek, Sheng-Li Holdings, and MND Holdings, and are established for a variety of reasons and purposes. Ventures such as the National Iron and Steel Mills, Jurong Shipyard, and Sugar Industries of Singapore were established to encourage private investors to take the plunge during Singapore's early years of industrialization.

Singapore's state-owned enterprises, whether wholly or partially owned, are operated as profit-making concerns reflecting the government's stand against public subsidies (except for housing, health care, and education). Together they employ over one-fifth of the island's labor force of 1.2 million. Their turnover in 1983 was S$8 million and their profits amounted to close to 10% of turnover, a high rate of return compared to that of most private firms.[8]

Lately, there are proposals to privatize government-owned companies in a bid to stimulate the local economy. A public sector Divestment Committee was set up in January 1986 to work out guidelines on the plan to sell government companies to the private sector.

NATIONAL ECONOMIC AND PHYSICAL ENVIRONMENT

Economic Structure

Restructuring is an ongoing process in any dynamic economy and Singapore is no exception. The Singapore economy has undergone structural transformation in the course of the past 25 years.

The most important sectoral change lay in the rapid emergence of the manufacturing sector. In 1960, this sector contributed only 11.9% of the GDP but in 1985 it constituted 24%, making it the second largest sector in the economy. The economic restructuring within this sector is worthy of further examination. Subsectors like food and beverages, paper products, fabricated metal products, wood products, and furniture have undergone relative decline, whereas subsectors like chemical products, petroleum, machinery, appliances, and transport equipment have shown very rapid expansion. The change is from manufacturing simple products requiring simple process to more sophisticated, capital-intensive, and higher technology products. In terms of labor utilization, labor intensive, low value-added activities have given way to less labor-intensive and high value-added activities.[9] Since 1983, strong expansion in new, high value-added industries such as computers, electronics, machinery, printing and pharmaceuticals have provided the impetus for growth.

Another important sector that has developed rapidly since independence is finance and business. In 1968, there were only 36 commercial banks with a consolidated asset value of $3,674 million. In 1985, the number of banks increased to 130 with an asset value of $70,618 million. The Asian dollar market in Singapore now reached an asset value of US$1.3 billion. As in the manufacturing sector, mechanization and computerization are also taking place in this sector, which is one of the only two sectors recording growth in 1985. The finance sector now accounts for 33% of GDP, about 1.5 times the manufacturing share.

In the trade sector, the entrepot subsector has changed drastically from dealing with natural produce like rubber and timber to oil and manufactured goods, particularly manufactured capital goods. The commerce sector has replaced the manufacturing sector to become the largest employer, with total employment of over 300,000 or 25% of the total workforce. There is overcapacity in this sector and a shakeout appears inevitable.

The construction sector, aided by acceleration in the private and public sector construction programs, used to be an important sector, contributing an average of 2.3% to GDP growth each year in the early 1980s. By mid-1984, a property glut became apparent, caused by unpredictable demand, excessive supply, and a loss of market confidence. The construction sector is now in a severe slump, contributing 2 percentage points to the fall in CDP in 1985. No short-term recovery is expected.

The recent slowdown in the Singapore economy, particularly in 1985 when real GDP fell by 1.7%, reaffirmed the need for restructuring toward an economy based on high value added activities. This is where Singapore's comparative advantage lies, given its scarce manpower and limited resources. Further growth of Singapore as a manufacturing center, a financial center, a tourist center, a center of transport and communication, and a healthcare center can be expected.

Income Distribution

As a result of two decades of rapid growth, in 1983 Singaporians enjoyed a per capita national income of US$6,620 per year. This ranked Singapore 22nd in the world.

A household expenditure survey carried out from 1982 to 1983 by the Singapore Department of Statistics (see Figure 3) revealed that more Singapore families have moved from the lower to the middle and upper income groups. The average family income in-

Figure 3 Income Distribution

Total Household Income	1982/83	1977/78
Below $500	4.8%	21.5%
$500 - $999	26.3%	40.4%
$1,000 - $1,400	21.6%	19.0%
$1,500 - $1,999	14.8%	9.0%
$2,000 - $2,999	15.7%	6.3%
$3,000 - $3,999	7.0%	2.2%
$4,000 - $4,999	3.8%	0.8%
$5,000 & Over	6.0%	0.8%
Average total household income	$2,029	$1,066

Source: **Department of Statistics**

creased from S$1,066 a month in 1977/78 to S$2,029 in 1982/83. In short, Singapore has reached a developed country's income level, before becoming a completely developed economy.[10]

Physical Resources, Logistics, and Physical Distribution

Singapore is a small island with total land area of 620 square meters, measuring 42 kilometers across and about 23 kilometers from South to North. Approximately 48% of the land in Singapore is developed for residential, commercial, and industrial purposes, and another 9% for agriculture. Land is therefore a scarce and precious resource in Singapore. The total population of Singapore numbers 2.5 million. Manpower is the Republic's major resource for development and growth. The labor force totalled 1.2 million, and about 35,000 enter the labor market each year.

Located at the crossroads of east-west trade routes, Singapore has long been renowned as a leading world port. In recent years, it has become an increasingly important air junction with its pursuit of a nonprotectionist "open-skies" policy and maintenance of a high quality airport services.

Activity at the port is brisk. Singapore is one of the busiest ports in the world and is also a major distribution center. In 1984 alone, the number of vessel arrivals and departures was about 60,000, registering shipping tonnage of about 527 million gross registered tons. To meet the continued growth of containerized cargo, facilities of the Port's container terminal are being expanded with nine berths being serviced by 18 quay cranes.

A mass rapid transit railway is being constructed to complement the existing comprehensive network of roads and expressways. The system will link major population centers in public housing estates with the industrial estates and the Central Business District. Road transport in Singapore is not a problem as public transport services are easily available and inexpensive.

Singapore boasts a sophisticated telecommunications infrastructure which keeps abreast of the latest technology. Singapore's telecommunication infrastructure comprises a network of satellite earth station antennae, submarine cables, microwave links, and radio circuits which provide direct links to most countries of the world.

SOCIOCULTURAL ENVIRONMENT

Cross-Cultural Differences

Singapore drew its early population mainly from Southern China, India, and the Malay Archipalego. This gives the Republic an ethnically diverse population comprising 76.3% Chinese, 14.9% Malay, 6.4% Indian, and 2.3% others.

Singapore has a rich cultural heritage evident in the colorful variety of the customs and festivals of the different ethnic groups. While retaining their traditional cultures and lifestyles, most people have gradually acquired a distinct identity as Singaporeans.

Racial harmony exists in Singapore and the government takes a serious view against racial discrimination. The official languages are Malay, Chinese, Tamil, and English. Malay is the national language while English is the language of administration. Major religions like Buddhism, Taoism, Islam, Christianity, and Hinduism exist side by side with other minor religious groups like the Sikhs, Jews, Jains, and Zoroastrians. Ethnic integration is further enhanced by the public housing program which allocates renting or purchasing of public housing units on grounds of citizenship and income and not ethnic affiliation. People from different ethnic backgrounds are relocated into the same public housing estates and they live side by side harmoniously.

Culture Conditioned Consumer Behavior

Although Chinese make up more than 75% of the population, it is incorrect to assume that Singaporeans are Oriental in nature. Due to Singapore's open economy, open particularly to Western values and ideas, Singaporeans are increasingly Westernized. This applies especially to the younger populace, regardless of their ethnic background. The shift in lifestyle toward preference for Western things (which range from fast-food to self service-stores) is also reflected in the shift to English language education.

What activities comprise the Singapore lifestyle? A recent survey (see Figure 4) showed that most Singaporeans enjoyed watching television. They generally prefer individualized and passive entertainment to the more social and active pastimes like eating out, shopping, and visiting friends and relatives, regardless of age, sex, race, or income.[11]

The heavy exposure to the various media and the preference for television watching have serious implications for marketers in Singapore. Singapore consumers are well-informed of recent developments in consumer products and are becoming sophisticated in their choices of product. Marketers have to brace themselves against a more discerning (in terms of tastes and values) group of consumers. The role of the print and television media in product or services promotion will become more important.

Figure 4 Top 10 Sunday Activities

TV viewing	88%	Shopping	40%
Reading	80%	Visiting	37%
Radio	63%	Cinema	17%
Marketing	44%	Jogging	12%
Eating out	44%	Parks/beaches	10%

Source: Research & Information Department, Straits Times.

Business Behavior

Singapore has a low proportion of indigenous investment in the manufacturing sector. Out of this sector's total investment commitments of S$1.1 billion in 1985, only 30% came from local investors. This was because "we do not have the techniques, the markets, the organisations to make a factory and then to sell their goods. . . ."

Most of the local manufacturers are small business concerns, often employing fewer than 100 people. These concerns have recently been criticized for their "reluctance to expand beyond the comparatively simple assembly-production stage to more complex operations such as design and engineering — a key aim of hi-tech investment strategies."[12] Low spending on research and development is another characteristic of local enterprises. There is, therefore, a vast difference between local and multinational companies in the manufacturing sector. Among Singapore companies, labor costs made up 20% of production costs. The figure is only 7 to 8% for the more efficient multinationals which have international experience and management expertise.[13] Even the Prime Minister, Mr. Lee Kuan Yew, admitted that "unfortunately most of the inefficient ones were Singaporean firms with old styles of management."[14] There is an urgent need for Singapore firms to give up old ways of doing business by changing their attitudes and methods of operations.

Overall, entrepreneurial spirit is low among Singaporeans. While historically not risk-averse, Singaporeans have developed a society with "a low tolerance for failure, an atmosphere hardly conducive to risk taking."[15] The appeal of well-paying public and private sector jobs also play a part in discouraging entrepreneurship.

POLITICAL AND LEGAL SYSTEMS

Basic Political and Business Values

The People's Action Party, the ruling party, has been in power since 1959. This is the party which is responsible for obtaining self-government from the British in 1959 and for achieving independence from the Malaysian Federation in 1965. This government sought and obtained the general mandate from the people in seven consecutive elections from 1959 to 1984.

The government is not shackled by any particular ideology or dogma. The main policy guideline has been rationality and not ideology. Rational pragmatism, more than anything else, underlines the government's politicoeconomic doctrine in steering the main course of action for Singapore. The real test has been whether or not the policy can work in the special context of Singapore.

The attitudes of the leaders also played an important role in shaping the economy. They believe in efficiency, productivity, competition, meritocracy, a corruption-free society, and growth with equity. Singapore has been able to develop most impressively in the past 25 years because of the existence of an honest and efficient, but certainly not faultless, government that has provided the leadership and chosen the right policy in bringing about a life for Singaporeans.

In the international arena, Singapore strives to maintain, consolidate, and develop friendly ties with all countries, regardless of ideology and social system. As with other free market economies in the world, Singapore shares a commitment in preserving free trade principles.

Powers of Constituencies

The Republic of Singapore has a parliamentary system of government. The President who is the head of state is elected by Parliament every four years. Political power rests with the Prime Minister and his cabinet ministers who are collectively responsible to the unicameral Parliament. Members of Parliament are elected by the people in single-member constituencies. Executive power is vested in the cabinet led by the Prime Minister who is appointed by the President as the Member of Parliament who commands the confidence of the majority of Members of Parliament.

The cabinet consists of a council of ministers who are responsible for administrating the country and providing Parliament with the policy for making decisions. Ministers are appointed by the President among Members of Parliament on the advice of the Prime Minister. There are 13 Ministers in charge of Communications, Community Development, Defense, Education, the Environment, Finance, Foreign Affairs, Health, Home Affairs, Labor, Law, National Development, and Trade and Industry.

Political Stability

Political stability has been and will continue to be an important factor in Singapore's economic development and its development as an international financial center. Singapore is singularly fortunate that throughout the 26 years since self-government in 1959, she has been ruled by one government. In five general elections in which a number of the 20 or so registered political parties contested, the People's Action Party (PAP) was returned as the government, winning all the parliamentary seats in the 1968, 1972, 1976, and 1980 elections and all but two seats in the 1984 election. It is this able and efficient government, ruling with general consent and which has enjoyed a most enviable corruption-free record throughout the years, that has given Singapore continual political stability since independence in 1965.

The 1984 election was a watershed election as it marked the transition to a new and younger political leadership. Several younger men have been appointed ministers and are taking a leading role in the government. These younger leaders have been consciously groomed by veteran PAP leaders and are expected to provide continuance to the political stability in Singapore.

Laws and Regulations Affecting Business

Singapore is a free enterprise economy. Generally speaking, there is no restriction on the types of businesses one can set up, except for certain regulated industries such as finance, communication, and defense, etc. The conditions for the issue of a license are governed by the Control of Manufacture Act (Cap 241).

All businesses in Singapore must be registered with the Registry of Companies and Businesses. The Business Registration Act (1973) and the Companies Act (Cap 185) are the two acts regulating businesses and companies in Singapore.

There are nonantimonopoly laws in Singapore. There are no hard and fast requirements for local equity participation in foreign businesses set up in Singapore. The Economic Incentives Act incorporates all fiscal incentives for foreign investors in Singapore.

In terms of employment, there are several legislatures of which a foreign investor in Singapore should be aware. The Employment Act stipulates the minimum standards governing the terms and conditions of employment in Singapore.

There are no capital gains tax, general sales tax, value added tax, defense surcharges, etc. in Singapore. The types of direct taxes levied are income tax, property tax, payroll tax, estate duty, and stamp duty. Company tax is at the flat rate of 33% (effective year of assessment, 1987) on income after deductible expenses, depreciation allowances, trading losses, and donations to approved charities. Tax credit is available for profits distributed to shareholders in the form of dividends. For personal income tax, income accruing in or derived from Singapore and income received in Singapore from outside are liable to tax charged on a sliding scale ranging from 3.5% to 33% (effective in year of assessment, 1987) after deductions.

TECHNOLOGICAL ENVIRONMENT

Material Culture

With a per capita national income of US$6,620 per year, Singaporeans are ahead of most developing countries. The standard of living is high with an average life expectancy rate of 72.3 years, which is comparable to the developed countries. The rise in the quality of life can also be seen from the daily newspaper circulation figures, which increased to 249 per 1,000 persons in 1984. The number of radio and television licenses also increased to 188 per 1,000 persons in the same year. The proportion of people having telephones increased steadily from 84 per 1,000 in 1966 to 396 per 1,000 in 1984. Travel overseas by Singaporeans increased to 263,006 in 1984. A Singaporean worker with some secondary education can afford, before he is 30, to buy a government built flat using his Central Provident Fund savings, without even needing to draw upon his take-home pay.[16]

Other changes arising from material affluence are the greater number of women seeking gainful employment outside the home, the change from low-rise to high-rise living, and the change from the traditional extended family system to the nuclear family system (a small family or no children at all).

Social preference and the government's respect for academic brilliance have also influenced occupational aspirations of Singaporeans. There is a general preference for white-collar jobs and Singaporeans generally shun occupations like domestic service, building and construction, and other relatively low-skill or unskilled jobs. Increasingly too, Singaporeans tend to "take as their old model the risk-averse, wealth-managing scholar-bureaucrat rather than the risk-taking, wealth-creating entrepreneur."[17]

Human Resource Skills and Availability

Deprived of natural resources, Singapore's sole asset is its human resources. The education level of the population has risen considerably over the past two decades. For example, the number of secondary school children in 1984 (185,800) was 3.1 times that in 1960 (59,244). Similarly, the number of students in tertiary institutions increased by four times in the corresponding period. The illiteracy rate has decreased from 28.0% in 1970 to 14.4% in 1984.

Despite Singapore's progress in education, the workforce on the whole is still less educated than those in the United States, Japan, and even Taiwan. Currently, only 5% of Singapore's workforce have tertiary education compared to 19% in the United States and Japan and 6% in Taiwan. About 63% or more than half of Singapore's workforce have no education or at most primary level education, compared with 16% in the United States, 36% in Japan, and 46% in Taiwan. Moreover, there is a limited pool of R & D manpower and a lack of industrial capability in many areas, although Singapore is keeping abreast of the latest development in new technologies.

However, the heartening news is that the quality of the workforce has been on a steady increase. The proportion of professional, technical, and skilled manpower has increased steadily from 13.6% of the total labor force of 1.2 million in 1980 to 16.2% in 1985. At the same time, the proportion of production workers and transport equipment operators declined from 38.8% in 1980 to 36.3% in 1985.[18] This trend is likely to continue as part of the government's deliberate effort to admit more students into the university and poly- technics to meet the acute shortage of professional and technical skills. There is a drive toward greater automation and mechaniza- tion in factories to achieve higher productivity.

ORGANIZATIONAL CULTURE

Organizational Forms

While local companies outnumbered foreign companies in 1983 (there were 70,000 local companies versus 5,000 foreign compan- ies), many of the local companies are small or medium-sized, i.e., employing less than 50 workers. However, local companies do play an important role in Singapore's economy. They account for 30% of Singapore's exports and they form the supporting industries, pro- viding intermediate inputs to the multinationals in Singapore.

Decision-Making Patterns

Foreign companies in Singapore are known for their in-built mar- kets and technological strength, whereas local Singaporean firms tend to be characterized by the freewheeling commercialism of the traditional Chinese businessman. They also appear to differ in man- agement practices, particularly in decision-making. Peter S. Low,[19] in a study of Singapore-based subsidiaries of U.S. multinationals and Singaporean firms, noted that authority and responsibility for each staff level was clearly spelled out in the majority of the U.S. companies, whereas authority rested more at the top management level in a majority of the local firms. "Major policy decisions were made mostly by chief executives alone in the Singaporean firms, whereas their American counter-parts, in many cases, encouraged personnel at various levels in policy decision making." The study concluded that foreign companies could be characterized as decen- tralized in nature as opposed to the authoritarian leadership style of local firms.

Such findings perhaps could help to explain the difference in per- formance between the two categories of firms in Singapore. The

Economic Committee acknowledged in its recent report[20] that the performance of local companies, both large and small, has generally not matched that of foreign-owned companies, and one of the contributory reasons is that "local firms have lower overall business efficiency."

Labor Management

Singapore has a harmonious industrial relations climate. In 1984, for the seventh successive year, there were no industrial strikes or lockouts.[21] However, there is still room for improvement in labor relations. The National Productivity Board in its promotion drive for productivity through harmonious labor-management relations identified several obstacles that hinder achievement of its aim. The greatest problem, especially among middle management, is the fear of losing power or control. Management has traditionally been in control, made all the decisions, and directed the affairs of the company in matters ranging from working conditions to long-term planning and forecasting. Very few managers would agree to workers' participation in decision-making even in areas which directly concern their employees.[22] Impatient managers tend to abandon their attempts to improve relationships with their subordinates and revert to traditional management styles, it has been observed. On the other hand, union leaders who were used to the confrontation approach of solving conflict with management have difficulty in accepting the new relationship.

Much remains to be done to change the attitudes of management, union leaders, and workers. The team-building program developed by the National Productivity Board, which involves bringing management and workers together to interact on common problems and explore ways of cooperation, is a step in the right direction.

NATIONAL CONTROL OF INTERNATIONAL TRADE

Foreign Trade Policy

Singapore's foreign trade policy has evolved over the last two decades, from one of import substitution in the 1960s to active export promotion in the 1980s. The Trade Development Board's

Trade Policy Division plays a major role in Singapore's trade development drive, monitoring, defending, and expanding Singapore's trade interests internationally. The objective is to help facilitate market access for Singapore products in the world market through mediation and negotiations with the various foreign governments, or through close monitoring of developments on international trade issues and participation at regional and international forums.

Singapore trades with most countries in the world and is committed to the principles of free trade.

Tariffs

There are no export duties on goods exported from Singapore. Machinery, equipment, and raw materials not obtainable locally for industrial enterprises in Singapore may be imported free of duty on application. Generally, many are not dutiable. Import duties, in fact, are levied only on a limited range of goods in Singapore. They consist mainly of revenue duties applied to three broad categories of goods, namely, intoxicating liquor, tobacco, and petroleum products. There are also a limited number of protective duties on consumer products such as clothing, nonessential foodstuffs, and motor vehicles. In view of Singapore's outward-looking development strategy, its traditional entrepot role, and the use of import duties as an antiinflationary device, there is decreasing reliance on import duties.

Nontariff Methods of Trade Control

In accordance with the United Nations Resolutions, Singapore prohibits any kind of imports from South Africa. Importation of goods such as lighters in the shape of pistols or revolvers, toy currency notes, toy coins, and firecrackers are strictly prohibited for security reasons. From time to time, a limited number of goods are subject to a certain amount of control for reasons of health, security, and social or personal safety of the users.

Other than those mentioned, most goods can be imported freely into Singapore. Only goods originating or consigned from Albania, East Germany, Socialist Republic of Vietnam, Peoples' Republic of Mongolia, and People's Democratic Republic of Laos require import licenses. Rice, Singapore's staple food, and air conditioners of certain power and capacity are also subject to import licensing.

There are nontariff forms of control of Singapore's exports. Scarcity of commodity resources in Singapore called for licensing of any export of granite, sand, and steel bars of certain specifications. However, Singapore's textile and garments exported to Canada, EEC countries, Norway, Sweden, and the United States are subject to quantitative restrictions.

Free Trade Zones and Postponement of Duty Liabilities

Under the ASEAN Preferential Trading arrangement, Singapore, like other member countries, enjoys "across-the-board" tariff cuts for intraregional trade, to all product items with export values exceeding US$10 million a year. The tariff cut was also increased to 50%, thereby bringing a total of 12,225 products eligible for the more favorable preference margins.

In terms of international trade, as a developing country Singapore is able to enjoy duty-free access to eligible exports under the various GSP programs offered by the developed countries. The concession by the United States, for example, was renewed for another 8-1/2 years from January 1985.

BUSINESS OPPORTUNITIES

National Plans

Singapore's 10-year Economic Development Plan for the 1980s was to achieve real GDP growth of 8-10% per annum. Implicit in this plan was the need to maintain a productivity growth of 6-8% per annum, which called for drastic restructuring of the Singapore economy.

A policy package for economic restructuring proposed by the 10-year plan involved the following:

1. A three year wage correction policy to bring wages into line with market levels and to induce more efficient use of labor.
2. Tax incentives to encourage greater automation, mechanization, and computerization.

3. Investment promotion strategies aimed at attracting higher value-added and skill-intensive activities.
4. Increased output of skilled manpower from the training and education institutions and greater emphasis on skills development.

This plan worked well for Singapore during the first half of the 10-year period, i.e., 1980-84, when Singapore's real GDP growth rate averaged 8.5% per annum. However, by the end of 1984, the Singapore economy began to slow down, and by 1985, real GDP fell by 1.7% for the first time. A number of adverse trends, internal and external, caused this severe downturn. External demand conditions have changed and Singapore's cost competitiveness in international markets has been eroded. All these factors reaffirmed the need to restructure the economy, to move toward one that is based on high-value-added activities. "This is where our comparative advantage lies, given our scarce manpower and limited resources. It is the only way to have high and rising living standards for our people."[23]

Industry Trends

Based on real GDP performance in 1985, the industry which shows the most promise is international services (transport, communications, banking, finance, and business services) which registered a growth rate of 13% per annum and which now accounts for 33% of GDP of S$35,138 million. World service trade has been growing twice as fast as merchandise trade and this trend is likely to continue. Singapore has a comparative advantage in exporting services and the demand for financial services in the Asia-Pacific region will continue to expand as the region has been identified as a high growth area in the coming decades. Financial services identified as having potential for growth center around fee-based activities such as fund management and new financial instruments such as financial futures.

The manufacturing sector performed poorly in 1985, registering a 7% drop in industrial output. The decline was largely due to weak demand from the United States and a loss in competitiveness of the export-related industries such as the electronics, electrical equipment, refineries, machinery, and transport equipment. Industries such as printing and publishing, chemical products, and industrial chemicals continued to enjoy growth in industrial output. However, recent signs show that one industry in particular is picking up again. Signs of recovery for the electronics industry, evident in many companies' (such as Data General, Siemens, and Silicon Systems) advertising for workers and workers working overtime indicate that the recession may be bottoming out for the electronics manufacturers.

The slump in the construction industry contributed by unpredictable demand, excessive supply, and a loss of market confidence will continue. However, given the scarcity of land in Singapore, it is believed that "in time, the property glut will be absorbed."[24]

Singapore will continue to face problems in exporting as protectionism grows and external demand continues to be sluggish. However, third-country trade and countertrade have been identified as areas of growing importance for Singapore. Third country trade in commodities such as crude oil, rice, sugar, and other products is estimated to be worth about S$45 billion annually while study shows that countertrade currently accounts for 8% and 10% of world trade.[25]

Market Trends

The Finance Minister, Dr. Richard Hu, in his 1986 Budget Speech warned Singapore traders to be "nimble and adapt to new developments and changes in world markets."[26] This is particularly so when over the last few years, other newly industrialized countries (NICs) have become Singapore's prime competitors. For instance, during the 1980-1984 period, Singapore's external demand growth dropped to 5% per annum while the other NICs continued to grow at 11% per annum. In fact, during the last six years, Singapore's competitive position has weakened 50% against Hong Kong, 15% against Taiwan, and 35% against Korea.[27]

Until the industrialized countries restore the health of their economies and increase employment, protectionism will continue to be rife in these traditional markets for Singapore's exports. Singapore traders need to be more aggressive in their marketing strategy and look toward nontraditional markets such as Latin America, Africa, and South Asia, while at the same time making greater efforts to expand the traditional markets closer to home.

SOURCES OF INFORMATION

International Sources

Singaporeans enjoy a high degree of access to newspapers, news magazines, and radio and television programs from all parts of the world. The population can tune in to overseas broadcast stations like BBC World Service, the Voice of America, Radio Japan, Radio Moscow, and Radio Beijing.

There are about 80 correspondents based in Singapore representing 61 foreign news agencies, news magazines, newspapers, and broadcasting stations.[28] Reuters, United Press International, AP-Dow Jones Economic Report, Associated Press, etc. are based in Singapore. Well-known daily newspapers and magazines also set up bureau in Singapore. Examples are: *Asahi Shimbun*, *The Times* (London), *The Asian Wall Street Journal*, *The Far Eastern Economic Review*, and *US News and World Report*.

The Australian Broadcasting Corporation (ABC), the British Broadcasting Corporation (BBC), Nippon Hoso Kyokai (NHK), German Radio and Television (ARD-NDR), the Kansai Telecasting Corporation, and All India Radio are represented in Singapore.

Information on overseas markets is also transmitted via the Trade Development Board's Worldwide centers, to countries like the United States, Europe, Japan, Korea, People's Republic of China, Bahrain, Australia, and others.

National Government Source

Singapore's Ministry of Culture, through its Information Division, disseminates government information through newspapers, magazines, radio, television, and other media.

The Division's press section liaises with the various government departments and with the press to facilitate the flow of information. Government statements are normally issued to news organizations via a telex broadcast. The press section also arranges interviews, press briefings, and other facilities for local and foreign media.

The Division's publications section produces a range of publications: *The Singapore Yearbook, Singapore Facts and Pictures, The Mirror* (a current affairs fortnightly), *Singapore Bulletin, Singapore Statement Series, Speeches,* and *Singapore Heritage.*

In the area of technical information, the Industrial Technical Information Services (ITIS) offered by the Singapore Institute of Standards and Industrial Research has a computerized on-line information retrieval service which enables companies here to have direct access to overseas databases.

The Trade Development Board's subscription to the on line database provided by DIALOG enables Singapore businessmen to have instant access to international databases. In addition, the Board's Trade Information Unit and the Trade Reference Library provide good information sources for business opportunities and trade regulations of countries. The Trade Development Board also publishes a Directory of Singapore Manufacturers which contains profiles of 2,100 companies in various product and industrial sectors.

The Ministry of Foreign Affairs "Diplomatic and Consular List," which is for sale to the public, contains details of diplomatic missions and trade representations in Singapore as well as Singapore's missions overseas.

Other Sources

There is no lack of information in Singapore. Besides the government bodies, firms and organizations in the private sector publish a host of directories, annuals, and listings. The Singapore Manufacturers Association publishes annually, the *Singapore Manufacturers' Association Directory, The Singapore Manufacturer,* and a *Directory of Packaging Industries in Singapore.* Alternatively, one can refer to the various directories published by the four chambers of commerce in Singapore, i.e., the Singapore Chinese Chamber of Commerce and Industry, the Singapore International Chamber of Commerce (SICC), the Singapore Indian Chamber of Commerce, and the Singapore Malay Chamber of Commerce. The SICC is particularly active in disseminating and publishing trade information.

It has, to its credit, an annual trade directory known as "Showcase: Singapore Products and Services" and it also publishes an economic journal, *The Economic Bulletin*, which contains latest trade statistics, trade enquiries, company registrations, and a digest of economic and financial news. The Stock Exchange of Singapore facilitates local investors with its publication of the *Companies Handbook* which provides information on the companies on official listing. Its monthly journal, the *Stock Exchange Journal*, provides review and development news on the Stock Exchange in Singapore and Malaysia. The Institute of Bankers' quarterly publication, *Singapore Banker*, provides up-to-date information on the local financial sector. Other institutions such as the Singapore Professional Center have their own directories and publications.

Besides these trade bodies and institutions, private publishers also contribute to the pool of information in Singapore. Times International publishes quarterly the *Banking and Financial Review* and Times Periodicals publishes an annual *Times Business Directory of Singapore*. Anyone needing help or information regarding legal firms in Singapore can refer to Calton's *The Legal Profession Directory of Singapore* (annual). A merchant bank, Singapore International Merchant Bankers Limited, publishes annually a directory of all financial institutions in Singapore, entitled *SIMBL Directory*.

METHODS OF ENTRY INTO NATIONAL BUSINESS

Exports to the Country

Singapore is a free enterprise economy with few trade restrictions. Exports from countries all over the world find their way into the Singapore market, either to meet local consumption needs or for entrepot trade purposes. Major items of imports range from food to steel bars.

Although there is a government-owned national trading company (Intraco Limited) involved in the import and export trades, there is no state monopoly on importation of goods. There is no central importing body like those existing in some socialist countries. Even for importation of a staple item like rice, it has been left totally to the private sector.[29] Overseas manufacturers or traders export goods either directly to the importing parties in Singapore or through the appointment of sole agents or distributors. Food items such as edible oils, instant noodles, and canned foods are directly exported to import-export companies (who often act as wholesalers) as well as retailers in Singapore. Alternatively, the overseas party can appoint a distributor, with or without formal distribution agreement, to sell the products in Singapore. For example, Seiko, a Japanese watch manufacturer, appoints several distributors in Singapore for its Seiko watches. An overseas manufacturer who wants more control over the sale of his product in Singapore can appoint a sole agent here for product distribution. There will be formal agreements with respect to the right to distribute goods in geographical areas, and in turn there are obligations expected from the local agent in terms of continuity of supplies, maintenance of a complete range of products to be carried, advertising and promotion, after-sales services, spare part stocks, and credit to the retail trade. Thus manufacturers of branded products, from consumable products like Aramis perfume to ostentatious durables like Gucci watches, appoint sole agents or exclusive distributors in Singapore on contractual terms. However, lately this form of distribution has been plagued by parallel importing, whereby sole agents have to compete with other importers who buy direct from the manufacturer and hence are able to distribute the goods at a much lower price than the sole agent because of lower landed costs. The official attitude, from one point of view of the Consumers' Association of Singapore, is that it "would like to see both the parallel import system working side by side (with the sole agents) for the benefit of the consumer."[30]

Wholly Owned Subsidiary

Any foreigner, or for that matter any person, can establish a business in Singapore provided it is properly registered with the Registrar of Companies. Foreign investments are welcome in Singapore and a host of fiscal incentives are available, ranging from pioneer status to tax incentives for research and development expenses. For example, the American multinational Sperry Corporation is setting up a subsidiary in Singapore and has been granted a seven-year pioneer status as well as skills development fund support.

There are no hard and fast requirements for local equity participation in foreign businesses set up in Singapore. Overseas manufacturers can set up wholly owned manufacturing outfits in Singapore to take advantage of the conducive economic and investment climate, or set up a subsidiary here as a spring board to Asia-wide trading. Oceano Instruments, a privately owned French Company with branches in Britain and the United States, recently set up a wholly owned company in Singapore as its Far East headquarters. "The plus factors, Singapore geographic location and set up and the help offered by the Economic Development Board, more than compensated for the high cost of doing business here."[31] Interestingly, most of the U.S. multinational corporations are already in Singapore. Apple Computers set up a manufacturing operations in Singapore in July 1981, while Newton Private Ltd, the American tool and die maker, had invested in a factory in 1970 to manufacture watch components and will be setting up a high tech complex scheduled for completion in early 1989.

Joint Ventures

Local capital is readily available for joint ventures. The Singapore government welcomes foreign investors' participation in joint venture projects with Singaporean firms, particularly in high-tech and high value-added industries. The petrochemical complex in Singapore (comprising the Petrochemical Corporation of Singapore [Pte] Ltd, the Polyolefin Company [Singapore] Pte Ltd, Philips Petroleum Singapore Chemicals [Pte] Ltd, and two other firms) is a joint venture between Singaporean and Japanese firms, with Sumitomo Chemical playing a leading role in setting up the complex. Government's support of such foreign and local joint ventures can also be seen in the recent agreement reached between Singapore and Italy, which calls for greater cooperation in high-technology industries including those manufacturing military helicopters and ornaments.[32] As a result, two public-owned Italian firms are discussing with their Singapore counterparts the possibility of the joint production of defense equipment.

Joint ventures are not only beneficial to Singapore, but to other ASEAN members as well. Singapore has become the first ASEAN country to offer facilities for repairing rotor blades through a joint venture with an American company. This meant lower costs of repair for Malaysia and Indonesian helicopter operators who incurred high freight charges for blades sent to the United States for repair.

With the opening up of the China market, more foreign companies are keen to combine their advanced technology with Singapore's traditional marketing links with China in order to penetrate the China market. Foxboro and Airbus are two of the companies that have recently tied up with Singapore companies for projects there. The Singapore companies active in such joint ventures include Wah Chang International, United Industrial Corporation, Lum Chang, and Wannian Holdings. "Singapore is a good partner—because of the number of Mandarin speaking Singapore Chinese who are familiar with Western business practices."[33]

Franchising

Franchising is very popular in Singapore, particularly in the fast-food industry. Major American fast-food manufacturers like McDonald's, Burger King, Wendy's, and Kentucky Fried Chicken have established franchise outlets in Singapore. Imported soft drinks like Pepsi and Coca-Cola are also being bottled and distributed by Singaporean bottlers, under franchise from the overseas manufacturers. Franchising as a form of business entry into Singapore is not restricted to food business but includes all facets of business. Show America Inc., one of the largest companies in the U.S. providing promotional robots, has granted franchise to a local distributor to promote the product in Singapore and, it is hoped, to other ASEAN countries in the near future.

Overseas or for that matter any manufacturers who wish to have more control over their products (especially patented and high-tech products) but who nevertheless would like to penetrate the local market could do so by supplying goods under a licensing arrangement. For instance, Northern Telecom, the Canadian telecommunications giant, is responsible for supplying push-button telephones to the Telecommunications Authority of Singapore over the next three years. The push-button phones are to be manufactured by a South Korean factory under license from Northern Telecom. The information technology industry (covering all sorts of information flow using computer technology, telecommunications, and office systems) is also taking shape in Singapore through various licensing arrangements with overseas manufacturers.

Contract Manufacturing

The Singapore Trade Development board is intensifying its efforts to promote multinational corporations to source products in Singapore, particularly electronics products. Annually, more and more buyers are visiting Singapore for this purpose. In 1985, a Canadian telecommunications giant and an American multinational involved in high-tech sourced a total of S$70 million worth of electronics products in Singapore. Universal Data System, a subsidiary of Motorola, recently contracted its modern manufacturing to a local printed circuit board assembly company (automated assembly). The contract was worth S$5 million[34] and this speaks well for the quality and competitiveness of Singapore-made products.

AREAS OF CONFLICT

Direction of Industrial Growth

Singapore has outgrown its pursuit of low wage, low-skill industries to concentrate on higher wage, higher-skilled industries. However, it is constrained by the need to price its output below the developed countries as well as some of the NICs like South Korea and Taiwan. There is a need for Singapore to find a niche where it can be economically as developed as the West yet maintain its international competitiveness. The direction of growth will be toward an international business center for manufacturing and services.

This direction flow calls for altering certain policies and building on existing strengths to maximize Singapore's advantages.

National Control of Key Sectors

The Singapore government in the past has done more than set rules and decide policies. It has also through government-owned companies directly invested in some sectors of the economy—airline, banking, and defense industries, to name a few. These companies have contributed to the growth and development of the Singapore economy. However, as the economy gets more complex and as Singapore moves toward the desired direction of growth, there are doubts as to whether the government should continue to own and control these companies (except for national security reasons) and whether the government should continue to venture into new businesses. However, the government has made it clear that it has no parochial interest in the existing companies it owns. It will be willing to divert ownership of these companies and give up management control at the right time. The government recognizes that "the impetus for growth must lie with the private sector, whether local or foreign," for the government is "likely to have the detailed and omniscient grasp of all sectors to identify which project to put money on."[35]

Credit and Pricing Policies

Government budgeting surplus, central provident fund contributions, and other factors were responsible for the contraction in Singapore's domestic liquidity conditions. The high domestic interest rate, in particular, is heavily influenced by Singapore's low inflation rate and external interest rates (especially the U.S. interest rate). Although domestic interest rates are on a declining trend, they are still relatively high in real terms when compared to other countries. The Monetary Authority of Singapore thus plays an important role in maintaining domestic price stability on the one hand and ensuring that adequate liquidity is reinjected into the domestic banking system for economic expansion on the other hand. There has also been increasing pressure to internationalize the Singapore dollar, which is resisted by the Monetary Authority. The Authority rationale is that the size of the Singapore economy is too small to allow large-scale use of the Singapore dollar. "If there is a lot of Singapore dollar denominated paper floating around the market then it could create instability if for whatever reason, investors get nervous about Singapore."[36] The Monetary Authority had to stabilize the value of the Singapore dollar against the risk of affecting its export competitiveness.

Singapore's price competitiveness is increasingly eroded because of the high cost of doing business. Statutory boards which provide many services such as port services, warehousing, telecommunications, utilities etc. for business use through their pricing policies have substantial influence on the cost of doing business. It is therefore imperative that there is a balanced approach in pricing policies so that services can be provided at competitive prices while enabling the statutory boards to recover costs and earn a fair return on the assets employed.

Research and Development

In 1984, Singapore spent only 0.6% of its GDP on research and development, which is low by international standards. However, the trend is to research and development expenditure as Singapore attempts to keep abreast of the latest development in new technologies.

There is however, a limited pool of R & D manpower and Singapore lacks industrial capability in many areas. This explains why most of the research is applied rather than basic in nature. This imbalance in approach needs to be corrected, particularly if information technology is to be one of Singapore's growth industries.

There is a also clear-cut distinction between private and public sector's interest in R & D. The public sector concentrates mainly on transport, telecommunications, defense, engineering, medicine, and the natural sciences, while the private sector pays more attention to electronics and electrical products which have "immediate commercial applications."

Human Resource Development Policies

The quality of the workforce has risen steadily in the past five years, thanks to the government's effort in manpower development. Currently, Singapore spends about 4% of its national income on education annually. Besides formal education, vocational and industrial training are given equal attention by the Singapore government. The overall emphasis is to upgrade the educational level of Singapore's population to meet the challenges of the high-technology-based economy.

However, there is a limit to the number of skilled manpower Singapore can produce in the long run, given a declining population growth rate. It has been estimated that Singapore's workforce can increase only by 1% per annum by the year 2000. And as more young people stay longer in formal education and training institutions, the size of the labor force is expected to remain small. The emphasis on human resources development policies is therefore to educate each individual to his or her maximum potential. "What we lack in quantity we must more than make up for in quality."

Taxation

Fiscal incentives play an important role in attracting foreign investments, which are necessary for Singapore's economic growth. However, such selective incentives contain certain biases in that they cater mainly to manufacturing activities. The corporate tax rate, until recently, has been high, at 40% compared to most of Singapore's competitors, particularly the NICs.

Recognizing that high taxes blunt Singapore's competitive edge and that Singapore, being an open economy, is dependent mainly on human resources, the government strives to ensure that the tax burden is not so high as to become a disincentive to work and enterprise, hence the recent (1986) budget announcement of reduction in corporate and personal tax rate. The top marginal corporate tax rate has been reduced to 33% and there is an across-the-board rebate of 25% tax rebate for income earners. Also, approved companies are allowed to set aside up to 20% of their taxable income as an R & D reserve which will be tax-exempt if spent within three years. Other fiscal incentives announced in the 1986 budget include tax credit, up to full amount of equity invested in approved venture-capital projects, for any loss arising from the sale of shares in the approved project company. The intention of this series of tax reforms is to eventually move toward a broad-based, low-tax regime.

However, as such direct taxes are lowered to meet competition, the government needs a compensatory source of revenue and consumption tax will be implemented for this purpose. The public is generally not in favor of consumption taxes as these are seen to be "unwieldly, inflationary and bad for tourism." Nevertheless, the government deemed that such taxes are inevitable and have to be seen in the larger context of Singapore's economic goals. Efforts will be made, however, to ensure that the side effects are lessened.

RESOLUTION OF CONFLICTS

Parties to Conflicts

Differences in opinion and approach are inevitable in an open economy like Singapore with its free enterprise system and diversity in business interests. As revealed by the report of the Economic Committee,[37] there are certain conflicts in policy practices and issues between the government and private sector and between local and foreign companies in the private sector. Besides these, one can also classify workers (and or union leaders) and management as parties to conflicting attitudes toward harmonious industrial relations. On the international front, other countries have questioned the developing status of Singapore's economy. The World Bank in particular has been threatening to graduate Singapore to developed nation status.

Types of Conflict

Government intervention in business has always been the bone of contention between the private and the government sectors in Singapore. "Public versus private competition unfair" sentiment is expressed by the private sector, particularly the local businesses, which cited several specific areas of "unfair competition."[38] The national trading company Intraco was accused of losing sight of its original objectives as it engaged increasingly in businesses in direct competition with the private sector. The same accusation was also levied at the Post Office Savings Bank whose original objective was to inculcate thrift among depositors in the lower-income group but which now became a major competitor of banks and finance houses. The government has indicated that there should not be any rush in privatizing government-owned companies, particularly during this recessionary period, as it will reduce private sector liquidity.

Conflicts can also occur in joint ventures formed between local and foreign firms. A 1982/83 study[39] of selected joint venture firms in the manufacturing sector in Singapore revealed, among other things, that transfer pricing of the products, royalties, and commissions to be paid to the parent companies; target market definition; allocation of the percentage of ownership between partners and distribution of control; composition of expatriates and locals; industrial relations with trade unions; and speed and willingness of technology transfer are the more significant issues contributing to conflicts between local and foreign partners.

Although Singapore has a calm and peaceful industrial relations climate, "the relationship between union and management at the enterprise level is by and large one of mutual tolerance rather than active cooperation."[40] Conflicting attitudes of union and management are responsible for this scenario. Management's fear of lowering power and control and management's lack of long-term perspective discourage some of them from practicing a participative form of decision-making. On the other hand, some union officials tend to distrust management's intention in instituting cooperative management programs. This distrust in some cases could be a result of union leader's unwillingness to give up an important source of power in the union: the respect gained through victories against management. Old timers who have made a career of "fighting management" also found it difficult to accept a participative management approach.

Singapore's high standard of living and high GNP per capita classify it as a developed nation. This means that many of its GSP benefits will be withdrawn. As it is, in April 1986, the U.S. government announced that from 1 July 1986, Singapore's exports of radio antennae and transceiver parts will be stripped of their duty-free status. However, in terms of education level of the population and the maturity of the structure of firms in the economy, Singapore has yet to achieve the status of a developed economy. Two-thirds of Singapore's adult population have no more than primary education. In the long run this conflicting situation has to be resolved.

International Business Diplomacy

In an effort to improve trade relations and encourage economic cooperation, bilateral trade talks and agreements are actively engaged by the Singapore government with other countries. The latest is the general agreement reached with the Italian government for greater cooperation in high technology industries during the Italian Deputy Minister for Foreign Affairs' visit to Singapore in March 1986. Such general agreements often pave the way for more private

joint ventures, as was the case for the Italian agreement, which led
to negotiations between two Italian public-owned firms and their
Singapore counterparts regarding joint production of defense equipment.

At the private level, chambers of commerce, industrial bodies,
and manufacturers' associations often conduct trade study missions
abroad to have a better understanding of overseas markets. Besides
participating in trade missions, such trade bodies also play host and
hold discussions with foreign trade missions visiting Singapore.
These activities allow firms to explore new markets as well as expand and consolidate existing ones.

International business diplomacy of this sort therefore help in
achieving greater understanding in international trade relations between Singapore and its trading partners.

Resolution Options

The word "conflict" often conjures negative thoughts and feelings. Yet conflicts are inevitable as we have discussed in the previous section. However, it is not enough just to identify conflicts;
one must also resolve them.

In regard to the government versus private enterprise issue, the
government has set up a Public Sector Divestment Committee in
January 1986 to work out guidelines on divestment. At the same
time, the Singapore government has also appointed a high-level
committee (Business Enterprise Committee) to foster greater business enterprise in the Republic by reducing government controls
and introducing greater flexibility in the implementation of government policies and regulations. These actions reflect the government's flexibility in policy decisions and keenness to revolve issues
causing conflict between public and private interest.

Aware that conflicts do exist in joint ventures, there is a need for
all foreign and local corporations to understand and recognize the
drawbacks and contributions of joint ventures. Both parties must be
realistic in evaluating their bargaining position and work toward the
achievement of the national goal. There is also a need for local
partners to understand the different management styles of the foreign partner against a diverse racial and cultural background. To

resolve the conflicting labor-management attitudes, there is a need for team-building in companies to enable labor and management to interact to understand the problems faced by both parties so that they can cooperate with each other for mutual benefit. The National Productivity Board has been spearheading this move by promoting a number of labor-management programs to help build team spirit and to improve labor-management relations in business organizations. The setting up of quality control circles and work improvement teams are but some means of fostering better labor-management relations. The government is also advocating the formation of house unions because they foster company loyalty and make it easier for workers to accept job enlargement and multifunctional assignments that are unique to the individual company.

The maturity and level of development of the Singapore economy must change in order to match its developed status as reflected in the high GNP per capita. Changes have been proposed and some have already been undertaken. A good case in point is the reduction in the employer's Central Provident Fund contribution by 15%, as a cost-cutting effort to improve Singapore's competitiveness.

CORPORATE STRATEGY AND PLANNING FOR FOREIGN FIRMS

Strategic Option

The Economic Development Board is promoting Singapore as an international business center for manufacturing and services. Foreign investors therefore have several strategic options open to them as far as direct and capital investments are concerned.

Foreign investors can continue to take advantage of the political stability, the efficient economic infrastructure, the skilled manpower, the attractive fiscal investment incentives, and the free enterprise climate to set up manufacturing base in Singapore. The plants in Singapore can produce or assemble items designed elsewhere and the final output can be reexported home, locally distributed, or exported to countries all over the world. The strategic location of Singapore, at the crossroads of Asia, could be exploited by foreign investors to set up regional headquarters in Singapore. The regional office not only manufactures the product to satisfy the region's demand, but it can also be used to provide after-sales service and maintenance services to customers in the region. Singapore can also be used as a trading base for Asia, particularly for the China market. Thus, despite the fact that Hong Kong is closer in proximity to Mainland China, several multinationals have made their headquarters in Singapore. Davenport, Campbell and Partners, an Australian space planning and interior design firm, recently shifted its 3-1/2-year-old Asia headquarter in Hong Kong to Singapore. The regional director was quoted as saying that the move has enabled the company to look for opportunities throughout Asia; "Singapore, more than Hong Kong, gave the company the reach it needed."[41] In terms of research and development activities, service-oriented and research-based companies can set up service and research centers in Singapore. Such facilities not only provide training and technical support to firms in Singapore but to firms in the region as well.

Planning Frameworks

Long-term strategic planning in Singapore is facilitated by the government's concern toward long-run interests of the country. Long-term policies necessary for economic growth are often committed even at the expense of short-term discomfort. Constant dialogue between the government and the private sector helps in formulating economic policies for future growth. The stable political and social climate also contribute to making long-term planning a less uncertain process.

Input for operational and strategic planning is easily available in Singapore. The annual budget statement often provides the private sector with directions of economic growth and priority areas of development, besides the usual facts and figures on government expenditure. The annual economic survey carried out by the Department of Statistics are for sale to the public, and it often provides businesses with the economic data much needed for forecasting purposes. Monthly economic statistics are also available from the Department of Statistics and the Monetary Authority of Singapore.

Corporate planning is also facilitated by the wide range of computer software packages developed by the computer industry in Singapore. These planning tools allow for more sophisticated forecasting and control.

Financial Options

Foreign firms that qualify for the listing requirements of the Stock Exchange of Singapore can tap the stock market for funds, through public listing of shares, or issue of bonds and debenture. The Asian Dollar Bond market is another source.

Bank credit facilities are readily available through the 130 local and foreign banks in a number of currencies such as the U.S. dollar, Japanese yen, Swiss franc, and German mark. Debt instruments such as revolving underwriting facility and note issuance facility form the package of debt securitization options open to borrowers in Singapore.

The Asia-Pacific region has been identified as a top growth region and foreign investors can look toward Singapore's off-shore financial markets, the Asian Dollar Market, and the Asian Dollar Bond market, both as sources of funds for investment or as alternative instruments of investment besides direct investments in plants and machinery.

CORPORATE ORGANIZATION AND CONTROL FOR FOREIGN FIRMS

Organizational Options

Foreign investors can establish businesses in Singapore by registering as a sole proprietorship, a partnership, or a limited company either wholly owned or jointly with local interests. The company can also be incorporated as a private or a public company. If the company is incorporated overseas but the foreign investor wishes to carry out business in Singapore, it will have to be registered as a foreign company. However, it must be noted that "carrying on business in Singapore" does not merely mean maintaining a bank account in Singapore, performing sales through a Singapore contractor, or investing in local property. Whether a foreign company is deemed to be doing business as a branch in Singapore will depend on the nature of the activities involved. Last but not least, if the company in Singapore is to be used only as a promotional base and no business transaction is to be carried out, it can be registered as a representative office with approval obtainable from Singapore's trade development office.

Control Systems

The regulatory environment is generally conducive to foreign firm's investment. There is no restriction on share ownership, although in the appoint of directors and secretaries, the foreign firm must ensure that at least one director and one secretary is a resident in Singapore.

There is no requirement for filing annual accounts if the foreign firm is a sole proprietorship or a partnership. However, control comes in the form of annual renewal of business registration. There is no restriction on the repatriation of profits after tax.

There are no regulations regarding management control of foreign firms in Singapore. Most of the multinational corporations in Singapore have top management staffed by personnel from the overseas parent company. However, in an effort to ensure more technology transfer, the Singapore government is inclined to issue employment passes only to expatriates who possess the necessary expertise or technical knowledge. Although Singaporean employees literally "grew up" in an environment governed by an authoritarian style of management, this does not mean that a democratic style of management cannot be practiced in Singapore. So long as such practices are congruent with local conditions, higher worker morale can be achieved. In fact the Singapore government encourages the adoption of more participative and less authoritarian forms of management, which contributes to productivity of firms.

In terms of organizational controls, Singaporean employees are familiar with the formally designed feedback systems and the formal performance appraisal system usually found in foreign firms, particularly the U.S. firms.

FUTURE BUSINESS OPPORTUNITIES
AND SCENARIOS

Trends in the world economy and developments in the region indicate that Singapore must reposition itself in the world market and develop a new niche to meet the challenges of the 1990s.

There will be increasing competition not only from Asian Newly Industrialized Countries but from developed countries as well. Indications are that by 1990, Singapore's existing niche as an offshore manufacturing base for developed countries will be taken over by emerging industrial powers like South Korea and Taiwan.

Protectionism will continue unabated, if not become worse, as the developed countries continue to be troubled by high unemployment rates, and economic structural adjustment. What is more troublesome is the trend toward market investment. Increasingly, capital exporting countries like Japan are setting up factories in countries where the goods are sold and where production cost is competitive in order to avoid tariff and nontariff barriers. Investments will be harder to come by for Singapore.

Uncertainty characterizes the growth prospect of the Southeast Asia region, particularly ASEAN. A current downturn in the economies of commodity-exporting countries brought about by low commodity prices is likely to continue as the long-term outlook for commodity prices is uncertain. This means that Singapore can no longer depend on these traditional sources of growth.

However, all is not lost. The future scenario can be promising if the policy changes and economic restructuring measures advocated by the government are carried out successfully.

The Asia-Pacific region has been identified as the top growth region, at least for the next decade. Singapore can therefore benefit from this development.

The government has identified a new niche for Singapore: that of an international business center for manufacturing and services. Singapore will move beyond being just a manufacturing base to enticing foreign companies to establish operational headquarters here, to manage subsidiaries in other parts of the world, to manage their treasury activities and funds, to carry out product development work, and to produce goods and services to be exported to other countries.

Singapore's comparative advantage in services has to be fully exploited to develop Singapore into a major exporter of services. Locally based services such as tourism and banking as well as offshore services will be heavily promoted. Foreign firms in service lines will be attracted to set up branches in Singapore. Singapore can play the role of a regional middleman in the growing information technology industry.

Therefore, opportunities abound in Singapore, particularly for foreign investors. Attractive incentives are available to nonresident investors in the financial services sector, particularly for fund management and fee-based activities. Post-pioneer status tax incentive, tax-deferred R & D reserve, and venture capital incentives are some examples of a host of incentives awaiting high value-added foreign investments in Singapore.

A stable political environment, a corruption-free and efficient government, a pool of skilled manpower, an efficient network of infrastructure, a free enterprise economic system, and a strategic geographic location complete the attractive and conducive business climate any investor can expect in Singapore.

ENDNOTES

1. See Chow Kit Boey, "ASEAN Economic Cooperation and Singapore," in You Poh Seng and Lim Clong Yah (eds.), *Singapore: Twenty Five Years of Development*, (Singapore: Nan Yang Xing Zhou Lianhe Zaobao), pp. 341-363.
2. See Chow Kit Boey, "ASEAN Economic Cooperation and Singapore," in You Poh Seng and Lim Chong Yah (eds.), *Singapore: Twenty Five Years of Development*, (Singapore: Nan Yang Xing Zhou Lianhe Zaobao), pp. 341-363.
3. *Business Times* (Singapore), 2 April 1986.
4. *Business Times* (Singapore), 14 March 1986.
5. *The Mirror* (Singapore), 27 June 1977.
6. *Straits Times* (Singapore), 17 May 1986.
7. *Straits Times* (Singapore), 18 February 1986.
8. *Straits Times* (Singapore), 15 March 1986.
9. For a more detailed discussion on changes in the manufacturing output and exports and reexports, See Lim Chong Yah, *Trade in Manufactures: A Singapore Perspective*, a paper presented at the Conference of the Pacific Corporation Task Force on Trade in Manufactured Goods, June 1983, Seoul.
10. *Straits Times* (Singapore), 4 March 1986.
11. Same as 10.
12. *Far Eastern Economic Review*, 27 March 1986.
13. *Far Eastern Economic Review*, 27 March 1986.

14. *Straits Times* (Singapore), 12 February 1986.
15. *Straits Times* (Singapore), February 1986.
16. *Report of the Economic Committee*, Ministry of Trade and Industry, Singapore.
17. See Pang Eng Fong, "Entrepreneurship and Economic Development in Singapore," a paper presented at the AIESEC Symposium on Entrepreneurship, November 1985, Singapore.
18. *Economic Survey Report 1985*.
19. Peter S. Low, "Singapore-Based Subsidiaries of US Multinationals and Singaporean Firms: A Comparative Management Study," in *Asia Pacific Journal of Management*, September 1984.
20. Same as 16.
21. *Singapore 1985*, published by the Information Division, Ministry of Communications and Information.
22. *Productivity Digest*, February 1984.
23. *Singapore Economic Bulletin*, February 1986.
24. *Straits Times* (Singapore), 8 March 1986.
25. *Straits Times* (Singapore), 8 March 1986.
26. *Straits Times* (Singapore), 8 March 1986.
27. *Far Eastern Economic Review*, 27 March 1986.
28. *Singapore 1985*, published by the Information Division, Ministry of Communications and Information.
29. *Straits Times* (Singapore), 8 March 1986.
30. *Sunday Times* (Singapore), 14 June 1985.
31. *Sunday Times* (Singapore), 26 May 1985.
32. *Straits Times* (Singapore), 7 March 1986.
33. *The Singapore Manufacturer*, October 1985, Vol 8, No 1.
34. *Trade Development Board*, annual Report, 1984/85.
35. Speech by Brig-Gen Lee Hsien Loong, "Singapore's Economic Policy: Vision for the 1990s," at the conference "Singapore: Towards the Year 2000;' held at the Commonwealth Institute in London, January 1986.
36. *Business Times* (Singapore), 1 January 1986.
37. *Report of the Economic Committee*, Ministry of Trade and Industry, Singapore.
38. *Straits Times* (Singapore), 1 January 1986.
39. Koh Seng Kee, "*Conflicts in Joint Ventures*," Academic Exercise, School of Management, National University of Singapore, 1982/83.
40. *Productivity Digest*, February 1984.
41. *Sunday Times* (Singapore), 26 May 1985.

Chapter 15

International Business Climate in Turkey

Osman Ata Atac
Nizamettin Aydin

Strategically located between southeastern Europe and western Asia, the Republic of Turkey is the only land route between Europe and the Middle East, and the only country that controls the single waterway from the Black Sea to the Mediterranean.

This country, characterized by trade, maritime, and military importance has a population of 53 million in 67 provinces, and a land area of more than 300,948 square miles administered by a centralized government. Its bordering neighbors are Greece, Bulgaria, the Soviet Union, Iran, Iraq, and Syria.

The Republic was founded in 1923 after the collapse of the Ottoman Empire following World War I. Since its inception the Turks, under the leadership of Ataturk ("Father of the Turks," 1881-1938) who became the first president after leading the Independence War, embarked on a number of reforms. The reforms were aimed at Westernization of the dominant culture. A wide variety of reforms including the introduction of the Latin alphabet were carried out. As a consequence, the present sociocultural environment in Turkey is a unique blend of Eastern and Western cultural elements. This cultural setting has important implications for business relationships with Turkey and the Turks. Since its inception the Republic has pursued a policy of economic and military alliance with the Western democracies. In this context, Turkey has been a member of NATO, the Organization for Economic Cooperation and Development, the

European Parliament, and is an associate member of the European Economic Community.

POLITICAL AND LEGAL ENVIRONMENT

Turkey's government is a secular, constitutional, and parliamentary democracy. Its legal and political system is heavily influenced by the experiences of the Western countries. Its predecessor, the Ottoman Empire was the Vatican of the Islamic world for 400 years, and as such the law of the land was the Islamic law. Consequently, when the Republic was founded in 1923, Turkey did not have a history of secular codification. The founders vigorously pursued a radical program of far-reaching reform and modernization, including secularization of the state and abolition of Islamic courts. As a result of this secular orientation, most of the major laws in Turkey are adapted from various Western codes. Turkish civil law comes from Switzerland, the criminal code comes from Italy, and the commercial code from Anglo-Saxon laws. For the Western businessman, the codification in Turkey should not create insurmountable problems.

LEGISLATIVE, EXECUTIVE, AND JUDICIAL POWERS

During the period from 1923 to 1946 the Republic had a one-party regime. The one-party system ended with the founding of a second party in 1946. Numerous other political parties were subsequently formed and the multiparty democracy continued with three brief military interventions in 1960, 1971, and 1980. Today, various political views are represented by a multitude of political parties. The formation of parties advocating radical political systems including communism and theocracy are prohibited. However, there are and have been various political parties tacitly supporting the extreme right, extreme left, and orthodox religious points of views. In spite of this proliferation, the Turkish parliment has been dominated by two major political views since 1950. One represents the populist-liberal point of view and the other the social democratic point of view. The 1960 constitution provided an opportunity for the parties with extreme right, left, and religious philosophies to win seats in the parliament and enabled them to share power in coalition goverments. Furthermore, the escalating struggle between the populist liberals and social democrats has enabled the extremists to gain disproportionate representation in cabinets, resulting in various unsuccessful coalition governments and political turmoil, hence inviting the military interventions of 1982 and 1980.

The 1982 Turkish constitution mandates the principle of the separation of powers, meaning that the legislative, executive, and judicial branches are separated. Presently the House of Representatives, whose 400 members are elected for a tenure of five years, is vested with the legislative power. Under the 1982 constitution, the executive power is shared between the president and the cabinet. The president is elected by the parliament for one seven-year term. The president is empowered to appoint the prime minister. The president's approval is needed for the appointment of the directors of certain state institutions including the Central Bank and state broadcasting organizations. The president is also empowered to dissolve the National Assembly and to declare a state of emergency entailing rule by decree. The 1982 constitution strengthened the power of the President to provide political stability.

The judicial branch is independent of the executive and legislative branches of the government except for the State Security Courts. Inherent in the judicial system is the specialization of courts. Major courts are: civil, criminal, taxation, juvenile, with appeal courts for each, and the Supreme Court. Business disputes are generally handled by the civil courts and tax disputes are handled by the tax court.

POLITICAL FORCES AND PROCESS

The major power groups in Turkey are the urban population, the rural population, the military, the intellectuals, and the business community. Political parties must balance the preferences of these groups in order to remain in power.

Approximately 54% of the population live in rural areas. This group tends to be conservative and dependent upon government price support and credit. Their main interest is in the economic infrastructure of the rural areas such as irrigation, transportation, energy, and more importantly the government agricultural price support policies. They traditionally vote for the populist-liberals.

Twenty-five percent of the urban population is concentrated in the three cities of Istanbul, Izmir, and Ankara, the capital city. The main interests of this group center around infrastructure, cost of living, and political ideologies. In general the social democrats seem to be favored by this group. Views advocated by the extremist organizations also find supporters in these urban areas.

The "intellectuals" include the press, university community, top bureaucrats, and professionals. They tend to favor social democrats and socialists. In spite of their small size, they constitute a major political pressure group.

The military commands a great deal of respect and plays the role of "guardian of republicanism." Its major role in the political arena is neutralization and pacification of extreme political polarization. The military has traditionally been important in the determination of the political structure. Military intervention in 1960 and 1980 resulted in new constitutions and political restructuring.

ECONOMIC, FINANCIAL AND PHYSICAL ENVIRONMENT

General Economic Structure

The existing economic structure has evolved as a result of five different periods of experimentation:

Political and Economic Restructuring (1923-1932): Hopes for private enterprise initiative fails under conditions of low savings, lack of experience and know-how, and the absence of protective tariffs. Establishment of the State Economic Enterprises (SEEs).

Etatism (1933-1950): The state takes an active role in economic life through "state economic enterprises." The beginning of World War II affects growth negatively, control of private sector increases.

Mixed Economy (1950-1963): Attempts to reduce state involvement and encourage private investments fail under excessive credit expansion, high price supports for agricultural products, high level of public investment, and excessive issue of currency.

Planned Import Substitution (1963-1980): Initiation of five-year development plans and intensification of import substitution. Planned economic policy falls short of attaining objectives with respect to consumption expenditures, investments, sectoral growth, price stability, and balance of payments, but attains overall growth objectives. Balance of payment crises, high inflation, shortages of imported inputs characterize this period.

Liberalization (1980 to Present): Liberalization and export-oriented growth. Reduction of state involvement and controls, preparation for the privatization of the SEEs, support for exports, removal of protective measures, support for big business and concentration.

In spite of the recent liberalization attempts, Turkey is still a planned-mixed economy where development plans guide the activities of the private sector and the state economic enterprises. The SEEs have been playing a major role in the economic life of the country, and presently account for about 45% of the productive capacity. Current plans call for this traditional etatist economic policy to shift to privatization of the SEEs and reduce the role of the public sector in the economy.

The State Economic Enterprises

The SEEs engage in the production and marketing of a wide variety of goods and services. Tobacco, air, sea and rail transportation, postal and communication services, sugar, tea, petrochemicals, hard coal, paper, steel, petroleum, lignite, fertilizers, and banking are some of the fields of operation. They have been crucial in the initial industrialization of the country. Since the 1930s the SEEs have been a major development vehicle. They have served important economic and social functions. Particularly during the period 1930 to 1950, they were either the sole or major providers of various goods and services that could not be provided by the private sector, and were the only investors in many major industrial projects. Their social function included providing goods and services at prices that were affordable to the medium-to-low income groups, and providing employment and training. In a sense, the SEEs laid the foundations of whatever industry the country has today. They still hold an important position in the economic and social life of the country. As of 1982, the SEEs accounted for 41.4% of total production, and 38.7% of the value added in manufacturing alone. Even though the expressed policy of the present government is to privatize the SEEs, their contribution to Gross Domestic Product increased to 14% in 1985 from 12% in 1979 in 1968 factor prices.

The privatization of the SEEs is authorized by Law No. 3291 which was enacted in 1986. Attempts at privatization are likely to be only partially successful for various reasons. The market value of the shares of those SEEs that are not profitable are likely to be much lower than their worth. Such SEEs will not be appealing to private investors. On the other hand, profitable SEEs seem to be attractive to private investors as indicated by the warm reception given to the sale of the shares of the state in TELETAS. TELETAS, which was a state economic enterprise in the telecommunications industry, had 40% of its shares controlled by the state. The second largest shareholder was Bell Telephone Manufacturing of Belgium with 39% control. Early results of reducing the shares of state to 18% seem controversial because of disagreements about the management of the corporation. Similar attempts at privatization in the telecommunications industry in Great Britain have not been successful for similar reasons. Moreover, privatizing the profitable SEEs means considerable loss of revenue for the government which may not be recovered through tax gains. Furthermore, in most cases, privatization will just reduce shares held by the state and will not mean complete divestment. This leads to revenue sharing with no tangible benefits to the economy.

National Income

Under Turkey's five-year development plans designed to improve the standard of living, the economic growth rate has increased faster than the average growth rate for developing countries. Conversely, the share of the agriculture sector in gross domestic product shrank to 19% in 1983 (Table 1) despite the fact that it still employs over 50% of the labor force (Table 2). As economic development continues, the GDP share of the agricultural sector will decrease further. The labor force in this sector will also decrease but at a slower rate because the growth in other sectors will not be enough to absorb both the disguised unemployment and the new additions to the labor force.

Employment and Wages

Turkey's high unemployment rate translates into a large and inexpensive labor force, with a minimum wage rate of less than $100 a month in U.S. currency. Real wage rates have been steadily decreasing since 1980. It is estimated that agricultural wage rates have declined 36% from 1985 to 1988. Unemployment has risen steadily since 1982 when it was 15.6%. By 1985 (last available data) it had risen to 16.72%, a 7% increase in three years. These figures do not account for a high degree of disguised unemployment. Labor shortage will not be a problem in the foreseeable near future.

Table 1   Gross Domestic Product by Sectors of Origin (%)

Economic Activities	1965	1983	1985
Agriculture	34	19	19
Industry	25	33	35
Manufacturing	16	24	25
Services	41	48	46
Distribution of GDP (%)			
Public Consumption	12	10	9
Private Consumption	74	73	75
Gross Domestic Investment	15	21	20
Gross Domestic Savings	13	16	16
Exports	6	16	19

Source: World Development Reports 1985, 1987, World Bank

Table 2   Percentage of Labor Force by Sectors

	1965	1983	1986
Agriculture	74	54	58
Industry	11	13	14
Services	15	33	28

Source: World Development Reports 1985, 1987 World Bank; and Economic Report, Istanbul Chamber of Commerce, 1986.

Prices

Structural inflation, aggravated by the 1978 oil crisis, has been a major problem in Turkey. Consequently, the country has been experiencing very high levels of inflation since 1978 (Table 3).

Prior to 1973, the annual inflation rate averaged 10.5% for approximately eight years, whereas from 1973 to 1983 it increased to 42%. Recent economic policies aimed at reducing the rate of inflation have only had a moderate and temporary effect. In fact, the long-term effects of the recent policies seem to be inflationary. As of June 1988 the official forecast of the yearly inflation rate was around 72%. The monthly increases in the wholesale and retail prices continue to be around 4.5% and 4.2%, respectively. As a result, the consumer price index increased from 410.3 in 1982 to 1,561 in 1986. Inflation continues to be a serious problem for the economy.

Energy

From 1960 to 1977 the most significant trend was the increasing share of petroleum in the total consumption of energy. In 1985 per capita energy consumption was estimated as 35.7 tons of oil equivalent. Oil is not plentiful in Turkey but hard coal and other energy reserves are. Turkey meets approximately half of her total energy needs from domestic sources but still has petroleum-based energy needs, and spends most of her export revenues on petroleum imports. For example, the percentages of the revenues from exports of merchandise spent on energy imports were 12% in 1965 to 66% in 1983. Due to declining oil prices this figure decreased to 44% in

Table 3   Inflation Rate (1980 = 100)

1975	13.84	1981	136.58
1976	16.24	1982	174.69
1977	20.64	1983	237.51
1978	29.98	1984	352.41
1979	47.58	1985	510.86
1980	100.00		

Source: International Financial Statistics, IMF, 1986.

1985. Turkey's expenditures on crude oil imports, however, jumped from $1.8 billion in 1986 to $2.7 billion in 1987 due to increased consumption. Although a series of major hydroelectric projects are underway, energy is likely to continue to be a problem area in the near future. Turkey is also exploring the possibilities of nuclear energy as well.

Public Finance

The current budget policy is to reduce government spending, increase revenues, and improve the performance of the State Economic Enterprises. The breakdown of central government expenditures is given in Table 4.

The major expenditure item "economic services" includes subsidies for the various economic activities including the State Economic Enterprises.

Taxes

Turkey has been making radical changes in its tax laws since 1980. New taxes have been levied and procedures of taxation have been changed drastically. A 10% value added tax (VAT), and the 6% petroleum consumption tax are the most important new taxes. All taxable corporate entities must be registered either as full or

Table 4   Central Government Spending

	1972	1982	1985
Total Expenditures (% of GNP)	21.8	23.3	25.7
Expenditures (% of total):			
Defense	15.4	15.2	10.9
Education	18.2	16.2	10.0
Health	3.3	2.1	1.8
Housing, social welfare	3.3	8.9	3.6
Economic Services	41.9	25.7	19.6
Other	17.9	31.3	54.1

Source: World Development Reports 1985, 1987, World Bank.

limited liability taxable entities. A full liability entity is taxed on worldwide income. Important changes have also been made in corporate tax policies after 1980.

The major sources of government revenues are:

1. Income tax
2. Corporate tax
3. Duties and fees
4. VAT (value added tax)

A recent change allowed the corporations to reevaluate the book value of their assets. The adjustment is now done on the basis of the average increases in the wholesale price index. There has been a number of recent tax reductions. To reduce the cost of borrowing, tax on financial transactions was reduced to 3% from 15%. Similarly, withholding tax on interest income was reduced from 20% to 10%. For holders of certificates of deposit, the reduction was from 30% to 10%. In order to reduce the cost of borrowing from abroad, a decree issued in March 1984 eliminated the withholding tax on interest payments for all kinds of loans. The foreign investment has certain exemptions from these taxes which shall be discussed under investment opportunities.

Money and Banking

The financial system in Turkey consists of the central bank; commercial, investment, and development banks; and the domestic capital markets. As of 1988, the banking industry was the most dynamic and profitable industry in the country. Banks increased their profits 13-fold within the last five years, mainly due to exorbitant interest rates in lending.

The Central Bank, established in 1930, carries out the state's fiscal policy, holds foreign exchange reserves, regulates capital market functions and institutions, maintains the value of the currency, provides financing to the treasury, supplies credit and loans to the SEEs, sets discount rates, and provides advance payments to commercial banks.

At present there are around 50 banks in Turkey. Forty-six of them pursue commercial banking activities, while four others concentrate on investment and development projects. The 1980 liberalization measures made it possible for Turkish banks to open branches abroad and eased the restrictions on foreign banks to open branches in Turkey. As of 1987, a number of foreign banks from various countries established operations in Turkey (Table 5).

A number of banks from Iraq and other countries are still in the process of approval. In addition, a number of banks also have representative offices in Turkey. At the same time Turkish banks have started to expand overseas (Table 6).

The money and credit policy of Turkey's governments in the 1980s has been shaped by a problematic choice between antiinfla-

Table 5
Foreign Banks in Turkey

Ottoman Bank	Italian – since 1863
Banco diRoma	Italian – since 1911
Holantse Bank Uni	Dutch – since 1921
American Turkish Foreign Trade Bank	USA, Turkey – since 1964
Arab Turkish Bank	Libya, Turkey – since 1977
Citibank	USA – since 1980
American Express	USA – since 1980
BCCI	Luxembourg – since 1980
Bank Mellat	Iran – since 1982
Habib Bank	Pakistan – since 1984
Turk Bankasi	Cyprus – since 1983
Chase Manhattan	USA – since 1983
Middle East Bank	United Arab Emirates
First National Bank	USA
Manufacturers Hanover Trust	USA – since 1984
Chemical Mitsui Bank	Japan – since 1985
Saudi-American Bank	Saudi Arabia – since 1985

Table 6
Foreign Branches of Turkish Banks

Ziraat Bankasi	New York, USA
Is Bankasi	Frankfort, West Germany
Is Bankasi	Berlin, West Germany
Is Bankasi	London, Great Britain
Yapi ve Kredi Bankasi	Bahrain, UAE
Akbank	London, Great Britain
Garanti Bankasi	London, Great Britain (Representative office)

tionary measures on the one hand, and the weakening liquidity position of the banking system and industry on the other. Through agreements with the International Monetary Fund and the World Bank, Turkey has been trying to control the money supply and rate of inflation since 1980, at times to the detriment of corporations and commercial banks. Such efforts usually end in changes in regulations. The Turkish Banking Industry has been broadly revised in 1983, and certain additional changes were made in 1988.

Capital Markets

The Turkish capital market is in the initial stages of development. A Capital Market Board, founded in 1981, regulates the capital market. Bonds, equity shares, and participation certificates are some of the instruments. However, the major source of capital for the private firms continues to be loans from investment and commercial banks and is likely to be so in the foreseeable future. The public sector, however, possesses additional means of raising capital. For example, since 1984, the government has been able to raise funds through a new public instrument, "Certificates of Revenue Partnership" (CRP). Under the present regulations the Housing Development and Public Participation Administration may issue CRPs for the revenues of public utilities and other state holdings and the SEEs to raise capital. The CRPs do not carry any voting or ownership rights. CRPs of the Bosphorus Bridge and Keban Dam were sold in 1984 and were well received by the investing public.

Balance of Payments

Like many other developing countries, Turkey has been experiencing deficits in its overall balance of payments. To finance its deficits, governments borrowed heavily from international capital markets, international development organizations, and foreign governments. Turkey was one of the first indebted developing countries to go through the debt renegotiation and restructuring process that others are presently experiencing.

Turkey has increased its debt burden since 1980. Turkey's medium and long-term foreign debts increased to more than $30 billion in 1988 from $8.8 in 1980. Short-term debt increased to more than

$10 billion during the same period. Debt to GNP ratios jumped from 28 to 58 during the period from 1980 to 1987. Interest burden on this debt is more than $7 billion, of which over 15% of this total is due to the private sector borrowing. Treasury obligations are around $13 billion. In addition, an outstanding 27 billion foreign debt to be paid in Turkish currency with an interest burden of 6 billion Turkish lira worsens the picture. According to the World Bank, Turkey ranked 22nd in the world in terms of the absolute amount of foreign debt, and 84th in terms of debt service as a percentage of total exports in 1986. The debt service ratio in terms of the exports of goods and services increased from 51% in 1985 to 84% in 1986. Because the outflow of capital (financial outflow) is controlled, the major cause of the Turkish balance of payments deficit is rooted in its import account (Table 7). Furthermore, most of the goods imported are for investment needed for development and cannot be reduced without crippling the development effort. Therefore, the way out of the balance of payments problem lies in its ability to accelerate its foreign exchange earnings. This is particularly important in light of the increasing debt payments and import liberalization.

Three major sources of foreign exchange earnings are: (a) exports of goods and services (except tourism); (b) workers remittances; and (c) tourism. Turkey's export-import performance will be discussed further in the section "Doing Business With Turkey."

Although the current account deficit is relatively large, the net current account balances are much lower because of a significant amount of worker remittances. The number of Turkish workers in Europe and especially in the EEC countries is approximately 1.3 million. The worker remittances is a significant item in the current account (Table 8), and is close to 20% of total exports (see Table 7).

Turkey hopes to improve its balance of payments situation by generating more income from tourism. With clean beaches and historical riches, Turkey has the potential to become one of the most attractive spots in international tourism. Although income from tourism has been steadily increasing (Table 9), it is still far below potential.

Turkey adopted a floating exchange rate system in May, 1982

whereby exchange rates are adjusted daily. The Central Bank establishes daily "central rates," commercial banks then determine their buying and selling prices within a specified range of the central rate.

Physical Resources

Turkey is well endowed with physical resources. Its location is a natural resource in itself by virtue of its being a natural bridge between Europe and Asia and the cradle of numerous civilizations. In addition to a rich supply of natural resources, with 7,110 kilometers

Table 7   The Balance of Payments 1987 (In Millions U.S. $)

Foreign Trade	
Exports	9154
Imports	-11896
Foreign Trade Balance	-2742
Other Goods Services and Income: Credit	3561
Tourism and Travel	1188
Other Income	2373
Other Goods Services and Income: Debit	-3681
Tourism and Travel	-391
Foreign Debt Interest	-2119
Other Expenditures	-1171
Balance Foreign Trade and Other Goods Services	-2862
Private Unrequited Transfers: Credit	1934
Workers' Remittances	1851
Other	83
Private Unrequited Transfers: Debit	-18
Official Unrequited Transfers	301
Current Account Balance	-645
Capital Excluding Reserves	1627
Direct Investment	106
Other Long Term Capital Activity	804
Short Term Capital	746
Net Errors and Omission	-625
Exceptional Financing	0
Counterpart Items	171
Overall Balance	528
Depletion of reserves	-528

Source: Review of Economic Conditions 1987, Turkiye Is Bankasi A.S., Ankara 1988.

Table 8   Worker Remittances (Millions of U.S.$)

1982	1983	1984	1985	1986	1987
2140	1513	1807	1850	1534	1851

Table 9   Tourism Income (Millions of U.S. $)

1982	1983	1984	1985	1986	1987
373	420	548	1094	2300	2373

of coastline surrounded by the Black Sea, the Marmara Sea, Aegean Sea, and the Mediterranean Sea, Turkey has rich marine resources as well. With an area of 781,000 square kilometers, most of which is suitable for many industrial and cash crops, Turkey ranks 7th in wheat production, 9th in barley, 7th in cotton, 6th in raisins, 6th in tobacco and wool, and first in hazelnut production in the world. A rich variety of mineral deposits adds to the physical resources; Turkey ranks 3rd, 5th, and 8th in chromium, antimony, and in magnetite reserves, respectively. The country also possesses rich deposits of lignite, borax, titanium, tungsten, molybdenum, copper, and aluminum. Turkey is self-sufficient in strategic elements and is an exporter of some. Although the country's mineral resources are rich in quantity and variety, their ore content is relatively low which results in high exploitation costs. Recent studies indicate rich reserves of rare earth elements such as lanthanum and samarium. These elements are essential ingredients in high technology and petroleum refining processes.

SOCIAL, CULTURAL, MATERIAL
AND ORGANIZATIONAL ENVIRONMENT

The Dominant Culture

The origin and sociocultural roots of the Turks are traced back to Central Asia. Despite this origin the present Turkish sociocultural setting cannot be labeled as Eastern in the strict sense of the word. It is a blend of various cultures. The Ottoman Empire (1299-1919) ruled a diverse group of nationalities, religions, and races from Central Europe in the West to Iran in the East, and from Crimea in the North to North Africa in the South, including the whole Middle East. As a result the emerging Ottoman culture was a unique synthesis of various cultures.

One of the distinct attributes of the Turkish culture is its shame consciousness. The expression *ayip* (shame on you) is engraved in the culture as the social sanctioning mode securing conformity to societal norms. This is in contrast to the guilt-conscious postindustrial Western culture. In a shame culture, members of the society will try to avoid situations that will create embarrassment and shame. In that sense, in a given social situation, what the others think may be more important for an individual than his/her own evaluation of the situation. This norm of social sanctioning is extremely powerful within peer and reference groups. This general characteristic reflects itself in consumer behavior and business negotiations.

Consumer behavior is essentially conformist. The consumption is other-directed, and a disproportionate amount is usually spent to conform to reference and peer group norms.

Stereotyping is also common. This stereotyping is especially prominent when purchasing imported products, that is, there is considerable "effect of the country of origin." For example, German products are believed to be of excellent quality. This has important implications for product and brand positioning strategies.

The dominant culture is authoritarian. Its roots can be traced back to the patriarchal extended family structure. Although economic pressures make it difficult to preserve the extended family structure, the typical family is still patriarchal and extended.

Turks are socialized with a very strong sense of pride and group orientation and expect a strict conformity to group norms. Deviant behavior is rarely approved. The openness of social interaction depends on the perceived closeness of the individuals, although outsiders are usually met with warmth.

The dominant culture is also quite homogeneous with only minor language or religious differences. Generally fatalistic in nature, the dominant culture exhibits many characteristics in common with Islamic and other Eastern cultures.

One cannot make similar generalizations about the material culture in Turkey. Because of inequitable income distribution, material wealth is usually disparate in different segments of the society.

By most objective standards, Turkey is at best a "developing" country as reflected by the "innovativeness" indicators. The R & D expenditures in 1982 were about $100 million. The same expenditures are over $80 billion in the U.S.A. The number of patents issued is indicative of the lack of support for innovativeness. For example, in 1983 there were 511 patent applications, of which 300 were found to be worth patenting. The total number of patents in the country is about 5,833. This is in sharp contrast to the industrial countries. For example, in 1983, 34,691 applications were filed in the U.K., of which 28,254 were approved and patent rights were granted; there were already 229,519 patents outstanding.

The illiteracy rate is still high. The percentage of illiterate in the population 15 years of age and older was about 31% in 1980. This basically means that about 10 million people are illiterate. About 7 million of this group are female. By comparison, the illiteracy rate in Singapore, for example, was only 17% in the same year.

However, Turkey has a significant pool of educated human resources and compares favorably to other countries. For example the number of teachers per thousand is 2.17, compared to 0.81 for Singapore. The number of pupils per thousand is 17 in Turkey versus 8 in Singapore. Turkey has a total of 10,436 scientific personnel of which 7,747 are scientists and engineers, and 2,689 are technicians. Most of the technicians are trained on-the-job through the apprentice system that has prevailed in the country since Ottoman times. Turkey, with 23 scientists per thousand, ranks higher than Japan where this number is 20 per thousand. The number of scientists is 33 per thousand in the U.S.A. and 14 in the Philippines. Despite this, the potential of the scientific community is not fully utilized because of the lack of resources allocated to R & D. A large number of scientists seek opportunities in other countries. In contrast to the availability of scientists, there exists a need for more trained technicians. This is because the educational system emphasizes general education over technical and vocational education. On the other hand, it is unlikely that there will ever be a shortage of semiskilled workers and top-level technocrats.

Organizational Culture and Management Behavior

The state-owned economic enterprises play an important role in Turkish organizational culture. Although not major, there exist certain differences in organizational culture and management behavior in privately owned firms and state enterprises.

The structure of the private sector shows a bimodal distribution of organizational forms. On the one hand, there are a large number of family-owned small-to-medium size businesses, and on the other, a few very large conglomerates which are again family-owned. This family ownership of business is a dominant structural characteristic of the whole economy. Even the large conglomerates are closely controlled by members of a family. Corporate names find their origin with the last names of the founders such as Sabanci, Koc, or Cukurova. Consequently, decision-making in privately owned corporations is quite centralized. Most important business negotiations are carried and concluded by the top executives who are usually the "owners." In many cases professional managers basically work as staff although their titles may indicate a line of authority.

A small number of large holding companies dominate the industrial sector. Their dominance is expected to continue in the future with new additions. One of the major reasons for the dominance of large firms is the absence of a well-developed financial market for both equity and debt financing. For example the Istanbul Stock Exchange has only 36 members listed. Consequently, banks are the major sources for equity capital. Collateral requirements by banks against credit and loans and the lack of a venture capital market perpetuate the domination of a few conglomerates in new investments. This trend is likely to continue, especially in light of the new liberalization policies which provide additional advantages to big businesses.

Turkey has an excellent pool of professional managers. Most of them are fluent in at least one foreign language. English, German, and French are popular languages. Universities such as the Middle

East Technical University in Ankara, Bogazici University, and Istanbul University in Istanbul are well known in the region for their excellent business administration programs. In the Middle East Technical University and Bogazici University, the medium of instruction is English. Quite a few of the executives hold MBA and MS degrees from European and U.S. schools. Most of these professionals are employed by big businesses, further disadvantaging smaller and government-owned companies. Recently, however, the public sector employment of educated professionals for managerial positions has increased sharply due to changes made in the government personnel and compensation policies.

The numerous state-owned companies in Turkey are the largest producers and employers. Most of the State Economic Enterprises were founded during the period from the 1920s to 1940. As such they were the first institutions in the country where professional managers, scientists, and technicians were trained. These state-owned organizations are formal in structure and follow a seniority system. Almost all of the upper level executives are promoted from within and are familiar with all aspects of the operations of the organization.

These same managers, however, are the targets of political manipulation. Since these organizations are the major employers and producers, political parties have been using them as instruments to gain power. For that reason, top management, especially the composition of boards, changes frequently. Continuity in middle management cannot be secured often. With the pending privatization, some major changes are expected in this regard.

INTERNATIONAL BUSINESS OPPORTUNITIES IN TURKEY

Turkey is a promising market for export, import, and foreign direct investment. First, opportunities exist for buying goods and services from the Turkish firms. Many of the agricultural and manufactured products of Turkey as well as her natural resources provide attractive options for buyers in terms of variety, quality, and availability. Second, with growing production in most sectors and recent emphasis on exports, Turkey provides opportunities for exporters as well. The import content for most local production is rather high and Turkey still depends on imports for capital goods. These coupled with the recent emphasis on liberalization and internationalization increase Turkey's attractiveness as a potential export market for both consumer and industrial goods. Finally, Turkey's new laws and procedures encourage foreign direct investment.

Turkey has implemented a strategy of import substitution for decades. Under this strategy, the government tried to provide protection to domestic industry by using taxes, barriers, quotas, and bans on imports. Various procedural restrictions were placed on exports, as well. Although exports were encouraged in general, the regulatory framework was restrictive, especially on financial transactions. Since 1980, however, Turkey has been liberalizing the economy and changing most of the regulations governing international transactions and has begun actively pursuing an export-oriented growth strategy. The import restrictions and regulations have gradually been liberalized and an elaborate export promotion scheme has been implemented. Consequently, international trade has started to play an important role in total economic activities. The volume of foreign trade accounted for about 19% of GDP in 1980, whereas the volume reached 37% in 1985 (Table 10). Although the share of imports in GDP is still considerable due to the export promotion policies, the export performance of Turkey has shown a greater improvement (Table 11).

Foreign direct investment (FDI) activities in Turkey have had

Table 10   Role of Trade In GDP (%)

	1980	1985
Exports to GDP	5.2	15.3
Imports to GDP	14.2	21.6

Table 11   Exports and Imports of Turkey (Billions of U.S. $)

	1960	1970	1980	1981	1983	1984	1987
Exports	0.8	1.3	2.9	4.7	5.7	7.1	10.1
Imports	1.6	2.1	7.9	8.9	9.2	10.1	14.1

three distinct phases: (a) legacy of the Ottoman Era, 1923-1950; (b) the 1950-1980 era; and (c) 1980 to present. Prior to 1923 almost all utility, transportation, and banking companies of the Ottoman Empire were owned by foreign corporations, mainly from France, England, and Italy. The young republic founded following the war was very sensitive about foreign investment for the reasons that will be discussed. Consequently, during the 1923-1950 period foreign direct investment was not given prominence in the development of the Turkish economy. Although certain initiatives were taken to attract foreign direct investment during the 1950-1980 period, FDI did not play a significant role in this period, which primarily followed an import substitution strategy. Since 1980, Turkey has been actively pursuing FDI by increasing incentives and relaxing the existing restrictions. Despite these measures, however, the inflow of FDI into the Turkish economy has generally been less than expected.

TURKEY AS A SUPPLIER

Export Performance of Turkey

Since 1980 the goverment has formulated and implemented policies aimed at streamlining the red tape and promoting exports. As a result of these policy changes, the volume of exports as a percentage of GDP increased from 5.2% in 1980 to 15.3% in 1985. During the same period export volume increased from $2,910 million to $7,958 million, reaching $10 billion in 1987. This was an appreciable increase in exports during the time when the world economy was experiencing a considerable slowdown. Although intensive and sustained export promotion policies are shown as the prime reason for this increase, it also appears that the continuing depreciation of the Turkish Lira played an important role. As Table 12 indicates, the indexed unit values of exports in U.S. dollars decreased from 100 in 1980 to 74.4 in 1984, a depreciation of more than 25%.

The sectoral distribution of exports has also been going through a major change. Agriculture, other raw materials, and mining have been decreasing in importance while industrial goods have been gaining (Table 13).

The share of manufacturing in exports climbed to 79% in 1987 from 36% in 1980. The share of this sector would have been even higher had it not been for the import quotas imposed by the EEC countries and the U.S.A., especially on textile imports.

Another kind of shift is observed in the destination of exports. Exports have shifted from industrial countries and the nonmarket economies to the Third World countries, neighboring Islamic countries. In 1965, 71% of exports were destined to industrial countries, whereas by 1984 this number was about 50%. On the other hand, Turkey's exports to the Middle East region have witnessed a dramatic increase, reaching 35% of the total in 1985. During the 1980s Turkey strengthened its relationship with the Islamic countries. However, exports to this group of countries are fairly concentrated. Turkey has been a beneficiary of the Iran-Iraq war, supplying nonmilitary supplies to both parties. Saudi Arabia and Libya have also been major importers of Turkish goods and services. Although exports to Iran and Iraq may not maintain the same level after the war, these countries are expected to remain major buyers. Turkey's ex-

Table 12   Export Performance of Turkey (Figures in U.S.$)

	1965	1970	1975	1980	1985
Volume (1) (millions)	467.7	588.5	1532.2	2910.1	7957.9
Volume Index (1) (1980 = 100)		91.0	93.4	100.0	273.5
Unit Values (1) (1980 = 100)		31.6	59.5	100.0	74.4
Destination (%) (2)					
Ind. Countries	71.0			56.6	53.7
Developing	14.0			29.8	43.1
Middle East				21.6	35.3
Non-Market	15.0			13.0	2.9

Source: (1) International Financial Statistics, IMF, 1986.
            (2) Direction of Trade Statistics Yearbook, IMF, 1986.

Table 13   Exports by Sector (%)

	1980	1985	1987
Agriculture	57.4	21.6	18.2
Mining	6.6	3.1	2.7
Industry	36.0	75.3	79.1

ports by sectors illustrate the structural changes that have been taking place as well (Table 14). Particularly important is the impressive performance of textile, leather, and hide products, and the products of iron and nonferrous metals, all three exceeding the $1 billion level, with textiles reaching close to $2 billion.

Manufacturing in Turkey is dependent on imports for approximately half of its input needs. As the country grows and tries to manufacture "export quality" merchandise, the need for imports of intermediary goods will also grow.

Implications of Export Performance

Turkey has been trying to reach the lucrative markets of Western Europe and North America for a long time. Bilateral agreements have played an important role in the Turkish exports. As in the past, the present government has also been actively pursuing such bilateral agreements. However, the major focus is still on the EEC market, and the U.S. market. Turkey has been an associate member of the EEC and has formally applied for full membership.

Turkish manufacturing and specifically textile industries have recently become attractive to a variety of Western buyers. Leather goods and textile products have been particularly popular. High quality workmanship and attractive designs of these products have a well-deserved reputation in many fashion centers. In this way Turkey can be a major and dependable supplier of textiles, garments, and leather goods, as well as a variety of manufactured products.

Turkish construction companies have successfully been exporting their services, especially to the Middle Eastern markets, for a long time. With its proximity to the lucrative Middle East markets, Turkey can also offer invaluable services through the recently established free trade zones.

TURKEY AS A MARKET

Import Performance of Turkey

Imports still play a significant role in the economic life of Turkey. Turkey is a potentially lucrative market for exports of manufactured, consumer, and even agricultural goods and services.

The growing population of Turkey, estimated to be around 50

Table 14   Exports by Sectors (Million U.S. $)

	1981	1982	1983	1984	1985	1986
Agricultural Products	2219	2141	1881	1749	1719	1097
Crops	1923	1699	1485	1382	1441	853
Cereals	110	130	187	92	63	2
Fruits	735	581	526	565	528	360
Vegetables	60	72	65	81	96	97
Others	1018	916	707	644	754	394
Animal Products	258	390	362	323	244	210
Livestock	233	351	305	238	176	170
Wool, animal hair	18	29	23	20	17	7
Others	7	10	34	65	51	33
Sea and Water Products	27	24	20	20	21	24
Forest Products	11	28	14	24	13	10
Mining and Quarrying	193	175	189	240	244	175
Stone Quarrying Products	161	149	156	199	190	138
Metal Ores	32	26	32	40	53	35
Fuels	--	--	1	1	1	2
Manufacturing	2291	3430	3658	5144	5995	3954
Agro-Industry	412	568	670	809	647	458
Food Industry	367	497	569	650	550	387
Others	45	71	101	159	97	71
Petroleum Products	107	344	232	409	372	143
Other Manufacturing	1772	2518	2756	3926	4976	3353
Cement	198	207	81	56	44	21
Chemicals	94	148	120	173	266	260
Leather and Hide	82	111	192	401	484	221
Textiles	803	1057	1299	1875	1790	1333
Ceramic and Glass	102	104	108	146	190	120
Products of iron &						
non-ferrous metals	130	408	486	662	1084	618
Machinery and Equipment	64	116	103	118	378	183
Vehicles and Parts	117	110	126	135	147	64
Others	182	257	241	360	593	533

Source: Economic Indicators of Turkey 1981-1985, Turkiye Is Bankasi A.S., Ankara
           1986.

million in 1986, creates a sizable market in consumer goods as well. With increasing urbanization and a large population segment 16 years of age and under Turkey is an attractive potential market with "willingness" to buy.

Although Turkey is a net exporter of agricultural goods, imports of agricultural goods create opportunities for foreign exporters as well. This is because agricultural output still depends on favorable growing conditions and government subsidies, and at times imports are needed to stabilize prices and secure market equilibrium.

Turkey's major suppliers are the EEC and the Middle Eastern countries. Energy from the Middle East is the largest single item in Turkey's import portfolio. This is in spite of the fact that Turkey tries to curb energy consumption sometimes using mandatory measures such as planned electricity interruptions. Energy use in Turkey climbed to 35 million metric ton coal equivalent in 1983 from 24 in 1974 although electricity production in the same period was doubled. Turkey still imports electricity from her neighbors. As to the imports from the EEC countries, West Germany is by far the biggest supplier. The U.S.A. is another major supplier (Table 15).

CONSUMER MARKETS

The demand for imported consumer goods in Turkey has traditionally been curbed through import barriers, ranging from import bans to high tariffs and heavy taxes. Imports of most consumer goods were not allowed until 1980, but there was always a small black market for such goods. With the trade liberalization policies of the 1980s, imports of consumer goods in selected categories increased significantly (Table 16). However, the absolute volume was rather small and accounted to only 8% of the total imports.

Table 15   Imports by Origin (%)

	1981	1982	1983	1984	1985	1986
EEC	28.2	27.9	28.1	27.6	31.3	43.5
Germany	10.5	11.7	11.4	10.9	12.1	19.4
Italy	4.2	4.7	5.5	0.8	5.8	7.8
France	4.5	3.0	2.4	2.3	4.5	4.0
UK	4.9	4.9	4.8	4.1	4.1	4.5
Netherlands	1.9	1.8	2.0	2.0	1.9	3.0
Belgium-Luxembourg	1.7	1.7	1.6	1.8	2.1	2.6
Middle East & North America	39.9	41.4	39.6	35.6	32.2	34.6
Iraq	17.5	14.8	10.3	8.8	10.0	7.4
Libya	8.8	10.4	8.6	6.1	5.5	1.8
Iran	5.8	8.5	13.2	14.4	11.2	7.6
Saudi Arabia	4.6	5.4	2.9	2.2	1.6	4.8
USA	6.6	9.2	7.5	10.0	10.1	7.4
Switzerland	6.0	3.7	2.9	2.2	1.6	2.2
USSR	1.8	1.2	2.6	2.9	1.9	1.9
Japan	2.3	4.0	3.8	3.8	4.5	1.3
Others	15.2	12.6	15.5	17.9	18.4	8.9

Table 16   Imports of Consumer Goods (Millions of U.S. $)

1979	1980	1981	1982	1983	1984	1985	1987
96	170	179	181	242	474	905	956

In addition to the trade restrictions, other factors have been instrumental in inhibiting the demand for the imported consumer goods. First, the purchasing power of the general population is quite low: per capita income in 1985 was only $1080. However, this average figure hides inequitable income distribution which results in a bimodal market. Consequently, the potential market is much larger than the per capita income indicates. World Bank figures show that traditionally, the top 10% and 20% of the households accounted for over 50% of national income. The situation has deteriorated further since then. High inflation, coupled with the policies of liberalization which favor big businesses, lowered the share of the middle class in total income and further distorted income distribution. The indications are that the middle class has further lost its share of the total income since 1980. This maldistribution of income creates a sizable group of affluent consumers from the upper strata who are concentrated in big cities such as Istanbul, Ankara, Izmir, and a few others. Shopping behavior and preferences of this group are similar to behavior of the comparable consumers in the developed high income countries. In fact, it may even be more sophisticated since the consumers in this group are quite familiar with and favorably disposed to various brands and products from a variety of high income countries. If the liberalization of trade continues, it is likely that this group will be a lucrative market for a wide variety of consumer goods.

Another factor that will affect the demand for imported goods is the migration from rural to urban areas. The newcomers tend to emulate the consumption pattern of the urban population. Even in rural areas, the preference for foreign manufactured consumer goods has increased substantially. One factor which contributed to this is the demonstration effect provided by the Turkish "guest workers" abroad.

The number of Turkish workers and their family members in

Western Europe amount to about 2.3 million. An overwhelming majority come from the rural areas and they pay frequent visits to Turkey. They bring along a variety of consumer goods into even the remotest villages. This process has exposed a large number of consumers to the variety, quality, and brand names of goods available to the European consumers. This process creates a latent demand that could easily be turned into an effective demand as the purchasing power increases.

Industrial Markets

As expected, imports of manufactured goods are the largest share of total imports. Most of the imported manufactured goods fall in the categories of investment goods and raw materials. This is mainly because Turkey's manufacturing industry is still import-dependent. Although exports of the manufacturing industry have increased substantially since 1980, the trade deficit in this sector makes up about 40% of the the total trade deficit (Table 17).

Chemicals, iron and steel products, and machinery are the three major importing industrial sectors (Table 18). Turkey will continue to depend on imports in these manufacturing sectors as well as in investment goods.

Agricultural Markets

Although agriculture has historically been a major source of export earnings, Turkey imports close to half a billion dollars worth of agricultural products. Periodic shortfalls of crop and government price stabilization efforts are major factors. Cereals and leguminous

Table 17   Manufacturing Trade Balance (In Millions U.S. $)

	1982	1983	1984	1985
Manufacturing:				
Exports	3430	3658	5144	5995
Imports	4927	5655	6695	7342
Sector Trade Deficit	(1497)	(1997)	(1551)	(1347)
Total Deficit	(3097)	(3507)	(3624)	(3386)
Percent of Total Deficit	48	57	43	40

seeds, and wool-animal hair are the two major imported categories (Table 19). However, the agricultural sector in Turkey will not be a major importer and is likely to continue to be a major export revenue generator.

MARKET FOR FOREIGN DIRECT INVESTMENT

Historical Perspective

The Ottoman Empire had granted various licenses, commonly known as "capitulations," to foreign firms. The French, Italian, German, and later British firms were granted various capitulations. The FDI activities were mainly concentrated in utilities (electricity, water, telephone, gas) and transportation (railways and urban). During the latter part of its existence, particularly during the early

Table 18   Imports by Sectors (Millions of U.S. $)

	1981	1982	1983	1984	1985	1986
Agro Industry	230	175	205	434	487	355
Petroleum Products	621	221	423	264	290	152
Chemicals	1199	893	1146	1340	1294	1056
Machinery	1189	1316	1449	1618	1551	1571
Iron & Steel Products	607	592	818	862	1060	751
Elec. & Electronic						
Machinery & Appliances	403	376	402	573	663	622
Transport Vehicles & Parts	360	605	448	517	813	598
Rubber & Plastic Goods	243	236	252	359	343	270
Products Non-ferrous	141	122	200	220	224	178
Textiles	78	103	98	117	146	125
Others	259	288	214	391	471	361

Table 19   Agricultural Trade Balance (In Millions U.S. $)

	1981	1982	1983	1984	1985	1986
Exports	2214	2141	1881	1749	1719	1097
Imports	125	176	138	418	375	352
Cereal & Seeds	58	105	33	286	183	133
Wool & Hair	41	41	65	63	63	45
Raw Skin & Fur	5	6	9	27	32	48

20th century, the Empire had a rather bad experience with the foreign corporations. Especially from 1911 to 1923, these corporations were used as instruments of foreign policy by the governments of their country of origin with which the Ottomans were at war. Following the Independence War of 1919-1922, the new Republic became concerned about the dominance of foreign firms and embarked upon a policy of "etatism." Therefore, during the period from 1923 to 1950, the existing foreign investments in utilities and transportation were nationalized by negotiation and with compensation, and except in some selected areas (mostly in services in the form of representative offices), practically no new FDI was allowed. The bulk of the new investment activities were carried out by the State Economic Enterprises. The generations who grew up in this period were constantly taught and reminded of the horror stories regarding FDI. The origin of the negative attitude toward FDI which still prevails in some quarters dates back to this era.

Early in the 1950s, a new legal framework was designed to attract FDI. Although there were very few restrictions imposed on foreign capital, no substantial incentives were offered either. Starting in 1963, the country embarked on a planned development policy. Although the private sector was encouraged, dominance of the public sector continued. The period from 1960 to 1980 witnessed periodic political instability. Consequently, the inflow of foreign investment remained far below expectations.

1980 to Present

Following the attempts at liberalization in 1980, the laws and regulations governing the FDI have changed considerably. Presently, there are three groups of statutes regulating FDI.

The first group is composed of the Laws that are general in nature and do not necessarily relate to FDI. Included in this group are the Petroleum Law No. 6326 and the Tourism Law No. 2394 (in recent years there have been frequent changes in these laws as they apply to FDI through government decrees).

The second group of regulations stemmed from the Law on the Preservation of the Value of the Turkish Currency No. 1567 which was enacted in 1930. This law regulating the international financial transactions of private and public organizations carries severe penalties for violators. The implementation of this law, which restricted the flexibility of foreign and local corporations in their international transactions, has been changed considerably since 1980, and many of its restrictions are relaxed.

The third group of regulations directly related to FDI fall within the framework of Law No. 6224, the Encouragement of Foreign Capital (first enacted in 1954, then modified through decrees, see "Current Practices"). As the name implies, this law has the specific purpose of increasing FDI in Turkey. However, it was not until 1980 that Turkey started to actively solicit FDI. The results of these efforts are summarized in Table 20.

The manufacturing sector has attracted most of the FDI in the country, as shown in Table 21. Presently, West German, Swiss,

Table 20   FDI in Turkey 1950-1984 (In Millions U.S. $)

	Prior to Law 6224	Under Law Annual	Under Law Cumulative	Number of Firms
1950-1953 (1)	2836			
1954-1972 (1)			108,468	110
Before 1980 (2)			228,100	91
1980		97,000	325,100	100
1981		337,500	662,600	127
1982	167,000	829,600	170	
1983	102,700	932,300	185	
1984		271,000	1,203,300	267

Source: (1) Mehmet Sahin, Turkiyede Yabanci Sermaye Yatirimlari, Ekonomik ve
               Sosyal Yayinlari A.S., Ankara, Turkey 1975. Figures represent actual
               amount brought in.
          (2) State Planning Organization. Figures represent amounts specified in
               the approved investment proposals.

Table 21   Sectoral Distribution of FDI Number of Firms 1984

Manufacturing	167
Service	94
Mining	3
Agriculture	3

and U.S. corporations lead others with 40, 40, and 26 firms, respectively. Total U.S. investment in Turkey was $224 million as of 1985.

Current Practices

The Foreign Capital Framework Decree (No. 86/10353, March 13, 1986) designates the State Planning Organization (SPO) as the sole government agency in charge of regulating FDI that falls under the laws numbered 6224 and 1567. To serve this end a Directorate of Foreign Capital (DFC) was created within the SPO. This decree aims to reduce red tape and centralizes the evaluation and approval procedures.

In general, the DFC is authorized to approve all FDI proposals except investment proposals in excess of $50 million. The proposals above $50 million require the approval by the cabinet pursuant the DFC review. There is no longer any restriction on ownership and type of operation so long as the investment does not constitute a monopoly and is in a field open to the Turkish private sector.

Turkey offers attractive incentives to encourage foreign investment in areas that fall outside the domestically provided services and products. Once cleared by the State Planning Organization, a foreign investor becomes eligible for a series of incentives based on the type and the stage of the investment. The major features of the provided incentives are summarized below. (These incentives change in kind and magnitude quite frequently, and the reader is advised to check with the authorities.)

1. *Customs exemption:* All investment goods imported to Turkey are exempt from import duties. All investment in less developed regions also benefit from this clause even if the general nature of the investment is not included in the incentives table.
2. *Subsidized low-interest domestic and external loans:* Under normal conditions commercial credit and loans are quite expensive. The government provides cheaper sources of credit to foreign investors.
3. *Exemptions from duties and charges:* The foreign investments are exempt from various duties and charges.

4. *Exemption from construction charges:* All factories, mills, manufacturing workshops, shipyards, and all other business ventures in industrial sites, hotels-motels, and tourism facilities are exempt from construction charges that are normally levied.

5. *Foreign exchange allocation:* Preferential foreign exchange allocations are made for imports of machinery, parts, and raw materials.

6. *Exemption from miscellaneous fees and taxes:* For investments with a commitment to exports, if and when the export targets are achieved or exceeded any or all taxes involved in bank procedures, notary expenses, registry, etc. are exempted.

7. *Imports of used equipment:* In principle, used equipment cannot be imported. However, it is possible to relax this requirement if need can be demonstrated.

8. *Reduction of corporate taxes:* A specific deduction is applied on the corporate taxes on revenues derived from new investments. This advantage is provided for a specific period.

9. *Exclusion from the financing fund:* This fund is a facility utilized in the financing of investments from which withdrawals can be made, and is in the nature of "tax deferrals."

10. *Investment support premium:* Involves cash assistance to investors with projects above a certain level (approximately $75 million).

11. *Low interest loans:* Investments backed by incentives can use lower interest medium- to long-term loans.

12. *Real estate tax exemption:* Real estate and other taxable buildings are exempted for a specific period.

13. *Accelerated depreciation:* Normal rates of depreciation on fixed assets may be increased during the initial years of operation.

14. *Allocation of infrastructure and real estate:* particularly for tourism projects, leasing and infrastructure options are offered.

15. *Lower tax rates for personal income:* In general, employees in less developed regions enjoy special deductions.

16. *Tax exemptions on housing and start-up work:* Law No. 2982

provides for exemptions from any or all taxes levied on transfers, leases, purchase, sale, rent, restraints, acquisitions, recovery, and other modifications during the purchase of real
estate.
17. *Full access to foreign liquidity:* For financing investment
projects, entrepreneurs may use foreign credits channeled
through commercial banks in Turkey.

The implementation of the current laws and regulations regarding
FDI is distinguished by its high degree of flexibility. This flexibility
is provided by a constitutional clause which empowers the government to issue decrees with the same enforceability as laws enacted
by the congress. Consequently, the government is able to respond
quickly to changing circumstances.

TURKEY AS A MARKET: CONCLUSIONS

Imports reached a $14 billion level in 1987. Over $9 billion of
this sum is spent on various raw materials, machinery, and supplies. Investment goods make up the remaining $3.8 billion. The
growth of Turkey as a potential market has been impresssive since
1980. However, part of these imports are financed by external public debt. Therefore, unless exports and invisible income from tourism and workers remittances are increased, it is not likely that Turkey can sustain the same level of import growth in the future
without increasing the debt burden.

So far as FDI is concerned, Turkey is an attractive market. With
geographical proximity to a number of lucrative markets and with a
relatively developed infrastructure, Turkey is fast becoming an attractive investment location. The present laws and regulations are
extremely conducive and encouraging. Unlike the previous practices, the foreign direct investors are now allowed and encouraged
to reinvest their earnings in related or other areas including production of consumer goods for domestic consumption. The limitation
on foreign equity share ownership has also been removed. Foreign
investors do not need prior permission for any kind of investment,
including investments in the State Economic Enterprises. Export
requirements and the restrictions on profit remittances have also

been eliminated. If inflation can be controlled, Turkey's attractiveness for FDI will increase markedly. The service sector, especially tourism, is one of the promising areas. During June of 1988 the government shifted considerable support from export-oriented activities to tourism.

Presently, Turkey has also concentrated on establishing free trade zones. Free Zone Statute No. 3218 went into effect June 1985 and two free zones (one in the south and the other on the west coast) are already in operation. In these zones, transactions may be conducted in foreign currencies hence reducing foreign exchange risks. Infrastructure is provided by the state, and foreign investors enjoy the same rights as local businesses.

DOING BUSINESS IN TURKEY

As is true with many countries in the Third World, doing business with Turkey is an investment. A stable and mutually beneficial relationship must be realized in stages and usually takes time.

Information is a vital and essential component of international business. Although macro-information is already available there still exist shortcomings in specific information categories. Private investments and plans for capital expansion are not generally publicized. Since most companies are family owned, secrecy can be maintained by most organizations. In that sense, information about the plans of the private industry is always "privileged information." The public sector is quite different, however. Their new investment and expansion plans are known at least a year in advance. In fact, all public investments and expansion are guided by the five-year development plans.

The five-year development plan and sectoral programs provide valuable information for those who are interested in doing business in the country. These plans and programs outline which new investments or capital expansions are encouraged, and with what incentives.

Another source of information is the feasibility reports. A feasibility study and report is a must if a project is to benefit from the incentives provided by the state. This is particularly true if the project is required to be in compliance with the development plans and the accompanying programs. However, the suppliers are already determined by the time the feasibility report is prepared, therefore it may be too late for a supplier to successfully bid after the feasibility report is publicized. Companies should make their offers known before or during the feasibility study.

Successful suppliers (exporters) gather information through their exclusive representatives. These representatives should have an excellent reputation and good connections since most initial contact and intelligence is through informal channels. Once intelligence is received, the seller must try to influence the preparation of the feasibility study by providing information and technical assistance through representatives or preferably through company staff. Such influence usually leads to successful bidding since the technical terms and conditions are written in compliance with the company's offering.

Turks tend to be serious in business negotiations. They are usually quite reserved and professional in attitude. They are well prepared for negotiations and do not waste much time in socializing. Most Turks are quite selective in their choice of friends.

Turkish buyers are usually loyal to their suppliers. One supplier may be preferred over others just because of past relationship. However, increasing contact and familiarity with many suppliers from a variety of countries and escalating competition among suppliers are sensitizing Turkish buyers to price and quality differences.

The Turkish private sector is fairly well organized. The developed country counterpart of chambers of commerce, industry, agriculture, and maritime trade can be found in most commercial and industrial centers. These, in turn, are represented by an umbrella organization, the Union of Chambers of Commerce, Industry, Agriculture, and Maritime Trade, located in Ankara. Other noteworthy business associations include the Association of the Turkish Industrialists and Businessmen and the Turkish Confederation of Employers' Union which are both located in Istanbul. Through these organizations as well as the commercial attaché in Turkey of one's own country and the Turkish commercial attachés, enough information can be gathered about prospective exporters, importers, and joint venture partners.

Chapter 16

Business and Marketing Dynamics in the United States of America

Eugene J. Kelley
Lisa R. Hearne

The United States market is one of contrasts, extremes, changes, and opportunities. Americans live in a nation of contrasts and diversity. The scale of the United States is difficult for its own citizens to fully comprehend, let alone an international marketer. In this chapter, we assess the changing nature of the United States marketplace; we provide an overview of its economic, commercial, and governmental activities; and we describe the form and conduct of business in the United States. The discussion emphasizes regional differences and similarities in American values, and their relevance to U.S. commerce. Finally, a "market focus" approach is suggested as a key to successful U.S. market entry.

AN OVERVIEW OF UNITED STATES GEOGRAPHY

Taken as a single unit—3,000 miles long, 1,500 miles wide, and 3,615,122 square miles in area—it is impossible to distinguish a single national topography or climate in the United States. As early as mid-September the Northern Great Plains states of Montana, Wyoming, and the Dakotas may be experiencing blizzard conditions. Meanwhile, the Southern coastal states are bracing themselves for hurricane season, the trees of the Northeastern portion of the country are ablaze with early autumn foliage, and the desert Southwest blisters under the 200° F sun.

Between the tree-covered mountains of the East Coast and the Rocky Mountains of the West Coast lies mostly farmland and desert prairie. When viewed as a whole, visitors are surprised to learn that much of this nation's vast territory is virtually unpopulated. Americans tend to cluster themselves along the northeastern and southern border states, around the five Great Lakes, and along a thin strip of the West Coast. According to the 1980 Census of Population, almost three out of four U.S. citizens live in cities or suburbs while most of the rest live in small towns with rapidly growing populations.

Marketing, of course, is more than geography. Figure 1 represents a visual conceptualization of 10 major components which influence the dynamic United States marketing process within its national environment. As the two-way arrows connecting elements throughout the system indicate, this process may be characterized as an interactive one. The resulting interdependency among these various components makes it difficult to explain each one separately without discussing its relationship with other system elements.

CHANGING NATURE AND STRUCTURE OF THE UNITED STATES MARKET

A Regional Approach to the United States

Consistent with the marketing concept, the central component of Figure 1 consists of the consumer and business markets of the United States. Fawcett and Thomas[1] have characterized American society as sharing a "rich and varied sameness." Since the marketing concept emphasizes the needs and desires of customers, and since these needs and desires tend to vary from one section of the country to another, this discussion of American markets will borrow from the regional approach proposed by Garreau *The Nine Nations of North America*[2] (see Table 1). Garreau's work does not specifically address marketing issues; however, an examination of the characteristics and trends within each region suggest certain implications for global marketers. (Table 2 lists some key characteristics for each major region within the United States.) While a review of the marketing implications of all eight "nations" relevant to the

Figure 1: Environmental Influences Which Impact on the U.S. Marketing Process

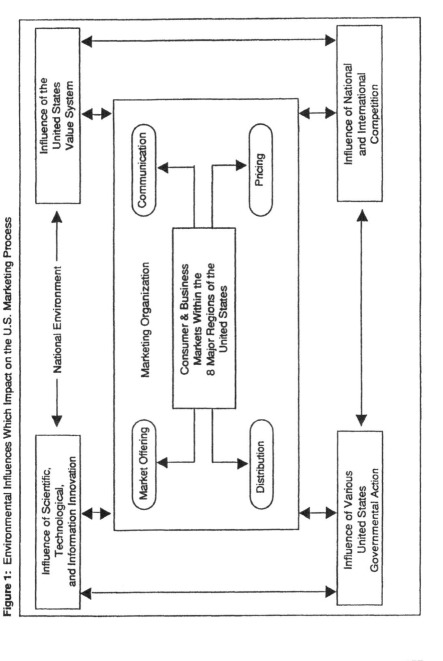

United States is beyond the scope of this chapter, the usefulness of the approach to global marketers can be readily illustrated by comparing the similarities and differences of just a few regions.

TABLE 1.
Geographic Description of the Eight
Major Regions of the United States

1. *New England*

The New England region is located in the northeastern corner of the United States. This area is composed of the states of Maine, New Hampshire, Vermont, Massachusetts, and Rhode Island in their entirety. Most of the state of Connecticut is also included except for the southeastern third of the state which belongs to the Foundry.

2. *The Foundry*

The Foundry region extends from the Middle Atlantic coast northward to the Canadian border and westward around the Great Lakes. The major portion of this region is formed by the states of New Jersey, New York, Pennsylvania, Ohio, and lower Michigan. In addition, the northern portions of Delaware, Maryland, Virginia, West Virginia, and Indiana, as well as the northeastern half of Illinois and the Lake Michigan coastline of Wisconsin are also included in this region.

3. *Dixie*

The Dixie region covers the southeastern portion of the United States between the Atlantic Ocean and the Gulf of Mexico. Included in their entirety are the states of North and South Carolina, Georgia, Alabama, Mississippi, Louisiana, Arkansas, Kentucky, and Tennessee. Along its northern borderline, the region includes southern portions of the states of Delaware, Maryland, Virginia, West Virginia, Indiana, Illinois, and Missouri. The southeastern corner of Oklahoma and the eastern portion of Texas form the western boundary of this area. In addition, Dixie also includes most of Florida except for the southern tip of the state.

4. *Mexamerica*

The region of Mexamerica occupies the southwestern corner of the United States. This area extends from the Gulf of Mexico along the Mexican border to the Pacific Ocean. The eastern border contains the southern and western portions of Texas. Most of the states of New Mexico and Arizona as well as the south-central section of Colorado are also included. The western boundary of Mexamerica follows the Pacific Coast up to Point Conception, California. From here, this region includes the section of California known as the San Joaquin Valley which lies between the Coastal Range and the Sierra Nevada Range, and extends northward to Sacramento.

5. *Ecotopia*

The region of Ecotopia occupies a narrow strip along the Pacific coastline in the Northwest corner of the United States. This area extends from Point Conception, California in the south, up through Oregon and Washington State, then northward to Homer, Alaska. The Sierra Nevada and the Cascade Mountain Ranges form the eastern boundary of Ecotopia.

6. *The Empty Quarter*

The Empty Quarter is located in the west-central portion of the United States. Included in their entirety are the states of Nevada, Utah, and Idaho. The southern boundary of this area cuts across central Colorado and then drops further south to include the northwest corner of New Mexico, and the northern section of Arizona. The 100th meridian forms the eastern boundary of the Empty Quarter, traveling northward across Colorado, Wyoming, and Montana to the Canadian border. The Sierra Nevada and Cascade Mountain Ranges form the western border, extending from California through Oregon to Washington State. In addition, most of the state of Alaska also belongs to the Empty Quarter.

7. *The Breadbasket*

The Breadbasket covers the central portion of the United States from Texas to the Canadian border. This area is composed of the states of Kansas, Nebraska, Iowa, North and South Dakota, and Minnesota. The western boundary of the Breadbasket is formed by the eastern section of the states of Montana, Wyoming, Colorado, and New Mexico. This region also contains most of Oklahoma, Missouri, Illinois, Wisconsin, and the Michigan Peninsula as well as the west-central portion of Indiana.

8. *The Islands*

The smallest of all the regions, the Islands region is located on the southern tip of Florida. This area also includes the United States territories of Puerto Rico and the Virgin Islands.

TABLE 2.
Characteristics of the Eight
Major Regions of the United States*

1. *New England*

The climate of this region may be described as cold in the winter, comfortably cool in the summer, with plenty of precipitation year-round. Representative cities of this area are Boston, Hartford, New London, and Portsmouth. This region's general characteristics include a declined economy; high taxes; liberal-

*Source: Garreau, *The Nine Nations of North America*.

ism; an educated, intellectual population which enjoys reading; ecology-mind-edness; highly skilled, dexterous labor force; the "Yankee" tradition; Puritan frugality and caution; and a European orientation.

2. *The Foundry*

The climate of the Foundry may be described as cold in the winter, warm in the summer, with plenty of precipitation throughout the entire year. Cities which are representative of this are Detroit, Chicago, Indianapolis, New York, Cleveland, Pittsburgh, Philadelphia, St. Louis, and Baltimore. This region may be generally characterized as being heavily industrialized; densely populated with people of diverse ethnic backgrounds; and as having a declining economy, many cities surrounded by large maturing suburban areas; and a fast-paced lifestyle where the work-ethic and blue-collar unionism is still highly valued.

3. *Dixie*

Dixie's climate may be described as mild in the winter, hot in the summer, with plenty of precipitation throughout the entire year. The representative cities of this region are Atlanta, Charleston, Durham, Montgomery, Knoxville, New Orleans, Jacksonville, and Dallas. Dixie's general characteristics include a rapid, "catch-up" growth rate and significant social change; a combination of rural agriculture and industrialization utilizing low-wage, unskilled labor; an eye to the future which has resulted in new prosperity; a probusiness attitude; and a leisurely, hospitable lifestyle which emphasizes a family frame of reference.

4. *Mexamerica*

The climate of Mexamerica may be described as hot, and desertlike, with very little precipitation throughout the year. Cities which are representative of this region include Los Angeles, Phoenix, Albuquerque, Santa Fe, Pueblo, San Antonio, Austin, and Houston. Mexamerica's general characteristics include spectacular growth in population and wealth; a strong Mexican influence and bilingual culture; large numbers of illegal immigrants from Mexico; competition for fresh water; a low-wage and plentiful labor force; large-scale agribusiness through long-distance irrigation; and heavy emphasis on entertainment and tourism.

5. *Ecotopia*

Ecotopia's climate may be described as temperate and foggy with large amounts of precipitation year-round. The representative cities of this region are San Francisco, Portland, Seattle, and Juneau. This region's general characteristics include a "back-to-nature" quality of life; bipartisan politics; an economy based on planned growth, renewable sources of energy, and recyclable resources; a receptive attitude toward new ideas and a high degree of social homogeneity; a small-scale, regional agriculture; Asian-oriented trade; a fervent zeal for environmentalism; a relatively small population of mostly Northern European descent; and an emphasis on health and fitness through recreation and leisure.

6. *The Empty Quarter*

The climate of the Empty Quarter may be described as extremely cold in the winter, comfortable in the summer, with very little precipitation throughout the year. Cities which are representative of this area are Denver, Salt Lake City, Las Vegas, Spokane, Boise, and Casper. General characteristics of the Empty Quarter include an extremely sparse population; vast and undeveloped oil and mineral deposits; ultra-conservative Republicanism, remote isolation with few towns or cities; an economy based largely on ranching and ski resorts; and an"Old West" Anglo-American, cowboy culture.

7. *The Breadbasket*

The Breadbasket's climate may be described as very cold in the winter, hot in the summer, with moderate amounts of precipitation throughout the year. Representative cities of this region are Kansas City, Fort Worth, Wichita, Omaha, Minneapolis, Madison, Cedar Rapids, and Springfield. The general characteristics of this area include vast expenses of fertile farmland; an economy based almost entirely on agricultural and livestock farming, an increasing rate of farm mortgage foreclosures; a relatively small population which is mostly of Northern European heritage; conservative, Protestant values; and widespread interest in world affairs and export issues.

8. *The Islands*

The climate of the Islands may be described as tropical, with high temperatures and lots of rain year-round. The smallest of the eight U.S. regions, the cities which are representative of this are Miami, Fort Lauderdale, and San Juan. The general characteristics of the Islands include a strong Hispanic and Caribbean influence; economy based on international trade, tourism, and illicit drugs; a densely populated, bilingual culture; and an excessively high crime rate.

For example, at first glance, there are some striking similarities between New England and Ecotopia. Both possess mountainous terrain with rocky coastlines, and both are blessed with plentiful rainfall and fresh water supplies. In both regions, fishing and forestry play an important role in parts of their respective economies.

The people of these two regions share a common cause of environmental protectionism — New Englanders and Ecotopians are both opposed to the use of nuclear power. These people have a high regard for the coexistence of mankind with nature. For New En-

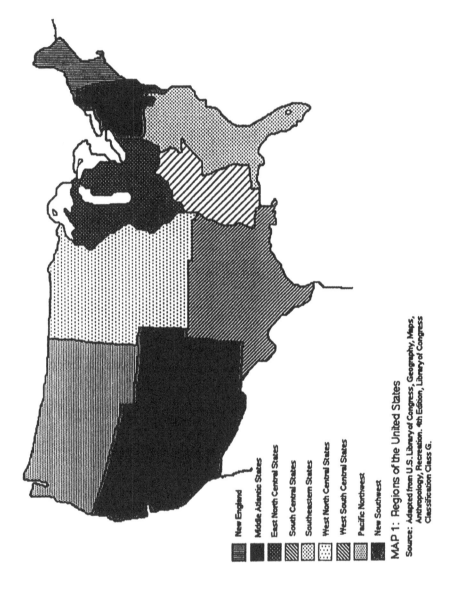

MAP 1: Regions of the United States

New England
Middle Atlantic States
East North Central States
South Central States
Southeastern States
West North Central States
West South Central States
Pacific Northwest
New Southwest

Source: Adapted from U.S. Library of Congress, Geography, Maps,
Anthropology, Recreation. 4th Edition, Library of Congress
Classification Class G.

582

glanders, this perspective is a reaction to the destruction of much of its ecology at the hands of the region's bygone industrialization, and is marked by the desire to conserve that which remains untouched. For Ecotopians, ecological concerns are derived from the determination that economic development and growth will not take place at the expense of the surrounding environment, and is marked by the desire to preserve the existing "quality of life" which is so precious to its residents.

Since neither New England nor Ecotopia is especially prosperous relative to other regions of the United States, it is likely that the people of both these regions engage in what Resnik, Sand, and Mason[3] have referred to as "smart consumption." This type of consumption pattern emphasizes the purchase and use of fewer but higher quality goods and services. Such buying behavior may involve trade-offs between various products (e.g., the willingness to purchase "generic" groceries in order to save for a personal computer or a foreign-built automobile), and can be summarized by the ethic "smaller (or fewer) is better."

Both New Englanders and Ecotopians exhibit an esteem for health and fitness through leisure-time recreation, though Ecotopians to a greater extent than New Englanders. This health-mindedness extends to the mind as well as the body. It is interesting to note that both regions possess internationally renowned centers for higher education—Harvard University and the Massachusetts Institute of Technology in the Boston area, and Stanford University in the San Francisco area—and both are vying for world leadership in high-tech industries.

New Englanders tend to be more intellectually sophisticated than Ecotopians. Boston is certainly one of the most cultural and cosmopolitan cities in the United States. Ecotopians, on the other hand, are more open-minded, are more bipartisan in their political beliefs, and, as a result of these two factors, a higher degree of social homogeneity is found in this region. In contrast, New Englanders are, for the most part, staunchly Democratic. The excessively high tax structure characteristic of this region tends to have a leveling effect on the disposable income of its residents. Despite this fact, there is a greater degree of social stratification in New England than in Ecotopia. This is probably due to its longer history and older culture.

Mexamerica contrasts sharply in comparison to either New England or Ecotopia. Warm and sunny year-round, lower tax rates, a lower cost of living, and the widespread use of air conditioning are helping to make this area one of the fastest growing regions in the United States. Despite large-scale, long-distance irrigation projects, rapid growth in population and industry has made water scarcity a politically charged issue between this region and its neighbor, Ecotopia.

The mild, dry climate and casual, relaxed lifestyle attract many people – both young and old – who seek overnight success and personal fulfillment in this "land of milk and honey." This has led some critics to describe this region as transient and decadent. The employment opportunities created by rapid growth have also attracted an increasing number of illegal aliens from Mexico. As a result, a large portion of the region's population is Spanish-speaking. Bilingual communication strategies will continue to be an important consideration for marketers who wish to target audiences in this region.

Core Values in the United States

Hand-in-hand with this regional approach, it is important to remember that U.S. society, like any other, comprises groups of individuals and market segments. The nature of its market potential may be best understood through the characteristics and behavior of individuals as supported by their framework of fixed principles. Thus, another recurrent, underlying theme of this chapter involves the core values of the United States. This is depicted in the upper righthand corner of Figure 1 as the "Influence of the United States Value System."

Values are beliefs: they serve as a basis for how people think and behave on both individual and collective levels. As such, the elements of the American value system (outlined in Figure 2) provide an important starting point for the discussion of the remaining eight components of the U.S. marketing process shown in Figure 1.

Rooted in the combined heritages of the Judeo-Christian ethic and Classic Secular Humanism, Figure 2 illustrates that the United States value system grew out of the principles of life, liberty, and

Figure 2   Foundations and Components of the United States Values System

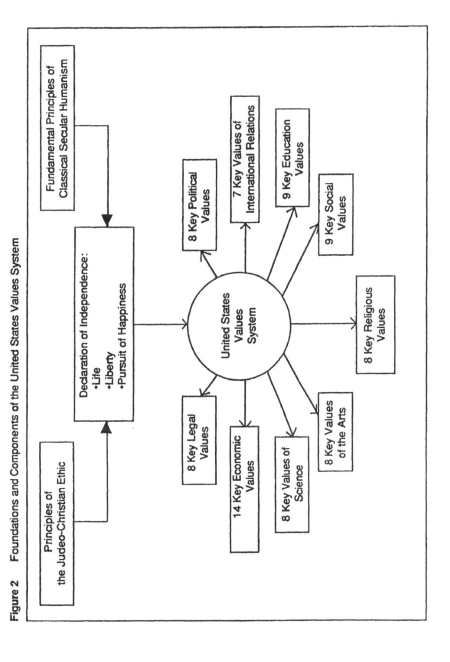

the pursuit of happiness contained in the Declaration of Independence. This value system is composed of nine subsystems: (1) political values; (2) legal values; (3) religious values; (4) social values; (5) educational values; (6) values in the arts; (7) values of the sciences; (8) economic values; and (9) values of international relations. A description of each of these nine value subsystems is provided in Table 3.

The various subsystems of values form the ethical foundation for American society, government, and commerce—providing guidelines for thought and behavior regarding the structure, development, and conduct of our public and private institutions. United States democratic philosophy is expressed throughout this value system and revolves around the dignity and importance of the individual person as a unique center of value and power. This respect for the individual is reflected by comprehensive political and legal rights and civil liberties; by freedom of individual expression in the arts, the sciences, and religion; and by regard for the principle of free enterprise (which extends to cultural and economic exchange between nations of the world).

This last point is particularly significant for international marketers interested in the United States market. The U.S. government values free trade and favors foreign investment, whether direct or portfolio. Governmental policy regards foreign capital on an equal basis with domestic capital (i.e., the government treats both forms of capital the same).

When compared to some other societies and cultures, Americans are, on the whole, accepting and adaptive to changes in their social, political, and economic environment. But this acceptance and adaptation does not always come easily. It involves a continual and selective process of sorting ideas and alternatives. It involves a willingness to compromise and reconcile "old notions to new realities."[4] The core value of respect for the individual inspires confidence in the American people that while they may not be able to alter the pace of environmental change, they can influence, individually or collectively, the direction and impact that various changes will have. In the aftermath of the social upheaval which accompanied U.S. involvement in the Vietnam War, the Civil Rights and

Women's Liberation movements, it is interesting to observe the current wave of U.S. conservatism. The recent return to many of these traditional values emphasizes how germaine they are to the American way of life.

TABLE 3.
The United States Value System*

Political Values

1. The responsibility of the state to provide for the general welfare and common defense of its people.

2. The right and responsibility of the adult citizen to vote and to thereby have a voice in his/her government.

3. The existence of a free press to provide a variety of information to citizens, except when such knowledge would endanger the common defense.

4. The freedom of speech, including both oral and written opinions, concerning social, religious, political, or economic matters.

5. The protection of the citizen from unlawful invasions of privacy by governmental officers or agencies.

6. The right of free citizens to assemble peaceably.

7. The principle that civil authority is the decision-making power and the military is the instrument to be used, when necessary, to implement civil decisions.

8. The concept of the American Federation as a permanent union of permanent states, firmly established after the Civil War, maintained by judicial enforcement of the Constitution and forbidding nullification or secession on the part of the states.

Legal Values

1. The concept of a "government of law and not of men," as exemplified by the supremacy of the law over governmental officers and agencies.

2. The concept of an evolutionary law which must be adaptive to the developmental needs of society.

---

*Source: U.S. National Commission for UNESCO, "Traditional Values in American Life," in *American Values, Continuity and Change*, Ralph H. Gabriel, ed., (Westport, CT: Greenwood Press, 1974).

3. The freedom of citizens, unless convicted of a crime, to choose their own location and occupation, subject only to the general law.

4. The right of each citizen to be informed specifically of any charges made by the state against him, to a speedy and public trial, to compulsory process for obtaining witnesses, and to legal counsel assuring his equal protection of the laws.

5. The right of each citizen to refrain from testifying against himself.

6. The right of every citizen to a trial by a jury of his peers when the United States government brings the charges.

7. The protection of citizens from being tried more than once for the same offense or, if convicted, from "cruel and unusual punishments."

8. The protection of citizens from governmental punishment through the use of any "ex post facto" law.

Religious Values

1. The principle of separation of church and state.

2. The freedom to believe and worship according to one's own conscience.

3. The responsibility of believers to assume the duty of supporting their organization of worship.

4. The widespread, if not universal, conviction that theism provides a framework for understanding the meaning of life.

5. The widespread, if not universal, conviction that theism provides ethical standards for personal conduct.

6. The moral duty of churches to offer their resources for errands of mercy, to assist social development toward a higher quality of life, and to promote peaceful cooperation among all people of the world.

7. The concept that acts of charity contribute to the well-being of individuals and societies, and are thus worthy of merit.

8. The responsibility of the state to respect the conscientious objector's right to refrain from direct participation in bloody conflicts of war.

Social Values

1. The dignity and importance of the individual person as a unique center of power and value.

2. The freedom of thought and action of the individual person to express his/her own dignity and significance.

3. As much as possible, the freedom of equality for the individual to make of his life what his unique abilities and opportunities will allow, and the expectation

that his status in society will derive from his personal qualities and accomplishments.

4. Regard for group activity and voluntary association as a means to develop the individual personality and enlarge the possibilities for effective action.

5. Regard for the family as the basic social unit as exemplified by the protection in law and custom of the privacy and mutual loyalty of its members — one spouse may not be compelled to testify in court against another spouse.

6. Regard for work leading to recognizable achievement — professional preferment, the accumulation of property — as a normal aspect of the good life which is expressed by the fact that having a job gives in itself a kind of social status.

7. Concern for the physical and mental well-being of the community which is exemplified by the numerous public health organizations, regulation, and activities in existence.

8. Regard for voluntary public service by private individuals. This manifests itself in the willingness among many citizens to contribute money to institutions and causes which further the general welfare. This value is also expressed by the willingness of many private citizens to serve without compensation in the management and promotion of these institutions and causes.

9. The wide, if not universal, acceptance of change as a normal aspect of social life and regard for the social sciences as instruments for gaining understanding of society and for the formulation of improvements.

Educational Values

1. The idea that effective self-government requires a sufficiently educated electorate who are able to adequately inform themselves about issues of importance.

2. The freedom of equality of educational opportunity for all citizens.

3. The responsibility of the state to provide educational opportunities from kindergarten through the university, and to enforce school attendance into the early teens.

4. The idea that the combination of both state supported and independent, privately supported schools, colleges, and universities bring to the educational system a diversity and variety which furthers the general welfare.

5. A regard for education which trains specialists to work in a society which emphasizes specialization, and which increases the opportunities for the individual to find a useful place in the community and to earn an income commensurate with his abilities.

6. The principle that the educational system exists for the training of a social being as well as the cultural and intellectual enrichment of the individual mind.

7. At the university level, the idea that general education should precede or pace

side by side with the training of the specialist so that the individual will possess breadth of view and flexibility of mind along with a particular competence.

8. The idea of academic freedom which asserts that teachers in higher education should be free to search for and to teach the truth as they see it without compulsion from the State, the church, the business community, or the administrative authorities of the institution and to this end should enjoy security of tenure.

9. The concept of education as a lifelong process as exemplified by the variety of postschool training available to adults.

Values of the Arts

1. Regard for the creation and presentation of music, reflected in the multiplication of composers, the growth of musical organizations, and the popularity of recorded music.

2. Regard for the collection of and making available to the public in museums painting, sculpture, and the crafts, both traditional and contemporary.

3. Regard for the quality of design in the artifacts of everyday life.

4. Regard for creative literature as an instrument for the fuller and deeper understanding of life.

5. Regard for the drama and the dance as presented in stage, film, and television as instruments for enriching human life.

6. Regard for tradition and for innovation in painting, sculpture, and the crafts and for popular and mature participants in these arts.

7. Regard for tradition and innovation, together with the principles of form and function, in the architecture of a rapidly evolving civilization.

8. Regard for criticism by scholars and specialists in the various arts to encourage discrimination by the public in evaluating performance and recognizing excellence.

Values of the Sciences

1. Regard for the rational and critical approach to the phenomena of nature and society, combined with the ongoing effort to reduce these phenomena to more consistent, orderly, and generalized forms of understanding.

2. The right and responsibility of men to uncover the secrets of nature to the extent that their abilities permit.

3. The obligation of men to assume responsibility for the use of whatever new power increased knowledge brings.

4. The conviction that the method of science, combining precise reasoning with accurate observation and controlled experimentation, should achieve new knowledge through an ethical code of creative thought.

5. In the search for new knowledge, the scholar should have the freedom to explore, to reason on the basis of discovered facts, and to present his findings and conclusions on the basis of those facts.

6. In the communication of scientific findings, the scholar is responsible to honestly report his method and observation.

7. Regard for an objective approach to problem-solving as exemplified by the willingness to accept evidence as well as to reject disproved hypotheses.

8. Regard for the application of scientific knowledge through technology to the affairs of business, education, and society.

Economic Values

1. Regard for the ethic of work as a normal aspect of life, and as a means of providing individuals' honorable status within society.

2. Regard for the economic well-being of the individual as a cornerstone of a sound economy and stable society.

3. Respect for property and sanctity of contract as a necessary prerequisite for dependable and orderly economic relations.

4. Regard for the increasingly efficient production of goods and service as a foundation for economic vitality and growth.

5. Respect for private enterprise and the opportunity it provides individual entrepreneurs to achieve creative and economic fulfillment.

6. Regard for the profit system because only where there are profits can private enterprise survive.

7. Regard for public- and private-supported social security as a means of ensuring the economic well-being of individuals and the community.

8. Regard for government assistance (such as minimum wage rates or agricultural subsides) as a means of furthering the economic prosperity of the community.

9. Regard for the principle and practice of competition in the production and distribution of goods and services.

10. Respect for the principle of collective bargaining, enabling the worker to negotiate with the employer on more nearly equal terms.

11. Regard for the opportunity of the individual to rise in the management of an enterprise through promotion based on demonstrated ability, providing for the mobilization or maximum capability in enterprise management.

12. Regard for the role of government in facilitating stable economic growth and preventing excessive economic inequalities.

Values of International Relations

1. Rejection of violence as an instrument of policy and the principle that relations between nations be conducted peacefully.

2. The principle of national sovereignty under international law for all nations, which includes the right to the security of territory, and to self-determination regarding government, economy, and foreign and domestic policy.

3. The value of collective security of organized nations as exemplified by the United Nations, and a recognition of the fact that no nation can enjoy prosperity in isolation.

4. Regard for the observance of international law and international treaties and commitments formally undertaken as the responsibility of a free nation.

5. Respect for the use of international adjudication to settle legal disputes which arise between nations.

6. The concept that free nations should practice neighborliness and that the stronger and more advanced among them should help those who are struggling in time of need.

7. The concept that government should encourage and support cultural exchange among peoples, on the grounds that increased understanding among diverse civilizations and mutual appreciation of their art and their values furthers the cause of peace among men of good will.

Characteristics of the U.S. Population

Of the 235 million living Americans, most were born in the United States. Only about 6% are naturalized citizens who were born in other countries. The South and West (i.e., Dixie and Mexamerica) account for nearly all of the nation's current population growth. Although this may be partially explained by the increasing number of people attracted to the warm climate and new industries these two regions offer, the major reason for this population growth is that both of these areas have a larger share of young people of childbearing age. Just as the U.S. was disproportionately young during the 1960s, it has become unusually middle-aged during the 1980s. In addition, advances in health care and medical technology continue to increase life-expectancy.[5] As a result, the fastest growing age categories are the 35-44 and the over-65 groups.

As mentioned earlier, most Americans today live in cities and towns, or their surrounding suburban areas. The 1980 Census reported 38 metropolitan areas with over a million inhabitants, 41 with over 500,000, and 211 with over 100,000. Over the past decade, metropolitan areas have grown faster than nonmetropolitan areas. In addition, there has been a steady decline in suburban growth. This trend is especially evident throughout the Foundry and New England regions, where the "homesteading" projects characteristic of urban redevelopment continue to attract large numbers of "urban pioneers" seeking inexpensive dwellings.

As of March 1987, there were over 89 million households [6] in the United States. The median income of these households was $24,897 per year; mean annual income for these households was $29,066.[7] Approximately 65% of the American population owned their own home. Only about 2% of total U.S. households were farms.

Most Americans are of European descent. As such, they are predominantly Christian and English-speaking. Freedom of worship is constitutionally guaranteed in the United States. Religion is an important component of the U.S. value system as Figure 2 and Table 3 illustrate. Approximately 60 % of the population are members of an organized religion. Of this group, 95% are Christian, mainly Protestant and Roman Catholic. Of the remaining number, about 4% are Jewish. In addition, a small portion of the population are affiliated with various Eastern religions. As previously mentioned, there are significant groups of Spanish-speaking people across the United States. Both New York City and Chicago have large Puerto Rican populations; Miami has a sizable Cuban population; and Mexamerica and the southwest part of Dixie have a substantial number of Mexicans.

Characteristics of the U.S. Labor Force

The U.S. civilian labor force currently numbers over 117 million, representing almost 50% of the total population. About 20% of the labor force are involved in manufacturing, 20% in wholesale and retail trade, and about 30% are involved in various service industries. Of the remainder, a third are in transportation, communications and other public utilities; a third in construction; over a sixth in public administration; less than a sixth in agriculture; and 1% in mining. Roughly a quarter of the labor force are managerial and professional specialty by occupation, with close to another third being technical, sales, and administrative support personnel.

One of the most distinguishing features of the American labor force is its level of vocational training and academic education. In order to ensure freedom of equality of educational opportunity, public education, — at the primary and secondary levels — is free of charge to all children up to the age of 18. The individual states are responsible for organizing their own systems of education, and individual communities are responsible for the administration of the public schools within local districts. In most states, school attendance is required by law until 16 years of age.

Approximately 75% of American workers have high school diplomas, representing 12 years of formal education at the primary and secondary levels. Of this number, about 1% pursue some sort of postsecondary vocational training, while an additional 19% continue into college- or university-level education. During recent years an increasing number of technical and managerial personnel have opted to pursue postgraduate education on either a part-time or full-time basis, earning advanced degrees in areas relating to their specialty and employment.

OVERVIEW OF THE UNITED STATES GOVERNMENT, ECONOMY, AND COMMERCE

The United States government was established in 1787 when the 13 original States of the Union ratified the United States Constitution. Since that time, the Constitution has been amended several times and 37 new states have joined the Union. Today, the United States of America is a federal republic of 50 states. The federal government is composed of three branches: the executive, the legislative, and the judicial. The U.S. political system is based on two political parties: the Democratic party, and the Republican party.

The President of the United States is the official Head of State, and is responsible for the administration of the executive branch of government. This branch consists of several executive departments of the civil service. Some of these include the Departments of State, Defense, Labor, and Commerce. The Secretaries, or head administrators of these various departments are appointed by the President and, unlike other parliamentary democracies, they are not members of the legislative branch. Department secretaries are collectively referred to as the President's cabinet. Members of the cabinet periodically meet with the President to discuss and assist in the formulation of various executive policies.

The legislative or parliamentary branch of the government, known as the United States Congress, is divided into two chambers: the U.S. Senate and the U.S. House of Representatives. Members of the U.S. Congress are elected through the popular vote of their respective state constituencies. The Constitution allows for two senators from each state; thus, there are currently 100 members in the Senate. Membership in the House of Representatives is limited by the Constitution to a total of 435. The number of representatives allotted to each state is determined by population. With the shift of population density to the regions of Dixie and Mexamerica, much of the political dominance in the House of Representatives which was traditionally held by the populace of New England and the Foundry is diminishing.

The judicial branch of government is composed of a system of federal courts located throughout the country. This system is headed by the United States Supreme Court which is presided over by 12 justices. These justices are appointed by the President and approved by Congress. The function of the Supreme Court is to rule on the constitutionality of various laws on appeal from the lower courts. Since it is the highest court in the nation, there is no appeal against the Court's decision. Certain rights and freedoms are guaranteed to the nation's citizens by the U.S. Constitution. All adult citizens, 18 years of age or older, have the right to vote and to thereby have a voice in their government. Americans have been provided with freedom of speech, freedom of the press, and freedom to assemble peaceably; and they are protected from unlawful invasions of personal privacy by the government. Other rights of American citizens may be found under "Political and Legal Values" in Table 3.

State governmental systems are generally patterned after the federal governmental system. Each state elects state legislative senators and representatives, and a chief executive, known as the Governor. Like the federal system, power is divided among three branches: the executive, the legislative, and the judicial. Legal jurisdiction is confined to each state, and is limited to those domains not already covered by the U.S. Constitution (the laws and regulations of the federal government).

Characteristics of U.S. Economic Growth and Development

The economic system of the United States is built on the policy of free enterprise. Due to this fact, there is no nationalization of commercial endeavor in the United States. As a result, a distinguishing feature of the nation's economy is the small proportion of government expenditures relative to other nations of the world. As of 1987, federal budget outlays (or expenditures) represented 24% of United States GNP. In addition, outstanding gross debt represented approximately 50% of GNP.[8]

American capitalism derives from several important economic values (shown in Table 3). First of all, the economic well-being and fulfillment of the individual is regarded as an essential ingredient of a sound economy and stable society. Economic vitality and growth as a national goal is exemplified by the continuing drive toward increasingly efficient production of goods and services. Accumulation of capital, ownership of property, and sanctity of contracts are regarded as necessary prerequisites for orderly and dependable economic relations.

The emphasis which is placed on the production and marketing of goods and services has facilitated the development of a distinctly American"consumption culture." Despite several periods of recession and high inflation during the past decade, Americans, for the most part, have continued to enjoy and improve upon an enviable standard of living. "Visitors from Western Europe, even today, continue to gape at college students with electric typewriters, children with home computers, FM radios in rental cars, ten-speed bicycles, jogging uniforms, eye clinics for pets, computer chess sets, and refrigerators as big as Volkswagens."[9] The mean income of all households was $29,066 in 1985.

GNP exceeded $3,436.2 billion at the end of 1983. Real GNP grew at a rate of 2.7% between the third quarter of 1981 and the fourth quarter of 1984, and is projected to grow at an average rate of 3.9% through the fourth quarter of 1990. Reduction of the budget deficit, defense spending, and unemployment will continue to be major challenges for both the President and Congress in the upcoming years. During fiscal 1984, the U.S. budget deficit was a record $195.4 billion. Estimates for fiscal 1985 are only slightly more promising with a budgeted deficit in the neighborhood of $179 billion.

Since the Great Depression of the 1930s, growth in real GNP has been a national policy goal in the U.S., and increased productivity has been considered essential to the growth process. Productivity in the nonfarm business (NFB) sector of the economy rose at an annual rate of 1.9% between the third quarter of 1981 and the fourth quarter of 1984. Since then it has slowed a little but are projected to rise at 2.0% per year for the rest of the decade. At the same time, the average hours worked per week is projected to decline at an annual rate of 0.2% through 1990.

The combined effect of these two projections suggests that output per hour worked should continue to increase as it has, at varying rates, during the past. One reason for the optimism regarding productivity involves the acquisition of advanced knowledge and improved skills by the "Baby Boom Generation,"[10] which began to enter the labor force during the 1970s. Other reasons include recent trends toward increased business investment, deregulation in certain major industries such as transportation and telecommunications, a lower, more stable inflation rate, and the elimination of certain inefficient government programs.

During the Reagan Administration, interest rates dropped from a record 21% in 1980 to below 8% in early 1988. By the end of 1987, inflation had declined 9.4% age points from a high of 12% in 1981. This Administration attempted to increase business expansion by promoting exports and encouraging further deregulation.

Resources: Natural and Human

Economic productivity is closely related to the efficient allocation of both material and human resources. The United States has an abundance of both and it has traditionally been successful, through its policy of competitive free enterprise, in encouraging resources to find their most valued uses. "The nation has seen enormous reallocations of resources; out of agriculture and into other industries; from the Northeast (New England and the Foundry) to the South (Dixie) and the West (Mexamerica)."[11] The American labor force is exceptionally mobile—one out of every six American moves each year.[12] In search of more productive and personally satisfying employment, young people will frequently move from one job to another whether they are in the same or different regions of the country.

United States mineral resources include gold and silver, coal, natural gas and petroleum, bauxite, copper, iron ore, lead, phosphorus, potash, uranium, zinc, and a variety of different types of building stone. Much of the nation's mineral wealth is located in the vast territory of the Empty Quarter. Due to federal restrictions or lack of water required for extraction, many of these deposits are currently inaccessible.[13] As a result, the U.S. currently imports large amounts of antimony, asbestos, bauxite, cadmium, chrome, cobalt, iron ore, manganese, nickel, tin, and zinc. In 1986, 29% of the nation's petroleum requirement was imported from abroad. In addition to its mineral resources, the U.S. also has vast regions of fertile soil and forests, and large sources of water supply and power.

In a broad sense, the United States is largely self-sufficient when it comes to natural resources. Nevertheless, it is a strategic government policy not to exhaust all of the nation's natural resources. Besides this, some of the nation's natural resources are too expensive to extract and utilize at this time. When combined, these two conditions encourage the importation of a variety of resources from abroad.

Union Membership and Foreign Investment

Although union membership has steadily declined over the past decade, 5144 labor unions remain an important force in the U.S. economy. In 1986, almost 18% of the total employed wage and salary work force included union members. In that same year, approximately 30% of union membership was in the manufacturing sector (as compared to about 41% in 1974), and approximately 33% was in the governmental or public administration sector (as compared to about 14% in 1974). The remaining 37% union membership in the private sector include the following: mining; construction; transportation, communications, and public utilities; wholesale and retail trades; finance, insurance, and real estate; and services.

Unions typically engage in three levels of operation: local, national, and in association with other national unions. Many national unions are affiliated with the American Federation of Labor and Congress of Industrial Organizations (AFL-CIO). "The AFL-CIO concerns itself primarily with defining the jurisdiction of national unions, disciplining affiliated unions, and attempting to influence federal legislation of interest to it."[15] During recent years, union lobbyist activities in Congress have been routinely thwarted by the influence of the Business Roundtable, which represents the most powerful of America's "Big" businesses. "The Reagan White House remains aloof from the AFL-CIO, treating it with the same disdain fellow conservative Margaret Thatcher shows toward the British Trades Union Congress."[16] Not only are unions losing more of their registration drives, but more employers are winning decertification elections organized to get rid of unions.

Labor's attitude toward foreign investment is generally neutral depending on particular industries and economic circumstances. "It is when the economy is depressed, unemployment high, and foreign imports appear to compete unfairly in the domestic market that concern can become vocal at the national and local level."[17] Other than this, labor's attitude toward investment can be quite favorable, especially when such investment provides increased employment opportunities and fair competition with domestic industries.

Agricultural Policies

During the 1970s, U.S. agricultural exports increased fivefold due to several factors, including global economic growth, depreciation of the U.S. dollar, modifications in Soviet import policies, and crop failures in several areas around the world.

These conditions together with inflation dramatically raised farm income and, with expectations of inflation and low real interest rates, set in motion huge investment to expand the productive capacity of U.S. farming and agribusiness. Total U.S. farm debt rose from $49 billion to $155 billion during the 1970s and the average price of farmland more than threefold.[18]

But the global recession of 1981 combined with the rising value of the U.S. dollar, depressed world agricultural trade and reduced the competitiveness of U.S. agriculture in world markets. To compound the problem, the rigid price supports established by the Agriculture and Food Act of 1981 has lead to U.S. commodities being priced out of the world market.

Over the past five years, market conditions and U.S. agricultural policies have benefited other exporting countries, enabling them to expand their global markets at the expense of U.S. agriculture. As farm exports have become less competitive abroad, the number of U.S. farm failures has risen at an alarming rate, the number of agricultural workers have steadily declined, and excess capacity among U.S. agricultural producers has increased substantially.5194 Yet, despite their reduced global competitiveness, American farms and agribusiness remain highly mechanized and highly productive. U.S. agriculture continues to produce 50% of the world's -18- corn, about 30% of its oats and cotton, and about 15% of its wheat. In response to large surpluses of agricultural inventories, the Reagan Administration initiated a payment-in-kind program in early 1983 which was designed to encourage a voluntary reduction in planted acreage. As excess capacity subsides and as market conditions improve, it can be expected that U.S. agriculture will begin to regain a strong competitive position in world agricultural markets.

American Manufacturing

Although employment in the manufacturing sector has been steadily declining, the American manufacturing sector contributes approximately one-fourth of the nation's total output.

While employment in manufacturing has risen only 1.25 times what it was in 1947, the sector has expanded its output 3.5 times its 1947 level. It has done so by maintaining the growth of its productivity at a strong, average annual rate 2.6%.[20]In 1982, the U.S. gross manufacturing product was $630.9 billion.

The nation's largest industry involves food processing, followed by the coal and petroleum products industries. It is interesting to note that the Exxon Corporation, a U.S. petroleum producer, is ranked the largest corporation, according to annual sales, in the world. "The United States produces about two-fifths of the world's aluminum, about one-fifth of the automobiles, and processes about one-fifth of the world's meat. It is a leader in aeronautics, space, and computer technology."[21] Other major industries in the U.S. manufacturing sector include: machinery, chemicals, metal products, transportation equipment, paper and allied products, textiles and apparel, primary metals, and printing and publishing.

Of the goods and services produced in the U.S., about two-thirds of the total output is bought for personal use by individuals and households. The remainder is purchased by business, institutions, and government. Of U.S. personal consumption expenditures, some 15% are spent on durable goods (mainly automobiles), 20% on food, 20% on other nondurables, and the balance on services (largely housing and household operation).

Communications and Transportation in the United States

Communities throughout the United States are connected by a highly sophisticated telecommunications system which is fast, convenient, and efficient. The break-up of American Telephone and Telegraph (AT&T) has lead to increased domestic competition and subsequent reduction in long-distance telephone rates. Despite these recent developments, direct-dialed calls continue to be connected with split-second speed and accuracy. Telex communications are almost universally used throughout U.S. business and commerce. In addition, with the reduction in costs brought about by the advent of fiber optics technology, computer networking is gaining wider acceptance by American industry.

The U.S. transportation system is extensive, linking major metropolitan areas with other towns and cities as well as remote areas across the country.

> The major domestic airlines connect the major airports to smaller cities. Airlines and highways have reduced the importance of railroads as passenger carriers, but railroads continue to be the primary means of transporting freight. U.S. roads and highways cover nearly 4 million miles (6.4 kilometers); over 143 million motor vehicles use the system.[22]

Coastal waterways connect the ports along the Atlantic seaboard. The St. Lawrence River and the Great Lakes provide ocean-going vessels access to inland ports such as Cleveland, Toledo, Detroit, Chicago, and Duluth. In addition, the Mississippi and Missouri River basins connect the heart of the nation to New Orleans and Houston in the Gulf of Mexico.

America's Economic Vitality and the Services Sector

Over the past 30 years, the American economy has been gradually shifting from the production of goods to the production of services. Today, for every person employed in the manufacturing sector, there are three employed in the service sector. This represents about 70% of the more than 117 million workers in the U.S. labor force.

> Productivity gains in farming and manufacturing, which created more goods with less labor, have freed workers to provide services that a poorer society could not afford—more education, more health care, more financial services, more travel, more professional sports, more meals outside the home.[23]

Service industry employment is expected to increase at twice the rate of manufacturing jobs into the 1990s,[24] and this estimate does not even include the numerous service jobs which are already a part of the manufacturing sector.

Despite the fact that "the welfare of a society depends very importantly on the size of its GNP, economic welfare is not measured solely by the quantity of goods and services produced . . . A substantial part of the growth in the potential output of goods and services has historically been taken not in the form of greater actual output but in increased leisure."[25] By increasing output per hour, it has been possible for Americans to enjoy more time for consumption as well as more time for leisure.

Today, most Americans spend more years in school, work fewer hours per week, and enjoy earlier retirement than previous generations. Their accumulation of knowledge and skills, as well as the other ways they invest to improve their quality of life, are not readily reflected in Census data or statistical tables. Yet, as the U.S. Council of Economic Advisors points out, these trends are as integral to U.S. economic vitality as growth in real GNP.

CLIMATE FOR INTERNATIONAL TRADE WITH THE UNITED STATES

Foreign Investment and the Current U.S. Trade Deficit

As previously mentioned, the U.S. government has historically had a favorable attitude toward foreign investment (whether direct or portfolio in nature) and toward foreign trade. Throughout American history, foreign investors have enriched the U.S., aiding its growth and development through continued contributions of capital, technological innovations, labor, jobs, and cultural diversity. When viewed as a whole, "international trade contributes about 10% to the well-being—to the life, work, comfort, problems, and happiness—of Americans."[26]

In 1986, exports of goods and services combined were $372.8 billion, while total combined imports were $498.5 billion. Since 1984, the U.S. has experienced a dramatic decline in its current account position—the difference between exports and imports of merchandise and services, less net transfer payments made to foreign residents—which resulted in a deficit of more than $141 billion in 1986. The merchandise trade deficit alone increased by approximately $120 billion from 1980 "to reach an all-time high of over $144 billion."[27]

Three major factors are usually cited for the current trade deficit: the strong U.S. dollar, the faster rate of economic recovery and growth of the U.S. relative to its trading partners, and the reduction of U.S. exports to heavily indebted countries. Because of the dependence of each of these factors, it is inherently difficult to estimate their contribution to the dramatic increase in the U.S. trade deficit. Some recent trends regarding each, however, suggest their relative importance to the current U.S. economic climate.

American economic growth has exceeded most of its major industrialized trading partners (except Japan) by approximately two-thirds of a per cent per year since 1981. This rapid growth has accelerated spending, resulting in increased U.S. purchases of both domestic and imported materials and products. Slower growth in U.S. exports is partially attributable to the financial constraints of certain debt-ridden nations which have thereby been obligated to reduce their imports. Another reason for slow export growth is the fact that, until recently, American industry, unlike the industry of Japan or Western Europe, has never had to be export-oriented because of the huge size of its own domestic market.

By the end of 1984, the value of the U.S. dollar was almost 65% above its 1980 average (the last year that the U.S. international trade account was nearly in balance), and "at its highest level since flexible exchange rates were adopted in 1973."[28] Although it has fallen significantly since then, it is still strong. The strength of the U.S. dollar[29] has yielded some important benefits to the U.S. economy. During the dollar's rise, inflation and interest rates have declined dramatically, encouraging higher levels of investment and growth.

In many industries, particularly those in the manufacturing sector, increased foreign competition has encouraged increased expenditures on physical plant and equipment as well as research and development. In addition, international competition has motivated more companies to further reduce costs. The net result of all this activity has been the stimulation of industry-wide production, even in sectors less affected by international trade.

Trade Protectionism in the United States

The size of the current U.S. trade deficit has resulted in increased calls for trade protection and other forms of market intervention. This issue is the source of heated political debate between those who are for and against it.

> Despite unusually strong protectionist pressures, the Congress and the Administration put in place an omnibus trade law that generally supports freer trade. The major provision of the Trade and Tariff Act of 1984 renews until 1993 the Generalized System of Preferences, which eliminates tariffs on eligible imports . . . (notably textiles) are not included . . . Countries with a per capita gross national product exceeding $8,500 (a figure indexed to one-half the rate of U.S. economic growth) are ineligible for the program.[30]

During 1984, President Reagan rejected import relief in the case of the copper industry, citing the potential for serious damage to the copper fabricating industry as his major reason. In addition, he also rejected import relief for steel production, opting for negotiations of voluntary restraint agreements (VRAs) over the next five years instead.

Nevertheless, U.S. businesses and industries, particularly those which have been most adversely affected by foreign competition in domestic markets, are represented by professional lobbyists who continue to exert pressure on Congress in favor of more stringent protectionist measures. New interim regulations covering U.S. textile imports were announced in August 1984. Designed to help the U.S. Custom Service determine the country of origin of imported textiles, these regulations respond to "claims by domestic producers that foreign suppliers were circumventing relevant export restrict agreements by shipping parts of garments to other countries for superficial processing before final shipment to the United States."[31] With no immediate or significant improvement in the U.S. trade deficit in sight, protectionist "fever" has continued to build during 1985. Protection of current or potential American markets is one reason why more global marketers are considering direct foreign investment in the United States.

Percent import and export totals according to major commodity groupings are given in Table 4. By the end of 1986, the estimated value of foreign direct investment in the United States was about $209.3 billion. For the same year, total foreign assets in the U.S. (excluding banks) were approximately $855.5 billion.[32]

Governmental Administration and Control of Commerce

Foreign capital is admitted into the U.S. with no federal requirements for registration, and is treated in the same manner under the law as domestic capital. Foreign investors and importers are free to bring their own foreign funds into the U.S., or they can borrow from U.S. banks. They are also allowed to repatriate any capital and profits earned in the U.S.[33]

> With few exceptions, there are no restrictions on foreign ownership of U.S. corporations—public or private—and no restrictions on the acquisition of existing companies owned by U.S. shareholders. The restrictions that do exist are imposed for national security reasons in the areas of defense, communications, air transport, coastal shipping, and atomic energy.[34]

Foreign investors involved in businesses related to these restricted areas may wish to contact the International Trade Administration in the U.S. Department of Commerce.

Various governmental agencies regulate certain business and industry activities, such as the sale of investment securities to the public; compliance with antitrust and tax laws; foods, drugs, and other pharmaceutical products; consumer protection and occupational safety; environmental protection and pollution control; and labor relations. In addition, there are federal and state agencies responsible for the regulation of certain industries like banking, insurance, and utilities. Some of the major regulatory agencies are listed in Table 5.

There are a number of governmental agencies that provide information and technical assistance to foreign investors interested in entering the U.S. marketplace. Through its "Invest and the USA"

Table 4

Exports and Imports by

Major Commodity Groups 1986

	In United States Dollars (Millions)	
	Exports	Imports
Machinery	60,809	87,549
Transportation equipment incl. Motor vehicles and parts	34,026	74,013
Food and live animals	17,303	20,802
Chemicals	22,766	15,001
Crude materials (inedible), excl. fuels	17,324	10,432
Other manufactured goods	30,034	105,569
Mineral fuels, lubricants, etc.	8,114	37,310
Beverages and tobacco	2,920	3,866
Oils and fats, animal and vegatable	1,015	516
Others	13,065	14,903
Total	207,376	369,961

Source: U.S. Department of Commerce, Survey of Current Business, (October 1987).

program, the International Trade Administration (ITA) of the U.S. Department of Commerce provides information regarding markets, industries, financing, and other related topics. This agency can also help the international marketer to make contact with domestic firms seeking joint ventures, licensing and other franchise agreements, or other investment arrangements; and with other public and private agencies such as state industrial development agencies; and investment bankers seeking new business opportunities and enterprises for specific localities within the United States.

The U.S. Department of Commerce may be contacted through its Commercial Officers at the U.S. Embassy or U.S. Consulates in

Table 5
Major Regulatory Agencies Governing
United States Business Activities

1. Monopoly and Antitrust -- the Federal Trade Commission and the Antitrust Division of the U.S. Department of Justice.

2. Stock Exchange -- the Securities Exchange Commission (SEC).

3. Imports and Exports -- the U.S. Customs Office.

4. Foods and Drugs -- the Food and Drug Administration.

5. Pollution Control -- the Environmental Protection Agency.

6. Interstate Transportation -- the Interstate Commerce Commission.

7. Interstate Communication -- the Federal Communications Commission.

8. Banks -- the Federal Reserve System, the Federal Deposit Insurance Corporation, and state banking authorities.

9. Patents and Trademarks -- the U.S. Patent Office.

10. Copyrights -- the Copyright Office, Library of Congress.

Source: Price Waterhouse, <u>Doing Business in the United States.</u>

their native countries. Other incentive programs are offered to investors, both domestic and foreign, by the federal government through the U.S. Department of Housing and Urban Development, the Economic Development Administration, the Small Business Administration, and the U.S. Department of Agriculture.

Individual state and local governments compete for new business investment, domestic or foreign, by offering a variety of services. Some of these include industrial revenue bond financing for new plants or existing plant expansions, private development credit organizations, state funds for industrial park site development, and state funds for the training or retraining of local labor.[35] State and local industrial development agencies, particularly those with vacant factory space and/or high unemployment, are eager to attract foreign investment as a means of economic rejuvenation. One example of a successful match between a community and global marketer is the Nissan manufacturing facility in Smyrna, Tennessee.

The U.S. government operates 104 Foreign Trade Zones (FTZs) distributed throughout 42 states. These secured areas, equivalent to international free trade zones, enable both foreign and domestic goods to be imported, stored, exhibited, manufactured, or assembled, then cleared for export without formal customs entry. Any customs duties or quotas are only applied if or when the goods enter the U.S. market.

CONDUCTING BUSINESS IN THE UNITED STATES

Market Entry and Forms of Business Enterprise

The most direct way for international marketers to enter the U.S. market is to export finished goods to the United States. Foreign imports cannot clear customs without a predetermined consignee who is responsible for employing a licensed customhouse broker.[36] In addition, the consignee must present a bill of lading from the foreign exporter and a designated customs entry form in order for any goods to be allowed to enter the country.

Unless specifically exempted, all goods entering the United States are subject to import duty. In most cases, duties are applied according to the "transactional value" or the actual price the buyer pays the importer for the imported goods. If, for any reason, the transactional value cannot be determined, U.S. Customs will apply a duty based on equivalent merchandise. Other special duties, determined by the U.S. International Trade Commission, may be applied in cases where foreign imports are subsidized by their native governments, or when foreign goods are being sold at less than fair value.

> If a foreign enterprise does not presently trade with the United States, various import barriers, such as tariffs, quotas, and differing methods of customs valuation . . . add to the cost of market testing in the United States by means of preliminary export operations. These import barriers are of particular importance to the foreign enterprise that envisions the establishment of a U.S. sales subsidiary to market foreign- produced products.[37]

With the distinct possibility of increased U.S. protectionism in the coming years, the existence of import duties and trade barriers is another incentive for the international marketer to consider other methods of U.S. business operations and market entry.

United States law recognizes several forms of business enterprise which are formed and controlled under the laws of individual states. With minor differences, these state laws are fairly uniform throughout the nation. The most common forms of business enterprise conducted in the U.S. include: (a) franchising and licensing; (b) joint ventures; (c) sole proprietorships; (d) general partnerships; (e) limited partnerships; (f) branch of a foreign corporation; and (g) U.S. corporations.

Franchising and Licensing

Franchising involves a system of distribution in which a series of business establishments are operated as part of a regional or national "chain." The International Franchise Association defines franchising as a system whereby one company – the franchisor – grants the right and license – the franchise – to sell its product or service to another business – the franchisee.[38] Thus, the franchisor retains control of the distribution chain, whereas the franchisee is responsible for the daily operating functions of the business.

There are three types of franchising. "Trade name franchising" grants the franchisee the right to use a brand name. "Product distribution franchising" licenses a franchisee to sell specific products or services under the franchisor's brand name. "Pure franchising" allows the franchisee to use the franchisor's complete system of business.[39]

Franchising is a significant part of the U.S. economy. For example, in 1987, this form of business accounted for $591.3 billion or over 40% of U.S. retail sales. Today, a wide variety of products and services are marketed through franchises in the United States. Examples of traditional areas of franchising include automobile dealerships such as Chevrolet, Oldsmobile, and Lincoln-Mercury; gasoline stations such as Mobil, Exxon, and Texaco; soft drink bottlers such as Pepsi-Cola and Coca-Cola; fast-food restaurants such as McDonald's, Elby's, and Howard Johnson's; and hotel chains such as Holiday Inn and Ramada Inn. During the past few years, franchising has begun to expand into other areas such as personal computers, audio and video products, energy products, health foods, sporting goods, beauty salons, real estate, and even certain professional services.

Joint Ventures

A joint venture is an enterprise involving two business parties where each party shares in the profit of a specific business project or a single transaction. Depending on which provides the most favorable taxation position agreed on by both parties, the joint venture takes the form of a partnership (as in the proposed joint venture between South Korea's Pohang Iron & Steel Co. [Posco] and U.S. Steel Corp.) or a corporation.[40] Most joint ventures take the form of a special partnership[41] which is formed for a single project or transaction. Once the project is complete, the joint venture agreement terminates and the "special" partnership is dissolved. In other instances, two or more investors called joint venturers may either agree to purchase stock in an existing company or organize a new corporation.

In any joint venture, the degree of control held by each partner will be determined by the amount of equity contributed, the level of involvement or activity in the venture, or the degree of technical expertise, production capability, or innovativeness. If the joint venture is a 50-50 proposition (as in the proposed joint venture between Germany's Siemens AG and GTE Corp.[42]), each joint venturer contributes equally to the project. Joint ventures are particularly beneficial when the parties involved can contribute special expertise or complementary abilities which enable each to profit from the other's strengths.[43]

Large companies are advised to consult with the Federal Trade Commission (FTC) and the Antitrust Division of the U.S. Department of Justice before entering into a joint venture agreement. The U.S. federal antitrust laws are administered and enforced by the FTC and the U.S. Department of Justice. These laws are composed of several broadly worded statutes and decisions designed to limit the growth of monopoly, to encourage free competition in the marketplace, and to protect the existence of small businesses in the U.S. economy. Antitrust laws restrict joint ventures, mergers and acquisitions that will lessen free competition – particularly mergers and acquisitions of companies in the same line of business, companies that are sources of supply, or businesses that are current customers.

The successful establishment of a joint venture, merger, or acquisition will not prevent a subsequent investigation or challenge to its legality. "The FTC is empowered to initiate investigations, interpret questions of law, and issue orders for the cessation of actions in restraint of trade."[44] Thus, it behooves foreign investors to analyze the competitive environment of the U.S. market, and to submit any plans for joint venture investment to either the FTC or the Justice Department prior to making any final decisions or commitments.

Sole Proprietorships

Since virtually any individual may operate a sole proprietorship, it is the most common and energetic form of business enterprise in the United States. American business magazines repeatedly feature sensational accounts of basement/garage to Triple-A credit-rating success stories. Sole proprietorships are generally required to obtain various state and/or local permits. The sole proprietor is subject to unlimited liability such that all of his/her assets – business or personal – may be taken for debt incurred by the business.

Partnership

Partnerships are usually formed through contractual agreement between two or more parties. There are two basic types: general partnerships,[45] and limited partnerships. Each partner in the general partnership shares in the rights and obligations of all other partners; therefore, all are subject to unlimited liability for the partnership's debts. In the limited partnership, at least one partner must be designated as a general partner or personally liable for the partnership's debts. The limited partners do not participate in the management of the business and are, thus, only liable up to and including the amount of their capital investment in the partnership. Depending on the complexity of the partnership agreement, this type of business formation is generally inexpensive and expedient.

Branch or Division of a Foreign Corporation

Rather than operate as a U.S. subsidiary of a foreign parent company, the foreign investor may choose to operate as an American division or branch of the foreign firm. Although a foreign-owned branch usually involves a U.S. office or plant, branch operations may also be conducted by merely sending employees or agents to the U.S. on an occasional basis. Wandel & Goltermann, Inc., the United States subsidiary of Wandel & Goltermann Gmbh & Co., Eningen, Federal Republic of Germany, began to market products in the U.S. in the early 1960s through an agent.[46] (By 1966, the U.S. subsidary was officially incorporated as W&G Instruments.) Under U.S. law, the parent company may be held liable not only for the acts of its U.S. branch, but for its own acts, such as antitrust, securities regulation, and product liability, outside of the U.S. territory.

Incorporating in the United States

In contrast to a U.S. branch, the foreign parent company may opt to incorporate its U.S. business as a subsidiary of the parent firm. As implied in the preceding paragraph, U.S. incorporation will insulate the foreign parent company from any liability arising from its U.S. subsidiary operations. U.S. incorporation will require the parent firm to comply with the formalities of local law; but, it may also increase its ability to obtain local financing.

Once a year, *Forbes* magazine publishes a list of the 100 largest foreign firms in the United States. The top 10 from 1985 included Seagram Co. Ltd. (Canada), Anglo American of South Africa, Royal Dutch/Shell Group (Netherlands/United Kingdom), British Petroleum Plc., Mitsui & Co. Ltd. (Japan), EAT Industries Plc. (United Kingdom/Canada), Flick Group (Germany), Nestle (Switzerland), Regie Nationale des Usines Renault (France), and Tenglemann Group (Germany).[47] It should also be noted that some foreign investors prefer to enter the U.S. market through acquisition of existing U.S. companies. One example of this is Sweden's Electrolux, which acquired Tappan Corporation in 1979 and, more recently, White Consolidated Industries.[48]

Corporate operations are preferred by most large business enterprises, both domestic and foreign. U.S. law recognizes the corporation as a legal entity. As a result, the only debt liability incurred by the corporation's owners (or shareholders) is the amount of their investment in the corporation. In addition, the parent firm is not liable for the debts of its U.S. subsidiary.

Corporations are formed under the laws of the individual states. In general, laws governing the formation and existence of corporations are the same throughout the nation. To obtain a Certificate of Incorporation, the founding firm (domestic or foreign) is required to file articles of incorporation and bylaws with the appropriate state officials. These documents contain the name of the firm, its place of business, the objectives of the enterprise, the proposed amount of capital stock, and other information. The foreign firm has the option to retain 100% ownership of the subsidiary or to sell stock to domestic and foreign investors.

Once a year each corporation is required to file an annual report with the state of incorporation. This report describes various information about the corporation, such as its authorized shares, its outstanding shares, officers, and directors. Annual report information requirements and their due dates vary according to the state of incorporation.

> A corporation organized in one state must make certain filings with the appropriate authorities in other states before beginning to do business in those other states. Once those filings have been made, the corporation is usually required to file annual reports and pay franchise taxes in the other states in which it has qualified to do business.[49]

Information provided by corporations to states become matters of public record.

Business Climate and Corporate Culture

Free enterprise and the competitiveness that accompanies it are "The American Way." Directly or indirectly, business touches every facet of American life, and its vitality is closely aligned with the well-being and progress of the nation as a whole.[50] After spending more than a decade on an economic roller-coaster, Americans are becoming increasingly preoccupied with business. Economic and business news that would have been relegated to the back, of our newspapers 10 years ago, are today's headline. The nightly news frequently begins with updates on the consumer price index, current unemployment levels, and interest rates as well as the latest trends in international trade, corporate acquisitions, and business mergers.[51]

Part of the intrigue that business holds for many in the United States is "the American dream of the self-made man who rises from poverty to wealth and success. Another part of our fascination resides in a love-hate, attraction-revulsion attitude toward business and businessmen."[52] The courage, enthusiasm, and hard work which is required to expand a small business into a large, successful corporation is deeply admired and respected in the United States. "It is a residual strength of the American economy that it throws up so many risk-takers with an insatiable drive for success."[53] Despite this admiration and the importance of business to national livelihood, many Americans are intimidated by the power which the business, particularly the larger multinational corporations, wields over the nation.

Small businessmen and independent entrepreneurs are still vitally important to the United States economy. In 1984, 640,000 new businesses were formed in the United States as compared with 93,000 in 1950. Thus, the rate of new business formation has doubled nearly six times in less than 30 years. Nevertheless, American "Big Business" gets most of the business news coverage, even though the Fortune 500[54] list of the largest U.S. corporations has contributed few new jobs in recent years.[55] The nations new jobs are now created mostly by new and small businessmen.

Upon first introduction, the size of some of the companies in "Corporate America" is as mind-boggling as the size of the markets they serve.

> At General Motors and at many other giant American corporations the test of senior managers, and the test of a chief executive's success or failure, is to prevent the bureaucracy from stifling itself. General Motors employs more than 700,000; General Electric more than 400,000; IBM more than 300,000; AT&T close to a million.[56]

In most corporations, ownership has been divorced from control for the past 50 years. Today, the majority of both service and manufacturing corporations are managed by highly trained professionals. These employees are paid salaries and rewarded with bonuses for meeting specific objectives, and they are fired by the corporations' directors if they fail to produce desired results.

Today, U.S. managers are plagued by several major criticisms. One of the most scathing regards the overemphasis, on the part of American management, on short-term profits. Thanks in part to increased foreign competition, the times are changing as a steadily increasing number of U.S. management teams develop long-term strategic plans for corporate growth and profitability. In order to facilitate the implementation of long-range goals, corporations have also begun to explore new motivational reward systems, and human resource development programs.

Like other corporations around the world, American corporations have long had a tradition of business philanthropy. Many of the old barons of U.S. capitalism (for example, the Wharton, Colgate, Ford, Cornell, Rockefeller, Carnegie, Mellon, and Vanderbilt families, to name just a few) have set up nonprofit foundations to act as patrons of arts and letters, provide funds for community projects, and endow educational institutions. Despite this history, certain public constituencies such as consumer activists and ecologists have called for greater corporate social responsibility.

In response to this outcry and to avoid further government regulation and intervention, some companies are turning part of their creativity to the areas of innovation and improvement to social problems. A good example is Dow Chemical Company.

> By fine-tuning production processes and by recycling wastes to recover raw materials, Dow has been able to pay for its pollution control devices out of the profits from recovered chemicals while simultaneously reducing air and water pollution.[57]

By rising up to this kind of social responsibility, companies can satisfy the needs of their community, earn public esteem, achieve corporate goals, and profit.

The way to success in most U.S. corporations is to work hard, to display undying loyalty to the company, and to please upper-level management by demonstrating an outstanding ability to achieve desired objectives. Although the founders of many U.S. companies are still household names, today's chief executives are all but anonymous to the general public. Yet, U.S. corporations still retain their own distinctive subcultures. IBM is well known for its emphasis on courteous and efficient customer service. It is also well known for the conformity it demands from its employees.

> Levi Strauss and J.C. Penney are motivated by enlightened self-interest, assuming that customers will remain loyal if they get their money's worth. . . . An overly fat profit is seen as unfair to customers and so against the chain store's interest. In recessions, employees at J.C. Penney are not laid off since the store believes loyalty is a two-way thing. Most of this would be regarded as sentimental softheadedness at Donald Kendall's Pepsi Co, where the average executive tenure is ten years, versus thirty-three at J.C. Penney.[58]

The differences between U.S. corporations are, however, less striking than the similarities. Despite the increasing numbers of women and minorities entering the workplace, American management continues to be overwhelmingly white, male, and Christian. Virtually all businesses work an eight-hour day, Monday through Friday, allowing for a one-hour lunch break in the middle of the day. Americans, particularly businessmen, are very time conscious.

Adherence to timetables and punctuality are the rule rather than the exception.[59]

American business has traditionally been product-driven, emphasizing short-term profit. The economic displacement created by increased imports and other forms of foreign competition has thrust U.S. industry into a period of transition, forcing manufacturers to compete for market share in a more demanding marketplace. As a result of this upheaval, American commerce is entering a period of "restructuring" which, according to DeVittorio,[60] will be characterized by three broad industry-wide trends: (a) internationalization; (b) industry realignment; and (c) incremental implementation of computerized systems such as MRP II, MIS CAD/CAM, and CIS.

The most distinguishing feature of this latest transformation is that it is heavily market-driven. During this restructuring process, manufacturers, suppliers, and distributors will have to reevaluate and rationalize their entire approaches to marketing. In order to increase customer satisfaction, marketing strategies will need to emphasize improved quality, greater variety, and reduced costs.

A MARKET FOCUS APPROACH
TO U.S. MARKET ENTRY

The characteristics of the United States — the vast size of its population and territory, the diversity and sophistication of its consumption demands and tastes, the affluence of its standard of living, the receptivity of its people to changes and innovations — continue to make it the most lucrative marketplace of the world, and one which continues to be attractive to international marketers and investors. However, for those who wish to enter the United States market, the same characteristics which make it so attractive can also make it somewhat intimidating.

How can the risk associated with U.S. market entry be minimized? Knowledge of the mechanics of market entry — the options, the procedures, the regulations, the competitors — is certainly valuable yet, by itself, not sufficient enough to ensure success. Experience has shown, in numerous cases, that a low-cost, innovative, and technically outstanding product (or service) does not necessarily guarantee increased profits or market share for its producers.

Fancy features and price leadership will not compensate for the failure to meet customer requirements or expectations.

Among all of the companies in any industry (be they product-producing or service-producing) there are always a few which, through their superior competitive performance in the marketplace, maintain a leadership position. Gustin has noted the common characteristic among these leading companies"is their overwhelming market focus – a focus that enables them to identify and meet the needs of major customer groups in ways that earn them first place in their markets."[61] The competitive edge provided by a well-defined market focus can enhance market entry and penetration.

The establishment of market focus requires that planning and implementation of marketing strategies become customer-driven rather than product- or service-driven. For many companies, particularly those traditionally driven by their research and development activities, the shift to market focus will also require a reversal of corporate "mind-set." Because return on investment (ROI) on production-oriented investments are more readily estimated and demonstrated than ROI on market-oriented investments, many firms are more willing to spend on new plants, production equipment, and technologies than they are on marketing.

To become market-focused, these production-oriented companies must *first* distinguish between "marketing" and "sales." Marketing is a process which involves the identification of current (and/or future) needs and desires of target customers, and the development of products and related services consistent with those needs and desires.[62] The process of marketing should involve every functional area within a firm – from the initial conceptualization of the product offering to final delivery to the customer.[63] Sales is one function of marketing. By definition, it is the process by which a specific product line is "sold" to individual customers in targeted market segments. Other marketing functions include product development, packaging, advertising, promotion, distribution, and customer service.

Companies which have a market focus "mind-set" understand that the essence of marketing involves listening to existing and potential customers. By distinguishing between marketing and sales, these firms are able to tailor their products and services to the needs and desires of their target market. This, in turn, simplifies the sales effort — enabling the sales force to promote product features which are meaningful and beneficial to customers.

Leading companies are market-oriented. They recognize that, in most cases, increased expenditures on marketing can have a more positive impact on corporate profitability than increased expenditures in engineering and production. For global marketers, the need to invest in market research cannot be overemphasized. Although market research can be expensive and time-consuming, it provides management with valuable insights regarding market opportunities and challenges. Management can then use this information to fine-tune and update its market objectives and strategies. These modifications may involve increased expenditures in other areas of the firm's marketing effort, such as product redesign, sales force expansion, or a new advertising campaign.

Leading companies rely on ongoing market research to continually identify and define the most important market segments for their products, and to develop and provide the product specifications required by key customers within each targeted segment. Meaningful market segments are based on the specific buying characteristics of the customers within each sub-division. The markets for consumer products are usually segmented according to various demographic, socioeconomic, and psychographic characteristics. Segmentation of industrial products is frequently based on end-use application, production economics, and size and location of customer firms.

Customer-driven segmentation enables creative companies to differentiate their products from those of their competitors. Global marketers who wish to begin U.S. market entry on a small scale may wish to look for highly specialized segments. These segments usually possess unique traits and needs which have either been overlooked or ignored by competitors. Marketers who pursue this "niche" strategy are typically able to "sustain premium prices for their products based on the product's differential value — that is, its worth to the customer as a result of its special features."[64] Thus, differences in product specifications are the marketing tactic used to gain competitive edge.

The utilization of ongoing market research during the segmentation process can provide valuable input for the development of marketing objectives and strategies. For example, information obtained from this process can help the international marketer to prioritize target segments and to identify key customer accounts within each segment. Knowledge of the nature and characteristics of strategic accounts can provide insights regarding which channel (or channels) of distribution will most effectively deliver the firm's goods and services to its key customers.

Effective segmentation schemes provide a customer-oriented framework around which marketing activities can be organized. Market-focused companies organize their strategic market units (SMUs) around their priority segments instead of their product lines. Each unit has its own sales force and market manager. This type of arrangement facilitates the coordination of marketing and sales efforts. Rather than an end in itself, segment-based organization is a means of attaining strategic goals — such as increased market share, profit performance, and competitive advantage — by becoming more responsive to the dynamics of the marketplace.

Successful entry into the United States marketplace is not so much a problem of exporting or selling, as it is a marketing challenge. Those who have achieved success have acquired an understanding of the structure and nature of this nation and its society. More importantly, they have also acquired a customer orientation which has enabled them to become market-focused rather than product-driven. Leading companies in the American marketplace understand that the perceived value of any product (or service) does not rely exclusively on the sophistication of its design or the innovativeness of its technology. Instead, the perceived value, and thus the inherent marketability, of a product depends more on the compatibility of product design and technology with the requirements of customers within targeted segments.

Entering the American marketplace is a broad objective which must be converted into a comprehensive plan of action. By following detail-oriented, investigative steps in the development of marketing strategies, global marketers can achieve a differential advantage and competitive position in United States markets.

ENDNOTES

1. Edmund Fawcett and Tony Thomas, *The American Condition* (New York, NY: Harper & Row Publishers, Inc., 1982), p. 11.

2. Joel Garreau, *The Nine Nations of North America* (Boston, MA: Houghton Mifflin, 1981). Garreau's perspective, is by no means, the only regional approach to understanding the United States. The U.S. government uses a variety of regional schemes. One example is shown in Map 1. For a review of various regional approaches, see Raymond D. Gastil, *Cultural Regions of the United States* (Seattle, CA: University of Washington Press, 1975).

3. Alan J. Resnik, Harold E. Sand, and J. Barry Mason, "Marketing Dilemma in the '80s," *California Management Review* 24 (Fall 1981), pp. 49-57.

4. Ben J. Wattenberg and David Gergen, "Attitudes," in *Reflections of America: Commemoration of the Statistical Abstract Centennial*. Norman Cousins, Honorary Ed. (Washington, DC: U.S. Government Printing Office, 1980), p. 22.

5. It should be noted that the term "life expectancy" does not refer to the current average life span, but rather to the expected duration of life at birth.

6. According to the U.S. Bureau of the Census, all persons occupying a single housing unit (such as a house or an apartment) are referred to as a "household." All persons living in a household who are related to each other (by blood, adoption, or marriage) are regarded as one family. Thus, while all families are households, not every household is considered to be a family.

7. U.S. Department of Commerce, Bureau of the Census, *Statistical Abstract of the United States 1988*, 108th Edition (Washington, DC: U.S. Government Printing Office, 1988), p. 444.

8. U.S. Department of Commerce, *Statistical Abstracts of the United States 1988*, p. 304.

9. Fawcett and Thomas, pp. 50-51.

10. The "Baby Boom Generation" consists of the 76 million Americans born between 1946 and 1964. In contrast, the "Baby Bust Generation" refers to the generation directly following Baby Boomers.

11. U.S. President *Economic Report of the President, Together with the Annual Report of the Council of Economic Advisors* (Washington, DC: U.S. Government Printing Office, 1985), p. 42.

12. Price Waterhouse, *Doing Business in the United States* (New York, NY: Price Waterhouse, 1985), p. 34.

13. Garreau, p. 302.

14. The overall decline in union membership in the United States may be attributed to the combination of several recent trends or factors. These include:

1. The increasingly sophisticated and enlightened labor management practices have hindered many of the recent union registration drives, and in some instances, have even led to union decertification

2. The introduction of new technologies, (e.g., microprocessors, robotics,

CAD/CAM) has made certain jobs obsolete, particularly in the heavy manufacturing sector of the economy, where unions have been historically more prevalent

3. According to the U.S. Industrial Outlook 1985, most of the new jobs in the United States are being created in the services sector of the economy — a sector which U.S. labor unions have never fully penetrated

4. During the past decade a significant number of industries and population have moved to the Sunbelt areas of Dixie and Mexamerica — regions which are characterized by a conservative work ethic of rural independence and anti-union sentiment

5. With increasing levels of education and vocational training, a greater proportion of the labor force identifies with management viewpoints than ever before

6. The increasing numbers of the labor force seeking second-income employment on a short-term or part-time basis, are less interested in the labor movement than full-time, long-term workers.

15. Price Waterhouse, p. 52.
16. Fawcett and Thomas, p. 80.
17. Price Waterhouse, p. 15.
18. U.S. President, p. 36.
19. Ibid, and Price Waterhouse.
20. J. M. DeVittorio, "The Restructuring of Corporate America," (University Park, PA: MBA Association, November 26, 1985), p. 2.
21. Price Waterhouse, p. 9.
22. Price Waterhouse, p. 10.
23. DeVittorio, p. 3.
24. Alexander B. Trowbridge, Jr., "Business," in *Reflections in America: Commemorating the Statistical Abstract Centennial*, Norman Cousins, Honorary Ed. (Washington, DC: U.S. Government Printing Office, 1980), p. 30.
25. U.S. President, p. 39.
26. J. A. Livingston, "International Trade," in, *Reflections of America: Commemorating the Statistical Abstract Centennial*, Norman Cousins, Honorary Ed. (Washington, DC: U.S. Government Printing Office, 1980), p. 128.
27. U.S. Department of Commerce, *Statistical Abstract of the United States*, 1988, p. 422.
28. *Ibid*, p. 103.
29. From 1980 through 1984, the real rate of exchange for the U.S. dollar (the nominal exchange rate adjusted for consumer price levels in the U.S. and abroad) rose by about 60%. This increase was only slightly less than the dollar's nominal rate of exchange. The combination of several factors contributed to the strength of the U.S. dollar by the end of 1984. These include:

1. Beginning in 1979, U.S. real interest rates rose — with a brief interruption in mid-1980 — until they peaked in 1982. Although interest rates abroad were also increasing during the same period, they did so at a lower rate than those

in the United States. Since 1982, U.S. interest rates have declined, but despite this fact, they are still relatively at high levels.

2. The tighter U.S. monetary policy initiated in 1979 lead to subsequent declines in U.S. inflationary rates, as well as to increases in the expected real return on U.S. dollar assets.

3. The Economic Recovery and Tax Act of 1981, when combined with reduced inflation, helped to raise the real return on U.S. business investment. The increases on this type of ROI carried over to returns on dollar-denominated assets in general, but more specifically to the U.S. dollar itself.

30. U.S. President, p. 111.

31. *Ibid*, p. 113.

32. U.S. Department of Commerce, *Survey of Current Business* (Washington, DC: U.S. Government Printing Office, October 1987).

33. U.S. Department of Commerce, International Trade Administration, *Invest in the USA: A Guide for the Foreign Investor* (Washington, DC: U.S. Government Printing Office, 1981), p. 32.

34. Price Waterhouse, p. 14.

35. For additional information about state and local assistance programs, refer to the International Trade Administration's *Invest in the USA: A Guide to the Foreign Investor* and to Price Waterhouse's *Doing Business in the United States.*

36. Although U.S. customs regulations do not require a license to import merchandise into the United States, the Customs Service is required to enforce licensing requirements which are imposed by other U.S. government agencies. These requirements may apply to specific products, certain quantities of specific products, or products which originate from specific countries. Some of the products subject to these import license requirements include cotton, dairy and agricultural products, certain drugs, lead and zinc, liquor, meat and meat products, plants and animals, petroleum products, sugar, products covered by the Philippine Trade Act of 1946, and products which originate in certain communist countries.

37. Price Waterhouse, p. 39.

38. Norman M. Scarborough and Thomas W. Zimmerer, *Effective Small Business Management* (Columbus, OH: Charles B. Merrill Publishing, Co., 1985), pp. 88-90.

39. For information regarding the laws which govern franchising, refer to Ronald A. Anderson and Walter A. Kumpf, *Business Law: Principles and Cases* (Cincinnati, OH: South-Western Publishing, Co., 1975), pp. 923-928.

40. William C. Symonds, "To Beat the Foreign Competition, U.S. Steel Joins It," *Business Week* (December 30, 1985-January 6, 1986), No. 2927, p. 55.

41. In general, joint venture agreements are subject to the same state laws that govern partnerships and corporations. For further discussion, see the "Partnerships" and "Incorporating in the United States" sections.

42. John Williamson, GTE-Siemens Venture Heats Up Competition in Switch Systems," *Telephony* (January 27, 1986), Vol. 210, No. 4, p. 13.

43. For more about joint ventures, seen Anderson and Kumpf, pp. 928-934.

44. Price Waterhouse, p. 21.

45. Each state has its own general partnership statute: however, many states have modeled their statutes after the Uniform Partnership Act (UPA). For additional information on partnerships and the UPA, see Anderson and Kumpf, pp. 876-878, 879-901, and 907-915.

46. Larry Lannon, "Wandel & Goltermann Dedicates U.S., HQ,"*Telephony* (April 1, 1985), Vol. 208, No. 13, pp. 21-22.

47. "100 Largest Foreign Investments in the U.S.," *Forbes* (July 29, 1985), Vol. 136, No. 3, pp. 180-185.

48. "White Finally Bows to Electrolux,"*Business Week* (March 24, 1986), No. 2938, p. 42.

49. Price Waterhouse, p. 42.

50. Daniel A. Wren, "Business: The Changing Scene,"in *Issue and Ideas in America*, Benjamin J. Taylor and Thurman J. White, eds.(Norman, OK: University of Oklahoma Press, 1976), p. 63.

51. Fawcett and Thomas, 1982.

52. Wren, p. 63.

53. Fawcett and Thomas, p. 60.

54. This listing of the 500 largest U.S. corporations is published annually by *Fortune* magazine.

55. John Naisbitt, *Megatrends* (New York City, NY: Warner Books, Inc., 1982).

56. Fawcett and Thomas, p. 66.

57. Wren, p. 87.

58. Fawcett and Thomas, p. 68.

59. For more about U.S. corporate culture, See Terrence E. Deal and Allan A. Kennedy, *Corporate Cultures* (Reading, MA: Addison-Wesley Publishing, Co., 1983).

60. DeVittorio, p. 10.

61. Bernard H. Gustin, "Achieving Strong Market Focus: A Challenge for Top Management," *Price Waterhouse Review* (No. 3, 1985), p. 3.

62. The American Marketing Association defines "marketing" as "the process of planning and executing the conception, pricing, promotion, and distribution of ideas, goods, and services, to created exchanges that satisfy individual and organizational objectives."

63. Thomas J. Peters and Robert H. Waterman, *In Search of Excellence* New York, NY: Harper & Row Publishers, 1982.

64. Gustin, 1985, p. 4.

BIBLIOGRAPHY

American Marketing Association, (1985). American Marketing Association Board Approves New Marketing Definition, *Marketing Educator* (Spring), 4.

Anderson, R. A. and Kumpf, W. A. (1982). *Business Law: Principles and Cases*, Cincinnati, OH: South-Western Publishing Co.

Deal, T. E. and Kennedy, A. A. (1982). *Corporate Cultures*, Reading, MA: Addison-Wesley Publishing Co.

DeVittorio, J. M. (1985). The Restructuring of Corporate America. A speech presented to the MBA Association, College of Business Administration, University Park, PA: The Pennsylvania State University (November 26).

Garreau, J. (1981). *The Nine Nations of North America*, Boston MA: Houghton Mifflin.

Gustin, B. H. (1985). Achieving Strong Market Focus: A Challenge for Top Management, *Price Waterhouse Review*, (3).

Kelley, E. J. and Hearne, L. R. (forthcoming). The New Rules for Marketing Leadership: Managing for Today and Tomorrow in World Society, *Fruits and Problems of the Japanese Way of Marketing*, Tokyo: Japan Marketing Association.

Lannon, L. (1985). Wandel & Goltermann Dedicates U.S. HQ, *Telephony*, (April 1), 208 (13), 21.

Livingston, J. A. (1980). International Trade. In: Norman Cousins (Honorary Ed.) *Reflections of America: Commemorating the Statistical Abstract Centennial*, U.S. Department of Commerce, Bureau of the Census, Washington, DC: U.S. Government Printing Office.

Library of Congress (1976). *Geography, Maps, Anthropology, Recreation*, 4th edition, Library of Congress Classification G, Washington, DC: Library of Congress, Cataloging Distribution Service Division.

Micklos, J., Jr. (1986). Ten Trends That Will Change Delaware Business Forever, *Delaware Today* (January), 55-80.

Naisbitt, J. (1982). *Megatrends*, New York, NY: Warner Books, Inc.

Naisbitt, J. and Aburdene, P. (1985). *Re-inventing the Corporation*, New York, NY: Warner Books, Inc.

Peters, T. J. and Waterman, R. H. (1982). *In Search of Excellence*, New York, NY: Harper & Row Publishers, Inc.

Pinchot, G., III (1985). *Intrapreneuring*, New York, NY: Harper & Row Publishers, Inc.

Price Waterhouse (1985). *Doing Business in the United States*, New York City, NY: Price Waterhouse.

Resnik, A. J., Sand, H. E., and Mason, J. B. (1981). Marketing Dilemma in the '80s, *California Management Review* (Fall), 24, 49-57.

Scarborough, N. N. and Zimmerer, T. W. (1984). *Effective Small Business Management*, Columbus, OH: Charles E. Merrill Publishing Co.

Symonds, W. C. (1986). To Beat the Foreign Competition, U.S. Steel Joins It, *Business Week* (December 30-January 6) (2927), 55.

Trowbridge, A. B., Jr. (1980). Business. In Norman Cousins, (Honorary Ed.) *Reflections of America: Commemorating the Statistical Abstract Centennial*, U.S. Department of Commerce, Bureau of the Census, Washington, DC: U.S. Government Printing Office.

U.S. Department of Commerce (1984). *Survey of Current Business*, Washington, DC: U.S. Government Printing Office (October).

U.S. Department of Commerce (1982). International Trade Administration, *Attracting Foreign Direct Investment to the United States: A Guide for Government*, Washington, DC: U.S.Government Printing Office.

U.S. Department of Commerce (1981). International Trade Administration, Office of Export Marketing Assistance, *Invest in the USA: A Guide for the Foreign Investor*, Washington, DC: U.S. Government Printing Office.

U.S. Department of Commerce (1985). International Trade Administration, Office of Trade and Investment Analysis, *United States Trade: Performance in 1984 and Outlook*, Washington, DC: U.S. Government Printing Office.

U.S. Department of Commerce, Bureau of the Census (1985). *Statistical Abstract of the United States 1985*, 105 Edition, Washington, DC: U.S. Governmental Printing Office.

U.S. Department of Commerce Bureau of the Census (1985). *U.S. Industrial Outlook 1985*, Washington, DC: U.S. Government Printing Office.

U.S. National Commission for UNESCO (1974). Traditional Values in the United States. Reprinted in Ralph H. Gabriel (Ed.) *American Values, Continuity and Change*, Westport, CT: Greenwood Press.

U.S. President (1985). Economic Report of the President, Transmitted to Congress, February 1985: Together with the Annual Report of the Council of Economic Advisors, Washington, DC: U.S. Government Printing Office.

Wattenberg, B. J. and Gergen, D. (1980). Attitudes. In: Norman Cousins (Honorary Ed.) *Reflections of America: Commemorating the Statistical Abstract Centennial*, U.S. Department of Commerce, Bureau of the Census, Washington, DC: U.S. Government Printing Office.

White Finally Bows to Electrolux, *Business Week*, 24, 1986) (2938), 42.

Williamson, J. (1986). GTE-Siemens Venture Heats Up Competition in Switch Systems, *Telephony* (January 27), 210 (4), 13.

Wren, D. A. (1976). Business: The Changing Scene. In: Benjamin J. Taylor and Thurman J. White, (Eds.) Issues and Ideas in America, Norman, OK: University of Oklahoma Press.

Part 3

The Future

Chapter 17

Epilogue

V. H. (Manek) Kirpalani
Eugene J. Kelley
Erdener Kaynak
Lisa R. Hearne

International businessmen need a view of the future and more knowledge of a number of factors in order to develop their strategy and plans effectively. Therefore this final chapter addresses the prospects for the world marketplace in the early 21st century and comments on the trends. Next, it proceeds to look at global marketing and global strategy management. It then concludes by discussing countertrade, since this is most helpful for international business. A caveat is in order: no one may forecast the future with certainty. Please read the following with that caution in mind.

PROSPECTS AND TRENDS
IN THE WORLD MARKETPLACE

The world economy is predicted to become more affluent over the next few years. Gross world product (GWP) should increase from half again to double its present size by 2001 A.D. This implies a real growth rate of 2.3% to 4% a year. The post-World War II rate has been between 3 to 4%. Almost all countries are encouraging population control and certainly in Western nations population stabilization may be achieved early in the 21st century. Furthermore, in many LDCs rising living standards, education in birth control, and other measures have started to reduce the birthrate. For example, the People's Republic of China has over 1 billion people, roughly a quarter of the world population.[1] The government has decreed that each couple should have only one child. If a couple has more than one child the working parent(s) will not receive promotion and will lose some housing entitlements and other state-given benefits. This policy is already slowing the birth rate. The combination of an increasing GWP and slower population growth implies that on average, world per capita real economic growth by 2001 A.D. is expected to reach a level some 25% to 50% above that which prevails at present. Furthermore, a continuation of the historical relationship between economic growth and international trade since World War II will then result in world exports continuing to expand at an average 5% to 7% per year.

The only national economies that are gaining world economic share are Japan and a group of fast-growing, middle-income nations: Brazil, Hong Kong, South Korea, Taiwan, and the ASEAN group. The OPEC nations looked as if they were also going to gain, but the oil price drop of the early 1980s caused by conservation plus world recession and the growth in new oil and natural gas supplies seems to have removed them from the fast track. The remarkable growth record of Hong Kong, South Korea, and Taiwan may also slow somewhat.[2] These smaller nations, unlike China and India, do not have large enough national markets to allow for self-sufficient economic growth. Also, in the recession of the mid 1980s, Western markets had turned protectionist and Western labor had raised strong protests against MNCs transferring technology and subcontracting work to countries with lower cost labor.

Two other factors have become very important. First is the advancement of computer aided design/computer aided technology. This may lead Western MNCs to move some operations back home; evidence of this already exists. Factories in which hundreds of poorly paid workers patiently make and assemble pieces may soon be obsolete; wages are rising in the middle-income Southeast Asian countries. Second, a few LDCs may become significant in world economic terms. China may be one because it has the world's largest cheap labor force and has an oil surplus. Similarly, Brazil and India have large populations and strong resource bases, although both are presently oil importers.

World Trade and Foreign Direct Investment

What of the global marketplace? If the world economy is expected to grow, then part of that growth will be caused by significant growth of the international marketplace. The factors are in place. Within the Organization for Economic Cooperation and Development (OECD), tariffs are very low for most products and nontariff barriers are gradually being lowered. Capital is flowing relatively freely across the OECD countries. The LDCs are being drawn by this vortex. Most of the nonoil LDCs are heavily borrowing external finance to sustain growth. This external finance has to be serviced by foreign exchange, which means that these LDCs have to increase their exports. Further, as growth occurs in LDCs, their imports will rise due to higher demand for capital equipment, plus demand for some intermediates from the newer exporting industries. For example, many OPEC nations are continuing to build infrastructure and industry and their imports will keep climbing.

The directions and flows of products are changing. For example, it is now accepted that economic revival in the West is not going to produce a boom in steel production, but the industry will be transformed in the next few years as international trade in semifinished steel opens up. Ore producers such as Brazil want to upgrade their own output on the spot. Brazil and Mexico already have surplus steel capacity which they aim to use to earn foreign exchange. Similarly, producers of bauxite and other ores for nonferrous metals are already building their own smelters. Usually this is done with the help of MNCs which are not expanding in OECD nations due to the high cost of production there. The transfer of technological expertise around the world coupled with the comparative advantage of low labor costs in LDCs have led to a rapid decline in heavy industries such as steel and shipbuilding in the industrialized West. There has also been more competition from LDC exports in many mature product industries. Therefore, the richer nations will have to restructure their industries into high productivity sectors where a comparative advantage exists for advanced technology and skilled labor. Some of these sectors will emerge from the new advances in electronics. The West also has an advantage in the service industries, particularly financial services and transportation.

Another trend is that the industrialized countries are becoming much more interdependent in the manufacturing sector. For example, U.S. imports in the early 1980s accounted for 19% of its steel, 28% of its autos, 55% of its consumer electronic products, and 27% of its machine tools demand.[3] This heavier import pattern is repeated in most of the industrialized nations. It takes just months for Japanese companies to analyze and copy the American microchips that drive the latest computer. They then export the copies to the U.S.

The trend in foreign direct investment across the rich nations is likely to continue as exporters will always be concerned about the possibility of more protectionism as these economies restructure their mature industries. Thus, for the foreseeable future, MNCs are probably going to prosper. Foreign direct investment in the U.S. has tripled over the past five years, and 10% of all recent takeovers in the U.S. have been by foreign MNCs. Foreign-owned firms now generate about 3 to 4% of American jobs, 4 to 5% of sales and, in some industries, 10% of production, although direct foreign investment in the U.S. at $100 billion is still less than half the value of U.S. MNC investment abroad.

Global Consumer Trends

This section builds on changes that are sweeping the U.S. marketplace and are extending themselves across the Western world. Nothing is more certain about life in America and the U.S. market than its ongoing change. As part of the New World, America always seems to be on the verge of being completed, and yet, is somehow never quite finished. This is a young country relative to other nations in the world and, as a result, Americans tend to keep their backs to the past and their faces to the future. This is perhaps one reason why America is so adaptive to change. Whatever the reason, receptivity to changes and innovations is a unique feature of U.S. "consumption culture" and one which broadens the scope of opportunities for imaginative and innovative marketers. Today this emphasis on consumption is permeating the world as media reaches all over the globe and affluence grows. Eight key trends are currently transforming the U.S. business and consumer marketplace. Similar trends are affecting the other industrialized economies.

1. An Evolving Economy Stimulated by the Rapid Growth of the Service Sector

The United States is seeing the dawn of a new economic era where rapid increases in the numbers of white-collar workers herald the development of an economic system which produces more services and information than hard goods. This same trend is sweeping across all the industrialized nations. John Naisbitt,[4] author of the bestseller *Megatrends*, has suggested that while the LDCs continue to take over labor-intensive industries such as textile and steel production, the emerging U.S. economy will be based more on knowledge and savvy than on sweat. In the near future, the number of professional workers, e.g., lawyers, physicians, managers, accountants, and consultants, is projected to exceed the numbers in any other job category.[5] Growth in the size and diversity of the service sector has been accompanied by a corresponding increase in worker compensation. Service wages are currently growing, and should continue to grow, faster than manufacturing wages.

As employment in service-related jobs has grown, employment in manufacturing-related jobs has steadily declined. New technologies, such as computers, microprocessors, and cybernetics, have made increases in productivity and efficiency possible, while increased competition, both domestic and international, have made them necessary. As a result, manufacturing in the advanced industrialized nations will continue to play a major role in the economy but will operate with a leaner, more highly skilled labor force. It should be remembered that much of the growth in service-related jobs has actually taken place in the manufacturing sector as new technologies and increased competition have also necessitated the hiring of highly educated managers, researchers, technicians, and other support personnel. For international businessmen this implies a growing global market in the transfer of technology between the advanced service economies and the manufacturing based LDCs.

2. Increasing Value of Information and Technology in a Competitive Marketplace

As the computer and telecommunications age has shifted into high gear in the United States, it has been accompanied by an information explosion and technological revolution. The main labor force of the emerging economic era consists of everyone who is involved in the business of dispensing advice, communicating knowledge and information, or solving problems. This force includes electronics manufacturers and retailers, telecommunications operators and technicians, network and cable broadcasters, professional managers and administrators, educators and researchers, as well as consultants in a variety of different fields and disciplines.

Millions of Americans currently use computers in work, at school, and at home; their numbers will continue to grow as software improves and hardware prices drop. This is happening across the Western world and Japan. Computer industry sales are expected to continue growing in the future. Much of this increase will be subtle as microcomputers continue to be incorporated as components in other systems. Some examples include microprocessor thermostats, boiler controls, refrigerators, microwave ovens, and automobiles; and computerized process control, air conditioning, and security systems. Robotics is likely to experience more rapid growth as industries seek further improvements in productivity and manufacturing efficiency. In Japan and Sweden, there are proportionally more robots than in the U.S. Another potential growth area is artificial intelligence which involves the computer accumulation and application of expert knowledge in a specific field of inquiry.

These trends suggest that in the advanced economies, much of today's paperwork will ultimately be replaced by the electronic distribution of information. The offices of tomorrow will become highly computerized and white-collar employees will access computers as easily as they currently access telephones.

3. Growth in Entrepreneurial and Intrapreneurial Activities in Commerce and Industry

The rapid growth of services and information has created numerous opportunities for entrepreneurs and small business development. The U.S. exemplifies what is happening throughout the Western world. Although big business is better known through established company names and brands, growth in new jobs is being fueled by the accelerating number of new small businesses being formed. This is not to say that big business is stagnating, only that the small business sector is taking off. Some examples of businesses which have begun to capitalize on new technologies and trends in society include computer and video outlets, health and fitness centers, day-care centers, and financial consulting.

Self-employed professional consultants represent a significant portion of new businesses in the services sector. Many of these consultants are retirees who work on a part-time basis to supplement their retirement income. Most, however, are highly skilled and educated members of the "Baby Boom" generation – the 76 million Americans born between 1946 and 1964 – who are turning to entrepreneurial activities in response to a tightening job market. In 1975, approximately 10 people competed for every mid-career position available, and, by 1995, an estimated 30 to 40 will compete for the same mid-level jobs. This partially explains the growing trend toward entrepreneurship by Baby Boomers. Unable to obtain traditional advancement in corporate settings, increasing numbers of them turn to consulting or open their own businesses in order to achieve their financial and career objectives.

Companies are becoming increasingly reliant on outside consultants as they seek ways to reduce their total personnel and the exorbitant expense associated with employee benefits, which currently range between 35 and 44% of worker compensation. As long as benefit costs remain high and there is a sufficient supply of educated experts, U.S. companies will continue to rely on consultants and small businesses.

With continued reductions in state and local government expenditures, once-public services are becoming privatized. Opportunities for private enterprise in this area include services such as garbage collection, road and street maintenance, day-care centers, retirement and nursing care, and public transportation networks.

In the face of increased competition both at home and abroad, and the information overload which has accompanied rapid technological advances, American management's traditional hierarchical structure is becoming obsolete. This conventional management style of vertical communication will be replaced by a bottom-up network-style of management which will emphasize horizontal and diagonal as well as vertical communication.[6]

One goal of this new management style is to enable the organization to selectively acquire and utilize only that information which is critical to the corporation's missions and goals. A second goal is to stimulate creativity and initiative within the organization by encouraging the development of intrapreneurial qualities among employees and members of management. Thus both employees and management profit. "The intrapreneur gets the company's good name, contacts, resources, and money, while the company keeps a creative person who may otherwise leave to start a new business."[7] In addition, intrapreneurship can lead to more efficient and effective operations, and even to potential new businesses in which the firm can become involved. This trend is probably more advanced in the U.S. with its upward mobile society than elsewhere, although it is emerging in Canada and Western Europe. The movement creates economic vitality and, for international businessmen, a variety of opportunities.

4. Evolving Role of Women in the Workplace

During the last 10 years, the number of women in the American workplace has steadily increased. The former U.S. family stereotype of the 1950s and 1960s, where the husband was the sole income-earner and the wife stayed home to keep house, is rapidly becoming a bygone lifestyle. The traditional family, with a working husband, homemaker wife, and two children currently represents only 7% of all U.S. families. The latest labor force projections estimate that about two-thirds of America's mothers will be wage-earners by 1990.

Despite their apparent invasion of the working world, women only earn $0.64 for every $1.00 earned by men. It is sad to note that things have not changed much in 35 years: in 1950, women earned only $0.60 for every $1.00 earned by men. Experts have suggested that this inequality is likely to change in the near future as the result of economic necessity. It is reasoned that as the U.S. economy continues to expand, the total number of young workers will decline. This reduction in the size of the young labor force will take place as the "Baby Bust" generation—the generation directly following the Baby Boomers—reaches adulthood. This, in turn, should lead to greater competition in the area of employee recruitment. As future employers scramble to attract and keep the most capable and best qualified personnel, any remnants of sex, race, or age discrimination are expected to disappear.

Women of today possess certain advantages and certain qualities which will enable them to advance and to succeed in the emerging service/information sector of the U.S. economy. For the first time in this nation's history, the number of female college undergraduates exceeds the number of male undergraduates.[8] American women are becoming better educated than men. In an economic sector where the most important requirements are literacy and knowledge, the significance of this trend is readily apparent.

With the growth of the service/information sector, the manager's role has begun to shift to that of human developer. The new managerial requirements will include the ability to nurture, to instruct, and to act as a mentor of promising personnel. This new management role emphasizes interpersonal skills that women are socialized almost from birth to possess. It has been suggested that the successful corporate style of the future will combine the personality assets of women managers with those of men.[9]

As the educational levels of women have steadily risen, so too have the pressures on women to continue their careers after marriage and childbirth. Aside from the need for ego satisfaction or intellectual stimulation, there are important economic considerations involved here. It is much more difficult for a family to sacrifice the $25,000 (or more) per year earned by a professional woman than it is for the same family to do without the $12,000 per year earned by a less educated wife and mother in a less skilled job.

The advent and rapid growth in two-career families is transforming the business world. The increased number of working women is also providing new opportunities in the marketplace. For affluent, single, and dual-income households, time has become as important as money. The businesses which will benefit most from this fact are those which will provide labor or time-saving goods and services to these households. The restaurant, travel, leisure, and recreation industries are among those which have already benefited. Manufacturers of frozen foods, food processors, microwave ovens, and other convenience appliances, as well as housekeeping, lawn, automobile services, and even "Dress for Success" consultants should also prosper. In addition, there should be an increasing demand for day care, private schools, after-school care, and baby-sitting services for children. In industrialized Western European economies the proportion of women in the workforce has since World War II exceeded that in the U.S. This happened because of the loss of men through the war, the need to rebuild the economies, and the training women had received during the war as support personnel. The dual income family has been common. Consumption affluence is a prominent feature. But the movement of women toward higher education there and in Japan is not so apparent. Also, in Japan, although many women work in their early 20s and later in their 40s and 50s, after the childbearing and nurturing years, they are generally in lower paid jobs.

5. Emphasis on Esthetics, Experiences, and Quality in Consumption

More than ever before, American consumers seem to emphasize esthetics, experiences, and quality in their purchase of goods and services. In the realm of business and institutional markets, this emphasis will become increasingly apparent as shrewd buyers seek the highest quality and value in products and services purchased.[10]

One reason for this increasing sophistication of consumer tastes is the nationwide decline in family size. In 1950, average U.S. family size was 3.54. Today's typical U.S. family size is 3.24. Average U.S. family size is expected to become even smaller by 1990. With smaller family size, there are fewer household costs and family expenses, as well as more disposable income.

Another reason is the saturation of the U.S. market for durable items. Nearly all Americans own at least one television, one car, and a variety of miscellaneous household appliances; most American families own more than one of each. Thus, the market for consumer durables is becoming limited to replacement sales. In addition, while mean family income has steadily increased, the prices of many durable goods have remained relatively stable. The net result of these two factors is that a smaller portion of family income is required for purchase of replacement durable items. This leaves larger amounts of disposable income for the "finer things in life," such as personal enrichment, recreation, and leisure.

Increased consumer expenditures in these finer things have contributed significantly to the recent boom in the service and high-tech sectors of the U.S. economy. While old standards like movie-going, bowling, and picnics in the park will continue to thrive, new and exciting recreational alternatives are becoming available everywhere. For example, many consumers can go on champagne balloon flights, hire clowns for their children's birthday parties, head for a tanning salon, lounge in a hot tub, watch cable television or video tapes, or listen to music on compact disc players. At the beach, the consumer can go jet-skiing, para-sailing, or wind-surfing. Fifteen years ago, most of these activities would have been mostly inaccessible — if not incomprehensible — to most Americans, but not so today. Several industries are benefiting from the emphasis on experiential qualities in the consumption of services. Among these, as mentioned earlier, are entertainment, restaurants, and travel. With the recent advances in satellite and telecommunications technology, cable television is becoming widely accepted across the United States. This has spawned and contributed to the growth of "pay channels" such as Home Box Office (HBO), the Cable News Network (CNN), Music Television (MTV), the Lifetime Network (LIFE), and the Entertainment Sports Programming Network (ESPN). The ever increasing demand for newer and more varied viewer entertainment has led several of these pay channels to produce their own movies, situation comedies, and special/feature programs.

One interesting characteristic of the maturing U.S. society — with its increasing affluence and leisure — is the renewed interest and curiosity in this nation's cultural and ethnic heritage. One manifestation of this is the recent boom in hometown entertainment including cultural and ethnic fairs; local arts and crafts shows; and bluegrass, jazz, and folk music festivals. The growth in the popularity of amusement parks such as Disney World, Busch Gardens, Hershey Park, and King's Dominion is yet another illustration of this trend.

The rise of dual-income families and affluent retirees is also contributing to the development of the travel industry. Ten or 15 years ago, most American families vacationed by car and few traveled very far from home. Today, families are taking more exotic trips, traveling greater distances, and relying more heavily on air transportation. The increasing number of American retirees is already providing a lucrative market for many businesses including resorts and travel agencies. The fact that many older people prefer to travel during off-peak seasons makes them particularly attractive to resort owners. Travel agents have responded to this by designing special group tours for the affluent senior set. Growth in these two industries seems destined to continue; the U.S. Bureau of Labor Statistics is projecting a 44% increase in the number of U.S. travel agents by 1995.

In the past, restaurant cuisine was limited to traditional American, Italian, French, and Chinese. As a result of the recent growth and development of the restaurant industry, restaurants now offer a wide array of cuisines—from Middle Eastern and Vietnamese to gourmet vegetarian. In today's restaurant business, the quality of the eating experience is becoming as important as the quality of the food and table service. Some restaurant chains, like Showbiz Pizza Place, emphasize this to an extreme by relying on unique mealtime entertainment to draw customers. As the restaurant business has become more popular and competitive, greater attention is being paid to atmosphere and decor. This has led to a consequent surge in business for interior designers.

Western Europe has always been ahead of the U.S. in these trends, mainly because of its older culture combined with greater affluence when measured over the past 100 years. Western Europe has in fact been a more mature society. For international businessmen there is obviously a semiglobal market in products designed to appeal to esthetics, experiences, and quality consumption.

6. *Impact of the "Baby Boom" Generation*

To anticipate some of the major market trends in the year 2000, one needs to target the potential interests of Baby Boomers, who account for nearly 45% of the adult U.S. population. By that time, the largest single age group in America will be 45-year olds. From birth, Baby Boomers have been, and will continue to be, important trendsetters. Because of its sheer size, the Baby Boom generation affects all areas of U.S. economy, commerce, culture, and society.

As Baby Boomers progress through various stages of life and the family life cycle, certain businesses and industries experience periods of prosperity or hardship. For example, manufacturers of acne products and record albums began to suffer as the members of this generation entered adulthood. In contrast, the market for residential real estate is expected to surge as more and more Baby Boomers enter their home-buying years.

Baby Boomers currently account for 53% of all professional and managerial positions, 56% of college graduates, and 53% of dual-income families.[11] Baby Boomers are typically characterized as well-educated, sophisticated, and affluent. They frequently eat out, like to travel, participate in sports, and enjoy attending movies, theater, and other cultural events. Affluent Baby Boomer parents, many of whom have postponed childbearing in order to firmly establish their own careers, demand the same high quality standards in items for their children as they do for themselves.

Current projections estimate that by the turn of the century, 25 million U.S. households will have annual incomes which exceed $50,000, in 1985 dollars. A significant portion of these households will comprise Baby Boomers and their offspring. At that time, Baby Boomers will be middle-aged; thus, industries which rely on discretionary income should prosper. Some of these might include gourmet dining, international travel, fine clothing and accessories, luxury cars, investment real estate, and financial services. Again the pattern is similar in Western Europe, thus the international businessman can service a very large semiglobal market of this Baby Boomer generation.

7. Impact of the "Sunset" Generation

As a result of advances in medicine and improved standards of living, Americans are living longer lives. To illustrate, average life expectancy at the turn of this century was 49 years. Today it is 74 years. There are 25 million U.S. citizens over the age of 65, and this figure will grow dramatically as Baby Boomers pass into and through middle-age. By the year 2020, senior citizens will probably number 40 million. What's more, the population of people aged 85 or older is expected to double over the next 20 years.[12] Thus, another significant characteristic of the maturing U.S. society is the aging of a major portion of its population.

The increasing ranks of the Sunset generation are providing even more opportunities for contemporary marketers. In addition to Social Security benefits, many Americans receive generous pensions on their retirement. Some retirees choose to supplement their income by engaging in part-time work, consulting work, or even private enterprise. Compared to the Baby Boomers, the Sunset generation is becoming as important a consumer group, if not in size, then certainly in buying power.

It is the increasing affluence of America's seniors that makes them such a lucrative market segment. Not only do they have money to spend, but they also have the time to spend it. One indicator of this is the growth of membership in organizations such as the American Association of Retired Persons (AARP), which sponsors group packages and rates on insurance, travel, recreation, and other social gatherings for retirement-aged people. The AARP also publishes a monthly magazine, *Modern Maturity*.

In addition to the recreation, travel, and leisure industries, day-care centers for the elderly — where a dependent parent or spouse can be cared for during daytime hours — should become more common. The future should also bring continued growth and development of various housing arrangements for seniors, such as independent retirement homes and condominium complexes, as well as continuous-care nursing homes. Producers of over-the-counter and prescription pharmaceuticals and other home health care products should also continue to prosper.

In Western Europe one sees the same pattern of the growing size and economic impact of the Sunset generation, for much the same reasons. Therefore the Sunset generation in North America and Western Europe provides another semiglobal market segment for international businessmen to cater to with similar products and services.

8. New Era in Health Care

During the past decade, there has been a dramatic increase in the awareness of and interest in health care on the part of the U.S. public. One manifestation of this new sense of self-responsibility is that more people are devoting their time, energy, and money to good nutrition and physical fitness in an effort to prevent illness and injury. The market for home health-care products is projected to jump from its current $7 billion to $30 billion by the year 2000. The popularity of physical fitness has created a large demand for health and fitness clubs, nutrition and diet centers, and aerobics and weight-lifting classes. Just as low-sodium, low-fat, and other low-calorie foods are no longer popular among dieters alone, organic health foods are not just for vegetarians.

The conventional health care delivery system offered by American hospitals has been thrust into competition with more contemporary health care services. These nontraditional services include in-home hospice care, where terminally ill patients receive medical care at home; and maternity centers, where licensed nurse-midwives deliver babies in a home-like environment. In addition, there has recently been rapid growth in health maintenance organizations (HMOs) and private clinics which offer various services, for example, diagnostic, outpatient, and emergency care, that were formerly the exclusive domain of hospitals. As a result, many hospitals have added more sophisticated services and facilities to remain competitive. Some have even turned to advertising in order to attract more patients. Health consciousness is probably greater in North America and Scandinavia than it is in Central Europe, but many opportunities abound for international businessmen to service this expanding need with world-class products. However, cultural traditions of families looking after their aged may well constrain a global approach.

GLOBAL MARKETING
AND GLOBAL STRATEGY MANAGEMENT

At the beginning of the 21st century, the world will depend more than ever on international communications, and the blurry lines between national economies will become fainter. Traditionally, international business has been based on the differences between people and nations. Global marketing emphasizes the similarities. The modern global corporation contrasts powerfully with the aging MNC. Instead of adapting to differences within and between nations, it will seek sensibly to force suitably standardized products and practices on the entire globe.[13] They are likely to be accepted if they come with low prices, quality, and reliability.

The world marketplace is developing a convergent commonality through improved communication, transport, and travel. This results in the new commercial reality of emerging global markets for standardized consumer products. Firms geared to this new reality benefit from enormous economies of scale in production, distribution, marketing, and management. By translating these benefits into reduced world prices, they can decimate competitors. Examples of such world-class products are those of McDonald's, Coca-Cola and Pepsi-Cola, Revlon cosmetics, and Levi jeans. The most effective global competitors sell in all national markets the same kind of product sold in their largest market. They compete on the basis of appropriate value: the best combinations of price, quality, reliability, and delivery for products that are globally identical with respect to design, function, and even fashion.

The global consumer-product development can be illustrated by an example. Driven by improved washing machine technology and the increased popularity of relatively fragile synthetic and colored fabrics, West European laundry habits have converged. Every major nation now washes a majority of its wash loads in under 60°C water. This created a common need for a product that performs well under these circumstances. The result has been the marketing of single brands with a common brand name, product formulation, and positioning across the whole of Europe.[14]

Today global marketing is little more than a concept. However, it is ripe with promise because television soon will be available to serve as global marketing's instrument of consumer access. Communication satellites can now provide relatively inexpensive television service anywhere in the world. The World Administrative Radio conference in 1977 allocated various channels to individual countries' government agencies for Direct Broadcast Satellite Service (DBS). This is expected to begin in Western Europe during this decade. Traditional satellite delivery is still open to entrepreneurs. Furthermore Luxembourg, which already has a far-reaching commercial radio service, has proposed various schemes to blanket Western Europe with commercial television. It is in fact beaming TV programs at the lucrative West German market. Throughout the international broadcast community there seems to be agreement that the dynamic of progress is irreversible. The number of channels will multiply, and private television will grow. Also, advertising time will expand and flourish on both private and public broadcasting systems. Moreover, the widespread penetration of video cassette recorders means that programs will increase and improve.

Global Strategy Management

International business in the past produced and sold for a local market. Many MNCs did this too, and therefore organized as a group of regional firms with a corporate headquarters. Thus MNCs accommodated local market needs, their local management was decentralized, and they were successful. However, as outlined earlier, global trends are increasingly creating a global shopping center for many consumer, industrial, and service products. Coca-Cola was one of the first to market a global brand. Today there are a growing number of global industries: aerospace, automobiles, semiconductors, telecommunications equipment, and television.[15] More will come in the future. International businessmen who wish to develop superior companies will have to think globally, and then adapt to the extent necessary. A decade ago, Black & Decker Corporation (B & D) was the unchallenged leader in power tools. It is a U.S. MNC with about 45% of its sales coming from foreign markets. In France, U.K., and West Germany its brand is as well or better known than in the U.S. However, Makita, a small Japanese manufacturer, embarked on a major program to take its power tool products global. Makita now is No. 1 in Japan and a major world player. Black & Decker realized they had to globalize to compete.[16]

The globalization attempt by B & D can serve international businessmen as an example of the prospects and problems of such an undertaking. They found that a global approach looks for similarities among markets while their previous multidomestic approach ignored similarities. Today B & D is out not to market lowest common denominator products but to act as a unified company designing products which can be sold in as many markets as possible. B & D has 16 plants outside the U.S. and has a large foreign network with production, distribution, marketing, and advertising advantages, plus the ability to commercialize their technology. Globalization offered economies of scale, less duplication of R & D effort, and new products that could be introduced more quickly. Previously B & D's country approach had resulted in product proliferation. The biggest problem was determining how to corral competing energies within the MNC and to get them to pull in the same direction. B & D has been striving to retain their strong geographic presence in each country while at the same time asking their managers to think and act globally. This is being achieved by headquarter marketing, engineering, and manufacturing executives being supportive of operating unit global initiatives. Computer-aided design is helping coordinate the efforts of product-design teams around the world, and consolidation is reducing duplication. Their worldwide advertising now is being handled by two agencies; previously it was 20. Similarly styled, multilingual product packaging has replaced hundreds of different packages. Power tools now come in only four colors, compared to almost 30 before. B & D thinks it will take 10 years to institute a global approach; in professional power tools they place themselves in year six, and in consumer power tools in year three.

The B & D example illustrates that global strategic management is obviously the process of developing and administering a strategy and structure for offering a world-class product to a global market segment that crosses national boundaries. The success of a global business rests on integrated operations and a highly coordinated strategy. Effective management of a global business also requires a means of gathering and internally distributing pertinent information about the world business environment. The firm must also share resources and experience throughout the enterprise.

Every international businessman should examine whether in his industry foreign sales and profits are a significant proportion of the total sales of the industry. If so, he must be prepared to deal with foreign competition and should investigate foreign market opportunities. This analysis should lead him to discovering segments that can be catered to through a global marketing strategy. Also the assessment should focus on identifying the potential advantages a global competitor could have over an MNC or other locally oriented firm. One advantage could be lower cost, since fixed costs can be spread across a larger volume of fewer products. Another advantage would arise from the experience curve as skill resources can be transferred and utilized across the system. Yet another advantage would lie in cheaper sourcing of materials and components because of larger purchasing volumes and production runs. Still another advantage should be from superior global information networks, which also enable identification and evaluation of the implications of competitors' and users' activities. Monitoring global environmental trends and events also yields information of commercial significance which can enable the firm to position itself in anticipation of happenings and to predict the impact of global events on local national markets. Moreover, the firm in a global market with a world-class product can sequentially concentrate its resources on a single national market, achieve a dominant position, and then transfer its resources to the next geographical target. At the operational level, a firm that intends to implement a global strategy should make sure that the following basic steps have been taken:

— Strategy evaluation including market segment scope
— A global product name
— A global product formulation
— Multilingual package copy and instructions
— Global package sizing
— Global pricing

It must be realized that developing a global strategy takes time and probably cannot be successfully accomplished in a hurry. However, it is the way of the future.

Another important operational trend that international businessmen must know in order to be successful in getting more world market share is countertrade.

COUNTERTRADE

Countertrade is the modern version of barter. This way of doing business has become one of the most rapidly growing elements of world trade. Forecasts of it range up to 20 to 30% of world trade.[17] The sheer shortage of convertible currency reserves in the LDCs and centrally planned economies forces barter. Among industrialized countries also, recession and unemployment are forcing barter. "I'll buy from you if you buy from me." Sweden recently won an agreement from General Electric Co. (GE) to buy Swedish products as the counterpart of a contract to GE to build engines for Sweden's JAS fighter.[18] Barter should not be done by an LDC if the products bartered by it could otherwise be marketed for convertible currency. In the instances where such barter does take place, the receiver of the goods has the benefit of unloading them on the world market and reaping the harvest of convertible currency. The supplier loses in two ways: one is the loss of convertible currency it could have gained, and the other is the real harm to its direct marketing of these products abroad, because the bartered products are probably sold at a reduced price and this tends to lower the usual price buyers are willing to pay. Such barter occurs mainly under the barter forms known as counter purchasing and switch trading.

Forms of Barter

Countertrade is the general name given to all forms of barter. The simplest is classical barter, which is a one-time direct exchange of goods between two countries with no money or credit required. This was too restrictive and gave way to cooperative barter in which more than two countries are involved. Neither of these forms offered flexibility in terms of the timing of the exchange. The most frequently used form of countertrade today is counter purchase or parallel barter.[19]

Counter purchase is sometimes referred to as bilateral trading, buy-sell, compensation trading, cooperation, countertrade, offset trade, parallel barter, or reciprocal trading. In this form of barter, each transaction is paid for in convertible currency and the transactions do not have to be simultaneous. The basic principle of counter purchase is that Party A, in order to be paid convertible currency for its products immediately or over time by Party B, enters into an undertaking to purchase, or have purchased by third parties, products from Party B with a value equal to a certain percentage of the value of the Party A product. Two separate but linked contracts are signed for a certain time period: one for the sale of Party A product and the second for the purchase of Party B's products, which are often a number of products rather than specific ones.

Counter purchase has grown since most Western countries will only provide export credit to LDCs if payment for Western products is finally received in convertible currency. The Western exporter under a separate arrangement agrees to purchase goods for export from the LDC. Thus, the convertible currency is provided with which the LDC can repay the export credit for the products it bought.

Switch trading is mainly a by-product of intergovernmental barter through clearing areements. There are 83 countries that maintain at least one clearing agreement with one or more countries. These clearing agreements are particularly suitable for centrally planned economies. Most of the trade within Eastern Europe, and almost 60% of the Soviet bloc trade with the LDCs, is done on this basis. The procedure is that two governments decide which goods they want to exchange, at what prices, and in what volumes. The books are balanced once a year either by payment in nonconvertible currency or by a transfer of goods to the next year, or switch trading takes place as surplus barter goods are switched to other countries by the stronger party who wants to earn convertible currency. A fair amount of the latter occurs. Bilateral clearing agreements have disadvantages, such as trade usually stopping for one partner as soon as it reaches its volume ceiling. An improvement would be triangular or multicountry agreements.

Another form of barter is the buy-back or compensation arrangement for dealing with MNC investors. This is often part of coproduction, turnkey, or technology assistance agreements. The MNC barters technical knowledge to build, or actually builds a plant, in return for an agreement to purchase some of its output. The LDC is guaranteed a certain demand for the plant's output while the MNC often finds the arrangement a relatively efficient way of expanding its operation. Buy-back is growing very rapidly, especially with the Soviet Union.[20] However, buy-back is not as prevalent as counter purchase since buy-back requires an initial decision to invest and a further decision to exercise quality control on the production in the foreign country.

In insisting on countertrade, the LDCs are trying to achieve two main objectives:

- to minimize outlays in hard currency for their imports
- to find additional outlets in hard currency for products that are otherwise difficult to export.

In addition, countertrade sales of LDC products to developed countries may at times circumvent protectionist measures.

From the viewpoint of the industrialized countries, countertrade facilitates their exports to markets which would otherwise not purchase. This enlargement of their export markets enables them to import more directly; or by disposing of the LDC products elsewhere, gives them the convertible foreign currency to purchase goods of their choice. It is worth noting that often the international businessman can negotiate and obtain a certain amount of convertible currency, and only the remaining percentage of the contract value in LDC products. Moreover, it has become customary to allow the international businessman to pay a penalty in the event of his being unable to honor his counterpurchase obligation.

Barter: By Firms, MNCs, and Barter Houses

Even if the price is higher, East European Foreign Trade Organizations usually buy from a Western company that accepts payment in barter goods rather than from another firm that insists on receiving hard currency. A Western exporter who agrees to barter is ordinarily asked to choose from a list of available goods. Often, many such products are unsuitable because of inferior quality, bad design, or lack of Western consumer interest. Industrial products can present some problems because of limited after-sales service.

In counter purchase, the amount is often about 40% of the value of the delivery of products. Almost all counter-purchase agreements stipulate a bank guaranteed penalty, ranging from 10 to 20% of the value of the counter-purchase goods, that must be paid if the obligation is not fulfilled. It should be emphasized that an MNC signing a counter-purchase contract must include a clause specifying that the obligation can be transferred to a third party.[21]

A number of MNCs that buy large quantities of products from Eastern Europe have set up special departments to handle barter and resale arrangements. Examples include Bayer and Thyssen of West Germany, SKF and Alfa Laval of Sweden, Renault of France, Fiat of Italy, and the large Swiss chemical companies. MNCs that do not have such departments usually get in touch with a professional barter agent. Most Western banks have connections with one or another barter house. The chambers of commerce in Western Europe also provide lists of barter houses upon request. Barter houses generally prefer deals over $1,000,000 because the commission on small deals is not adequate compensation for the amount of work involved in selling barter goods. One example of barter deals illustrates the range.

Switch Trading Example

Switch-trading transactions are more complicated than barter deals. A U.S. firm had negotiated the sale of textile machinery to Bulgaria and was offered 70% in hard currency and 30% in barter goods. It found nothing suitable among Bulgaria's commodities. The Bulgarians then offered switch-accounting units usable only in Pakistan. The U.S. exporter, through a switch trader in Zurich, found an importer in Spain who was willing to buy Pakistani jute for hard currency. The Bulgarians gave the U.S. exporter an irrevocable letter of credit authorizing it, or a third party, to purchase jute in Pakistan on the Bulgarian account. The jute was shipped directly to Spain. For its efforts, the Swiss dealer received a 12% commission on the value of the jute shipment, 10% of which it had to give to the Spanish buyer. The U.S. firm was able to add this cost to the price of the textile equipment.

A Proposal Using Countertrade to Increase Trade

The present model of export credit trade is outlined with an example.

Let us assume I_p is an Indonesian importer willing to import a capital good from Canada and needs to finance such a transaction.

The Canadian exporter (E_c) applied to the Export Development Corporation (EDC) in Canada for financing. The EDC is a Government of Canada Crown Corporation which gives export credits. EDC, after consideration of whether the case meets the criteria, particularly the Canadian content, will agree to finance the export at relatively favorable terms if a major Indonesian bank (I_B) guarantees the buyer's credit and repayment. Figure 1 displays the usual model of flows.

As can be seen, E_c will ship the goods and present the shippings documents to EDC, which pays E_c in dollars. The Indonesian importer (I_P) will start the repayment of the amount to I_B on the agreed terms. I_B will be receiving payment of the capital plus interest from I_P in Indonesian money. As I_P repays, I_B remits dollars to EDC. But the Indonesian buyers have learned the hard way that long-term loans in dollars are very risky because whenever there is a devaluation they have to pay more Indonesian money to obtain the amount of dollars I_B has to pay to EDC. The exchange risk can be so high that the Indonesian buyer refuses to import Canadian products. Consequently, exports of these Canadian products to Indonesia do

Figure 17-1

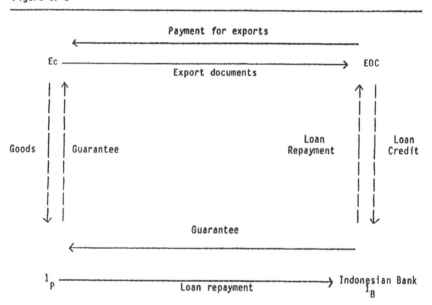

not occur, while the line of credit available through EDC is unused. At the same time Indonesian authorities are desperately looking for new credits from the IMF, World Bank, and/or private banks.

The proposal[22] would increase trade over and beyond what is otherwise possible through the reduction of commercial and financial risk. In the proposal, EDC gives the dollars to the Indonesian Bank instead of giving them to the Canadian exporter. The Indonesian bank then gives a Trading House a line of local currency credit, which it is agreed will be extinguished as the Indonesian importer pays the Bank for the Canadian goods. The Trading House now buys Indonesian products and exports them. The dollars earned thereby are paid to the Canadian exporter. When this transaction is over, the Indonesian Bank returns to EDC the dollars it received originally from EDC.

The proposal has a number of advantages:

— The Indonesian importer is able to acquire Canadian equipment at a fixed price in Indonesian currency. Thus he eliminates his currency risk.
— The Canadian exporter is paid in dollars and therefore is not affected.
— The Indonesian Bank has use of an untied dollar loan at concessionary EDC terms. It can make an interest return on this loan: the difference between the market rate and the concessionary EDC rate.
— The Indonesian Bank has the dollars to return to EDC once the transaction is fully completed. The currency risk is eliminated. Besides the Bank fulfills a role in stimulating Indonesian exports.
— The Trading House does more business.

SUMMARY AND CONCLUSIONS

Doing international business is necessary for success today and in the world of the future. The gains from greater awareness and knowledge of international business are immense for nations, MNCs, trading companies, exporters, and all entrepreneurs. For international businessmen this epilogue has drawn a picture of the prospects and trends in the world marketplace. Further, it has emphasized the importance of developing a global marketing approach and implementing global strategy management. The era of the MNC, the multidomestic corporation, is gradually declining, except in special situations. Increasingly the emphasis will be on developing world-class products that will reach global market segments arching over national boundaries. In this attempt the international businessmen will be supported by communications and broadcast technologies. Future products for global transfer will be more and more mass market, reasonably priced, good quality products, and services of all kinds including, most importantly, technology.

This epilogue concludes with an emphasis on a rapidly growing operational vehicle, countertrade, for expanding international business. Three-quarters of the world population live in nations which are short of foreign exchange reserves. For economic growth they need foreign trade and investment, and one of the major vehicles to expand such foreign interfaces is through countertrade. It behooves the international businessman to investigate its possibilities. In so doing he will add meaningfully to his knowledge of the world marketplace and the possibilities of competing successfully in it.

REFERENCE NOTES

1. *U.N. Monthly Bulletin of Statistics* (1983), New York: United Nations, various issues.

2. Sharpe, William D. (1983, May 30), Asia's Growth-Minded Group of Four, *The Asian Wall Street Journal Weekly*, p. 10.

3. Buying Up America (1983, May 21), *The Economist*, pp. 104-105.

4. This whole section on trends draws heavily on Naisbitt, John (1982), *Megatrends*, New York: Warner Books Inc.

5. U.S. Department of Commerce (1985), *U.S. Industrial Outlook, 1985*, Washington, DC: U.S. Government Printing Office.

6. Naisbitt, John and Aburdene, Patricia (1985), *Re-inventing the Corporation*, New York: Warner Books Inc.; and Pinchot III, Gifford (1985), *Intrapreneuring*, New York: Harper & Row.

7. *Op. cit.*, Naisbitt (1982), p. 228.

8. U.S. Department of Commerce, Bureau of the Census (1985), *Statistical Abstract of the United States, 1985*, 105th edition, Washington, DC: U.S. Government Printing Office.

9. *Op. cit.*, Naisbitt and Aburdene (1985).

10. Kelley, Eugene J. and Hearne, Lisa E. (forthcoming), The New Rules for Marketing Leadership: Managing for Today and Tomorrow in World Society, in *Fruits and Problems of the Japanese Way of Marketing*, Tokyo: Japan Marketing Association.

11. Micklos, John (1986, January), Ten Trends that will Change Delaware Business Forever, *Delaware Today*, p. 68.

12. *Ibid.*, p. 70.

13. Levitt, Theodore (1983), The Globalization of Markets, *Harvard Business Review* (May - June), 61 (3), 94.

14. Saatchi & Saatchi (1984), quoted in International Advertising Association Global Media Commission, *Global Marketing: From Now to the Twenty-First Century*, New York: International Advertising Association, p. 16.

15. Multinationals vs. Globals (1984, May 5), *The Economist*, p. 79.

16. Farley, Laurence J., Chairman and C.E.O. of Black & Decker Corporation (1985, October 11), quoted in Global Approach seeks Similarities in Markets, *Marketing News*, pp. 12-13.

17. U.S. Department of Commerce (1980), *Countertrade Practices in East Europe, the Soviet Union and China — An Introductory Guide to Business*, Washington, DC: U.S. Department of Commerce; and Kirpalani, V.H. (1985), *International Marketing* (p. 493), New York: Random House, Inc.

18. New Restrictions on World Trade (1982, July 19), *Business Week*, pp. 118-122.

19. Kaikati, Jack (1981), International Barter Boom: Perspectives and Challenges, *Journal of International Marketing*, (1), 29-38; Welt, Leo B. (1980, July 14), Countertrade Gains Popularity as International Trade Tool, *Business America*, pp. 14-16; and Sebuster, Falko (1978), Bartering Process in Industrial Buying and Selling, *Industrial Marketing Management* (April), 119-127.

20. Lange, Irene and Elliott, James P. (1977), U.S. Role in East-West Trade: An Appraisal, *Journal of International Business Studies* (Fall-Winter), 5-16; and Stroh, Edward H. (1978, June 19), Countertrade — Not for Everyone but Worth a Look, *Commerce America*, pp. 2-4.

21. Mandato, Joseph; Skola, Thomas J. and Wyne, Kenneth L. (1978), Counterpurchase Sales in the German Democratic Republic, *Columbia Journal of World Business* (Spring), 140-146.

22. The proposal draws heavily on Kirpalani, V.H. and Librowicz, M. (1986), Countertrade: Limits and Possibilities; Examples from Canada-ASEAN Trade. In V.H. Kirpalani, W. Lazer and C.T. Tan (Eds.), *Proceedings of the American Marketing Association — National University of Singapore International Marketing Conference*, (pp. 246-252), Conference held at the National University of Singapore (June, 16-18).

Index

ANDEAN COUNTRIES

CENTRAL AMERICA

CHINA

Name Index

Abbondante, P., 416
Abu Naba'a, A., 415
Aburdene, P., 626,656,657
Acker, C., 411,412
Ackes, C., 413
Aharoni, Yari, 334
Aida, Yuji, 371
Al-Dabbagh, A.T., 192,229
Alden, Vernon R., 371
Alganhim, K., 413
Almaney, Aduan, 61
Anastos, D., 411,413
Anderson, Charles A., 371
Anderson, Ronald A., 624,625
Angus, C., 413
Apgar, M., 413
Arbose, J., 201,229
Artisien, P.F.R., 302,309
Athose, Anthony G., 372
Ayubi, N.M., 202,229

Badawy, M.K., 201,229
Bair, Frank, 392,410,411,415
Baldridge, Malcolm, 63
Bangsbert, P.T., 189
Baranson, Jack, 371
Barone, Saun, 61
Basck, John, 62
Bavisli, Vinod, 62
Bedos, A., 411,413
Benedek, G.I., 275,310
Bennett, Peter D., 62
Benson, Soffer, 60
Beracs, J., 296,310
Berkman, Harold W., 61,62
Blank, Stephen, 62

Boddewyn, Jean J., 62
Boey, Chow Kit, 536
Bownas, Geoffrey, 372
Bradbury, Frank R., 60
Bradley, David G., 61
Brophy, Hugh, 62
Buckley, P.J., 302,309

Campbell, D.I., 413
Cardoso, Fernando Henrique, 94
Christopher, Robert, 371
Clement, C., 413
Cline, William, 94
Connan, B., 413
Connolly, S.G., 412,413
Corcoran, Kevin, 412,415
Counsell, A., 413
Courdy, Jean C., 371
Cousins, Norman, 622,623,626
Cracco, Etienne F., 62
Crane, Keith, 449
Csillag, I., 310
Czinkota, M.R., 225,229,231

Daniels, John D., 63
Davidson, WIlliam H., 371
Davies, M.H., 203,204,229
Davies, R.L., 138
Dawson, J.A., 138
De Fontaney, P., 310
Deal, Terrence E., 625,626
Delene, L., 200,230,385,410
Destler, I.M., 371
DeVittorio, J.M., 618,623,625,626
Doz, Yves L., 62
Dunn, D.T. Jr., 226,229

For Product Safety Concerns and Information please contact our
EU representative GPSR@taylorandfrancis.com Taylor & Francis
Verlag GmbH, Kaufingerstraße 24, 80331 München, Germany